THE HISTORY OF AN
OBSESSION

THE HISTORY OF AN
OBSESSION

German Judeophobia and the Holocaust

KLAUS P. FISCHER

CONSTABLE · LONDON

Published in the United States of America 1998 by
The Continuum Publishing Company, New York
First published in Great Britain 1998
by Constable and Company Limited
3 The Lanchesters, 162 Fulham Palace Road
London W6 9ER
Copyright © Klaus Fischer 1998
ISBN 0 09 479030 2
The right of Klaus Fischer to be identified as author of this work
has been asserted by him in accordance with
the Copyright, Designs and Patents Act 1988

A CIP catalogue record for this book is available from the British Library

Printed in the United States of America

Contents

Acknowledgments

Not too long ago, I had a nerve-wracking nightmare about the Holocaust. It began when I was asked to give a lecture to a large audience of
what appeared to be prominent people. As I began to speak, I found
myself completely alone, microphone in hand, in a ghastly charnel-
house museum chock-full of hideously tortured, mangled, and deformed
Jewish victims. I ran through this horror chamber in panic, frequently
bumping into grotesquely disfigured bodies, all of whom were carrying
descriptive signs attesting to the nature of their deaths. Gasping for air,
I tried to explain to my invisible audience that what I was seeing and
describing was real and that they should trust my testimony. Just as I
was communicating this message, the walls, ceiling, and floor of the horror chamber began to slither and change position. The floor turned into
blood-soaked corpses. In great horror, I tried to run over the corpses in
hopes of finding the exit. At this point, I woke up in a cold sweat.

The nightmare suggested two things: recognition that I was dealing with evil in its most pristine form and a feeling of creeping doubt
whether I would be able to work through, comprehend, and explain that
evil to others. Fortunately, throughout the writing of this book I had
a great deal of emotional support from my family, especially from my
wife, Ann, and from good friends and helpful intellectual critics. Without the benefit of Leonard Marsak's encouragement and our ongoing,
open-ended dialogue of what it means to be a Jew, my understanding
of the Jewish experience would have lacked important insights. Similarly, if I had not had Jeffrey Burton Russell as a sounding board on
evil and human aggression, I would have fallen far short of capturing
the quintessential nature of evil in general and Nazi evil in particular.
Throughout the writing of this book, he was a steadfast and demanding
critic. I knew that I was on the right track when his marginal comments
on key issues were often in the form of anguished confessions that he
was literally trembling while reading about some of the worst instances
of Nazi cruelty and mendacity.

I would also like to express my gratitude to Roger Lydon and Gerhart Hoffmeister, both of whom read sizable sections of the manuscript
and made helpful suggestions. Thanks are also due to Gary Bierly, my
good friend and colleague at Allan Hancock College, to my students at
several institutions who helped me in clarifying my ideas and arguments,

and to Sheila Harmon, who proved invaluable in the preparation of this manuscript. Frank Oveis, my editor at Continuum, proved to be an incisive critic and sensitive guide; his support and helpful suggestions are much appreciated.

In writing this book, I have personally experienced what I have known intellectually all along, namely, that the painful past is never far below the surface of the present, and that our instinctual way of dealing with it is to repress it. This was particularly apparent during my travels through Germany, Austria, Hungary, and Poland, where the topic of Jewish suffering and the Holocaust continues to be taboo for many people, including some of my own relatives who deliberately avoided discussing the subject. I sincerely hope that my book makes a small contribution in highlighting the urgent necessity of coming to terms with the sort of radical evil that defined the Holocaust in order to spare future generations from having to relive similar horrors.

Abbreviations and Acronyms

Gestapo	Geheime Staatspolizei (Secret State Police, the Nazi political police)
KdF	Kanzlei des Führers (the Führer's private chancellery)
Kripo	Kriminalpolizei (Criminal Police)
NSDAP	Nationalsozialistische Deutsche Arbeiterpartei (National Socialist German Workers' Party, political party of National Socialism mass movement)
OMGUS	Office of the Military Government for Germany, United States
OKW	Oberkommando der Wehrmacht (High Command of the Armed Forces)
Orpo	Ordnungspolizei (Order Police)
RKFDV	Reichskommissariat für die Festigung des deutschen Volkstums (Reich Commission for the Strengthening of Germandom)
RSHA	Reichssicherheitshauptamt (Reich Main Security Office)
RuSHA	Rasse und Siedlungshauptamt (Race and Settlement Main Office)
SA	Sturmabteilung (Assault Division, storm troopers, or brownshirts, a paramilitary organization of the Nazi Party)
SD	Sicherheitsdienst (Security Service, an SS intelligence department)
Sipo	Sicherheitspolizei (Security Police)
SPD	Sozialdemokratische Partei Deutschlands (Social Democratic Party of Germany)
SS	Schutzstaffel (Protective Squadron, the black-uniformed elite corps of the Nazi Party)

Introduction

The state-sponsored murder of six million Jews, commonly referred to as the Holocaust, was the greatest crime of the twentieth century, and, given the vicious and calculated brutality that was inflicted on its innocent victims, historians of the future could well label it the greatest crime in history. Recognition of this fact has necessarily led historians to ask two key philosophical questions: how could such evil have erupted in the midst of what many regarded as a progressive western culture, and why did the Germans, who gave the world some of the most brilliant scientists, musicians, philosophers, theologians, and writers, stoop to a level of bestiality no sane person could have predicted in 1900? This book tries to answer such apparently inexplicable questions.

Any who hope to explain an event of this magnitude should state at the outset what assumptions they hold and what sort of personal commitments inform their work. One of the major principles that guides this book is the attempt to avoid the two extremes often encountered in such narratives: Germanophobia and apologetic revisionism. Fifty years ago, in the wake of the horrible atrocities inflicted on the Jews of Europe, it was understandable that many people wanted to indict all Germans for the evils unleashed by the Nazi regime; but since a blanket indictment, implying universal guilt, would have amounted to tarring all Germans with the same condemnatory brush, such a racist approach in reverse was quickly dropped by the Allied Powers. It was understood by humane and thoughtful people that you could not indict a whole people with a crime committed by its criminal leadership without engaging in the same irrational thinking that inspired the Nazis to murder six million Jews.

Yet, under the spell of the sheer magnitude of this crime, some historians continue to assert, openly or by way of clever insinuation, the thesis of universal, original German guilt.[1] In its most extreme formulation, such as one that this author heard during a presentation on the Holocaust at an annual meeting of the American Historical Association, the thesis asserts that the Germans were unique, that they did what they did because they were by nature racists and militarists. As one of the speakers asserted, it was probably some chemical abnormality in their blood that made the Germans commit such heinous crimes. A similar view was echoed by an anonymous letter received by this author in 1989 arguing that the reunification of Germany must never be permitted because we must then immediately "brace ourselves for WW III.... Germany has honestly earned the right to remain on its knees and suffer permanent disability. After all, doesn't society mete out 'life imprisonment without possibility of parole' to those whose antisocial behavior warrants such a lifelong sentence?" If one starts with the assumption that all Germans were evil, as these extreme views hold, then one will be predisposed to look for and invariably find selective evidence in German history to support this thesis. In this form, however, it is just another variation of the Nazi theme that the Jews were evil, which in turn stems from the racist credo that some human groups are solely guilty because of their genetic make-up — a credo that no humane and civilized person could affirm in the wake of the Holocaust because it would amount to giving Hitler his ultimate victory.

Admittedly, such extreme views are not stocks-in-trade of respectable historians today, any more than the rantings of Holocaust deniers who claim that the killings never happened or the glib assertions of clever sophists who insist that the vast majority of Germans did not know or were forced to follow orders. There are still some apologists who believe that Hitler and his henchmen alone were responsible, and that, in any case, atrocities were committed by many other nations, making them just as bad as the Germans. By every conceivable tactic, ranging from simple denial, obeying of orders, mitigation of circumstances, victimization (we, too, were victims of Hitler), to comparative trivialization (you were as bad as we were), some revisionist historians have tried to whitewash the record by claiming that the Nazis, though perhaps misguided, wanted the best for Germany and did not commit most of the heinous crimes attributed to them by their opponents.[2]

If one approach may be termed condemnatory and the other exculpatory and both are obviously unacceptable, what other explanatory strategy is more likely to move us to an approximation of the truth? It must be understood that, given our different intellectual investments, even scrupulously honest historians are bound to differ in their evaluative judgments. Historians who are intellectually and morally invested in the Jewish experience, no matter how fair they try to be to the Germans, are likely to push in the direction of greater German guilt, whereas German historians are likely to try to lessen that guilt. The debate in recent years has been over the question of how many Germans actually knew and participated in the mass murder of the Jews. It is, so far, primarily a one-sided debate because the Germans, one feels, appear to be sick and tired of the Nazi debate; they want to go on with their lives and forge a new unified and prosperous Germany. In the words of many, they want a *Schlusstrich,* or final line, to the whole sordid affair; they do not want to be bothered by those who want to ladle out a steady and indefinite dose of guilt. It makes no difference to them whether more Germans were involved in the Holocaust than was previously supposed. They ask what ideological agenda motivates some studies that seem to implicate as many Germans as possible in the murder of the Jews.

A related question involves the guilt of ancestors — that is, to what extent were previous generations of Germans responsible for the Holocaust? Several books in the Anglo-American community have recently revived the concept of "national character," some well meaning, others ideologically and morally suspect.[3] This consists in the construction of long chains of historical causation in which personalities and movements are linked as antecedents that inevitably result in certain consequences. Ideas, indeed, have consequences, but Luther's ideas caused the Reformation and not the Holocaust. Indicting every major thinker in German history with "anti-Semitism," a term that is inherently ambiguous on both linguistic and historical grounds, may establish mild, moderate, or extreme hostility to Jews, but torn from its past cultural context, this "guilt by association" does not establish a causal relationship to the event that still needs to be explained. All too often such approaches transform German history into a laboratory of alleged aberrant ideas and behavior; they assume the German past to be a unique continuum, distinct and different from that of other nations, and therefore pregnant with abnormalities that point to the Nazi outcome, which was as logical as it was inevitable.

According to this view, Judeophobia was not only a necessary but also a sufficient cause for the occurrence of the Holocaust. Anti-Jewish utterances are collected from hundreds of years of Judeophobia and shown to be a prefiguration of Auschwitz and the swastika. In this form, which still prevails in too many studies, it amounts to little more than the slippery slope argument, the unwarranted assumption that a proposed course of action will lead, by a series of steps, to an undesirable or even catastrophic outcome. Thus, by taking the first fateful step in 1543 when he wrote *On the Jews and Their Lies*, Martin Luther, judged by some as "a racist, pure and simple,"[4] set in motion certain ideas which, like links in a chain, led to others of a similar nature (Fichte, Arndt, Jahn) and those to others (Dühring, Marr, Wagner, Stöcker) until, at length, the falling dominoes came to their bitter end in Hitler and the Holocaust. Quite apart from draining German history of anything resembling normality, and thus libeling a whole people, this approach, as will be shown later, does not yield even a minimal understanding of why the Holocaust happened in Nazi Germany.

Did Judeophobia, defined as an irrational fear of, prejudice against, and hatred toward Jews, cause the Holocaust? The answer depends, among other things, on what kind of Judeophobia or anti-Judaism — Christian, xenophobic, social-discriminatory, or biological-racial — we are talking about and the level of intensity in which it expressed itself. It is my contention, however, that no single strain of Judeophobia by itself was a sufficient reason for what happened in Nazi Germany. As generally understood in Germany and other countries, to be anti-Jewish meant being prejudiced against the Jews and wanting them excluded from public office and reduced to the status of an underprivileged minority. This conception of anti-Jewish prejudice, however, is not a sufficient explanation for the occurrence of the Holocaust. It is only when hatred of Jews has moved beyond a prejudice to a pathology, when it has combined hostility to individual Jews with intense irrational hatred of Jews in the abstract, that we can begin to establish causal connections to the Holocaust.

In trying to grasp this deeper connection, it is also important to ask how Judeophobia was institutionalized in Germany and in what form. For example, was it church-sponsored and therefore ecclesiastically sanctioned? Was it state-sponsored and therefore legally sanctioned? Was it embodied in political parties, civic or commercial associations, special interest groups, or cultural traditions? Was it promoted and reinforced by educational institutions?

In examining these questions, one discovers that the German record was not a very good one, that Judeophobia was deeply embodied in German life and thought, but neither was it, compared to Russia or eastern European countries, the worst record, because German Jews were rapidly assimilated into German society in the nineteenth century. This was also true, as will be shown, of eastern Jews (*Ostjuden*), who looked to Germany as both a refuge from persecution and the country of their loftiest spiritual aspirations. In other words, the historical record does not support an annihilatory intention before 1933. There is no direct causal link between popular discriminatory Judeophobia and the Holocaust, no chain of anti-Jewish causes that lead from Luther to Hitler. The real antecedents to annihilatory thinking are to be found in the racist thinking of the *Gründerzeit* generation, the founding generation of the Second Reich, for it was on this seedbed of racist delusion and paranoia that Hitler's generation drew. The watershed of modern Judeophobia was World War I, which greatly intensified Judeophobia in Germany. The war and the terrible consequences of defeat opened the floodgates of political extremism and nurtured the hard-core Nazi mentality — a mentality that was pathologically anti-Jewish to the core. In other words, after 1918 hatred of Jews intensified in Germany more than in any other country, attaching itself to right-wing movements, especially the Nazi Party, and becoming the personal obsession of its leaders (Hitler, Himmler, Goebbels, Rosenberg, Heydrich, Bormann, etc.), all of whom were murderous Jew-haters.

Between 1933 and 1939 this type of annihilatory Judeophobia became state sponsored, and its aim during those six years was to strip German Jews of their civil rights, their livelihood, and their homes in Germany. World War II, which brought millions of additional Jews under Hitler's control, ushered in the actual annihilatory stage. It is this "Final Solution" to the Jewish problem, as the Nazis euphemistically termed the murder of the Jews, that needs, above all, to be explained, and the chief question here is whether the German people as a whole desired the annihilation of the Jews. To what extent did the Nazi leadership actually succeed in indoctrinating the German people into supporting such a monstrous project? The answer to this question, presented in a later chapter, is that a conclusive answer is impossible on principle because, even with hindsight and more information, we cannot know with any certainty what was on the collective mind of the German people, especially in a totalitarian setting and in times of total war. In addition, there is something morally objectionable to indicting a whole people for the crime committed by a criminal regime and its helpers. Recent attempts to widen the circle of perpetrators and claiming that those who murdered the Jews were "representative" of the whole German population, which must have consisted of equally murderous Jew-haters, commit two major logical fallacies: the fallacy of composition, which claims that what is true of the parts is true of the whole, and the related error of unrepresentative generalization that attempts to reason from the composition of the Holocaust murderers to the population as a whole, which must have been equally murderous, if not in fact then in intention. The purpose of this book is neither to indict nor to exculpate, neither to devise spurious logical traps to ensnare every German of murderous Judeophobia nor to devise escape hatches to insulate the Germans from accepting moral responsibility. The German people as a whole did not desire the annihilation of the Jews, nor were all of them indoctrinated enough into supporting the Holocaust. It will be found that the veil of strict secrecy surrounding the Holocaust, a veil that admittedly had holes because information about German atrocities against Jews leaked out early, justifies our thesis that the Nazis had grave doubts that their genocidal project would be accepted by the German people. That more people knew about the Final Solution than was previously assumed or that German institutions were directly or indirectly implicated does not invalidate the fact that the Nazi leadership believed that the German people would not support such a gigantic murder project.

There remains the fact that the Nazis had established a vast terror machine, that this machine found many willing helpers, and that relatively few Germans openly and decisively worked to undermine and destroy it. All too many Germans lent a willing hand to mass murder. The key question in this study is why this happened. What went on in the thinking of the mass murderers, especially the architect of genocide — Adolf Hitler? Were these men, Hitler included, mentally deranged or did they suffer from delusional thinking in only this or related areas? My contention, which is not designed to clear the German people, of responsibility, is essentially "no Hitler, no Holocaust."[5] Hitler was the undisputed dictator of the German people and he made a unilateral decision to annihilate the Jews of Europe. There can be no dispute on this question; the only question still remaining, to which historians have given varying answers, is when Hitler gave the order to annihilate the Jews. Some would argue that he harbored annihilatory intentions all along; others that he ordered the mass murder of the Jews only after he believed that the war was lost, so that the act of annihilation symbolized, in his twisted mind, a final act of racial redemption out of which the seeds of future German greatness could germinate.

Hitler may have been the devil incarnate, but the German people gave him unconditional support to the very end. How do we explain why "decent," civilized, and well-educated German officials cooperated with a murderous regime? Our focus in this discussion will rest on anthropological or cultural traits exhibited by the members of the German people, specifically on such cultural traits as authoritarianism, extreme ethnocentrism, and preference for militarism, and certain psychological habits of extreme rigidity, arrogance, and compulsive orderliness. These cultural traits, in turn, are linked to certain psychological traits that characterized not only the fanatical Nazi leaders and the institutions they created (Gestapo, SS, SD, etc.) but also a substantial number of ordinary Germans who shared these traits to some degree and allowed themselves to be deluded by aberrant thinking.

Most disturbingly, how can it be explained that many killers performed their duties with a good conscience? Our focus here will be on certain defense mechanisms (dehumanization, splitting, projection, numbing, derealization), on distorted ideological thinking, and on sheer sadism. The collective act of mass murder, it will be shown, conforms to a certain pattern of human behavior that has recurred throughout history, a pattern that has also, in part, been replicated in various psychological experiments. There is, indeed, a logic to inhumanity in terms of its motivation, content, and structure.[6] All humans are potential killers; we kill each other individually and we organize mass killings among each other. War is the highest organization of human killing. The Holocaust was also a war, but a war of a unique sort because the enemy was a noncombatant, which defied traditional military thinking. Yet, to Hitler the Jews were combatants of a particularly malignant and destructive nature. It is for this reason that he saw himself waging two simultaneous wars — one a conventional military war and the other a racial war, with the latter being as important as the former. It therefore follows that, without World War II, which Hitler initiated, there would have been no Holocaust. The peculiar mentality that could have envisioned and launched such an apocalyptic war, the aberrant personalities which were needed to carry it out, the psychological and institutional mechanisms that were required to indoctrinate, entrap, taint, and justify mass murder — all these require detailed explanation if this event is to be even remotely understood.

Finally, every Holocaust historian is confronted with the question concerning the "uniqueness" of the event. Was the Holocaust sui generis, without parallel in history, or was it merely the epitome of previous genocidal destructions in human history? Moreover, are these two positions — one claiming uniqueness and the other asserting recurrency — mutually exclusive? Isaac Deutscher spoke for uniqueness when he asserted:

> For the historian who attempts to understand the Holocaust of the Jews, the most important obstacle is the absolute unique character of this catastrophe. It is not only a matter of time and of historical perspective. I doubt that in a thousand years people will better understand Hitler, Auschwitz, Majdanek and Treblinka than we do today. Will they have a better historical perspective? It may be, on the contrary, that posterity will understand all that even less than we do.[7]

The opposite position has been advanced by Ernst Nolte in his controversial position that the deeds of Nazism, including the Holocaust, must be seen in relation to other totalitarian systems that engaged in similar genocidal activities. Nolte argued that by labeling the Holocaust as absolutely unique and as the highest perfection of evil, historians will forever be condemned to treat this event as absolutely singular, which runs against the conventional historical credo that every event exists in time and place and reflects recurring human characteristics rather than singular German, Jewish, Chinese, or Indian qualities.[8] One unstated but often assumed corollary of the thesis that the Holocaust was unique in history is the assertion that it must have been caused by something unique in the German character. For some recent historians the thesis of singularity entails the thesis of German singularity, so that those who believe in this explanatory theory must find a quality or set of qualities that only the Germans and no other people exhibited. The Holocaust for such historians thus establishes the existence of original sin in only the German group.

This book attempts to avoid both extremes by arguing that the Holocaust was indeed unique in its genocidal scope and intensity, but that it must also be accepted as a historical manifestation of *human evil* that existed in the past and is therefore likely to repeat itself in the future. That it was perpetrated by the Germans requires an analysis of the specific German conditions that made it possible, but it would be too comforting for those of us who are not German to suppose that these conditions were inherently German. Related genocidal deeds over the course of human history belie this thesis of a peculiar German disease. It is more likely that the Germans of that time were a compulsively obedient and orderly people with a genius for collective organization who allowed their murderous leaders to implicate and even motivate many of them into a collective project of ethnic discrimination, exclusion, and annihilation that showed unmistakable touches of German thoroughness so lethal that it dwarfed all previous genocides.

In explaining and describing the events that led to the Holocaust it is important at the outset to state one's intellectual and moral presuppositions. The book takes its point of moral departure from the values of the eighteenth-century Enlightenment, which are taken to be a belief in reason, freedom, human dignity, toleration, government by consent of the governed, and the pursuit of truth through the application of scientific humanism. At the same time, on both Christian and Kantian grounds it must also be asserted that "from such crooked wood as man is made of nothing perfectly straight can be built."[9] Five thousand years of recorded history demonstrate that humans are anything but good, let alone perfectible, a truth well-known to most eighteenth-century thinkers. If properly indoctrinated, bribed, and corrupted, the majority of human beings will lend a willing hand to almost any crime, even genocide. Evil is a reality in history; it is neither a part of our primitive heritage nor is it socially conditioned. Evil is rather a moral flaw that arises out of twisted instincts and perverted desires: "it squats in the deepest part of our conscience, exuding hatred of God and love of death. Deadly sin lies in associating ourselves with this nothingness."[10]

Underlying the narrative are also several explanatory assumptions and strategies. The first is that there is a correlation between rhetoric and action, between what a person believes and what that person does. Adolf Hitler and his henchmen were true believers, and among the things they believed was that Jews were a mortal danger to Germany and therefore had to be expelled and exterminated. What Hitler said about his "granite foundation" of faith, especially his Jew-hatred, he sincerely believed and acted upon. Second, there can be absolutely no doubt that Hitler and his henchmen were murderous Jew-haters. Third, we assume that the Nazi leadership was deviant and inherently manipulative. The Führer set the tone with a management style that was at once manipulative and distrustful: "I only tell somebody just as much as he needs to know"; and, worthy of the most scheming criminal, he once said that "it is an old maxim of life: whatever one can discuss orally one should not write down."[11] It follows, therefore, that in judging the veracity or truthfulness of Hitler and his intimate circle one should always err on the side of extreme caution since one is dealing with psychopathic liars. Moreover, since deceit was institutionalized in Nazi Germany, extreme caution must be exercised when we examine "official" Nazi documents. Documentation, of course, is the flywheel of historical reconstruction, but preference for official or governmental documentation can be a big snare. The Holocaust was perpetrated by a criminal regime whose official sources are to be distrusted *on principle* because they are polluted by lies and all the other thought disorders common to the criminal mind — omissions, circumlocutions, exaggerations, concealments, euphemisms, etc. It follows that a wider and less tainted net of information, including diaries, autobiographies, literary, pictorial, journalistic, and a host of other interdisciplinary sources must be cast over this complex and painful event.

Although the following approach is interdisciplinary in the broadest sense, using concepts and principles derived from psychology, sociology, literature, philosophy, and history, its emphasis is always on human choices and human actions rather than on abstractions that frequently tend to become reifications. It is true that while we see or experience particulars, we usually think in universals. This is the price we have to pay for explaining events and assigning a meaning or purpose to them. The act of reconstructing a complex historical event requires a host of explanatory principles, but these aids to understanding sometimes become ends in themselves, driving the narrative and enshrouding it in a cloud of abstractions. The Holocaust should not be dissolved into an abstraction of either a linguistic or statistical nature. Abstractions are not responsible, but humans are. Victims, perpetrators, and bystanders were not embodiments of social, religious, economic, or psychological categories; they were human beings who made choices and decisions, active or passive, that made them victims, perpetrators, heroes, collaborators, or bystanders. Concepts are aids for understanding reality, which they represent but do not reproduce. It is hoped that despite the use of many abstract terms the human element always takes center stage in the following account, for it is only in this way that the Holocaust can attain significant meaning in our collective memory.

Chapter 1

The Rise of Judeophobia:
The Evolution of an Obsession

Ideological Delusion and Fanatical Hatred

On September 1, 1939, Adolf Hitler launched two world wars simultaneously — a conventional military war against Poland and its western allies and a biological-racial war directed primarily against the Jews of Europe. It was the second war that would lead to the greatest crime in modern history, a crime without parallel because it involved the assembly-line annihilation of over six million people by a modern industrial state. Never before in history had a whole group of people been singled out for extermination because its members — men, women, and children — were officially judged to be subhuman, carriers of deadly social bacilli, and in league with Germany's enemies to destroy the German people.

How do we explain this monstrous crime? Who was responsible and how did the murderers justify the deed to themselves, the German people, and the world? Confronted with the sheer magnitude and singularity of this crime, some historians have wondered whether this event can be explained at all. Jean-François Lyotard, for example, posed the question: "how do we measure such an earthquake which has destroyed all instruments of measurement?"[1] He seems to be implying, as Nietzsche's madman did in his anguished cry about the Death of God, that the Holocaust was the death of meaning, the destruction of all moral connections by which we have unchained this earth from god and plunged the human race into a dark abyss. In this sense, the Holocaust was both a historical and an ontological tragedy because it not only killed six million innocent people but also because it shattered ancient moral taboos and deconstructed the western belief in the existence of normative laws of reason, the possibility of discovering objective truths, and, by extension, the attainment of a better world.

If the Holocaust was essentially a monumental eruption of irrationality, can we ever hope to explain it in rational terms? In other words, is it true, as one Holocaust survivor has confessed, that this crime was not just an inversion of values, in which case it would be intelligible in rational terms, but an "amorality beyond all categories of evil"?[2] This would certainly be true if our categories of evil were insufficient to account for its reality or if our methods of explanation were too narrow to enable us to understand the nature of the irrational. The perpetration of the Holocaust was surely not "amoral" but "immoral" because it was committed by human beings who planned and justified it. The Holocaust was a moral failure of tragic proportion in the German leadership and in many ordinary Germans, a failure that was quite extensive because it involved, besides a persistent prejudice against Jews, a collective failure on the political and social level to protect civilized values against the onslaught of barbarism.

In a discussion of the Holocaust it is not appropriate to introduce categories of "amorality" because the deed was perpetrated by human beings who knew exactly what they were doing and why. Their actions are therefore subject to moral criteria of right and wrong as understood by any of the major moral traditions of the human race. By no standard of human morality that has passed the test of time could it be said that the mass murder of six million innocent people was, in the words of one of its perpetrators, a noble deed that should forever be recorded for posterity on bronze tablets. Odilo Globocnik, who made this immoral judgment, justified his participation in the Holocaust by appealing to an annihilatory racial ideology that was, in turn, based on delusionary thinking patterns peculiar to himself, the hard-core Nazi mentality, and, tragically, a large number of Germans who had assimilated anti-Jewish prejudices as social norms.[3]

Within this delusional or chimerical pattern of thinking that for the Nazis amounted to a passionate faith, there was, of course, a certain "logic" that inspired and justified acts of mass murder; but since it is a logic of delusion without a rational foundation in reality, it cannot be allowed to function as normative and binding for all human actions. The deconstructionist logic that today seeks to undermine the western belief in the existence of a knowable and objective world, dissolving every moral judgment into mere assertions of subjective perception, must itself be ranked among the dangerous delusions of our chaotic world.

The Nazis were only the latest in a long line of people who have been gripped by delusions of the most destructive kind. In the year 1096, before the crusaders embarked on their first holy war, some of the more zealous crusaders, gripped by a special kind of Jew-hatred that sprang from their own Christian fears and doubts, descended on various Jewish communities in northern France and Germany and indiscriminately massacred thousands.[4] They justified this because the Jews, they claimed, had murdered Christ, had not recognized the errors of their ways by converting to Christianity, and had stubbornly persisted in their unholy ways: "behold the time has come to avenge him who was crucified, whom their ancestors slew. Now let not a remnant or a residue escape;

even an infant or a suckling in the cradle."[5] Contemporary documents even indicate that killing Jews was seen as a worthy Christian act because "anyone who kills a single Jew will have all his sins absolved."[6] Jews who had lived for years in peace with their Christian neighbors were betrayed, abandoned, and turned over to murderous fanatics who acted out their ideological zeal in addition to their sadistic predilections. In the face of such intense feelings, normal restraints that were ordinarily imposed by worldly or ecclesiastical authorities completely collapsed; in fact, the authorities and behind them the ordinary burghers or peasants became active participants in mass murder. The violence was ideologically grounded, and the only reason that it was not even more lethal was that Jew-hatred was just gathering force and was at this point a specific expression of the crusading message of Pope Urban II.[7] As Salo W. Baron has pointed out, however, the year 1096 was a real turning point in the development of this growing delusion:

> The trail of blood and smoldering ruins left behind in the Jewish communities from France to Palestine, ... for the first time brought home to the Jewish people, its foes and friends, the utter instability of the Jewish position in the western world. ... From the First Crusade on, anti-Jewish persecutions exercised a dangerously contagious appeal, which in periods of great emotional stress degenerated into mass psychosis transcending national boundaries.[8]

Another mass psychosis that transcended national boundaries was witchcraft. In studying episodes of anti-Jewish rages or witchcraft manias, we can already catch a glimpse of the various elements that would also compose the theory and practice of National Socialism in Germany. In the case of witchcraft, those who were gripped by this delusion believed that some human beings were in league with the devil to overthrow God and his worldly government. This belief, in turn, was sanctioned by appeal to the Bible, especially the passage in Exodus (22:18) which stated that one should not "suffer a witch to live." If the Bible is the literal word of God and he commands the believers to kill witches, then it follows that a good Christian must kill witches. The belief created its own reality in the form of entirely innocent people who were identified, tortured, and killed as witches. By way of intellectual delusion a chimerical world became flesh and blood; and its fabricators embellished this world in some extraordinary terms. It was in this way, for example, that books like the *Hammer against Witches* (*Malleus Maleficarum*, 1486), a convenient reference guide to witch detection, came into being — a handbook that contained dreadful sexist assumptions that witches are likely to be on average female because "they were weaker, more stupid, superstitious, and sensual."[9] It was in this way, too, that institutions like the Inquisition came into being, institutions that monitored heresy and inflicted untold cruelties on totally innocent people. At its height in the later Middle Ages, witch-hunting was the scourge of Europe; it killed "hundreds of thousands of men and women, terrorized millions, defiled the minds of the best thinkers for centuries, and left a hideous blot on the record of christian society."[10]

Nazi beliefs about Jews represented a twentieth-century reversion to witchcraft because it shared similar delusional ideas and patterns of behavior; its primary object, to be sure, was not literally the stereotypical witch that obsessed people in the sixteenth century but the "witchified" Jew who became the centerpiece of Nazi diabolism. As Norman Cohn put it, the energy to exterminate the Jews sprang from a "quasi-demonological superstition" rather than from economics or political motives of the perpetrators.[11] It appears that many Germans, particularly those who had been indoctrinated by Nazi institutions such as the party, the Hitler Youth, the SA, or the SS, received extensive immersion in diabolist thinking reminiscent of the witchcraft craze of early modern times. Some Germans confessed this quite openly as soon as the obsession had dissipated after World War II, notably the philosopher Karl Jaspers when he said that

> during the past twelve years something has happened to us that seems like the remolding of our entire being. To put it in the form of an image: Devils have been raining blows upon us and have swept us away, together with themselves, into a chaos which has robbed us of sight and hearing.... We have experienced something like the witchcraft madness of the later Middle Ages.[12]

The source of the ideological motivation that led to the Holocaust must be located in human delusion and its behavioral corollaries — fear, paranoia, projection, scapegoating, and aggression. If seen in this light, the Holocaust forces us to reinstate an archaic truth about ourselves that we seem to have repressed in modern times — namely, that humans are, in part, inherently prone to mass delusions and will cling to them with stubborn tenacity despite evidence to the contrary. Recurring episodes of mass delusional behavior also seem to prove that the majority of humans, provided that they are indoctrinated by their culture with unrealistic fantasies and dangerous illusions, will lend a willing hand to almost any grotesque activity, including mass murder. This is especially true when a malignantly destructive belief has been enshrouded in the form of religious or secular beliefs and given broad institutional support. Spinoza once wrote that of all the hatreds "none is more deep and tenacious than that which springs from extreme devoutness or piety, and is itself cherished as pious."[13] Ironically, it should be of more than passing interest, that Spinoza was discussing Jewish hatred toward other nations, which, he argued, resulted in hatred against the Jews that was just as intense. Enlarging by analogy on Lord Acton's famous dictum about power corrupting and absolute power corrupting absolutely, it could also be said that the hatred that springs from faith corrupts and the hatred that springs from absolute faith corrupts absolutely. If faith is the moral equivalent of power, the greatest corruption of human fraternity may be said to occur when two faith systems, each claiming to be "chosen by God," clash in absolute and implacable hostility, as they have throughout the last two thousand years.

Arno J. Mayer has drawn attention to the recurring spiritual upheavals of the past, especially the crusades and the religious wars of the period extending from 1550 to 1648, arguing that the Holocaust was the outcome of a second Thirty Years War, a more gruesome and destructive repetition of earlier genocides.[14] This argument, though it seems to diminish the singularity of the Holocaust to some degree, has merit in that it correctly diagnoses as a primary cause of genocide the fanatical spiritual zeal that motivated the genocidal perpetrators on all sides. Mayer is also correct in pointing out that the cultural energy invested by Europeans in various holy wars such as the crusades, the subjugation of infidels in the new world, or the wars of religious annihilation during the age of the Reformation (1517–1648) did not diminish with the end of the Wars of Religion (1648), but was reactivated or merely redirected in a different form after a short lull in the eighteenth century. In fact, one could argue that the energy unleashed by misplaced faith was not only redirected but secularized, attaching itself during the past two centuries to such ideologies as socialism, communism, or fascism. In the past fifty years, we recall, the communist east and the democratic west have waged an ideological hot and cold war that involved on both sides the total mobilization of human and natural resources for the expressed purpose of converting hearts and minds or, alternatively, destroying their other (evil) side. During this conflict we have also witnessed the recrudescence of religious patterns of consciousness, though now grafted onto secular causes and secular forms of salvation.

It appears that the cultural energy invested in spiritual or ideological conflicts always has the potential of generating mass delusions that quickly turn into mass aggression.[15] From time to time whole communities have been seized by unusual types of irrational thinking. In the worst of times, when everything seems to conspire against a given group, a collective regression to prelogical or mythical forms of consciousness takes place. Events are no longer seen as natural occurrences, subject to the normal process of cause and effect, but as manifestations of hidden and capricious forces that are allegedly active *behind* the chaotic world in which the disoriented community perceives itself adrift and rapidly sinking. When a whole community or a significant number of its members sees itself threatened, either by real or by imaginary enemies, a repertoire of previously dormant thought patterns appears to be triggered and subsequently permeates the thinking of the whole group in such a way that ordinary, normal, and intelligent people are not only ready to believe the most outlandish claims but also willing to act upon them.

The human record, as historians well know, is embarrassingly full of such irrational eruptions — from belief in demons and witches, to redemptionist theologies or ideologies. It is a serious mistake to assume, however, that such irrational patterns of consciousness operate only in preliterate or preindustrial societies; on the contrary, they could be said to have been most intense and destructive in the twentieth century.

We still do not know enough about the human mind to be able to identify the psychological or physiological processes by which irrational thought patterns are activated. All we know is that the mind has the creative capacity to imagine a thousand different worlds and to conceptualize them in strikingly different ways. Our thought patterns and the symbolic form in which we articulate them approximate but do not embody the reality they are intended to encapsulate. At the same time, however, we have discovered through painful experiences that the rational organization of consciousness enables us to gain a much better understanding of and a more effective adjustment to the real world.

The organization of consciousness is to a large extent a symbolic or cultural process, but it is also shaped by irrational fears, paranoid delusions, and unbridled emotions. Just as individuals deemed to be ordinary, sane, and decent can often slip into irrational modes of thinking, the same is true of whole communities. The structure of consciousness is never wholly rational, and under the impact of "mind-bending" forces it can be transformed, partially or wholly, into a mythical or chimerical type of consciousness with a radically different perception of reality.

Philosophers and psychologists have not always paid sufficient attention to such irrational types of consciousness because they have been interested, for the most part, in the logic rather than the psychology of consciousness. The emphasis in our western tradition has been on the logic rather than the psychology of knowing — on rationality rather than irrationality. Since Aristotle the western world has invested most of its cultural energies into the development of rationality, and the rewards we have reaped from this investment have been to a large extent equivalent to our mastery of the physical world and exploiting it to our material benefit. On the other hand, that the evolution of rationality is linked organically to selfishness and the irrational is not generally admitted, nor is it commonly understood that there is a logic to the irrational with its attendant symbolic representations.

In order to forestall several objections commonly raised against explanations that try to account for the irrational by taking recourse to psychology, sociology, or anthropology — in short, multifaceted explanations — it is necessary to remember the extent of evil and suffering that humans, individually or in groups, have perpetrated in history. Hegel was surely right when he called history a slaughter bench on which the happiness of people and nations has been sacrificed.[16] Five thousand years of history and well over fifteen thousand wars attest to the reality of radical evil in history. It therefore follows that understanding evil requires more than its description, which is historical, but also its analysis and its meaning, which is philosophical, sociological, or psychological.

Knowledge of causes, by whatever means, does not always entail understanding of their consequences, nor does it excuse the behavior of those who have caused great suffering. In the end, most human evils are the result of conscious choice, which is itself based on a variety of motives ranging from gross selfishness, craving for domination, delight in cruelty, belief in spiritual absolutes, to perverted idealism or sheer delusion. Unfortunately, it is also the cunning of evil that it sometimes springs from apparently noble intentions. There is no transparency in the human as there seems to be in the animal world; we are rarely what we appear to be and we combine at any given time a great many life-enhancing qualities with a disconcerting number of life-denying ones. In order to reinforce the former against the destructive consequences of the latter, the human race has invented civilization, which in its ideal form entails the institutionalization of decency, cooperation, and social order, but just as individuals become deluded, corrupted, or destructive, the same is true for the order of civilization itself. The Holocaust was the ultimate degeneration of German civilization; and in order to understand this corruption, it is necessary to comprehend, to the best of our abilities, the thinking patterns of its members, to elucidate why a sizeable number of Germans who subscribed to the Nazi mentality accepted irrational ideas and how they organized their ideas into a delusional system of thought that compelled them to view the Jews as subhuman and demonic and for that reason to be exterminated as a whole race.

Belief in such a delusional system, including its component elements, is not uniquely German but has recurred, as previously mentioned, throughout human history. Before discussing its peculiar Nazi dynamic in the following chapter, a few general observations about its characteristics, based on various historical manifestations, are in order.

A social disaster that strikes any community with a great destructive force is bound to evoke panic responses and great mental anguish. The resiliency of the response in coping with the impact of the crisis depends upon the institutional stability of the community that experiences it. All societies are perched on a volcano because they are always exposed to potentially wrenching changes from both within and without, and the fabric of their institutions is rarely so strong that they can withstand sustained disasters and hardships. Throughout history human communities have experienced frequent traumas, and the response to some of them has been in the form of self-defeating coping mechanisms that exacerbated rather than diminished the problem.

Whenever people are struck by an apparently incomprehensible disaster, they almost instinctively tend to "give in" to their emotions. If the crisis persists, their normal thinking patterns will probably be distorted by these traumatic experiences. Idiographic studies, conducted by social psychologists, have shown how individuals and entire communities have reacted to crisis situations. It has been demonstrated, for example, that the members of a community are held together not only by common institutions or traditions, but also by a characteristic organization of public consciousness. The outer structure is a measure of its mental interior. In the history of most human communities in the past the content of this mental interior, the psychic substratum, was strongly permeated by spiritual, mythic, and imaginative themes and processes. It should therefore not be surprising that the intellectual responses to crises or disasters, though usually accompanied by common sense and survival instincts, were also cast in a frame of meaning that drew upon the common psychic substratum consisting of myths, legends, heroic epics, and religious beliefs. This is why in the consciousness of many communities in history the key to secular history was always to be found in its sacred history. Events were colored or decoded in and through mythic symbols.

Public reactions to great disasters, past or present, are generally accompanied by irrational patterns of thinking, but sometimes the patterns persist beyond the crisis itself because the community is in denial about the real nature of the crisis, develops willful defense mechanisms to deny the truth, and uses inadequate coping mechanisms in trying to heal the disease. History is full of such examples, some of which have been brilliantly recaptured by Otto Friedrich in his book *The End of the World,* in which he recounts the various reactions to calamities that were so intense that people at the time believed that the end of the world was near. The events in question were the Sack of Rome in 410 c.e., the birth of the Inquisition (1209–44), the Black Death (1347–50), the apocalyptic visions and disasters centering around Thomas Münzer and other Reformation sectarians who wanted to create a "New Jerusalem," the Lisbon Earthquake of 1755, the Russian Revolution of 1905, and Auschwitz. We might add to this list the witchcraft mania, the crusades, and medieval millenarian heresies. It is important to realize however, that societies are afflicted by great stresses that are not necessarily in the form of obvious catastrophes such as a virulent plague, a devastating famine, earthquake, or war. The trauma may also have been caused by times of wrenching social changes during which old cultural traditions dissolved, but new ones had not taken shape to replace them.

In most of these crises the first reaction seems to be intellectual dissociation; there is a feeling that the world is out of joint or even coming to an end. Events of the sort just experienced must have been initiated by hidden forces of great power and malignity. In religious communities such events give rise to apocalyptical anxieties that God is punishing the community, or alternatively, that satanic forces are on the loose. It may be that at this point in the disaster syndrome some collective human memory is triggered, setting in motion a number of mythic thought patterns that, in turn, stimulate primordial, fearful, and haunting images.

Since the catastrophe is perceived to be of immense proportion, it is assumed that it could not be the work of ordinary people or knowable physical causes, but must be the work of hidden and as yet unknown forces or perpetrators. At this stage of the disaster syndrome, as James Rhodes referred to the Nazi reaction to defeat in war and the economic collapse that followed, the affected members see themselves as helpless victims, displaying psychological symptoms that are typical of such reactions: they feel violated and raped, wallowing in self-pity and bemoaning their fate. Almost simultaneously, however, they lash out hysterically at presumed perpetrators or, in the religious language of the past, "fleshly malefactors."

In studying such disaster syndromes exhibited by religious communities in the past and the Nazis in our century, James Rhodes has identified several common responses: first, total disorientation, then intense fear of group annihilation, followed by the unmasking of evil-doers, the revelation of the truth, and the triumph of good over evil.[17] The object of fear, at first, may be entirely chimerical in the form of the Great Beast of the Apocalypse, Mephistopheles, or the Great Whore of Babylon. Gradually, however, the chimera takes on flesh and blood in the leering Jew or in other totally innocent people who are presumed to be guilty because they are foreigners, heretics, witches, lepers, and the like. This work of unmasking the guilty often falls to marginal intellectuals or visionaries who claim to possess a special (gnostic) way of knowing that goes far deeper than mere rationality or formal analytical processes. On the grounds of a *better* form of knowing, based on visionary powers, mystic illumination, or psychic insights, these self-proclaimed specialists in salvation begin to pronounce to the community what really ails it and what must be done to heal it. In Nathan Adler's suggestive words, these visionaries respond to the crisis by "becoming drunk with illusions,"[18] bypassing established political and social powers, appealing directly to a gullible multitude, and seeking justification in recited mythologies. Adler writes that "an apocalyptic ethos of decline, destruction, and renewal is central to their orientation, and they either respond with zeal or hyperactivity or surrender as passive spectators; they may become arrogant supermen and scornful self-actualizers or populists rediscovering the people."[19]

A host of such types, including religious visionaries (Joachim of Fiore, John Wycliff, Peter Waldo, Savonarola, Thomas Münzer) and their secularized counterparts (Robespierre, Marx, Danilewski, Jahn, Langbehn, Lagarde, Mussolini, Rosenberg, Hitler) have claimed special revelations, telling their followers that they are not vanquished but a chosen people singled out by God (or history) to smite their tormentors. The encounter with the tormentor, whether Satan, Jew, nobleman, or capitalist, will be of titanic proportions in coming battles of Armageddon.[20] There is in all this a pervasive feeling of urgency, a sense that the forces of evil have almost gained the upper hand.

From feelings of victimization and despair, the affected community has now moved, by way of certain psychological increments, to a collective focus on the real perpetrators and how they might be defeated. The scales, so to speak, have fallen from the victim's eyes, and the annihilation anxiety, though still strong, has been significantly diminished. With the malefactors unmasked and the gospel of liberation proclaimed, the ontological battle can now begin. If radical evil has been exposed to be at the root of things, squatting like a Jewish "maggot in a rotting corpse," as Hitler put it, then radical measures are needed to remove the cancerous abscess. In other words, since the enemy is the incarnation of evil and seeks to exterminate the members of the afflicted community, it follows that the evil must be purged from the community by the most radical procedures. Every paranoid distortion of reality based on extreme fear of annihilation is bound to entail annihilatory tactics as the only therapeutic release from suffering.

In the coming battle between the forces of good and the forces of evil, as envisioned by this sort of thinking, the future of the world will be decided once and for all. It is characteristic of such a faith that its effectiveness rests on projecting a hopeful, utopian future. As Eric Hoffer put it, "no faith is potent unless it is also a faith in the future; unless it has a millennial component."[21] With the destruction of evil a new age will dawn in the form of a New Jerusalem, a Workers' Paradise, a Thousand-Year Reich. The intellectual formulations of such beliefs display a definite and recognizable structure that is generally couched in millennial terms — that is, language by which social conflicts are endowed with transcendental significance.[22] As Norman Cohn has shown, this type of belief structure motivated the many apocalyptical movements of the Middle Ages, such as the crusades, the Brothers and Sisters of the Free Spirit, the theology of Joachim of Fiore, the Taborites, and the Anabaptists of the Reformation.[23] We might add that both the structure and the eschatological message embedded in such movements was later secularized in various philosophies of history (Condorcet, Comte, Hegel, Marx) and in redemptionist political ideologies on both the left (Marx, Lenin) and the right (Moeller van den Bruck, Rosenberg, Hitler).

The roots of the Nazi system of hate must be located in the fringe movements of popular delusion, in delusional (chimerical) systems of ideas that did not originate in the minds of well-known thinkers but in the minds of alienated and often marginal individuals who sometimes rose out of obscurity in times of extreme change, galvanized a large following, and proclaimed a religious or pseudoreligious message in which intense feelings of hate and hope were intermingled. It was out of a demimonde of delusionary ideas, "churned out by crooks and half-educated fanatics for the benefit of the ignorant and superstitious,"[24] that the myth of the Jewish world conspiracy, a central myth in Nazi ideology, emerged in the postwar period. The Nazi ideology and its basic mentality were an outgrowth of the crisis of consciousness produced by the First World War; Jew-hatred did not cause it but became a significant element in it because the stereotypical Jew was blamed for the evils that allegedly had ruined the German people. That the Nazis were able to persuade a significant number of Germans that this was true was due to a long-standing tradition of Judeophobia in European culture in general and German culture in particular.

Varieties of Jew Hatred: The Western Perspective

History records no other people like the Jews. Admired and scorned, feared and persecuted, despised and demonized, they have been the obsession of a long succession of people during the last three thousand years. The Pharaohs enslaved them in Egypt, the Assyrians grabbed their northern kingdom (Israel), Nebuchadnezzar of Babylonia destroyed the rest of their kingdom (Judah) and carted off ten thousand valuable Jewish captives into "Babylonian Exile," the Greeks and Persians oppressed and despised them, the Romans deprived them of their homeland in Palestine and dispersed them all over the ancient world, Muslim fanatics periodically descended upon them, Christian crusaders slaughtered thousands of them before embarking on their holy mission, the Inquisition expelled them from Iberia, Poles and Russians viciously massacred them in genocidal pogroms, and the Germans consummated this long harvest of hate by annihilating six million of them in the Holocaust. Yet, throughout this three-thousand-year ordeal, the Jews have clung to their religious beliefs and ethnic practices. In Hugh Trevor-Roper's suggestive phrase, the Jews are the "indigestible people,"[25] the greatest nonconformists in history; for by every sociological law they should have disappeared from the stage of history a long time ago, as did all ethnic groups before them who were uprooted from their native land or, alternately, were conquered and assimilated by stronger groups.

This historical fate did not happen to the Jews because they had evolved a unique monotheistic belief in one God who revealed himself to them and made a pact by which he designated them his chosen people. Their sacred scriptures, the Hebrew Bible (Old Testament), later elaborated during the course of Jewish suffering in a series of books of rabbinical commentaries, precepts, glosses, and instructions called the Talmud, became the foundation of their unique sense of religious and ethnic identity. They clung to their 613 commandments and prohibitions with stubborn tenacity and institutionalized them in customs, rituals, and religious holidays, thereby managing to preserve their historical existence without existing as a unified political people. They became a nation within the nations, strongly adhering to their sacred laws and ancestral customs, surviving but also suffering terribly at the hands of people to whom their beliefs sounded strange and offensive. To many other powerful people of the ancient world, who also had a strong sense of mission like the Egyptians, Greeks, Persians, or Romans, it was especially galling to learn that the Jews regarded themselves as the chosen people of God, for this seemed to imply that if only the Jews were chosen, all the other people were unchosen and therefore inferior.

The Jews, for the most part, avoided suggesting such implications. They insisted that their religion was a universal one, open to all who wanted to join. Moreover, they pointed out that their sense of being chosen meant having a religious and moral duty to fulfill the standards that God expected them to meet and to be a shining moral beacon to the rest of the world. Whether it was due to ethnic or religious prejudices on both sides, barriers between the Jews and their hosts would become, save for a few exceptions and accommodations, a permanent condition of their cultural relationship. The fact that Jewish religion and culture significantly enriched both Christian and Islamic civilization and that Jewish commercial activities brought prosperity to even the remotest village in Poland or Russia did not lead to the removal of such barriers. Differences separate, and perceived mutually exclusive differences tend to separate greatly. At a time in history when consciousness of tribal differences (tribalism) was intense, the Jewish response of exclusivity, coming as it did from a position of political weakness, invited endless mistrust and persecution. We know a great deal about the suffering the Jews were exposed to at the hands of their tormentors in history; what is less frequently examined is the effect such persecutory treatment had on their own inner development — that is, their ability or rather inability to rediscover a homeland and to forge a sense of potential unity beyond the fragmented and insulated world dominated by rabbinical rule and thought. This was especially true after the Jews were forced by the Persians and then by the Romans to live outside their homeland in Palestine, to be scattered throughout foreign lands, particularly after their unsuccessful revolt against the Romans (66–70 C.E.). This is the meaning of the word "diaspora," from the Greek "a scattering" of Jews outside their homeland. Over time the word "diaspora" would also take on additional meanings as implying a way of life induced by being "homeless" or being an "outsider" in foreign communities with attendant problems of losing one's own identity and culture.

They became a nation without a nation, a loose consensus of different communities dwelling within other nations. Jewish historical development took a fateful course when the majority of the Jews, especially those who later lived in western and eastern Europe, followed the religious and ritualistic practices of the Jewish community of Babylon (Mesopotamia) rather than that of the other powerful Jewish community of Alexandria. The Alexandrian approach, later practiced in Moorish Spain and by modern reform Judaism, followed Philo of Alexandria, a contemporary of Christ, who tried to bridge the gap of cultural differences by showing that there was a close affinity between Hebraic and Greek (Platonic) wisdom, which represented a noble effort not only of interpreting Jewish faith to the world but forging a cultural dialogue that would enable Jew and gentile to live together rather than apart from each other. By contrast, the rabbinic approach, which would become the predominant one for most Jews until the nineteenth century, demanded the continuation of the strictest Pharisaical Judaism; its aim, expounded at length by the rabbinical writers of the Talmud, was to insulate and therefore to isolate the Jewish community from the outside world, tying believers so firmly to a daily routine of scriptural rules and practices that they would end up living in a world within a world, limiting their conduct with the outside world to purely economic relations.

Accepting such a restrictive life of religious and cultural isolation in order to avoid external pressures to conform or assimilate may have enabled Jewish communities to survive as distinct religious units, but it also condemned its members to a somewhat fossilized cultural existence. Isolation in any case did not mean independence because Jews still lived within a larger Christian community which did its best to oppress them. An important consequence of this separateness within a context of social and political inferiority was psychological. In a world where Jews were permanent and weaker aliens their identity was fixed by the people who controlled them, so that they became the invention of the society that produced them. Having no autonomous power to define themselves, they were forced to behave according to the negative stereotype set over them by the society that dominated them. In an ironic sort of way, it could be said that the Jews have indeed been chosen by the people of the world as the chosen people — that is to say, they have been unfairly singled out for special treatment because their enemies believed that their sense of being chosen meant to be superior rather than religiously different in the eyes of their God.

As previously mentioned, Judeophobia has had a long history because the Jews survived the destruction of their kingdom and managed to perpetuate their religious and social traditions while living in exile in the communities of other people. Inevitably, the existence of an alien minority within the various ancient states aroused much hostility, giving rise, in turn, to an evolving tradition of Judeophobia to which each people added its own distinct contribution, while at the same time drawing upon already existing hatreds. A great deal of scholarly work has been expended on defining the nature of this peculiar hatred and its various dimensions: the source of this peculiar hatred, its latent and manifest function in terms of a society's preoccupation with it, and its intensity at any given place and time. The term used to describe Jew-hatred, "anti-Semitism," has itself come under intense scrutiny because of its ambiguous nature. The term was actually not coined until 1879, when Wilhelm Marr, a second-rate German journalist and founder of the League of Anti-Semites (Antisemiten Liga), used the word as a political slogan that was designed to unite as many Germans as possible behind a nonpartisan movement to fight the detrimental influence allegedly exerted on German society by organized Jewry.

Although a standard scholarly term today, "anti-Semitism" is ambiguous enough on several grounds to make us use it sparingly and cautiously because it stems from the counterfeit coinage of the oppressor who claims in the prefix "anti-" simply to be opposed to "semite," an equally ambiguous term because it can refer to people who are Arabic, Aramaic, Babylonian, Assyrian, and Ethiopian, as well as Jewish. Weaned on racist beliefs, Wilhelm Marr and the generation that embraced this ideology confused linguistic and ethnic terminology — as evidenced by their fondness for contrasting the terms "Aryan" and "Semitic" — and they committed the primary fallacy common to all racists, namely, the belief that biological inheritance explains and determines cultural differences.[26] Their sleight of hand was to disguise their hatred as reasonable opposition based on scientific considerations.

Any discussion of the Holocaust should be aware of linguistic snares and not allow itself to be dominated by the terminology of its perpetrators. Whenever the context demands it, the terms "Judeophobia," "Jew-hatred," "anti-Judaism," or "anti-Jewish prejudices," rather than "anti-Semitism," will be used; in other words by choosing clinical or more descriptive labels and attaching them to the purveyors of hatred, the onus of responsibility can be shifted where it really belongs, thus removing doubts as to its destructive potential. It is also important to be aware of the fact that we are dealing with an evolving historical hatred that, while exhibiting common features, also expressed itself in different historical terms, depending upon the specific relationship that existed at various points in time between the Jews and their opponents. It would be, for example, totally inappropriate to project Marr's racially tinged terminology back into time and use it as an explanatory device to describe the hostility of Christians toward Jews. In short, Judeophobia has had a long history and its meaning requires, beyond sociological or psychological understanding that tells us what the Jew-hater felt or did also a historical understanding that shows us how the hatred originated and how it evolved over time, changing and adapting itself to new conditions while also retaining its essential hateful character.

In sociological terms, the Jews represented a distinct outgroup, marked by strict adherence to different religious and customary practices, in every community in which they resided. In general human terms, hostility toward any outgroup expresses itself in the form of prejudice, a word that originally came from the Latin *praeiudicium* and meant a judgment based on a series of past decisions considered to be true or binding, as in the legal context of setting a precedent. The legal sense of precedent, in fact, continues to operate in the linguistic usage of the word "prejudice," because it means a prejudgment based on insufficient and distorted evidence that is itself based on certain precedents that have been uncritically accepted over time. Social psychologists have shown that people who prejudge are prone to overgeneralize, to think in stereotypes, and to accept uncritically the beliefs of their tribe (ethnocentrism). A prejudgment, in Gordon Allport's view, becomes a prejudice only if it is not reversible when exposed to new knowledge.[27] Customary habits and beliefs, as is well known, do not change easily, particularly when they have been institutionalized in certain "characteristic codes and beliefs, standards and 'enemies' to suit their own adaptive needs."[28] The more insulated the community, the less likely it will be to change its fundamental categories, except under extreme pressure, self-interest, or exceptional open-mindedness.

Social psychologists have discovered that prejudice is functionally related to both personality development and cognitive expression; they have also identified a "prejudiced personality," an "authoritarian personality," or an "open-and-closed mind," and mapped out the cognitive-linguistic categories by which prejudiced people structure their consciousness and interpret the world accordingly.[29] Despite the discovery that prejudiced people think differently from nonprejudiced or tolerant people, that prejudice is a human as well as a group-centered (ethnic) phenomenon, and that it must be distinguished from merely erroneous generalizations by its irreversibility, it remains a fact that we have no sure way of preventing biased judgments because humans are still divided politically, culturally, racially, and linguistically into thousands of different and opposing groups and also because we do not possess a value-free and apodictic method by which we can assess the truth value of generalizations we make about other groups. All of us are condemned to speak evaluatively from our own point of reference, but at the same time intergroup hostilities have taught us how to recognize, if we are honest, that some judgments we make about other groups are either realistic — that is, in conformity with empirical reality — or prejudiced in the sense of being based on hearsay, stereotypes, self-serving beliefs, or personal animosities. If these judgments are of the latter variety, they can further be broken down into popular-stereotypical, xenophobic, and chimerical and measured socially by their intensity. The expression of anti-Jewish hatred, it will be found, has been most intense in proportion to the organization of that hatred in a delusionary system of thought that has become intractable to change and manifests itself as a major obsession and with great intensity at a certain point in time.

In plotting the trajectory of Judeophobia historically, we can identify several distinct phases: (1) a relatively mild hatred of Jews in ancient times; (2) a gathering momentum with the coming and expansion of Christianity, which condemned the Jews as Christ killers and frustrators of redemption, marked at certain moments by outbreaks of great violence in the crusades or the Inquisition and accompanied by the rise of delusional thinking in various individuals and groups; (3) a short ebb during the Wars of Religion (1540–1648) and the ensuing age of toleration and enlightenment (1650–1815); (4) a new rising tide of

Judeophobia in a potentially destructive form under the impact of nationalism and racism in the nineteenth century; (5) and a final tidal wave, set in motion by World War I and the Nazi movement, which culminated in the Holocaust. From a metahistorical point of view, one could argue that the evolution of Judeophobia conformed to a linear pattern — that is, developed from a starting point (*terminus a quo*) and moved to a final end (*terminus ad quem*) — from popular dislike, prejudice, and hate, to annihilatory rage, while on the other hand one could argue, in a cyclical fashion, that Judeophobia repeats itself in various forms and levels of intensity from age to age and society to society, exhibiting no particular inevitable progression from mild prejudice to murderous genocide. The two philosophical views are not necessarily mutually exclusive because a prejudice that has been hardened into a movement of hate can progress across societies and cultures by feeding upon past hates and accentuating their lethal potential, as the Nazi movement certainly proved. At the same time, the contingency of historical events is such that few movements exhibit the sort of inner necessity whose unfolding can be genetically predicted. A narrative structured to predict the event to be explained by retrodicting the past, assembling unrelated and only remotely similar past events and straining them into a procrustean bed to make them fit the theory, could be particularly tempting in the case of the Holocaust; but for that very reason, as previously mentioned, such a narrative should be resisted because it often results in distorted perceptions and tendentious judgments of the past. The following sketch of Judeophobia is therefore designed simply to illustrate patterns of past Jewish prejudices, without suggesting that, like links in a chain, they inevitably culminated in the Holocaust.

Christians and Jews during the Middle Ages

Although the Jews were deprived of their national autonomy as early as the sixth century before Christ, the people of the ancient world continued to look at the Jews as constituting a "Jewish nation" and possessing a specific national and religious character. As a result, the relation between the Jews and their pagan neighbors was marked by tensions and animosities, rising at various times to a level of genocidal fury. The book of Esther, for example, documents this resentment against the Jewish community in exile, and it features in the figure of Haman the first architect of Jewish genocide in history, a kind of archetypal inquisitor who would later undergo a series of historical incarnations in other Jew haters just like him — Torquemada, Eisenmenger, Marr, Fritsch, Chamberlain, Drumont, Eckart, Rosenberg, Streicher, Himmler, and Hitler. Haman's order to "destroy, to kill and to cause to perish, all Jews, both young and old, little children and women" was luckily averted by the Persian king, who had fallen in love with the beautiful Esther. The king foiled the genocidal plot, hanged the wicked Haman, and allowed the Jews to eliminate their enemies.

Neither the Persians nor the Romans, however, treated the Jews any differently than they did other subject people, illustrating the fact that anti-Jewishness in ancient times did not possess a strong religious and definitely not a racial framework.[30] Intergroup hostility, of course, was sometimes quite high, and many examples from pagan writers could be cited to illustrate the existence of anti-Jewish prejudices. The Egyptian priest and historian Manetho, for example, tried to refute the biblical story of the Exodus and spread the legend that Moses was really a renegade priest who spearheaded a revolt of outcasts, including Jews, blacks, and lepers, aimed at overthrowing the government and replacing it with a wicked alien religion. The legend was subsequently embellished by the Alexandrian Apian and was, suitably trimmed, impressed to do service for Freud in *Moses and Monotheism* (1938). The Greek and Roman intelligentsia frowned on Jewish culture as sterile and superstitious, and from time to time the Jews were denounced for their supposedly barbaric practices. It was said, for example, that the Jews were "strange," that they worshiped asses, that they conducted secret human sacrifices in their temples, or that they engaged in other mysterious activities. Such accusations were quite common, but they were never organized into a coherent anti-Jewish ideology sponsored by the secular or religious branch of any state in ancient times.

It was not until the coming of Christianity that the Jews were automatically singled out not only as a suspect people, as an alien nation, but also as a guilty people — guilty because they had killed Jesus, the Son of God. Jesus, of course, was a Jew, and so were his immediate followers, who were rebellious and heretical Jews. From a small heretical Jewish sect, however, Christianity expanded into a world religion, a feat that was due, in large degree, to one man: Saul of Tarsus, or St. Paul, a Greek-speaking Jew from Tarsus in Asia Minor, who converted to Christianity, served as its greatest missionary, and imposed on it a sophisticated theological framework that probably would have startled its founder. Beginning with St. Paul, two decisive changes in Christianity can be detected: one was the movement's departure from insisting on an exclusive Jewish membership and reaching out to all believers; the other was to shift the blame for Jesus' crucifixion from the Romans to the Jews. Because they were blamed for killing the Son of God, the Jews were increasingly seen by Christians as an accursed people, as is evident in the famous outcry attributed to the Jewish crowd in the New Testament: "His blood be upon us and on our children" (Matt. 27:24ff.).

St. Paul, a Jew himself, was hardly a despiser of his own people, but he obviously believed that Judaism was a superseded religion, and he therefore made strenuous efforts to persuade his fellow Jews to convert to Christianity. In the Epistle to the Romans, we find him repeatedly and urgently pleading with the Jews to convert: "Brethren, my heart's desire and prayer to God for Israel is that they might be saved" (Rom. 10:1); and yet the Jews remained "ignorant of God's righteousness" (Rom. 10:3). Paul even has God saying: "All day long I have stretched forth my hands unto a disobedient and gainsaying people" (Rom. 10:21). The Jews adamantly refused to acknowledge that Jesus was the Messiah, and they stubbornly clung to their erroneous beliefs. This stubbornness of the Jews in refusing to be converted to Christianity, together with their growing belief that they were guilty of killing Christ, infuriated Christians and prompted periodic outbursts of hostility. As Leon Poliakov has argued, "for the organization of Christianity, it was essential that the Jews be a criminally guilty people."[31] Some of the early church fathers fulminated against the Jews, as did Origen when he insisted that "we may thus assert in utter confidence that the Jews will not return to their earlier situation, for they have committed the most abominable of crimes, in forming this conspiracy against the saviour of the human race."[32] Gregory of Nyssa was even more condemnatory, denouncing the Jews as "murderers of the Lord, assassins of the prophets, rebels and detesters of God . . . companions of the devil, race of vipers, informers, calumniators, darkeners of the mind, pharisaic leaven, Sanhedrin of demons, accursed, detested, lapidators, enemies of all that is beautiful."[33] Even the great St. Augustine fired off a broadside against the Jews entitled *Contra Judaeos,* in which he depicted the Jews as a reprobate people who had been superseded by a new chosen people.[34] This notion figured even more prominently in his seminal work, the *The City of God,*[35] which became one of the great milestones of Christian theology with its theme of two cities, the city of God consisting of those who live in the Christian spirit and the city of man consisting of those who live after the flesh (pagans, Jews, unbelievers). It was also St. Augustine who elaborated on a theme of St. Paul's that the conversion of the Jews signaled the end of the world, the implication being that Jewish stubbornness would delay the Second Coming and frustrate the redemptive hopes of Christian believers.[36]

Although one can collect many vile outbursts against the Jews by the early church fathers, one should not forget, as Steven Katz reminds us, that no Jew was persecuted by the church in this formative period.[37] As soon as the state became Christian, however, legal restrictions against Jews began. Starting in the late Roman empire and continuing under Christian rule in the early Middle Ages, many ancient Jewish privileges were suspended, proselytizing was prohibited, rabbinical jurisdiction was curtailed or abolished, sexual relations with Christians were forbidden, and most legal protections were removed. Yet before the First Crusade in 1096, few outbreaks of specific, popular anti-Jewish activities took place. Jewish colonies were established all over Europe, especially within the Carolingian empire, where Jews were very active as merchants, officials, physicians, artisans, and even landowners. At the official level, involving bishops and rabbis, the relationship between Jew and gentile was marked by toleration and sometimes even cordiality. In Muslim countries their treatment was even better because of the closer racial, religious, and cultural resemblance of Jews and Arabs. Jewish traders followed on the heels of the Arab conquerors who were spreading the world of Allah and setting the stage for the expansion of Islamic civilization from the Pyrenees to India and from Morocco to China. It was arguably in Moorish Spain that the Jews found one of the few havens in their long and troubled history, although it would not survive the Christian reconquest of Spain in the fifteenth century.

The decisive shift in the direction of popular Jew-hatred set in, as previously mentioned, with the First Crusade in 1096. Before proceeding on their trip to the holy land to smite the infidel, marauding bands of fanatics massacred about ten thousand innocent Jews in northern France and Germany, igniting the sort of irrational Jew-hatred that would later replicate itself under the impact of various crises that Christians were unable to resolve.[38] What was so unusual about 1096 and subsequent crusades or upheavals in medieval Europe, as Gavin Langmuir has shown, was the "chimerical" nature of the hatred that was showered on the Jews, a hatred that was entirely based on a growing number of delusional beliefs about the Jews and their wicked ways.[39] The authorities, both secular and ecclesiastical, were officially opposed to such outbreaks of popular violence, but their inherent hostility to the Jews caused them to be aloof and ambiguous in a crisis and therefore unable or unwilling to stem the tide of murderous anti-Jewish activity. The papacy vacillated between the view expressed by Gregory I, who had insisted that nonbelievers should be treated kindly and persuaded by clear reasoning "pleasantly presented," a view subsequently enshrined in papal bulls that Jews had a right to live as Jews in Christian societies,[40] and the more strident pronouncements of popes like Innocent III or Lateran councils that declared the Jews as slaves of Christians (Third Lateran Council, 1179) or socially segregated Jews from Christians, forcing them to wear distinct attire and calling them "blasphemers of the Christian name" (Fourth Lateran Council, 1215). Working hand-in-glove, both secular and ecclesiastical authorities prohibited the Jews from owning land, excluded them from the guilds, and restricted them to despised and marginal occupations such as money lending, hawking, and trafficking in second-hand goods. By the time of the Black Death (1347–50), which added the myth of "well poisoning" to a stock of already existing black legends about the evil ways of the Jews, the chimerical nature of the Christian stereotype about the Jew was already in place, so that, in Langmuir's view, Jews were no longer killed as side effects of the crusades but by mobs organized to avenge entirely delusional instances of well poisoning, host profanation, or ritual child murder.[41]

It is important to focus at some greater length on these delusional elements within the evolving system of Judeophobia because some of them were later modernized and transmogrified to serve the Nazi delusion about Jews. There are at least ten such delusions, most of them firmly in place by the end of the Middle Ages:

1. The stubbornness of the Jews

2. The Wandering Jew (Ahasuerus)

3. The Jews in league with the devil

4. The mephitic smell of the Jews

5. Jewish carnality

6. Blood libel and ritual child murder

7. Host desecration

8. A Jewish world conspiracy

9. Well poisoning

10. The unproductive Jewish parasite

The theme that Jews are stubborn, as previously seen, referred to their refusal to convert to what to Christians seemed self-evident truths, notably the belief that Jesus was the Messiah. Their refusal to convert was particularly infuriating to self-righteous Christians because of a widespread belief that the Second Coming presupposed, among other occurrences such as the coming of Elias the Tishbite and the rule of the Antichrist, the conversion of the Jews. In the words of Leon Bloy, "the salvation of all peoples was, by their malice, diabolically suspended."[42] Connected to this myth of Jewish pig-headedness was that of the Wandering Jew, a myth not formally articulated in written form until 1602 but known since ancient times in several variations and perpetuated throughout the Middle Ages.[43] At the heart of this myth is once more the stubbornness and guilt of the Jews, except that it is now embodied in a mythical figure, later called Ahasuerus (or Ahasverus), who was supposedly present on the day they crucified Jesus and mocked him on his way to Golgotha; in return, the redeemer condemned him to wander the face of the earth, forsaken and unhappy, until he returned to usher in the Final Judgment and the end of the world. To the gullible, the myth of the Wandering Jew(s) seemed confirmed by actual empirical evidence because Christians throughout the later Middle Ages witnessed the fact that Jews were hounded from place to place, wandering from city to city without having any settled home in any land. Suitably embellished over many centuries, the myth took on flesh and blood in 1542 when a Lutheran minister, Paulus von Eitzen, encountered a bearded vagrant in a Hamburg church by the name of Ahasverus and judged him to be the Jew who cursed Jesus on Golgotha and was, in turn, cursed by Jesus with the words "go on forever till I return." The tale based on the legendary story and Eitzen's encounter with a man called Ahasuerus was finally published in 1602 as *Kurze Beschreybung und Erzählung von einem Juden mit Namen Ahasverus* (Brief description and tale of a Jew named Ahasverus) and became so popular that it went through nearly fifty editions in just a few years.[44]

By metaphoric extension, the curse of Ahasuerus was, of course, a curse on the whole Jewish race, not only for their stubbornness but also for their demonic nature. In an age in which the devil was a reality to the people who believed in his existence because they believed in the existence of radical evil, the unbeliever or Jew must be in league with him. If Jesus was the Messiah, the only person the Jews could be waiting for was the Antichrist.[45] It was in this way that Christian writers spread the legend that the Jews were the supporters of the Antichrist. During the last days, this Jewish parody of Christ would resurrect the temple and briefly preside over a new Jewish empire before being destroyed by Christ. According to Robert S. Wistrich, the Antichrist myth, contributing to the massacres of the Jews at the time of the crusades, foreshadowed the millenarian thinking that would grip the Germans during the 1930s and that visualized Adolf Hitler as a secular German Christ who came to purge Germany of the real source of evil: the Jews.[46]

The association of the Jews with the devil can already be detected in the New Testament and in the writings of the early church fathers like Gregory of Nyssa or St. John Chrysostom, who portrayed the Jews as embodying Satan's synagogue.[47] One consequence of this diabolizing of the Jew was the projection of fearful and hateful impulses harbored by Christians onto the Jew. In medieval folklore and art the Jew is sometimes depicted as a sow, *Judensau,* and is portrayed as swarthy, hook-nosed, curly headed, and foul-smelling. In various woodcuts we see him sporting a devil's tail and a goatee, riding a billy goat.[48] Jews are seen as sorcerers and magicians, capable of performing a variety of black arts. In a basically illiterate world, these iconographic images had a powerful impact on gullible people whose basic source of information was either the spoken word or the visual arts. In looking at the visual documentation ranging from the Roll of Essex (1277), depicting Aaron as the son of the devil, the sixteenth-century series of prints known as *Juden Badstub* (Jewish bathhouse), depicting the devil assisting Jews in bathhouses, seventeenth-century prints showing the devil attending a synagogue and participating in Jewish ritual, the endless cartoons that portray Jews as hook-nosed, ugly, leering, and contemplating one hideous deed after another, to Philippe Rupprecht's perfection of these libelous arts in the pages of Julius Streicher's *Der Stürmer*—looking, in short, at all this massive accumulated material of visual Jew-hatred, it should not be surprising that the stereotype was accepted by so many people as reality.

If the Jews are disciples of the devil, it would also follow that they must possess certain characteristics associated with him. Since the devil gave off a foul smell, for example, the Jews must also give off a foul smell, a "mephitic odor." In one of the devil's distinct incarnations, he is referred to as Mephistopheles. Although not medieval, the name was drawn from various Greek elements such as *mē*, or not, *phōs*, or light, and *philos*, or love — that is, "he who is not a lover of light," a parody on Lucifer the lightbearer.[49] The most interesting particles of the word, however, are *mephitic*, which is Latin for pungent, sulfurous, stinking, and the Hebrew *tophel*, or liar. The devil, of course, is all of these things; and by implication, so is the Jew. Thus, if the devil smells, so does the Jew. In fact, the belief that the Jews emitted mephitic odors was so strong that it persisted through the ages and prompted German scholars to investigate the nature and origin of Jewish farts (*foetor judaicus*). The Nazi racialist Hans F. Günther strongly subscribed to this belief and promised to study it with the help of chemical analysis.[50]

There is in all this, as Leon Poliakov has shown, a great deal of sexual projection. Jews are shown to be hypervirile, obsessively carnal, and therefore a deadly threat to Christians who had made spiritual purity, unaffected by desire, a prerequisite for salvation. The devil is the Lord of matter, and he uses the human body as a vehicle for his temptations.[51] The Christian ideal was that of Jesus and the saints who transcended the physical temptations of the body and aspired to spiritual purity. As is well known, sexual renunciation became the loftiest ideal in Christian faith; conversely, sexual indulgence was denounced as wicked and the church drew a veil of shame over all sexual expressions by excluding erotic words, images, actions, and people in order to enshrine its basic belief that "love of God is better than love between man and woman,...that chastity is higher than wedlock, and that virgins are holier than wives."[52] The body was often degraded to a foul and repulsive object, the seat of many lusts or unbridled desires. As a medium of sexuality it could forge relationships to others that might seriously jeopardize one's relationship to God. The devil came to be strongly identified as a source of "sexually symbolized needs" that helped to turn Christians from devoting themselves to God.

Behind the devil came the carnal Jew, which explains why Judeophobia always exhibits a strong sexual coloration. In reality, this projection of sexuality onto devil or Jew can be explained as externalizing forbidden impulses within the self, impulses that are not only sexual but may also be feelings of disguised protest against the authorities that are thwarting them — church and God.

Connected to such sexual fantasies were equally irrational beliefs that the Jews, despite their apparent virility or potency, were also constitutionally weak and sickly people who required periodic infusion of strong Christian blood to maintain their health. Among the many afflictions they suffered from were copious menstruation hemorrhages and hemorrhoids.[53] Jewish men, it was believed, menstruated because they were circumcised, requiring Christian blood for rejuvenation. The most potent Christian blood was the blood of young children; thus by sacrificing young children and drinking their blood the perpetrators would be invigorated with magical potency. It is in this way that the ancient myth of ritual murder found a new form of expression in the myth of ritual Jewish child murder. The first alleged child murder was reported in England in 1144. On the eve of Good Friday the body of a young apprentice was discovered in the woods near Norwich, and rumors quickly spread that the local Jews, supposedly acting on rabbinical instructions, had committed the foul deed in order to mock the Passion of the Savior. The local authorities, however, put no credence in the rumor and the sheriff of Norwich tried to protect the local Jews, unsuccessfully as it would turn out, because riots erupted in the city during which a Jew was murdered by a knight who was his debtor. The city subsequently made a cult out of "St. William," as the young apprentice was called, by erecting a profitable shrine that attracted many pilgrimages.[54] The Norwich case, in turn, prompted a whole spate of ritual child murder cases all over Europe, each time resulting in slanderous accusations, riots, and pogroms of innocent Jews. When the rages threatened to get out of hand, the emperor Frederick II of the Holy Roman Empire convened a commission of high dignitaries, including converted Jews, to investigate the rumor that Jews murdered Christian children and mixed their blood into their unleavened bread during Passover. The commission reported back that there was no shred of evidence confirming this belief, that, on the contrary, Jews abhorred the shedding of blood, as their dietary and religious laws made abundantly clear.[55] In 1236 Frederick II released a major golden bull in which he explicitly cleared the Jews of this accusation; but by that time, as Leon Poliakov has shown, the rumor had seeped so deeply into the collective consciousness that not even Frederick's imperial edict could reverse the damage.[56]

The accusation of ritual child murder was connected to two other delusions: host desecration and the belief that the Jews of the world were organized and controlled by a secret and mysterious society of rabbinical conspirators who plotted to undermine Christian civilization. The allegation that Jews profaned host wafers arose in the thirteenth century when the Fourth Lateran Council (1215) confirmed the dogma of transubstantiation, the belief that by a perpetual miracle Christ's flesh and blood became present in the consecrated host and wine in the sacrament of Holy Communion (Eucharist). At the end of the thirteenth century, Jews were accused of "mutilating" and "torturing" the transubstantiated body of Christ by desecrating or profaning host wafers. The myth of a Jewish world conspiracy, later surfacing in the famous nineteenth-century documentary fraud called the *Protocols of the Elders of Zion,* had already appeared in the wake of the Norwich case when the accusers claimed that the ritual murder had been planned by a conclave of rabbis at Narbonne in France. A converted Jew had supposedly revealed that the Jews of Spain convened every year at Narbonne to select a Christian victim for the annual sacrifice prescribed in their religious writings. The reason given for this practice was that the Jews strongly believed that they could attain their freedom and the return of their homeland only by mocking Christ and annually shedding blood by sacrificing a Christian.[57] Accordingly, each year the Jews of Spain, where the seat of their power and influence was greatest, supposedly met in Narbonne in southern France and cast lots that would decide in which city Christian blood was to be spilled.

Although patently absurd, as Frederick's commission indicated, this delusion of rabbinical evil-doers plotting sacrificial murder of Christian children continued to operate so strongly that it replaced the crusades as a justification for mass extermination. The craze spread quickly throughout Europe, and it often involved Christians in criminal actions because lies had to be deliberately fabricated and, under scrutiny, covered up or protected not only by individuals but also by whole communities. There were also cases where Christians themselves either hid or kidnapped children and then blamed the Jews for having done it, thus providing the pretext for more actions that resulted in the pillaging of Jewish homes and the killing of innocent Jews. Wherever the alleged crimes occurred, popular shrines were built, pilgrimages arranged, and supposed victims canonized. In the wake of the Endinger ritual child murder of 1462 in Bavaria, for example, a famous play and popular theater, called the *Endinger Judenspiel* (Endinger Jewish play) was annually performed to large audiences. Tourists can still visit the *Kinderfresserbrunnen* (Child-devouring fountain) in Berne, Switzerland, dedicated to a young boy who vanished from the city in 1294; with him disappeared all the Jews of Berne who were blamed for killing him.

In 1315 a terrible famine swept through Europe, and in its wake marauding bands of starving peasants massacred thousands of Jews, especially in the French southern duchy of Aquitaine. It was here that another accusation, later reinforced by the Black Plague, arose — that of Jewish well poisoning. The rumor was probably started by a leper who was captured on the estate of the Lord of Parthenai and confessed that a Jew had given him a bag of poison, consisting of human blood, urine, three secret herbs, and powder from a consecrated host, and instructed him to drop it into a well.[58] This episode set in motion the slanderous accusation that Jews were poisoning wells and springs, an accusation that received considerable reinforcement by the Black Plague (1347–50), which unhinged people's minds and made them receptive to all sorts of irrational beliefs. In Leon Poliakov's view, the year 1347 was comparable to that of 1096 because it sealed the fate of the European Jews in many parts of Europe; for besides the usual cosmic forces that were seen to be responsible in the form of a wrathful God, Satan, or both, it was clear to many impressionable people that demonic forces were on the loose, polluting the air and poisoning the waters. If Satan operated with the help of his usual minions, "where could he recruit them if not from the dregs of humanity, among the outcasts of all types, the lepers — and above all, from among the Jews, the people of both God and the Devil? Thus the Jews were promoted on a grand scale to their role of scapegoat."[59]

In order to bolster the Jewish stereotype, based largely on irrational thinking — to make it, so to speak, invulnerable to empirical reality — it was necessary to reduce Jews to positions of social inferiority. It was in this way that the Jews fulfilled the vicious logic of the self-fulfilling prophecy, which defines outgroups as inferior and proceeds in practice to oppress them to make them fit the mental image one had of them all along. The ultimate success of the self-fulfilling prophecy occurs when the victims believe it themselves, as did a Polish rabbi who reportedly told his flock during an SS roundup to obey the Nazi killers, saying, "Did we not kill Christ, and did we not ourselves cry out, 'Let the blood be on our heads?' "[60] Whatever Christians considered to be socially unsavory, they handed over to Jews. Prohibited from owning land, the real source of power in the Middle Ages, and also excluded from the guilds, the Jews were economically forced to engage in occupations that Christians considered to be not only inferior but also immoral, especially the practice of money-lending. Jews who engaged in this practice fulfilled a very important and useful economic function, but they also exposed themselves to many vicious accusations, notably of being bloodsuckers. This accusation, repeated in every part of Europe for centuries, possessed a grain of truth because Jews lent money at exorbitant rates, amounting at times to a hundred percent of the loan they extended, but they did so because they always operated from a position of social weakness. With no legal standing in most parts of Europe and little power of enforcement, they often had to count on the good word of their Christian debtors. Few contemporaries appreciated the tragedy of the Jewish double-bind; they preferred to call the Jews bloodsuckers or parasites who lived off the productive labor of their Christian neighbors. This accusation forms the background to the final myth of the "unproductive parasite," which also originated during the Middle Ages. Repeated in various versions over the centuries, the myth held that Jews, unlike Christians, did not engage in productive or soil-bound occupations but preferred to live off the fat of the land in urban centers where they engaged in purely speculative or abstract money manipulation. The abbot of Cluny, Peter the Venerable, already charged the Jews in the twelfth century with being an urban people living off the labor of hard-working Christian peasants and cheating them in unfair money transactions. What the abbot and all those who were making this accusation did not mention was that Jews could not engage in occupations where one "worked with one's hand." As Moses Mendelssohn justly protested later, "they bind our hands and then complain that we do not make use of them."[61]

By the end of the Middle Ages most of the elements of modern Judeophobia had been formed, a hatred that, in the end, sprung from the weaknesses and insecurities of Christian culture itself. From a psychological point of view, Judeophobia was the expression of the Christian believers' inner doubts about the truth of their own religion; and one way of assuaging this doubt was to nail the Jew to the cross and to project on them internal Christian doubt, fears, and loathings. In Steven Katz's judgment:

> Fear of disease, fear of pollution, fear of the unseen, fear of the unknown, fear of uncontrollable powers, fear of demons and monsters, fear of witches and wizards, fear of the malignant forces of nature and supernature, fear of devils and fallen angels, fear of sin, fear of theological corruption, fear of theological untruth, fear of sexuality both licit and suppressed, fear of self, fear of psyche, fear of primal needs and their outer manifestations, fear of economic competition and its consequences, fear of political defeat and conquest — all this and more was projected onto "the Jews."[62]

Yet, by removing the Jews, even teaching them a terrible and periodic lesson, the Christians could not still their own uncertainties, for as long as the Jews were present and active in Christian society, they were a living reminder of nonconformism and religious opposition.

Ideas have social and political consequences, in this case in the form of social stigmatization, ghettoization, expulsion, and even extermination. In order to mark them off from ordinary, decent folk, the Jews were forced to wear distinct garments and special insignia such as the yellow circular patch in France, called *rouelle,* which resembled a coin and suggested, in its color and form, the idea of jealousy, greed, and wickedness. In Germany Jews were required to wear a canonical hat (yellow or red), in Poland a pointed green hat, in Italy and Spain a yellow patch.[63]

Hand in hand with such personal stigmatization went physical segregation and expulsion. In 1290 the Jews were expelled from England by Edward I, not to return until the middle of the seventeenth century. During the following decades they were also expelled from France and from many towns in Germany. During the final Christian reconquest of Spain in the late fifteenth century, the Jews along with the Moors became the targets of the Inquisition, which was formally set up in Spain in 1479 to identify and try the infidels as well as Christian heretics; its first grand Inquisitor, Thomas Torquemada (1420–98), unleashed a reign of terror in which many Jews were killed. The Inquisition kept a close watch on the converted Jews, popularly called *marranos,* or pigs, many of whom had moved up into high social positions in Spanish society. Spanish mistrust of these converted Jews revealed a deep suspicion of Jews in general and brought out ugly and novel stereotypes, particularly the belief that Jewish blood was bad (*mala sangre*), caused bad character, and was irreversible because it was transmitted by heredity from one generation to the next. It is in this way that biological racism made its first appearance in history, admittedly still in inchoate form but vicious enough to dispel the belief that the Nazis were the first to be obsessed with blood pollution and blood purity. Only thirteen years later, when the Christian reconquest of Spain was completed, Ferdinand and Isabella expelled the Jews from Spain, and Portugal followed suit in 1498. By 1500, all of western Europe, with the exception of a few areas in Germany and Austria, was free of Jews (*judenrein*).

By the end of the Middle Ages "the Jew" had been lifted from actual human existence and transformed into a "dehumanized" mythic figure of great evil. Hatred of Jews was therefore regarded as a virtue; in fact, as Steven Katz reminds us, the more one hated Jews the more pious one was.[64] The Nazis therefore did not create the belief that the Jew was spiritually perverse; the church had already shown the way. What the Nazis added to this mythic belief was a different interpretation of its origins, which they saw as residing in "Jewish blood" rather than Jewish religion, and a different method of dealing with it — extermination in the here-and-now. The medieval answer to the Jewish question, as it would later be called, was either conversion or expulsion; and failing that, the Jews were permitted a marginal existence as ghettoized outsiders, branded and despised wherever they went.[65] The reason Christian Europe did not resort to genocidal activity in solving the Jewish question was that its Christian ethic, based as it was on love and forgiveness of sin, did not permit the perpetration of such a godless deed.

Migration and Ghettoization

By 1500 the cultural center of world Jewry had shifted from southwestern Europe (Italy, Spain, Portugal, France) to northeastern Europe (Poland, Western Russia). The great Jewish golden age, associated with the Jewish-Muslim-Christian symbiosis of Iberia, had immensely enriched the world both economically and culturally, thus confirming Franz Boas's observations that "advances of culture depend upon the opportunities presented to a social group to learn from the experience of their neighbors."[66] But by now this golden age had come to an end. The Jews of Iberia fled, finding refuge in Turkey, Palestine, Syria, and even the New World. The Jews of the Near East were called Sephardim, and they took with them pride in their Iberian heritage, their highly mystical and speculative theology, their esoteric folklore, and their advanced commercial skills. The Jews in the northern area moved in large numbers to Poland and western Russia, taking with them their highly developed sense of cultural literacy and commercial acumen that would benefit the many backward villages of eastern Europe. These eastern European Jews, known as Ashkenazim, spoke a compound dialect of German and Hebrew called Yiddish, subscribed to strict rabbinical rules, and lived a segregated life in their own communities. Those Jews who remained scattered throughout Austria and Germany were forced to live in segregated quarters called ghettos, usually located in the worst parts of town in terribly overcrowded conditions. The life of these segregated ghetto Jews was strictly regulated by the Christian communities. Jews had to pay arbitrary and excessively high taxes and wear a special yellow badge or hat; they were prohibited from socializing with Christians and restricted to their quarters at night.

For well over three hundred years (1500–1800), the exact duration depending on the locations, the Jews remained essentially isolated and ghettoized, but the winds of change also buffeted their insulated and anxiety-ridden existence. The Christian Wars of Religion (1540–1648), which turned all of Europe into a battleground of intense religious hatred, also impinged on the Jews of Europe and especially on those who were still living in the German lands. The father of the Protestant Reformation, Martin Luther, was a neurotic genius with an essentially medieval cast of mind who saw the world in stark and unambiguous opposites that sprang from a deep need for absolutes. He loved and hated with equal intensity; and once he found the truth, as he saw it, he condemned every point of view that did not fit his own with biting sarcasm and disdain. Luther could serve as a textbook model of the split and unintegrated man. As Heinrich Heine said of him:

> He was at once a dreamy mystic and a practical man of action. His thoughts had not only wings, but also hands....He was both a cold, scholastic wordsifter, and an inspired, God-drunk prophet. After a long day spent in laboriously working out dogmatic distinctions, at evening time he would take his flute and go out to gaze at the stars, and his soul would dissolve in melody and devotion. This same man, who could scold like a fishwife, could also be as sensitive as a maiden.[67]

Luther initially reached out to the Jews because he identified emotionally with the suffering they had been exposed to by a church he had come to despise as demonic — the Roman Catholic Church. He reminded his fellow Germans that Jesus was a Jew who taught a pure gospel of love and that it was therefore their Christian duty to treat the Jews with love and compassion, particularly in view of the fact that Catholics had been unable to live up to this Christian ideal. In a pamphlet entitled *Jesus Christ Was Born a Jew*, written in 1523, Luther said:

> If the Apostles, who were also Jews, had dealt with us Gentiles as we Gentiles deal with the Jews there would never have been a Christian among the Gentiles....We in our turn ought to treat the Jews in a brotherly manner in order that we might convert some of them....We are but Gentiles, while the Jews are of the lineage of Christ. We are aliens and in-laws; they are blood relatives, cousins and brothers of our Lord.[68]

This was written in 1523, at the height of his struggle with the Catholic Church; exactly twenty years later, in 1543, following a lengthy period of struggle, both within and outside his own Lutheran camp, a far more conservative, indeed reactionary, Luther vented his spleen against the Jews by denouncing them as insidious parasites who "stuff themselves, guzzle and sit around the stove...fart and roast pears....They fleece us of our money and goods."[69] Adding more serious moral charges to these stock-in-trade cliches of Jewish material greed, Luther reminds his readers of their criminal guilt for killing Christ and trafficking with Satan. He recommends:

> First, to set fire to their synagogues or schools....
> Second, I advise that their houses also be razed and destroyed....
> Third, I advise that all their prayer books and Talmudic writings, in which such adultery, lies, cursing and blasphemy are taught, be taken from them....
> Fourth, I advise that their Rabbis be forbidden to teach.
> Fifth, I advise that safe conduct on the highways be abolished completely for the Jews.
> Sixth, I advise that all cash and treasure of silver be taken from them....
> Seventh,...let whoever can, throw brimstone and pitch upon them.
> ...Let them be driven like mad dogs out of the land.[70]

Such vitriol, rising at times to scatological heights, as many of Luther's outbursts did in moments of fanatical frenzy, have convinced some historians that the "first great national prophet of Germany and the forger of the German language itself...shaped the overwhelmingly pejorative, indeed demonic, significance of the word *Jude*,"[71] that Luther heaped more vile attacks on the Jews than could be found in Hitler's *Mein Kampf*,[72] and that his whole apocalyptic thinking, in which Jews are children of the devil, was the first major step on the road to the Holocaust.[73] There is some truth to these charges because Luther's vile outbursts against the Jews have no counterpart in any medieval theologian; even St. John Chrysostom's anti-Jewish outbursts, made at a time when both Jews and Christians were more equal and competed with each other for converts, appear in retrospect far milder by comparison. True, Martin Luther caused the Reformation and not the Holocaust, but he did share with Adolf Hitler, if not the same world, the same passionate hatred of Jews, a hatred that showed definite demonological characteristics. Luther, however, was a Christian and not a racist, who did believe — some outbursts to the contrary notwithstanding — that Jews were human beings, created in the image of God, and salvageable. He did not shape the world or the mindset that produced Adolf Hitler any more than Muhammad produced the mindset that spawned the Ayatollah Khomeini.[74] What Luther and his supporters did, however, was to amalgamate already existing medieval Jewish prejudices, perpetuate them into the future, and, when the Nazis perpetrated the Holocaust, contribute to that blunting of conscience that is always necessary if evil is to flourish.

The Reformation that Luther initiated brought about an intensification of religious fanaticism that could only exacerbate already existing anti-Jewish attitudes. The fact that Christians were intent upon annihilating each other, however, meant that the annihilatory rage previously reserved largely for Jews was displaced and therefore slightly diminished. The exception was eastern Europe, where the Jews had found refuge in the later Middle Ages and built up a firm nation within a nation. Over the objection of the Catholic clergy, the kings of Poland had given the Jews of Poland such preferential treatment that a papal legate was astounded to learn in 1565 that "in these regions, masses of Jews are to be found, who are not subject to the scorn they met elsewhere.... They own land, engage in commerce, study medicine and astronomy. They possess great wealth and are not only counted among respectable people but sometimes even dominate them.... In short, they have all the rights of citizens."[75] This situation, however, was not destined to last. When the Polish state began to decline in the seventeenth century as a result of Polish inability to create a strong centralized nation state, internal divisions erupted into serious disturbances. The most ominous came in 1648 when the Russian peasants of the Ukraine, most of them Eastern Orthodox, revolted against their Polish landowners and the Jewish financial agents who had been representing their interests. The uprising of the Russian peasants, who rallied to the cause of Bagdan Chmielnicki, resulted in widespread pogroms against both Jews and Poles, eventually led to a Russo-Polish war in which Sweden also intervened, and degenerated into a free-for-all in which well over a hundred thousand Jews were killed.

The Jews of eastern Europe responded to these pogroms, generally considered to be the worst since the crusades, by retreating into their well-regulated, insular world and digging in behind walls of strict Talmudic learning, especially in Lithuania and White Russia. An exception to this fundamentalism, however, occurred in southern Poland and the Ukraine, where Judaism took on an emotional turn similar to the evangelical Christian movements in Europe such as German Pietism or English Methodism. In addition to embracing a more liberal interpretation of the Talmud, Jewish believers also rediscovered the rich mystical traditions of the Kabbala and of Jewish folklore and poetry. They spontaneously discovered a religion of the heart that ignited fervent messianic hopes, culminating in the charismatic preacher Israel ben Eliezer (c. 1700–1760) of Moldavia whose followers, called Hasidim (Pious Ones), gave their name to the great mystical form of modern Judaism called Hasidism.

Enlightenment and Emancipation

In western Europe a fundamental change in the perception and treatment of Jews occurred during the age of Enlightenment, which was itself the culmination of three centuries of opposition to ancient religious and secular authorities. The broad thrust of the Enlightenment was to "demythologize" the world and to redefine it as nothing but matter in motion subject to rational processes that could be understood by the human mind. Armed with the new principles of science and a broader humanistic perspective they had gained through the rediscovery of the values of classical antiquity, the "Enlighteners" (*Aufklärer*) attempted to formulate a new humanistic cosmology in place of the old religious one and to change the world accordingly. Radiating from its French center, the Enlightenment became an international movement of ideas, supported primarily by a vanguard of intellectuals (*les philosophes*) who articulated the values of the rising commercial classes of the advanced countries of Europe. These values, sustained by broad cosmopolitan and middle-class interests, asserted that all humans were created free and equal and should be liberated from traditional and arbitrary forms of control. For some, this new gospel of human liberation with its resonant words and phrases — such as "reason," "progress," "human dignity," "government by consent of the governed," and "free enterprise" — became almost a secular millenarian movement aimed at rebuilding the Heavenly City of medieval times with more updated material.

The transmutation of the Christian millennial spirit into its secular equivalent is undeniable, but what was different was the instrument by which such earthly salvation was to be attained. The eighteenth century was not, as Carl Becker suggested, a mere reenactment of the thirteenth century but a radical shift in the axis of western civilization — a shift away from God and the supernatural to human beings and their secular hopes and aspirations. The means of salvation also differed; science replaced religion as a means by which the age-old enemies (ignorance, superstition, poverty, war) could be conquered and the new secular heaven attained. The Enlightenment, in other words, was a major reorientation of human consciousness; it was also, just as importantly, a psychological shift in mood because it spoke a more optimistic and a more tolerant language, claiming that all humans were essentially good, that the good life should be sought in the goods of this life rather than in some other life to come, and that all this could be achieved through significant social and political change.

The spirit behind many assumptions of the Enlightenment was the new science, which its supporters claimed to be a cooperative, cumulative, empirical, and progressive enterprise; its self-correcting principles would permit the correction of error in a way that the old theology never could because, unlike faith, based as it was on dogmatic and unexamined premises, the new science appealed to empirically verifiable facts. Given this faith in science, it was bound to happen that faith in religion would seriously diminish, which, indeed, was the case. From initial efforts by John Locke and the English deists to formulate a purely "rational" religion shorn of miraculous or mysterious elements, the Enlightenment moved steadily in the direction of philosophical skepticism, secular humanism, and unbelief. Religion became increasingly more rationalistic and correspondingly less mystical, emotional, or otherworldly. Although the eighteenth century remained committed to the Christian tradition, its philosophical avant-garde (Voltaire, Hume, Rousseau, Kant, Lessing, Jefferson) embraced essentially deistic and skeptical ideas. They counseled broad religious toleration and, ideally, looked to a separation of church and state.

Like all oppressed minorities, the Jews welcomed the blessings of the Enlightenment; moreover they became one of the chief beneficiaries of the new values when the ideas of the Enlightenment were translated into practice during the so-called age of democratic revolution (1776–1848). The Jews were slowly emancipated from civil disabilities. In 1781 Joseph II of Austria, one of the more enlightened rulers of the eighteenth century, released his first Patent of Toleration on the grounds that it was the Christian thing to do and that it was useful to the state. Indeed, the Jews were increasingly tolerated because it was not only right but economically useful, as the king of Prussia, Frederick William I, had informed his estates long before when he told them that "the Jews and their business seem not harmful but rather useful to us and the country."[76] It was, in fact, in Prussia that a hunchbacked Jew, Moses Mendelssohn, opened up a window to the larger world and initiated, almost single-handedly, a remarkable cultural dialogue with ruling intellectual leaders in Berlin and the rest of Germany, chiefly with the playwright and philosopher Gotthold Ephraim Lessing, whose great drama *Nathan der Weise* (Nathan the Wise), represents one of the enduring documents of universal toleration and compassion. Mendelssohn's friend, the Prussian civil servant Christian Wilhelm von Dohm, set off a contentious debate not only in Germany, but also in France with his book *Bürgerliche Verbesserung der Juden* (The civil improvement of the Jews, 1781), which indicted society for its mistreatment of Jews and recommended full citizenship and equality. In 1789 the French Revolutionary Assembly granted the Jews full citizenship, and all the regions that came under French domination, such as the Rhineland, Westphalia, Switzerland, and Northern Italy, did the same. Bavaria, Baden, and Württemberg followed the Austrian model by granting citizenship while at the same time retaining certain restrictions. The state of Prussia, defeated by Napoleon in 1806, undertook its own internal reforms and in 1812 granted the Jews economic but not political emancipation.[77] By the end of the Napoleonic wars all the Jews of western and central Europe had been emancipated from most previous disabilities by becoming citizens or subjects in the nations in which they resided.

The lure of emancipation, which tempted many Jews to leave their ghettos, was a double-edged sword on several accounts. In the first place, it raised the religious and cultural problems associated with assimilation, which, in turn, posed the danger of undermining Jewish religion and culture. In the second place, assimilation meant that Jews were expected to adopt the qualities deemed necessary to become full-fledged

French, German, or Italian citizens, and it raised the thorny question whether the national community in which Jews resided would accept them as full-fledged nationals and be willing to grant them, in return for making this concession, the additional right to remain Jewish. In the third place, would the Jews of Europe themselves be able to make concessions in order to live peaceably with their Christian neighbors?

When the march out of the ghetto began under the impact of emancipation and the tidal wave of capitalist expansion, the Jews discovered quickly that wealth was one of the major determinants of social standing. Skillful as traders and money-lenders and having little to gain by defending the old feudal order, the Jews quickly became the great agents of modernization. Even before the age of democratic revolution, they had served as court Jews (*Hofjuden*) managing the financial affairs of princely courts throughout Europe. Their cosmopolitan mentality, together with their ability — acquired by sheer necessity over many centuries — to speak different languages enabled them to forge international business ties that were the envy of their competitors. The rise of the international house of Rothschild is perhaps the best and most spectacular example of this Jewish breakthrough in the age of capitalist expansion. The founder of the house, Meyer Amschel Rothschild (1743–1812), started his career as a minor bank clerk in Frankfurt and later set up his own business in the city's *Judengasse* dealing in coins, medals, and antiques. During the Napoleonic wars he amassed a huge fortune, set up his five sons in five major financial capitals of Europe — Frankfurt, Paris, London, Naples, and Vienna — and still managed to serve simultaneously the governments of Germany, France, Britain, Italy, and Austria. The five sons, in turn, refined the shrewd business acumen and remarkable timing of their father and made the House of Rothschild the most admired and despised financial operation in the world. The Rothschilds swore by their policy of buying below market price and selling above it; they specialized in the buying and selling of international currencies on several markets in order to take advantage of price differences — a tricky venture that required intimate knowledge of local financial and political conditions and perfect timing.[78] Their agents were carefully picked and reported so accurately on local conditions that the House of Rothschild became a better informed institution than any news agency.

The Rothschilds became not only a symbol of legendary wealth and power but also the Jew-haters' favorite target, for where else, as Hannah Arendt observed, "was there better proof of the fantastic concept of a Jewish world government than in this one family, nationals of five different countries, close cooperation with at least three different governments...whose frequent conflicts never for a moment shook the solidarity of interest of their state bankers? No propaganda could have created a symbol more effective for political purposes than the reality itself."[79] For our purposes, however, it is also important to look at the obverse of this financial success — that is, in what it did to the Jewish family and its exposure to the lure of assimilation and nationalization. Although Meyer Amschel Rothschild succeeded in successfully ensconcing his five sons in different European capitals, he also contributed to the eventual weakening of family unity because the Rothschilds became nationalized as Germans, Austrians, French, or English. Though unabashedly Jewish, as Fritz Stern has said of them, they also vied fiercely for national honors and recognition, moved with relative ease in the highest national circles, and often displayed markedly cautious and conservative attitudes. Meyer Carl von Rothschild, Amschel Meyer's grandson, was a member of the North German Parliament of 1867 and served in the Prussian upper house; Baron Salomon of Vienna moved in the highest court circles in Vienna, gaining a fifty year's concession in financing the Northern Austrian Railway; Baron James of Paris and his son Alphonse became equally prominent in French society; and Nathan Meyer's son Lionel Rothschild became the first Jewish member of the British House of Commons, and his son Nathaniel was made a hereditary peer by Queen Victoria in 1885. Such identification with national governments put a premium on both family and ethnic loyalties, although the Rothschilds tried to follow strict customs by keeping the family and its business Jewish.

Unlike the Rothschilds or later the Bleichröders, most Jews still lived on the socioeconomic margin; only a few rose to prominence because of their economic usefulness to the state. All of them, however, were vulnerable to constant discrimination and, beginning with emancipation, to what Fritz Stern called "the anguish of assimilation,"[80] which involved the dilemma posed by divided loyalties — the sort that often pitted their patriotism against their religious or family allegiances.

The fortress of the Jews, amid the danger and temptations of the gentile world, had always been the family, for it was here that a set of Jewish patterns — religious, moral, and ethnic — had been internalized. Jews had always seen themselves as an ethnic minority, and they looked to each other as an extended family. Would emancipation dissolve these bonds and weaken the very fiber of the Jewish community? The vanguard of the Jewish community — that is, its leaders and success stories such as Moses Mendelssohn, Ludwig Börne, Heinrich Heine, Felix Mendelssohn, the Rothschilds — were pulling in the direction of assimilation, modernization, and secularism. In order to avoid the dangers of anti-Jewish prejudice and still-existing restrictions, an increasing number of Jews began to convert to Christianity, as did Karl Marx's father, Heinrich, who brought up his family more in the enlightened tradition of the eighteenth century than in his own Jewish faith.

Even within the Jewish religion itself certain fissures developed in the early nineteenth century when some Jews who had embraced the Enlightenment, especially the Jewish variant called Haskala, broke with orthodox Judaism. The Reformists challenged two ancient traditions, the predominance of the Talmud and the rule of the rabbis, and they insisted that Judaism had to adapt itself to the modern world by taking into account the contribution of non-Jewish philosophers such as Locke, Kant, and Hegel. In 1818 reform-minded Jews founded the Wissenschaft des Judentum (Science of Jewry), an educational and religious institution whose academics taught a very broad (latitudinarian) theology with strong humanistic overtones, and they encouraged a cultural dialogue with non-Jews. Reform Judaism began in the German synagogues, where reform-minded rabbis simplified synagogue worship, eliminated references in their sermons to the coming of the Jewish Messiah or the resurrection of the dead, installed organs and choirs, and sang hymns in the vernacular rather than in Hebrew. This concession to modernity, strongly challenged by Orthodox Judaism, culminated in 1843 when the radicals in the Reform movement declared:

> *First,* we recognize the possibility of unlimited development in the Mosaic religion. *Second,* the collection of controversies, dissertations, and perceptions commonly designated by the name Talmud possesses for us no authority from either a doctrinal or practical standpoint. *Third,* a Messiah who is to lead back the Israelites to the land of Palestine is neither expected nor desired of us; we know no fatherland but that to which we belong by both birth and citizenship.[81]

This remarkable statement represents the broadest concession by religious Jews in history, a concession, as it would turn out, that was not accepted by the majority of the Jewish community, nor did its affirmation of Jewish willingness to identify itself with non-Jewish nationalities evoke widespread approval. Most religious Jews were beginning to see themselves as both Jewish and German, French, or English, and they wanted complete legal emancipation, to be considered citizens while at the same time being allowed to practice their religion. The degree to which the European nationalities were willing to concede this request would determine the relative degree to which the Jews of Europe would be integrated, assimilated, or tolerated by the national community in which they resided.

Jews in the Age of Nationalism and European Racism

There were lengthy debates in many European communities in the post-Napoleonic era about the integration and toleration of Jews, and they were most vocal and intense in those areas where the Jewish population was larger and had reached a higher degree of social awareness, chiefly in France and the German-speaking territories. The question that seems to have preoccupied thinkers more than any other was whether the Jewish national character was compatible with German or French national character, variously defined in religious, ethnic, and cultural terms. The French, who had a far more cohesive sense of both their cultural and religious identity, took objections to Jews primarily on religious and later on economic grounds. The French Jewish population was numerically much smaller than elsewhere, amounting in the late eighteenth century to little more than fifty thousand, and limited geographically largely to Alsace and Lorraine in the eastern departments.[82] French anti-Jewish prejudices were voiced mainly by reactionary Roman Catholic writers, by Jewish apostates who actively turned against their former coreligionists, and by socialist critics who attacked the Jews for promoting capitalistic practices. The German response, however, was far more intense on several grounds: first, because Jews had never been completely expelled from the German lands as they had from England and France, thus constituting a real presence and not one that was merely embedded in folklore or art; second and following from the first, Judeophobia constituted a continuous and persistent tradition; and third, the Germans lacked a cohesive sense of national identity, fell more strongly under the spell of nationalism, and ended up defining themselves so exclusively along narrow cultural and later irrational racial lines that a growing number of them refused to accept the idea of integrating any non-German ethnic or religious minority, especially the Jews.

A flood of pamphlets inundated the German territories after the Napoleonic wars, debating the "Jewish question" — a debate, as will be seen in the next chapter, that had a profound influence on the development of Judeophobia in the late nineteenth century. Before the 1870s the debate was still conducted within a traditional Christian and cultural framework. On the anti-Jewish side, its point of departure was the indictment of the Judaic religion and its practices by Andreas Eisenmenger, whose book *Entdecktes Judentum* (Uncovered Jewry, 1706), a massive two-volume study of Jewish belief and alleged misconduct, furnished all the ammunition Jew-haters needed to discredit their opponents: namely, that Jews belonged to an absolutely different nation, that they showed contempt for other beliefs, that they followed two different standards of morality — one for themselves and the other for external purposes — that they engaged in ritual murder and host desecration, and the like.[83] The extent of Eisenmenger's research, his knowledge of Hebrew, Aramaic, and Arabic, his clever insinuations and twisted interpretations — all these made his book a primary source of Jew hatred until its argumentative framework was radically altered by the biological and racist views of the late nineteenth century; but until that time, Eisenmenger's book, which had no counterpart elsewhere, remained the point of departure for German Judeophobia. Eisenmenger still hoped to convert the Jews to Christianity or, failing that, to drive them back into their ghettos. The same appeared to be the case with those critics in the early nineteenth century who wrote under the influence of romantic nationalism, particularly at the time of the anti-Jewish Hep! Hep! riots that swept over a number of German cities (Würzburg, Bamberg, Bayreuth, Frankfurt, Hamburg), combining traditional Christian Judeophobia with a new strident nationalism born of political frustrations and anti-capitalist sentiments.[84] Contemporary Jewish observers referred to this German rage as a New Teutomania, a new form of romantic xenophobia that was unleashed by the right-wing of the romantic movement (Arndt, Jahn) and that rejected the notion that Jews could ever be a part of the German *Volk* because they lacked the required Christian-German spirit. Yet many anti-Jewish critics still believed that conversion to both was possible, as did the broad middle class and the leaders of the German states. The Hep! Hep! riots were ruthlessly put down and Jewish assimilation continued to make progress, although in the form of grudging concessions rather than full-blown legal and social emancipation. The Frankfurt Assembly of 1848 went on record as advocating that the Jews be granted full equality, which was simply a reassertion of the democratic belief of the eighteenth century in the natural rights of man.

During the last quarter of the nineteenth-century, however, a new form of Judeophobia emerged that not only stirred up a wave of hatred throughout Europe but also produced the soil on which the Nazi mentality would be nourished. This was the emergence of biological racism based on the pseudoscientific theories spun out by the followers of Darwin, who extended and misinterpreted his biological findings to fit their ideological agendas. Biological racism, in turn, converged with a new belligerent type of nationalism and imperialism. Most ominously, however, late nineteenth century thinkers, especially those living in undemocractic or illiberal societies such as Germany, Austro-Hungary, and Russia, began to abandon the values of the Enlightenment by turning their backs on equality, democracy, natural rights, and rationality itself. It was a profound cultural shift with important implications for modern Jewry.

Racism is rooted in ethnic prejudices, which had a long and ugly history in Europe.[85] The European continent is a hodgepodge of widely diverse ethnic groups and the tensions between them reach back over thousands of years. The rise of nationalism exacerbated these tensions because ideals of national self-determination and expansion, now ideologically bolstered and raised to the level of a quasi-religion, even millenarian in nature, threatened to erupt in renewed conflicts. The most acute ethnic tensions existed between German and Slavs, particularly in that part of Europe lying within the long, wide belt from the Baltic Sea to the Black Sea, where centuries of shifting conquests had splintered these areas into a multiracial, multilinguistic, and multireligious confusion.[86] It was also in this part of Europe that the majority of the Jews resided and that nationalism, later augmented by racial themes, produced the greatest harm. Additionally, the growth of pan-Slavism or pan-Germanism in these regions served as a strong force in breaking up multiethnic empires and in reviving imperialistic dreams among the ruling elites.

The most insidious influence that ethnic conflicts invariably encouraged was racism, which in the nineteenth century evolved from a personal or social bias to an all-embracing ideology claiming to possess a master key to world history. In extolling the racial superiority of their tribe, racial ideologues appealed primarily to the new science of biology and the social implications purportedly to follow from it. Public discussion was intensely focused on such magical Darwinian terms as "natural selection," "heredity," "struggle for existence," and "survival of the fittest," with a veritable flood of printed material dedicated to racial stocks, racial behavior, racial breeding, and racial improvement. In the light of Darwin's discoveries, the public naturally wanted to know which societies and which nations were fittest and why. Invariably, ethnocentric researchers jumped to hasty and self-serving conclusions that skin color was the chief determinant of biological and, therefore, social superiority. It was merely a question of elucidating the racial traits of the strongest (fittest) and the weakest (least fit) nations and demonstrating, by way of comparative anthropology, which qualities promoted survival and which did not. The general consensus was that competition, boldness, bravery, and assertive (aggressive) qualities promoted survival, while weakness, compromise, pacifism, in short, passive traits, were sociobiologically undesirable.

This kind of thinking linked up with the emerging eugenic movement, which originated in England and was spearheaded by Darwin's cousin, Sir Francis Galton, who became a powerful advocate for the belief that heredity rather than environment molded individual characteristics. Together with his friend Karl Pearson, he called for a concerted national effort to breed a superior race of people by encouraging the fittest to procreate and by discouraging, by sterilization if necessary, the procreation of feeble, incompetent, and sickly types. It was in the course of these discussions about social eugenics that Pearson and others promoted the ideal of National Socialism in a form that was not too unlike that of the Nazis fifty years later. Pearson, for example, described the nation using the analogy of an individual organism and warned that no nation could survive in the struggle for existence unless it was a homogeneous whole. Class conflicts are, therefore, utterly divisive and must be rooted out in the new socialist state in which every individual, regardless of social rank, cooperated with others for the common good and in which, by way of appropriate eugenic measures, the strongest and most intelligent attained positions of leadership.

Of all the racial theorists, the two most persuasive evangelists of racism were the French Count Arthur de Gobineau and the Englishman Houston Stewart Chamberlain. Gobineau is often seen as the first spokesman of "Aryan" (white) superiority, and his four-volume essay entitled *Essay sur l'inégalité de races humaines* (Essay on the inequality of human races) (1853–54) is widely regarded, along with Chamberlain's *Die Grundlagen des neunzehnten Jahrhunderts* (The foundations of the nineteenth century), as one of the major ideological cornerstones of twentieth-century fascism. Both men were cultural conservatives with decidedly reactionary attitudes about the social ills of modern industrialization and democracy. Both also attempted to explain the rise and fall of civilization in racial terms, arguing that the creative growth gene that makes civilization possible resides in the racial superiority of the Aryan people, a label that both men uncritically and falsely transposed from linguistics to biology. Both were also profoundly anti-Jewish and saw in the Jew not only a racially inferior type but also a subversive social force. If the Aryans or Teutons are the culture creators, the Jews are always its destroyers, for once the Jews have put their stamp on any movement, its vital force will be sapped. Christianity, Chamberlain pointed out, was a case in point because of its double-faced appearance: half Jewish and half Aryan. Its Aryan face is profoundly rich in symbolism and mythology, while its Jewish face is strongly colored by rigid adherence to ritual and law. Thus, what was best in Christianity — its primitive vigor and childlike faith — became distorted by Jewish elements into an intolerant creed emphasizing sin, guilt, and punishment rather than redemption, love, and divine grace. In the course of these ruminations, Chamberlain's deep antipathy toward the Jews led him to the amazing conclusion that, given his heroic (Aryan) qualities, Jesus must have been an Aryan rather than a Jew.

Two other similarities between Gobineau and Chamberlain should be noted. The first is that their works, though pretending to be scientific or scholarly, were really racist tracts with a political agenda; in this they represented an emerging literary genre that was made up of texts pretending to be works of academic scholarship while belonging more properly in the demimonde of popular advocacy. Second, their works were most popular in Germany. Gobineau's racial theories were promoted in Germany with great success by the composer Richard Wagner. In fact, Gobineau and Wagner struck up a close friendship after discovering that their aesthetic sensibilities were much the same. In the Wagner circle at Bayreuth, Gobineau's racial doctrines were enthusiastically promoted, and in 1894, Ludwig Schemann, who translated Gobineau's book into German, founded the Gobineau Vereinigung in Freiburg. Chamberlain, too, had a close connection to Wagner and Germany. A transplanted Englishman and scion of a wealthy family of scholars, explorers, and soldiers of the British empire, Chamberlain was attracted to Wagner's music, settled in Germany, and married one of Wagner's daughters, becoming the focal point of radical Germanism and violent antimodernism.[87] His *Foundation* sold well over a hundred thousand copies by the outbreak of World War I and various pan-German and anti-Jewish groups enthusiastically endorsed its beliefs. Moreover, Chamberlain moved in highly influential circles, counting the German kaiser as his friend, and his ideas were sanctioned by members of the ruling elite. During the 1930s Chamberlain actively supported the Nazis, who considered him one of their own and hailed his book as a *Kampfbuch* (Battle book), a beacon lighting the way to victory for the party.

In the late nineteenth century, racism cross-fertilized with several other disturbing attitudes. A decisive reaction set in against formal, classical and rationalistic modes of thought that profoundly undermined the equilibrium of western culture. The primacy of reason, which had been the hallmark of the Enlightenment, was increasingly challenged by speculative writers who emphasized the predominant role of will, the irrational, the subjective, the intuitive, or the unconscious in human life. Historians have called this intellectual counterrevolution "vitalism," "irrationalism," "neo-romanticism," or "neo-mysticism" — labels that are suggestive but also misleading. The revolt against reason was primarily directed against the spirit of industrial civilization, and this involved a profound dissatisfaction with urbanism, technical rationality, and the generally tame, unexciting, and unheroic routine of bourgeois life. By some instinctual logic there was a sudden convergence of archaic patterns that, from diverse literary and philosophical quarters, began to challenge axiomatic middle-class (Enlightenment) assumptions about human rationality and the perfectibility of the social order through science, capitalism, and parliamentary democracy.

Fritz Stern has called this mood, once it became articulated and organized socially and politically, the "politics of cultural despair,"[88] and noted its profound reactionary and antimodern attitudes. Decrying the dehumanizing tendency of technology, the danger of "lower-class" politics, the rapacity of capitalism, and the decline in aesthetic taste, many intellectuals and young people adopted a profoundly antidemocratic, elitist attitude with very strong anti-Jewish coloration. Instead of mastering the forces of the modern world for human benefit, they preferred to run away into a world of mythology and archaic customs, which only further served to alienate them from the modern world. In its most extreme form, this manifested itself in a strong underground movement in Germany called the *völkisch* ideology.[89]

Given these fissures in western culture, it should not be surprising that there were violent eruptions of Judeophobia in the late nineteenth century. Jew-baiting became a popular pastime in almost every part of Europe. Arguably the most prolific Jew-baiter of this period was the Frenchman Edouard Drumond, who churned out a steady stream of vitriol that made others look mild by comparison. In his two-volume work *La France juive* (1886) and his numerous commentaries in *La Libre Parole*, which he founded in 1892, Drumond flung accusation after accusation against the Jews, saying that they were physically and mentally different, smelled bad, exploited the French financially, undermined French culture, and betrayed the country to the Germans. Two events in the 1890s intensified Judeophobia in France: one was a public scandal that involved extensive bribing of government officials by the Jewish banker Jacques de Reinach and the blackmailer Cornelius Herz, and the other was the Dreyfus Affair, arguably the greatest *cause célèbre* of the *fin de siècle*. Of these the Dreyfus Affair was of much greater significance because it revealed that there was widespread anti-Jewish prejudice in the French military and among Roman Catholics and right-wing conservatives. At the same time, it also revealed that the anti-Dreyfusards were confronted by an even larger and, as it would turn out after Zola's *J'accuse,* a more powerful bloc of Dreyfusard republicans and socialists. The Jews in France and Britain were citizens of advanced liberal democracies. In France, the ideas of the Enlightenment were much stronger than elsewhere, and Jews were well assimilated into French intellectual life, as is shown by the careers of Bergson, Benda, and Durkheim. The French generally recruited their future intellectual leaders without regard to their religion or race. As a student of Péguy noted: "We had always lived with our Jewish comrades in the same intimacy as with those who were Christians; it did not enter our heads that they could be different from us; and the idea that a man should have to suffer for his religion and his race seemed intolerable to us."[90]

By contrast, Judeophobia was much stronger and more institutionally reinforced, as we shall see, in Germany and the Austro-Hungarian empire. The most dangerous place in the world for a Jew, before World War I, however, was in eastern Europe and Russia rather than in Germany. It was here that governments actually passed discriminatory legislation against the Jews. In Romania, for example, the government initiated severe legal restrictions against the country's roughly 250,000 Jews, curtailing their right to vote and to hold public office. The most destructive measures against eastern Jews, however, were initiated by the Russian government in the 1880s. Judeophobia had always been very strong in the Christian west, except that in Russia the Jews confronted a cohesive force in the form of the tsarist autocracy and its spiritual underpinning — the Eastern Orthodox Church. It was not only the Caesaropapist nature of the Russian state that represented a threat to Russian Jewry, but the highly messianic nature that undergirded it. Muscovite ideology, with its adopted Byzantine symbol of the two-headed eagle, had proclaimed Moscow as the Third Rome, a New Jerusalem, and the logical successor to Rome and Constantinople as the true center of Christianity. A country that envisioned itself as religiously chosen was bound to clash with a people that subscribed to a rival claim of being divinely chosen. The resurgence of Russian nationalism, which retained strong apocalyptical and messianic expectations, only sharpened this sense of Russian exclusivity and, by implication, its long-standing Judeophobia. Interestingly enough, the Russian landscape was so highly charged with messianic thinking that it encouraged considerable theological cross-fertilization, stimulating parallel messianic expectations among Russian Jews in the form of populism and Zionism.

Discrimination and pogroms against the Jews had been systemic in the Russian system for centuries. Active government discrimination against the Jews intensified in the early 1880s under the reign of Tsar Alexander III, who gave in to his Slavophilic extremists by passing a series of ordinances that prohibited Jews from buying landed property (1881), restricting admission to universities and secondary schools, and forcing those Jews who lived in the interior of Russia to move to the western provinces — the so-called "Jewish Pale" (1890), where they were forbidden to own land, systematically spied upon, harassed, and physically attacked. It is estimated that more than five million Jews lived in Russia at the end of the nineteenth century, most of them in the Pale and generally under deplorable economic conditions. Starting in 1881, mob violence, often instigated by tsarist officials, erupted against the Jews of Russia ostensibly for their alleged role in the assassination of Alexander III, but actually to hound them out of the major Russian cities and towns into the pale of settlement and to feed a growing mood of Judeophobia that had long defined broad sections of the Russian population. It was in the wake of this popular Jew-hatred that one of the most vicious documents ever published against the Jews, the *Protocols of the Elders of Zion,* originated and found willing believers in Russia and elsewhere. Forged by the tsarist secret police, the Okhrana, and based on the literary and political tracts of Maurice Joly and Hermann Goedsche, the document consisted of twenty-four "Protocols," or speeches, by alleged Jewish leaders who explain how they would use the subversive forces of liberalism, socialism, and atheism to undermine western civilization and set the stage for a Jewish world government.[91] First published in 1903, the *Protocols* and hundreds of similar anti-Jewish tracts were widely circulated in Russia and later exported to western Europe by refugees from Bolshevism, including Alfred Rosenberg, Max Erwin von Scheubner-Richter, and thousands of tsarist loyalists, where they would feed the flames of hate that went into the Nazi movement.

The combined effect of economic privation and political persecution explains why the Jews of Russia fled the country in large numbers. Some of these exiles had been captivated by the rising Zionist movement that urged the Jews to re-create a Jewish state in Palestine, but others looked to the west and the United States as a better place to live. Many looked to the recently unified Germany for a permanent haven; they were attracted by its advanced technology, its superb educational institutions, its world-renowned reputation as a land of great poets, philosophers, and bold speculators, and its standing as a *Rechtsstaat* (legal state) that had recently granted Jews full civil rights. In 1871 a Jewish member of the Prussian lower house remarked with a sigh of relief after the Jews had been legally emancipated, "finally after years of waiting in vain we have landed in a safe harbor."[92] From a post-Holocaust perspective, this tragic error in judgment cries out for an explanation.

Chapter 2

German and Jew, 1700–1871

The Jewish Problem as a German Problem

Thousands of visitors to Germany, past and present, have been struck by the country's picturesque and perfectly maintained villages and towns, its friendly and tidy people, its smooth functioning transportation system, and above all, its atmosphere of conviviality (*Gemütlichkeit*). For such visitors there are lingering impressions of *biergartens* with waitresses in dirndl skirts and lace-trimmed blouses clutching great *biersteins* while oompah bands play merry tunes, of coffee houses with their rich pastries, or of meticulously organized displays of high culture (*Kultur*) in the great museums, theaters, and opera houses. But the visitor with a sense of discernment and a knowledge of the language, sooner or later, is bound to stumble on the less attractive features of the land and its people — the discovery, for example, that Germans do not like foreigners very much, especially those who have decided to settle there; that they are remarkably provincial and ethnocentric; do not take criticism of their values or mores very kindly; allow their compulsive need for competition to get the better of them to the point of bad sportsmanship; and cannot admit that other people in the world or their institutions could be any better than their own.

In the past, far more than today, there was also the annoying German habit of always deferring to authority and obeying instinctively without questioning. Obedience was considered a virtue and children were brought up so strictly and according to such unbending rules that they either obeyed by force of habit or mimicked polite behavior so convincingly that one could not tell the difference. This habit of obedience to authority, bred into the German people over centuries by secular and ecclesiastical authorities — by church, state, family, school, and the armed forces — probably constituted one of the greatest blindspots in the national character of the German people. The historian Gordon Craig, who visited Germany in 1935 as a student, had a discussion with the American consul in Munich, a man called Hathaway. Wondering why the Germans, who had expressed such irrepressible individualism as philosophers or theologians, had bowed down so willingly and abjectly

to worldly authority as citizens, he received a most revealing reply from a
man who had evidently come to appreciate and understand the Germans:

> Oh my yes, I live in a little village south of Munich, and the people there
> are hardworking and friendly and not interested in politics in general, and
> they and I like and respect each other. But if someone in uniform came to
> them and said, "March!" they would march. And if he said, "Go and cut
> off Hathaway's head! He is a bad man!," they would reply, "We didn't
> know that!" But they would cut my head off all the same.[1]

We have since come to appreciate that Hathaway's funny remark contained a deadly truth about the Germans, their own self-image, their
cultural traits, and their relations with other people. Hathaway's remark
to Craig was not unlike the impression an English psychiatrist carried
away from an interrogation of an SS concentration camp guard who
did what he did because the regulation said so: "Right from tomorrow
we have a new class of enemy — the Jews: the regulations say so."[2] Of
course, the Germans had been taught for centuries that Jews were an
enemy, but the regulations in the Nazi period constituted the official
blessing the Germans have always needed to transform their belief or biases into official practice. The organizational, collective genius that the
German people possessed for getting things done extraordinarily well
added a particularly deadly component to their Jew-hatred.

The intellectual trajectory of German Judeophobia in the modern
world runs from Andreas Eisenmenger's book *Entdecktes Judentum,*
published in 1700, to Adolf Hitler's hate book of 1925, appropriately
labeled *Mein Kampf* (My battle), a book in which fanatical, even murderous, hatred of Jews constitutes one of his central obsessions. In
between these two dates, one cannot help but notice an ongoing conversation, ebbing and flowing, simmering, and then rising to a fever pitch,
about the Jewish question, a topic that to many Germans was always
aktuell, or timely. The Enlighteners wanted to "improve the Jews" so
that they could become good citizens, the romantic nationalists wanted
them to convert to the values of the German *Volk,* to its *volksgeist;* the
liberal assimilationists counseled intermarriage and pledging higher allegiance to universal human values than to Judaic religion, family, or
ethnic community; and *völkisch* nationalists of the late nineteenth century wanted to drive them back into their ghettos, strip them of their
civil rights, or even exterminate them.

This German preoccupation with Jews and the Jewish question was
both persistent and obsessional, out of all proportion to the actual numbers of Jews who lived in the German territories in modern times. In
Eisenmenger's time, there were no more than 50,000 Jews in Germany;
a little over a century later, in 1820, the total Jewish population was
about a quarter of a million, most of whom lived in Prussia; by 1871,
when the German empire had been founded, the Jewish population
stood at 383,000 (1.5 percent); in 1925 it rose to 564,000 (.9 per-

cent); and by the time of Hitler's seizure of power, it was 503,000 (.76 percent).[3] These figures reveal that the rise in Jewish population was relatively modest and actually shows a steady decline in comparison with that of the general population between 1871 and 1933. Some historians have argued that the Jews, though numerically small, were highly visible because they lived in large cities and were overrepresented in certain occupations such as the "free professions" — business, commerce, law, medicine, journalism, and the arts. They undoubtedly took advantage of the opportunities afforded them by emancipation by attending the elite secondary schools (Gymnasia) and universities in proportionally much larger numbers than native Germans and benefiting accordingly. Their creative contributions, as will be seen, were nothing less than spectacular but therefore also caused consternation, misgiving, and envy in many Germans. At no time, however, could it be said that the Jews constituted a threat to the prosperity or spiritual well-being of the German people. Never well organized politically and seeing themselves, in fact, acculturated as Germans, the Jews posed no real threat.

As previously mentioned, however, Judeophobia was never based on reality in the first place, but on false perceptions, stereotypes, and delusions. This being the case, the Jewish question was really a German question or problem, and its understanding requires, first and foremost, the unmasking of this problem in the Germans themselves. In short, it was not the Jews who were deluded but the Germans. The nature of this problem resides in certain historical developments that have shaped the Germans' perception of their Jewish compatriots, chiefly a long-standing Christian tradition of Judeophobia, as indicated previously, distinct cultural and moral blindspots that can be attributed to the romantic movement, especially its extreme *völkisch* wing in the late nineteenth century, the obsession with biological racial utopias, and the inability of the German people, individually and collectively, to define their role as Germans in a humane ecumenical sense that was inclusive and tolerant of different religious and ethnic groups. In order to understand the Holocaust, several additional German "cultural traits" must be added — namely, an exaggerated sense of order with corresponding habits of obedience to authority (authoritarianism); undue admiration of the military and its way of life (militarism); an exclusive sense of ethnic superiority and corresponding prejudices against foreigners or "unassimilated elements"; and a strong need, rooted in past religious and philosophical traditions, for all-embracing ideological explanations in the form of worldviews.

German and Jew in the Age of Emancipation

In one of Friedrich Nicolai's works entitled *Sebaldus Nothanker* (1776), a witty and ironic *Bildungsroman* loosely patterned on Voltaire's *Candide,* the chief protagonist is called upon to write a patriotic essay on the glory of the "fatherland" and is at a loss to know what fatherland he should write about. The story illustrates a problem Germans have been wrestling with for the greater part of their history; it concerns their inability to forge a common national identity. In fact, one could argue that one of the major leitmotifs of German history is this search for national unity and identity.[4] Throughout the past five hundred years the Germans have suffered from internal religious and political divisions. By the end of the Middle Ages, Germany was a geographical expression, and its ramshackle empire — the Holy Roman Empire of the German Nation — was torn apart by centrifugal forces that left the real political power in the hands of feudal princes safeguarding a decentralized state administration at the very time other European countries had moved in the direction of centralized control. The Protestant Reformation added religious division that further weakened the development of a homogeneous nation state and erupted in the Wars of Religion, which left the country economically devastated, internally divided into 1,789 independent principalities, and at the mercy of more powerful nations.

As a result of the Thirty Years War, Germany suffered a population decline of about 35 percent — from 21 million to about 13.5 million. Some parts of Germany, mostly in the north and northcentral east (Prussia, Saxony, Hamburg) were less affected; others suffered terrible losses. Württemberg, the Palatine, and Bohemia suffered catastrophic losses in population, especially in the last phase of the war when the Swedes cut a long swath from Sweden in the north to Bavaria in the south, destroying and plundering as they went. In the last eighteen years of the war some eighteen thousand villages along with fifteen hundred towns and two hundred castles were destroyed.[5] Except for World War II, there was no instance in modern warfare when the population suffered as much as it did in the Thirty Years War. The end result was the triumph of the petty or princely nobility and of political absolutism, sanctified by religious authority. In both the Protestant north and the Catholic south, the German people were habituated to the strictest sense of obedience to princely or ecclesiastical authority. This was particularly true of the Lutheran tradition, which followed Martin Luther's compromise with worldly powers by limiting freedom, defined in purely religious or spiritual terms, to the inner life and exhorted believers to subordinate themselves in all other matters to the power of the prince. The motto Seid unterthan der Obrigkeit (Be subservient to authority) was preached by countless Lutheran ministers from their pulpits. In an eighteenth-century work on popular enlightenment (Volksaufklärung), a Protestant clergyman reminded his good parishioners: "God wills that I obey authority [Obrigkeit], and that I fulfill the tasks I am given. If I fail to do so, I sin against God because authority has not materialized by accident; it was placed there by God himself."[6]

These habits of authority, sanctioned by church and state, were also reinforced strongly in the home and in the school system. They survived the winds of revolution in the eighteenth century and were perpetuated institutionally, especially by the militaristic Prussian tradition, into the nineteenth century until, at length, they formed the basis of the new German empire in 1871. The wave of democratic theory and protest that swept over the western world, of course, also affected Germany, but it did so on a much smaller scale because the Enlightenment was much weaker and the feudal authorities remained much stronger in Germany than elsewhere in western Europe. The established authorities were able to absorb the protest through a compromise with their relatively weak, insecure, and economically dependent intellectual classes.[7] Only the Protestant north was significantly affected by the egalitarian ideas of the Enlightenment, and even here it was limited largely to a few cities such as Berlin, Hamburg, Leipzig, Halle, and Göttingen, and to a few leading intellectual circles. It also lacked a strong economic spine in the form of an increasingly assertive middle class that could have carried through economic and political changes, as happened in England or France.

The center of the German Enlightenment was Berlin, especially under the reign of Frederick the Great (1740–86), the philosopher king, sometime friend of Voltaire, lover of French culture, and supporter of the sciences and the arts. The Prussian king invited Voltaire to Berlin as his poet in residence, encouraged the propagation of the ideas of the French encyclopedists, and promoted the works of the Berlin Academy under the aegis of its president Maupertuis, a French scientist and philosopher. On the popular level, enlightened ideas were promoted by a group of "Popular Philosophers," of whom Friedrich Nicolai (1733–1811), a Berlin book dealer and popular writer, was the most vocal and influential. Nicolai espoused a somewhat simplistic and, for German intellectuals, a distinctly too optimistic philosophy that was later much satirized by many well-known intellectuals, including Goethe and Schiller; but there is no doubt that his literary efforts, expressed in novels, satires, essays, and travel books, reached a fairly wide audience. Nicolai's most famous collaborator was the Jewish philosopher Moses Mendelssohn (1729–86), who had come to Berlin in 1743 unknown, unwanted, and speaking only broken German, and through dint of hard work and mental tenacity had reached a position of intellectual preeminence enjoyed by few other Jews in Europe at the time.[8] When he first walked through the Berlin Gate in 1743, we are told, the custom's official recorded in his watchbook: "Today there passed six oxen, seven swine, and a Jew,"[9] which sums up the popular attitudes shown to Jews at the time.

A generation later, this picture had changed dramatically, owing to a large extent to Mendelssohn's efforts. By that time the Jewish population, invited into Prussia by Frederick the Great's predecessors — his father Frederick William I, Frederick I, and Frederick William (the Great Elector) — had risen from a mere 1,850 to about 4,245.[10] Mendelssohn had advised Jews to liberate themselves from the spiritual shackles of the ghetto, divest themselves of some of their obsolete rituals, and accept German culture. Mendelssohn himself remained a pious Jew all his life, and he resisted a variety of intrusively clumsy efforts to make him convert to Christianity. His cultural role was that of a mediator who opened up a dialogue with educated and cultured Germans. It was a role that put a considerable burden on this gentle and hunchbacked Jew who made his living by working as an accountant in a silk factory and who, like his solitary predecessor the lens-grinder Baruch Spinoza in Amsterdam, still found enough time and energy to philosophize and cultivate a circle of important people. Like Spinoza, he was also, despite his gentleness and distaste for controversy, a remarkably courageous man; he had the nerve, for example, to tell the king of Prussia, Frederick II — a man who habitually ridiculed German culture, refused to include any German books in his library, and surrounded himself with French advisors — to recognize and honor the importance of German cultural accomplishments. How portentous but also how ironic that it took a Jew, side by side with a number of rising German talents, to point out the importance of an indigenous German culture!

Among the new rising literary talents destined to forge a new humanistic tradition in German culture, shaping the classical Weimar synthesis of Herder, Goethe, and Schiller in the next generation, was Gotthold Ephraim Lessing (1729–81), a very close friend of Mendelssohn. Shortly before coming to Berlin and being personally introduced to Mendelssohn by the Jewish physician Gumpertz, Lessing had already struggled with the problem of fanatical faith, on both the believer's *and* the unbeliever's part, and reached the conclusion that only understanding and tolerance could solve age-old problems of intergroup hatreds and bigotries. It was in this spirit that he had written a light comedy, *Die Juden* (The Jews, 1749), in which this theme was presented to the German public in a deliberately witty manner in order to make it more acceptable. The story was simple: a baron and his daughter are attacked by bandits and saved by a brave and gallant traveler (*Der Reisende*). In return for his courageous intervention, the baron offers him his daughter's hand, only to be told by the traveler that, regretfully, he had to decline because he was a Jew:

Traveler: I am a Jew

Baron: A Jew! What cruel mischance....

Lisette: A Jew!

Fräulein: What difference does it make?

Lisette: Shush, Fräulein, I'll tell you the difference afterward.

Baron: So there are cases when Heaven itself prevents us from being grateful.

Traveler: It would be superfluous because you wish it to be.

Baron: But I wish to do at least as much as fate allows me....

Traveler: This offer is in vain for the God of my fathers has given me
            more than I need. As sole reward all I ask is that in future
            you judge my people more kindly and do not generalize. I
            did not conceal myself from you because I am ashamed of
            my religion. No! But I saw that you looked favorably on me
            but unfavorably on my people. And a man's friendship...has
            always been irresistible to me.

Baron: I am ashamed of my behavior....Everything I see of you fills
            me with rejoicing....How estimable the Jews would be if
            they were all like you!

Traveler: And how praiseworthy the Christians if they all had your
            qualities!

            (*Curtain*)[11]

The traveler, as one German literary scholar has observed, was the
first cultivated Jew in German literature,[12] a Jew, to be sure, who still
suffered from the indignities and restrictions placed upon his people,
but also a Jew who, in the eyes of his German inventor, deserved to be
treated as an equal. Exactly twenty years later in 1779, Lessing lifted
this topic of Jewish legal and social oppression to a much higher intellectual level in his drama *Nathan der Weise* (Nathan the Wise), a
lofty philosophical poem that highlights the German Enlightenment's
vision of *Humanität* (humanity). In the famous ring parable of the
third act, Lessing evoked the ideal of universal religious toleration. All
nations, at all times, Lessing indicated, have produced good people regardless of religious differences. The evil that lurks in the human heart
stems from self-love and ethnic bigotry. And only an inner transformation of the heart through love-of-other (*Nächstenliebe*) can ultimately
change that propensity for human hatred. Lessing's appeal, in other
words, is not in the form of calling the Germans to the barricades, to
arouse them to change themselves through the force of legislation, but
to their sense of moral decency. By employing the tools of literary pedagogy, Lessing hoped to change hearts and minds, which expressed the
more cautious approaches of the German *Aufklärer* who believed that a
change in consciousness could be effected without revolutionary changes
in social conditions.

   This hope for a fundamental change of heart, unaccompanied by disruptive or violent changes in society, was not fulfilled. Lessing and his
generation of Enlighteners undoubtedly prepared the way for greater tolerance and respect for religious difference, and this can be demonstrated
by the fact that the plight of German Jews was increasingly recognized
by educated people, many of whom were also seriously reaching out
to integrate Jews into German life and culture. It was surely a sign
of progress when in 1788 the actor who was playing the character of

Shylock in Shakespeare's *Merchant of Venice* explained in a prologue
to his predominantly Jewish audience in Berlin that the Jews enjoyed
great esteem and should not be offended by the views his part forced
him to express.[13] Jews began to forge closer social ties with Germans
through shared cultural interests, intermarriage, and conversion. Mendelssohn's own six children are a case in point. His two older sons,
Joseph (1777–1848) and Abraham (1776–1835), remained Jewish and
set up a bank, while his youngest son, Nathan (1782–1852), converted
to Lutheranism and became an official; of his three daughters, the el-
dest, Dorothea Mendelssohn Veit (1764–1839), led the most interesting
life because it included two marriages, a conversion to Protestantism,
and a prominent role as a host to many well-known literary and public figures. Henriette (1774–1831), the youngest, also made a mark on
the social world by opening a boarding school for Parisian society girls,
where she also conducted a salon that attracted people like Madame de
Staël, Benjamin Constant, and the composer Gaspar Spontini. The third
daughter, Recha (1767–1831), remained Jewish and appears to have led
a relatively uneventful life.[14]

Dorothea Mendelssohn, who presided over a literary salon in Berlin in the 1780s that attracted a number of Berlin writers and assorted
wives and daughters of Jewish merchants, married a Jewish banker
named Simon Veit and had two children. In 1795, she met the passionate romantic poet Friedrich Schlegel at the leading Jewish salon
held by Henriette Herz, fell madly in love with him and scandalized
Berlin with her openly conducted affair, which furnished both with
enough literary material to be able to launch two novels into the public
limelight: Schlegel's *Lucinde* (1799) and Dorothea's equally tantalizing
Florentine (1801). Dorothea converted to Protestantism in order to "legitimize" her union with Schlegel and then followed him to Vienna,
where both converted to Roman Catholicism. Henriette Herz, the wife
of Dr. Markus Herz, a friend and correspondent of Immanuel Kant, was
another prominent Jewish woman; she gathered around her a large social circle of Berlin luminaries who flocked to her salon and admired
her wit and beauty. The theologian Friedrich Schleiermacher looked at
her as his "soul mate," and Friedrich Nicolai sang praises to her beauty
and intelligence.

It was Rahel Levin (1771–1832), however, who held out the greatest
fascination to her contemporaries and whose inner struggles with her
Jewishness provide us with the most poignant insights into the Jewish-
German relationship.[15] Rahel Levin (1771–1832), the daughter of a
Jewish banker, plain looking in appearance but blessed with great intelligence and social graces, suffered the bane of being both a woman
and a Jew, never fully able to resolve within herself the differences between them. For decades, the most brilliant luminaries of Germany,
men and women of different social classes and religious beliefs, attended her literary evenings in her little garret room in the Jägerstrasse.

Present at these literary evenings were, of course, her Jewish friends, including the sons and daughters of Moses Mendelssohn and Henriette Herz, and an interesting array of guests, statesmen such as the brothers Wilhelm and Alexander Humboldt, and the poets Friedrich Schlegel, Ludwig Tieck, Adalbert von Chamisso, Clemens von Brenteno, and later the young Heinrich Heine, whom she nurtured like a second son and who, in turn, called her the *geistreichste Frau des Universum*— the richest female spirit in the universe. Present at her gatherings were also government officials like Friedrich Gentz, the Swedish ambassador Gustav von Brinckmann, and even the nephew of the great king himself, Prince Louis Ferdinand of Hohenzollern. Rahel's real inner struggle with her identity, however, took place in her solitude and her letters to a wide array of correspondents. These letters chronicle her long and tragic struggle with her Jewishness, which, on the one hand she wanted to "extirpate" in herself even if it meant complete uprootedness. But on the other hand she encountered it again and again until, at length and following a conversion to Christianity and a marriage to a Prussian diplomat, she seems to have reaffirmed it spiritually after becoming tired of constantly having to legitimize herself in vain as a bona fide German.

Rahel's life and struggle are indicative of educated Jews who were turning to German culture for a new sense of meaning and identity, finding increasingly less and less inspiration in their own religion. This was particularly true in the wake of the romantic movement and its emphasis on feeling and emotional sensibility. The German Enlightenment, as previously mentioned, was limited largely to a few intellectuals and remained apolitical, cautious, and metaphysical in orientation. The German *Aufklärer* did not develop an ideology of resistance to royal absolutionism, as did their English or French counterparts; their ethical speculations were still rooted in precapitalistic assumptions that condemned excessive risks and profits and warned against active political involvement. The German Enlightenment postulated a lofty philosophical ideal of *Humanität* and *Bildung* (humanity and self-cultivation), but it envisioned this ideal as a model of individual self-improvement on a purely aesthetic and spiritual plane, neglecting the importance of simultaneously changing the political system that presupposed its fulfillment. Additionally, the German Enlightenment did not produce a strong civil rights tradition, as did the French or the English tradition. German political and legal theory emphasized the duties of the individual in relation to the state rather than the protection of individual liberties. Inasmuch as German thinkers contemplated the idea of freedom at all, they tended to see it in Lutheran terms as freedom of individual conscience, as a spiritual process of self-discovery that had very little to do with external political authority, which was to be strictly obeyed.[16]

In a collective sense, however, the Germans became increasingly aware of their political impotence and their overdependence, culturally and politically, on foreign powers, especially the French. The Thirty

Years War, as previously mentioned, had devastated Germany in more
than just economic terms; it caused deep psychic scars that would hem-
orrhage its cultural life for well over a century. In reconstructing the
devastated cultural scene, the *Aufklärer* at first looked to France for
role models, following Frederick the Great's prejudice that good culture was synonymous with French culture. In his *Critische Dichtkunst*
(Critical art of poetry) Germany's literary preceptor, Johann Christoph
Gottsched (1700–1766), had recommended adherence to strict classical
French models, laying it down as a law that "what the Greeks were to
the Romans the French are to us."[17] A simultaneous borrowing occurred
in philosophy, which through much of the eighteenth century followed
Cartesianism rather than English empirical philosophy. As late as the
middle of the eighteenth century, a self-conscious Lessing could still say
"compared to the French, the Germans are still barbarians, more barbarian than our most barbarian forefathers."[18] Such confessions of cultural
backwardness were only too conveniently reinforced by malicious foreign commentators like Jakob Mauvillon, a French literary critic, who
taunted the Germans and dared them to name a single German endowed
with creative genius, a single German with an international reputation.
He conveniently forgot Leibniz, of course, and the Germans would soon
prove him wrong by launching a series of great movements, ranging
from *Sturm und Drang,* romanticism, Weimar Classicism, to Philosophical Idealism, and the grand musical tradition that encompassed Bach,
Handel, Haydn, Mozart, and Beethoven. Lessing and Mendelssohn's
generation, in fact, had nothing to be ashamed of, particularly since
they provided the intellectual foundation on which future generations
could build.

There is no denying the fact, however, that the Germans tried to define their own distinct cultural style out of opposition to foreign models,
particularly the French. The great intellectual fermentation in Germany,
in fact, coincided with the French Revolution and the enlightened ideas
on which it was based. The French Revolution challenged the Germans
to come to terms with their own identity and their own sense of nationality. Initially, educated Germans responded enthusiastically to the call
of liberty, equality, and fraternity, planting liberty trees and challenging
their own authorities to make liberal concessions, but gradually misgivings set in when the French revolutionaries plunged their nation into
violent upheavals and used the slogans of freedom as excuses for imperialistic expansion. The Napoleonic conquests of Germany confronted
thinking Germans with the painful fact of their national weaknesses. Although Napoleon claimed to create a United States of Europe founded
on the cosmopolitan ideals of the Enlightenment, his actual conquests
proved otherwise. Napoleon also released or rekindled ancient tribalism
in the form of strident assertions of nationalistic supremacy. This was
particularly true in Germany, where an aroused wave of nationalistic
fervor greeted the Napoleonic conquest and domination of Europe.[19]

German opposition to French rule was twofold: it prompted a nationalistic uprising against Napoleon, spearheaded largely by Prussia, and it set in motion an intellectual counterrevolution, already underway since the preromantic *Sturm und Drang* period (1770–85) that was directed against the very ideals that the French Revolution was based on: enlightened ideas of reason, universal fraternity, and the democratic rights of man. This counterrevolution, exceedingly complex in its various expressions, was the romantic movement. As Jacques Barzun noted long ago, romanticism has exhibited both perennial as well as uniquely temporal characteristics because it expresses human traits or human needs that recur from age to age, while at the same time taking on a specific temporal association, as it did in the period 1770–1830, usually labeled by historians as the age of romanticism.[20]

In the late eighteenth century, the romantic impulse was revitalized and greatly enriched by German writers, artists, and musicians, but it must also be remembered in the context of this discussion of anti-Jewish prejudices that German romanticism, reacting very strongly against what it perceived to be mistaken in the Enlightenment and in French cultural ideals, expressed itself in strident terms. An earlier generation of historians has even labeled the more extreme expressions of German romanticism as a revolt against the "west." Since no one knows with certainty what the "west" really is or whether it can be defined univocally, it seems intellectually unproductive to revive wartime models of Germany's *Sonderweg* (special path) or departure from western values. The truth is that romanticism was primarily an aesthetic movement, limited to literature, music, and the fine arts, with only peripheral and poorly focused political aims. If it had a general political thrust, especially in Germany, it was as an anti-French resistance movement prompted by Napoleon's occupation of Germany between 1806 and 1813 and as a counterthrust to French ideas and practices. Tragically, however, there was also a very shrill party in the German romantic movement that proclaimed a belligerent message of Germanic racial superiority. Although this was only a noisy wing, its historical significance was far more serious because it later grafted itself on German militarism, nationalism, and Judeophobia, thus posing a serious threat to the people of Europe.[21]

The beginning of German nationalism has often been dated to 1807 when the philosopher Johann Gottlieb Fichte (1762–1814) delivered his stirring patriotic lectures, *Addresses to the German Nation,* to a divided people that had just recently been humiliated and conquered by Napoleon. In these addresses, delivered to an enthralled audience in Berlin and under the very eyes of the French occupation, Fichte blamed the selfishness and patriotic unconcern of all citizens and called for a regeneration of the nation's greatness through dedication to the loftiest ideals and the most stringent discipline. Reminding the Germans that they were descended from a divinely chosen race, and therefore possessing the moral right to fulfill their historical destiny, he proposed the creation of an all-powerful state based on a regulated economy and system of education that would educate Germans in the highest form of patriotism. What it meant to be German was still not entirely clear to a people divided into well over thirty major principalities, speaking numerous dialects, separated from each other by surviving social and occupational distinctions, and still smarting from the great fault line of the Reformation that had divided them along religious lines.

Fichte and his generation tried to resurrect, amid all their differences, the substratum that they believed to be uniquely German: the unity among the multiplicity, so to speak. This quintessential nature, they argued, was the *Volk*, a concept that had been enshrouded for some time by the romantics in a highly mythical form. The philosopher Herder, for example, had argued in his *Ideas for a Philosophy of the History of Mankind* (1784–91) that history revealed the imprint of God, who was seen by both Herder and later by Hegel as a divine educator teaching the human race, sequentially and over a lengthy period of time, to attain a higher stage of consciousness and creative potential. God manifested his will through the instrument of his historical design: the *Volk* (people). Each *Volk* was charged, so to speak, with enacting a certain part of God's design; each *Volk* was absolutely unique, not because it was racially or biologically different, but because it had attained a unique sense of itself as a result of its idiosyncratic interaction with its native soil, its peculiar climate, and its relations with other people. A *Volk*'s unique nature was the product of its unfolding cultural experiences, particularly those embodied in its mythology. The most creative moments of peoples (*völker*) could be found in their myths, epics, or folk songs. These creations were symbolic representations of their collective existence as well as psychic bonds that integrated its members into a cohesive community. Herder made no ethical judgment about the relative merits of different people; in his view, each *Volk* had its own center of gravity and should be allowed to fulfill its divine potential.[22] This generous outlook, which respected the distinct cultural contributions of different nations and favored the free unfolding of national self-identity, had a profound and beneficial effect in rekindling ethnic pride and historical achievements throughout Europe. In Germany, it stimulated a new historical consciousness (historicism); a corresponding retrieval of ancient folklore, as in the Grimm fairy tales, the *Nibelungenlied* (Song of the Nibelungen), Arnim and Brentano's collection of folk songs (*Des Knaben Wunderhorn*); and a creative outpouring of poetic and musical compositions.

Unfortunately, such celebration of the *Volk* contained a number of disturbing features because it was frequently couched in zealous religious and millenarian terms. In the works of Ernst Moritz Arndt (1769–1860) or Friedrich Ludwig Jahn (1778–1852), the German *Volk* was no longer one of many different and equally worthy people, but a unique and chosen people better than any of the others. In the face of French domination, all Germans must therefore be taught to love their country as they would love their God. In Arndt's words, "the highest form of religion was to love the fatherland more passionately than laws and princes, fathers and mothers, wives and children."[23] The Enlightenment, he felt, had been wrong in teaching universal brotherhood and spreading the poison of equality, a radical error that could have only been sown by the Jews: "Cursed be the humanitarianism and cosmopolitanism you brag about.... Cursed be that Jewish one-worldism which you hail as the summit of human education."[24] In countless poems, especially the famous hymn *Das deutsche Vaterland* (1813), Arndt formulated an exclusive and aggressive type of German nationalism with definite racial colorations, expansionist ideas, and paeans to heroic leadership.

Even more strident in expressing his nationalistic convictions was Friedrich Ludwig Jahn, whom generations of Germans later venerated as the founder of the popular gymnastic associations that combined competitive sport with fervent nationalism. "*Turnvater* (Gym Father) Jahn," as Germans affectionately called him, taught young Germans to cultivate both their bodies and their *Deutschtum*, or Germanness, which to him meant Prussian order and duty (*Ordnung und Pflicht*), love of the fatherland, and the rekindling of ancient and therefore "real" German character traits such as plain-speaking honesty, unabashed frankness, and unflinching loyalty. Whether by nature or by design, there was always something about Jahn that reminded people of the country bumpkin who disliked refined manners or speech and preferred to be in the company of ordinary folks because they were unpretentious and uncomplicated. Indeed, Jahn was a kind of reactionary populist with a distaste for civilization, which he associated with the decadent French; his strident gospel of Germanic superiority sounded no different from that of the Nazis. Jahn's dream was the creation of a Germania or Teutonia, racially pure, socially integrated around a fervent patriotism, and politically governed by a great "Führer who was cast of iron and fire."[25]

Jahn's type of xenophobic nationalism definitely foreshadowed the sort of racially exclusive nationalism that would later be referred to as *völkisch*. The romantics did not endorse such strident ideas, any more than they did some of the perverted Nazi values later attributed to them by some historians. The romantic movement, however, provided some of the emotional and symbolic forms of representation that would predispose the German people to certain types of public persuasion, especially of an aesthetic, emotional, and patriotic kind. Since the romantic movement was the defining moment in the cultural consciousness of modern Germany, penetrating very deeply into the fabric of German life, its beliefs and values became an intimate part of the nation's persona, persisting far beyond the feudal and preindustrial world into the machine age. The historical significance of German romanticism, in fact, is that it preserved, in part, a rural, archaic, and preindustrial form of consciousness that was giving way rapidly to a different material world and therefore a different consciousness. German romanticism, reacting against the rationalism of the Enlightenment, attempted to "remythologize" the world and to redefine it once more as romance, magic, myth, legend, and the wonders of the imagination — a laudable enterprise so long as it did not confuse imagination with empirical reality or elevate the former at the expense of the latter. The extreme subjectivists among the romantics as well as the German philosophical idealists are an example of this tendency to separate feelings, emotions, sentiments, or ideas from their attachment to concrete reality and to treat them as autonomous powers. In his *Monologe* (Soliloquies, 1800) Schleiermacher essentially argued that the real is the imaginary and the imaginary is the real; and even if our greatest love is torn from us, we can still possess her in our imagination:

> The impossibility of outward accomplishment does not prevent an inner process.... As long as we belong to one another, she and I, imagination will transport us, though we have not actually met, into our lovely paradise.... Oh that men knew how to use this divine power of the imagination, which alone can free the spirit and place it far beyond coercion and limitation of any kind! For me imagination supplies what reality withholds.[26]

In a similar vein, this penchant to prefer fantasy to objective reality, one's inner feelings to their external point of reference, was expressed by Ludwig Tieck, who saw it as his task not to describe the world but to luxuriate in the feelings that were aroused by his perceptions: "I do not wish to write about these plants or mountains, but about the sentiment or mood which governs me at this very moment." Philosophy converged with literature on this point, for it also effaced the subject-object relationship by redefining or mystifying the object as nothing but the perceiver's subjective idea. In Fichte, for example, objective reality was centered entirely in the mind that was perceiving it, so that the ego was the world itself.

It was not overly helpful to mold public consciousness in terms of traditions that celebrated the preeminence of feelings and endowed them with greater cognitive merit than reason, or that elevated imagination over empirical testing. Nor was it healthy to confuse history and mythology. The Germans have given the world some of the great conceptual tools and practices of historical understanding, but they have not always perceived themselves realistically or honestly.[27] In the public arena, their collective sense of themselves was always strongly influenced by the power of mythology. Those who believed in the educational value of mythology argued that a people's shared perception of the past always created its own truth, which was independent of the objective reality of an empirically knowable past; and since the past could never be known or validated objectively, it was more useful to a society to see itself in relation to a great heroic past. This need to drink at the fountain of myth may have been for some Germans a defense mechanism by which they tried to evade reality, which was a world of political and social fragmentation.

One of the most potent myths of the German collective psyche was the belief in a hidden savior (*Führer*), a man of superhuman strength and vision who, in times of great national peril, would save the German people from oppression and bondage to foreign rule and usher in a glorious national rebirth that would last a thousand years. This theme, as is well known, was embodied in the myth of the savior king in the form of Frederick Barbarossa, the medieval emperor, who really did not die but merely slumbered on a seat next to a big oak table deep in a cavern in the Kyffhäuser mountain. Legend had it that the king's red beard kept on growing during the succeeding centuries of unrest and turmoil, and once it encircled the whole table and Germany needed him most, the king would awake from his slumber, galvanize the German people into a united force, destroy the oppressor, and usher in a glorious new Reich. The myth enchanted generations of Germans, particularly Adolf Hitler, who believed that Barbarossa slumbered in the mountains near his home at Berchtesgaden. That he actually saw himself as a savior king was subsequently proven when he embarked on his great crusade against Russia under the banner of "Operation Barbarossa."

Many nations, of course, have their mythologies, and one could study American history in terms of several seminal myths — the myth of the New Adam, of the New Jerusalem or City on a Hill, of the Frontier, of Manifest Destiny, of the Self-Made Man, of Equality, and the like — but the content of the myth in terms of its ennobling message and the influence it has on the people who believe it is the decisive factor. And what the myth of Barbarossa, of Siegfried and the Nibelungen, of Valhalla and its warrior heroes, of a glorious Thousand-Year Reich, of some ultimate world conflagration (*Götterdämmerung*) tells us is of a troubled and torn people, obsessed by haunting images of death, who often prefer fantasy for reality and see themselves historically victimized by forces of truly demonic proportions. The romantics did not create this perception — it was deeply embodied in Germanic legend and folklore — but what they did was to solidify it in the spiritual life of the German people. They also reinforced the German sense of being torn or split by deep psychic and social divisions, a theme that figured prominently in the nation's greatest cultural representations — from the various permutations of the Faust legend in Goethe or Thomas Mann, E. T. A. Hoffmann's story about a *Doppelgänger*, or double, in *Elixiere des Teufels* (The devil's elixir), "the two Germanies" embodied in the contrasting symbols of Weimar and Potsdam, the split nature of Germany's religious existence as Catholics and Protestants, the sociological dichotomies of

Gemeinschaft vs. *Gesellschaft, Kultur* vs. *Zivilisation,* to the wall that separated East and West Germany.

The romantics also dwelled on several other obsessions: the reality of radical evil, the power of the irrational, and the dark side of life in the shadow of death. The reality of radical evil has had a long history in European consciousness, but in few other countries was it as sharply accentuated as it was in Germany. In the collective memory of the German people the belief that they dwelled in a world of great evil was present at crucial moments of their history. It constituted a key role in Martin Luther's vivid and troubled perception and in his Protestant followers, it was embodied in the artistic perception of Dürer and the Baroque artists, in the glamorization of death by several romantic poets (Novalis, Tieck, Kleist) and their *völkisch* epigoni, and it was also a powerful factor in the stylization of death in the German armed forces during two world wars.

Finally, the romantic movement postulated an essentially reactionary worldview in its celebration of the unspoiled countryside and the time-honored medieval tradition of social hierarchy. Some of this nostalgia for medieval society was a reaction to the odious consequences of modern industrialization with its grimy cities and dehumanizing workplaces. This theme of alienation under capitalism, of course, was also prominent in the social protest that inspired the liberal and socialist movements. Unfortunately, in Germany it also linked up in the late nineteenth century with the extreme *völkisch* movement and its reactionary attitudes of blood and soil and the stereotypical association of the Jew with the worst excesses of industrial capitalism.

The darker sides of the romantic movement that have been described did not fully manifest themselves until the end of the century, and then in a perverted form that most romantics would have rejected. In the early nineteenth century most Germans and Jews saw the movement as a liberating one and strongly identified with its positive features: its emotional sensibility, poetic and musical beauty, and psychological depth.

The Jewish Response to Emancipation

The Jewish response to emancipation and to the great golden age of German culture between 1780 and 1848 was in the nature of a powerful attraction, and for many young Jews it almost amounted to a seduction.[28] From a political point of view, emancipation was still half realized because the Prussian Edict of 1812, which promised the Jews full equality under the law, was riddled with loopholes, was significantly curtailed in the wake of Napoleon's defeat, and was not fully implemented for all of Germany until 1871. Nevertheless, a window of opportunity had been opened for the Jews of Germany, and many of them saw definite glimpses of the promised land. Throughout the first half of the nineteenth century, Jewish acculturation to German society continued unabated — so much so, that it not only raised concern for Germans but for many anguished rabbis who became convinced that too many of their young people were becoming ashamed of their faith. During the Napoleonic occupation many Jews strongly supported the German cause, and some young Jews fought in the Prussian army. One of them was Meno Burg, who served as a geometry instructor in the artillery branch during the Napoleonic wars and who became the first and, for a long time, the only Jewish officer. Burg's career was seriously hindered by his Jewishness, which exposed him to periodic anti-Jewish biases and delayed his promotion from lieutenant to major until 1847, thirty-four years after he had enlisted.[29]

Similar limitations were experienced by Jewish students who sought admission to the institutions of higher learning. In 1810 the University of Berlin, founded by Wilhelm von Humboldt and presided over by J. G. Fichte as its first rector, opened its door to its first entering class of 247, of whom 16 were Jewish. Only three years prior, the first Jewish magazine published in German, *Sulamith*, made its appearance; its editor, David Fränkel, appealed to the Jews of Germany to support a modern system of education if they wanted their children to enjoy a meaningful, productive life. Many Jews already knew what Fränkel was telling them, namely, that advancement in society required education. In fact, they eagerly grasped at the new opportunities and organized their own schools or, more commonly, sent their children to the German Gymnasiums and universities. Jewish learning was increasingly separated from the synagogue and attached itself, with alarming implications, to secular institutions. By the middle of the nineteenth century, a new generation of university-trained Jewish scholars, impressed by the prospect of western learning, began to reexamine its Judaic heritage, just as the philosophes and later the Higher Critics were doing on the Christian side.

In late 1819, just when the anti-Jewish Hep! Hep! riots erupted in Germany, a group of avant-garde Jewish intellectuals founded the Verein für Cultur und Wissenschaft der Juden (Society for the Culture and Science of the Jews), which was dedicated to a reexamination of Judaic beliefs and practices, a process that had already begun with Moses Mendelssohn, the German-Jewish Haskala (enlightenment), and the spread of Reform Judaism. What was interesting about the founding of the Verein in 1819 was not its novelty or even its stated effort to reexamine Judaic beliefs, but the fact that two important founders — Eduard Gans and Heinrich Heine — converted to Christianity shortly after helping to found the society, which gave added poignancy to Friedrich Schleiermacher's conviction that Judaism was dead. Indeed, throughout the early nineteenth century there was a veritable *Taufwelle*, or baptismal wave, by Jews into the Christian faith. In some communities whole families converted, as did the Marxes in Trier and many families in Berlin.[30]

Although the traditionalists undoubtedly overreacted when they feared for the survival of the Jewish faith, there is no denying that German culture exerted a very powerful pull on the Jews — so much so, as Gershom Scholem observed, that many of them "began casting yearning and furtive glances at the realm of German history as a possible replacement for the Jewish realm."[31] What was it that led to this German-Jewish symbiosis or cultural dialogue, as some prefer to call it. Gordon Craig used the analogy of a "family resemblance"[32] in referring to the German-Jewish relationship because both groups, as a result of loosely similar historical and cultural experiences, shared a surprising number of similar values: a strong sense of family, hard work, commitment to religion, and great respect for education. Since the majority of Jews in modern times, especially the eastern Jews (Ashkenazim), first encountered the Germans in moving toward the western world, they acquired a mentality and intellectual framework that was distinctly German.[33] They attached themselves so closely to the German mentality that, to use another metaphor, they often became *Doppelgänger,* half Jewish and half German, unable to integrate the two sides because the Germans would never let them do so.

It may be one of the supreme ironies of history that the Jewish-German affinity, forged by the accidents of history, would turn out to be the most explosive in a long line of similar pairings of gentiles and Jews. In trying to get to the bottom of this German-Jewish affinity and interpenetration, Erich Kahler once observed that the relationship was more volatile because it followed a long and winding period that, through accordance and discordance, touched the very nerves of existence in the sense that both people came under the spell of a peculiarly deadly love-hate relationship.[34] The German cultural historian Friedrich Sieburg described both German and Jews as two people who are

> admired and hated... both equally unable to make themselves liked, equally ambivalent between servility and arrogance, equally indispensable as well as troublesome to the world, equally aggressive, equally inclined to self-pity, equally vilified without distinction and admired for the boldness of their thinking; musical, talented for speculative thinking, but hopelessly different in one point: in their attitude toward violence. How deeply they were interwoven with our life![35]

The similarities alluded to by Sieburg are accidental results of historical experiences rather than innate predispositions, and in many instances they were the consequence of the historical misfortunes that befell both peoples. Both never fully defined their character in political terms because they existed for most of their past as transnational people, unable until recently to integrate themselves into a cohesive national community. Buffeted by historical setbacks, both compensated for their lack of identity by cultivating spiritual rather than political pursuits. Until the middle of the nineteenth century, German intellectual life was largely preoccupied with metaphysical questions relating to the meaning of existence, the relationship between human beings and God, the problem of evil and suffering in the world, and the role of the transcendent in art, literature, philosophy, and history. The poet and critic Friedrich Schlegel, husband of Dorothea née Mendelssohn, addressed himself to young Germans by telling them, "Do not waste culture on the mundane realm of low politics, but offer up your innermost being to the divine world of scholarship and art, in the sacred fire of eternal *Bildung.*"[36] Madame de Staël's description of Germany as a land of poets and philosophers was therefore not entirely overdrawn. During the first great intellectual fermentation that seized the country between 1770 and 1848, Germany was indeed a land of philosophers and poets (*Denker und Dichter*), but that was because the still prevailing feudal system made it difficult for Germans to direct their creative energies into political channels. Thus, just as the Jews found the only outlet for their abilities in a few officially sanctioned fields, the German intellectuals also tended to express their creative abilities in the "safe" realm of abstract speculation.

German and Jew, therefore, were forced to displace vital energies, and so it came about that they turned these energies into similar academic or speculative pursuits. In the unpolitical German intellectual of the eighteenth century, as previously shown, the Jew encountered a sympathetic partner and explored the possibility of cultural dialogue. The friendship between Moses Mendelssohn and Lessing, one representing the Jewish and the other the German Enlightenment, furnishes the highest examplar of the German-Jewish cultural dialogue. Lessing's great drama *Nathan der Weise* reflects not only this common meeting ground of German and Jew in the humane values of the Enlightenment but also the lack of concrete experience which informed its noble rhetoric. Being apolitical, both Germans and Jews could conceptualize a new heaven and a new earth; they could project religious-philosophical abstractions against concrete reality, but had to leave it up to others to carry them out politically.

The unpolitical German has been the subject of considerable discussion, but far less has been written about the unpolitical Jew. Walter Laqueur, however, has drawn attention to this fact several times, arguing that Jews "have shown great ability on the level of abstract thought, but politics also involves instinct, common sense, wisdom, and foresight, and in this respect their record has not been impressive" — a judgment that has also been made about the Germans.[37] Even when both people have concerned themselves with politics, they have done so in speculative form by viewing politics in teleological terms as the inevitable manifestation of immanent principles or laws. Much of nineteenth-century thought, for example, centers around the philosophy of Hegel and Marx, the former viewing the historical process from the perch of his lofty idealism and the latter from a secularized Judeo-Christian millenarianism.

Not only did Germans and Jews encounter each other in similar thought patterns; they also expressed themselves in the same language. Beginning with Mendelssohn, Jewish writers in Germany almost universally used the German language to express their innermost thoughts, and they would carry this German intellectual framework with them all of their lives, including into their eventual exile. Theodor Herzl, one of the spiritual founding fathers of the state of Israel and leader of the Zionist movement, wrote his book *Der Judenstaat* (The Jewish state) in German. Eastern European Jews looked to Germany as a land of opportunity, eagerly assimilating German language and culture. In the words of one eastern Jew:

> The writings and thoughts of the representatives of German intellectual life were highly spread among the Jews of the east. The ideal of many young Jews was to sit at the feet of German professors, to learn their language, and to enjoy Germany's freedom and culture.... Even those who could not travel felt attracted by Germany. And when my heart longed for the spirit of the people, I was driven toward Germany — I might almost say, to the mother country of my language.[38]

The close linguistic tie between Germans and Jews was embodied in the Yiddish (*Jüdisch*) dialect, the language of many lower-class Jews in eastern Europe. Yiddish was an offspring of medieval high German dialects with additional words drawn from the Hebrew and Slavic languages, written in Hebrew characters and widely spoken by Jews in their eastern and western communities. Most Germans had little difficulty in understanding or appreciating parts of Yiddish speech, though as the animosities between the two people intensified, the Yiddish dialect became a stigma to the person speaking it in German society. Even among the educated urban Jews, who were speaking Yiddish, Hebrew, and German, the Yiddish dialect rapidly declined after 1830.

The German-Jewish affinities just described often fostered some fundamental distortions about the real nature of both ethnic groups. Jews themselves tended to contribute to this cultural misunderstanding by believing in the ideal of the humane, tolerant, and civilized German, embodied for many Jews in the overidealized image of the poet Friedrich Schiller, who "was more real than their encounter with actual Germans."[39] We may call this idealized image the "Weimar stereotype"; it involved the belief that Germany, at its highest, exemplified the spirit of Schiller, Goethe, Herder, Bach, Beethoven, and the classical *paideia*. Such views, however, were unrealistic because Weimar culture did not exist outside the small and unpolitical circles of poets and writers who created a brief, but ephemeral, enclave of civilized refinement in the early nineteenth century. The Jews either mistook this kind of Germany for the real one or they assumed, throughout their troubled relationship with the Germans, that the classical-liberal tradition within German culture would gradually gain the upper hand over an emerging neoromantic and illiberal Germany. The larger Germany, as it was gradually defining itself in the nineteenth century, would become the Prussianized Germany of Bismarck and the kaiser, the land of "blood and iron," not the country of poets and philosophers.

Saul Ascher (1767–1822), a Jewish bookseller and scholar, was one of the first to recognize the danger of this other Germany when he referred, as early as 1815, to the recent wave of xenophobic nationalism as Germanomania. Ascher was reacting to a change in mood concerning the Jews. Just how dramatic this change was can be gauged by the fact that in 1820 Berlin audiences, listening to a musical performance of *Hebrew Melodies,* had to be told that the lyrical treatment of Jews was really not as fond as it appeared to be, a dramatic reversal of generational attitudes, for it will be recalled that only twenty years earlier public apologies were issued to audiences not to assume anti-Jewish intentions through the performance of Shakespeare's *Merchant of Venice.*[40]

This shift in mood can be attributed to the rise of romantic nationalism and its espousal of a pure German national character, which, of course, implied the removal of all alien elements. Christian Friedrich Rühs (1781–1820), a Berlin historian, set off a lengthy and heated public debate about the German national character in relation to the Jewish national character, formulating the discussion in such dogmatic terms as to leave no doubt in anyone's mind that Germans and Jews were unalterably different and therefore could not coexist in a German national community: "A people cannot become a single whole [*ein Ganzes*] except through the internal coalescence [*inniges Zusammenwachsen*] of all the traits of its character, by a manner of their manifestations: by thought, language, faith, by devotion to its constitution."[41]

This radical formulation of the German-Jewish question, affirmed by a whole group of German intellectuals such as Fichte, Jakob Friedrich Fries, Karl Wilhelm Friedrich Grattenauer, and others, made it difficult for the Jews as Jews to find a safe home in Germany. What this small band of xenophobic nationalists, in essence, was saying was that the Jews had to purge themselves of their Jewishness and become German. It is also quite clear that they did not mean by this that the Jews only had to convert to Christianity; rather they had to become members of the German tribe and accept the whole panoply of its values and customs. Before Germany was unified in 1871, there was no such being as a "German citizen"; there were only Prussians, Bavarians, Württembergers, Saxons, Austrians, and the like. The universal quality "German" thus did not mean citizen but member of an ethnic group. As long as the Jews remained religiously and ethically distinct, they could never be accepted as full Germans in the eyes of a growing number of intellectuals and ordinary Germans who believed in a mystical fatherland based on ancestral blood ties.[42]

Those who conceived of the fatherland as a mystical community of ancestral blood ties in the early nineteenth century already doubted that

either conversion or acculturation to German values could redeem the
Jews from their Jewishness. Fichte angrily remarked that changing the
Jews would probably mean that "the only way to give them citizenship
would be to cut off their heads on the same night in order to replace
them with those containing no Jewish ideas."[43] The reactionary Hartwig
von Hundt-Radowski went one step further by demanding either the liquidation or sterilization of Jewish men in order to rid Germany of the
Jewish vermin. Few were willing to endorse such exterminatory ideas
in the nineteenth century, and Hundt-Radowski actually was imprisoned for his political activities and later publicly apologized to the Jews
for his Judeophobic remarks.[44] But it was becoming alarmingly clear to
many Jews that, no matter what they did — convert, assimilate, become
more perfect than the Germans — there would always remain a gnaw-
ing doubt in the mind of their German counterparts that "once a Jew,
always a Jew."

How Jews agonized over this stubborn refusal to be accepted as
equals may be illustrated by the careers of four interesting Jewish
converts: Friedrich Julius Stahl (1802–61), Eduard Gans (1798–1839),
Ludwig Börne (1786–1837), and Heinrich Heine (1797–1856). The first
two converted to Christianity out of convenience in order to pursue their
academic careers as university professors, which essentially required a
Christian affiliation as a prerequisite for appointment. Stahl, whose real
name was Jolson, became a conservative Christian defender of Prussian-
ism and the patriarchal state. In his *Die Philosophie des Rechts nach
geschichtlicher Ansicht* (The philosophy of law in historical perspective, 1830), Stahl decisively rejected notions of abstract rights based
on natural law in favor of tradition and custom, coming to the ed-
ifying conclusion, probably reinforced by his rabbinical training, that
law must be a reflection of a nation's religious traditions and its corresponding ethical and customary practices. Stahl belonged to a growing
number of Jewish apostates who decisively rejected Judaism and went
so far as to argue that unconverted Jews had no place in a Christian
German state. As professor of law at the University of Berlin and later
a member of the Prussian Upper House, he became an influential philosophical mouthpiece of the Prussian Conservative Party. His predecessor
at the University of Berlin, Eduard Gans, also converted to Christianity and became a right-wing Hegelian, editing the master's *Geschichte
der Philosophie* (History of philosophy) and *Rechtsphilosophie* (Philosophy of right) and playing an important role in university affairs. Like
Stahl, he was uncomfortable with his origin, avoided association with
Jews, and in 1838 signed a petition circulated by the law department
that called for excluding Jews from obtaining law degrees.[45]

Unlike Stahl and Gans, who seemed to shed their Jewishness with
a cool detachment one would expect of nimble legal minds, the poets
Börne and Heine found it far more difficult to integrate themselves,
socially and psychologically, into the mainstream of German society.

Ludwig Börne, originally called Juda Loew Baruch, had gone from Frankfurt to Berlin in order to study medicine under Markus Herz, but he quickly fell more under the influence of Henriette Herz and through her circle under the spell of Berlin cosmopolitanism and religious skepticism. Shifting from medicine to law, he studied at various German universities until finally receiving a law degree from the University of Giessen in 1808. Shortly afterward, he obtained a post in the municipal government of the city of Frankfurt, a post from which he was unceremoniously dismissed because of his Jewishness in the wake of the new restrictions that were reimposed in 1815. Three years later, he converted to Christianity, adopted the name Ludwig Börne, and reinvented himself as a writer, publisher of a new magazine, *Die Waage* (The scale), and passionately promoted the cause of human emancipation. As Karl Marx and Heine would also discover, Germany was not a hospitable place for liberal critics. Plagued by ignorant censors and uninterested readers, Börne suspended publication and went to Paris as a political and cultural exile. His carefully crafted essays are little gems that went unappreciated by his fellow Germans, many of whom directed a steady stream of anti-Jewish invectives against him. Some could never forgive him for his attacks on Goethe and Schiller, the two towering German icons, but Börne's purpose was to arouse the Germans to move beyond the Olympian heights that Goethe and Schiller had cultivated and to commit themselves to liberal change. In return he was branded an unpatriotic Jew, to which he replied:

> It is like a miracle! A thousand times have I experienced it and yet it is eternally new to me. Some reproach me because I am a Jew; others excuse me for it; a third praises me for it. But all of them think of it. They are as though they are fixed by the spell of this magic Jewish circle and no one can get out of it. I also know quite well where this evil charm comes from. The poor Germans! Living in the lowest floor, oppressed by seven floors of the upper classes, their anxiety is made lighter by speaking of people who are still lower than they are and who live in the cellar. No, the fact that I was born a Jew has not embittered me against the Germans and has never deluded me.... Yes, because I was a bondsman, I therefore love liberty more than you.... Yes, because I was born without a fatherland my desire for a fatherland is more passionate than yours.... I want to be completely free again, I have built my house of freedom from the bottom up; do as I have done and do not feel content with covering the roof of a rotten political edifice with new tiles.[46]

Börne died in exile, neglected and forgotten. A somewhat similar fate befell Heinrich Heine, with the difference that the Germans, try as some of them might, could not afford to dismiss a man who is widely acknowledged as the greatest lyric poet next to Goethe. His career followed a similar pattern we have already seen in Börne and to a lesser extent in Stahl and Gans. Born in French-occupied Düsseldorf (1797) and destined for a career in business, Heine originally pursued a legal

career, studying at Bonn, Göttingen, and Berlin, but discovered a taste
for literature instead. In 1825 he converted to Christianity in order to
obtain, as he later put it, "an entrance card to European culture." His
conversion, however, would touch a raw nerve that never healed, for
Heine quickly discovered, as he freely admitted, that he had entered a
hollow space moving about as neither a Christian nor a Jew, and despised by both. His romantic attachment to Germany, more ideal than
real, inspired some of the greatest poems in German literature, notably
Die Lorelei, which like so many of his poems evoked passionate and
yearning feelings for the native soil, its people, and the past. It was characteristic of his vindictive German critics until the Nazi period to doubt
his pedigree and to attack his lyrical powers as artificial and marred
by typically satirical blemishes common to the Jewish mind. The truth
is that Heine was both a poet and a satirist, uniquely so because his
love of country, its people, and its rich tradition inspired a genuine
longing, while at the same time prompting him, as a Jewish outsider,
to perceive its tragic blindspots. Few critics of the German condition
have therefore been as objective and honest as Heine, which may explain why the Germans could not stomach him after he satirized their
cultural pretensions and their exaggerated nationalism. To the Germans
he was a disturber of the peace, a gadfly who both praised and criticized the best and the worst in their traditions. After realizing that the
Germans took themselves too deadly seriously, refused to examine their
sacred pieties, and showed little interest in democratic freedom, Heine
became a permanent exile in France, where he threw barbs at the Germans in a vain attempt to arouse the smug German philistines from
their dreamy and unpolitical existence and make them join the world
of freedom and democracy.

Heine's dream of a free and democratic Germany would be long delayed; in the meantime, he preferred to love his country from a distance,
confessing that he would respect its flag if the Germans lived up to
the lofty pretensions of their great thinkers. A young German-Jewish
socialist, who assisted Heine in launching his Deutschland, ein Win-
termärchen (Germany, a winter's tale) in Paris, a man called Karl Marx,
the father of modern communism, had passed through very similar
experiences in wrestling with his German-Jewish conscience.[47]

Born in 1818 in the Rhenish city of Trier, a recent acquisition of
Prussia, Marx was descended on both sides of the family from a long
line of rabbis who had only recently left the narrow confines of the
Jewish ghetto. His father, Heinrich Marx, had been one of only three
professional men in Trier who faced dismissal from their positions when
the Prussian authorities reimposed some of the old legal provisions that
barred Jews from holding government or civil service positions. In order
to retain his legal appointment at the provincial court, Heinrich and
his family converted to the Lutheran Church, a step that eventually
earned him the title of Justizrat and with it a comfortable life, free of

financial worries, as a prominent member of the community.[48] Heinrich remained a cautious, timid, and grateful Jew all his life, but his oldest son, Karl, who early on displayed a fiercely independent mind, great energy, and extraordinary will power, made his way in the world as one of the greatest social trailblazers in modern times. The history of Karl Marx was a peculiarly German-Jewish history because the philosophical system that he launched into the world in the form of communism was essentially an intellectual fusion of German (Hegelian) idealism and Jewish-Christian millenarianism.

In his younger student years Marx had studied law and philosophy at the Universities of Bonn and Berlin, assimilating Hegelian idealism and moving in the company of young liberals, many of whom were Jewish like himself. His affiliation with progressive and critical thinkers at the university, notably the critic Bruno Bauer, prevented him from obtaining an academic appointment after he received his doctoral degree in 1841. The tenuous social standing of a German Jew, even a recently emancipated one, had been on Marx's mind since his days as a Gymnasium student when he had written an essay for his finals in German composition, entitled "The Reflections of a Youth before Choosing a Profession." In this highly revealing essay, the course of Marx's life is remarkably foretold in that it speaks about overcoming selfishness and serving humanity, while at the same time, as though conscious of the limitations that would await an idealistic Jew, it interrupts the flow of idealism by saying that "we cannot always take up the profession for which we feel ourselves suited; our relations in society have begun to crystallize more or less before we are in a position to determine them."[49]

In 1841, if not much earlier, young Marx realized that the social relations in a Prussian-dominated society were not conducive to a free spirit, not even in the universities, which were state controlled and at that time under the watchful eye of reactionary ministers like Johann Eichhorn. Marx then did the next best thing to taking a university position: he went into journalism by joining the liberal middle-class newspaper *Rheinische Zeitung* (Rhenish Gazette) as an investigative reporter and, after only a year of service, became its chief editor. Working closely with Moses Hess, another Jewish journalist and the man who showed him the way to socialism, Marx wrote a series of penetrating articles on civil rights, in which he castigated the illiberal proceedings of the Rhenish diet and its high-handed decrees aimed at restricting freedom of speech. He also displayed the first flashes of that famous moral outrage, delivered in a form that combined penetrating scholarship with contemptuous sarcasm, that we associate with his later works and that found an outlet in his rousing defense of exploited peasants and wine growers in the Rhineland.

Marx's newspaper work brought him face to face with the reality of power in a conservative Christian age, including its vested interests, social pretensions, and ideological justifications. While he worked for the

Rheinische Zeitung, the Jewish question was extensively discussed by Marx and his circle and it found its way into two contentious articles, one by Bruno Bauer and the other by Marx. In his pamphlet *Judenfrage,* an intellectually reckless attack on the whole Judeo-Christian tradition, Bauer tried to undermine the intellectual basis on which both religions rested, naively assuming that in having dealt a mortal blow to religious consciousness, the social conditions for complete liberation and freedom would be automatically created. Marx responded with an essay of his own, entitled *On the Jewish Question* (1843), by arguing that the elimination of religion, however praiseworthy, would not automatically involve a corresponding elimination of the political system to which it was connected, nor to the removal of the real obstacle to "human" emancipation — the economic and social relations that are embodied in modern capitalism. Bauer was particularly mistaken, Marx thought, in identifying the Jewish problem with the Jewish religion rather than the Jewish national character that had defined itself by the way Jews were making a living, primarily through huckstering (*Schachern*) and money-lending.[50] The truth is that Jewish personality had become a mere reflection of the worst elements in modern capitalism — that is, selfishness and greed. Marx's identification of the Jews with capitalistic greed and his sweeping assertion that the social emancipation of the Jews was really nothing but the emancipation of society from Jewry have sometimes been referred to as examples of Jewish self-hatred, and there is no doubt that Marx, like many secular Jews, was probably ashamed of his Jewishness, embarrassed to encounter it in the economic system he despised, and eager to disavow his connection by attacking both. On the other hand, it seems unlikely that Marx was so consumed with Jewish self-hatred that he tried to purge that hatred by displacing it onto capitalism, which would lead to the absurd conclusion that the primary motivation for his communistic convictions must be sought in his inability to resolve some deep-seated psychological problem.

If Marx's attack on the Jews cannot so easily be regarded as an instance of Jewish self-hatred, it can certainly be regarded as an instance of an emerging secular strand of Judeophobia, prominent at the time among the young Hegelians and later among certain sections of the socialist movement. This strand, as seen in Marx, holds the Jew primarily culpable for having internalized the egotistic values of modern capitalism and only secondarily guilty for sticking to a fossilized religion with a cruel, vengeful, and selfish God.

Marx's newspaper career was cut short in Germany when the authorities suppressed *Die Rheinische Zeitung* in 1843 for espousing radical ideas. By that time Marx had already moved beyond liberalism to socialism and was about to take a series of decisive steps that would put him on a collision course with political authorities throughout Europe. Marrying his childhood sweetheart, Jenny von Westphalen, the daughter of a Prussian state official in Trier and his father's superior at the provincial court, Marx said goodbye to Germany, bitterly complaining after his dismissal from the *Rheinische Zeitung* that he was "tired of the hypocrisy, stupidity, and the brutality of the authorities and of our submissiveness, pliancy, evasiveness, and hairsplitting. The government has given me freedom once more.... In Germany I can do nothing more. One only debases oneself here."[51]

We know the rest of the story: Marx first went to Paris, where he became a confirmed communist, and then after his expulsion from France, settled for three years in Belgium, teaming up with Friedrich Engels to write the first significant formulation of communism and its political goals in the *Communist Manifesto* (1848). Marx's provocative pamphlet was hardly off the press when the Revolution of 1848 broke out in Paris and subsequently spread to the great capitals of Europe — to Berlin, Vienna, Prague, and Budapest. With most of the conservative-reactionary governments on the run, Marx's opening lines of the *Manifesto* seemed to become a reality: a specter was indeed haunting Europe, but Marx miscalculated in thinking that the specter was communism when it was really a weak bourgeois liberalism. Still Marx flitted back to Germany, reissued the old *Rheinische Zeitung* under the title *"Neue" Rheinische Zeitung* and tried to promote a revolutionary reconstitution of society. Unfortunately, the great hopes of the reformers for a united and democratic Germany went up in flames and decisively changed the future of Germany, Karl Marx, and the Jews of Germany. The established regimes, as it would turn out, still had the support of the majority of the German people and, more importantly, the armed forces. They quickly staged a counterrevolution that put an end to the democratic Frankfurt parliament, which had managed to write a democratic constitution for a united Germany.

It is almost painful to read this story today, to watch the ridicule heaped upon the representatives of the liberal delegation from Frankfurt as it tried to offer the crown of the new proposed Germany to Frederick William IV of Prussia, only to be told by him that he could not accept such a crown from the gutter — that is, from the people — but only from his fellow princes. The liberal delegation was quickly shooed out of Berlin, ridiculed by the conservative newspaper *Kreuzzeitung* as "beggars and bankrupt speculators in cast-off popular sovereignty."[52] Karl Marx was also chased out of Germany for good in the wake of the counterrevolution; in the autumn of 1849, he arrived in London, where he would remain for the rest of his life, writing his seminal works and organizing the international Communist movement.

In following Marx's life, we can trace the career of a secularized and radicalized Jew that would later repeat itself in the lives of such well-known German socialists as Ferdinand Lassalle, Eduard Bernstein, Karl Kautsky, Rosa Luxemburg, Gustav Landauer, and Kurt Eisner. Given a tradition of persecution and oppression, together with a strong religious belief in universal justice, Jews could more readily empathize with the underdog, and they could perhaps also provide a keener intellectual framework in articulating their protest.[53] Although eager to adapt to Christian values, as did Gans or Stahl, many young Jews with a social conscience drifted almost instinctively into liberal and, more often, radical causes, not only in the obvious political sense but also in the intellectual sense of being radical innovators in the arts, the sciences, or the social sciences. Their position as outsiders, even when they thought they were insiders, gave them a degree of detachment throughout their history that enabled them to perceive the strengths and flaws of the respective societies in which they lived with a remarkable degree of clarity that was often concealed to those who were immersed in it. Conversely, it brought on them a constant shower of denunciation from communities that could not stomach criticism and misunderstood, as was the case with the Germans, even the mildest form of national criticism as subversive.

Modern Jewish social conscience expressed itself in the great democratic movements of the nineteenth century — particularly democracy and democratic socialism. The tragedy for both Germans and Jews was that Germany pursued an undemocratic path, beginning with the Second Reich (1871–1918) and then, after a failed experience in the Weimar period (1919–33), consummating the experience with authoritarian and illiberal traditions in the totalitarian system of the Third Reich (1933–45).

Chapter 3

German and Jew in the Second Reich

On September 30, 1862, Otto von Bismarck marched into the Prussian Lower House, where the Budget Commission had been deliberating on how to break the constitutional deadlock that had developed between the king and the legislature over army appropriations. He delivered an aggressive speech in which he contemptuously waved aside the possibility of a constitutional solution and high-handedly declared that "the great questions of the time will be decided not by speeches and resolutions of majorities — that was the mistake of 1848 and 1849 — but by blood and iron."[1] Over the next nine years Bismarck made good on this declaration by breaking the constitutional deadlock in unconstitutional ways, expanding the power of the Prussian state, and delivering on a boast he had made to Disraeli that he would "declare war on Austria, dissolve the German Confederation, subjugate the middle and smaller states, and give Germany national unity under the control of Prussia."[2] The "Iron Chancellor" had indeed unified Germany by a combination of clever diplomacy as well as "blood and iron," and on January 18, 1873, after the defeat of France, he celebrated his remarkable achievement in the Hall of Mirrors in the palace of Versailles, where he staged an elaborate ceremony attended by the major princes of the German state and proclaimed King William of Prussia the emperor of the new, unified Germany.

Most Germans were swept away by patriotic fervor, and writers, musicians, and artists rose to the occasion by idealizing the great event, captured in all its romantic grandeur by the painter Anton von Werner in a gigantic historical canvas. Not all Germans, of course, were ecstatic with the prospect of a Prussianized Germany: the rulers of the individual states, some of whom had to be cajoled or bribed to join the union, Catholics who feared that a Prussian state would mean a Protestant state, liberals who still had reservations about the reactionary leanings of the Prussian elite, socialists who not altogether without good reason suspected a reign of repression. The Jews, too, had good reason to be cautious, despite the fact that some seven thousand of them had fought with distinction in the German army during the Franco-Prussian

War. The chief Jewish newspaper in Germany, the *Allgemeine Zeitung des Judenthums,* reacted to the news of unification by cautiously reminding its readers that the Jews had struggled very hard to achieve human dignity and equality under the law, that they had come a long way, but also that they had not yet reached their goal.[3] On the positive side, the newly unified Germany granted Jews full legal equality; painful experiences, however, had taught the Jews that laws could easily be rescinded, violated through numerous restrictions, or undermined through various forms of social discrimination. Although they were treated as citizens in a legal state (*Rechtsstaat*), the acquisition and interpretation of citizenship remained in the hands of the individual states and its officials; it would therefore be more accurate to speak of Prussian or Bavarian citizenship, which was a prerequisite to German citizenship. Some state governments, as it would turn out, made naturalization practically impossible.[4]

It was heartening, of course, that Germans appeared to accept and tolerate the Jews on both the legal and social levels, but the treatment they often received from Germans and the ambiguous signals they picked up as they interacted with them were such that they could never dispel a certain feeling of unease or skepticism. Even the language of the emancipators was laced with hidden assumptions and did not seem to be inspired by Enlightenment beliefs in a pluralistic society in which the natural rights of all citizens would be protected. From the beginning of the empire until its end, the Jewish question simply did not go away and most Germans assumed that the Jews would eventually be assimilated and abandon their separate status as Jews.[5] Their refusal brought on surprise, misgivings, outright discrimination, and, at its most extreme, calls for expulsion. What stood between the Jews and their mistreatment by Jew-haters was ultimately the German state; and as long as it was a civilized state, observing equitable and humane principles, the Jews could count on being treated with relative decency. The German state was a civilized state until Hitler came to power in 1933; from that moment on Germany was no longer civilized. There are, however, degrees of civilization, as any comparative perspective of different societies reveals. In the context of the late nineteenth century, the German state was not the best but neither was it among the worst. In trying to understand the eventual breakdown of the civilizing elements of German government and society, it is essential to expose the weaknesses of the system, to identify its specific features, and to indicate just how it affected the Jewish population.

Although the Holocaust could not have taken place in imperial Germany, there were three major structural weaknesses that undermined the essential stability of the German state and gave rise, under the additional trauma of a lost war, to the kind of forces that would sweep Hitler into power and enable him to legislate his murderous Jew-hatred into political existence. These structural preconditions were:

1. A hybrid and unintegrated social system, half-feudal and half industrial, with long-standing militaristic and authoritarian traditions.

2. The nationalization of the masses as an instrument of social control and international aggression.

3. The respectability of biological and racial beliefs among many sections of society.

A Hybrid Social System: The Second Reich, 1871–1914

Bismarck unified Germany by imposing the militaristic-authoritarian character of Prussian institutions on the rest of the country. Thus, the Hohenzollern king of Prussia became the German emperor, the Prussian capital of Berlin became the German capital, and Prussian institutions and habits of mind began to pervade all aspects of the nation's consciousness. This new Prussianized Germany, of course, had many good qualities, as even its most severe critic, Friedrich Nietzsche, freely admitted: a respect for authority, a strong dedication to duty (*Pflicht*) and hard work, and an ingrained sense of good order. At the same time, the militaristic traditions of Prussia, which glorified the ethos of soldiering and elevated officers over any civilian to the highest level of social esteem, were not always compatible with civilized existence. The historian Friedrich Meinecke, who would later agonize over his own Prussian origins and their impact on the Third Reich, sadly acknowledged in his old age that there had always existed two tendencies in the Prussian character: one that was capable of culture and the other that was not. The former, he believed, was humane and individualistic, the outgrowth of the Protestant conscience; the latter was brutal and collectivist, the result of long-standing militaristic tradition.[6] The Prussian spirit of subservience to authority, symbolized by the semidivine status still accorded the emperor, penetrated many aspects of life during the Second Reich (1871–1918).

The new Prussianized Germany was militaristic in the highest sense, closely approximating Alfred Vagts's classic definition of militarism as "the domination of the military man over the civilian, an emphasis on military considerations, spirit, and ideals and scales of values,...the imposition of heavy burdens on a people for military purposes, to the neglect of welfare and culture, and the waste of the nation's best manpower in unproductive army service."[7] In short, the new Germany institutionalized and perpetuated archaic military feudal values in a way that no other European country was doing; it indoctrinated young Germans with the idea that to be "German" meant, above all, to be a courageous and loyal soldier. The only other country that idolized the warrior as a cultural role model was Japan.

In fact, in imperial Germany the military establishment stood above all other institutions and enjoyed the kind of reputation that was accorded only to ecclesiastical orders in former times. The officers' corps was venerated like an idol, as evidenced by the popular saying that "the human being begins with the lieutenant." Anyone who put on the *Kaiserrock*, the kaiser's coat, was instantly elevated above ordinary mortals. As a member of an exclusive caste, every German officer was immune from civilian control; his obedience was, first and foremost, to the emperor. The military caste had its own code of honor and law, the military court of honor; but since the military was not subject to civilian control, it represented a law unto itself. Sir John Wheeler-Bennett has justly remarked that the German officers' corps stood to the kaiser in the relation of the Praetorian Guard to the Roman emperor.[8] It goes without saying that the military caste, drawn almost exclusively from the aristocracy, recruited itself and would never suffer a single Jew to join its ranks.

The young emperor William II epitomized the German delight in military affairs. Contemptuous of civilians, to whom he disparagingly referred as *Schlappe Zivilisten* (flabby civilians), the kaiser put his trust in the army rather than the Reichstag or the constitution. His public rhetoric was deliberately pitched to a high military or martial tone, which, to foreigners or Germans used to a more melodious romantic German, sounded intolerably provocative. Addressing the German contingent of troops detailed to help in suppressing the Boxer rebellion in China (1900), the kaiser ordered them to take no prisoners and conduct themselves like Huns — a phrase that was later used with great effect by Allied propagandists to characterize all Germans as fiendish. William's saber-rattling rhetoric, imitated across the length and breadth of Germany by drill sergeants or officials barking at their underlings, was replete with such words as "smash," "war to the knife," "unbending will," and so on. He also loved to impress his people with inflated expressions of regal authority, coupled with menacing threats that he would not tolerate opposition to his sovereignty. Those who knew the emperor realized that most of these statements were hyperbole designed for public consumption; at the same time it is socially significant that martial language and attitudes were considered to be worthy of the highest form of imitation.

Friedrich Nietzsche, who watched this militarization of German life and culture with great misgiving, feared not only for the musicality of the German language but also for the feeling and sensibility that had sustained it in earlier generations of Germans. Nietzsche was not overreacting to what he perceived to be an almost malignant intrusion of rigid military habits into the everyday life of German citizens. Military habits of strict obedience, martial language, compulsive order, unflinching loyalty, narrow rank-consciousness, and similar military fetishes began to replicate themselves in how mothers brought up children, fathers barked out orders to their families, employers organized their businesses and treated their employees, or state officials managed the public domain.

Yet the aura of authority that was conveyed by this new martial empire was basically illusory. Beneath the grandeur of Hohenzollern power lurked many social forces that were incompatible with the pretensions of a feudal monarchy. In times of rapid industrial growth, the German monarchy adhered to the traditional values of its preindustrial past. The social perpetuation of an obsolete feudal regime in the midst of rising capitalism had caused the downfall of the *ancien régime* in France less than a century before. Was there any reason to assume that Germany would escape the dire consequences of a similar cultural lag? Prewar Germany, like prerevolutionary France, was a hybrid society that saw the persistence of feudal political institutions within the context of modern capitalism and machine technology.

Politically, the new Reich contained a number of anomalies and discordant voices. Bismarck's constitution established a thinly veiled autocracy in which the emperor, as the chief executive officer, was empowered to appoint and dismiss the chancellor and other officials; to control the whole of foreign policy; to serve as commander-in-chief of the armed forces; to declare martial law in case of social unrest; to deprive dissident member states of their territorial integrity; to summon, prorogue, and dismiss the Reichstag; to publish and supervise the execution of federal laws; and to interpret the constitution.[9] These sweeping discretionary powers, which may have been more appropriate in the age of absolutism, were not suitable to an industrial age in which shared power or, at the very least, countervailing powers proved more effective in blunting social conflicts. Countervailing powers, of course, developed in the form of a bicameral parliament, the growth of political parties, the rise of labor unionism, powerful business cartels, and the like. Unfortunately, neither Bismarck nor his successors trained the German people for political democracy, opting instead for makeshift pragmatic alliances and the formation of special interest groups in solving political problems. Under the empire the Reichstag was largely excluded from the major decision-making process because the ruling conservative elite succeeded in maintaining and even enlarging its preponderant Prussian influence in the new Reich. Despite appearances to the contrary, the political reality of the new Reich consisted of a powerful Prussian state with a virtual monopoly on military power, a predominant role in the upper house (Bundesrat), and an illiberal state electoral process that favored the wealthier classes.

Germany, of course, did not escape the pressures of popular sovereignty, but genuine demands by the people for popular democratic participation were either blunted or co-opted by the feudal-conservative establishment. That such tactics succeeded may be attributed, in part, to centuries of subservience by many Germans to higher authority (*Obrigkeit*), and the rationalizations of the sacredness of the powers-that-be by religious or philosophical spokesmen (Luther, Fichte, Hegel, Treitschke). Opposition to the ruling autocracy remained relatively ineffective also because the best elements of the nation chose not to serve in parliament and because political parties evolved into narrow economic interest groups rather than national parties that could successfully address the important social issues of the day: the widening gulf between the feudal elites and the working population, the new diplomatic role of Germany in the European community of nations, and the arrogant exclusivity of a military establishment that saw itself as standing above the law of the land.

Although in practice political life in imperial Germany was relatively free and social democracy made steady progress, as evidenced by the fact that the Social Democratic Party became the largest party in the Reichstag by 1912, the sad fact was that meaningful participation in politics was still exclusively controlled by a narrow and often arrogant elite bent upon perpetuating its rule into the twentieth century. Those who had created the Second Reich, though doffing their hat ceremoniously to popular sovereignty, made it unmistakably clear that power was to remain in the hands of the feudal classes. It did not escape the notice of vigilant Germans of ordinary backgrounds, especially the Jews, that their constitution made no mention of fundamental civil rights in the form of a "Bill of Rights" or a "Declaration of the Rights of Man and Citizen."[10]

Economically, the autocratic spirit of the new Prussianized Germany manifested itself, as Ralf Dahrendorf put it, in a "fruitful misalliance" between industry and the feudal state.[11] As soon as Germany was unified, the state managed the industrial process from above by granting loans without interest; tolerating large syndicates, trusts, and cartels; and owning vast property and enterprises (coal mines, blast furnaces, utilities). The state administered these enterprises through an intricate network of well-trained and efficient civil servants. Thus, in Germany free enterprise was displaced by state enterprise; industrial expansion, the most dynamic in Europe at the time, was the result of government planning and control. Even the odious consequences of industrialization — unemployment, sickness, accident, poor working conditions — fell under the protective mantle of the state. Having traditionally displayed a paternalistic attitude toward the average citizen, the feudal state saw no contradiction in extending progressive welfare measures to its citizens in the industrial world. As a result of its patriarchal traditions and also its basic fear of radical socialism, the new Prussianized Germany undertook measures that would make it the most progressive welfare state in Europe, while at the same time maintaining its feudal façade. In a curious way, therefore, the state was a hybrid: it was both socialistic in a patriarchal sense as well as capitalistic.[12]

Paternalism on such a scale, however, conditions a population to obedience and dependency, fostering the illusion that nothing great can be accomplished without state intervention and that the individual is insignificant apart from the state. This is what Oswald Spengler later referred to as the Prussian instinct that prompts the good citizen to work for the common good rather than for private or selfish good.[13] In this sense, the Prussian goal aims at promoting both nationalism and socialism; it is in a curious way a prefiguration of National Socialism. Unquestionable obedience and loyalty to the state are expected of every citizen; and in return, the state rewards such total commitment with generous social benefits such as old age pensions, unemployment insurance, disability protection, and health care. The social expectation was that all Germans would define themselves as obedient Germans who would serve the needs of the state and who, in turn, would be judged by the state by performance, talent, and loyalty to the state.

Yet these beliefs remained wishful thinking because, in practice, the ruling conservative elite was not willing to include the majority in a larger share of the expanding resources, and no amount of paternalism could gloss over the disparities in distributive justice in the Second Reich. Class conflicts therefore abounded; and instead of building bridges to the growing working class, the imperial elite, as Fritz Stern so aptly put it, preferred to build moats.[14] Moreover, the imperial leadership increasingly expressed its insecurity in hostile terms by relying on a mindset that was becoming all too familiar to Germans of all kinds — that of dividing the world into friend or foe. The ascension of the politically inept and in many ways clownish Emperor William II (1888–1918) symbolized the weaknesses of the new Germany: the young posturing kaiser, immature and insecure, was Germany writ large, for he represented a nation that had not found a stable identity, trying instead to cover up its weaknesses by irritating posturing and dogmatic self-assertion.

The German intellectual elite, the guardians of *Kultur und Bildung* (culture and education), mirrored the tensions and anomalies embodied in the institutions of the new Reich.[15] Bismarck had forged the new Germany by "blood and iron"; and in so doing, he had flung an obvious, even taunting, challenge to the intellectuals. How did the nation of poets and philosophers respond to the new militarized Germany? Far from speaking truth to power, the intellectuals quickly surrendered to it. Surprisingly, even most of Bismarck's former liberal critics surrendered to his successes; they performed an astonishing *volte-face* after the triumph of Prussian arms and abandoned their peaceful democratic ideals as unrealistic pipe dreams. The vision of a spiritual state (*Staat des Geistes*) associated with Goethe and the romantic poets, which many educated Jews ironically still admired as the "real" Germany, was rapidly giving way to the new vision of a military power state (*Machtstaat*) in which, as an imperial staff officer observed, "militarism is the state of mind of the civilian."[16]

Impressed by the successes of Bismarck's Machiavellianism, which also appeared to be supported by Social Darwinism and the general respectability of struggle, competition, and force in leading academic circles, many German intellectuals became convinced that the essence of life resided in power. Even Friedrich Nietzsche, who had warned his fellow Germans that power politics, unaccompanied by spiritual depth, would stupefy and brutalize the German people, nevertheless consecrated his own life to what he termed "the will to power" — a phrase later used with much fanfare by the Nazis. He also suggested that "where the will to power is lacking there is decline," and, as an antidote, he urged the Germans to rediscover their vital roots, to transcend decadent bourgeois materialism through heroic "self-overcoming," and to uplift the rule of a noble caste of supermen "without pity for the degenerate."[17] Nietzsche's highly allusive and aphoristic philosophy lent itself to a great deal of crude misinterpretation, and its concepts of the will to power or the superman (*Übermensch*) could, and subsequently would, merge with crude Darwinian notions of struggle and survival of the fittest as well as with neo-romantic beliefs in the power of myth, the role of a charismatic hero, and visions of glorious conquests.

Nietzsche's spiritualization of power, in other words, differed only in kind from others that were less subtle and far more aggressive. In the words of *völkisch* nationalists the will to power was quickly adulterated from Nietzsche's belief in "spiritual transcendence" into brutal domination and unbridled aggression. The belief in myths, which was to link people to their communal past, could easily turn into collective delusion and incitement to revolution. Breeding a higher type of man, the *Übermensch,* far from assuring the education of "a Caesar with the heart of Christ," could, under the influence of crude Darwinian biology and "racial hygiene," result in state-sponsored programs of human stud farms and elimination of the unfit through sterilization or extermination. German intellectuals, high- and low-brow alike, were almost luxuriating in their celebration of power, viewing it as the ultimate source and sanction of reality rather than as a pragmatic tool for the attainment of certain specific goals. Similarly, they saw the state in Hegelian terms as the manifestation of the divine will on earth rather than as a conventional set of human institutions. From this it followed, as the historian Heinrich Treitschke, who would later coin the phrase "the Jews are our misfortune," so repeatedly insisted, that every German citizen must submit in pious devotion to the state (*fromme Hingabe an den Staat*).[18]

Among a sizable section of the German intellectual community of the prewar period we can detect a strong antidemocratic prejudice and a preference for political absolutism — attitudes that were often at odds with moderation or compromise. These antidemocratic prejudices were strongly built into the expanding system of German education during the Second Reich. On the surface, Germany had one of the most impressive educational systems in the world, providing a free comprehensive education to more young people than any other country. From a purely technical point of view, it was a good system because it taught its young people how to read, write, and compute so well that these skills became ingrained habits and formed the foundation for either an excellent vocational or academic career. The organization of German education, however, took place within the context of rigidly authoritarian and elitist beliefs and practices. The educational system deliberately aimed at producing conscientious, well-trained, and obedient servants of the state; it decidedly did not encourage in its young people individual initiative, creativity, or nonconformity. Whereas in a democracy education ideally encourages the art of self-discovery, in the German elitist state it required the mastery of officially approved knowledge for the purpose of serving the state.

Some German conservatives, though proud of the fact that German youngsters could read and write and, therefore, could make good workers in an increasingly industrial world, also wondered whether they might not turn to radicalism or other ways to dilute the quality of high culture. The fear of the "vulgar" masses was a common theme in the late nineteenth century, and it figured prominently in the works of reactionary writers such as Paul de Lagarde and Julius Langbehn. Such fears, however, were greatly exaggerated because the German school system remained in the hands of state authorities with decidedly conservative and authoritarian leanings that emphasized strict discipline, sound order, and obedience to authority. This was especially true of the elite secondary schools, the Gymnasiums, and the universities which educated a small percentage of the population, consisting largely of students from the well-to-do middle and upper-middle classes. It goes without saying that it was not an education in democracy but in careerism and what the Germans call *Bildung,* which was officially advertised as a well-rounded general education but actually came to mean the acquisition of a cultivated, often supercilious, façade of classical learning that one exhibited in order to prove one's social superiority. The Gymnasiums were loosely and falsely patterned on Greek and Roman models; they neither taught the values of classical antiquity in any real depth, instead stressing the mechanics of grammar without instilling a delight in the work itself, nor did they produce the physically and mentally well-rounded citizen. What these schools produced was often bookish, elitist, and provincial minds — good technicians, civil servants, productive scholars, but rarely socially or politically engaged citizens. The students they produced would later be called, and called themselves proudly, the "unpolitical Germans," passive followers or obedient servants of any political system that controlled them.

Since the German educational system maintained its authoritarian and undemocratic foundation, refused to reform itself when it had the opportunity during the Weimar Republic, and eagerly assimilated anti-Jewish prejudices, it must be regarded as one of the major institutional culprits of the Holocaust, either by default in the sense of refusing to teach the truth or by actively instilling in its young people neo-romantic mythologies, chauvinistic beliefs, and racist doctrines. Even the better side of the educational equation — the German men of learning who enriched so many fields of knowledge in the modern world — contributed to the rise of a narrow "German mentality" that defined itself by what it opposed in the democratic values of the eighteenth century.

This clearly emerged in 1914, when a galaxy of great German intellectuals committed themselves to what Johann Plenge, a professor of sociology at the University of Münster, called "the ideas of 1914."[19] The intellectuals in question, who included, ironically, both Germans and Jews, consisted of such people as Werner Sombart, Adolf von Harnack, Thomas Mann, Paul Ehrlich, Fritz Haber, Max Liebermann, Friedrich Naumann, Max Planck, Walther Rathenau, Ernst Troeltsch, Friedrich Meinecke, Max Scheler, and others. Despite their philosophical or scholarly differences, these thinkers agreed that Anglo-American liberalism was without a real moral spine and wittingly or unwittingly reinforced various forces of social decay with its gospel of moral relativity, affluence, and universal happiness. In place of middle-class liberalism and its materialistic values, they stressed a more conservative way of life in which a sense of tradition, honor, love of country, and consciousness of the past would be predominant. In social terms this meant an organic community without class divisions, a society in which each individual or group worked for the common good. German sociologists such as Max Weber, Ernst Troeltsch, and Ferdinand Tönnies hoped that Germany would not become as atomized and rootless as Anglo-Saxon societies; they stressed the importance of *Gemeinschaft* (communalism) rather than *Gesellschaft* (class society), an organically integrated folk community rather than an agglomeration of selfish individuals pursuing their hedonistic desires.

Friedrich Naumann, in a highly influential book called *Mitteleuropa* (1915), proposed an international order in central Europe under the political umbrella of Germany that would serve as a socioeconomic alternative to western models of laissez-faire liberalism. Naumann and his group not only championed the cause of German nationalism but also toyed with notions of socialism in order to integrate the working people into their national folk community. Some of these intellectuals were revisionary socialists who stressed class cooperation rather than class war and argued that ties of nationality are always more important than ties of class. Already at that time there was much talk of "National Socialism" in order to avert social disruption, national weakness, and alienation among classes. When Adolf Hitler spoke a somewhat similar but far more racist language in the 1920s and 1930s, he simply repeated ideas that had long circulated among the intellectuals of the imperial period.

The Nationalization of the Masses

In order to integrate the hitherto disenfranchised masses into the conservative social order, the ruling classes of the German empire envisioned a strong central Europe under German control, an expansionist policy in the east, and the acquisition of a colonial empire abroad. Rapid industrialization had not been accompanied by democratization; and by excluding the working population from any meaningful participation in politics, the ruling elite had only managed to deepen the social divisions that had been sown into society by the industrial revolution. This gaping social problem made it imperative to develop sound social policies by which the widening "gap of tragedy" between the rich and the poor could be narrowed. Unfortunately, the social gap was not narrowed through genuine reforms, but through stopgap measures aimed at blunting or even co-opting radical demands. Bismarck, for example, approached domestic politics in the same way he had handled foreign policy: he cleverly manipulated parties or interest groups to advance his own shifting aims, which he egotistically assumed to be identical with the good of Germany. This objective was not so much to bring about a lasting harmony of social order, which would have required the abolition of privileges on the part of the old order, but short-range alliances, makeshift rapprochements, or artificially contrived crusades such as the cultural battle (*Kulturkampf*) against the Catholics or the campaign to destroy the socialistic enemies of the Reich (*Reichsfeinde*).

Although Bismarck carefully avoided overseas entanglements on the assumption that the new Reich had not been politically stabilized, his successors, who were faced with acute social problems, began to invoke tribal nationalism and imperialism in order to gain the support of the working classes and to integrate them, if not economically or politically then psychologically, into a homogeneous national community. In the Wilhelminian era, the German people were exposed to the white heat of publicly orchestrated causes in the form of popular imperialism, the naval race, and the rise of patriotic associations or interest groups. A succession of influential leaders such as Johannes Miguel, Admiral Alfred Tirpitz, Karl Bülow, and the kaiser himself advocated policies of internal mobilization and external expansion that foreshadowed the Nazi crusades in everything except emotional intensity.

The German emperor, who saw himself as a reincarnated Caesar, wanted to transform his country into a world power surpassing even the British empire. He must have known that such imperial grand designs would put him on a collision course with Great Britain and other major powers. He was, by birth, half English and half German; his mother, Princess Victoria, was the daughter of Queen Victoria of England and Albert of Saxe-Coburg. When he came to the throne in 1888, following the brief reign of his reform-minded and liberal father Frederick III, he was eager to chart a new course for Germany, dismissing Bismarck and

supporting a new *Weltpolitik* (world politics). Steeped in the literature
of late nineteenth-century imperialism, he dreamed of a greater German
empire whose future lay in overseas colonies. The kaiser admired imperialistic authors and adventurers such as Rudyard Kipling, Cecil Rhodes,
Admiral Mahan, and above all Houston Stewart Chamberlain, whose
theories of Germanic superiority captured his imagination and greatly
stimulated his aggressive rhetoric.

The kaiser, in turn, galvanized others to the imperial call. Alfred
von Tirpitz, secretary of the navy, was instrumental in building the second most powerful navy in the world and in orchestrating a brilliant
public relations campaign on behalf of imperialistic politics. He also
propounded the popular conservative "risk theory" that called for a
powerful German fleet that could deter even the strongest sea power
in the world, thus enabling Germany to pursue its colonial aims and to
safeguard its supply lines. These imperialistic views were disseminated
by a host of popular associations, most notably the Pan-German League
(Alldeutscher Verband), the Naval League (Flottenverein) the Colonial
Union (Kolonialverein), and the Army League (Wehrverein) — organizations that popularized, indeed, glamorized war as a noble cause,
celebrated the struggle for existence, demanded living space (*Lebensraum*) for the German people, and proclaimed the Germans the master
race (*Herrenvolk*) of the future.[20]

Among these social imperialists, who included a very broad section not only of the ruling Prussian elites but also prominent members
of industry and academia, we find some interesting supporters or fellow travelers of the later Nazi movement, including Alfred Hugenberg
(1865–1951), the cofounder of the Pan-German League; Gustav Krupp
von Bohlen und Halbach (1870–1950), industrialist and arms mogul;
court councillor Dr. Heinrich Class (1867–1953), a student of Heinrich Treitschke and a confirmed anti-Jewish bigot who later opened the
door of the Pan-German League to Hitler; Fritz Thyssen (1873–1951),
the wealthy industrialist who would later extend financial assistance to
the Nazi Party; and Emil Kirdorf (1847–1938), another wealthy icon
and coal magnate who poured money into the Nazi coffers. These men,
however, were just the tip of an emerging nationalistic iceberg that en-
gulfed broad sections of German society, including the lower-middle and
middle classes, academics, students, and even portions of the workers.
From a larger international perspective, it was a very dangerous and
naive jingoism that was badly informed by knowledge of the world
and by an inflated ethnocentric belief that Germany could afford and
maintain the biggest army and navy in the world.

Few institutions were so full of this kind of megalomania than the
Pan-German League, whose members championed wild expansionist
policies, proclaimed the superiority of the Nordic race, called for living space in the east, and anxiously awaited the coming of a messianic
leader who would deliver Germany from the Jewish menace.[21] In exam-

ining the Pan-German League and similar associations that claimed to speak for Germany, it quickly becomes apparent that these groups projected a very narrow and brutal message to the rest of the world, a vision that did not even pretend to liberate humanity or fight for human freedom but spoke unabashedly in terms of conquest and subjugation. In other words, the Germans, as a nation, did not try to carry a generous, humane message to the world. Some Germans, it is true, were sometimes moved to repeat Goethe's maxim: "Am deutschen Wesen soll die Welt genesen" (The world shall flourish on the German nature); but the real German call to the world would be the first lines of Hoffmann von Fallersleben's national anthem, "Deutschland, Deutschland über alles" (Germany, Germany over all). Implied in the national anthem was a rousing assertion of national superiority rather than the Enlightenment credo embodied in Schiller's "Ode to Joy" that "alle Menschen werden Brüder" — that all men will become brothers. This message, a belief of a bygone age, was now passé in imperial Germany. There undoubtedly were many Germans who stressed the better qualities of the nation's contributions as measured by its rich cultural legacy and its impressive scientific and technological advances, but this was increasingly drowned out by belligerent assertions that Germany was great because the Germans were the greatest. Compared to previous missionizing people who at least claimed and sometimes delivered on some of their claims regarding a "Pax Romana," "Liberty, Equality, and Fraternity," "National Self-Determination," or "Making the World Safe for Democracy," "the Germans alone," said Hans Kohn, and that was certainly true between 1871 and 1945, "had nothing to offer but self-centered power and self-glorification."[22]

There was no shortage of Germans who did not fail to notice this national weakness and wished, as J. Fröbel expressed it, that they did not constantly use attributes praising their own character: "German energy, German faithfulness, German love, German seriousness, German song, German wine, German depth, German thoroughness, German diligence, German womanhood, German virgins, German men."[23] For the sake of his people's spiritual self-growth, Nietzsche hoped that the Germans would not turn themselves into a nationalistic monument but would instead "de-Germanize" themselves by becoming good Europeans — a hope that would not be fulfilled, as Nietzsche himself suspected when he observed that with the Germans "the question what is German never dies out."[24] The consensus during the Second Reich appears to have been that a genuine German belonged to an ethnic blood community and subscribed to shared nationalistic convictions that proclaimed the superiority of German life and culture. Connected to this ethnocentric belief, which had potentially ominous implications for the Jews, was a growing conviction that the best society was culturally and ethnically homogeneous rather than diverse or pluralistic. Such visions are always narrow, exclusive, and ungenerous because they have no place for foreigners, nonconformists, or ethnically diverse people.

The Respectability of Racism and Ethnic Prejudices

Jews in the Second Reich

One of Karl Marx's favorite metaphors, especially in his earlier works, was to "strip away the veil of illusion" — that is, to penetrate beneath a society's mystifications in the form of established myths and social pretensions and to lay bare its essential dominating agencies. This is precisely what Marx proceeded to do in his ruthless dissection of capitalism and capitalists by exposing the system as a monstrous organization of human greed and exploitation. Far from being entirely detached and analytical in his critique of capitalism, Marx's writings rise to a high level of self-righteous moralism and abound in apocalyptic and demonological images.[25] The figure of the worker is lifted from a flesh-and-blood human being and turned into a mythological Sisyphus and Prometheus; whereas the capitalist is stripped of his humanness and becomes Gorgon and the Furies, a monster "that vampire-like only lives by sucking living labor" and possesses a "vampire-thirst for the living blood of labor." Elsewhere, he referred to capital's machines as giants and ogres and to the capitalists as ghouls who coin children's blood into capital.[26] By the time the reader has finished with Marx's indictment of the capitalist system and its standard bearers — the bourgeoisie and its lackeys — a whole new world of abstractions has been created for the purpose of political action, propaganda, and revolutionary change. People are stripped of their individual human qualities and treated, as Marx explicitly acknowledges, as nothing but "personifications of economic categories, embodiments of particular class-relations and class-interests."[27]

Was this procedure of stripping the veil of illusion and finding the head of Medusa behind it so different from the anti-Jewish critic who saw grasping Jews behind every financial operation that failed or social crisis that developed? It may be objected that Marx exposed real social injustices and real oppressors, whereas the Jew-hater only trafficked in delusions. Even if it contains a measure of truth, this objection does not touch on the real issue at hand, which is not the relative truth embodied in the two positions, but the kind of thinking that sustains them both — a kind of thinking, I contend, that makes illegitimate use of such potential mental aberrations as stereotyping, personifying, or reifying individuals in order to prove either a delusion, as in the case of the Judeophobe, or a sociological theory, as in the case of Karl Marx.

Just what was real and what was delusionary about the Jews in imperial Germany? Although it is possible to write a group portrait of the Jews, it is not possible to treat them as an abstraction with a single will or purpose. In general terms, the Jews of Germany formed a distinct group on account of their religion, customary practices, and occupational or professional affiliations. For historical reasons they generally preferred to live in towns or cities — the larger the city the greater the Jewish presence — and engage in those occupations, the free professions, that were open to them. This accounts for the fact that they were highly visible in business, law, medicine, journalism, and those fields that began to cater to a new mass audience. Most ordinary Germans interacted with Jews, both in town and country, in the retail and wholesale trades, because the Jews had become the middlemen who moved the goods. Many had become independent shop owners, small-scale entrepreneurs, and, in the case of a few outstanding talents, large-scale entrepreneurs who operated banks, newspapers, publishing concerns, major businesses, and industrial plants. The latter class of Jewish financial successes was especially visible, at once envied and despised.

Of these new men, one of the most fascinating was Emil Rathenau, an engineer who formed the German Edison Company in 1883 after personally witnessing Thomas Edison light up an electric bulb at a Paris fair in 1881 and then negotiating with the American inventor to market the new technology in Germany. Rathenau's company, which at the time of his death employed seventy thousand people, was largely responsible not only for electrifying most of Germany but many parts of the world that the company was serving around the turn of the century.[28] Rathenau's son, Walther Rathenau, became director of his father's electrical trust (A.E.G.S.), helped to organize Germany's war economy in 1916, and later served as foreign minister in the Weimar Republic, falling victim to an assassination by right-wing Jew-haters.

Rathenau belonged to a rising group of Jewish talents who had received excellent scientific training in the universities and technical schools of Wilhelmine Germany and applied that knowledge in building up new industrial concerns. One of the founders of the I. G. Farben chemical trust was Heinrich Caro, a Sephardic Jew whose discoveries in the field of aniline dyes helped propel his company to world prominence as a manufacturer in the fields of synthetic dyes and synthetic substitutes for rubber, oil, and nitrates. Another Jewish chemist, Adolph Frank, discovered the usefulness of a potash derivative as fertilizer and exported his product to the United States. Probably the most interesting Jewish chemist, however, was Fritz Haber, a converted Jew from Breslau, who developed a process for synthesizing ammonia from atmospheric nitrogen and later helped the German war machine in manufacturing its own nitrates for explosives and also in developing poison gas. As Fritz Stern has observed, in 1914 he could not have foreseen that "the Germans for whom he produced poison gas would use another kind of gas for the killing of millions of his own people."[29]

Haber, like many German Jews, was a successfully assimilated German whose career could serve as a textbook example of Jewish upward mobility and success as inventor, director of the kaiser Wilhelm Institute, state privy councillor (*Geheimrat*), and Nobel Prize laureate. Yet even this great achiever and defender of German life and culture would discover, painfully and tragically, that all of his patriotic services were meaningless under Nazi rule. In 1933 Haber was dismissed from all of his academic posts and reluctantly went into exile where he died a broken man only one year later.

The most visible Jewish success stories, of course, could be found in the financial and banking fields because the expansion of modern business enterprises required the mobilization of large-scale capital. As mentioned previously, the Jews enjoyed a historical advantage in this field, having served over the past five hundred years as money-lenders to peasants and princes and therefore having gained knowledge and insights that would place them at the "cutting edge." Some of the well-known Jewish families who operated major banks were, besides the Rothschilds already mentioned, the Mendelssohns and Bleichröders of Berlin, the Warburgs of Hamburg, and the Oppenheims of Cologne. Individual Jews also played a prominent role in founding other important German banks. One of the founders of the Deutsche Bank was Ludwig Bamberger, later a Reichstag deputy. Another Jewish banker, Eugen Gutmann, expanded the Dresdener bank into a nationwide operation.

Fritz Stern has documented the close partnership between the banker Gerson Bleichröder and Otto von Bismarck, showing in great detail how the lives of the Jewish banker and the Iron Chancellor were intertwined and how Jewish financial know-how contributed to the founding and greatness of the German empire. It is a highly revealing study that conclusively demonstrates the financial importance that the Jews played in a positive sense, but it also lays to rest two anti-Jewish mythologies — namely, that Jews enjoyed not only great wealth but also used that wealth to gain undeserved political influence and power.[30] Stern shows, on the contrary, that even Bleichröder's wealth fell short of significant political influence because it did not move the levers of power in the Prussian system. Although Bleichröder had access to Bismarck's private financial affairs, which he carefully managed, and he frequently served the chancellor by providing him with shrewd information and advice, he never moved in Bismarck's social circles, remaining, at best, a prized and honored outsider who had to be content with the limitations prescribed for him by the German system.

Jewish gold helped significantly in financing the very sinews of the Empire of Blood and Iron, just as it had helped in the recovery of Germany from the devastating Thirty Years War. Jewish bankers risked their capital in many industrial ventures during the *Gründerzeit* period, and of particular importance to the economic health was the expanding transportation system. Abraham Oppenheim of Cologne financed and subsequently managed one of the first railroad companies in Germany, the Rhenish Railway Company, whose rails connected Cologne and

Antwerp. Baron Maurice de Hirsch, nicknamed *Türkenhirsch,* received a contract from the Turkish government in 1869 to build a railroad line connecting Vienna and Constantinople; the first train of this Orient Express left Vienna in 1888. By that time Hirsch had become one of the wealthiest entrepreneurs in Germany, but he was also a very generous and socially involved man who gave away millions to worthy causes, particularly those aimed at supporting the millions of Russian Jews who were fleeing to the west in the wake of tsarist oppression.[31]

Another tycoon was the flamboyant Bethel Henry Strousburg, a converted Prussian Jew who lived on his wits and talents, seeking fame and fortune in England, the United States, and his native Germany. Strousburg was a bit of a *Luftmensch* (a man who lives on air) who never invested his own but rather other people's money and lived on future promises; but he was quick-minded and charming enough to talk serious investors, including foreign governments, into investing in his grand projects. After helping English investors to launch a railroad in East Prussia, he branched out and constructed railway lines in Germany, Russia, and Hungary, amassing a huge paper fortune that became the catalyst for further ventures. His empire finally collapsed in 1873 when the Rumanian government defaulted on the payment of a railroad line he was supposed to be building in Rumania. For once, his timing had been disastrously bad because 1873 was the year the market crashed in Germany, ushering in a lengthy depression that wiped out many investors who, like Hirsch, had been living on inflated financial values and risky ventures.

The greatest Jewish success story in the shipbuilding business was Albert Ballin, who rose from the position of manager of the passenger department of the Hamburg-Amerika Line to become the company's general director. Ballin distinguished himself by showing brilliant organizational skills in transporting millions of Jewish immigrants from eastern Europe to their final destination, generally the United States. Like Hirsch, Ballin was a man with a strong social conscience who went out of his way to accommodate his customers, even to the point of drastically improving their quarters before and after they embarked on their journey to the new world. He set up miniature villages, replete with churches and synagogues, before sending his passengers on their way. Ballin turned the Hamburg-Amerika Line (HAPAG) into one of the major carriers of the world, utilizing his ships even during the bad winter months for pleasure cruises for the rich and famous. Ballin himself moved in the company of the elite, counting the kaiser among his friends. Both the kaiser and Ballin loved ships, but the emperor preferred battleships over passenger ships and refused to heed his friend's advice to steer a moderate course in international affairs. It was Ballin who ultimately informed the kaiser that the war was lost. The kaiser departed Germany and Ballin departed this world by taking an overdose of sleeping pills.

In addition to being prominent in banking, business, and transportation, the Jews were also much in evidence in the emerging mass media enterprises revolving around the publication of newspapers, journals, and books. The Jews are the people of the book in more ways than one. For over two thousand years they have lived by the word, and it is therefore no accident that they would take to printing like fish do to water. Although they were disproportionately overrepresented in this field, they did not even remotely dominate it as their detractors believed. Here, again, it was a matter of stereotypical perception; outwardly, a few Jewish press barons seemed to dominate the market, notably in Berlin and Frankfurt, but for every Jewish-controlled newspaper, there were hundreds that were non-Jewish. Nor was it true, as Jew-haters insisted, that the "Jewish press" was a radical one or even a "Jewish" one. In the newspaper or publishing business, as elsewhere, the Jews actually tended to gravitate to the moderate center rather than either the conservative or socialist extremes of the spectrum. Moreover, Jews rarely propagandized a "Jewish" position — that is, they did not publicly advocate Judaic religious ideas; but to the Jew-haters, as will be seen, this made no difference because they would quickly invent a whole imaginary catalogue of Jewish "traits," "convictions," "spirit," and the like. In the long run, it would prove impossible to defend oneself against pernicious accusations of holding a Jewish position or exhibiting a Jewish spirit.

The father of modern Jewish journalism was Leopold Sonnemann, who founded the liberal *Frankfurter Zeitung* in 1866. Sonnemann had two great counterparts in Berlin: Leopold Ullstein and Rudolf Mosse. Ullstein purchased the *Neues Berliner Tageblatt* in 1877 and then added a morning paper called *Berliner Morgenpost*. Joined by his five sons, the House of Ullstein became one of the great publishing concerns until it was broken up by the Nazis. Even more influential, especially in reaching a mass market, was the House of Mosse, whose founder, Rudolf Mosse, brought out the *Berliner Tageblatt* in 1871, the first newspaper that was financed largely by advertisers rather than by readers. Mosse increased his empire by also founding two cheap daily newspapers that catered primarily to the working population: the *Volksblatt* and *Morgenblatt*. By 1914 the combined circulation of the Mosse papers had reached 250,000 copies in a population of roughly four million people.[32] Jewish presence was less visible in the book publishing business, but here, too, one could find some notable publishers such as Samuel Fischer and Kurt Wolff, two substantial publishers who reached out to a mass audience while at the same time maintaining very high literary standards.

Next to the "Jewish" press or bank, the one institution that always formed an important element in the Judeophobe's mental universe was the much maligned department store. The Nazis, in particular, never ceased ranting against the demonic department store that allegedly sucked the life out of many small German stores and left them dying on the vine. The reality, again, was quite different; the department store, especially in the nineteenth century, was a marvel of innovation because it combined a great many goods in a central location and tempted the customer with attractions hitherto unknown in the form of elegant surroundings, reading and lounging rooms, restaurants, and often bargain-basement prices. The department store should have demolished the stereotype of the haggling Jew because it dealt in fixed prices, but the mutability of hatred for Jews was such that it quickly replaced the old stereotype with a new one — namely, that the Gerson, Grünfeld, Tietz, Schocken, or Wertheim stores were part of a larger Jewish economic conspiracy aimed at taking over the German economy.

This kind of resentment of Jewish economic success often sprang from socioeconomic groups that were being rapidly bypassed by modernization and that blamed Jewish bankers or Jewish wholesale dealers for their economic plight. They lashed out at what they perceived to be rootless, pushy, and unsentimental Jews climbing the economic ladder of success without regard for the damage they supposedly inflicted on their innocent victims. Such feelings were particularly strong among the peasants in various parts of Germany. Despite the progress that was being made during the Second Reich in setting up various lending institutions that could serve the farmers, traditional patterns of Jewish money-lending in the countryside continued unabated. Farmers had fashioned centuries-old traditions of dealing directly with Jewish middlemen not only in financial transactions but also in much broader commercial relations that involved trading in cattle, wheat, hops, wool, leather goods, and wood. In some parts of Germany, notably in Franconia, Hesse, and Westphalia, Jewish commercial dealers retained their leading position; three-fourths of the cattle dealers in these areas were Jewish.[33]

Throughout the late nineteenth century and beyond, German agriculture was in a constant state of crisis because German farmers proved unable to adjust to the latest scientific methods of production and management, thus becoming noncompetitive in the world market. Many farmers became heavily indebted to Jewish money-lenders, with whom they preferred to deal because it was considered less shameful to owe money to a Jew than to a respectable German institution, and they were often forced to sell their overmortgaged farms to their Jewish debtors. Resentment reached a high level of anti-Jewish hatred in the countryside whenever Jews made profits from auctioning off the indebted properties of their clients. It was this resentment that anti-Jewish agitators like Otto Böckel and Hermann Ahlwardt would organize politically in the late nineteenth century. Despite rapid industrialization and modernization, the persistence of agricultural and preindustrial trades remained very strong in Germany, and it was among those groups that were displaced or threatened by modernization — farmers, traditional craftsmen, noncompetitive businessmen, indebted Junkers — that anti-Jewish prejudice ran very high.

The cultural counterpart to this kind of anti-Jewish economic resentment was the accusation that Jews were polluting the purity of German culture by infecting it with the crass materialistic values of their Jewish mentality. Being the agents of modernization without necessarily having imbued the cultural implications of modernism, the Jews, in Peter Gay's suggestive phrase, became both the masters and the victims of their historical position. In the field of culture, as in every other field, Jews were highly visible to Germans not so much as artists, writers, or musicians but as Jewish artists, writers, or musicians; in addition, many were also branded with pejorative labels or negatively associated with avant-garde movements that were despised by cultural conservatives as un-German or decadent. But what was a Jewish "writer" or a "Jewish spirit," and how could one objectively distinguish a German from a Jewish artist? As Max Liebermann, one of Germany's greatest painters of the period and also a Jew, observed: "What does painting have to do with Judaism?"[34] And like countless Jewish Germans, he asserted his belief in a strong humanistic conviction that saw no moral incompatibility between showing respect for human dignity and pride in one's ethnic or religious affiliation. "All of my life," he said, "my first question was: What kind of human being are you? But never, Are you a Jew, Christian, or heathen?"[35] This did not alter his self-image as a Jew because he wryly admitted that he was born a Jew and would die a Jew.

Many Jews, in fact, increasingly believed that there was no reason why one could not be both a Jew and a German. Among the educated Jews of Germany the process of either assimilation or adaptation to German culture proceeded with remarkable speed. Educated Jews eagerly embraced German *Bildung* and proudly displayed its emblems in the form of a good general education, artfully decorated homes with ever-present pianos and bookcases, and obligatory visits to museums, theaters, or the opera. Quotations from the *Klassiker* (Schiller, Goethe, Kant), both in private conversation or public discourse, became one of the ways by which many Jews validated their Germanness. They did this so well that they were often better guardians of German high culture than many Germans themselves. For example, no complete work by Bach was printed between 1750 and 1800 because the German musical elite regarded Bach as an out-of-date musical pedant. Even by the 1820s little of Bach's music was in print. The Jewish composer Felix Mendelssohn Bartholdy (1809–47), the grandson of the great philosopher Moses Mendelssohn, learned about the St. Matthew Passion from his great-aunt Sara Levy and the musical director Karl Friedrich Zelter, who possessed a complete manuscript of the work. Zelter had great doubts that the work could be performed, but when Mendelssohn arranged a private performance in his house in 1827, Mendelssohn convinced Zelter that the work should be revived. While Mendelssohn and the actor Edouard Devrient labored on Bach's immense work, editing and cutting it down to manageable performance standards, the young Jewish composer remarked: "To think that a comedian and a 'Jew Boy' must revive the greatest Christian music in the world!" On March 11, 1829, Bach's St. Matthew Passion, conducted by Mendelssohn, was performed to a packed audience in Berlin. Afterward, there was a grand party for Berlin luminaries at Zelter's house. Story had it that Frau Devrient whispered to Mendelssohn: "Do tell me, who is this stupid fellow sitting next to me?" Mendelssohn whispered back behind his napkin: "The stupid fellow next to you is the philosopher Hegel."[36]

Jews were also upholders of German culture in other areas. The members of the George Kreis who fluttered around the poet Stefan George and cultivated the purity of German language and culture with an almost fanatical zeal were predominantly Jewish. The back-to-Kant movement that sought to prove both the epistemological and moral relevance of Kant's doctrines began with Otto Liebmann's provocative polemic *Kant und die Epigonen* (1865). It was carried on throughout the late nineteenth century by Hermann Cohen and the students he groomed at Marburg University, including the great Ernst Cassirer, who "breathed high German culture with his every breath."[37] These writers continued the Enlightenment tradition and its vision of human freedom and toleration; in Peter Gay's view, they turned to Schiller or Kant because they "supplied ringing, eminently quotable pronouncements; and Kant's critical philosophy provided a rationale for a religion of reason that permitted emancipated Jews to fit their own religious views into a universal — they hoped universally respected — scheme."[38]

Cohen's dream that Germany would become a cultural melting pot in which Jews and Germans would become one was not fulfilled, but it represented the hopes of many Jews of his generation. Cohen was one of the few Jewish professors who rose to a full professorial position, which generally required religious conversion for those who sought admission to the tenured ranks. Freud was never admitted into the professoriat, and many other great talents, converts or nonconverts, encountered constant forms of discrimination. Chances of employment in elementary or secondary schools were even worse; the same was true for other types of government employment. Jews were effectively barred from the upper echelons of the civil service, from cabinet posts, and, above all, from the pinnacle of national respectability — the officer corps. No unbaptized Jew could become an officer in the Prussian army nor in Prussian-dominated regiments in other states. As Fritz Stern has said, there was no Dreyfus affair in Germany because there was no Dreyfus.[39]

Yet, despite these still existing forms of discrimination, the Jews of Germany, as revealed in so many of their own observations and personal confessions, felt themselves German and identified with Rabbi Leopold Stein's assertion:

We are Germans and want to be nothing else! We have no other fatherland than the German fatherland and we wish for no other! Only by our

faith are we Israelites, in every other respect we belong with devotion to
the state in which we live.[40]

If we look back on the Second Reich and the Jewish perception of
what it was like to live there, it emerges clearly that, despite the many
slights and humiliations visited upon individual Jews, they felt at home
in Germany, raising families and participating in German life and culture. Their commitment to Germany can be gauged by their immersion
in its culture as well as their financial investment in its economic greatness. The rewards they reaped were not inconsiderable because more
than three-fourths belonged to the substantial *Mittelstand,* the petit
bourgeoisie who enjoyed a level of income comparatively higher than
the average German's. Their houses and mansions were visible signs of
their material success; they were not visible reminders that they expected
to be eliminated at any moment or that their lives in Germany were
so precarious that they had to have their suitcases packed because they
might have to leave at a moment's notice. What, then, accounts for the
persistence of Jew-hatred in Germany, how did it express itself, and why
was it so potentially dangerous to the German Jew?

The Varieties of Anti-Jewish Prejudices in the Second Reich

Anti-Jewish prejudices in the Second Reich may be compared to eddies in a stream of water, varying in intensity and always threatening
to engulf the Jewish people until, at length, the eddies became part
of a larger whirlpool of political and cultural stresses out of which
the monster of racial hatred emerged, transformed and lethal, in Adolf
Hitler and the Nazi movement. These eddies consisted of lingering anti-
Jewish Christian prejudices that condemned Jews as Christ killers and
charged them with committing various crimes against the Christian
community; nationalistic biases that accused them of being an "alien
presence," a state within a state; economic self-interests that accused
Jews of being bloodsuckers cheating honest Germans; popular discriminatory biases that were directed against individual Jews in various
humiliating forms (snubbing, exclusion, ridicule); and racial-biological
beliefs that stigmatized Jews as both racially inferior and a biological
health hazard to the community. These prejudices by no means operated in isolation but formed, in many instances, an interconnected set
or syndrome that operated in single individuals as well as larger groups.
Moreover, it was during the Second Reich that these anti-Jewish prejudices erupted publicly and became part and parcel of an organized
political movement.

Traditional Christian prejudices against the Jews still continued to be
strong in Germany, especially in the countryside, where religious convictions were more deeply rooted and people were more closely tied to
their religious institutions. The villagers of Oberammergau in Bavaria,

for example, were still reenacting a Passion Play every ten years that went back to 1633 and commemorated the resurrection of Jesus. Its essential theme, acted out in melodramatic moral terms, was the guilt of the Jews in crucifying Jesus. Although irreligious, the Nazis would retain this play as an example of genuine folkish culture; in reality what they found valuable in it was its anti-Jewish message, which they believed transcended its religious origins. Among superstitious peasants and deluded Judeophobes old religious myths still found a receptive audience. Between 1867 and 1914 there were twelve trials involving charges of ritual child murder in Germany and Austria; eleven of these collapsed and the twelfth resulted in a conviction for murder rather than ritual child murder.[41] To the credit of ecclesiastical authorities, it should be said that some clerics like the archbishops of Cologne and Breslau went on record in condemning age-old anti-Jewish libels, though it did not help when Pope Pius IX undermined such clerical enlightenment with anti-Jewish outbursts, as when he proclaimed that the Jews were "the enemies of Jesus, they have no God but their money."[42]

In an age of secular materialism, permeated increasingly by aggressive and hateful attitudes that were aroused by various ideologies such as Marxism, imperialism, nationalism, or Social Darwinism, it should not be surprising that anti-Jewish prejudices quickly adapted themselves to the new currents. The hatred, of course, was the same, but its language was nationalistic or racist. The Jews were now seen by xenophobic Germans as an alien people that could never be assimilated to the German *Volk*. The rise of extreme *völkisch* nationalism thus undermined an earlier belief that the Jews could belong to the German *Volk*. When Europe, particularly Germany, moved from religious anti-Judaism to tribal purification, Jews could expect little sympathy or mercy because conversion to Christianity or even allegiance to nation was of no use at all. Jews were Jews now and forever; they could never be German Jews or Jewish Germans, which to a racist was an oxymoron. In the racist perception of the Judeophobe Jews were inherently tainted by their "Jewish blood," which completely determined the way they behaved. As Peter Pulzer expressed it, "It is not morality that makes Jews bad, but the Jews make morality bad."[43] Pulzer rightly refers to this stage in the progression of Jew-hatred as the "bacteriological" phase. In an increasingly race-conscious world the Jews had now become a biological health hazard to the German (Aryan) community. The transition from traditional religious to racial Judeophobia can already be seen quite clearly in the works of several highly influential writers such as Julius Langbehn and Eugen Dühring.

Both Dühring and Langbehn saw the source of "Jewish depravity" in "Jewish blood" rather than in Jewish religion or culture. The charge, as previously mentioned, was connected to Darwinian biology, especially the emergence of the eugenic movement and its promise to produce a racially healthy stock of people. Members of the German academic community began to abandon doctrines of equality in favor of the intrinsic inequality that supposedly existed among the various racial groups. There was also a change in language with the appearance of biological metaphors and annihilatory words such as "parasite," "bacillus," "extermination" (*Ausrottung*), "annihilation" (*Vernichtung*), and "extirpation" (*Vertilgung*). The word *Ausrottung,* for example, was generally used in connection with the killing of parasites; and in their discussion of purifying the German *Volk,* several *völkisch* spokesmen advocated extermination of the Jews as the best method of ridding the German people of its parasitical intruder.[44] Lagarde, for example, rejected the notion of turning Jews into Germans, which he regarded as a futile approach, arguing instead that they should be expelled or even annihilated. In one of his books he referred to Jews as vermin and bacilli and declared that "with trichinae and bacilli one does not negotiate, nor are trichinae and bacilli subjected to education; they are exterminated as quickly and as thoroughly as possible."[45] That such ideas had consequences may be shown by the fact that in 1944 an anthology of Lagarde's work was distributed by the Wehrmacht (the regular army),[46] presumably to give aid and comfort to those who were exterminating Jews.

A similar message was delivered by Eugen Dühring, an influential economist and philosopher, who insisted that the Jews were a unique species with entirely different ethical beliefs and therefore incapable of being assimilated into German culture. In his various pamphlets on the Jewish question, especially his belligerent *The Jewish Question as Racial, Moral, and Cultural Question* (1881), Dühring revealed himself as a racist and an exterminationist by calling for *Ertötung und Ausrottung* (killing and extermination) of world Jewry (*Judentum*) and justified such genocidal ideas by reference to a higher law of history.[47] Langbehn and Dühring already expressed themselves in thought patterns of racial exclusivity; they perceived Jews as deadly foreign organisms having grafted themselves on their German host and therefore had to be removed surgically in order to save the national body. What was true of Germany was true of any nation that had been "Jewified" (*verjudet;*) such a nation had to be "de-Jewified" (*entjudet*) if it wanted to survive as a healthy nation. The traditional Christian method of "de-Jewifying" a country through baptism was useless because the Jew's destructive nature was genetically fixed and therefore unalterable. This racial Manichaeism predated the Nazi movement and its family tree was planted by Eugen Dühring, Julius Langbehn, Paul de Lagarde, Otto Böckel, and a host of noisy *völkisch* ideologues and inspired eugenicists.

Historians have speculated about the causes of such strident and irrational beliefs, attributing them to a number of different, yet also related, sources such as tribal nationalism, neo-romanticism, and racism. George Mosse, for example, argued long ago that a considerable number of Germans, particularly those belonging to the conservative middle classes and upper classes, as well as skilled artisans, were highly susceptible to an emerging populist ideology that combined various tribal notions of blood and soil with neo-romantic mythologies and racist utopias.[48] To some extent, the new *völkisch* ideology, as it has sometimes been called, was a reaction to modernization, a backlash on the part of alienated intellectuals and social classes that felt themselves threatened by the tidal wave of modern capitalism and liberal democracy. This backlash brought together various heterogeneous groups such as nationalistic teachers and their students, peasants, neo-romantic intellectuals, marginal occupational groups (small noncompetitive shopkeepers, unwanted artisans, shop or office clerks), and saber-rattling militarists and their popular lobbies. For many of them, as Otto Glagau would later say, the social question was the Jewish question. Rather than face the emerging world of big cities and the hectic pace of commercial enterprise, these groups tried to stage a Don Quixote-like counterrevolution aimed at recapturing a more primitive and rooted world that they imagined to have existed in the past. In other words, the values they cherished belonged to a preindustrial age; they revolved around rootedness in soil and country, social hierarchy, and the observance of time-honored customs and traditions. In their perception, the Jews embodied everything they despised: they were town dwellers and identified themselves with the forces of modern capitalism and democracy.

As previously shown, such neo-romantic protests against the alienating effects of modernization were quite widespread throughout Europe, but as George Mosse points out, "the chemistry of the German movement was quite different" because its reactionary thrust went much deeper into the national consciousness.[49] In Germany the *völkisch* counterrevolution became a national obsession, and many of its reactionary beliefs became institutionalized in the schools, the armed forces, the youth organizations, popular literature, and popular entertainment. Members of the educated middle class were especially susceptible to *völkisch* ideology, and the acculturation of young people often took place within a framework of elitist, undemocratic, anti-Jewish prejudice. A number of studies have focused on this stubborn illiberalism and on its völkisch ideology of "the politics of cultural despair." They have shown that sizable sections of German society, especially the well-educated middle classes, remained profoundly conservative and fixated on preindustrial values.[50] This was especially true of German students; unlike their counterparts in France or England, who strongly identified with social equality, social justice, and economic help for the underprivileged, German students tended to be elitists and cultural conservatives.[51] Students, professors, and a growing subculture of *völkisch* nationalists were busily engaged in researching their Teutonic roots and avidly speculating about the meaning of Teutonic legends, myths, and fairy tales. These groups pretended to find arcane wisdom in the *Edda,* the *Nibelungenlied,* or the runic symbols of the ancient Germans; they practiced various occult arts and tried to revitalize ancient Germanic folk customs such as open-air assemblies, theaters, and nature worship. The fine arts became a popular vehicle for the propagation of this tribal narcissism.

It is in this area that Richard Wagner's spectacular stage productions, combining music, theater, and Germanic narcissism, probably had the greatest impact in reinforcing tribal nationalism in the collective psyche of the German people. The effect of Wagner's music on Hitler, of course, is well-known, but it had a somewhat similar impact on millions of Germans who thrilled to its sounds and felt uplifted by its message of popularized romanticism with its symbolic evocations of Nordic superiority, the quest for a pagan holy grail (*das Reich*), the celebration of knightly conquests, and the stout hails to victory — *Sieg! Sieg! Sieg! Heil dir Heil!*[52] As is also well known, Wagner and his circle were parlor racists and Judeophobes; the master himself penned a poisonous pamphlet against the noxious influence of the Jews in music, entitled *Das Judentum in der Musik* (1850), in which he accused the Jews of lacking musical sensibility because they supposedly lacked feeling for the German soil and its people. The Jews, he claimed, merely simulated creativity by eclectic borrowing from the culture of others. There was no hope for them, either as artists or as citizens, unless they ceased being Jews and became part of the folk community. What ceasing to be a Jew really meant or how it could be effected was never spelled out by the capricious composer or by any fanatical Judeophobe because it would have meant that he had to give up his own anti-Jewish prejudices, which he was not prepared to do. Curiously enough, some of Wagner's closest supporters and friends were Jewish, notably his favorite pianist, Joseph Rubenstein, and his "alter ego," the conductor Hermann Levi — both of whom tried to soft-pedal the master's anti-Jewish outbursts as really stemming from "the most noble motives."[53]

The celebration of heroic Teutonic man and woman also became a popular theme with sculptors and painters, notably with Karl Höppner, who churned out a steady stream of paintings of sun-drenched muscular youths under the pseudonym Fidus. The visual arts, in turn, linked with the popular gymnastic associations that had been inspired by Turnvater Jahn. By the end of the century, the German gymnasts became role models for the young; they touted physical strength and beauty, celebrated *völkisch* ideas, and excluded Jews as un-German.

Not all of these *völkisch,* neo-romantic beliefs, of course, preached a rabid anti-Jewish message of expulsion or elimination, but the cumulative effect was a heightening of popular discriminatory Jew-hatred. These ranged from literary stereotypes of haggling and dishonest Jews to more sinister diabolizing images of Jews as deadly bacilli. They encompassed the world of high-brow culture as well as the demimonde of crankish and half-demented pamphleteers. The influential novelist

Gustav Freytag, for example, created the negative literary portrait of the Jewish financial bloodsucker in Veitel Itzig — the shameless, physically ugly, and dishonest Jew who tries to subvert the straightforward and honest morality of the everyday German. A similar portrait can be found in Wilhelm Raabe's famous novel *Hungerpastor* (Hunger pastor) in which Raabe contrasts two men, a German and a Jew, and how they try to make their way in the world. The German pursues an honest path and becomes the pastor of a poor seaside parish, whereas the Jew sets out on a reckless and dishonest course of self-aggrandizement and ends up drowning in a river. As a sop to the Jewish community, however, Raabe introduces a "good Jew" who earnestly strives to overcome the weaknesses of his race so that he can become an honest German. This literary technique of contrasting two mentalities or cultural traits — one German and honest and the other Jewish and dishonest, with attendant physiognomic contrasts of blondish good-looking Aryans and curly-haired, swarthy, hook-nosed Jews — became a widespread practice among popular novelists and artists. In Gordon Craig's estimate probably some twenty million Germans derived their spiritual nourishment from low-brow trashy novels that appeared in weekly installments and taught them to look at Jews as usurers, well-poisoners, child murderers, and master criminals.[54]

It is generally agreed that these various types of Judeophobia did not converge into an organized political movement until the last quarter of the nineteenth century. The causes appear to have been primarily twofold: the first centered on the financial crash of 1873 and the ensuing depression and the second on the steady influx of east European Jews (*Ostjuden*) into Germany and Austria. In the early 1870s economic liberals passed a number of economic reforms, the most important being a law that limited liability of investors in enterprises to the actual amount of money they invested rather than their own assets. This measure encouraged a flood of investments by venture capitalists and created, at least temporarily, an impressive economic boom; but since the new investments were not regulated, many fraudulent speculators also participated in this orgy of frenzied expansion. In 1873 the financial market collapsed, many enterprises failed, and the public looked for scapegoats. Bethel Strausbourg, who had been a leading culprit along with other reckless Jewish investors, was singled out as an example of a larger Jewish conspiracy. Conveniently forgotten was the fact that two Jewish Reichstag deputies, Lasker and Bamberger, had repeatedly warned the business community against the reckless and fraudulent practices that had led to the crisis or that Bleichröder, who had kept his distance from the frenzied promoters, intervened personally to prevent the crisis from becoming worse than it already was.[55] That just as many Jews as Germans were involved and ruined in the crisis was not commonly recognized; the public wanted not just scapegoats but Jewish scapegoats, and this is what the public received.

It was, in fact, in the wake of the 1873 crash that political Judeo-phobia emerged and was organized by several militant rabble-rousers. One of the first spokesmen of the anti-Jewish cause in Germany was the imperial court chaplain Adolf Stöcker, who founded the Christlich-Soziale Partei (Christian Social Party) in 1878 in order to rescue the working classes from the clutches of Marxian socialism. The son of a sergeant, Stöcker combined a military and ministerial career. He served first in a poor mining parish and then in the army as a military chaplain before being appointed to the court. He had witnessed the rough conditions that workers had been exposed to and became alarmed by the possibility that their loyalties to church and state were rapidly disintegrating. Sensing the importance of mass appeal, the fiery preacher hoped to create a right-wing counterpoise to the threat he saw developing on the political left. As a chaplain of the imperial court, Stöcker enjoyed the blessing of the Hohenzollern dynasty, and his relations with the conservative *Kreuzzeitung* gave him access to the molders of public opinion. He also cultivated a close contact with the lower classes in his capacity as director of the Berlin City Mission, a charitable organization of the Lutheran Church that ministered to the needy. Stöcker's anti-Jewish campaign was motivated by opportunistic political and personal reasons rather than by intellectual convictions. Representing an economically displaced lower middle class, threatened by an increasingly well organized working class from below and by feudal interests from above, he used the Jews as a convenient scapegoat for the ills recently caused by the depression of 1873 and by a series of financial scandals connected to it. Stöcker also insinuated that "Jewish capital" supported only big corporate interests but not small German business owners. He identified himself with the common complaint of small business owners who claimed that they had been ruined by corporations and bankers; and since these large institutions were in the hands of Jews, all the misfortunes suffered by small businessmen must have been caused by Jews. There was just enough credibility in this false kind of reasoning to make it attractive to the half-educated and the gullible, for as Hannah Arendt observed, many of the bankers were Jews and, more importantly, the general figure of the banker bore definite Jewish traits for historical reasons.

Stöcker's party failed miserably, polling only 1,422 votes in Berlin during the general Reichstag's election of 1878,[56] but his anti-Jewish rhetoric found a receptive audience among conservative circles, particularly among such conservative newspapers as the *Kreuzzeitung* and *Germania*. In a series of highly charged articles, the *Kreuzzeitung* attacked the government's fiscal policies by dubbing them bankers' policies made by and for Jews. It singled out Bismarck's close financial confidant, the banker Gerson Bleichröder, as the chief culprit of economic distress in Germany. The same allegations were made by the leading Catholic paper, *Germania,* which embarrassed Bismarck by reprinting a speech he had delivered against Jewish emancipation over a quarter of a century before. *Germania* also cast aspersions on the motives of German Jews, insisting that Jews were overrepresented in lucrative businesses and underrepresented in "productive" enterprises, and advising good Catholics that the disproportionate number of wealthy Jews in Germany might be offset by a boycott of Jewish businesses.

Stöcker's anti-Jewish campaign not only resonated throughout Germany, hitting responsive cords in various places, but it also revealed a certain pattern. Some militant Jew-haters used Judeophobia in order to promote their own causes; others fashioned it into a political strategy of integrating Germans into a common unit bound by a strong sense of nationalism and anti-Jewish convictions.[57] The integrative-political approach was especially popular with ultraconservative nationalists, who found in the historian Heinrich Treitschke the most persuasive spokesman of gold-plated, academic Jew-hatred. In 1879, only one year after Stöcker had founded the Christian Social Party, Treitschke launched his intellectual campaign against the Jews in the pages of the elitist conservative journal *Preussische Jahrbücher* by using a slogan that the Nazis would repeat endlessly — namely, "the Jews are our national misfortune." Treitschke's attack was motivated primarily by nationalist rather than by racist convictions; it proceeded on the assumption that Germany could be great only if it melded into a cohesive national community with a single will and purpose. He violently denounced any form of double nationality (*Doppelnationalität*) or dual loyalty, demanding strict adherence to a romanticized nationalism peculiar to himself and many other educated Germans.

For decades, this historian-mythologist was carried away by intense and impassioned outbursts of inspired national zeal, protected by his deafness from ever hearing the other side; he succeeded not only in indoctrinating many young minds who were exposed to him at the University of Berlin but also in making anti-Jewishness a respectable position.[58] Treitschke proudly proclaimed that "the fatherland of modern anti-Semitism is Germany, where the systems were thought out and the slogans coined. The German literature is the richest in anti-Jewish writing."[59] Whether Germany was, in fact, the most anti-Jewish country in the world was a matter of opinion, but Treitschke and like-minded Jew-haters were doing their best to make it so. Although Treitschke's clarion call to the anti-Jewish cause brought forth a blistering rebuttal by some of his colleagues, notably the historian Theodor Mommsen, it became quite clear during and after this academic exchange that the majority of Treitschke's colleagues in academia held to similar anti-Jewish convictions.

Stöcker and Treitschke were beginning to articulate, each in his own particular way, an increasingly resentful and intolerant position regarding the Jews. Treitschke spoke for the conservative elite, Stöcker for the socially or economically displaced. One could argue whether the former was more influential than the latter, but for the coming of the Nazi movement, which was a broad populist movement, it is especially important to examine anti-Jewish outbursts that expressed themselves, as they did with Stöcker, in populist and highly charged emotional forms. In the 1870s and later this kind of Judeophobia was often the resentful expression of displaced social groups who suffered most from economic depressions and blamed Bismarck or Jewish liberalism for their problems. Another articulate spokesman of these pent-up frustrations and resentments was the journalist Wilhelm Marr (1819–1904), who coined the word "anti-Semitism" in 1879 and wrote two influential books, *Der Judenspiegel* (The Jewish mirror, 1862) and *Der Sieg des Judentums über das Germanentum* (The victory of Jewry over Germandom, 1879). Marr used the psychological approach of insinuating scare tactics into the anti-Jewish campaign by suggesting that the Jews, far from being weak or politically impotent, were in fact powerful and insidious people, bent upon sapping the racial strength of the German people as a prelude to their real and diabolical aim — the establishment of a new Palestine in Germany. Marr's anti-Jewish message already bore definite apocalyptic and millenarian features; he saw Germans and Jews locked in mortal combat, warning that the hour was late and that only a concerted counterattack against world Jewry could stay the doom of the German race.

Wilhelm Marr's shrill warning was by no means an aberrant exception. In 1874, *Die Gartenlaube* (The Gardenhouse), a literary magazine that catered to middle-class readers, published a series of anti-Jewish articles on the stock exchange and speculation frauds in Berlin. Written by Otto Glagau (1834–89), these articles reflected the grievances of the lower middle class — artisans, small businessmen, merchants, minor civil servants — who blamed Jewish bankers and politicians for their plight. The chief recipient of their paranoid fears more often than not was Bismarck's friend and confidant, the Jewish banker Gerson Bleichröder. As Fritz Stern put it,

> He embodied all that the socially aggrieved came to detest: he was a Jew with legendary wealth and power, a parvenu and plutocrat unsettling the traditional order of rank. He seemed to fit all the stereotypes of the anti-semites: the Jew as promoter and plotter, as corruptor and perpetual wirepuller, the Jew, in short, as a man of devious power — and it was Jewish power that made gentiles uneasy and anti-semites frantic. He had amassed his fortune by stock jobbing in defiance of that sacred principle that a man should earn his daily bread. There was a violent anti-capitalist element in the new anti-semitism; Bleichröder, the international banker, the respectable usurer, was proof of all the iniquities of Jews and capitalists.[60]

Germans who thought this way were likely to belong to the *Mittelstand,* the petit bourgeois order that felt especially threatened by the recurring economic fluctuations under capitalism. Such groups felt unrepresented and neglected, scarcely knowing which way to turn. As Paul Massing pointed out, liberalism had nothing to offer them but noble rhetoric about free enterprise, conservatism was too remote and too elitist to persuade them, and socialism wrote them off the books as doomed by the laws of history. It took National Socialism to mobilize their frustrations.[61]

These diverse resentments were eventually organized politically by several anti-Jewish rabble-rousers. In 1879 Wilhelm Marr founded the Bund *der Antisemiten* (League of Anti-Semites); in 1880 two new parties, the Social Reich Party and the German Reform Party, came into being; both made anti-Jewish resentments and prejudices their chief platform. In 1881 Max Liebermann von Sonneberg, a minor aristocrat who was always suffering from major financial embarrassments, and Bernhard Förster, Friedrich Nietzsche's embarrassing brother-in-law, founded the Deutsche Volksverein (German People's League), dedicated to combatting parliamentary democracy and the Jews. Förster, a slightly deranged and cashiered schoolteacher, later emigrated to Paraguay with the intention of founding a pure Aryan colony called New Germania. His bizarre experiment in utopian racialism, however, failed miserably and he committed suicide in 1889. Liebermann, Förster, and Ernst Henrici, the founder of the Social Reich Party, gathered the "Anti-Semitic Petition" in 1881, signed by 225,000 people, which called for a suspension of immigration and the exclusion of Jews from public office, and submitted it to Bismarck. The petition was turned down by the chancellor's ministers with the laconic reply: "The government intends no action to deprive the Jews of their rights."[62]

Nevertheless, the Jewish question would not disappear; in fact, in the last two decades of the nineteenth century, Germany was inundated by a proliferation of anti-Jewish books, magazines, parties, and public speeches. The clearinghouse for anti-Jewish activists of all kinds was the League of Anti-Semites; and one of its cofounders, Theodor Fritsch (1852–1933), would become one of the most influential Jew-baiters of modern times. Fritsch, who was later hailed as a master teacher by the Nazis, published a stream of anti-Jewish broadsides, starting with *Antisemiten-Katechismus* (Anti-Semitic Catechism) in 1887 and culminating in his pernicious Jew-baiting magnum opus, *Handbuch der Judenfrage* (Handbook of the Jewish question) in 1907. He also founded his own publishing house in Leipzig, the Hammer Publishing Company, which promoted anti-Jewish books and deftly exploited popular racial prejudices through its periodical magazine called *Hammer.* The theme in these publications was always the same: the Jews, in connivance with other conspiratorial groups such as Freemasons, Catholics, and Jehovah's Witnesses, were secretly conspiring to gain control over the reins of power throughout the world. A tone of paranoid urgency rang through most of Fritsch's writings; and in his *Handbook of the Jewish Question,* he went so far as to append a detailed list of Jews he considered responsible for major crimes such as murder, treason, forgery, and rape. Such Jew-baiting would later be much appreciated by Julius Streicher and Adolf Hitler.

In 1887, Otto Böckel, a librarian at the University of Marburg, spokesman for the Hessian peasants, and author of a notorious Jew-baiting work called *The Jews: Kings of Our Times,* became the first official "anti-Semite" to be elected as an Independent to the Reichstag. Böckel was one of several self-appointed populist leaders who would use Jew-hatred as a means for his own political self-aggrandizement. His platform called for a radical separation of Germans and Jews along with treating Jews as foreigners with limited rights. Although Böckel eventually lost his seat and faded from public view, he left behind him the seeds from which future anti-Jewish activities could sprout.

An even more unsavory anti-Jewish rabble-rouser was Hermann Ahlwardt, a former schoolteacher who had been dismissed for embezzling funds earmarked for poor students and had also spent some time in prison for spreading libelous stories about Bismarck and Bleichröder. Like Böckel, Ahlwardt fished in troubled social waters, organizing the disaffection of peasants and artisans in Saxony and insinuating the most malicious smear tactics into his crusades against Jews and socialists. In 1892 he was elected to the Reichstag on the Conservative Party ticket. In the same year, Ahlwardt's noisy lower-class followers pressured the Conservative Party into accepting a new program, the Tivoli Program, that began with the statement: "We combat the widely obtruding and decomposing Jewish influence on our popular life."[63] Although the program was intended to capture a mass following, neither popular anti-Jewish sentiments nor the rabble-rousers showed much political staying power. The Antisemitische Volkspartei (Anti-Semitic People's Party), founded by Otto Böckel in 1889, showed a steady but unspectacular growth from 12,000 votes in 1889 to 264,000 in 1893 and to 350,000 on the eve of World War I. The various one-issue, anti-Semitic parties never managed to elect more than twenty deputies to the Reichstag, and Böckel and Ahlwardt lost their own seats and faded into obscurity. Yet these parties, their interest groups, and the men who led them illustrate the existence of a widespread Jewish hatred, a monstrous Hydra with many ugly heads. Anti-Jewish agitators, however, always managed to put a shiny veneer on their hatred by posturing as noble nationalists who claimed to represent purely national rather than narrow party interests.

This theme of representing national rather than provincial interests was even more pronounced in Austria, where ethnic conflicts were far more intense than in Germany. The Habsburg empire was a multiethnic, multireligious, and multilingual community — one in which the ruling German population saw itself in immanent danger of being displaced by other ethnic groups: Czechs, Hungarians, Slavs, Croats, Jews. The result was the growth of xenophobic Germanism with strident anti-Jewish overtones. When young Adolf Hitler arrived in Vienna in 1907, the city was governed by the anti-Jewish mayor Dr. Karl Lueger (1844–1910), whom Hitler later called "the mightiest mayor of all times." Lueger was a Christian Socialist who had been swept into office by his lower middle-class constituency during a period of economic hardship and financial scandals. He was basically a romantic reactionary who favored a return to a more organic racial capitalism. His aim was to remove Jews from influential professions and from public life in general.

Lueger's political rival was Georg Ritter von Schönerer (1842–1921), a landowner, member of the Austrian House of Delegates and one of the founders of the Pan-German Nationalist Party. Schönerer also founded the Los von Rom (Break with Rome) movement, which called for an end to the cultural and religious domination by Roman Catholicism and Judaism under the slogan "Without Juda, without Rome, we build Germania's dome." Schönerer's call for Austrian annexation to Germany, his rabid Jew-baiting, and his conservative nationalism made a deep impression on the young Hitler.

Indeed, Vienna was probably the most racially paranoid capital of Europe; it was here that fears of Slavic encirclement and rumors of Jewish conspiracies combined to produce a very volatile atmosphere that could be easily exploited.[64] It was also in Vienna that Theodor Herzl, having come to the painful recognition that Jews would never be fully accepted as equals in any non-Jewish society, articulated the case for a new Exodus and reinvigorated the cause of Zionism almost single-handedly. The Jewish population in Vienna had grown from a mere 6,217 in 1857 to 175,318 in 1910. Demographically, large numbers of Jews lived in the city's Leopoldstadt in the second district across the Danube Canal; the majority of these Jews, the so-called *Ostjuden,* came from Galicia in eastern Europe. Their treatment in German-speaking territories sheds an important light on the nature of German Jew-hatred, especially its ugly xenophobic and racial overtones.

The waves of east European Jewry washed ashore on two major German lands — eastern Austria and the eastern district of Prussia called Posen. Beginning in the late 1860s, there was a steady influx of east European Jews; initially, it was the result of various cholera epidemics and famines, but later it was also caused by Russian-sponsored pogroms. Although well over two million Jews fled to the west, the majority of these refugees moved on to France, England, and the United States rather than the German-speaking territories, as alarmed German immigrant-bashers seemed to believe. The German government, even more than the Austrian government, instituted harsh measures to prevent these migrants from settling in Germany. Every possible tactic, ranging from humiliating searches and harassment to forced resettlements, was employed to rush these migrants out of Germany. Even foreign Jews who did not plan to stay in Germany but were mere transients on their way to other countries were rounded up at key border areas, herded into barracks, subjected to humiliating delousing and disinfection procedures, packed

into sealed railroad cars, and shipped to port cities where additional
isolation in barracks and gratuitous insults greeted them before they
finally departed for their new homes. In her journey from Plotzk to Boston, Mary Antin got a preview of the later Holocaust at the hands of
supercilious German officials:

> We emigrants were herded, packed in cars, and driven from place to
> place like cattle....In a great field, opposite a solitary house within a
> large yard, our train pulled up at last, and a conductor commanded the
> passengers to make haste and get out....He hurried us into one large
> room which made up the house, and then into the yard. Here a great
> many men and women in white received us, the women attending to the
> women and girls of the passengers, and the men to the others. This was
> another scene of bewildering confusion, parents losing their children, and
> little ones crying; baggage being thrown together in one corner of the
> yard, heedless of content, which suffered in consequence; those white-
> clad Germans shouting commands, always accompanied with "Quick!
> Quick!" — the confused passengers obeying all orders like meek children,
> only questioning now and then what was going to be done to them. And
> no wonder if in some minds stories arose of people being captured by
> robbers, murderers and the like. Here we had been taken away to a
> lonely place where only that house was to be seen; our things were taken
> away, our friends separated from us; a man came to inspect us, as if
> to ascertain our full value; strange-looking people driving us about like
> dumb animals, helpless and unresisting; children we could not see cry-
> ing in a way that suggested terrible things; ourselves driven into a little
> room where a great kettle was boiling on a little stove; our clothes taken
> off; our bodies rubbed with a slippery substance that might be any bad
> thing; a shower of warm water let down on us without warning; again
> driven to another little room, where we sit, wrapped in woolen blankets
> too large; coarse bags are brought in, their contents turned out, and we
> see only a cloud of steam, and hear the women's orders to dress our-
> selves — "Quick! Quick!" or else we'll miss — something we cannot hear.
> We are forced to pick up our clothes from among all the others, with
> the steam blinding us; we choke, cough, entreat the women to give us
> time; they persist, "Quick!" "Quick!" — or we'll miss the train — Oh,
> so we really won't be murdered! They are only making us ready for the
> rest of our journey, cleaning us of all suspicions of dangerous sickness.
> Thank God![65]

With hindsight, too much can be made of such experiences, but
they illustrate the paranoid fear that Germans had of these foreigners. We now know that there never was a tidal wave of immigrants
swarming into Germany but only the perception of one — a perception, no doubt, that was partly based on the fact that east European
Jews stood out sharply because they clustered and wore distinct attire, spoke Yiddish, and annoyed Germans by their strange mannerisms.
Forming clannish communities, these eastern Jews created the impression in the minds of many Germans, including, ironically, the assimilated
German Jews, that an alien body amounting to a state within a state

was being implanted into the middle of German society. To many Germans, these eastern Jews presented an unpleasant sight as they seemed to scurry along the pavements of Vienna or Berlin in search of business. They were stigmatized as "unwanted elements," said to be "swarming" into Germany in great numbers, and bringing with them nihilistic ideologies. Government officials likened them to vermin bringing in the plague. Treitschke said that there was nothing German about these *Schnorrers* (tramps) with their "stinking caftans and obligatory lovelocks, except their detestably bad German speech." Even German Jews, who were trying hard to behave like Germans, were leery of their eastern coreligionists. In the words of one German Jew "their laziness, their perpetual readiness to cheat cannot help but fill the western European with . . . unedifying thought. . . . The evil wish arises that in some painless way the world might be rid of these disagreeable objects."[66] Walther Rathenau, himself an assimilated German Jew, could say with apparent sincerity that the Jews were becoming a "foreign organism in the German people's body,"[67] thus expressing, as Karl Marx had done before him, a deep-seated ambiguity toward the Jewish heritage within himself.

If Walther Rathenau, himself a Jew, was offended by the sight of certain *Ostjuden,* how much greater must have been Adolf Hitler's antipathies when he first encountered what he called these "beings clad in caftan, with black curls," whose "smell often made me ill."[68] Suddenly Walther Rathenau's foreign organism became, in the Judeophobic perception, a "poisonous abscess," a "ferment of decomposition," a "bacillus," and the battle to be waged against such a deadly virus required heroic measures comparable to those used by Pasteur and Koch. By 1914 Hitler and other racial Judeophobes had already moved sequentially from a perception that Jews were alien people to a belief that they were deadly bacilli and therefore had to be destroyed.

I do not want to suggest that Hitler's perception of the Jews in prewar Vienna was a common one, but the evidence shows that it was far more widespread among all sections of the community than is usually supposed. The negative stereotype of the unassimilated Jewish outsider, as Jack Wertheimer reminds us, also points to a perennial problem the Germans have had with foreigners in general: "At its core, the German approach to aliens was exploitive: not only did Germans not conceive of their homeland as a haven for the persecuted and needy, they evaluated foreigners solely on the basis of their utility."[69] The cynical treatment accorded to aliens in the Second Reich was going to have obvious relevance not only to Nazi Germany but to the postwar Federal Republic. If it is true that a willingness to assimilate alien groups and allow them to become citizens is one important measure of a nation's character, then it is clear that imperial Germany not only fell far short of that liberal measure but also created, in embryonic form, "the imagery and policies of the Nazi era."[70]

Prejudices against the *Ostjuden,* in other words, embodied the most virulent forms of anti-Jewish hate: xenophobic nationalism and biological racism. Before World War I such blatant anti-Jewish prejudices did not constitute a majority view, and they were still limited to extreme *völkisch* and racial circles. Yet these extremist circles and the cranks who dominated them would play a significant role in shaping future racist minds and policies. A case in point was Georg Lanz von Liebenfels, who gave Hitler many of his racial ideas.[71] In 1905 Liebenfels, a pseudonym for Adolf Josef Lanz (1834–1954), founded the Order of the New Temple (Ordensburg Werfenstein), whose membership was restricted to fair-haired, blue-eyed men, who were exhorted by the master to mate with equally endowed Aryan women in order to produce a new racial order in Germany. Liebenfels disseminated his racial ideas in his periodical *Ostara,* a magazine usually adorned with a swastika on its front cover. Copies of *Ostara* sold briskly in both Austria and Germany; in fact, circulation reached over a hundred thousand for the fall issue of 1908. In that year, Liebenfels produced his major work, entitled *Theozoology, or the Science of Sodom's Apelings and the Divine Electron: An Introduction to the Earliest and Most Recent World View and a Vindication of Royalty and the Nobility* — a rambling work that tried to show that history was a perennial conflict between the children of darkness (Sodom's Apelings) and the children of light (Aryans, or Heldlinge). Liebenfels claimed that the heroic Aryans possessed electric bodily organs and built-in electric transmitters, but their energies had been dissipated by centuries of accumulated racial impurities. He hoped to revitalize the heroic qualities within the Aryan race by means of purifying eugenics, thus helping the Aryans to rekindle their electromagnetic-radiological organs and become all-knowing, all-wise, and all-powerful. As to all lower races, particularly the Jews, Liebenfels recommended a state-sponsored policy of slavery, sterilization, and extermination.

Liebenfels was not only a mad crank but also an imposter; his real name was Adolf Josef Lanz, a former Cistercian monk in the Heiligenkreuz (Holy Cross) monastery in Austria. In 1899 he left the monastery, called himself "Baron," awarded himself a doctoral title, and otherwise obscured his origin. In addition to his literary activities, Liebenfels gathered like-minded cultists in a ruined castle at Werfenstein in upper Austria. There he gathered his disciples, hoisted a swastika flag, and chanted magical incantations to the Teutonic spirits. According to Wilfried Daim, who has traced Liebenfels's bizarre career, Adolf Hitler actually met Liebenfels on one occasion and asked him for some back issues of *Ostara.*[72] In fact, the swastika symbol, the racial theory of history, the Holy Grail of Aryan purity, extermination of ape-like humans (*Tiermenschen*) — all these mental aberrations were prefabricated for Hitler by Liebenfels.

It would be a grave mistake, however, to single out Liebenfels and racial cultists as the only purveyors of racial prejudices. There was considerable cross-fertilization of racial ideas and active cooperation between racial populists and academics. In 1900, for example, the arms manufacturer Friedrich Albert Krupp sponsored an essay competition on the subject, "What can we learn from the principles of Darwinism and its application to the inner political development and the laws of the state?" The panel of judges was chaired by the Social Darwinist Ernst Haeckel; the majority of the contestants were believers in Aryan superiority and endorsed some form of anti-Jewish discrimination. First prize in the competition went to a Munich physician by the name of Wilhelm Schallmeyer, who colored all human activities with a broad Social Darwinian brush of struggle and survival of the fittest and recommended benign neglect of the racially weak specimens. He strongly believed that the Aryan race represented the apex of human achievement and that stringent eugenic efforts, preferably state supported, would be required to keep the Aryan race pure and predominant.

Another contestant in Krupp's competition, Ludwig Woltmann, who was awarded the third prize, later received much renown by publishing a racial periodical called *Politisch-Anthropologische Revue* (Political-Anthropological Review). His journal was only one of several scholarly journals dedicated to racial studies. One of the most respectable was the *Archiv für Rassen und Gesellschaftsbiologie* (Archive for Racial and Social Biology), published by Alfred Ploetz, the founder of the eugenic movement in Germany. Ploetz's publication became a forum for avant-garde racial ideas. Ploetz later coined the phrase "race hygiene," founded a secret Nordic society (Ring der Norde), and was lavishly rewarded for his racial contributions by Adolf Hitler with a university chair. Some of the chief eugenicists and geneticists of the next generation — the scientists, in other words, who flourished under the protective mantle of National Socialism — were influenced by Woltmann and Ploetz. Among this group can be found Eugen Fischer, Fritz Lenz, and Otmar von Verschuer, the man who served as a mentor to the future "Angel of Death" at Auschwitz, Dr. Josef Mengele. The most zealous of this group was Eugen Fischer, who applied Mendelian genetics to racial hygiene. In 1934 Fischer boasted that he had been the first scientist to promote Woltmann's ideas within the academic community and to have "inflamed young hearts with enthusiasm for racial science."[73] Fischer's colleague, Fritz Lenz, was a disciple of Alfred Ploetz and a frequent contributor to his racial journal. Before the outbreak of the First World War, Ploetz's review was avidly read by many German academics; it became a clearinghouse for all sorts of racial doctrines, including the pseudoscientific ruminations of Fritsch and Lanz von Liebenfels.

Although Alfred Ploetz had tried to make it clear that he did not want racial hygiene to be deflected by anti-Jewish prejudices, which he condemned as superstitious, the movement moved precisely in this direction after World War I and cross-fertilized with extreme *völkisch* and nationalistic anti-Jewish prejudices, giving them a respectable scientific veneer.[74] Adolf Hitler's racial image of the world was not simply the product of his own delusion but the result of the findings of "respectable" science in Germany and in other parts of the western world, including the United States. When Hitler and other Nazis read Fritsch or Liebenfels, they merely absorbed ideas which were widely entertained in both academic and popular circles.

The message embodied in these doctrines was unmistakable: any living creature is engaged during its lifetime in a ceaseless struggle for existence and is doomed to extinction if it does not fight. Nations, like individuals, are also engaged in a never-ending conflict in which only the fittest survive. The fighting quality of a nation depends upon its racial and ethnic purity and its ability to breed the fittest specimens in the form of productive workers, savage fighters, and charismatic leaders. Those who defile a race of people — Jews, Gypsies, Asiatic inferiors, the mentally ill or physically disabled — must be eliminated through appropriate state measures. Of all the human stocks, the Aryan (white) race stands at the apex of human achievement; and since Germany is the homeland of the Aryan race, the German people have been entrusted with a secret mission — to multiply prodigiously and dominate the world. Racial mongrelization, however, has gone so far that the hour may be late indeed. Thus, only state-sponsored legislation can protect the Aryan race from being further infected by inferior races. In 1913 Eugen Fischer boldly prophesied "with absolute certainty" that white Europeans would become extinct unless governments, especially the German government, developed and implemented a coherent racial policy.[75] Adolf Hitler and the Nazi movement provided that policy.

No one could have predicted that development in 1914, certainly not in the forms the Nazis would shape it. Despite the ominous fault lines in German society previously discussed, the German state was a civilized *Rechtsstaat* protecting hard-earned Jewish rights. The Jews themselves, in Peter Pulzer's words, found "life tolerable in the Empire — for many it was distinctly good. They were at home, insofar as anyone is ever at home anywhere."[76] There were reasons to be alarmed, of course, because Jew-hatred had not only infected vulgar or ignorant people, as it had throughout history, but insinuated itself into the minds of educated people from all walks of life, in addition to having nestled itself into many social and political institutions. As tempted as we might be to draw vertical connections linking the Second with the Third Reich, there was no reason to assume in 1914 that the festering anti-Jewish infection would seize the whole society and plunge the Jews into a dark abyss. The eruption of World War I and its violent aftermath, however, provided the conditions that would aggravate the infection and transform it into a raging disease.

Chapter 4

The Rise of Pathological Judeophobia, 1918–33

World War I and Its Aftermath

On August 2, 1914, shortly before the "Guns of August" began to thunder, numerous war speeches resounded across the length and breadth of Germany. In Munich's Odeonsplatz thousands cheered when the declaration of war was read from the steps of the Hall of Field Marshals; in the crowd, not too far from the stone lions that faced out across the square from either side of the pavilion, stood a young man who appeared to be in a state of ecstasy, swept away by the excitement of the moment and, judging by his gaping mouth and shimmering eyes, he was fleetingly experiencing a premonition that destiny was beckoning him to greatness. The young man in the photograph was Adolf Hitler. In the words of Richard Hanser, "the picture freezes forever the precise instant at which the career of Adolf Hitler became possible. The war that was being proclaimed as the photo was taken would produce the social chaos indispensable to his rise."[1] Hitler was so swept away by the excitement of war that "those hours appeared like the redemption from the annoying moods of my youth...I am not ashamed today to say that, overwhelmed by the impassioned enthusiasm, I had fallen on my knees and thanked Heaven out of my overflowing heart that it had granted me the good fortune of being allowed to live in these times."[2]

Hitler's euphoria about the impending thrill of combat, real or vicarious, was shared by the majority of Germans in August of 1914. The nation was gripped by a veritable war psychosis, as young and old alike cheerfully welcomed the prospect of fighting for Germany. Decades of pent-up social frustrations, combined with intensely held nationalistic beliefs, erupted publicly and produced, at least momentarily, a strongly integrated people with a common goal and purpose. The parties of the left joined with their political antagonists by pledging themselves to suspend civil dissent until victory was achieved. The emperor proudly proclaimed a Burgfrieden, a halt of party strife within the nation, and said, "I no longer recognize parties; I recognize only Germans."[3]

Intoxicated by this pervasive mood of nationalistic fervor, most Germans looked upon war as an exciting diversion, perhaps even a redemption from years of dissatisfaction, alienation, or failure, and expected it to be all over by Christmas. The young men, egged on by their parents, teachers, or loved ones, could hardly wait to go to the front. One future Nazi storm trooper later recalled: "I sensed within myself the urge for the front. The craving to be allowed at last to participate in this holy struggle grew stronger and rose to a nearly pathological height."[4] Young Germans, weaned on the lofty ideals of manly courage and self-sacrifice for the fatherland, while harnessed at the same time to a cultivation of hatred unknown since the Wars of Religion, jubilantly marched off to the front, cheered on by adoring women and rousing marching bands and feeling psychologically empowered by a fanatical resolve.

This also included the vast majority of German Jews, who seized upon the moment to prove their loyalty and to validate their Germanness. "All Jews," one association announced, "must do their duty, but the German Jews must do more than their duty."[5] Many Jews welcomed the war for the same reasons as their fellow Germans, but perhaps especially because it provided them with the opportunity to prove convincingly that, by laying their lives on the line for Germany, they were loyal German citizens. This they did in numbers all out of proportion to their actual standing in the population. Although only 3,500 Jews had served in the German army before 1914, a total of about 100,000 Jews served in the armed forces between 1914 and 1918. Of these, 80,000 served in combat, 35,000 were decorated for bravery, 23,000 earned noncommissioned rank, and 2,000 became officers. All in all, 12,000 German Jews lost their lives in World War I.[6]

The youngest of all volunteers was a thirteen-year-old Jewish teenager named Joseph Zippes, who lost both of his legs at the front; the first Reichstag deputy to volunteer, Ludwig Frank, was also Jewish.[7] Leo Baeck, who was emerging as one of Germany's foremost Jewish intellectual leaders, served as a *Feldrabbiner* (field rabbi) on both the western and the eastern fronts, consoling Jewish soldiers and ministering to their religious needs. Fritz Haber, head of the kaiser Wilhelm Institute, a man usually not given to displays of chauvinism, lent his name to the "Manifesto of Ninety-Three," a public statement signed by ninety-three famous intellectuals that justified the German invasion of Belgium, denied all charges of German war atrocities or violations of international law, and boldly affirmed that the German army and the German people were one. Other Jewish intellectuals who signed this chauvinistic document were Paul Ehrlich, Ludwig Fulda, Paul Laband, Max Liebermann, and Max Reinhardt — a very impressive group of intellectual luminaries.[8] Fritz Haber quickly put his institute on a war footing and lent his own chemical knowledge to the production of poison gas. Along with two other well-known Jewish scientists and future Nobel laureates, James Frank and Richard Willstätter, Haber was responsible for developing a variety of chemical weapons and even personally conducted actual assaults on the front. Haber was not alone in his patriotic zeal. The Jewish poet Ernst Lissauer (1882–1937) wrote the most aggressive hate poem of the war, entitled *Hassgesang gegen England* (Hymn of hate against England), which brought him instant fame:

> Hate by water and hate by land;
> Hate of heart and hate of the hand;
> We love as one and hate as one;
> We have but one foe alone — England.[9]

The Viennese poet was not alone in making such war-mongering remarks in the Jewish community of Vienna. Even Sigmund Freud, at least initially, exclaimed that "my libido is given to Austro-Hungary," confessing that for the first time he felt himself to be an Austrian.[10] Freud's patriotic ardor cooled off quickly because his three sons were all called to duty and saw heavy action; his Jewish colleagues, too, were being called up: Max Eitington was excited by a quick prospect for victory, Karl Abraham was detailed to a surgical unit near Berlin, and Sandor Ferenzi was sent to the Hungarian Hussars.[11] There were other Austrian Jews who also quickly came to the service of their country. Stefan Zweig, writer and later pacifist, initially wrote propaganda pieces for the Austrian war effort, and Ludwig Wittgenstein, who would revolutionize philosophy in the twentieth century, hurried back from Cambridge to volunteer as a gunner in the Austrian army, despite a double hernia that entitled him to an exemption.[12]

Many of the idealistic young men who marched off to battle in August of 1914 would never return; the war that everyone assumed would be over by Christmas quickly turned into a seesaw battle of attrition with such staggering losses in men and materiel that even cold-hearted militarists gasped when they saw the casualty lists. The home front, so solid in 1914, soon began to crack. The parties on the left, having reluctantly voted for war appropriations, expected significant social and political concessions from the conservative ruling classes; but when these concessions did not materialize, political dissension reopened with a vengeance. It is remarkable, however, that support for the war effort continued as long as it did, a fact that could only be attributed to an excessive delight in war, official insensitivity to suffering, and a misguided belief on the part of many Germans that their leadership would richly reward them with the fruits of victory.

The fact that the German High Command lacked a strategic plan for coordinating a war fought on several fronts and faced an enemy of decided numerical and productive superiority made it highly unlikely that Germany would be able to win a long war of attrition. This became increasingly apparent by 1916 and was compounded by exceptionally poor decision-making by the team of Paul von Hindenburg and Erich Ludendorff. Having crippled the Russians at Tannenberg and the Masurian Lakes, Hindenburg and Ludendorff became superhuman heroes in the eyes of most Germans, and their reputations so dwarfed that of the emperor or any civilian that few dared to question the wisdom of their policies. As long as the military could hoodwink the public into believing that victory was just around the corner, support for the war effort remained surprisingly strong.

The truth was that Germany's military autocrats, including Field Marshal von Moltke, General Falkenhayn, and the team of Hindenburg and Ludendorff bungled from one disaster to another. In 1914 their much-vaunted Schlieffen plan had failed to deliver the promised knock-out blow in the west; in 1915 and 1916 they sacrificed a million men in futile battles of trench warfare on the western front; in 1916 their effort to challenge the British navy off the coast of Jutland failed. In 1917 they committed three blunders that almost certainly guaranteed defeat: they threw away whatever chances they had to conclude a moderate peace with the western powers, authorized unlimited submarine warfare and thus made inevitable the entrance of the United States into the war, and foolishly shipped Lenin from Switzerland into Russia to engineer the Russian Revolution. Finally, in 1918 they committed Germany's last reserves in a series of hopeless battles, and, facing certain defeat, they appointed civilians to arrange for a cease-fire and later blamed them for having "stabbed" the German army in the back.[13]

The tide of battle and the possibility of defeat had a profound psychological impact on the fighting forces and the German people who supported them. Four years of savage fighting, involving gruesome and heart-wrenching experiences, fundamentally remolded the personalities of many men who had gone into battle in "a rain of flowers to seek the death of heroes"; instead, they found a nightmare of endless sacrifice with no glorious victory at the end. What they did experience, as Robert Waite has pointed out, were three essential qualities of the totalitarian state that lurked just around the corner and that they would help to shape: total commitment, state coercion, and a new form of autocracy based on the well-being of the people.[14] With its inherent requirement for centralized planning, war for the German people would become a school for socialism and an education for authoritarianism.[15] Some referred to this later as "socialism of the trenches" because millions of men had met each other in the trenches and learned to trust each other as comrades rather than as members of unequal social groups.

The trenches also bred a new and frightening human being: unsentimental, emotionally desensitized, regimented, brutal, and violent. The poet Ernst Jünger would later glamorize this efficient killer as a higher type of human being, the "New Man" of the future whose cunning, strength, and ruthlessness, together with his fanatical single-mindedness, would break the back of a spineless bourgeois civilization. As Jünger correctly predicted: "This war is not the end but the new ascending of force.... New forms will be filled with blood, and might well be seized with the hard fist."[16] Having participated in a secular crusade and shared the "Front Experience" with its psychological bonding features of comradeship, storm attacks, and self-sacrifice, many young men would treasure these experiences throughout their lives and actively promote a replication of the soldier's community in peacetime. This was also Adolf Hitler's fondest dream, a dream he may have glimpsed on that day in the Odeonsplatz and that he later tried to realize in the Third Reich by perpetuating the feeling of soldierly fraternity into peacetime, extinguishing class differences and infusing the spirit of the trenches into everyday life.

The First World War was a watershed in the organization of human killing because it accelerated the pace by which modern nation states perfected the techniques of mobilizing a whole range of activities — scientific, technological, economic, bureaucratic, and psychological — for the expressed purpose of annihilating their enemies. In Omer Bartov's judgment, the First World War provided the motives and organizational techniques that became standard in later experiments of state-organized mass killings, including the Holocaust. The death camps, he reminds us, were architecturally and organizationally patterned on the experience of the Great War, "incorporating all the attributes of a military environment, such as uniforms and barbed wire, watchtowers and roll calls, hierarchy and order, drill and commands. The Holocaust was therefore a militarized genocide, made all the more effective both by killing *all* those targeted for murder and in being safe for *all* those who carried it out."[17] There is something demonic about modern industrial states transforming themselves into organized killing machines, whether the purpose is to save democracy, protect national self-interest, or, more disturbingly, annihilate racial enemies or fulfill romantic longings for heroism and death. In the case of many young Germans, the First World War provided the experiences that would predispose them toward a fascist way of life, including the glorification of a pseudoreligious nationalism and an exaggerated form of militarism.

While the First World War was for many young Germans a school for fascism, it was also a school for a virulent form of Judeophobia. As the tide of battle turned, latent anti-Jewish prejudices within and outside the armed forces began to emerge. In June of 1916 an anti-Jewish deputy in the Reichstag asked the minister of War an ominous question about how many Jews were actually serving at the front. Rumor had been circulating for some time that the Jews were *Drückebergers* — that is, shirkers who avoided frontline duties and deliberately chose safe and lucrative noncombatant positions. Hitler would later repeat these false allegations in *Mein Kampf,* claiming that Jewish soldiers were cowardly paper-shufflers behind the fighting front:

...the offices of the authorities were occupied by Jews. Almost every clerk a Jew and every Jew a clerk. I was amazed by this multitude of fighters of the Chosen People and could not help comparing them with the few representatives they had on the front.[18]

The upshot of such vicious rumors was that the War Ministry launched a full-fledged *Judenzählung* (Jewish census), but never released its findings, claiming that the results were intended only for internal information rather that public consumption. The reality, as previously indicated, was that Jews were carrying as much responsibility as their German counterparts, but that reality was deliberately suppressed by a collective desire for scapegoats; such scapegoating was both spontaneous and actively promoted by Judeophobic parties, associations, and interest groups. Among the populace one could pick up all sorts of disparaging anti-Jewish remarks to the effect that "the Jews have not yet earned enough, that is why the war has not yet ended."[19] As the war turned against Germany, the ruling elite, working hand in glove with anti-Jewish groups such as the Pan-German League and the Vaterland Party, deliberately stirred up Judeophobic feelings in order to deflect responsibility for the government's mismanagement of the war and to distract people's attention from the deprivations and inequalities suffered by ordinary Germans. Defeat made the use of these tactics even more widespread. Having been indoctrinated for four years that victory was just around the corner, the nation was stunned to learn the humiliating provisions of the armistice and the subsequent terms of the Versailles Treaty, which stripped the nation of its armed forces, its whole merchant marine fleet, and valuable territories in Europe and overseas, and exacted such harsh reparations that its future economic survival was seriously jeopardized. To make it worse, the nation was plunged into political chaos with the collapse of the monarchy, civil war, and years of political instability.

The shock of defeat, accompanied by a collective sense of disbelief, triggered a series of denials that obscured the real causes of the collapse and made it very difficult, in a climate of fear, suspicion, and recrimination, to reconstruct the nation's socioeconomic and political foundation on a democratic basis. Since the war had not been fought on German soil and its armies returned in relatively good order, many Germans believed that the army had never been defeated in battle but had been undermined at home by socialists, pacifists, liberals, or Jews. The generals, who were the most to blame for the defeat, subsequently blamed their failures on defeatism and sabotage at home. Adolf Hitler referred to the amorphous forces who supposedly "stabbed the German army in the back" as the November Criminals.

Amid the general collapse that followed the German defeat, few things were clear except that the Old Europe lay in ruins. The war had devoured almost two million Germans and permanently crippled as many more. A generation of young people had bled to death on the battlefields of Europe; and those who survived were permanently scarred by their wartime experiences, lacking the psychological resources needed to build a stable and peaceful society. With the collapse of the monarchy the German people became an orphaned people, splintering into numerous and often mutually opposed parties, associations, and interest groups. Out of the trauma of defeat and the disappearance of ancient symbols of authority came years of violence, civil strife, and extremism. It is against this postwar chaos, which extended into the 1920s and was rekindled by the Great Depression of 1929, that the growth of political pathology must be seen. In Germany, as elsewhere in Europe, a generation of political extremists roamed the political landscape in search of a messianic leader who could redeem them from meaningless sacrifices on the battlefield and restore a collective sense of purpose that had disappeared with the old authorities.

World War I also brought world revolution in the form of international communism. Just as in Russia, councils of workers and soldiers began to sprout in Germany, starting with a mutiny of sailors in Kiel in late October of 1918 and spreading throughout Germany. In Berlin a council of People's Commissars proclaimed itself the executive branch of the new government, and in Munich the Independent Socialist Kurt Eisner, supported by councils of workers, soldiers, and peasants, proclaimed a socialist republic. A reenactment of the Russian Revolution appeared imminent; in reality, the fear of communism was much exaggerated because Germany was not Russia. In Russia, the urban working class was proportionately much smaller than the German working force; it was also less skilled along formal union lines and lacked the tradition of skilled craftsmanship that predisposed the German worker toward a more conservative outlook. The radicalism of the councils of workers, soldiers, and peasants was quickly co-opted by the Majority Socialists, commonly called the Social Democrats, led by cautious trade unionists — Friedrich Ebert, Philip Scheidemann, Gustav Noske — who showed little interest in ideology and even less in subverting the social order for communism. They advocated a social democracy with primary focus on such bread-and-butter issues as higher wages, better social benefits, and better working conditions for their workers. During the collapse of the old ruling elite, power devolved, for the time being, on the forces of social democracy, especially the Social Democrats (Majority Socialists). In January of 1919 they beat off the only serious revolt by the revolutionary left, launched by the Spartacists under the leadership of Karl Liebknecht and Rosa Luxemburg, but they did so with the help of the military and its protofascist Free Corps units that had formed to resist the communization and democratization of German society. Friedrich Ebert's devil's pact with the traditional military elite may have saved the moderate socialists from the extremes of a communist revolution but it also doomed the new democratic republic that was being established at Weimar.[20] Ebert initially agreed not to tamper with the traditional structure of the army; what he did not know was that this also committed his party not to tamper with the traditional conservative order in the civil service, the universities, and big business. These institutions and groups despised the democratic process, and they became the rallying point for right-wing extremists who wanted to destroy the democratic republic.

From the beginning of the republic three major political forces could be identified: a revolutionary left, defeated in 1919 but continuing to promote the cause of world communism and despising the proportionally much larger Majority Socialists; the moderate Majority Socialists, who temporarily allied themselves with the Catholic Center and the democratic parties of the bourgeois middle and thus gave the Weimar Republic a tenuous lease on life; and a growing conservative right, initially stunned and paralyzed by defeat in war, but quickly recovering its strength and promoting itself as the genuine bearer of traditional German values.[21] Postwar politics was marked by these three forces, but the outcome was already decided in favor of the conservative right when Ebert and the Social Democrats made their pact with the traditional military-industrial elite in 1918–19, thus forestalling the possibility of any fundamental social change in the institutions and traditions of German society and also discrediting social democracy in the eyes of both the communists on the left and the conservatives on the right.

Between 1918 and 1923 Germany experienced such intense socioeconomic and cultural convulsions that it was unable to heal the many internal divisions and safeguard itself against the growing threat of right-wing totalitarianism. During these five years Germany was in a virtual state of civil war and economic depression. In the year 1923 alone the feeble republic was reeling from one crisis to another: the Ruhr was occupied by the French; Communist-Socialist regimes had taken power in Thuringia and Saxony; Communist insurrections plagued Hamburg; Bavaria had fallen into the hand of right-wing reactionaries who threatened to secede from the Reich; Germany's eastern borders were threatened by the Poles; and the German mark stood at 4.6 million to the dollar. Bourgeois civilization was on the verge of collapse, particularly after the German currency, and with it the German economy, collapsed under the impact of ruinous inflation. One historian, Konrad Heiden, referred to this economic apocalypse as "the death of money,"[22] the end of roseate visions of material affluence, and the end of secular faiths in progress. Many Germans who lived through this period also lost their faith in government, its good word, and its assurance that savings would be protected by law. For nine years they had sacrificed their lives and their savings to the government; in return, the government had squandered a third of the national wealth in a futile war as a result of which war loans, savings, and investments were now worthless. The social climate of opinion during these five years was ripe with rage and the desire to find scapegoats. This is why these years have rightly been called the incubation period of both National Socialism and a revitalized Judeophobia. Both phenomena were closely related, as they presupposed a "remystification" of consciousness among a growing section of the German population.

A Gathering of Judeophobes

In 1920 a member of the Forty-First Bavarian Guard Regiment in Passau, Hans Knodn, sent an urgent report to the Bavarian minister president Gustav von Kahr, entitled "Recommendations for the Solution to the Jewish Question," in which he offered solutions that were almost identical to those formulated by the Wannsee Conference in January of 1942. The young man, described by a prominent state assembly representative as a "thoroughly well-meaning and honorable young man" who was motivated by the most noble intentions of saving people and fatherland from misfortune, offered the following "humane considerations":

1. Jews were to report to designated round-up areas within a time frame of 24–48 hours and then to be transported to concentration camps.

2. Jews who resisted such measures were to be executed and their property was to be forfeited.

3. Germans who provided aid and comfort to Jews were to suffer the same fate.

4. In case of Entente reprisals, immediate measures were to be taken in the form of starving Jews to death. Actual invasion by the Allied Powers was to be answered by an immediate massacre of all Jews.

5. Internment of Jews would continue as long as Germany was threatened by internal and external enemies. In case the Jews should survive their internment and the internal and external enemies had been eliminated, the remaining Jews were to be completely pushed out [*abgeschoben*] of Germany into Palestine, forfeiting all their property and assets. The return to Germany by any Jew was to be made a capital offense.[23]

The young man's "honorable intentions" were summarily dismissed by the authorities as the rantings of a sick fanatic, but the extreme proposals he submitted were probably shared by far more people than the authorities were willing to admit. In the first place, pathological Judeophobia had taken firm roots among military circles in the wake of German defeat in November of 1918. By that time, Judeophobia had spread throughout the officers' corps and the ranks of the military administration. The disintegration of the imperial army did not diminish anti-Jewish prejudices because these were quickly transplanted into the proliferating paramilitary organizations that mushroomed all over Germany between 1919 and 1923. In fact, it was the Free Corps and the many affiliated ex-servicemen's associations, *völkisch* leagues (*Bünde*), and defensive associations that would serve as the breeding grounds of that hardcore Judeophobia that we associate with the Nazi movement.

The origin of the Free Corps (Freikorps) can be traced back to the revolutionary turmoil of the winter of 1918 when the collapse of the imperial government gave rise to a bitter power struggle between the revolutionary left and the forces of social democracy, the former trying to revolutionize German society and establish a communist system and the latter trying to arrange for a peaceful transition to social democracy. Neither of the two parties had sufficient power or support from the German people. As previously seen, the Social Democrats crushed the revolutionary left with the help of the army and its affiliated Free Corps units. In the winter of 1918 the imperial army was quickly self-destructing as a result of the defeat, loss of morale, and rapid demobilization required by the terms of the armistice and reconfirmed by the Versailles Treaty, which demanded that the size of the German army be scaled down to 100,000 men. The majority of the officers and enlisted men of the old imperial army saw themselves as embodying the heart and soul of Germany. Many of them refused to lay down their arms but continued to function as volunteer units, actively following their commanders into a variety of political adventures either against domestic enemies on the left or against the Poles or Lithuanians in the east. Having lost the war along with their warlord, the kaiser, these militarists thought they faced a bleak prospect under a socialist regime that was known to be hostile to the old military establishment. It is estimated that there were some 270,000 officers in 1919, many of whom came from the old nobility.[24] They had enjoyed virtual immunity from civilian control and exercised a degree of social influence that was the envy of ordinary Germans. Stunned by the shock of defeat, the loss of both their military and social privileges, and the prospect of a dreary "unheroic" life under socialism, they became outraged reactionaries desperately seeking a new imperial banner and enemies they could blame for their plight.

As Robert G. L. Waite has shown, these paramilitary forces were the vanguard of Nazism and they produced the Judeophobic mentality that subsequently defined Hitler's political foot soldiers — the storm troopers (the SA, or Sturmabteilung [Assault Division]).[25] The men of these units, many of them eventually finding their way into the Nazi movement, strongly believed in the leadership principle (*Führerprinzip*), despised democracy, hated the "philistine" values of the middle class, identified the Jews as their racial enemy, and called for a "Jew-free," remilitarized German Reich. Adolf Hitler would use these men as a battering ram against the democratic Weimar Republic. Out of their ranks would also come prominent Holocaust murderers such as Martin Bormann, Rudolf

Höss, Erich von dem Bach Zalewski, Erich Koch, Kurt Daluege, Hans Frank, and Reinhard Heydrich.

Many of these men had the mentality of freebooters who enjoyed plundering and pillaging; war was still in their blood and they would later create a whole neo-romantic mythology out of their violent experiences. As one of them later recounted his Free Corps adventures in the east:

> We roared out songs into the air and threw hand grenades after them. ...We saw red. The land where we had lived groaned with destruction. Where once peaceful villages stood, was now only soot, ashes and burning embers after we had passed. We kindled a funeral pyre and more than dead material burned there — there burned our hopes, our longings; there burned the *bürgerlich* tablets, the laws and values of the civilized world; there burned everything.... And so we came back swaggering, drunken, laden with plunder.[26]

This malignant mentality cross-fertilized with hateful attitudes from related social and political groups on the beleaguered conservative right that included civil servants, military officers, academics, and industrialists. After an initial shock following the German defeat, the radical right unleashed a hysterical campaign against its political opponents in which Judeophobia played a very prominent role. The initial impetus of this campaign came from Heinrich Class and his Pan-German League, supported by prominent military leaders and by an increasingly radicalized bourgeoisie. Class and his reactionary followers regarded the new democracy as poison from Jewish sources. The Jews, they contended, were poisoners not so much by freedom of choice but by inherent necessity, the implication being that they were biologically evil and should therefore, in Class's words, be beaten to death.[27] Class, a *Justizrat* (privy councillor), represented a numerically small and politically endangered feudal elite that was terrified of being displaced by the broad forces of social democracy. Class had already sounded the alarm before World War I in a violently anti-Jewish book called *If I Were the Kaiser* (1912), in which he denounced the elections that had propelled the Social Democratic Party into the majority as a democratic swindle engineered by the Jews. The lost war, for which his circle bore a major responsibility, provided him with additional self-serving ammunition by which he could continue blaming Jews for all of Germany's disasters. His Pan-German League, working hand in glove with the military, was instrumental in torpedoing the 1914 Burgfrieden and setting in motion a well-financed and politically organized campaign aimed at maligning various class and racial enemies — liberals, socialists, pacifists, and Jews.

At the very time that the democratic leaders were trying to lay the foundation of the New Republic at Weimar, Class's Pan-German League founded the Deutsche Schutz und Trutz Bund (German League for Protection and Resistance), a militant antidemocratic and Judeophobic action group whose purpose was to fight for the rebirth of the German *Volk* and to remove "the pernicious and destructive influence of Jewry."[28] This racist organization anticipated the Nazi movement in organizational skill and propaganda by organizing itself on the grassroots level into *Gaue* (districts) and *Ortsgruppen* (regional groups) and unleashing a blitzkrieg of propaganda throughout Germany. According to Alfred Roth, over 7,642,000 pieces of propaganda were distributed in 1920. In addition the league had its own newspaper, *Deutschvölkische Blätter* (German-Racial Papers) and its own "scientific" race journal, *Politische-Anthropologische Monatschrift* (Political-Anthropological Monthly); the logos on both publications was the swastika.[29]

As Robert G. L. Waite has pointed out, the Schutz und Trutz Bund not only prepared the way for Nazism, but also groomed some of its leaders, notably such Jew-haters as Julius Streicher, editor of the most notorious Judeophobic magazine in Germany between 1923 and 1945, *Der Stürmer;* Dietrich Eckart, mentor of the young Hitler and coeditor along with Alfred Rosenberg of the Nazi Party newspaper *Völkische Beobachter* (Racial Observer); and young Reinhard Heydrich, SS *Gruppenführer,* head of the Security Service (Sicherheitsdienst; SD), of the SS, and one of the major architects of the Holocaust.

Offering fraternal support to like-minded associations or interest groups, the Schutz und Trutz Bund also targeted all those who nursed grievances in the postwar period, and that included a sizeable number of socially displaced and economically impoverished Germans who, buffeted by war, revolution, and a vindictive peace treaty, genuinely feared for their country's future. It was in such troubled waters that the league and similar Judeophobic organizations began to cast their bait, deliberately provoking latent and manifest anti-Jewish prejudices. In the words of Class's colleague, General Konstantin von Gebsattal, the Jews were to be used as lightning rods for every injustice visited on Germany as a result of World War I.[30] And so it came to pass that a growing number of Judeophobes singled out the Jews as scapegoats for everything that had gone wrong.

In the first place, the Jews were blamed for having undermined the war effort by shirking their military duties, exploiting the national-economic resources for their own material gain, encouraging the influx of foreign Jews (*Ostjuden*) as cheap workers but actually as compatriots in their racial complicity to subvert German blood, and mobilizing their radical press to undermine the war effort. In the second place, Jews were blamed for giving aid and comfort to revolutionaries and to the vindictive statesmen who were enslaving the German people through reparations, territorial losses, and impudent slights and humiliations. In the third place, the Judeophobes rejected the democratic Weimar Republic as a "Jew Republic" because its constitution was written by a Jew (Hugo Preuss) and its democratic features were crafted in such a way as to benefit Jews. Finally, as the cultural changes released by the First

World War began to register on the lives of the German people, Judeophobes almost immediately began to blame the Jews for every negative repercussion, ranging from the perceived decadence of modernism to the socioeconomic misfortunes afflicting broad sections of the population.

It is difficult to disprove a negative rooted either in deliberate lying or delusion, and some Jews despaired of ever laying the Judeophobic ghost to rest. Shortly before committing suicide, Albert Ballin confessed that "one cannot control the forces now at work, but has to watch their development in a resigned way. I am gripped by a deep melancholy from which I am unable to remove myself."[31] Ballin's despair was premature but well-founded, for between 1919 and 1923 the sort of annihilatory Judeophobia that would cause the Holocaust was born. It had all the features of chimerical thinking previously mentioned: the release of disaster syndromes following the defeat and its consequences (Revolution, the Versailles Treaty, political chaos, and economic collapse), fear of group annihilation, received "revelations" and signs of election, the unmasking of radical evil, and the mobilization of redemptive political forces in order to create a new and revitalized Third Reich. It was in the circles of a small racist beerhall club called the German Workers' Party, later rechristened the National Socialist German Workers' Party (NSDAP), that this sort of thinking and belief took on a particularly virulent form and was subsequently projected on the whole political landscape.

The Rise of Nazi Judeophobia

The rise of pathological Judeophobia was a German rather than a "Nazi" phenomenon. "Nazis," after all, were Germans who believed in Nazi ideology of racial supremacy, a regimented and homogeneous social community, obedience to a charismatic Führer, conquest of living space, and the creation of a new Germanic Reich that would last a thousand years. How many Germans believed all, some, or none of these five essential features of Nazism cannot be established with any degree of certainty because we lack the necessary knowledge and the methodological tools that would allow us to offer definitive explanations. What can be established from polling data before the Nazis seized power and from the enthusiastic support given to their policies up to the time the war turned against them is that a sizeable number of nationalistically minded Germans of all social groups seem to have identified themselves with some or all of these Nazi principles. The reason they did hold these principles was the result of certain inherited cultural traits that had crystallized during the Second Reich and taught the German people unconditional respect for authority, admiration for the military way of life, superiority of all things German, and suspicion, if not contempt, for minorities and foreigners. The Nazis built upon these ethnocentric cultural traits by extending them far beyond the point of exaggeration they had already reached during the Second Reich. The passionate intensity they brought to already exaggerated forms of nationalism, militarism, or racism, together with the fanatical determination they mobilized to implement them, was something new and frightening to sober-minded Germans and foreign onlookers.

Once the Nazis had seized power, they mobilized all the resources of a modern technological state to indoctrinate the German people with their ideological delusions and to enlist them as agents of their designs. We now know that they succeeded in spreading their delusional net over the German people, but how close they came in involving them in their greatest crime — the Holocaust — will be left an open question until the last chapter. What must be said at the onset, however, is that the Nazis were Germans with a passionate faith and a fanatical determination to implant it in the German people as a whole. Their faith was not a complete aberration in the sense that it came out of the blue; it was rooted in a number of German traditions, which it built upon and exaggerated, traditions that were undemocratic and illiberal. Germany could have, of course, proceeded in a different direction — a democratic, humane, and peaceful one — but the democratic Weimar Republic did not develop the liberal institutions that would have been required to "reeducate" the German people in democratic values and practices. Instead, the Germans followed the path of delusion and destruction mapped out for them by Adolf Hitler and the Nazi Party.

The Nazi movement grew out of the postwar turmoil in Bavaria, where in the course of just six months (November 1918–May 1919) the state was torn apart by a series of political upheavals that included the fall of the Wittelsbach monarchy, the establishment of a socialist government under the leadership of Kurt Eisner, the rule of Schwabing "coffeehouse" anarchists, a reign of terror under a communist regime, and a counterrevolution of right-wing forces that would eventually prepare the ground for the incipient Nazi movement.[32] The fact that Eisner and the majority of the Schwabing anarchists as well as the Soviet-style radicals were Jewish would leave a lasting impression on ordinary Bavarians, reinforcing already latent Christian prejudices against Jews that had existed there for centuries. With the destruction of the radical left, the needle on the political compass in Bavaria pointed unmistakably to the radical right. The discredited experiment in socialism was condemned as the work of subversive agents of international communism and world Jewry, and many Bavarians would link these forces long before Hitler tried to pound the connection into their heads through his clever propaganda.

In sum, many Bavarians, already Judeophobic before the revolutionary upheavals of 1918–19, became convinced more than ever that left-wing revolutions, in the words of the founder of the conspiratorial-racist Thule Society, Rudolf Sebattendorf, had been "made by a lower race [the Jews] to corrupt the Germans.... From now on it must be an eye for an eye and a tooth for a tooth."[33] It was out of the Thule Society and similar racist organizations that the Nazi Party would recruit its early members. Starting in 1920, Bavaria, now governed by a right-wing government under Gustav von Kahr, became a magnet attracting all sorts of extremist groups that plotted to overthrow the democratic Republic. The Bavarian government generally turned a blind eye to paramilitary extremists on the right, including refractory Free Corps units that operated freely under the protection of the regular army. The Erhardt Brigade, having played a major role in the unsuccessful overthrow of the Weimar Republic during the Kapp putsch in March of 1920, found a refuge in Bavaria, as did the extremists who instigated the political assassinations of Matthias Erzberger and Walther Rathenau. The leading officers of the army district command in Munich openly sympathized with the Nazi cause and some, like the future chief of the brown-shirted storm troopers Ernst Röhm, would often roam the beerhalls of Munich or scour the ranks of the Free Corps and similar ex-servicemen associations for new recruits for the Nazi Party. These men saw themselves as harbingers of a revitalized Germany and as knights crusading against communism, democracy, pacifism, liberalism, internationalism, and the force they believed to connect them all— international finance Jewry. In order to combat these perceived evils, the men of the militant right planted demonic delusions in Bavaria and later in the rest of Germany that would corrupt the moral conscience of the German people.

It began with a small racist beerhall club, founded on January 5, 1919, that called itself the Deutsche Arbeiterpartei (German Workers' Party); its founders (Anton Drexler and Karl Harrer) and its early members were undistinguished workers who wanted to save the German working class from the clutches of international communism. Opposed equally to communism and capitalism, they envisioned a *völkisch* state, purged of all alien forces (Jews, pacifists, foreigners), that rested on broad middle-class and working-class support and exhibited a sound social conscience. Originally, the new party drew on four diverse groups for its membership: petit bourgeois nationalists with strong racist convictions, amateur intellectuals with bizarre panaceas for Germany's salvation, military men with decidedly conservative and authoritarian attitudes, and asocial characters with shadowy pasts who used the party for their own opportunistic purposes. Among the first group were the party's founders, Anton Drexler and Karl Harrer; among the second group were Gotfried Feder, Dietrich Eckart, Alfred Rosenberg, and Max Erwin von Scheubner-Richter; among the prominent military men were Ritter von Epp, Ernst Röhm, Alfred Ludendorff, and later Hermann Göring; and among the growing group of asocial bullies or con-men was Hermann Esser, who epitomized the type before Adolf Hitler replaced him in that role.

Despite their different social origins, these men were all profoundly disoriented by the sweeping and chaotic changes set in motion by the German defeat in war and its consequences: civil strife, revolution, economic calamities, and the despised Versailles Treaty. They were also, either by conviction or by social affiliation, strident nationalists and incurable militarists who regarded the new democratic changes as a deadly threat to their social existence. Above all, they were unabashed Judeophobes, blaming the Jews for every misfortune that had befallen their country. Gottfried Feder, the party's financial expert, accused the Jews of having caused Germany's economic collapse through their shameful war profiteering and their treasonable business connections with foreign powers. The Jews, he charged, were part of an international conspiracy aimed at unhinging the normal course of events and deliberately causing crisis, runs on banks, depressions — all for their own profit. Feder spoke for the economic little man who had been marginalized and impoverished by the dislocations of the war and felt betrayed and sold out by both big business and big labor, clinging nostalgically to a pre-industrial vision of a harmonious *Volk* community in which burghers, workers, farmers, and soldiers cooperated for the good of the fatherland. Hitler would later exploit the fears of marginal economic groups (handicraftsmen, small business proprietors, farm workers, domestics, semiskilled workers) and galvanize them into political action by using what Richard Hofstadter has termed in another context "the paranoid style in politics."[34]

Feder's Judeophobia was primarily economic in nature; but among the ideological stalwarts of the rising Nazi Party, Jew-hatred assumed far more virulent ideological dimensions. A major catalyst of annihilatory-racial Judeophobia was Hitler's political mentor Dietrich Eckart, a second-rate journalist, author of flowery patriotic plays, and self-inflated poseur. Eckart, like most members of the party's inner circle, was psychologically unstable, morally bankrupt, and politically dangerous. From 1918 to 1920 he published a highly inflammatory paper called *Auf Gut Deutsch* (In plain German), which specialized in anti-Jewish and anti-communist propaganda. He was also a prominent member of the racist Thule Society and therefore a midwife to the Nazi Party. His social connections enabled the German Workers' Party to acquire the *Münchener Beobachter* in December of 1920. Edited by Eckart, the paper was later renamed *Völkische Beobachter* (Racial observer) and became the Nazi Party's ideological mouthpiece. Eckart saw in Hitler Germany's redeemer, took the young inexperienced rabble-rouser under his wing, and furthered his political career. Hitler, in turn, looked up to Eckart as a role model and spiritual godfather of the Nazi movement, later dedicating *Mein Kampf* to his memory. Eckart's final legacy to the Nazi movement before he died in December of 1923 was to draft a poisonous and preposterous pamphlet, entitled *Der Bolschewismus von Moses bis Lenin: Zwiegespräch zwischen Adolf Hitler und mir* (Bolshevism from Moses to Lenin: A dialogue between Hitler and me), in which he cleverly served up every stock-in-trade anti-Jewish libel going back over two thousand years and presented his readers with the alarming revelations that the Jews were in league with the devil, seeking not only world domination but, more frighteningly, the actual annihilation of the world. The pamphlet, however, broke off with the reassuring judgment that, try as they might to destroy the world, the Jews would come up short and only destroy themselves

One day in 1919 a young Baltic German refugee from Bolshevism, Alfred Rosenberg, appeared in Eckart's office and inquired whether Eckart could use "a fighter against Jerusalem." The delighted editor, without blinking an eye, supposedly responded by saying: "Certainly."[35] This would launch Rosenberg on his infamous career as an expert on "the Jewish question," Bolshevism, and Nazi racial ideology. Rosenberg was born in Reval, Estonia, son of an Estonian mother and a Lithuanian father. Culturally, Rosenberg belonged to what the Germans call *Auslandsdeutsche* (foreign land Germans), to those ethnic Germans who lived in German communities in the Baltic states, Russia, or elsewhere in Europe or overseas. These "little Germanies" often cultivated an exaggerated sense of German ethnicity that displayed strong nationalistic and racial coloration. Although Rosenberg had pursued a technical career, studying architecture at Riga and Moscow, he had steeped himself so well in the intellectual demimonde of racist philosophy that when he met Hitler, the two men immediately recognized each other as soulmates. Rosenberg was a brooding, pedantic, and intolerant ideologue who has been called "a profoundly half-educated man."[36] Like Hitler's, his knowledge of the world was culled primarily from ethnic-racial tracts and numerous apocryphal sources and theories; and out of this mesh of self-serving doctrines of Aryan superiority, he had constructed a Weltanschauung that he would subsequently launch on the world in such works as *Die Spur des Juden im Wandel der Zeiten* (The trace of the Jews in changing times, 1920), *Unmoral im Talmud* (Immorality in the Talmud, 1920), and his magnum opus, *Der Mythos des 20. Jahrhunderts* (The myth of the twentieth century, 1930).

One of Rosenberg's most significant contributions to the dissemination of anti-Jewish prejudices was his work as chief editor of the *Völkische Beobachter,* one of the Nazi Party's most successful instruments of Judeophobic propaganda. He was also an important intellectual agent who transmitted the fanatically religious version of Judeophobia that had poisoned Russian culture for several centuries and surfaced in a particularly nauseous form in the *Protocols of the Elders of Zion.* Rosenberg had already steeped himself in the *Protocols* long before he appeared in Eckart's office; he subsequently persuaded Hitler that the document was absolutely genuine and true and then proceeded to publish his own edited version in 1923.

Rosenberg brought another Baltic German into the party called Max Erwin von Scheubner-Richter, an engineer and former member of the German diplomatic corps who had seen service in eastern Europe and Turkey during the war and had built up a diverse circle of prominent people that included members of the Bavarian royal family, captains of industry, high prelates, Russian emigrés, and army officers. One of his most important contacts was General Ludendorff, legendary war hero to the Germans and reviled war criminal to the allies. The general escaped the wrath of both the Allied Powers and the revolutionary socialists by fleeing to Sweden, where he wrote his self-serving memoirs and waited for a propitious moment when he could return to Germany. He did so right after the defeat of the Spartacists, returning to Berlin and dabbling in political intrigues under the very noses of the Allied watch-dogs of the Disarmament Commission, who were staying in the same hotel where the general was living under an assumed name. Still considered a national icon and sought out by various nationalistic circles, the general allowed himself to get involved in the Kapp putsch aimed at overthrowing the democratic republic he despised and whose leaders, as he told his wife, he hoped to hang with "a clear conscience and watch them dangle."[37] When the putsch failed, he quickly disavowed any responsibility and moved to the more hospitable right-wing haven of Bavaria, where a series of fateful events would involve him in Adolf Hitler's scheme to topple the government. His political judgments, which never equaled his military acumen, steadily deteriorated, particularly after he divorced his wife, Margarethe, and married Mathilde Kemnitz, a sinister and pseudointellectual quack who poisoned his mind with racist, pagan, and anti-Jewish prejudices. A major reason for the collapse of November 1918, Ludendorff came to believe, was the convergence of subversive forces — pacifists, socialists, Freemasons, Jesuits, and Jews — that stabbed the German army in the back. Writing in his *Lebenserinnerungen* (Life recollections), he said:

> Gradually I recognized the pernicious forces which had caused the collapse of the people, and in them the real enemies of freedom of the German race.... More and more plainly I became aware of the fungi within the structure of our society ... in the form of secret supranational forces, i.e., the Jewish people and Rome, along with their tools, the Freemasons, the Jesuit order, occult and satanic structures.[38]

Such language, using parasitical and demonological metaphors, would become a defining characteristic in the paranoid mindset of fanatical Jew-haters. It is also significant that these paranoid rantings did not only spring from socially dispossessed or from mentally deranged people, but also, as in the case of Ludendorff and many others, from brilliant and highly successful leaders. Ludendorff sincerely believed, as he put it in his own writings, that the Jewish people were fungi and vermin who, working hand in glove with both Bolshevists and international finance capitalists, wanted "to castrate us as men and people, so that others with a stronger national will can rule us."[39] Suspending all rational faculties, the general then invoked wholly chimerical reasons why the Jews were close to their goal, claiming that 1923 was for numerological reasons the year in which they would strike at the German Reich:

> It was...a "Year of Jehovah." Like the year 1914 the total sum of the digits (1+9+2+3) gives the number 15; this comprises the numbers 10 and 5, which according to the Jewish superstition are the first two consonants of the word Jahweh — Jehovah — and therefore makes the actions of the Jewish and Christian cabalists successful in such years.... The time to shatter the Reich had come.[40]

This sort of paranoid thinking that moved within a delusional and demonological framework was becoming alarmingly widespread between 1918 and 1923. It sprang from a sense of betrayal and a haunting fear of group annihilation, and it seems to have been most intense among the conservative and *völkisch* right, where it spanned a broad spectrum of different classes and occupations. Both Ludendorff and Hitler, general as well as corporal, believed that the German *Volk* organism had been infected by the Jewish bacillus; both used hysterical words to describe what was done to the German body: it was being raped, castrated, infected with syphilis, enslaved, and annihilated; both identified the Jews as fleshly malefactors; and finally, both hinted darkly that the annihilators, in turn, had to be annihilated by hanging or even gassing.

These fears were incessantly fueled by hyperactive militarists and by their well-financed publishing concerns. For them every crisis or catastrophe was instantly explained as yet another example of Jewish wrongdoing. Rumors were accepted as fact and the most extreme explanations were given more credence than rational or balanced judgments. A case in point was the widespread acceptance in many aroused nationalistic and Judeophobic circles of the *Protocols of the Elders of Zion*. The document was brought to Germany by Russian emigrés who had fled from communism. These exiles formed sizeable colonies in some of the major cities of Germany, especially Berlin and Munich, where they spent their waking hours spewing propaganda and plotting revenge.[41] In Berlin, for example, Fydor Vinberg, a former tsarist officer, published a daily Russian-language newspaper called *Prizyv* (The call) in which, among other proposals, he advocated as "the Final Solution" to the Jewish problem the actual extermination of all Jews. In support of this monstrous proposal, Vinberg disseminated the first copies in Germany of the *Protocols*.[42] As previously shown, the document purported to be the record of secret meetings of Jewish elders who pledged themselves to overthrow Christian civilization by infecting it with such subversive forces as democracy, liberalism, pacifism, and communism. The *Protocols* also outlined the technical means by which the establishment of a world Jewish state could be accomplished. The first German edition was brought out in July 1919 by Ludwig Müller von Hausen, using the pseudonym Gottfried zur Beek, under the imprint Auf Vorposten (Advanced Outpost), a publishing house owned by the League against Jewish Arrogance. The book went through thirty-three editions by 1933; and a cheap "people's edition," brought out by Fritsch's Hammer Verlag, had sold a hundred thousand copies by the time of Hitler's seizure of power.[43] On July 24, 1922, Walther Rathenau, Germany's foreign minister, was gunned down by right-wing extremists while being driven to his office in his open car. One of the youthful murderers, Ernst-Werner Techow, later testified in court that his group had been strongly influenced by the *Protocols* and that they were convinced that the Jewish foreign minister had been one of the three hundred elders mentioned in the Judeophobic document.[44]

The young men who had gunned down the foreign minister were by no means an aberrant exception. In 1920, a Jewish observer gave the following account of several meetings he attended on *The Protocols of the Elders of Zion:*

> The speaker was usually a professor, a teacher, an editor, a lawyer or someone of that kind. The audience consisted of the educated class, civil servants, tradesmen, former officers, ladies, above all students, students of all faculties and years of seniority.... Passions were whipped up to the boiling point. There, in front of one, in the flesh, was the cause of all ills — those who had made the war and brought about the defeat and engineered the revolution, those who had conjured up all our suffering. This enemy was quite close by, he could be caught by our hands, and yet he was the enemy who slunk about in the darkness... I observed the students. A few hours earlier they had perhaps been exerting all their mental energy in a seminar under the guidance of a world-famous scholar, in an effort to solve some legal or philosophical problem. Now young blood was boiling, eyes flashed, fists clenched, hoarse voices roared applause or vengeance.... If I had been recognized as a Jew, I doubt whether I would have got away without physical injury.[45]

This passage is highly significant because it correctly reveals that the intellectualization of Judeophobia was carried out in the minds of Germany's cultural elite. Although there were many common folks who believed in the traditional stereotypes of Jewish wrongdoing, Judeophobia was intellectualized by a significant number of professional people — university professors and their students, teachers, lawyers, civil servants, journalists, military officers and enlisted men, businessmen — who believed that the Jews were Germany's misfortune. The delusion, then, could be said to have trickled down from the top rather than moved up from the bottom of the social ladder.

In order to understand this social aberration, it is necessary to appreciate the painful fact that education does not always equate with enlightenment or the moral improvement of its recipients. Professors can and do teach hatred and bigotry; they have no monopoly on virtue. The strength and persistence of a delusion, in fact, depends on the tenacity by which it is held by its intellectual perpetrators. The rise and expansion of Judeophobia depended greatly on the intellectual elites who promoted it and the cultural and political agencies that reinforced it in everyday life. Even so, one still marvels at the wide persuasiveness that this vulgar, idiotic, and insane hatred held over the minds of educated people in modern Germany. Those who despair in seeing how this all added up might seriously consider, once having subtracted from their explanation of Judeophobia all the obvious causes — socioeconomic, political, cultural, psychological — that there might exist some irreducible radical evil that is periodically at work in history.

Certainly in Nazi circles this kind of paranoid Judeophobia was an ever-present force from the beginning of the party as a racist beerhall club, through its triumphs, to its violent end in the shattered rubbles of Germany's great cities, factories, and cultural landmarks. It forms a leitmotif in Rosenberg's *Völkische Beobachter,* Streicher's mad rantings in the pages of *Der Stürmer,* and the violent language of its top leadership, particularly the obsessive hatred displayed toward Jews by Adolf Hitler, Joseph Goebbels, and Heinrich Himmler. Arguably the most ugly display of Judeophobia occurred in the pages of *Der Stümer,* a racist tabloid published by Julius Streicher between 1923 and 1945. Streicher, who has been rightly called the "world's Jew-baiter no. 1,"[46] had joined the Nazi Party in 1923 because he saw in its Judeophobia a mirror image of his own prejudices and in Adolf Hitler the future savior of Germany. When he heard Hitler speak for the first time in 1922, he was so mesmerized by what he saw and heard that afterward he made his way to the podium and said to Hitler: "I am Julius Streicher. At this moment I know that I can only be a follower. But you are a leader! I give to you the popular movement which I have built in Franconia."[47] Streicher's encounter with Hitler, which was in the form of a revelation followed by a rapid conversion, was by no means an exception in the lives of many prominent leaders or undistinguished followers of the Nazi religion; it can be recorded in almost identical terms in the experiences of Göring, Goebbels, Himmler, Speer, and many others who came under the demonic spell of Adolf Hitler.

In 1923, Streicher founded what ultimately became the world's most notorious anti-Jewish tabloid — *Der Stürmer* (The Stormer), a luridly pornographic hate magazine that could serve as a mirror image of the twisted lives and deformed personalities of the Nazi leadership cadre and its political foot soldiers — the brown-shirted storm troopers. *Der Stürmer* also reflects Streicher's personal obsessions and aberrations: he was, by all accounts, a sexual deviate and a bully, habitually strutting about with a riding whip and later, as *Gauleiter* (district leader) of Franconia, taking great pleasure in beating up political prisoners. Gordon Craig remembers him lecturing in the Great Hall (*Aula*) of the University of Munich holding forth in the most disgusting terms on his favorite subject — the Jews. As Craig recalls:

> For three and a half hours, this gross bully, bulging in his brown uniform, poured forth floods of filth that I would not have thought possible in public oratory, let alone from a university lectern, and offered "scientific" evidence of the predatory nature of the Jews, at one point arguing insistently that, if one was attentive while visiting zoos, one would note that the blond-haired German children always played happily in the sandboxes while the swarthy Jewish children sat expectantly before the cages of the beasts of prey, seeking vicarious satisfaction of their blood-tainted lusts. The audience in the *Aula* was attentive, and many took notes.[48]

It has been suggested that the leering, sexually obsessed Jew Streicher conjured up in the pages of *Der Stürmer* was really a reflection of his own conduct, a form of conduct that was by most standards crude and uncivilized. In fact, it can be said of Streicher and many other members of Hitler's inner circle that they were shabby little bigots who delighted in each other's company, regarded women as sex objects, enjoyed a brawling fight with their political opponents, and distrusted what was "respectable" or "refined." The Nazi movement authenticated the brutal impulses of such asocial characters and allowed the Streichers of Germany to "normalize" their deviancy.

For over twenty years, Streicher dished up a steady stream of nauseating anti-Jewish articles in the pages of *Der Stürmer.* Never before or since have the black arts of racist prejudice reached such a perfection of rottenness. In its heyday, *Der Stürmer* reached close to half a million people per issue and titillated its anti-Jewish readers with hairraising stories about Jewish misconduct or crimes such as ritual child murder, rape, financial manipulations, sinister political plots, and the like. Philippe Rupprecht (pseud. FIPS), the tabloid's cartoonist, usually drew the Jews short, fat, ugly, unshaven, drooling, slouching, sexually perverted, bent-nosed, with pig-like eyes and protruding lips. In order to dehumanize the Jews, he also portrayed them as toads, vampires, vultures, insects, spiders, bacteria, and toadstools.[49] Other tactics of desensitizing the reader consisted of showing that Jews lacked any real human qualities such as love, laughter, loyalty, friendship, sympathy; depicting them as physically repulsive; insinuating that, therefore, they were morally tainted; and advocating, as a corollary of the above, that they were not fit to live in the company of decent Germans.

Streicher's conviction that the Jews were a biologically demonic race — devils in the beginning who took on a "quasi-human" appearance — was by no means an aberration but a growing belief among the *völkisch* right. In people like Streicher or Hitler this delusion seems to have followed a certain developmental progression, starting with popular discriminatory biases that Jews were alien outsiders one should distrust on account of their strange religious beliefs and sharp economic practices to the full-blown delusion that they were, in Goebbels's phrase, an *Unrasse,* or anti-race, forming an abscess on the body of Germany's sick folkhood.[50] Once the Jew-haters had made this transition from "popular discriminatory" prejudice, shared by many average Germans, to "biological-racial" Judeophobia, they had turned prejudice into a deadly psychological obsession.

In a little-known book called *Verkappte Religionen* (Masked religion, 1924), Carl Christian Bry has described this Judeophobic delusion as an expression of a perverted form of religious remystification, arguing that the Judeophobes were actually trying to replace the old Christian religion with a revitalized racial Christian religion of their own. Judeophobia constitutes a defining element in the new religion because it provides the explanation to all the evils of the world. Bry illustrates the mark of the obsessed Judeophobe with an analogy of a salt container (*Salzfass*) on the dining table. Normal people, he pointed out, would only see a simple salt container; the Judeophobe, on the other hand, after just a few remarks would propound the thesis that the Jews had already cheated in the salt trade in Phoenician times and that even today the proportion of Jewish employers in the saltworks was alarmingly high. Such a person, Bry argued, was positively incapable of seeing a simple salt container but had to give vent to his central and recurring obsession — the sinister influence of the Jews.[51]

Germans who were no longer able to see a simple human being but a demonic racial freak had fled from reality into a world of mythological fantasy; they had accepted an irrational religion with its own peculiar beliefs and liturgical rites. In examining the paranoid mindset of the Nazi leaders and their hard-core followers, James M. Rhodes argued that the dynamic that moved Nazism was a secular millennial faith analogous to the sort of apocalyptic consciousness found in the Bible, particularly the book of Daniel and the book of Revelation.[52] Those who exhibited this sort of consciousness believed themselves to be victims of mind-bending catastrophes, developed corresponding disaster syndromes, experienced mystical revelations that evil forces caused their afflictions, learned from their revelations that they had been chosen to confront and defeat the forces of evil in titanic battles of Armageddon, and reached the conviction that they would then usher in a paradisiacal order of being (New Jerusalem, Thousand-Year Reich). Rhodes shows convincingly that the Nazis, and to some extent many Germans, were totally disoriented by the catastrophic events unleashed by World War I and sincerely believed that malignant forces wanted to annihilate them. Relying on special revelations, based on what they believed to be nonrational forms of knowing, such as racial instincts, "call of the blood," and magical insights, they proceeded to unmask the veil of illusion and discovered, among other things, that the Jews were the primary tormenters of the German people. The Jew is a "many-headed hydra," the Nazis warned: one head is Jewish international finance capitalism; others are communism, liberalism, freemasonry, pacifism, and all the forces supporting the Weimar republic. The leaders of the republic, the Nazis believed, were either real or suspected Jews; they had inflamed the helpless and disoriented masses with a subversive ideology, brought down the Kaiserreich, and erected a corrupt political system that was in the hands of Jewish bankers, retailers, department store magnates, left-wing intellectuals, and press barons.

The path to salvation proceeds from the unmasking of the "Jewish evil" to its radical annihilation. In the minds of Hitler and his hard-core followers this involved not merely ridding oneself of the Jewish "infection" but the radical reconstruction of the German people along healthy racial lines. The Nazis actually believed that they could biologically create a new type of Aryan Man through racial eugenics, thus gaining a sort of self-deification and immortality.[53] A prerequisite for that sort of racial millennium, of course, was the end of racial pollution. Nazi racialists believed that German blood was polluted by sexual contact with the Jews. This delusion, of course, had already emerged before the First World War in the writings of Lanz von Liebenfels and other *völkisch* racists, but it was also relatively isolated and poorly organized. After 1918 the delusion spread quickly among significant sections of the German population. Even before it found its ultimate home in the Nazi movement, the delusion was already being spread through countless pamphlets and popular low-brow novels.

One of the most influential was Artur Dinter's novel *Die Sünde Wider das Blut* (The Sin against the blood, 1917). The story is about a scholar who discovers to his great horror that his family had been tainted by bad Jewish blood. Having been previously married to a Jew, the scholar takes as his second wife an Aryan woman who provides him with damaged goods in the form of a son who exhibits unmistakably "Semitic" traits. How can that be? Who could have tainted or spoiled his son? The answer reveals a terrifying conspiracy. As it turns out the father of his first wife had set up a boarding house that specialized in taking in young, blond, and innocent Aryan girls, including his second wife, and exposing them to seductive Jewish males. Once pregnant, the boarding house owner brutally expelled the "polluted" Aryan girls and quickly replaced them with new unspoiled virgins, thus starting the cycle of pollution all over again. Dinter's novel sold briskly; by 1934 it had reached over a quarter of a million in sales.[54] Dinter also met Hitler, fell under his influence, and was appointed *Gauleiter* of Thürigen for several years.

The theme of racial pollution was also promoted by the prolific Judeophobic publicist Theodor Fritsch, who spoke of "racial deformation" (*rassische Entartung*) and claimed in one of his books, *Das Rätsel des jüdischen Erfolges* (The riddle of Jewish success, 1919), that police files supposedly proved that Jews had a special sexual need to seduce Aryan women and that, tragically and often inexplicably, Aryan women succumbed to Jewish seduction:

Quite a shabby Jew encountered a woman of good middle-class standing. He looks at her and, paralyzed in her tracks, she turns and follows him. A similar incident occurred on a street where a red-haired Jew-clothier stood in front of his store. A young and proper girl, hardly out of her teens, walks by when the Jew whispers something in her ears; taken aback, she lingers at the store window and stares incessantly at the Jew behind it. It doesn't take long before she follows him into the store.... The question now arises: Are there secret Talmudic tricks at work? Some Jews are said to have perfected these acts to such a degree that they can compel women to shake and tremble as though they were seized by an electrical shock.... Who can solve these riddles? Is it the glance (perhaps what the Italians call *jettatura*) or does Talmudic cleverness and life experience perhaps know the secret of interpersonal relationships, notably the mysterious sympathetic forces? Or does Jewish energy also play a role in the way Jews are able to dominate female psychology?[55]

Unaware of their own sexual deformations and projections, these writers churned out a steady stream of titillating stories in which Jews, charged by an almost satanic sexual appetite, constantly harassed and threatened pure Aryan women. Next to Streicher's vile stories in the pages of *Der Stürmer,* such racial stereotypes were promoted prolifically by Hans Zöberlein's malicious and dishonest popular novels, notably *Der Glaube an Deutschland* (Faith in Germany, 1934) and *Der Befehl des Gewissens* (The command of conscience, 1937). Vignettes, like the following, that recount close shaves by Aryan women with Jewish sexual deviants are standard fare in Zöberlein's novels:

Love possesses unfathomable power; it stems from a place that only weaves in the supersensible. Love conquers all! It can sacrifice to the point of self-sacrifice, fight to the death, work without tiring, hunger and thirst without feeling anything.... "You are awfully smart," Hans laughs at Berta, while she is lying in the middle of a meadow among the flowers and recounts all about it.... And so they wander daily in the open air from morning to evening, returning home filled with wonderful experiences and revelations.... On a hot day they go to a lake for a swim. Hans is swimming far out as Berta watches him from the shore. Suddenly she feels the glances of the men who are lying about her; and while she proudly rebuffs them with her own glances, a lot of grinning cowardly Jew-faces are fixed on her, so that she shudders with disgust and wishes Hans could be with her.... Suddenly a sunburned Jew jumps up and blocks her way: "May I invite the charming lady for coffee or ice-cream. Please! You look fabulous, the veritable shape of the Venus itself." "Leave me in peace." "But why? A girl alone. It isn't so nice to be alone here." Grinning behind his horn-rimmed spectacles, he approaches like Satan. Berta steps back and pales, surrounded suddenly by Jews, one of whom tries to grab her hand and says insolently: "You're not going to give me the brush-off, sweetie, are you?" Waving to the others, he shouts, "Come on, let's go to the casino!" And the chorus screams, laughs, and roars, so that one cannot hear the pleas and cries of poor Berta. "Hans," she whispers quietly, "Hans, please help me." Horny hands paw over her body, pulling and pushing.... "What's happening?" Hans is suddenly there, soaking wet and out of breath. He looks at Berta, beholds the harvest of Satan and turns white as a sheet. His eyes become fixed and glittering-green, as the nearest Jew and then the second and third buckle under Hans's lightning blows. The others run away. He laughs with grim satisfaction as he regains his color.[56]

It is difficult to measure the precise impact of this and many similar hate books that were published in Germany before and after World War I. One thing is most certainly false, as claimed by some, namely, that such beliefs were limited to the lunatic fringe on the political right. Nor could it be argued that radical Judeophobia was a virtual monopoly of the Nazis alone, for the evidence clearly indicates that it had mutated beyond the circles of hard-core Nazis. On the other hand, it is indisputable that rabid Jew-hatred found its most lethal expression in Adolf Hitler, the man who translated his obsession into public policy.

Adolf Hitler's Judeophobia

In 1930, following several years of sly insinuations by his political enemies that he had Jewish blood in his veins, Adolf Hitler consulted his personal attorney, Hans Frank, and asked him to investigate these allegations in hopes of forestalling a potentially disastrous setback to his political fortunes. Having tied his political movement to an uncompromising hatred of Jews, Hitler clearly risked complete political credibility if it were discovered that the most vocal Jewish rabble-rouser turned out to be Jewish himself. Frank reportedly investigated Hitler's ancestral background and discovered that the Führer's father was the illegitimate child of Maria Anna Schickelgruber, who at the time her baby was conceived had been employed as a cook in a Jewish household in Graz. Frank later claimed that his research showed that the Frankenbergers, as the Jewish family was called, paid for the maintenance of the child almost from the moment of his birth, thus tacitly admitting that the child had been fathered by their nineteen-year-old son.[57] When confronted with this information, Adolf Hitler supposedly flew into a rage and denounced the story as a blatant lie, insisting that his grandmother had personally assured him that the story was false and that she only took the money from the Jew because she was so poor. If Hitler really made this statement to Frank, he was obviously lying because his grandmother had died more than forty years before he was born. What Hans Frank's account clearly reveals, however, is Adolf Hitler's obsession with Jews, including his paranoid fear that he himself might have been "infected" by Jewish blood.[58]

This fear of Jewish blood poisoning revealed itself even more remarkably in July of 1938, only a few months after he had annexed his Austrian homeland. In that month, the Austrian Land Registries Office received an order to conduct a land survey of Döllersheim and surrounding areas in order to determine whether the terrain was suitable for army maneuvers. The next year, the citizens of Döllersheim were forcibly evacuated and the village, along with its heavily wooded countryside, was blasted beyond recognition by mortar shells and thoroughly plowed over by army tanks.[59] The village of Döllersheim was part of the poverty-stricken Waldviertel, a section of Austria lying between the Danube and the Bohemian border. It was also the birthplace of Hitler's ancestors. Why would the triumphant conqueror of his native Austria encourage the obliteration of his ancestral roots, rendering the birthplace of his father and the site of his grandmother's grave all but unrecognizable, if he did not want to conceal his greatest shame — the possibility that he was Jewish?

Despite sixty years of research on Hitler's ancestral roots, no compelling evidence has yet surfaced that establishes the suspected Jewish link in Hitler's family tree. In the end, it would probably make little difference because the psychological link — the way in which Hitler himself viewed the matter of his and Germany's Jewish infection — is overwhelming. From Hitler's own writings, speeches, and personal remarks to a host of different people, it emerges that he was irrationally obsessed with Jewishness in general and his own potential Jewishness in particular. In virtually every public utterance he delivered on Germany's misfortunes, Hitler specifically singled out the Jews as one of the chief perpetrators; his use of the word *Jude* on such occasions took on a particularly vile tone that was expressive of his innermost hatred. In Robert G. L. Waite's judgment, Hitler "felt Jewishness to be an evil within himself, a poison to be purged, a demon to be exorcised."[60]

This hatred of Jews was at once personal as well as ideological. Hitler blamed Jews for his own failures as a rejected artist in prewar Vienna as well as for their supposedly poisonous influence on Aryan culture. As he moved through Vienna, unemployed, unattached, and unloved, he began to project his inner shortcomings and loathing on the city's sizeable number of *Ostjuden* who came to represent everything he hated. "One day when I was walking through the inner city," he recalled, "I suddenly came upon an appearance clad in caftan, with black curls."[61] He wondered whether this "appearance" — the German word *Erscheinung* can also mean apparition — was also a Jew like the more German-looking ones he had seen in his native town of Linz. His next thought, he tells us, was whether this strange being was also a German. The answer, Hitler said, was a resounding "No." Jews could never become German because they were racially and religiously different; and their difference was so vast, their character so alien, that they had to be removed from German society by every possible means. Hitler's perception of Jews as alien beings was emotionally heightened by his conviction that they smelled different and that their whole glandular system was putrid and offensive.[62] Having steeped himself in the literature of popular Jew-hatred, readily available in the popular tabloids such as the *Deutsche Volksblatt* (German People's Paper) or Lanz von Liebenfels's *Ostara*, the scales quickly fell from Hitler's eyes: Vienna's "foul-smelling" Jews were merely the tip of the iceberg, the most visible sign of a deeper social disease. Like leeches they had grafted themselves on the German social body and were now sucking out its blood. Thus, whenever we cut open a social sore, Hitler maliciously suggested, we "always find a little Jew, blinded by the sudden light, like a maggot in a rotten corpse."[63]

If Hitler blamed the Jews for every social ill, he also held them responsible for his own personal misfortunes. He probably blamed them for the death of his mother at the hands of her Jewish physician, Dr. Eduard Bloch, who was unable to cure her terminal breast cancer and who made her suffer excruciating pain by applying foul-smelling liquid iodoform gauze on her festering wounds. In October of 1918, while recovering from the effects of a poison gas attack on the western front which temporarily blinded him, Hitler relived his mother's martyrdom, rekindled by associating the similar smells of the poisonous iodoform that had riddled his mother's body with the poison that had blinded him.[64] He experienced a psychotic episode in which he saw the source of all evil and the means by which it could be combatted. Lying prostrate in his hospital bed in Pasewalk, Hitler relived his mother's final ordeal, except that this time, as Rudolph Binion has pointed out, it was his surrogate mother, or Germany, that was being defiled.[65] Once he had made the connection that in both cases the Jews had been responsible, Hitler discovered the solution to the Jewish problem. Dr. Bloch had been right in treating one poison with another; the time had come to apply the same treatment to Germany's disease — to poison the poisoners, or Jews. In *Mein Kampf,* his self-serving autobiography and justification of his ideological prejudices, Hitler blamed the Jews for stabbing the German army in the back and recommended that they be poisoned. And after initiating the real poisoning in the death chambers of Auschwitz, Belzec, Majdanek, Treblinka, and Sobibor, he openly admitted that "I gave the order to burn out the abscesses of our inner well-poisoning and of the foreign poisoning down to the raw flesh."[66]

No one knows exactly when Hitler had his primal revelation that the Jews were the source of every social malignancy in the world, nor is it clear how he arrived at this insight. It may have been the result of a psychotic episode during which he imagined that a Jew had raped and annihilated both his own mother, Klara, and his surrogate mother, Germany. It may have been the result of Germany's calamities between 1918 and 1923 that convinced him that Germany's major enemies — the communists and the western plutocracies — were both dominated by world Jewry. It may even have been a personal and painful experience with Jews in his own life, although no reliable evidence has surfaced to confirm this theory. In the end, Hitler's virulent Judeophobia may have been a manifestation of his insatiable need to hate, which itself sprang from and represented a projection of his own self-hatred.

Hitler was the embodiment of the self-contained man who was driven by a passion for domination and destruction; at the same time, he was a political genius who could infect masses of people with his own loathing through clever oratory and superb organizational skills. He also had an intuitive sense of how he could exploit the possibilities of mass democracy for his own sinister ends. Long before the age of mass communication had arrived on the scene, Hitler knew how to turn politics into mass theater and to use every available technology to merchandize his program and sell it to his audience in appealing images, symbols, and "sound bites." Later assisted by a host of "spin doctors," notably Joseph Goebbels, Hitler brilliantly merchandized himself as an ordinary and caring man who empathized with the suffering of the German people and promised them radical change. Masking his destructive intentions, he appealed to the loftiest ideals and traditions in German history. He soothed middle-class fears of lawlessness by promising to restore law and order, gratified conservatives with promises of a national resurgence, pleased the militarists by evoking visions of a powerful new army, and reassured workers that no one would ever go hungry under National Socialism. Above all, he absolved his listeners of personal responsibility by telling them that they were the victims of an evil conspiracy. He knew the agents of their suffering, could identify the culprits, and with the aid of the German people would wage a war of liberation, ridding the German people of the tormentors and leading them to a glorious future.

Neither the man nor the message were always transparently evil because Hitler knew, when it suited his political purpose, how to mask himself and his destructive prejudices. If he had been transparently evil, masses of people would not have followed him so willingly. Nazi propaganda cleverly disguised the fact that Hitler was a dangerous psychopath with a totally warped and unrealistic vision of reality. Few realized how dangerous he really was until it was too late. Yet it was not for any lack of evidence that many Germans chose to believe otherwise. They chose to believe the bombast and the illusions he tossed out, while at the same time willfully ignoring the destructive consequences that were bound to result if the nation acted on them. When Hitler stepped into the political limelight, he did so with a definite political program that he was determined to implement after he had assumed political power.

The details of Hitler's grand design are by now familiar to everyone, but the point often overlooked today is that they were well known from the beginning of his political career. In his *Kampfbuch* (Battle book), *Mein Kampf,* he made it abundantly clear that he would transform Germany into a world power; he also made it unmistakably clear that the Aryan race, being at the apex of biological and cultural evolution, was destined to dominate the world. Since Germany was the heartland of the

Aryan race, Hitler called upon the German people to take up the White Man's Burden by conquering the Eurasian world and to plant its seed for thousands of years to come. In Hitler's racially obsessed mind, the concept of race was intimately linked to that of space. A people's greatness depends, first and foremost, on its racial purity, but in another sense it also depends on its ability to reproduce itself more prodigiously than inferior races and to purge itself of race pollution by such inferior races as Jews, Gypsies, or Asiatics. Adjusting a growing race like the Germans to a limited space is to doom them to vassalage to stronger races. This is why Hitler demanded living space (*Lebensraum*) for the German people in the vast spaces of eastern Europe and Russia.

Hitler promised that Germany would either be a world power or there would be no Germany.[67] But how could a geographically and demographically small nation, situated precariously in the center of Europe, turn into a world power and compete with the Soviet Union, the United States, or the British empire? In Hitler's judgment, this required the rigid mobilization of all its material resources and the institutionalization of war-like and aggressive impulses in its human resources. Hitler wanted to breed a racially hard, callous, obedient, and determined youth that would delight in war and conquest. The motto of the future Hitler Youth would subsequently reflect this Spartan pedagogy:

> Der deutsche Junge muss schlank und rank sein, flink wie ein Windhund, zäh wie Leder und hart wie Kruppstahl. Er muss lernen, Entbehrungen auf sich zu nehmen, Tadel und Unrecht zu ertragen, zuverlässig, verschwiegen, gehorsam und treu zu sein....Das Ziel der weiblichen Erziehung hat unverrückbar die kommende Mutter zu sein.

> A German boy must be lean and mean, quick like a greyhound, tough as leather, and hard as Krupp steel. He must learn self-denial, to endure reproaches and injustice, to be reliable, silent, obedient, and loyal. ...The goal of female education must be without delay the future German mother.[68]

The chief aim of a Nazi state, Hitler told Rauschning, was to teach all Germans the habit of being brutal with a good conscience; only in this way, he insisted, could the German people attain historical greatness.[69] In Hitler's mind racial regeneration and conquest of living space entailed each other. Historians who have argued that Judeophobia played a secondary role in Hitler's grand schemes are mistaken on two counts: first, because Hitler believed in the absolute necessity of engineering a new Aryan racial type as a prerequisite for Germanic greatness; and second, because that belief entailed the elimination of the Jew as a racial type altogether. Judeophobia was therefore an integral part of Hitler's racial philosophy. These convictions can be traced to his earliest public speeches, and they form a central line of argumentation in *Mein Kampf*. In other words, the bedrock of Hitler's worldview, what he called his "granite foundation," was the belief in the biological and cultural superiority of the Aryan race.

The strength and weakness of man, Hitler boldly declared, rest solely in the blood.[70] There is superior blood and inferior blood. Hitler was a crude naturalist who believed that nature promotes "higher breeding" by encouraging propagation of the strong and discouraging propagation of the weak. Humans, however, have upset this natural design by allowing superior blood to be mixed with inferior and by artificially (socially) protecting the weaker types to live and to reproduce their kind. As an armchair sociobiologist, Hitler confidently asserted that the best blood is obtained when animals mate solely with representatives of their own species — titmouse seeking titmouse, the finch the finch, the stork the stork, the field mouse the field mouse, the wolf the wolf.[71] Any crossing between beings of not quite the same type produces inherently weaker or infertile types. Since human nature is a part of nature, the biological laws of racial purity are applicable. Here, too, nature encourages sharp separations between racial groups, while also promoting uniform characteristics within each group. Thus, white, black, or yellow persons seek their own kind. Since human racial groups are qualitatively different, it follows that cross-breeding undermines racial purity and produces inferior offspring. The worst blood-defiling occurs when the Jews mate with the Aryans, which Hitler regarded almost like mating across species — a biological absurdity because no human group has speciated.

According to Hitler's racial taxonomy, the human race falls into three distinct racial groups: Aryan culture-founders, culture-bearers, and culture-destroyers.[72] Only the Aryan, Hitler insisted, creates culture; he is the Prometheus of mankind "out of whose brightest forehead springs the divine spark of genius at all times" because only he possesses the creative "race nucleus." Asiatic people, he conceded, possess high culture, but this is only because the Aryans had provided the creative impetus for it. In the absence of continuing Aryan influence, the culture of the Japanese, for example, would "stiffen and fall back into the sleep out of which it was startled... by the Aryan wave of culture." Other racial groups are equally uncreative; and Africans are incapable of even being culture-bearers.

As to the Jews, he felt, they are without a genuine culture because they are incapable of creating one. Jews merely exploit what others have created; they are pure parasites feeding on the body of healthy cultures. Hitler's stereotypical *Jude* is "a sponger who, like a harmful bacillus, spreads out more and more if only a favorable medium invites him to do so."[73] The Jews always lived a furtive existence in other people's communities, where they secretly built up their own state under the guise of a religious community. Their great lie, Hitler insisted, is that they are only religiously different, while in all other respects being as German as the Germans. On the contrary, Hitler was convinced that the Jews were "always a people with definite racial qualities and never a religion."[74]

For well over two thousand years Jews have managed to preserve their racial and cultural traits to a far greater degree of purity that any other people in the world, but they have done so always at the expense of other people. Their role has been entirely parasitical and therefore destructive to the biological and social health of the community in which they resided.[75]

In drawing attention to the destructive influence of the Jews, Hitler, of course, trotted out the various Judeophobic arguments, starting with the corrosive damage they had supposedly inflicted on the economic well-being of their host nations. In one of his most demagogic speeches, given at a party meeting in Munich on April 12, 1922, and entitled "The Inciters of Truth" (*Die Hetzer der Wahrheit*), Hitler ruthlessly unmasked what he regarded as the real culprit of Germany's social crisis by asking how the guilty could be identified.[76] The answer, he suggested, was to ask who had benefited most from Germany's misfortunes. In other words, by identifying those who were doing well one could ferret out those who had caused all the ills. Stockjobbers, bankers, and similar agents of capitalism come to mind immediately, Hitler suggested, but if one really wanted to get to the bottom of the crisis, the veil of illusion had to be stripped completely; and if we did this, Hitler insisted, we would find the "tuberculosis of peoples,"[77] the "ferment of decomposition" — in short, the eternal Jew.[78] Hitler claimed that only the Nazi movement had been courageous enough to recognize this primal truth because it, too, saw itself as representing a chosen people with a mission to keep its blood pure. He saw himself as possessing a special method of knowing based on blood, a kind of *Blut-ernstes Erkentnis* (blood-serious cognition) by which he was able to unmask what was not biologically healthy to the German folk organism.[79] In addition, he saw himself as a latter-day Aryan Jesus turning out the money lenders from the temple, an inciter (*Hetzer*) against the false Jewish-money god.

Hitler's frequent references to biological, indeed parasitological images indicate strongly that he believed that the whole German people, including himself, had been "polluted" by Jewish blood. His thinking on such occasions rose to a high level of paranoid intensity, which also explains why he believed unconditionally in the existence of a Jewish world conspiracy, as foretold in the *Protocols of the Elders of Zion*. His habitual response to alleged evil-doing was always to attribute it to a scheming Jew, whether it was the rapacious money-lending Jew, the Jew as court svengali, the Jew as bleeding-heart liberal, the Jew as parliamentary democrat, the Jew as pacifist, or the Jew as Bolshevist. The end result, in Hitler's mind, was always the same: the Jew incites social divisiveness, hollows out a healthy community from within, and so prepares the way for the final takeover of the world.

Eberhard Jäckel has drawn attention to the fact that Hitler strongly believed that the racial value of a people was determined by its racial sense of itself, its form of leadership, and its ability to wage war.[80]

These three qualities are expressed in nationalism, the *Führerprinzip*, or leadership principle, and militarism. As he tried to articulate these assumptions for the purpose of incorporating them into a larger Nazi *Weltanschauung*, he began to realize that the Jew supported three counterprinciples — internationalism, democracy, and pacifism. In other words, Hitler believed that the Jews promoted principles that were calculated to undermine any healthy community. This led him to irrational ruminations that somehow nations were literally social organisms, and that like all organisms they were exposed to decomposers whose function it was under normal conditions to take all organic debris and break it down into its elemental components so as to be reusable by the producing system. The organism wards off attack through its own adaptive system, but sometimes the stresses are so toxic that they overcome and destroy the whole organism. The same is true of social organisms, which are also exposed to decomposers in the form of aggressors, outlaws, poverty, disease, class conflict, or war. According to Hitler, the most lethal decomposers of any social organism are the Jews; they are the social analogue of the most lethal pathogen and therefore inevitably undermine the whole social system.

The irrational logic of this argument led Hitler to conclude that the Jew, being a lethal pathogen, must be the personification of the devil, the spirit who always subverts what is healthy and good.[81] As a consequence of this delusional system of ideas, Hitler could literally envision "bow-legged Jew bastards" lurking behind the corners of dark alleys waiting to rape unsuspecting Aryan girls and defile them with their Jewish seed.[82] Such vile outbursts were by no means confined to his private circle but found frequent expression in his writings and in his public speeches. In chapter 10 of *Mein Kampf*, for example, where he described the "real" causes of Germany's defeat in World War I, Hitler quickly bypassed any realistic discussion of why Germany lost the war and plunged instead into dark ruminations about "moral poisoning" by the "bottomless lying of Jewry" and ended up, in the course of a curious psychotic passage on the evils of syphilis, blaming the Jews for having caused the syphilization of Germany's national body.[83] This passage and sizeable parts of *Mein Kampf* resound with shrill alarms about blood defiling and blood poisoning by demonic Jews. Hitler rants and raves about the hidden and "truly diabolic intentions"[84] of the Jews to bastardize the Germans and solemnly appeals to the nation's sacred obligation to keep the blood pure. Here are only a few samples (with corresponding page numbers from *Mein Kampf*) of Hitler's prejudiced epithets, describing the Jews as:

- Personification of the devil (447)
- Defilers of Aryan blood (448, 826–27)
- Ferment of decomposition (666, 952)
- Bloodsuckers and vampires (426–27, 451)
- Purveyors of prostitution and syphilis (78, 326–51)

- Rapists of Aryan women (448, 816)
- Harmful bacillus (420)
- Maggots (75)
- Poisoners (76, 312)
- Pestilence (76)
- Bow-legged bastards (619)
- Foul-smelling creatures (75)
- Spongers (420)
- Fungi (160)
- Regents of the stock exchange (930)
- Great Masters of lying (313, 412)
- Members of a different race (74)
- Wire-pullers (772, 911)

Hitler was absolutely convinced that a people's greatness depended upon the purity of its blood. A corollary of this racial belief was the fear that whenever a people permitted itself to become bastardized, it *"sins against the will of eternal Providence"* (emphasis added).[85] Elsewhere, Hitler called race pollution the original sin. Although the Jews have already undermined the quality of German blood, a sound racial policy, aimed at removing the poisonous Jews, can still reverse the disease and restore the German folk organism to sound health. The *völkisch* state, therefore, has a clear-cut mission: to breed the most racially pure, fertile, and healthy specimens, so that, at length, the entire national group participates in the blessing of a high-bred racial treasure.[86] From these strictures it is only a short step to Himmler's racial stud farms, the SS elite, and the extermination of inferior breeds (Jews, Gypsies, cripples, the mentally retarded, "Asiatic inferiors"). The only effective antidote to racial pollution, Hitler insisted, was to keep the German blood pure and to eliminate the Jews before the Jews destroyed the German. For Hitler, this was an "all or nothing" proposition because the Jew is the "great agitator for the complete destruction of Germany. Wherever in the world we read about attacks on Germany, Jews are their fabricators."[87] And it is not only Germany that the Jew is trying to subvert; the terrifying fact is that the Jew "tries to bring nations into a state of unrest, to divest them of their true interests, and to plunge them into reciprocal wars and in this way gradually rise to mastery over them with the help of the power of money and propaganda." The Jews' diabolical goal, Hitler concluded,

is the denationalization, the promiscuous bastardization of other peoples, the lowering of the racial level of the highest peoples as well as the domination of this racial mish-mash through the extirpation of the folkish intelligentsia and its replacement by the members of his own people.[88]

It follows by dire necessity that Germany had to take the lead in this global crisis by devising a state policy aimed at the complete elimination of the Jews. Already in *Mein Kampf,* Hitler clearly spelled out his strategy of how the Jews should be eradicated — that is, by poison gas:

If, at the beginning of the War and during the War, twelve or fifteen thousand of these Hebraic corrupters of the nation had been subjected to poison gas such as had to be endured in the field by hundreds of thousands of our best German workers of all classes and professions, then the sacrifice of millions at the front would not have been in vain. On the contrary: twelve thousand scoundrels opportunely eliminated and perhaps a million orderly, worth-while Germans had been saved for the future.[89]

It does not require hindsight to understand the significance of Hitler's ideas, especially the Judeophobic prejudices he repeated ad infinitum to anyone who came within earshot of his uninhibited tirades. What he thought of the Jews and how he would deal with them once he had attained power was a matter of public record. His opponents, both Jews and decent Germans alike, tragically miscalculated the seriousness of his Judeophobic intentions.

Chapter 5

German and Jew in the Weimar Period

Splits in the German Foundation

On the eve of World War I, a motion picture entitled *Der Student von Prague* (The student of Prague) introduced a disturbing theme to the screen that was already well known to generations of theater fans: the tragedy of split personality. The story of the motion picture, borrowed from E. T. A. Hoffmann, the Faust legend, and Edgar Allan Poe's William Wilson, told about a poor student, Baldwin, who made a pact with a sorcerer who promised the young man a good marriage and inexhaustible wealth in return for complete control over his mirror image. Having made the pact, Baldwin then falls in love with a beautiful countess, but is challenged to a duel by her suitor. The countess's father, however, tries to prevent the duel because the student is known to be an excellent fencer. Promising to spare the suitor's life, the student hurries to his rendezvous — prevented, of course, by the sorcerer from getting there on time — and discovers to his horror that his ghostly counterpart has already acted on his own and killed the suitor. The student is disgraced; his evil self has undermined his better self. The split is final and irreparable. In the attic place where he originally struck the devilish bargain the student shoots his reflection but ends up by shooting himself. Thereupon the sorcerer, who is actually a manifestation of the devil, enters the room and tears up the contract with its pieces dropping on the student's corpse.[1]

The theme of split personality introduced by *The Student of Prague* would obsess the German cinema in the postwar years and spawn a whole spate of "split personality" pictures such as *Der Andere* (The other) and *Januskopf* (Janus-faced). The theme of a Dr. Jekyll and Mr. Hyde in each of these pictures is a projection of two opposing tendencies dwelling in the same person. Awareness of being split, of course, questions the very foundation of the self because it involves the discovery that the "other" or darker side is not only displacing the better side, even taking over in its place, but also constitutes an integral part of the whole person. In the films *Der Golem* and *Homunculus* two additional themes, mirroring German society, are added: the creation of abnormal creatures in abnormal times who try desperately and unsuccessfully to lead normal lives, to overcome their loneliness, to be loved and admired; but when they encounter rejection, ridicule, and hate instead, they explode with homicidal rage. In the medieval legend, the Golem was a creature fashioned from clay by Rabbi Loew, who infused life in it by putting a magic sign on its heart. In the 1915 film version, workmen digging a well in a synagogue excavate the statue and give it to an antique dealer, who animates it with the help of Rabbi Loew's instructions, which he discovers in a book of cabalistic magic. The statue initially functions as an obedient and robotic servant, but then reveals definite traces of human feelings by falling in love with the antique dealer's daughter. When the frightened girl rejects his love, he explodes in rage and destroys everything in his way. In the end, the Golem plunges from a tower and scatters into his component clay pieces. Homunculus was another artificial creature who spread devastation and destruction upon discovering who he was and why he was rejected by everyone. Siegfried Kracauer tells us that the figure of Homunculus and his career of becoming a tyrant and despiser of humanity foreshadows in a surprising way the career of Adolf Hitler. Homunculus, like Hitler, externalizes his self-hatred by making himself dictator of a large country and "then sets out to take unheard-of-revenge for his suffering."[2] At the time the film *Homunculus* appeared, Kracauer points out, the philosopher Max Scheler was lecturing on the hatred that Germany's actions were arousing in the world and intimated that Germany resembled Homunculus in being the product of abnormal circumstances and suffering from a deep-seated inferiority complex and arrested social development.

If films show us the deeper psychological layers of collective mentality, as Kracauer believed,[3] we should look at these films of the German cinema between 1914 and 1933 as symbolic representations of the dissonances and deep divisions in the German psyche. What these films reveal, and history confirms, is that Germans responded to the postwar chaos with a variety of deeply troubling and inherently self-defeating attitudes. These attitudes ranged from passive-aggressive forms of withdrawal and resistance on the international front to the retrogressive activity of rebellion and submission on the domestic front. Although the Germans experienced a momentary sense of freedom with the disintegration of the old imperial order, their insecurities and inner divisions prevented them from reconstructing their social order in a genuinely democratic way. Their fear of modernity proved stronger than their love of freedom, and their hunger for wholeness, which they associated with authoritarianism, proved to be more powerful than individual creativity. In the end, they opted to escape from freedom, by endorsing first the paternal authority of Hindenburg the father and then the capricious authority of the bad son in the form of Adolf Hitler.

It was not inevitable, though highly probable, that a society so deeply at odds with itself even before the war would find it difficult to reconstruct a broken social system amid the chaos of defeat, humiliation, and economic ruin. Ironically, democracy, as the Germans would practice it, only helped to exacerbate already existing social divisions. The multiparty system, with its unstable coalitions and mediocre politicians, lacked a strong democratic spine in the form of committed republicans who did not confuse democratic practices with permissive attitudes that tolerated those who had sworn to destroy democracy. They neither had the intelligence nor the courage to act upon Voltaire's dictum that there was one case in which intolerance was a human right, and that one case involved those groups in society who were themselves intolerant and thus threatened the principle of toleration itself. In other words, wherever intolerance becomes socially destructive, the laws of a liberal society cannot tolerate it; if people are to deserve tolerance they must stop being fanatics.[4]

For fourteen years (1919–33) the Germans reluctantly tried democracy; but since that democracy was stigmatized from its inception by defeat and a sense of betrayal, it was never more than a feeble reed.[5] The democratic constitution itself was the work of Hugo Preuss, a Jew and a progressive liberal who had been a marginalized academic outsider before the war but, as the old order lay in ruins, rose out of obscurity in order to lend a willing hand to a new democratic Germany. In his single-minded effort to find the best arrangement for his war-torn country, Preuss picked eclectically from several sources: the American constitution, the best features of European parliamentarianism, and even the abortive constitution of the Frankfurt Assembly of 1848. Having to work with antagonistic parties and social interest groups, Preuss was necessarily forced to compromise; and the final document, after being meticulously revised several times, was in many ways a mirror image of the social dissonances of German society. On paper, however, it was a splendid democratic document, offering a wide array of liberties and progressive innovations which made it one of the most democratic constitutions in the world. Yet Preuss was personally skeptical about whether such a democratic constitution would work in the hands of a people that was neither psychologically nor historically prepared for self-government. He even wondered aloud whether such a system should be given to a people that resisted it with every sinew of its body.[6]

A democracy presupposes not only a democratic piece of paper, but also a society willing to democratize its major institutions — the civil service, the school system, the police, the armed forces — but this is precisely what most Germans were not prepared to do. The Hohenzollerns had been dethroned but not their generals or field marshals or even the broad middle class that, along with the military, still believed in the nationalistic illusions of the Kaiserreich. Although lawmaking passed into the hands of republican lawmakers, law enforcement remained in the hands of conservative and antidemocratic officials. The German elites had survived the winds of revolution, and they now opposed the republic at every step; the mass of ordinary Germans began to reject democracy after the Great Depression of 1929 made itself felt.[7]

The most profound split in the republic, which involved a war over the heart and soul of German identity, was a cultural struggle between conservatives who upheld traditional values and modernists who championed a variety of new, innovative, and radical ideas. Although the conflict had already surfaced in the Kaiserreich, it erupted with particular force and intensity in the postwar period. Modernism questioned the basic convictions of middle-class reality, particularly the belief in rationality and in the existence of objective standards of truth, beauty, and morality. Such cultural assumptions had formed the basis of good art, music, and literature during the empire. A good German artist or writer was expected to depict patriotic and uplifting themes that celebrated the natural beauty of town and country and reinforced Christian pieties. The desired art form was to be neo-romantic and sentimental on the personal level and appropriately neoclassical on the public level; it was to be, ideally, a noble blend of neoclassicism, with its aesthetic preferences for polished style and dignified restraint and the loftier strivings of romantic feelings and individual creativity. In practice, a country that had not found a permanent and secure political style was unlikely to discover one in the cultural sphere. Even before the war, several cultural styles, reflecting the deep socioeconomic divisions of the new nation, competed with each other: the traditional style of the feudal nobility, the values of middle-class Protestantism, the Catholic culture of the Rhineland and southern Germany, and the emerging culture of the working class.[8] In general, the tone fluctuated between grand spectacle and inner subjectivity, and it usually lacked political commitment.

The direction of German culture was strongly shaped by the forces of modernization and the traumatic impact of World War I. Modernization made new demands on culture because it involved the search for different forms of expression suitable to a mass audience rather than to a smaller cultural elite. The pull of modernization was in the direction of the new rather than the old, usually at the expense of ancient traditions and inherited patterns of life. Even under normal conditions this process is accompanied by widespread anxiety, but coming in the wake of a lost war and its chaotic aftermath the impact was far more acute in Germany than in most other countries.

Although Germany had experienced the impact of modernity during the imperial period, the floodgates of change did not really open until the Weimar Republic. This is why the republic, certainly in the perception of cultural conservatives, became associated with every threatening wind of change in fashion, mores, or intellectual attitudes. Intellectually, the 1920s were characterized by Einstein's theory of relativity and Heisenberg's principle of uncertainty. Both theories postulated a universe of flux and taught that all "facts" were simply fleeting perceptions of different possibilities. Truth now appeared to be a function of subjective perception and morality, merely an expression of group choice. The Roaring Twenties ushered in a new age of moral uncertainty, made all the more disturbing by the fact that a whole generation had been brutalized by four years of war and now seemed deprived of the moral standards that had guided the *Gründerzeit* generation. Many young people, especially those who had been traumatized by war, exhibited disturbing symptoms of maladjustment that involved depression, scapegoating, paranoid fears, aggressive behavior, and, above all, strong generational conflicts.

The revolt against the older generations, especially that of the fathers who sent their sons into World War I, constituted an important element in the growing pains of the young and not surprisingly expressed itself frequently in literary form. The young Jewish poet Georg Heym wrote in his diary: "I would be a great poet but for that swine my father" (*Mein schweinerner Vater*).[9] Parricide was not an uncommon theme on the stage, notably in Walter Hasenclever's *Der Sohn* (The son) and in Arnolt Bronnen's *Vatermord* (Father murder). When the son in Hasenclever's play asks his friend, "What shall I do," the friend replies: "Destroy the tyranny of the family.... Remember that the fight against the father is like taking revenge on the princes in a former age."[10] Such generational revenge was directed primarily against the country's cruel fathers who had suppressed individual creativity and forced their sons to participate in four years of senseless slaughter. Some young people sought refuge in nihilistic lifestyles; others searched for a messianic leader who would redeem their sacrifices and lead them to a glorious future. A Nietzschean mood of smashing old idols, including parental authority, pervaded the postwar period. In a world that was no longer stable and predictable, pious pronouncements about "the good old days" or self-righteous appeals to Christian morality now seemed somehow hypocritical, platitudinous, and hollow. This being the case, why not just live for today and party? After all, "Man lebt ja nur so kurze Zeit und ist so lange tot" (One lives but such a short time and is dead for so very long). Such attitudes, captured so well in the cabaret songs of Berlin, also expressed a simple human need to enjoy life after years of morbid fear, suffering, and death.

For ten years, until Hitler rang down the curtain on the Roaring Twenties, many Germans enjoyed a temporary triumph of *eros* over *thanatos,* experiencing a sense of liberation hitherto unknown in a land where strong discipline and public conformity had held sway for generations. The country was gripped by a veritable dance fever, and sex emerged from the hidden domain of taboo morality. Sexual expression ranged from quasi-scientific research institutes to nude shows and hard-core pornography, with Berlin becoming the capital of liberated sexuality, where cabarets, bordellos, and magazines enticed people with such titles as "Nights in a Harem," "The White Slave Traffic," "Women with Whips," and "Exotic Methods of Sexual Intercourse."[11]

In 1919 the actor Conrad Veidt portrayed an upper-class homosexual who was being blackmailed. The film concluded with a brief speech by Dr. Magnus Hirschfeld, founder of the Institute for Sexual Science, who told the audience that such mistreatment of a much maligned minority would soon be part of the past. The film caused a riot, and Hirschfeld, a Jew, was beaten up by a mob and excoriated by the conservative press.[12] Germans considered the stage a forum for public morality, and they were shocked by what the new radical playwrights, especially the expressionists, were offering them: marital infidelity, incest, rape, prostitution, patricide, fratricide. Between 1919 and 1933 intense battles were fought over the issue of sexuality, especially over the performance of a play called *Reigen* (round dance).[13] The play by Arthur Schnitzler, an Austrian Jewish playwright, consisted of ten self-contained parts, or dialogues, in which various couples from different stations of life were featured on the stage chatting before and after the sexual act. The sex act was represented simply by drawing down the curtain for six seconds, during which the audience was exposed to a few beats of a waltz or the sound of a rushing train. During "the before," the men usually gallop quickly to their goal, while the women display some hilarious tactics for slowing things down. During "the after" part, women typically want to know whether they were still loved, to which one character, a boorish soldier, replies: "Na, das musst doch g'spürt haben, Fräul'n Marie" (Well, you should have felt that, Fräulein Marie).[14] Although a witty sociological commentary on sexual mores, the play evoked a howl of protest wherever it was performed. In Vienna, protesters opened water hydrants and flooded the theater; in Berlin, young right-wing thugs hurled stink bombs on the stage, denouncing the play as a Jewish plot to subvert German decency. Such disruptions, especially of plays by Jewish playwrights, became commonplace during the republic.

Although cultural conservatives pretended to be shocked by the new sexual freedoms and delivered blanket condemnations, the stage or even the "vice industry" was not as malignant and ubiquitous as it appeared to be. As Walter Laqueur reminds us, a great deal of traditional piety and self-restraint continued to operate, even in sinful Berlin, where the famous "Tiller girls" traveled with a chaperon and had to say their prayers every night.[15] However, the perception of many conservative Germans was of a world out of joint, a Sodom and Gomorrah of rampant wickedness, an outcome, they believed, of the permissive republic and its liberal or "Jewish" policies.

What some historians have called the first "modern" culture was in fact a curious hybrid of conservative tradition and creative experimentation. In the 1920s German intellectuals, and that included many Jews, formed the vanguard of modernity and articulated the patterns of consciousness we still use in such diverse fields as psychology, philosophy, sociology, the fine arts, and the natural sciences. Avant-garde movements proliferated: psychoanalysis, the sociology of knowledge, expressionism, atonal music, Bauhaus architecture, existential philosophy, and quantum physics. In almost every field, Jews were prominent and in some areas even predominant. The Psychoanalytical Institute in Berlin, inspired by Freud, was founded by Max Eitington and supported by Hanns Sachs and Karl Abraham — all Jewish. The institute trained a host of brilliant analysts, many of whom were also Jewish: Karen Horney, Franz Alexander, Wilhelm Reich, and Melanie Klein. In the field of sociology, the Institute of Social Research, founded in 1923, espoused a critical Marxist humanism, and the scholars associated with it, most of whom were Jewish (Max Horkheimer, Theodor Adorno, Walter Benjamin, Franz Neumann), would provide the theoretical impetus in the social sciences for decades to come, particularly after the institute relocated to New York in the 1930s. In literature, a whole galaxy of bright stars, some traditional and some smartly avant-garde, lit the postwar sky, including the brothers Thomas and Heinrich Mann, Hermann Hesse, Bertolt Brecht, Robert Musil, Rainer Maria Rilke, Stefan George, Gottfried Benn, and Alfred Döblin. In music, too, there were new and novel approaches, many expressing a sense of disquiet, as in the discordant sounds of artists such as Arnold Schönberg, Paul Hindemith, and Kurt Weill. Architecture and art, now more closely related than ever, also experimented with new ideas and symbolic forms of expression. Walter Gropius and the Bauhaus architects stressed the union of art and technology and experimented with steel, glass, reinforced concrete, and plastic in order to achieve the ideal of pure form and function. Finally, out of theoretical physics and existential philosophy would emerge an indistinct, largely subjective, and ideational universe that reinforced an already pervasive feeling about the anxiety (*Angst*), uncertainty, and ambiguity of modern life.

Many traditional artists, craftsmen, writers, and cultural commentators condemned these avant-garde movements as a betrayal of the classical canons of the past. Their opposition, however, was not merely aesthetic but also political. When they saw painters like George Grosz apparently revelling in incoherent forms or ugliness, musicians like Arnold Schönberg throwing harmony overboard in favor of a cacophony of dissonant sounds, writers like Alfred Döblin taking their readers to the brink of the social abyss, sociologists or psychologists like Walter Benjamin or Wilhelm Reich denouncing German institutions as inherently unjust and repressive, they mounted vocal protests and delivered blanket indictments against the culture of modernity as a whole, a culture they variously condemned as materialistic, decadent, soulless, or "Jewish."

The fear of modernity by many Germans had deep socioeconomic and psychological roots, but invariably it was also connected to deep-seated prejudices against Jews because the Jews, it was claimed, were the agents of modernization who threatened to undermine the stable, though largely illusory, world in which conservative-minded Germans had invested so much psychological capital. Wherever they looked, conservative Germans saw radicalism and decay: sex and marital infidelity on the stage and screen, pacifism and ridicule of traditional German values of manliness and respect for authority in the novel, perverted and distorted themes and images in art, and so forth. Although the German Jews as a group were neither modernists nor radicals, right-wing cultural critics often succeeded in associating them with hateful anti-Jewish stereotypes from the past. The writer and theater critic Ludwig Marcuse frequently received letters and cards from outraged conservatives saying:

> You Jewish swine have the temerity to [criticize] those who protest against the weeds and filth of current productions. . . . You dare to call the sort of thing art that is put in front of us in "Love in the Country," "Soldiers Schweijk," "Danton's Death," "Marriage Made in Heaven," "Sickness of Youth." It is nothing but a big pigsty [*Schweinerei*] through which an already corrupted youth will be [plunged] even more into depravity and brutalization. . . . You are the sort of theatre critic who should be hanged. As a Jew, you naturally desire the destruction of German youth.[16]

Jews were caught in the extreme polarization between traditionalists, who preached the unity of a "German" style in all the expressions of culture, and the modernists, who welcomed the existence of divergent, even contradictory styles because they meant a more vibrant and creative spirit. The Jews were caught on the losing side of this battle, just as they were caught on the losing side of the political battle that pitted an aroused authoritarian party against a small and ever dwindling party of republicans. The cultural split was, of course, closely connected to the political split in the sense that the Nazis would use the cultural criticism of the conservative right as a stalking horse to power. As one historian has rightly observed, "The most consistent electoral support for the Nazi Party was concentrated in those social and occupational groups that harbored the greatest reservations about the development of modern industrial society."[17]

One of the most ominous implications of Germany's cultural split was that young people were increasingly won over to reactionary cultural views. Out of some 9 million young people, 4.3 million belonged to various youth organizations, and with few exceptions these organizations were opposed to the new democratic changes of the Weimar period.[18] Young Germans, especially young German males, were restless, disoriented, and alienated; they tried to forge, if only in a haphazard fashion, closer emotional bonds with each other. Unfortunately, these coping mechanisms were often reactionary and escapist in nature and contained, in embryonic form, certain features that the Nazi movement was to exploit and pervert shamelessly. These features took the forms of innocent attitudes and vague longings such as a pantheistic love of nature, a mystical love of fatherland, homoerotic friendships, romanticized longings for a world without greed and materialism, a strong need for group affiliation, and a cult of hero worship. These longings were strongly embedded in many Germans, not just young men; they reflected a deep hunger for wholeness, for some reintegration into a commonly shared culture. They involved also a utopian longing for a frictionless people's community (*Volksgemeinschaft*) in which the many divisions that had separated Germans from each other in the past would no longer exist.

Since many Germans, consciously or unconsciously, felt that the forces of modernity were undermining the nation's political and cultural center, holding the new democracy responsible for much of the nation's ills, they looked for solutions in the conservative and authoritarian values of their preindustrial past. It was a flight into an imaginary past and an inauthentic answer to the problems posed by modernization. What had shaped the hunger for wholeness was really a fear of modernity, and that fear also shaped the solution, which was the escape from freedom. Adolf Hitler intuitively knew how to mold these collective longings to his own perverse intentions.

It should not be surprising that a nation that was so deeply polarized would exhibit a number of disturbing social pathologies. In fact, deviance and crime tore at the seams of the Weimar Republic. According to Detlev Peukert, the postwar period witnessed the most dramatic increase in crime since the compilation of statistics began.[19] There was also a corresponding decline in ethical standards, giving rise to a "racketeering mentality."[20] Stories about Berlin in the 1920s usually contain accounts of dope peddlers and prostitutes, homicidal maniacs and notorious robbers. Endemic crime and political violence plagued the major German cities throughout the Weimar Republic:

> Berlin was in a state of civil war. Hate exploded suddenly, without warning, out of nowhere; at street corners, in restaurants, cinemas, dance halls, swimming-baths; at midnight, after breakfast, in the middle of the afternoon. Knives were whipped out, blows were dealt with spiked rings, beer mugs, chair legs or leaded clubs; bullets slashed the advertisements on poster-columns; rebounded from the iron roofs of latrines. In the middle of a crowded street a young man would be attacked, stripped, thrashed and left bleeding on the pavement; in fifteen seconds it was all over and the assailants had disappeared.[21]

It is important to understand these darker corners of German life in order to discover the clues to the Nazi future. Drawing on certain preexisting pathologies, the Nazis not only committed criminal acts but also tried to normalize them in the culture; they would "turn the law inside out and make illegality legal."[22] Crime, it has been said, is a kind of mirror that reflects the evils of a society; and we might add also that the type of criminal a society produces will be an indication of the type of crimes committed on a large scale when the leadership of that society has itself become criminal.

World War I and five years of civil unrest had brutalized and cheapened human life to such a degree that the public became desensitized to violence. Besides a widespread acceptance of violence there was also a disturbing toleration, even glorification, of the *Hochstapler* (confidence man). This preoccupation with swindlers and criminals, as Gordon Craig reminds us, figured prominently in the novels and plays of the Weimar period: in Hans J. Rehfisch's *Das Duell am Lido,* Thomas Mann's *Felix Krull,* Vicki Baum's *Menschen im Hotel,* Bertolt Brecht's *Dreigroschenoper,* and Franz Wedekind's *Marquis von Keith.* Brecht's *Threepenny Opera* was basically an anarchist play that glorified the gangster, Macheath, because he preyed on a social system that was already rotten to the core and therefore not really worth defending.[23] Interestingly enough, in the *Threepenny* novel, which appeared six years after *The Threepenny Opera,* Macheath has become the director of a bourgeois bank — an appropriate place for a crook in the eyes of many Germans who had been ruined by the inflation of 1923.

Criminality also featured prominently on the silver screen. In some of Fritz Lang's motion pictures, especially *M,* the world of the police and the criminal are often interchangeable, so that it is unclear to the viewer who is really good or bad. The motion pictures portrayed, in part, a world that was out of joint. Films such as *Das Cabinet des Dr. Caligari, Dr. Marbuse,* or *M* brought viewers face to face with insane authority, sex murders, prostitution, and insatiable lust for cruelty. In *M,* based on the Düsseldorf child murderer Kürten, the murderer (the character "M") has no rational explanation for his heinous crimes other than pathetically crying out that he could not help himself. *M* was in appearance the prototype of the German *Kleinbürger* (petit bourgeois): pudgy, submissive, and fastidious; he was perhaps also symbolically and prophetically the prototype of the future desk murderers of the Third Reich.

German filmmakers did not have to look hard to find manifestations of pathology in German society. In the 1920s several grisly serial murders were committed, some even implicating unsuspecting Germans in mass cannibalism because the murderers cut up their victims and sold the usable parts as "meat" to local butchers.[24] One of these serial murderers, a soft-spoken, innocuous, and apparently mild little man by the name of Georg Haarmann, preyed on young boys who needed help. He would befriend these boys by offering them food and drink, then invite them to stay overnight in his apartment. After tucking them into bed, he would sexually assault them and then kill them by tearing out their throats with his teeth. Haarmann could not remember anything relating to these attacks other than experiencing a violent rage and afterward finding himself in bed with another dead boy the next morning. He would then dispose of the corpses in a tidy manner by selling their clothes and reducing their bodies to nicely boiled, potted meat. Such corpses, attractively packaged as pork or veal, would fetch good prices on the black market.

When Haarmann was arrested he showed no feelings at all, not even at the prospect of his execution. When he was finally executed, people began singing songs about his wicked deeds. One particularly sick ditty, undoubtedly meant as a warning to naughty children, had this to say:

> Warte, warte nur ein Weilchen
> Bald kommt Haarmann auch zu dir.
> Mit dem Kleinen Hackelbeilchen
> Macht er Pökelfleisch aus dir.
>
> Wait, wait just a little while,
> And soon Haarmann will come to you.
> With his little hatchet
> He'll make smoked meat out of you.[25]

Such sick expressions are common in societies that have become desensitized to violence, societies in which brutality is often accepted in the form of callous remarks, malicious snickers, or foul racial jokes. German society had long harbored within itself dark corners, attitudes expressed in a fascination with morbid, demonic, putrid, and brutal themes. Even German fairy tales reflected this disturbing underside of the collective unconscious. Although everybody loves and admires the fairy tales of the Grimm brothers, it is appalling to learn, as Robert Waite reminds us, how much bizarre physical and psychic cruelty they contain:

> A queen boils and eats her own children; a young man is required to sleep with a corpse and keep it warm; a king's daughter is torn apart by bears and her mother is roasted alive; a wicked step-mother ... is put into a barrel filled with venomous snakes; a little girl's tongue and eyes are cut out; a pretty young girl is hacked to pieces and thrown into a vat filled with putrefying human remains; a little boy is chopped up, put into a pan, and made into a pudding which is eaten by his father.... The fate that awaited Hansel and Gretel, it will be recalled, was to be roasted and eaten.[26]

Fairy tales are not only the expression of the mythmaking function of the collective psyche; they are also powerful tools for shaping young minds because they are used as educative devices by parents and teachers. The lessons young Germans were taught to derive from such tales included obedience to authority, discipline, and distrust of strangers (Jews or foreigners). Nourished by a stream of high- and low-brow romantic literature, such authoritarian attitudes were taught to young Germans by their nurturing mothers and their stern fathers and were later reinforced by the public schools, the army, and the workforce.

In an effort to explain Auschwitz, Ralf Dahrendorf pointed an accusing finger at these "dark corners" of German society, particularly the role singled out for those who were not considered to be a part of the German tribe. Whoever did not conform to established rituals and beliefs or fell short of ideal physical expectations — the deformed, the handicapped, the foreigner — was immediately suspect. According to

Dahrendorf, German social life was characterized by an "extreme narrowness of permitted actions."[27] In every society, of course, there is a line that demarcates what is permissible, specifying what individuals are allowed to do and what society is allowed to stop them from doing. In Germany this line was drawn overwhelmingly in favor of collective or authoritarian habits. Outsiders, including Germans who fell short of rigid expectations, were often humiliated, rejected, ostracized, and, under the Nazis, arrested, tortured, and annihilated. That this could take place in an otherwise civilized country whose people were, in general, religious, law-abiding, and friendly has puzzled historians to this very day. It may be that the Germans, at certain points in their history, have displayed arrogant, supercilious, and aggressive cultural traits, made all the more destructive because they were motivated by closed systems of thought, religious or political, and reinforced institutionally in family, school, and work until they became habitual in everyday life. Would it then not be conceivable that even a Haarmann could be considered normal, provided that he externalized his lust for cruelty on outsiders such as Jews?

When Klaus Mann, son of the novelist Thomas Mann, was sitting in the Carlton Tea Room in Munich, he saw Hitler, who was sitting at another table, devouring three strawberry tarts in succession. As he scrutinized the Führer's face, he thought that the Nazi leader reminded him of someone whose picture he had recently seen in the newspapers, but it took him some time to make the connection:

> There was nothing but dim rosy light, soft music and heaps of cookies; and in the midst of this sugary idyll, a moustached little man with veiled eyes and a stubborn forehead.... While I called the waitress to pay for my cup of coffee, I suddenly remembered whom Herr Hitler resembled. It was that sex murderer in Hannover, whose case had such huge headlines.... His name was Haarmann.... The likeness between him and Hitler was striking. The sightless eyes, the moustache, the brutal and nervous mouth, even the unspeakable vulgarity of the fleshy nose; it was, indeed, precisely the same physiognomy.[28]

Splits in the Jewish Psyche: Integration, Self-Identity, Self-Hatred

It should not be surprising that the dangerous splits in the mainstream of German society, the sort that did enable Hitler to turn people into *Pökelfleisch,* exercised a decisive impact on the future of the small Jewish community that was living precariously within its midst. The fate of the Jews, as it would turn out, was intimately tied to the survival of the republic. Although every generalization about the Jews of Germany, just as about the Germans themselves, is subject to qualification — for there were Jewish communists and Jewish monarchists who disliked the republic — it is certainly true to say that to be Jewish in the 1920s was to be prorepublican. The Jews of Germany overwhelmingly supported the republic and eagerly took advantage of the new democratic freedoms it offered — so much so, that the culture of the 1920s was strongly shaped by their distinctive contributions.[29] In retrospect, they helped shape a vibrant culture, full of possibilities, yet tragically cut short by a resurgent counterrevolution that put an end not only to Jewish but German hopes of freedom.

During the Weimar Republic, just as in the Kaiserreich, the Jews essentially led lives parallel with their fellow Germans. The war and its aftermath, however, had brought about a very close encounter between the two people that was fraught with great dangers for the Jews. Yet, despite the constant chorus of right-wing prejudices that had been evoked by the defeat in war, the Jews quickly adjusted to the new postwar challenges and opportunities. Emancipation continued in full force under the legal protection of the democratic republic; it even looked as though the last barriers to full emancipation, especially those that had stubbornly remained in place in public service and the academic world, might be fully removed in the near future. The Jews of Germany, in fact, began to assume such an important role in German life and culture that there was every reason to hope that full emancipation would be attained with the help of the new democracy. Many Jews did not worry so much about the likelihood of full emancipation as they did about the impact such emancipation would have on Jewish identity and Jewish consciousness. With the fall of the monarchy, the German Jews were also forced to reexamine their role in a radically different and unpredictable world. At the very heart of the Jewish dilemma, now more than ever before, was the question of to what extent Jews could allow themselves to be integrated into German society without losing their distinct Jewishness. It was a question of integration and identity, a vexing problem for those Jews who, on both religious and psychological grounds, considered themselves to be Jewish. At the center of the Jewish group, writes Werner Mosse, there always is a core among whose members the preservation of ethnic identity supersedes considerations of integration into the mainstream of gentile society. Around this core, in concentric circles, are then ranged various forms of accommodation, becoming weaker and weaker as they move away from the inner core. On the very periphery one can find those Jews who are in the process of abandoning their Jewishness.[30] It goes without saying that the new democratic freedoms accelerated the process of Jewish emancipation.

Integration, as before, involved various strategies, most commonly conversion, gentile intermarriage, or simply secularization. Male Jews encountered strong obstacles in trying to shed their Jewish origins because it generally involved ethnic intermarriages over two or three generations, name changes, and full acceptance of German cultural norms.[31] As Eva Reichmann has pointed out, one of the major reasons for the sort of intergroup hostility that had existed between Germans and Jews had always been the fact that the two groups had been "objectively different,"[32] but such a difference was rapidly fading away during the Weimar Republic because Jewish assimilation was remarkably successful. Some objective differences, of course, remained in place because the Jewish core, though dwindling alarmingly in the eyes of orthodox believers, remained intact and would actually solidify under renewed Judeophobia. The irony of the German Jewish situation actually resided in the fact that German Jews had been assimilated and integrated more successfully in Germany than anywhere else in the world. One could even argue that the Jewish core would have been in great jeopardy under the continuing existence of the Weimar Republic.

Spokesmen of German Jewry, such as Leo Baeck, who was emerging as one of the most commanding talents of the Jewish core in the postwar period, constantly worried about reductions of core believers due to a declining birthrate, intermarriage, and secularization. In Berlin, where most German Jews resided, it is estimated that by the end of the 1920s one of every three Jews married outside of the Jewish faith.[33] In his study of the lives of six prominent Jews who decided to remain in Nazi Germany, John V. H. Dippel has shown that his six subjects had become so acculturated to German life and culture that they had great difficulty in rejecting their country once it had rejected them.[34] His six subjects include Richard Willstätter, a Nobel laureate in chemistry; Max Warburg, a leading banker; Hans-Joachim Schoeps, a right-wing youth leader and young philosopher; Bella Fromm, a Berlin gossip columnist; Robert Weltsch, Zionist editor of the *Jüdische Rundschau;* and Leo Baeck, a leading rabbi. What unites these six is that they all survived the Nazi Holocaust, stayed on for some or all of the time in Nazi Germany, left behind them a revealing record that was uncolored by the Holocaust, and often listened more to their hearts than they did to their heads, which may explain why they tragically miscalculated the terrible danger coming from the Nazi movement. Dippel compares the Jewish-German relationship to an abusive marriage, a family relationship that had gone tragically wrong. He quotes Richard Willstätter replying to Chaim Weizmann's urgent pleas that the chemist should flee his Munich home: "One does not leave one's mother, even when she behaves badly."[35] The tragic weakness of these German Jews was that their basic perception of life was bourgeois and rationalistic in a world that was being turned upside down and becoming increasingly irrational.

It is, of course, problematical to generalize from six lives to the whole population of German Jews, but the historical record seems to confirm that these six individuals were, if not typical, at least not atypical and therefore fairly representative of middle-class Jews in Germany. With the exception of Weltsch and Baeck, these German Jews were fully secularized and had either given up their Jewish faith or lapsed into becoming "three-day Jews" who attended synagogue only on the major holy days. All of them had become so acculturated to German society that their whole intellectual framework, their habitual way of seeing reality, was cast in an essentially German mold. This fact, along with the changed historical circumstances of the postwar period, led many Jews into a reexamination, at once urgent and worrisome, about the nature of Jewish life in the modern world. This reexamination was spearheaded by several remarkable Jewish theologians, notably Martin Buber, Franz Rosenzweig, and Leo Baeck, who tried to formulate a modern message from traditional Judaism without undermining either its essential theological premises or its institutional practices. Along with many other Jewish thinkers, religious and secular, they also agonized over the question of what it meant to be a Jew in the modern world.

Franz Rosenzweig (1886–1929), a noted philosopher and historian, was a fully assimilated German Jew, a follower of Kant and Hegel, who planned to convert to Christianity, only to rediscover his Jewish faith in a dramatic way. In 1913, while attending high holy day services at a Berlin synagogue, he experienced a kind of epiphany that revealed that closeness to God did not depend on the mediation of Jesus but was open to any Jews who opened their hearts to God. During World War I, while serving in the German army on the Balkan front, Rosenzweig wrote *Stern der Erlösung* (Star of redemption), in which he argued that Judaism and Christianity were two aspects of the same religious coin, speaking the truth in their own distinctive ways. His religious approach, destined to usher in a religious reawakening among educated German Jews, was a kind of existential humanism within a broad religious framework. It emphasized the importance of a direct, personal, and experiential encounter with God, unencumbered by either the Talmudic reliance on legalistic practices or the emotionality of Hasidism that often confused religious ecstasy with God himself. After World War I Rosenzweig moved to Frankfurt, where he opened the Freie Jüdische Lehrhaus (Free Jewish House of Learning), dedicated to helping Jews in moving from the periphery of their faith back to its core or center.[36] In 1922 he was afflicted with progressive paralysis, but heroically continued to pursue his life's work until his death in 1929.

Martin Buber (1878–1956) also offered a novel reexamination of classical Judaism, which was based on his personal experiences and philosophical insights. His thought influenced a variety of thinkers, Jewish and non-Jewish, beyond the German-speaking world. Although born in Vienna in 1878, Buber was brought up by his Jewish grandfather in Galicia, where he was influenced by the emotional tendencies of Hasidism. After receiving a doctoral degree in philosophy from the University of Berlin, he joined the Zionist movement and edited a journal dedicated to the sociology of religion. He also republished Hasidic tales and joined with Rosenzweig in calling for a more personal encounter with the divine in the religious life of the believer. The heart of Buber's message is contained in his most famous work, *Ich und Du*

(I and thou, 1937), in which he identified the presence of a collective or national soul in each human being. For Jews, the existence of this collective unconscious force consisted of four thousand years of shared historical experiences. These experiences, he believed, could be reactivated by all Jews provided that they acquired and practiced a constant form of historical reenactment; and by so doing, they would reexperience the presence of God within themselves. Our living encounter with God depends upon the maintenance of this shared historical experience. This is the meaning of the famous "I and Thou" relationship because, through faith, the I discovers the Thou within itself; it is a process of self-discovery that is one of intimacy, mutuality, sharing, and trust. In 1924 Buber became a professor of Jewish religion at the University of Frankfurt; he also became actively involved in the Zionist movement. In 1938 he fled Germany and settled in Palestine, where he continued his work as a teacher at Hebrew University.

Leo Baeck, a "German" rabbi from head to toe, professional in his bearing as well as in his learning, stayed forever loyal to his Jewish community, all the more so at a time when it came under increasing attack by the Nazis. In the 1920s Baeck was at the height of his career and his intellectual powers. Physically as well as intellectually, he was a commanding, almost aristocratic presence: tall, with his hair and beard graying, he walked assertively, always looking straight ahead as though he knew exactly where he was going. There was also a great deal of the penetrating, yet slightly distanced professor about him that spellbound most people who came in contact with him. His education had been, except for his rabbinical training, an immersion in German *Bildung,* first in the Gymnasium in Lissa in Posen and then at the University of Berlin, where he wrote a doctoral dissertation on the influence of Spinoza, which was supervised by the great historian Wilhelm Dilthey. Baeck, however, never forgot his origins at the crossroad of German and eastern European Judaism. Although his family was and felt itself middle-class German, his hometown of Lissa in the Prussian province of Posen had originally belonged to Poland (reverting to Poland again after 1919) and still exhibited strong characteristics of traditional Jewish ghetto life. Baeck understood both worlds, which would make him an important mediator between them.

In fact, Baeck's activities as one of the leading rabbis of Germany in the postwar world revolved around his efforts to mend the deep fissures that had developed within the Jewish community. Perhaps even more than Rosenzweig and Buber, he worried about the future of the Jewish community — the *Gemeinde* around which Jewish life in Germany revolved. When we speak of the Jewish community we should be careful not to confuse it with the concept of a homogeneous whole, institutionally centralized, doctrinally unified, or speaking with a common voice. The German word *Gemeinde* actually refers to an individual religious community that had been officially recognized and designated as a legal corporation so that it could be taxed and segregated from the mainstream Christian community. Dating back to the Middle Ages, as previously shown, the *Kultus-Gemeinden* were empowered over time by the German states in which they were located to hire rabbis, maintain and build synagogues, and organize activities related to the life of a religious community, including charitable work, schools, libraries, and newspapers. Every professed German Jew was required by state law to belong to the *Gemeinde* closest to his or her home.

The Jewish communities were never centrally organized, nor could they be, in a Christian state that saw no profit in organizing its opposition and therefore preferred to deal with individual Jewish communities and tax them as much as the traffic could bear. In addition to their heterogeneous nature, Jewish communities, as previously indicated, were also split along orthodox and liberal lines, with the upper hand having been gained in the 1920s by the Liberal Party. The Berlin *Gemeinde* was the largest in Germany; by 1900 it represented almost one-third of all German Jews.[37] Like other Jewish *Gemeinden,* it was also riven by internal dissensions — to the point that some orthodox rabbis refused to belong to it because they believed that it was contaminated by the liberal movement.[38] Although Leo Baeck often managed to smooth over the most disruptive disagreements, the essential split between the liberals, to whom he himself belonged, and the orthodox side could not be mended. Nor did Baeck succeed in bridging the gap between German Jews, whom he primarily represented and whose cultural assumptions he typified, and the growing number of *Ostjuden* (eastern Jews).

There was also a third divisive element that had developed in the Jewish community: the growing dispute between Zionists and non-Zionists. Few German Jews fully supported the radical proposals of the Zionists; their homeland was Germany and not Palestine. Although they listened to Buber, Weltsch, or Scholem, especially after the Nazi threat became ever more ominous, they preferred to think of themselves, as the title of their major defensive organization stated, as *Deutsche Staatsbürger jüdischen Glaubens* (German citizens of the Jewish faith). Leo Baeck, too, made this commitment to both Germany and his Jewish faith, but this did not prevent him from supporting some Zionist ideas and proposals because, like the Zionists, he realized that conditions in Germany could deteriorate to such a low point for German Jews that every avenue of hope, including exile in Palestine, should be seriously explored. This explains his membership in the Founding Congress of the Pro-Palestine Committee and his contribution to the Keren Hayesod organization, which collected funds for the development of Palestine as a Jewish homeland.[39]

Baeck's intellectual efforts reflect the temper of the man: they represent the best in both the German and the Jewish heritage. In the broadest sense, Baeck tried to fuse the *Menscheitsideal* (ideal of enlightened humankind: Goethe, Schiller, Kant) with the religious and moral

tradition of enlightened liberal Judaism. Baeck regarded Judaism as the
great ancestral religion of the western world; its ideal of humanity and
commitment to universal moral rules represent its enduring legacy and
serve as a shining beacon to the rest of the world. In his major work,
The Essence of Judaism, first published in 1905 but considerably revised
and expanded in 1922, Baeck provided a rousing defense of Judaism
against its Christian detractors. He was careful not to attack Jesus or
even Christianity itself, but rather to focus on what he believed to be the
erroneous, largely Pauline interpretations of the Judaic religion. Deni-
grating the Jewish faith to one of religious obsolescence and completely
distorting the meaning of Jesus have been, he argued, the two cardinal
errors of Christianity. Baeck also took issue with Christian ideas of salvation as something in no way earned but somehow bestowed in some
inexplicable way by divine grace. To a Jew, salvation implies not only individual and collective effort; it also involves an ongoing dialogue with
God who is the personal partner in salvation.

Baeck's religious approach was irenic. He believed that in addition to
Talmudic ritual and learning, Jews must also open their hearts to the
emotional warmth and mystery offered by their mystical traditions. He
believed that Jews not only have a right but also a responsibility to be
different; their religious traditions, in fact, required them to be moral
examples, to stand up and speak truth to worldly powers. As he put it,

> By its mere existence Judaism is a never silent protest against the assump-
> tion of the multitude that force is superior to truth. So long as Judaism
> exists, nobody will be able to say that the soul of man has surrendered.
> Its very existence through the ages is proof that conviction cannot be
> mastered by number.[40]

For Rosenzweig, Buber, and Baeck the overriding problem was to
save the Jews as Jews, to safeguard their existential place in the world
and to provide the theological strategies by which they could derive
continuous intellectual nourishment. For all three, it was the Jewish
community, or core, that was of vital importance; individuals, after all,
cannot extend themselves into the future without the community. The
spinal principle of historical continuity is found in a chain of generations bound to a central belief system whose doctrines and rituals are
forever renewed, shared, reinforced, and handed down to future generations. When the links in the chain, for whatever reason, begin to break,
the core begins to dwindle, the well of belief dries up, and the energy
needed for survival dissipates.

The question that some Jews began to ask themselves in the interwar
period was whether the Jews could be saved as Jews in Germany. During
the Weimar period, that question, of course, revolved primarily around
Jewish self-identification; it concerned the issue of what it meant to be a
Jew and, assuming that this question could be answered, whether and in
what sense such a Jew could participate in a community of like-minded

Jews. During the Nazi period, these questions, still open-ended during the republic, were taken out of the hands of the Jews and answered in explicit and dogmatic racial terms. The Jews had lost complete control to define themselves freely and participate in any meaningful way in German life and culture. Up until the very moment of Nazi control, however, the Jews of Germany never ceased asking what it meant to be Jewish, why this aroused so much animosity, and what they had to do to cope with their own sense of Jewishness. One could say that just as the Germans never stopped asking what it meant to be German, the German Jews, who were often German *Doppelgänger,* also endlessly asked what it meant to be Jewish.

To Rosenzweig, Buber, and Baeck, people who breathed their Jewish religion with their every breath, the answer was obvious: to be a Jew meant to be, above all else, a practicing observant of the Jewish faith, orthodox or reformed. From a statistical point of view, 503,000 of such *Glaubensjuden* (believing Jews) were officially recorded in 1933, which is less than 1 percent of the total population.[41] The *Statistik des deutschen Reiches,* the statistical compilation for the Reich, does not record those Jews who had converted to Christianity, declared or felt themselves secular, agnostic, or atheist, or had simply drifted away from their *Kultus-Gemeinden* and were no longer counted as Jewish. Yet all of them in some way still felt themselves to be Jewish or were conscious of belonging, symbolically or sentimentally, to the Jewish people, heritage, or religion. It is important to assess, inadequate as it may be, how assimilated Jews of that sort grappled with their Jewishness and how, consciously or unconsciously, that Jewishness shaped their mental world. What did Jewishness mean to assimilated Jews whose ancestors may have been Jewish but who now considered themselves to be fully German and were only dimly aware of their lineage while they lived their lives and followed their careers as doctors, lawyers, teachers, artists, writers, journalists, bankers, merchants, or workers?

The novelist Alfred Döblin, who had converted to Christianity and considered himself to be a fully assimilated German, discovered that he needed to know what it meant to be Jewish, suspecting that, having found an answer to that question, he would also find an answer to the question: "Who am I?" As he put it:

> I discovered that I had to inform myself about the Jews. I discovered that I really did not know any Jews. My relatives who called themselves Jews I could not call Jews. They were not so by faith nor by language; perhaps they were the remnant of a people who perished long ago and merged into their new surroundings. I therefore asked myself and others: Where do Jews exist? I was told: In Poland.[42]

Apparently taking this literally, Döblin went to Poland to find out. But what did he expect to find? That the identity of real Jewishness increases in direct proportion to the "objective differences" between two people who live side by side with each other, so that the differences are so great that identification can be easily determined since it comes down to mutually exclusive opposites — that is, black and white or apples and oranges? Although Döblin wrote a vivid and memorable account of Polish Jewry, he missed an important point that was obscured by his original false premise: namely, that "man kann ja kein jüdisches Leben führen, wo keins ist" (one cannot live a Jewish life where there is none).[43] He axiomatically assumed, taking his own assimilated position as normative, that one could not lead a Jewish life in Germany and that, therefore, only *Ostjuden* (eastern Jews) but not *Westjuden* (western Jews) could be real Jews.[44] Granted that Polish Jews differed substantially from their western coreligionists in many obvious ways — in their ghetto way of life with its distinctive attire, language, mannerisms, and rituals — but did this really mean that one group was more Jewish than another? Quite apart from missing an important anthropological connection by failing to examine the relationship of Poles and Polish Jews, to show how they interacted with each other in a cultural matrix, Döblin uncritically assumed that the existence of a pristine Jewish community had a greater claim to some assumed original than any other. His analysis failed the test of Jewish history, which teaches that Jewishness resides in its diversity, that a Jew in Germany, France, or England has as much of a claim to be Jewish as the *Ostjuden,* and that wherever a *minyan* (minimum of ten adult males necessary to perform a service) could be found, a Jewish community had come into existence.[45]

Döblin was not alone in misjudging the Jewish question even while trying to understand it honestly. He assumed that German Jewry did not exist as an entity, but his own need to know indicates otherwise: it shows that secularized Jews were also Jews whenever they felt themselves Jewish by virtue of belonging to the people of the Diaspora and sharing with them a sense of common history, a sense of history that, for some of them, is so vivid that the suffering, joys, and insights experienced by past generations of Jews appear as if they happened only yesterday. There was the additional fact that in Germany and Austria the mainstream political culture was obsessed with the Jewish question to such an extent that even assimilated Jews who no longer practiced the Jewish faith could not escape from the psychological pressures of their Jewishness.

Few German writers agonized over their Jewishness as persistently and, as it would turn out unsuccessfully, as the novelist Jakob Wassermann (1873–1934), a deeply troubled and split human being who had reached international renown through a series of novels in which the German-Jewish tragedy was a constant preoccupation. Starting with his first work, *Juden von Zirndorf* (The Jews of Zirndorf), and continuing in a series of related stories such as *Geschichte der jungen Renate Fuchs* (Story of the young Renate Fuchs, 1900), *Caspar Hauser* (1908), and *Gansemännchen* (Little goose men, 1915), Wassermann confronts

his readers with the anguish felt by various Jewish figures as they wres-
tle with the malicious hatred to which they are exposed and for which
they have few defenses, let alone few solutions. Their anguish, which
was Wassermann's anguish, sprang from their role as outsiders sincerely
seeking integration, only to be viciously rebuffed. Daniel Nothafft, a
character in *Gansemännchen,* is described as stretching out his hands,
only to be spat upon; his tormentors only take and take without ever
giving thanks. Wassermann saw himself and his people forever used,
rarely thanked, and never really considered good enough to be good
Germans. His own life was a struggle not only against a hostile and
whimsical world but also against insensitive parents and family members who expected him to pursue a business career for which he was
ill suited. Yet, like some of the protagonists in his novels, he struggled
painfully to be accepted and hated himself for having to employ insincere strategies to do it. Yet, out of this mesh of complicated personal
relationships, which are reflected in what Peter Gay calls the almost
Baroque quality of his involved stories, Wassermann extracted the essential dilemma of the tragic relationship between German and Jew. It
was particularly in *Gansemännchen,* as Peter Gay points out, that he
successfully relived "his own persistent confrontation: that of Jew and
Christian, Jew and German, in perpetual conflict and perpetual search
for harmony."[46]

Wassermann failed in his effort to be at once a reconciler and a healer,
a kind of secular saint inspiring both German and Jew to rise to a higher
form of enlightened consciousness, but he was remarkably successful in
penetrating to the root of hate that often seized quite ordinary Germans
when they confronted real or imaginary Jews. Since what he had to say
on this subject, especially in his autobiographical work *Mein Weg als
Deutscher und Jude* (My path as German and Jew, 1921), was so compelling in light of what would later happen under the Nazis, it deserves
to be examined at some length.

Although Wassermann realized that Judeophobia was a general western phenomenon and therefore existed in various degrees of intensity in
all western countries, it bore a distinctive signature in German-speaking
areas. It was *the* national German hatred. Its defining quality was its
superstitious nature — the fact that it was a delusion; but Wassermann
quickly added that it was a voluntary delusion rather than an invol-
untary one, a matter of choice rather than necessity. Embedded in this
delusion, he believed, one could find a cross-section of festering and displaced social fears, frustrations, animosities, jealousies, and hatreds. In
it, one could find a fear of demons, clerical insensibility, the rancor of
the disadvantaged, the deceived as well as the ignorant, the mendacity of liars. There is also a whiff of monkey-like malice (*affenhafter
Bosheit*) one often finds in religious fanaticism. Furthermore, Judeophobia contains greed and animosity, bloodlust, fear of being seduced
or tempted, the allure of mystery, and the lack of self-esteem.[47] In sum,

German Judeophobia is a fusion of all these elements, and as such it is impenetrable and irrational. When a Danish acquaintance once asked Wassermann, "What do the Germans really want to do with their hate of Jews?" and then added that "in my fatherland Jews are generally loved,"[48] Wassermann launched into a complicated explanation about the Jewish dilemma of divided loyalties, of double love (*Doppelliebe*), later realizing that what he should have told the curious Dane was that the Germans, riddled by internal divisions, simply needed the emotion of hate and a convenient scapegoat to absorb that hate. Every time the Germans suffered, after every defeat, in each tight spot, in each sticky situation, they displaced their blame and guilt onto the Jews. He agreed with the Dane that the Germans, certainly since the founding of the Kaiserreich, suffered from a singular lack of liberalism, but the intensity of their hatred also involved a general lack of imagination, freedom, and good will.

As long as the Germans made the Jews responsible for every social ill, as long as they believed that the Jews poisoned the German atmosphere, seduced its young people into "un-German" ways — commercial calculation, melancholy brooding, skeptical doubt, Asiatic sensuality — as long as the Germans believed these delusions, Wassermann argued, there would never be a cure for this German hate. He illustrated the irrationality of this German hatred with two particularly effective examples: one fictional and the other drawn from a conversation with a friend. Being a Jew in Germany, he said, may be compared to a worker who never receives his full paycheck, although his work is as good as that of his German co-workers. Whenever the Jew complains of such unequal treatment and demands his proper due, he is told that the reason he did not get his full wages was because he is pockmarked. Rushing home, he looks at his face in the mirror, but finding no evidence of pockmarks, he returns to tell his tormentors that his face is entirely unblemished. This does him no good, however, because the employer simply shrugs his shoulders and replies: "You were reported as pockmarked; therefore you are pockmarked."[49] If we put ourselves into the shoes of such a tormented creature, Wassermann pointed out, we would understand his mental confusion: here is a man who is denied basic rights under the pretense that he suffered some blemish he couldn't find, endlessly stressing himself to try to find it because it was officially reported to be there. Psychologically paralyzed after repeated attempts to fight for his rights, the branded Jew simply gives up his fight. As Wassermann put it, such treatment is "a cunningly conceived form of torture."[50]

This sense that there would always be a permanent barrier between German and Jew was brought home to Wassermann in a personal discussion of the issue with a good friend. What are the various reasons that separate Germans and Jews? he asked his friend. Specifically, what separates the two of us? Is it faith? Since both of us are neither Christian nor Jew, are we separated by blood? But who would dare to separate like blood from like blood? Surely, pure Germans do not exist; they mixed with French immigrants, with Slavs, Scandinavians, Spaniards, Italians, and most likely with Huns and Mongolians who flooded German territory over the course of two thousand years. If the difference between German and Jew cannot be found in the blood, he asked his friend, is the difference to be found in a different moral fiber or perhaps even a different human mold? His friend replied that this is probably what the answer was: Jews are different moral beings and therefore different human beings. When pressed whether he considered Wassermann to be a different human being, the friend wanted him to swear, hand on his heart, whether he "felt himself as a real Jew," but Wassermann hesitated because he wanted to know what his friend implied by his question. His friend laughed and said that he knew that it might be hard for him to admit feeling like a Jew because of the difficulty surrounding the term "Jew." Wassermann shot back that the same could be said of the term "German." His friend then shifted his line of questioning by wanting to know whether Wassermann's mother was definitely Jewish and whether there had been any crossings in his family tree? When Wassermann firmly stuck to the fact of his purely Jewish background, his friend shook his head and admitted that his case was unusual, a special case because a friend he liked and respected surely could not be purely Jewish. But Wassermann wanted no special dispensation, no special recognition that his case was an exception that entitled him to be declared an honorary German. He could only marvel at the ingrained nature of his friend's prejudice and at his own naive belief that anyone who was born on German soil, breathed its air, and assimilated its language and cultural norms, would automatically be considered a German. His friend's hesitation to accept him as an equal German was based on such deep emotional resistance that Wassermann came away from this experience forever doubting that a Jew could be accepted as being a German as well as a Jew. If a personal friend could feel this way, willing, at best, to make a condescending dispensation and, at worst, demanding an "either-or" choice, then it was clear to Wassermann that Jews were permanently stigmatized as aliens on German soil.[51]

Who, then, was Wassermann? A neurotic German Jew, as the Zionist *Jüdische Rundschau* claimed in 1928 after taking issue with one of his public speeches on the topic of Jewishness? The Zionist periodical criticized him for being egocentric and turning the Wassermann neurosis into a general Jewish neurosis; it denied him the right to speak on behalf of all Jews. Wassermann responded to such Zionist criticisms by arguing that the German-Jewish schism would only widen if the Zionists had their way because they, too, denied the possibility that Jews could be Germans; they regarded themselves as *jüdische Juden* (Jewish Jews) rather than *deutsche Juden* (German Jews). He would remain, he said, a German Jew, vulnerable, to be sure, since he did not completely embrace either of the two sides, but feeling confident nevertheless that his middle (liberal) position allowed him greater flexibility in pointing toward common ground.[52] Wassermann's depressing, almost pathetic revelations are symptomatic of the older generation of Jews who grew up under the Kaiserreich and despaired, under repeated waves of Judeophobia, of ever finding a way out of their dilemma because their fellow Germans could not resolve their own uncertain German identity. Wassermann and others who agonized over their Jewishness, insecure as both Germans and Jews, had to pay a special and devastating psychological price in the form of Jewish self-hate.

The term "Jewish self-hate" was coined by Theodor Lessing in his 1930 book *Der Jüdische Selbsthass* (The Jewish self-hatred), a curious work of self-diagnosis and description of a form of Jewish masochism that had its roots in traditional Judeophobia long before Lessing invented the term. Lessing was a tortured soul who had converted to Lutheranism before World War I and adopted a strident anti-Jewish position in order to root out whatever vestiges of Jewishness still remained in his thinking. Whenever he was unable to confront his Jewishness, he displaced it into Judeophobic prejudices, the most shameful example being a letter to Freud in which he denounced psychoanalysis as a typical abortion (*Ausgeburt*) of the Jewish spirit. Freud later recalled that at first he assumed that Lessing was related to the eighteenth-century philosopher G. E. Lessing, but when he learned otherwise he immediately terminated his correspondence. As a good clinician, always trying to act on the principle that nothing human must be alien to the analyst, Freud still marveled at this textbook example of Jewish self-hatred, calling it an "exquisite Jewish phenomenon."[53]

Lessing was indeed a troubled man: small and dark-skinned in appearance, he admired Germanic ideals of beauty and identified with patriotic causes. For a short time he found himself as the odd man out in the setting of one of Hermann Lietz's boarding schools that combined neo-romantic ideals of *Heimat* (homeland) and *Volk* with fervent nationalistic principles. When Lessing's Germanic faith, however, did not fit Lietz's narrow *völkisch* ideology with its Judeophobic underpinnings, he quarreled with the headmaster and was dismissed. The First World War converted Lessing from a strident Judeophobe to an equally assertive Zionist; it represented the disquiet over his Jewishness in a new form. During the war Lessing wrote a profoundly pessimistic book that indicted both his Jewish and his German heritage. Entitled *Decline of the Earth Spirit*, the book described the Jewish people as a desiccated and sterile race, forever condemned to lead a marginalized existence because it had no homeland, no contact with the creative forces of life that are always rooted in native soil and country. Their only hope was to escape from their bondage to Mammon and recover their native homeland. In the 1920s Lessing became a distinguished philosopher with a flair for making sweeping judgments that earned him the reputation of being a gadfly. During the 1926 presidential campaign he imprudently attacked Field Marshal Hindenburg, the icon of the *völkisch* right, as a "moronic zero who was paving the way for a future Nero," a remark that aroused the political right to such a frenzy that he essentially had to curtail his teaching activities at the Hannover Technical Institute and confine himself to private research. When the Nazis took over in 1933, Lessing fled to Czechoslovakia, where he was tracked down a year later and assassinated by Nazi killers.

Probably the most grotesque example of Jewish self-hatred, mentioned here only because its pathological dynamics would later generate a number of tragic suicides, was that of the Austrian author Otto Weininger, who achieved great notoriety with a book called *Geschlecht und Charakter* (Sex and character), in which the idea of bisexuality is linked to intellectual tendencies and turned into a measurement for calculating degrees of human perfection or imperfection.[54] According to Weininger, men and women are androgynous, each containing various psychological counterparts to the anatomical vestiges of the opposite sex. The ideal type, and the one who is responsible for all cultural achievements, is the masculine type in whom the feminine vestige exactly counterbalances the masculinity of the woman. Weininger believed that women, embodying the wanton urge toward sexual gratification, were the antithesis of male rationality, and that Jews were still lower because their racial-sexual quotient was the least balanced. The Aryan race, by contrast, represents the embodiment of the perfectly tuned masculine-creative principle. When he found out that he was branded by both the inferiority of Jewishness and a preponderance of the female element, the demented Weininger dramatically shot himself in the house where Beethoven had lived, an act that was later much applauded by Jew-haters who endorsed it as entirely commendable. While ruminating on the "Jewish bacillus" at Führer headquarters in December of 1941, Hitler recalled that Dietrich Eckart had once told him that he had known only one decent Jew, Otto Weininger, who had killed himself after recognizing that the Jew lives as a parasite on the body of other people.[55]

Weininger's Jewish self-hatred was undoubtedly a pathological manifestation of his own personality, but in an important way it also reflected the fact that it was strongly shaped by intense cultural prejudices. A culture that institutionalizes a set of powerful mystifications deludes everyone, German as well as Jew. Not even the strongest members of a minority will be able to slough off the stings of hate indefinitely. As to the weakest members, they often tried to escape from their Jewishness in some pathetic ways, ranging from hating themselves, posturing as fervent nationalists, or even identifying themselves with the aggressor. Jewish parents sometimes tried to teach their children to act in a more "German" and a less "Jewish" way, instilling all sorts of habits in their children that were assumed to be typically German. Walther Rathenau, in an essay directed toward Jews entitled "Höre, Israel"

(Hear, Israel), called upon Jews to give up their objectionable qualities and become authentically German.[56] The objectionable qualities he had in mind were, besides their supposed penchant for materialism, the habits and characteristics associated with the embarrassing *Ostjuden*. The novelist Wassermann, who lived for a time in Vienna, found these Jews to be foreign and deeply repellent, and he hoped that the German Jewish self-image would not be negatively affected by these dirty *Schnorrers* (tramps) who still reeked of the ghetto. In order to be accepted in German society, Jews were obedience-trained by their parents and teachers to be extra polite, pleasing, and accommodating so that they would be a pleasure to be with. Peter Gay points out that the quality that Jews were to emulate in order to please their German neighbors was *Liebenswürdigkeit* (amiability), even exaggerated amiability that the Germans call *hinreissende Liebenswürdigkeit*, or overwhelming amiability.[57] What this often meant in practice, however, was groveling self-abasement, the sort of behavior that describes the relationship between the socially superior insider and the socially inferior servant. It is an unhealthy relationship, a servile form of dependency used by the oppressors to build up their own egos by deflating those of their subjects.

It is difficult to assess how many Jews tried to escape from their Jewishness by mimicking supposedly cultivated German mannerisms, but managing only to be embarrassing and therefore doubly suspect of being Jewish. In Jewish intellectual circles this sort of conduct was much despised. Jewish intellectuals, in any case, did not constitute a coherent body with a uniform point of view, nor did they consciously accentuate their Jewishness. This does not mean that, as a group, they did not possess a recognizable family resemblance. For one thing, Jewish intellectuals tended to be liberal or socialist in their convictions, although the main body of German Jewry itself, being strongly middle class in composition, never moved to the extreme left. Although many Jewish intellectuals initially participated as left-wing militants in the revolutionary upheavals of the postwar years (1918–23), their participation in radical causes dwindled steadily thereafter. As Walter Laqueur has pointed out, few Jewish intellectuals worked through any political party; only a few Jews were active in the SPD (Sozialdemokratische Partei Deutschlands, the Social Democratic Party of Germany). The Communist Party initially attracted many Jews; by 1931, however, there was not a single Jew among the hundred communist deputies elected to the Reichstag in that year.[58]

It would be a grave error to assume that German intellectuals in general and German-Jewish intellectuals in particular wielded any significant influence over public policy in Germany. As previously shown, German intellectuals had contributed their share in separating *Geist* (intellect) and *Macht* (power) and prided themselves for being unpolitical. The result was that, historically, German intellectuals constituted a class of marginalized outsiders who had little influence over the course of politics. Lacking experience in working through the political culture, they withdrew into the realm of spirit: the arts, literature, philosophy, music. Jewish intellectuals, in addition to being politically ineffective, suffered from two other liabilities: that they were Jews in a country that distrusted them, and that they generally belonged to the political left and were perceived to be radical in their political convictions and modernist in their intellectual convictions. It is a fact that Jewish intellectuals were frequently in the vanguard of avant-garde movements; they formed a prominent part of the expressionist movement as writers, artists, theater producers, and leaders in the emerging motion picture industry.[59] They owned leading liberal newspapers. The Mosse chain, already mentioned, had cornered a significant part of the Berlin newspaper and magazine market. Its rival, the house of Ullstein, was even more successful, particularly after it acquired the respectable *Vossische Zeitung* and increased sales through journals, fashion magazines, and inexpensive books. Many publishers, editors, and critics were Jewish, including Samuel Fischer, Kurt Wolff, the Cassirers, Georg Bondi, Erich Reiss, and the firm of Malik.

The Nazis constantly raised the specter that German culture was being controlled by left-wing Jews who were "polluting" traditional German values with their decadent beliefs. The fact that Jewish intellectuals were generally liberal or socialist played into the hands of right-wing critics who specialized in exaggerating the political importance of a few famous Jewish radicals and tarring the majority with the same radical brush. The bogus perception of Jewish subversion was inadvertently reinforced by some Jewish writers who publicly excoriated what they regarded as destructive in German culture. Kurt Tucholsky, a brilliant Jewish satirist, managed to give the stereotype of the subversive Jewish literati a mighty boost by pouring out a stream of venomous essays on the foibles of German life. Charged by his opponents as unpatriotic, he nonchalantly brushed aside such criticism by saying, "The country which I am supposedly betraying is not my country; this state is not my state; and this legal order is not my legal order. I am indifferent to the color of their flag as I am to their provincially limited ideals. I have nothing to betray here because no one has entrusted me with anything."[60] In 1928 he stated publicly that "there is no secret of the German Army which I would not deliver to a foreign power, if this seemed necessary for the preservation of peace.... We are high traitors. But we betray a country which we repudiate, in favor of a country which we love, for the sake of peace and for our true fatherland: Europe."[61]

Did this mean that Tucholsky, a secularized Jew, was escaping from his Jewishness into an intellectual ideal, displacing his past into a new identity — that of a cosmopolitan citizen of Europe with progressive social convictions? Was it a rejection of both his German and his Jewish persona or was it merely an intellectual pose? Perhaps it was all of these things, because Tucholsky was a deeply split and annoying gadfly who ultimately despaired of finding an authentic escape from his past and killed himself in a Swedish hotel room.

Tucholsky was one of several prominent Jewish intellectuals who wrote for the *Weltbühne*, the most influential journal of the left. Others who were associated with the *Weltbühne* included Carl von Ossietzky, the journal's editor and later a Nobel Peace laureate as well as a victim of Nazi brutality, Ernst Bloch, and Walter Benjamin. The views and convictions of these writers belie the stereotypical judgment that condemned them as militant radicals and dangerous subversives; they were, in fact, kindhearted reformers who took up the cause of any downtrodden victim. Their intellectual weakness was the weakness of many politically inexperienced improvers of the world: a tendency to overreact to real or presumed injustices and to offer sweeping blueprints for human salvation. Tucholsky and his little band of cultural critics were deeply disenchanted and alienated intellectuals who could not forgive the Germans for what they regarded as a betrayal of the better side of their heritage, and that included cultural beliefs once considered the benchmark of a civilized German: a strong pride of country within a large cosmopolitan (European) framework and a commitment to the humane values of the Enlightenment. As the antidemocratic pressures against the republic began to intensify in the late 1920s, many Jewish intellectuals began to feel more and more like outsiders again looking in on a society that, in their estimation, had betrayed its better side.

It is difficult to determine just how influential these critics really were or whether their negative attitude toward the republic was not just another nail in its coffin. Since the republic failed to meet the test of their vague utopian longings, they generally kept their distance or voiced their condescension. It was perhaps their resentment of not being allowed to share power that led them to make absurd judgments, the most silly being that the Social Democrats were the most reactionary politicians in the world, a judgment that may have been prompted, as Walter Laqueur points out, by the fact that many of these intellectual critics looked down on the working class origins of the defenders of the republic, for President Ebert was, after all, only a saddlemaker, Severing a locksmith, Scheidemann a painter, Noske a basketmaker, and Wels an upholsterer.[62]

This would indicate that these Weimar writers perhaps did not know their country as well as they thought they did; and conversely, that their right-wing critics vastly overrated their influence on German culture. The Jews in general were still outsiders wanting to be insiders, but it was only in a few areas that they made a significant breakthrough, and that was in journalism, the theater, and the publishing world. Yet, even in these fields their influence was never a dominating one because their convictions were not "Jewish" but German. Although the Jews played a significant role in the newspaper world, the range of "Jew-

ish" papers was limited almost wholly to some of the bigger cities;
the prominent press remained in non-Jewish hands. The Mosse or Ullstein papers were more liberal than left-wing in their orientation, and
it was never clear what the Nazis really meant by the "Jewish press"
once the fact of their Jewish ownership had been removed from consideration. The truth is that the Nazis mistook their own prejudices
for the only real German values, lumping all of their opponents, especially the Jews, as disloyal and un-German. It was also characteristic
of them to denounce anything they particularly despised under the general pejorative term "Jewish," and that could mean anything modern,
avant-garde, pacifistic, democratic, communistic, cosmopolitan, liberal,
and, more vaguely, "corrosive," "rootless," "materialistic," "decadent,"
"skeptical," and even "clever." The quality of "cleverness," was flung at
Jews at every turn. In reality it was the perverse way by which the ignorant Nazis paid homage to the virtue of their opponents. "Skeptical,"
"clever," and "flippant" were no more than descriptions of quick-
witted Berliners in general. As Peter Gay reminds us, these epithets were
applied by Germans to Berliners who were admired for being *schlag-
fertig* — that is, quick-witted deflators of pomposity, self-importance,
and empty grandeur.[63]

In the final analysis, the epithet of the "clever" Jew had its real origin in the psychology of jealous Germans who envied the Jews for their
success and tried to discount it by sullying its motives and belittling
its fruits. The label "clever" Jew, of course, concealed a long-standing
psychological stereotype — that of the upwardly mobile, pushy, and unsentimental Jew who is coldly indifferent to venerable German customs
and prizes only material success. The stereotype could be found not only
in the rantings of the dogmatic Jew-hater but also in Werner Sombart's
academic writings and in the pages and cartoons of the satirical *Simpli-
cissimus*. Given their "pushy nature" and their "lack of spiritual depth,"
Jews were supposedly incapable of creating truly enduring works of
art, literature, or music. If it is true that great cultural achievements
have their source in the native soil and its people, as the *völkisch* right
claimed, would it not follow that the Jews, as marginalized outsiders,
can never aspire to create anything great anywhere in the world? The
premise was, of course, false on two grounds: most German Jews were
fully assimilated Germans no less "rooted" than other Germans, and
great achievements spring from individual geniuses whose creative talents transcend the culture in which they are active. Jewish intellectuals,
of course, made this point repeatedly, but this did not alter the perception of the prejudiced Germans who continued to equate anything
Jewish with un-German.

Walter Laqueur shows that this may have had a devastating psychological impact on Jewish intellectuals because it created an anomaly in
their personal as well as in their creative lives. They "were good Europeans, but they were also split personalities, divorced from the people

among whom they were living."[64] This split, he believed, may account for their inability to produce truly great works in literature or the arts, which required popular and national roots. In science, which knows no national frontiers, the Jews made great contributions. Whether Jewish contributions in literature or art actually fell short of first-rank quality could be challenged, but Laqueur's point about the profound split in Jewish intellectual life is well taken. It was felt by most Jewish intellectuals, even by those who, like Einstein and Freud, had made the greatest contributions to science. It is revealing to examine this split in the lives of these two scientists, especially the life and work of Freud because the psychologist by virtue of his psychoanalytical training provided an existential testimony that could not be equalled by a natural scientist.

Both Einstein and Freud were secularized Jews who struggled for many years, the former as a humble patent clerk in Zürich and the latter as a professionally isolated psychiatrist in Vienna, before they made their dramatic breakthroughs as scientists. Both proved that truth transcends culture because, on a higher level, it informs us about the natural world or the human condition; both men, however, became the brunt of Judeophobic criticisms that sought to invalidate their work because of its supposed Jewish origin. In the 1920s Einstein was exposed periodically to ugly attacks on both his person and his reputation. Jew-haters, in fact, made it a point to wait for his appearance at the Kaiser Wilhelm Institute and shout: "Jew-Science." His mailbox was filled with letters attacking his Jewishness. At one point, a gang of right-wing students disrupted his lecture at the University of Berlin, with one student shouting, "I'm going to cut the throat of that dirty Jew."[65] Attacking the relativity principle as a false Jewish principle, a group of pseudo-scientists calling themselves the Working Committee of German Natural Philosophy rented the Berlin Philharmonic Hall for a series of lectures aimed at exposing the "Einstein Hoax." Einstein was a man with a large heart and a great sense of humor who laughed off some of this silliness. To show that he was not intimidated by the antics of his detractors, he even rented a box at Philharmonic Hall and laughed at the proofs offered to invalidate his findings. Yet, even the self-deprecating Einstein had to admit that the Judeophobes got under his skin with their invectives, making it difficult for him to do his work. At one point, a demented Judeophobe even made a public threat on his life by offering a reward to anyone who would kill the scientist. It was a mark of the unreformed conservative legal system that Rudolph Leber, who had made this threat on Einstein's life, merely received a slap on the wrist by having to pay a paltry fine of sixteen dollars.[66]

What German nationalists with Judeophobic beliefs resented in Einstein, who became their favorite whipping boy, was what they hated in all intellectuals who questioned the foundation of their rigid worldview. Einstein, in Frederic Grunfeld's judgment, "robbed the German public of something it regarded as essential to its well-being — the categorical absolute that dinner is at seven and all's right with the world."[67] As previously shown, Germans had a positive aversion to what was culturally unfamiliar. They had made "nonacceptance of the unfamiliar" a normative response when confronted with different beliefs or lifestyles. Many Jews, on the other hand, were often indifferent to assumed eternal social truths or to the rigid German authorities that were trying to maintain them. Opposition to revealed social truths manifested itself early in the lives of many young German Jews, particularly at school. Einstein was constantly troubled as a student by the "convict atmosphere" and the "self-opinionated tone and customs"[68] of the German school system, where students were bullied, regimented, and often publicly humiliated by teachers who had taken on the habits of drill sergeants. For an uprooted Jew who also had a strong will to follow his own creative inclinations, there was no place in such a system; consequently, he did poorly in everything except mathematics and was dismissed from the Luitpold Gymnasium in Munich because his presence in class was disruptive and supposedly contaminated other students. We know the rest of the story. Einstein finished his education in Switzerland, continued to follow his "fanatical desire to be a free spirit," distrusted received scientific authority, and made his earthshaking discoveries in physics. It may well be that his Jewishness, combined with his natural tendency toward independent-minded thinking, made him particularly susceptible to the ambiguities of time and space that were the psychological prerequisite for understanding relativity.

Freud lived a more withdrawn existence in Vienna, but he, too, had been exposed to anti-Jewish prejudices all of his life, both as a student and as a professional man. Like Einstein, Freud was a secularized Jew who rejected all religions because he believed them to be illusions. Although his wife, Martha Bernays, had been brought up in a strict Jewish home, Freud refused to have anything to do with Orthodox Judaism. To his critics, however, Freud became a Jew precisely at the point where his doctrines became controversial. His work on infantile sexuality, for example, exposed him to vicious attacks, many of them with strong anti-Jewish coloration. He was accused of undermining Christian morality, and his psychoanalytical method, which was largely championed by Jewish psychologists (Karl Abraham, Max Eitington, Alfred Adler, Hanns Sachs, Wilhelm Reich), was widely rejected as a "Jewish Science." One conservative scholar said dismissingly: "What else do we need to know about Freudianism than that it was invented by a Jew?"[69] This sort of crude comment, of course, could be discounted, but far more painful was the reaction of Carl Jung, Freud's non-Jewish former comrade-in-arms and anointed crown prince, who, in the 1930s, appeared to flutter into the Nazi orbit, associated himself with a Nazi-controlled journal of psychiatry, and delivered weighty pronouncements that the Aryan unconscious has a higher potential than the Jewish and that it is a "quite unpardonable mistake to accept the conclusions of a Jewish psychology as generally valid."[70]

Such anti-Jewish attacks, which must have been a source of great anguish to Freud and Einstein, go to the very heart of the German-Jewish split; they also go to the heart of Jewish self-identity. In the case of Einstein, Freud, and many other intellectuals, such persistent anti-Jewish prejudices merely heightened their consciousness of being Jewish, at least in the sense of feeling Jewish or becoming more actively involved in organizations that promoted the interests of Jews. On January 6, 1927, the *Israelitisches Familienblatt* showed a picture of the Berlin Founding Congress of the Pro-Palestine Committee. Albert Einstein, along with Leo Baeck, was one of the figures in the photograph.[71] As early as 1895 Freud had joined the B'nai B'rith Society, a fraternal Jewish organization, in order to find social contacts with people who came from similar Jewish backgrounds and were tolerant of a broad range of opinions.[72] It indicates that Freud felt himself to be Jewish in the sense of sharing a cultural affinity with Jewish history and suffering. In Peter Gay's estimate, this identification was Freud's own solution to the problem of Jewish self-identity; it was a kind of "defiant pride" in being Jewish. Was it any more than that? Was there in Freud's work itself, discounting the obvious anti-Jewish libels, something that was indeed genuinely "Jewish," in addition to being archetypal or universal? The answer to this enormously complicated question is probably in the affirmative, and this may also provide an answer to Peter Gay's question of whether the German Jew's self-definition as a German was nothing more than a degrading infatuation.[73] The German-Austrian cultural situation, with its great intellectual accomplishments *and* its wretched and dark underside, was the indispensable condition that made Freudian psychoanalysis possible.

In 1926, Freud reportedly confessed to a German-American interviewer, George Sylvester Viereck, that "my language is German. My Culture, my attainments are German. I considered myself German intellectually, until I noticed the growth of anti-Semitic prejudice in Germany and German Austria. Since that time, I prefer to call myself a Jew."[74] It was not only his self-definition as a Jew that was molded by his Austrian-German surroundings but also his essential cast of mind, his ironic detachment as a critical outsider, and his penetrating dissections of cultural and political mystifications. Vienna, the city in which Freud grew to intellectual maturity, was a city of glaring contrasts: on the surface it was stage-managed, as it still is today by its tourist authorities, as a romantic city of Strauss waltzes, cafés, rich pastries, and carefree *Gemütlichkeit*. Beneath the surface, however, Vienna was a magnified Freudian psyche, a seething cauldron of instinctual and cultural dissonances.[75] Vienna was the capital of the Austro-Hungarian empire and royal seat of the House of Habsburg, one of the few remaining dynasties in Europe that did not rule over a homogeneous geographic, cultural

or ethnic nation. Rather the empire was made up of a disparate group
of ethnic minorities stretching over a geographical sprawl that at one
time included lands from the Baltic to the Black Sea, to the Carpathian
Mountains, to that hotbed of ethnic strife — the Balkans. The Habs-
burgs were originally archdukes of Austria, but their power was vastly
augmented when they inherited the title of Holy Roman Emperor in
the Middle Ages, a title they retained until Napoleon put an end to
the Holy Roman Empire in 1806. They continued to rule as emperors
of Austria and kings of Hungary throughout the nineteenth century,
tenaciously clinging to their dreams of imperial glory in an age of nationalistic ferment. The capital city mirrored the ethnic, linguistic and
religious tensions of this polyglot empire; it resembled a frozen monument curiously out of step with the forces of modernity. The head of the
Habsburg empire, Franz Josef (1848–1916), had ascended the throne in
1848 and lived long enough to witness the First World War that would
destroy his empire.

A visitor to the Austrian capital, then as now, cannot help but be
struck by the officially stage-managed style of grandeur. Both the Hofburg (the imperial palace) and the "little" country *Schloss* (palace) on
the edge of Vienna called Schloss Schönbrunn are huge, flamboyant,
and grandiose, yet, to the discerning visitors, more of a stage set than
places where people actually lived. It is in these stage sets that we meet
the people who, in retrospect, were so out of touch with reality. Of
special interest to the Freudian mind, of course, is Franz Josef, a man
who made a fetish of honor and duty, but had no visible sense of direction and apparently no sense of humor at all. In A. J. P. Taylor's
suggestive insight, he had one great and dubious strength, and that was
Sitzfleisch, or a tough behind.[76] He assumed that by sitting at least eight
hours behind his desk and signing documents he could make the empire work, trusting in official grandeur and his fifty odd titles — one
of which was "Duke of Auschwitz" — to do the rest. In A. J. P. Taylor's judgment, the fading luster of the baroque Austrian empire was
"grandiose, full of superficial life, yet sterile within; it was theater,
not reality."[77]

Not too far from the Hofburg, where the old emperor was pouring
over documents and holding "audiences," a different reality was coming into being at Berggasse 19, for it was here that Sigmund Freud,
revolutionized psychology and discredited the superstitions that were
still bolstering the authority of Franz Josef and the civilization he represented. It is instructive to ponder the role of these two men, especially
after one has visited both the Hofburg and Berggasse 19, to visualize
both the stodgy emperor and the creative genius living contemporane-
ously and in close proximity to each other, yet so far removed in their
perception of reality. The visitor to the Hofburg will notice that the emperor was in the habit of granting audiences, and one can still see the old
lectern with an audience book that recorded the names and signatures.

A copy of a list of such a royal audience shows the name of Sigmund Freud and it can still be found at the Freud Museum at Berggasse 19; it dates back to about 1902 when Freud, following an audience, received the title of "Professor Extraordinarius," a splendid title that, however, did not include a university chair. Freud later jokingly said that it was as though the emperor had officially "recognized the role of sexuality, and the Cabinet ratified the interpretation of dreams, or the necessity of psychoanalytical therapy in the treatment of hysteria had been passed by Parliament with a two-thirds majority."[78]

In reality Freud had invalidated the authority of the emperor and much more — all of which brings us to the heart of the Jewish-German symbiosis. Freud had seen behind the veil of illusion. He had gone to its psychological roots; and by so doing, he was playing with fire and stealing it from the gods. His Jewishness played no insignificant part in this drama, for it heightened his critical perception of the duality of existence in the Austria-Hungarian empire in general and civilization in particular. His joke about the "recognition of sexuality" presaged, of course, the furor that would later rage about his role in having unleashed a force that threatened the very foundation of a culture based on guilt and aggression, a Caucasian morality that in the words of Karl Kraus, the *enfant terrible* of Jewish-Austrian satire, had "built iron-clad ships but was performing a ritual dance round the fetish of the hymen."[79] In sum, a culture that had, in large degree, celebrated the death instinct, had made a fetish of aggression and death, could not easily countenance the liberation of sexuality; and it would further follow that the bearers of the old guilt culture would marshal every effort to defend such a culture against its detractors, especially if one of their leading intellects was a Jew.

Freud's life and career was an odyssey of self-discovery in which his sense of Jewishness constituted an indispensable part but in which the Austrian-German background also provided the psychological conditions that furnished him with the clues by which he tried to find the answers to human deception, suffering, and unhappiness. It could be argued that Freud's psychoanalytical method was his particular instrument of wrestling with his own deception and the deception of others; by using it he could perhaps unlock the hidden (veiled) causes of human suffering. That it was a historical method should not surprise us. Immersed in a city that lived in the past and drew strength from it, conscious of a Jewish heritage that connected him to a four-thousand-year tradition, Freud probably could not help but think historically. As Philip Rieff reminds us, Freud always seemed to collapse not only the present but also the future into the past.[80] The known does not arise from new experiences but from the remembered; in fact, the event of decisive importance has already happened in the past, either in the form of suffering and alienation experienced by the human race when it made that fateful transition from primitivism to civilization, free-flowing eros to civilizational repression, or in the form of individual repression suffered by its members in childhood. In both cases the repression occurred in the past and now squats in the unconscious from which it supplies both private and public history with its dynamic element. The recovery of such unconscious knowledge from the past by way of historical reenactment becomes the key to alleviating human suffering.

Freud's deep awareness of the tragic element in history, validated for him by both his Jewish and his German background, prevented him from following an optimistic path; in other words, awareness that we can become only what we have already been forecloses belief in radical change or salvation. This does not mean, however, that Freud was an unconditional pessimist who believed in endless historical recurrence. He was, after all, an heir of the Enlightenment who strongly believed that the human race had moved from barbarism to civilization, from killer to humanist, but he also believed that the human psyche was biologically and psychologically invariable (fixed) in its essential functions. Both the life instinct (*eros*) and the death instinct (*thanatos*) are in perpetual tension, so that regressions to the basest primitivism are to be expected as normal and routine in human history. War is therefore an intimate part in the circular motion of history, for it flows from an inclination to aggression that is original, self-subsisting, and instinctual in humans.[81] We are therefore condemned to live with our past; and the extent to which we come to terms with it will affect our mental health. Neurosis is the failure to escape from the past; and since all of us can never completely escape from our past, it would follow that we are, in varying degrees, neurotic. Although neurosis is a universal condition and therefore cannot be eliminated, the suffering it entails is treatable and can be psychologically alleviated. Freud was in this sense a cautious developmental progressive who believed that psychoanalysis could alleviate suffering by adjusting us to its reality, which was very much the belief of the mature Enlightenment and its hope in incremental progress through scientific humanism. As a clinician, Freud tried to free the patients from the burden of the past but not from the past itself, which will always hang on their shoulders.

Freud's affinity for history was not the only quality in his intellectual make-up that he may have owed to his Jewish self-consciousness; another was his highly developed analytical ability to strip the world of its illusions. What really counts in Freud is not the outer event but the *milieu interieur* — the substratum of psychic forces that shapes its exterior behavior. In other words, the outer event, individual or historical, operates in terms of its inner psychological articulations. These inner and largely unconscious forces provide the clue to the unfolding of the external event. Knowledge of things past, which provides the clues to things to come, resides in decoding and understanding those hidden unconscious forces that inhibit mature ego development and libidinal functioning. The past and its repressed events provide the answer to both the present and the future. Although Freud shared this model of time with Marx, his own prospective vision was different in that it delivered a pessimistic prognosis. Marx had secularized the Judeo-Christian millenarian tradition within the historical process itself. Freud, on the other hand, refrained from taking a utopian leap out of history in order to escape from its evidential record. We can only speculate why Freud remained so stubbornly resistant to "ultimate" answers, but it could be argued that it had a great deal to do with his Jewishness, his psychological resistance to utopian ideals, and his stoic temperament. This is why he ultimately viewed life as a little island of pain floating in a sea of indifference. This is why he also avoided the temptation of offering easy therapeutic answers to complex psychological problems. In fact, the expert on dreams counseled us to stop dreaming illusions and to limit ourselves to realizable goals that are consonant with our weaknesses, limitations, and talents.

The *Aufklärer* in Freud always wanted to confirm the world rationally, to strip it of its mystifications, and to educate individuals to its immutable conditions. As a stoic, he labored under no illusion that humans could perfect the world and find a cure for suffering; yet, as a psychologist, he also recognized the psychological need that drives individuals and societies to seek a cure for suffering. Investing hope in this psychological need is not misplaced if it stays within the bounds imposed on us by our limitations. And as Freud pondered the problems of his time, cognizant of the dangers that were approaching from all sides, he realized that the party of the Enlightenment would once again be forced on the defensive as the mass of people defected from its program and escaped into mass illusions. The gathering clouds of Nazi fanaticism indicated to Freud that hateful impulses had been aroused that would not so easily be repressed, and that the illusions all too many Germans were embracing were bound to lead to a collective hysteria with brutal consequences.

How was one to confront this impending irrationality? By continuing the work of Enlightenment? By marshalling one's forces and organizing resistance? By passively and patiently waiting until this latest anti-Jewish storm, just like all the others before it, had blown itself out? Freud himself continued his work of spreading Enlightenment even while his country was betraying it. That Freud's scientific work with its humanistic underpinnings had been conceived and sprouted roots, however feeble in its time and place, attests to the fact that the German-Jewish symbiosis was not an illusion but a viable possibility. That it was cut short was due to the fact that the roots of Enlightenment were not strong or deep enough to withstand the onslaught of irrationality. The triumph of the Nazi movement in Germany was possible because the Germans had lost belief in the universal human values of reason, love, compassion, and mutual toleration.

The Jewish Response to Judeophobia

The gathering of Judeophobic prejudices impinged upon the lives of most Jews; no one, including Freud or Einstein, was immune from being touched by it. In Germany one could not ignore the noisy and increasingly strident street thugs of the SA who delighted in provoking anti-Jewish outrages throughout the 1920s, outrages that became commonplace during the last few years of the declining republic. Hitler and his storm troopers believed in deliberate provocation; their tactics may be described as blatantly provocative, as this battle hymn of the SA clearly illustrates:

> Ihr Sturmkollonnen jung und alt;
> Nehmt die Waffen in die Hand
> Denn die Juden hausen fürchterlich
> Im deutschen Vaterland.

> Wenn der Sturmsoldat in's Feuer geht,
> Ja, dann hat er frohen Mut,
> Denn wenn das Judenblut vom Messer spritzt
> Dann geht's noch mal so gut.

> You storm troopers, both young and old
> Put weapons in your hand;
> For the Jews wreak havoc fearfully
> In the German Fatherland

> When the storm trooper comes under fire
> He feels courageous cheer,
> For when the Jews' blood spurts from the knife
> Good times are once more here.[82]

The antics of the Nazis could be and often were written off by Germans and Jews as the rantings of a noisy minority that had made Judeophobia the center of its political program. In the 1920s most Germans were more preoccupied with the economic, social, and political consequences of the war than they were with the Jewish question. It was not until the economic depression of 1929 and the political disintegration of the republic associated with it that Judeophobia gathered momentum, attached itself to the Nazi bandwagon, and subsequently continued to play a major role in German public life. Yet, even before 1929, as previously shown, Judeophobia played an important role in German society, certainly significant enough in its dangerous implications that German Jews felt it necessary to marshal opposition and to organize resistance. Since the early 1920s many Jews had kept a careful watch on the activities of right-wing nationalistic groups, especially Adolf Hitler and the Nazi Party. They knew very well that one of the major points of the Nazi program (point 4), publicly proclaimed on February 24, 1920, was that no Jews could be German citizens because they were not "racially" Germans.[83] In 1920, of course, most Jews did not know Adolf Hitler and the Nazi Party; by 1929, however, many of them knew very well who he was and what might be expected from him if he gained power. By 1932, when the Nazi Party had become the largest party in the state, few Jews had any remaining doubts as to what could be expected from the Nazis.

In that year Rabbi Alfred Wiener, writing in the pages of the *Centralverein Zeitung* (July 24, 1932), used the following headline question to alert his readers to the Nazi peril: "Programmerfüllung oder Agitation: Was würde eine Hitler Mehrheit tun?" (Fulfillment of a program or agitation: What would a Hitler majority do?). Wiener pulled no punches by warning his fellow Jews that "should the Third Reich come, then farewell to justice and prosperity, farewell to public spiritedness and free enterprise."[84]

Alfred Wiener was a member of the largest defense organization representing the Jews of Germany: the Centralverein Deutscher Staatsbürger Jüdischen Glaubens (Central Association of German Citizens of the Jewish Faith). Founded in 1893, the Centralverein (CV) was the first Jewish organization explicitly developed for the purpose of fighting Judeophobia, protecting the civil rights of Jews, and promoting the cause of Jewish-German self-identity. In the postwar years membership in the Centralverein fluctuated between sixty and seventy thousand, which was about 14 percent of the Jewish population in Germany. The Centralverein, however, claimed to represent almost 90 percent of German Jewry.[85] The driving force behind it consisted largely of socially active members of the free professions (lawyers, doctors, journalists, writers, businessmen) and students. The association also published its own paper, originally called *Im deutschen Reich* but renamed, after amalgamating with the *Allgemeine Zeitung des Judentums,* as *Centralverein Zeitung* (Central Association News). During the frenetic campaigns of the dying republic, the Centralverein published hundreds of books, distributed leaflets, and organized public forums aimed at enlightening German citizens about the life of real as opposed to imaginary Jews in German society. Again and again, the Centralverein documented the contributions Jews had made to German society and culture and refuted the lies that were still told about Jews by their opponents, ranging from the distortions of the Talmud, ritual child murder, and conspiratorial plots, to accusations of cowardly conduct by Jews during World War I. In trying to dispel the accusation that Jews were disloyal to Germany, Alfred Wiener pointedly asserted during a Jewish protest meeting in 1930 that "if there were a Nobel Prize for Germanism, the Jews of Germany would be the recipients."[86]

In addition to waging a program of public enlightenment, the Centralverein also tried to work through the German legal system in order to protect Jewish rights and reputations. Lawyers of the Centralverein, using paragraphs 130 and 165 of the German penal code (Strafgesetzbuch) dealing with personal and religious libel, scored a number of successes against blatant Judeophobes. The leading Judeo-phobic publisher Theodor Fritsch, along with several leading Nazis such as Joseph Goebbels, Gregor Strasser, Robert Ley, Karl Holz, and Julius Streicher, were ordered to pay minor fines for libeling Jewish individu-als.[87] The German legal system, as previously shown, was in the hands of conservative judges who disliked the democratic republic and often sided with its sworn enemies. On several occasions the legal system dis-played blatant anti-Jewish prejudices in its decisions. Although the law had made it an offense "publicly to vilify the constitutionally established form of government," the Supreme Court in 1923 found nothing wrong with epithets such as: "Jew republic! Shame, Jew republic!" because "the new legal and social order in Germany...was brought about in significant measure by German and foreign Jews."[88] The legal system was therefore a double-edged sword, quite apart from the fact that it often generously offered the publicity-hungry Nazis a public forum for their prejudices.

A second major defensive organization representing German Jews was the Reichsbund jüdischer Frontsoldaten (Reich League for Jewish Frontline Soldiers), founded on February 8, 1919, by forty Jewish vet-erans of World War I under the leadership of Captain Leo Löwenstein, who had distinguished himself during the war by developing a sonar de-vice for the military. Its original purpose was to defend the honor of Jewish soldiers against the Judeophobic accusation that the Jews had been *Drückebergers,* or shirkers, who avoided military service, especially on the front line. Although the organization officially tried to avoid get-ting entangled in the internal religious activities of German Jews, it went on record on several occasions that it opposed the divisive efforts of the Zionists because they threatened to alienate the German Jews from their homeland. The Reichsbund was a cautious and conservative or-ganization that avoided following a militant strategy, except on those occasions when Jewish veterans had been explicitly maligned. For ex-ample, it sued Hitler's mentor, Dietrich Eckart, over a boast he had made publicly that he would pay a thousand marks to anyone who could prove that a Jewish family had given three sons to the fighting front for a minimum of three weeks. The Reichsbund submitted dozens of names, took Eckart to court, and had him pay up.[89] Such successes, however, were rare and largely symbolic. Numerically the Reichsbund was a small but well-organized association of about 30,000 members, 14,000 youthful followers, 360 regional offices, and a central periodical called *Der Schild.*[90]

Another defensive organization with strong conservative views was the Verband Nationaldeutscher Juden (League of Nationalistic German Jews), founded in 1921 by Max Neumann, formerly a reserve officer in the German army. The organization followed its leader's belief that anti-Jewish prejudices stemmed from the perception that Jews were different from Germans. This being so, Jews must therefore prove that they were as loyal, patriotic, and nationalistic as the Germans. Neumann rejected both the Zionists and the *Ostjuden* because they reinforced the traditional negative image of the alien Jew, and he exhorted German Jews to give up being half-German and to become hundred-percent Germans.[91] Initially, Neumann admired the Nazis for their nationalistic convictions; he even tried to reach an accommodation with them, only to discover what every Jewish group was forced to recognize eventually, namely, that the Nazis had to reject Jewish support because they had demonized the Jews as a racial enemy.

For a loyal, patriotic, and conservative Jew, this was indeed a stunning and painful discovery, as illustrated by the young German Jewish youth leader Hans-Joachim Schoeps (1909–80). Young Schoeps came from a prosperous middle-class family of Prussian Jews who had become fully assimilated during the Kaiserreich and had brought up their son to think and feel as a German. Born in 1909, Schoeps missed the "front experience" but not its postwar effects. Like so many young patriotic Germans, he identified with the spirit of camaraderie shared by the veterans of the war, many of whom had also been part of the popular youth movements of the prewar period.[92] Always a bit of a rebel and fond of the company of young men, Schoeps was searching for something more meaningful than the regimented routine of middle-class existence. His search for identity, at once sexual and intellectual, took place very much within a typically conservative middle-class framework: it involved a generational rebellion against the bourgeois life of his parents, an escape into the neo-romantic world of the youth movement with its homoerotic and fraternal bonds, involvement in student fraternities at the university, and immersion in philosophical and religious worldviews. At the University of Heidelberg, Schoeps's forceful personality, Germanic good-looks, and intellectual depth attracted much attention; in 1930 he founded a new youth organization, Freideutsche Kameradschaft (Free German Comradeship) deep in a forest in Thuringia, while at the same time writing articles rejecting materialism and exhorting his young followers to seek existential meaning by turning inward to the spiritual.[93] If the Nazis had not come to power in Germany, Schoeps would probably have enjoyed a successful academic career no different from any other German scholar of his generation. Feeling himself to be a conservative German more than a Jew, he disregarded the danger signals coming from the Nazi camp; he even wrote off National Socialism in the early 1930s as being "of little difference."[94] When the Nazis made a big difference in 1933, he still believed that he could parley with them and receive their seal of approval for his newly founded Deutscher Vortrupp (German Vanguard), a conservative, authoritarian association of Jews who shared most of the Nazi ideology except its Judeophobia. As John Dippel has written, the "problem for Schoeps and other ultrapatriotic Jews was that they represented exactly what the Nazis did not want — a Jewry so in love with Germany they could not bear the thought of leaving it."[95] This was certainly true of Schoeps, whose bright academic career was cut short by the Nazis; he had to flee for his life in 1938.

Schoeps was by no means a rare exception to the way many German Jews saw social reality and responded to it. Jews often founded their own parallel institutions with essentially the same aims as their German counterparts, except for their anti-Jewishness. In view of the Nazi danger, many historians have later wondered why these German Jews were so naive or blind or both. The historian's temptation is to point out, with the benefit of hindsight, what they should have done but did not do; but as one German Jew has responded to such retrodictions, "Hinterher ist es leicht, weise zu erscheinen" — (In hindsight it is easy to appear wise).[96] Who could have known in 1933 what would happen at Auschwitz in 1943? Georg Salzberger, a rabbi from Frankfurt who survived the Holocaust, wrote about the problem of Jewish foreknowledge: "There were indications, yes. But not an expressed anti-Semitism. One could lead a normal life until 1933 when Hitler came to power, then everything changed. None of us could guess what his coming to power meant."[97] It is always useful to keep such reactions in mind, if only to correct a natural inclination to tell a story so internally consistent that only one outcome could have been expected. That most German Jews did not expect to become victims of genocide and acted upon the expectation that it was unthinkable is an important part of their history and must therefore be recorded on their behalf.

While the Jews of Germany did not misjudge the danger of Judeophobia, they certainly underestimated its intensity. Their organizations were too weak and too poorly coordinated to make much of a difference, reflecting the fact that German Jewry was not a very cohesive and self-consciously Jewish entity. Its members were not only well assimilated, but also highly diverse in their professional, intellectual, political, and religious convictions. Their defense organizations were equally diverse and sometimes internally divided, barely managing to find common ground even while all of them came under attack by the Nazis. Moreover, their leaders, with few exceptions, were timid men whose response to the danger of Judeophobia was generally to counsel patience and perseverance.

The Zionists were the exception to this rule. Robert Weltsch, Martin Buber, Kurt Blumenfeld, and Gershom Scholem accepted the *völkisch* belief that the Jews were a separate *Volk*, a different people, and that their real emancipation was not only from the ghetto but also from the lure of German or any other nationality. Such an emancipation, however, required emigration to Palestine. The Zionists believed, in short, that the Jews were ethnically different and would remain rootless and unwanted on German soil.[98] They accused the "German Jews" of flailing against windmills and sneered at their "wait-and-see" tactics, afterward congratulating themselves that their assessment of the German situation had been vindicated. Yet even the Zionists were not as far-seeing as they afterward claimed to be. Even those German Jews who had moved from a policy of total assimilation to one of total rejection carried too much German cultural baggage with them to live and act out their Zionist convictions. This explains why, despite their avowed goal to emigrate to Palestine, only two thousand German Jews had moved to Palestine by 1933.[99] Emigration to Palestine, with its inherent political obstacles, was not seen by most German Zionists as a realistic option for the majority of German Jews; it was, at best, a possible choice for those Jews who were willing to uproot themselves and had the patience and courage required to get there and stay there. Robert Weltsch, editor of the Zionist *Jüdische Rundschau,* and Karl Blumenfeld, president of the Zionist Federation, advised a flexible policy that saw emigration as a future possibility only and focused its efforts on organizing German Jews in such a way that they would eventually settle for an unassimilated existence in Germany. Their belief that this was possible and their own misreading of the Nazi peril show that they were no more prescient than other German Jews. It was not until late 1931, with the discovery of secret Nazi documents that revealed that Hitler intended to destroy the Jews, that leading Zionists woke up to the danger of Nazism, and yet even then they still discounted the possibility of a Nazi takeover or the dire consequences predicted if such a takeover did in fact occur. In retrospect, was Jewish confidence in the decency of German institutions and traditions completely misplaced? How intense was Judeophobia before Hitler and the Nazis manipulated it with all the power of a modern state at their command?

How Intense Was Judeophobia during the Weimar Period?

One of the most contentious controversies in recent years has centered on the question of how many "ordinary" Germans shared Hitler's obsession that the Jews were Germany's archenemies and must therefore either be expelled from Germany or be annihilated. On one end of the spectrum are those historians who agree that Judeophobia was never more than the obsession of a small but noisy group of Jew-haters who played an insignificant role in German life and culture until the Nazis seized power and turned their anti-Jewish obsessions into a public policy. These historians contend that Judeophobia was never more than a minor nuisance in either the Kaiserreich or the Weimar Republic. Although there were a few parties during the Wilhelmine period that had made "anti-Semitism" their primary mission, these parties never gained more than 1 percent of the popular vote and eventually faded into obscurity. Except for the Nazi Party, which was also a marginal racist party until 1930, no major party that made "anti-Semitism" an integral part of its program gained significant votes during the Weimar Republíc. Even during the years of its chaotic birth, it is pointed out, the entire Judeophobic vote never exceeded 8 percent of the total.[100] Moreover, it is often held that German voters were far more concerned with the cancer of inflation and unemployment, Germany's reduction to a third-rate power, the Versailles Treaty, or the threat of communism. It cannot be automatically assumed that everybody who voted for the Nazis hated the Jews.[101] If the political culture was not Judeophobic, these historians argue, the same is true for Germany's intellectual culture. Sarah Gordon, for example, insists that Germany's cultural heritage was not uniformly anti-Jewish, and she points out that even the conservative Prussian system was committed to upholding the law that guaranteed legal equality to all Jews. Between 1869 and 1933, she reminds us, not a single law was passed that rescinded Jewish rights.[102] During the Weimar Republic, according to these historians, radical Judeophobia was a virtual monopoly of the Nazis. The Weimar Republic, in Eugene Davidson's estimate, was an "open society with a high degree of religious toleration where political anti-Semitism had faded away to nothing."[103]

On the opposite side of the spectrum are those historians who argue that rabid Jew-hatred was deeply embedded in German life and culture for centuries. At its most radical, this argument, which was popular in Anglo-American circles during World War II, assumed that Germany had long deviated from the liberal and humane traditions of the western world and had institutionalized strident militaristic, antidemocratic, and imperialistic values with strong Judeophobic overtones. Among the historians who have advocated the theory of a German *Sonderweg* (special path), as it was later dubbed, are Peter Viereck, Edmund Vermeil, Rohan Butler, A. J. P. Taylor, and William Shirer.[104] These writers discovered a pattern of aggression in German history that inevitably led to Adolf Hitler. The Third Reich, with all its horrors, was for them simply "a logical continuation of German history";[105] and the Germans, as A. J. P. Taylor described them, "have always been exterminators and...no other people has pursued extermination as a permanent policy." From this it would follow, if Taylor is to be believed, that the Holocaust represented the deepest wishes of the German people.[106]

Such views, of course, are no longer fashionable in a world where former enemies have become friends, and so it is somewhat surprising that these Germanophobic views have recently resurfaced in several studies, most notably in Daniel Jonah Goldhagen's controversial book *Hitler's Willing Executioners: Ordinary Germans and the Holocaust* (1996). In this book, Goldhagen argues that "eliminationist" anti-Semitism was a central part of Germany's cultural heritage; it was taken in by ordinary Germans like "mother's milk."[107] Nazi anti-Semitism was integral to the beliefs of ordinary Germans and was widespread among all social classes. When the Holocaust was finally perpetrated, the Nazis had no trouble finding willing executioners whose crime became, so to speak, a sort of "national project."[108] Putting it sardonically, just as the

Egyptians built pyramids, the Germans built concentration camps and gas ovens.

Provocation or hyperbole, for whatever reason, is sometimes a useful means of shedding light on the truth. There is some truth embodied in all of these studies. The Holocaust did not emerge by spontaneous combustion: the roots of hate were deep and broad long before the Nazis made it a state mandate. Judeophobia was part of the German cultural tradition, and it had broad popular support. On the other hand, as previously shown, there were different types of Judeophobia expressing themselves in varying forms of intensity. Anti-Jewish prejudices, in other words, were not all cut out of the same cloth. Consider, for example, the different stereotypical images held by Germans at various times, some seeing the Jew as an economic bloodsucker, a subversive "cultural Bolshevik," an alien presence, a racial inferior, a Christ-killer, or simply a social inferior. The fusion of these images into a constellation or syndrome so that it became the central obsession of a Jew-hater's waking existence constitutes the sort of delusionary thinking that is essential for genocidal action.

How many Germans really shared this Hitlerian delusion? This is a question that must be constantly kept in mind, but it is also a question, I would contend, that cannot be conclusively answered. The reason for this is that hatreds, irrationalities, delusions, and similar mental states cannot be measured precisely because we cannot objectively determine what is on people's minds. Recourse to intellectual approaches that probe into the minds of Jew-haters, analyze various cultural traditions, or even focus on a "national" mind, mentality, habitus, or character shed important light on the problem but do not resolve it. The same is true of more quantitative approaches that seek to measure the phenomenon of Judeophobia by focusing on measurable units such as electoral votes, public opinion surveys, data pertaining to the mass marketing of books, newspapers, or periodicals, content analysis of speeches or public documents, and so forth. Since Judeophobia eludes exact measurement, this does not mean we should not try to measure it; similarly, since it also eludes exact cultural understanding, this does not mean we should give up using traditional methods of intellectual history in trying to explain it. Using all available tools, what can we conclude about the nature, scope, and intensity of Judeophobia during the Weimar Republic?

In trying to measure Judeophobia, four criteria have to be observed relating to its source, expression, intensity, and extent: where did it come from? how and by what means was it expressed? how violent was it? and how many people were won over by it? The sources of Judeophobia, dating back to the Middle Ages, have already been explored. These were religious, economic, political, cultural, and racial, varying in intensity over time, waxing and waning, but retaining strong popular support and, in some cases, showing disturbing pathological signs.

World War I and the chaotic years that followed led to a noticeable increase in pathological Judeophobia. In the previous chapter, extensive documentation has been provided to illustrate that this was true in radical right-wing circles. To what extent was this also true for other groups and for German society as a whole?

As this chapter has shown, the Jews of Germany were subject to two important facts of life: on the one hand they continued to receive the legal protection of the state, a state now also sworn to uphold a broad range of democratic rights, but on the other hand they experienced, in one form or another, constant reminders that they were alien and unwanted in Germany. Jewish self-identity, in all its ambiguity, was defined by the uncertainty produced by those two forces. Jews continued to be exposed to all sorts of anti-Jewish prejudices and actions in the form of name-calling, discrimination by employers or government officials, libelous attacks on their personal character and integrity (*Verleumdung und Beleidigung*), physical assault, desecration of synagogues or Jewish cemeteries, vandalism, and public riots. From an institutional point of view, anti-Jewish prejudices were strongly entrenched in the army, the civil service, law enforcement agencies, and the school system.

A great deal has already been said about the increase of Judeophobia in the military during World War I and its mutation into pathological Jew-hatred in the Free Corps and various right-wing ex-servicemen's associations. To realize how inhospitable the military was to German Jews, one should ponder the statistical fact that for most of the Weimar period there were less than a dozen Jews in the *Reichswehr* (German armed forces); in 1931, for example, there were only eight Jews in the German army and none was an officer.[109] A lot of embittered racists could also be found in the police forces of various German cities. The Hamburg police force heavily recruited its members from Free Corps units. According to one historian, most members of the Hamburg Ordnungspolizei came from a Free Corps called Schleswig Holstein.[110] The leaders of Germany's law enforcement agencies were generally conservative, if not reactionary, in their political persuasions.[111] Even the Berlin police force, which was under the control of the Social Democrats, was never democratized; its officers displayed marked conservative, reactionary, and often anti-Jewish attitudes. The same was true of the legal establishment, which harbored blatant anti-Jewish judges, perhaps not of the "rowdy" sort one could find among the ranks of Nazi storm troopers but more "cultivated" Judeophobes who preferred to cover their prejudices behind euphemistic legal phrases or supercilious, mendacious, or dismissive attitudes. The school system was also a very unfriendly institution for Jews. Michael Müller-Claudius observed in 1927 that there was not a single classroom in Germany where Jewish students were not constantly exposed to hostile and degrading remarks.[112] University students were especially susceptible to anti-Jewish prejudices throughout the 1920s. The universities remained as unreformed and antidemocratic as the army or the civil service; they were bastions of institutionalized conservatism and elitism. Access was still restricted to the upper classes and to graduates of the elite Gymnasia, while overall control remained in the hands of state authorities with decidedly authoritarian tendencies.

From the beginning to the end of the republic, there was continuous, at times even disruptive, Judeophobia in academia, exacerbated by the fact that academic positions, and jobs in general, were extremely scarce in the 1920s. There was also the perception that too many Jews attended universities out of all proportion to their standing in German society. Student associations repeatedly demanded quotas (*numerus clausus*) for Jews, limiting their enrollments to the number corresponding to their percentage of the population. The Nazis scored astonishing successes in student council elections in the late 1920s. In 1919 students at the University of Munich cheered at the news that Kurt Eisner had been assassinated; in 1920 a memorial service for Walther Rathenau, who had been assassinated by three young Jew-haters, had to be canceled at the University of Berlin because students threatened to disrupt it. In fairness, it should be recorded, however, that one million Berliners turned out publicly to mourn their fallen leader. In 1927 the Prussian student union took a poll that asked its members whether Jews should be allowed to join the union; the answer was ominous: 77 percent voted no.[113]

After the great Nazi breakthrough in the elections of September 14, 1930, anti-Jewish disruptions at German universities became commonplace. In 1931 anti-Jewish riots erupted in Vienna, Berlin, Cologne, Greifswald, Halle, Hamburg, Breslau, Kiel, Königsberg, and Munich.[114] On January 22, 1932 anti-Jewish students at the University of Berlin attacked members of the Jewish fraternity K. C. Sprevia with whips and leather belts, seriously injuring a number of the badly outnumbered Jewish students. Although the rector called the police and cleared the university, similar attacks on Jewish students were staged over the next four days, despite assurances from the authorities that such disruptions would not be tolerated. In the fall of 1932 students at the University of Breslau, supported by local SA storm troopers, tried to make good on a boast that had been made for some time in radical right-wing circles that no German student should sit at the feet of a Jewish teacher.[115] The students vented their Judeophobic spleen on Professor Ernst Cohn, a young legal scholar at the university, by shouting and chanting anti-Jewish epithets during his lectures. For weeks he was brutally shouted down by thuggish students, but he persevered in hopes that the furor of his appointment would die down and that his colleagues would rally to his cause. That this did not happen illustrates that the German professoriat, in addition to its unpolitical attitudes, harbored strong anti-Jewish prejudices. Although the Centralverein spent an inordinate amount of time on Cohn's case, regarding it as a textbook example of academic freedom, their efforts were undercut by the university authorities who relieved Cohn of his duty on the pretext that he had involved himself in political issues by telling the press that, under certain circumstances, he favored political asylum for Trotsky in Germany.[116]

Cohn's case reveals that anti-Jewish students had plenty of support from their anti-Jewish teachers. The argument made by some that the German professoriat was not anti-Jewish is seriously flawed. Professors were "cultivated anti-Semites" and, in a number of prominent cases, vocal Judeophobes. They rarely stood up to aroused students in either supporting appointments of outstanding Jewish professors or in defending their Jewish colleagues. The resignation of Richard Willstätter, the Nobel laureate in chemistry, from his university position in 1924 is a case in point.[117] As dean of the faculty at the University of Munich, he found himself at the center of ugly anti-Jewish outbursts in the early 1920s, with students breaking into faculty meetings and demanding the removal of Jewish professors. But what led to Willstätter's decision to resign was not so much the Jewish prejudices of the students but those of his colleagues. In 1924 the name of Viktor Goldschmidt, an outstanding geochemist, was proposed as a successor to Willstätter's colleague Paul von Groth, who was retiring from the University of Munich. Willstätter was an enthusiastic supporter of Goldschmidt, but he quickly discovered that his colleagues' resistance to Goldschmidt's appointment was not based on academic but on racist grounds. After considerable backdoor politics, the faculty voted down Goldschmidt's appointment on the pretext that he was a foreigner. Willstätter promptly resigned, stunning both his colleagues and his students. His resignation, he insisted, was based on principle and was irrevocable; he could not go along with a faculty that felt it necessary to make allowances for the "anti-Jewish tendencies of the times" because it sought to avoid disturbances at the university. Willstätter was the first Jewish intellectual who went into "internal exile" because of institutional racism.

It is important to document the prehistory of Judeophobic thinking in the German academy, if only to dispel once more the notion, comforting to intellectuals, that delusionary thinking is a virtual monopoly of the uneducated. The facts belie this assumption. Racial ideals were enthusiastically championed by numerous German professors. The new rector of the University of Berlin, Wilhelm His, revealed in his inaugural address that he was a firm advocate of racial hygiene.[118] According to Robert Proctor,

> Many of the leading institutes and courses on *Rassenhygiene* and *Rassenkunde* were established at German universities long before the Nazi rise to power. And by 1932 it is fair to say that racial hygiene became a scientific orthodoxy in the German medical community. In the winter semester of 1932–33, racial hygiene was taught in twenty-six separate courses of lectures in the medical faculties of most German universities.[119]

But it was not in medicine alone that this ideological obsession was being taught; it was also promoted by the anthropologist Hans F. K.

Günther and the philosopher Max Wundt at the University of Jena, the sociologist Johann Plenge at the University of Münster, the Berlin jurist E. von Möller, and the philosopher Hermann Schwarz at the University of Greifswald.[120] It is true that these outspoken anti-Jewish professors were not necessarily representative of the whole professoriat, but there can be no denying that their views were tolerated by their colleagues and widely shared by a new crop of radicalized students.

In addition to these institutional forms of Judeophobia one can also document the occurrence of numerous "hate crimes" in the form of desecrations of Jewish cemeteries and synagogues throughout the 1920s. It is instructive to read contemporary Jewish publications documenting the occurrence of such outrages. The Centralverein meticulously recorded hundreds of *Friedhofsschändungen* (desecrations of cemeteries) between 1923 and 1932;[121] similar records were kept by the Association to Resist Anti-Semitism. Although no pogroms occurred during the Weimar Republic, there were several riots and anti-Jewish provocations that could have easily degenerated into pogroms if the authorities had not intervened. In early November of 1923, anti-Jewish riots erupted in the Scheunerviertel in Berlin, where many Jews lived and worked. In a portent of Kristallnacht, howling mobs smashed Jewish store windows and ransacked their premises, screaming "kill the Jews."[122] In the same month, numerous Jews were attacked during the Hitler putsch in Munich. Nazi thugs picked apartments at random simply because their occupants had Jewish-sounding names such as Löwenthal, Löwenstein, Herz, or Crailsheimer; they then proceeded to ransack the premises and intimidated or beat up their owners.[123] Hitler's SA thugs chose their hostages from the telephone books, picking Jewish-sounding names and dispatching their storm troopers to pick them up. Rudolf Hess, in addition to "arresting" practically the whole Bavarian cabinet, also held the Jewish banker Ludwig Wassermann as a hostage and showered him with Judeophobic epithets.

It was a portent of things to come. Eight years later, when the Nazis already smelled victory, they picked the first day of the Jewish New Year, September 12, 1931, to schedule a pogrom against Berlin Jews. The plan, worked out by SA Leaders Count Helldorf and Karl Ernst, called for an ambush of Jewish worshipers on the Kurfürstendamm; but when the Nazi thugs appeared on the fashionable avenue, most Jewish worshipers had already gone home, which did not, however, deter the SA thugs from attacking "Jewish-looking" passersby, most of them, as it turned out, being Romanians or Armenians.[124] The repercussions of this incident are significant on three accounts: German pedestrians who witnessed the event were not particularly outraged and did not interfere; the police made only token gestures to round up a few suspects; and the courts subsequently cleared those few arrested suspects of any wrongdoing.[125] The fact that a court trial was held at all, of course, demonstrates that Germany was still a legal state in which citizens were guaranteed full civil rights, but that state was hurtling rapidly toward catastrophe under the impact of the depression and renewed political fanaticism.

Only two months after this incident in Berlin, compromising secret Nazi documents were released to the Frankfurt police which revealed what the Nazis planned to do in case of a national emergency. Drafted by the Hesse *Gauleitung* at a farmstead, the Boxheimer Hof, these documents outlined the emergency measures that were to be put into operation when the Nazis came to power and faced a communist takeover. These "Boxheim" documents revealed in no uncertain terms what might be in store for Germans once the Nazis had gained power: ruthless totalitarian control, seizure of state ministries by the SA, and death penalties for a variety of infractions. The documents also showed what was in store for the Jews: mass starvation and expulsion.

Hitler, of course, disavowed all knowledge of these documents and tried to distance himself from the radical proposals they contained. Being on the verge of political success, he could ill afford revelations of the truth, which was that his party was determined, given the right opportunity, to do exactly what the Boxheim papers proposed. In the meantime, he played his chameleon-like game with such consummate skill that he hoodwinked important business groups in German society into believing that his anti-Jewish policies were simply designed to diminish Jewish prominence in German society and that he had no intention of attacking Jewish persons as such. Yet, Robert Weltsch and other prominent Jews who read the Boxheim documents were shaken to the depths; they realized that this was not just demagogic phrase-mongering designed to gain political control, but a carefully crafted strategy for a future Nazi state.[126]

The Reich Supreme Court (*Reichsgericht*) suspended proceedings against the author of the Boxheim papers, Werner Best, on the grounds that these plans merely represented an exercise in utopian thinking. Such a political misjudgment illustrates once again that Germany's institutions were failing to protect the democratic republic against its sworn enemies; and, unable to fend off the threat against itself, it is not surprising that the republic was unable to defend the rights of a small Jewish minority residing within its jurisdiction. This degeneration of the democratic process illustrates the dilemma faced by those who supported the republic and its democratic constitution. It was among the ranks of the supporters of the republic that the Jews found their strongest allies. The parties of the moderate middle — the Democratic Party, the Center Party, and the German People's Party — strongly championed Jewish civil rights and opposed all forms of Judeophobia. By 1932, however, the moderate middle had virtually ceased to exist as a major factor in German politics. The parties of the left were adamantly opposed to Judeophobia, but they, too, were losing ground to the extreme right and despised each other almost as much as they did the Nazis. Historically, the leadership of the Communist and Social Democratic Parties was strongly opposed to all forms of Judeophobia, but this attitude did not always extend to the rank-and-file, who often associated Jews with capitalism and who also feared competition from Jewish immigrants (*Ostjuden*). The left was captive to its class-conscious mentality that saw Judeophobia almost wholly in economic terms — that is, connected to the economic interests of capitalist exploiters who used Jew-hatred as a means to deflect the attention of the working class from their economic hardships. Still, German workers with strong socialist convictions were never won over to the cause of Nazi Judeophobia.

As for the churches, their official position was to fight for the rights of their own believers before taking up the fight for anyone else. Like the many special interest groups and parties, the churches were self-concerned and often insulated within their own clerical walls. When outrages against Jews were committed from time to time, the church slept and rarely woke up.[127] German churches would perpetuate such self-defeating habits into the Third Reich, waking up too late to change the tragic outcome. Within the evangelical church itself a split had opened up when a noisy minority, calling itself "German Christians" (*Deutsche Christen*), accepted *völkisch* ideas that had convinced them that Jesus was an Aryan. The church as a whole, however, was strongly opposed to such anti-Jewish notions and continued to affirm the belief that redemption originally came from the Jews. Neither the Evangelical nor the Roman Catholic Church, along with the majority of their members, ever affirmed any violent form of Judeophobia that involved depriving Jews of their rights, expelling them from Germany, or annihilating them. Unfortunately, the churches never mustered enough political strength or courage to protect the civil rights of their own members, let alone the rights of their Jewish fellow citizens.

This, of course, was true of all civilized parties and groups in Germany; their differences proved stronger than their commitment to the common defense of civilized values. In the dying years of the republic, the political weight shifted away from the democratic left and middle to the extreme right, from a willingness to experiment with democracy to a strong collective desire for authoritarian control. Hitler was the beneficiary of this momentous shift; his political genius consisted in mobilizing the many discontents and in winning the support of apparently incompatible social groups. He knew that voting patterns in an age of mass democracy were shaped not only by class affiliation but by group prejudices. He reasoned that if he could successfully nationalize the masses, indoctrinating them with ethnic prejudices, he could effectively diffuse economic divisions and reintegrate heterogeneous elements into one national community (*Volksgemeinschaft*). He was right. Between 1923 and 1933 he created the basis for such a mass party (*Sammelpartei*), a concept so novel that it completely eluded the class conscious thinking of his political opponents, especially on the political left. Electoral patterns reveal that Hitler's appeal cut across all class boundaries; it was especially strong among middle- and upper-middle-class sections of society.[128] The thesis that Hitler drew most of his support from the lower middle class, from socially and economically displaced and marginalized *Kleinbürger*, is no longer tenable.[129]

The truth is that Hitler enjoyed widespread support from all sections of society; and though it is also true that the highest vote he ever received in a free election was only 37.3 percent — that is, only three out of every eight votes — that margin was higher than that of any other party, enough to enable him to gain the momentum he needed in order to break down his opponents and take the key to the chancellery. What came to Hitler's aid was the flawed split in the republic and its culture, specifically the mediocre leadership of opposition parties, the defects of the Weimar constitution, the universal hatred of the Versailles Treaty, a growing mood for authoritarian leadership, and a defection of key members of the ruling elite. Capitalizing on the tactical superiority of his party and his own manipulative talents, Hitler simply outwitted the only group that could still block him in 1932: the conservative clique around President Hindenburg. Once having done so, Hitler took a mere eighteen months to eliminate his most serious opposition and to set up the means of totalitarian control: police, government institutions, mass media, the economy, and the armed forces.

Germans who voted for Hitler were often more concerned about inflation and unemployment, the danger of communism, and the status of their nation than they were about the Jews. In retrospect, however, it is clear that a vote for Hitler was a vote against the Jews. It is impossible to determine how many Germans were fully aware of this fact in 1932. Whatever the answer, Hitler could draw upon a strong reservoir of German Judeophobia and exploit it for his own ends — the elimination, by whatever means, of Jews from German society. How far the German people were willing to support him in this policy would depend on their perception of his goals and their personal support and loyalty to him as their leader.

Chapter 6

The Nazi Racial State

Race and Politics

In a series of rambling monologues with various Nazi insiders, later reconstructed by Hermann Rauschning, the President of the Danzig Senate, Adolf Hitler freely ventilated a number of racial fantasies and obsessions that he would shortly try to implement in the Third Reich. At the time these conversations took place (1932–34), Hitler's racial ideas found a certain resonance with Rauschning, a conservative landowner and *völkisch* politician; but unlike other members of his class, Rauschning became quickly disillusioned by Nazism, fled the country in 1935, and published two penetrating studies (*Revolution of Nihilism* in 1938 and *Conversations with Hitler* in 1939) that captured the destructive essence of Nazism with a remarkable degree of accuracy. Rauschning's conversations with Hitler not only faithfully mirrored the Führer's racial obsessions but also captured the demonic essence of the man, including voice tone, facial gestures, and other disturbing mannerisms. In a curious and ironic sort of way, Rauschning's conversations with Hitler invalidated the main argument of his book *Revolution of Nihilism* that Nazism had no substance apart from its relentless need to oppress and dominate. The conversations with Hitler clearly belie this assumption, for they reveal that Hitler and his group were strongly motivated by a metaphysical racial belief that, while deluded and destructive, was anything but nihilistic.

A constant thread that runs through these bizarre conversations was Hitler's belief that the Jews represented the principle of evil in the world. He reminded Rauschning that the existence of Jewish evil could be comprehended only in racial terms; in fact, the key political questions of our time, he insisted, required a knowledge of "biological politics."[1] He wished that this salient fact were widely accepted, but he also confessed that only a handful of people, including himself and Julius Streicher, were fully alert to the global significance of racial issues. He believed that Streicher was doing the right thing in heightening popular consciousness of racial issues in the pages of *Der Stürmer,* but this was only the first step in the coming battle for racial world supremacy that would be conducted between German and Jew. As far as Hitler was concerned, the real political questions of the future were racial: "everything else is deceptive reality [*trügerischer Schein*]. Behind England, behind France, behind the USA squats Israel. Even when we have succeeded in expelling the Jew from Germany, he still remains our world enemy."[2]

When Rauschning asked whether this meant that the Jew should be eliminated completely, Hitler's sinister reply was: "No, we would then have to invent him. One needs a visible enemy, not just an invisible one."[3] He explained that the Roman Catholic Church, whose organizations and propagandistic techniques he greatly admired, had never been satisfied with the devil alone, but periodically focused on visible demons. As he put it, "the Jew always squats in us, but it is easier to fight him in physical form rather than as an invisible demon."[4] Hitler confided that he was on to this Jewish devil in all of his manifestations, revealing to Rauschning that he was absolutely convinced of the genuineness of the *Protocols of the Elders of Zion.* "There cannot be two chosen people," Hitler insisted. "We are the people of God. Doesn't this say everything?" Surely, Rauschning interjected, this talk about chosen people could only be taken symbolically. No, Hitler replied, "it is a basic reality one cannot evade. Two worlds stand opposed to each other! The God Man and the Satanic Man. The Jew is the Counter Man, the Anti-Man. The Jew is the creation of a different God. He must have grown from a different root of the human tribe. If I put the Aryan next to the Jew and call the former a man, then I have to call the other by another name. They are as far apart as the animal is from the human. Not that I want to call the Jew an animal. He is farther removed from the animal than the Aryan. He is a being foreign to nature and removed from nature [*ein naturfremdes und naturfernes Wesen*]."[5]

After this animated outburst on the essence of the Jew, Rauschning observed that Hitler wanted to say a few more things, but, judging from the "intensity of his overwrought face, his language failed him." His face, according to Rauschning, was "convulsively distorted." He cracked his knuckles in agitation and stammered that on this subject of Jews one could never learn enough. In another "discussion," which was, like all of Hitler's conversations, little more than a monologue, the Führer made it quite clear that he would root out the Jewish poison through appropriate state policies. He would practice biological politics and produce a new God-like human being in the form of New Aryan Man.[6] Indeed, if there was a genuine Nazi revolution, it did not reside in conventional socioeconomic changes but in the application of pseudoscientific racial principles to German life and culture. Hitler's political program consisted in the institutionalization of racial-biological principles through totalitarian means. The essence of all twentieth-century totalitarian regimes, of course, has resided in their claim that they would produce new revolutionary types of human beings — the New Soviet Man, the New Chinese Man, the New Cuban Man, but the new Nazi type of man was to be the product of biological rather than socioeconomic changes. He was to be genetically engineered rather than environmentally produced; his nature was to be biologically nurtured. All totalitarian regimes have aimed at human standardization; the Nazi regime aimed at racial standardization.[7] As Hitler told Rauschning, the aim of the Nazi racial state was to produce a new Godlike human being. This is why National Socialism was more than just a political movement, even "more than a religion; it is the will to create a new man."

Inside Germany, such fantastic ideas were taken very seriously not only by Hitler but by a growing number of racial enthusiasts who wanted to purify the German race by eliminating from its gene pool all harmful elements that had been injected into it by such poisonous carriers as the mentally ill, people with hereditary diseases, homosexuals, and alien inferiors — Gypsies, Slavs, and Jews. These racial fanatics, insinuating themselves into important positions in the party, in various state agencies, and in academic and medical circles, tried to develop a new standard by which human worth was to be measured. As it turned out, it was a pseudoscientific superstition, an essentially irrational standard that divided the human race into a new *scala naturae,* at the apex of which perched the Aryan race and at the bottom squatted the Jewish anti-race, the deadly bacillus that undermined all healthy races. By the standards of this new racial Darwinism, for the Nazis grafted race theories on popular notions of Social Darwinism, the Nazis abolished the principles of the French Revolution that had served as a shining beacon to human freedom and human dignity. As Joseph Goebbels, the Nazi propaganda minister, put it in a radio address to the German people on April 1, 1933, the day the regime announced a boycott against Jewish goods: "The year 1789 is hereby eradicated from history."[8]

In cancelling the principles of 1789 the Nazis actually believed that they could begin to heal the social and cultural divisions these "subversive" principles had allegedly contributed toward the weakening of German society and its defeat in World War I. They associated democracy and the whole democratic way of life with the economic interests of the wealthy (plutocracy) and the immersion in selfish materialism and decadent lifestyles. In their eyes, democracy was the invention of Jewish plutocrats whose real aim was to exploit, weaken, and destroy the German people. The Nazis equally despised communism because it, too, was an outgrowth of the "false" principles of 1789, except that it pandered to the working classes by offering them a deceptive message of economic equality in a one-party system. Some of the more conspiratorially minded Nazis, Hitler included, saw in both democratic capitalism and communism a common thread: the subversive influence of the Jews, who were manipulating the two systems for their own design, namely, the destruction of all nationalistic and ethnic cultures and their replacement by international Jewry.

Yet, it was not only Hitler and his Nazi followers who rejected the two contending political movements of the twentieth century. The conservative political and intellectual community shared with the Nazis similar antidemocratic convictions, which it expressed in equally strident nationalistic and imperialistic rhetoric.[9] The only difference was that the conservatives were traditional elitists whose wealth and social standing made them suspicious of the leveling doctrines preached by the left wing within the Nazi Party. On most issues, however, Nazis and conservatives found much common ground; they both rallied behind *völkisch* appeals to blood and soil, the need for strong authoritarian leadership, motherhood and family, German greatness, and the virtues of discipline, hard work, and sacrifice to the nation. The Nazi revolution, in fact, had largely depended on an antecedent conservative counterrevolution that had already rejected democracy as both an ineffectual style of governance and an inferior way of life.

Among people of Hindenburg's generation and their younger camp followers — men like Heinrich Brüning, General Kurt von Schleicher, Franz von Papen, Edgar J. Jung — western democracy represented a totally ineffective instrument of governance because it encouraged political divisiveness to the point of paralysis and prevented the implementation of nationally beneficial goals. These men believed that the guardians of the nation should not have to submit themselves to the shifting and conflicting claims and counterclaims of selfish interest groups and parties; they should function as nonpartisan state civil servants, empowered by the authoritarian state, preferably in monarchical form, to make decisions based on expertise rather than party affiliation or economic self-interest. The conservative elite put its trust in the authoritarian civil service state, a state in which they tried to persuade themselves decisions would be made by dedicated, well-educated, and nonpartisan *Beamten* (civil servants) who placed the good of the country over the good of any party. The role of parliament, in their view, should be restricted to the formulation of legislative rules, while the executive function should be in the hands of an authoritarian government and its administrative branch — the civil service and the army.

The conservatives not only undermined Weimar democracy; they also conspired behind the backs of the German electorate to appoint Hitler to the chancellorship, hoping to use the popular dynamism of Nazism as a means of consolidating their own antidemocratic counterrevolution. They quickly discovered, however, that Hitler refused to become a pliant pawn; rather, he quickly checkmated their political strategies with a few bold moves. Although their own revolution had gone awry, the conservative elite became quickly corrupted by the political or military positions Hitler tossed their way. So long as Hitler kept his radical brownshirts in abeyance, which he certainly did after the Röhm purge, rearmed the nation, restored economic prosperity, smashed communist opposition, created the appearance of Germanic greatness — even if it was cinematic illusion — as long as Hitler was able to do these things, the conservatives could fool themselves into believing that the Nazi revolution had also been a conservative revolution. It was only when Hitler's war was failing and the full impact of Nazi tyranny began to impinge directly on their lives and careers that the traditional elites began to defect, but by that time it was too late. Except for a few early defections and ineffective protests, the conservative elite remained loyal to the Nazi state and, above all, loyal to an authoritarian value system that made a fetish out of obedience to higher authority, technical rationality, and martial virtues.

The traditional elites, it was true, were sometimes perturbed by the pseudodemocratic slogans the Nazis used when they claimed that they had created a harmonious community of the people (*Volksgemeinschaft*) in which past divisions had been resolved and leadership was firmly exercised by a popular charismatic Führer who represented the sovereign will of the people. These rhetorical shibboleths could be easily disregarded, particularly since the Nazis themselves were often unabashedly honest in trumpeting their elitist convictions. Their elitism, of course, was of a slightly different form because, outwardly at least, it claimed to be based on race rather than class. Doctrines of racial superiority were flattering and attractive to many Germans, especially to those who had been weaned on *völkisch* beliefs, as so many conservative-minded Germans had been for well over a generation. Racial doctrines also served as a means of social integration, as a political strategy by which real social problems could be obscured under the cover of empty slogans that were designed to bolster collective self-esteem. National Socialism was largely a system of such a smoke-and-mirror approach to social reality because it invented shared enemies (Jews, communists, liberals, pacifists, Gypsies, Jehovah's Witnesses) and covered up social problems by using such integrative strategies as extreme nationalism, racism, welfare statism, artificially contrived crusades, and war. What was not smoke and mirror, however, was the brutal reality of a sociopathic leadership and a terroristic police system to browbeat everyone into line who opposed these official deceptions and delusions.

In tracing the trajectory that led to the Holocaust, the most significant delusion in the Nazi system was also its most revolutionary component — race. The Nazi leadership pursued racial politics in ways that went far beyond rhetoric or integrative social strategies. Racism was a metaphysical belief system that rejected the essential equality of all humans and affirmed, to the contrary, that inequality among racial groups was an inherent fact of life. Racists offered no scientific evidence for this belief other than their convictions that Aryans were racially and therefore also culturally superior to Jews, blacks, or Asians. Intense self-serving ethnocentric conviction generally substituted for rational scientific proof. Failing to convince by rational argument, Nazi racial fanatics retreated to the proposition that might makes right, that Aryans

are superior because they have superior force on their side. In short,
Nazi racists measured superiority by ethnocentric convictions and the
rule of force: they believed themselves to be superior and tried to prove
it by bludgeoning their opponents into submission by superior force.

It would be a mistake, however, to assume that such brutal attitudes
revealed themselves for the evil they really stood for; on the contrary,
racist beliefs were taught as noble ideals that required the support of
idealistic, dedicated, and honest people. The Nazi regime tried to instill,
especially in young people, the ideal of a homogeneous racial community that had been purged of all alien elements and had succeeded in
producing a new race of supermen (*Übermenschen*), for only in this
way could the nation's military might be reconstructed, the defeat in
World War I avenged, and the Thousand-Year Reich attained. In teaching these amorphous and grandiose ideas, which were always pitched
in the highest key of idealism, the Nazi regime found many enthusiastic believers. It did so because many Germans had lived through more
than a decade of crisis, could look back to years of economic hardship and suffering, and saw in Nazism a movement of regeneration and
hope. It did so also because its rhetoric appealed especially to young
people, to their sense of self-sacrifice and their longing to find meaning in life. What few Germans saw at the time was that Hitler, who
seemed to embody these longings, was actually channeling the idealism
of German youth into brutal and warlike ends, exploiting an already
perverted form of militarism, revitalizing tribal nationalism by grafting
onto it a biological-racial dimension, romanticizing cruelty and irrationality, and carrying authoritarianism to its ultimate conclusion —
blind obedience.

The Nazis cloaked these perversions under the cover of lofty ideals
and seductive rhetoric. Hitler was a combination of soldier-politician
and artist who had a keen eye for the aesthetic and who knew that
persuasion required conversion, and that such conversion, at its deeper
psychological level, was emotional rather than cerebral.[10] Hence the
constant, indeed relentless, appeals to masses of people; hence also the
persistent efforts to strip Germans of their individuality and to seduce
them into believing the officially proclaimed mythology.

The most dangerous delusion in this politics of mass seduction, dangerous because it destroyed German and Jew alike, was the myth of
Aryan racial supremacy. Belief in this myth not only fueled the war
against the Jews but also the assault on people with mental or physical
disabilities, on Gypsies, black "Rhineland Bastards," homosexuals, and
later also on Slavs and other "Asiatic inferiors," except the Japanese
who became "honorary Aryans." As previously shown, racial beliefs
had been "respectable," especially in right-wing intellectual circles since
the late nineteenth century, but it was not until the Nazi seizure of
power in 1933 that these racial beliefs were officially sponsored and
publicly institutionalized by a modern technocratic state that was being

quickly transformed into a totalitarian state with all the features typically associated with it: a charismatic dictator, a single mass party, a terroristic police force, a mass media monopoly, a weapons monopoly, and a planned economy.[11]

A great deal has been written about the Nazi state, and historians have offered conflicting judgments as to whether it was a dual state, a totalitarian state, a polyocracy of competing private empires, an old-fashioned tyranny, or even a nonstate comparable to past oriental courts or sultanates.[12] Some historians have even wondered whether Hitler was actually in charge of the institutions of the Third Reich, claiming that he was a weak and ineffectual leader who was relatively absent in his government, was unable to deal with routine bureaucratic tasks, encouraged endless competition and rivalry, and thus caused a vast amount of wasted energy and sufficient confusion to have cost him his victory.[13] Such attempts to downplay the role of Hitler in the Third Reich will forever be doomed to failure. Nazi Germany was a one-man dictatorship, and as such it enjoyed widespread popular support and loyalty — so much so, that Hitler's power was never seriously challenged, not even in July of 1944 when a small and ineffectual group of officers miserably failed in killing the dictator and in galvanizing public opposition against him. As Norman Rich rightly put it, "Hitler was master in the Third Reich."[14] It is true, of course, that Hitler delegated power to a host of subsidiary Führers, that he encouraged competition among his chief paladins, even caused inefficiency and confusion, but his power was always recognized as inviolable by the vast majority who served under him. German soldiers, civil servants, and all those who served in any Nazi organization swore a personal oath to him, which meant that they agreed unconditionally to carry out any order he might issue, and that, it would turn out, involved many criminal orders. The supremacy of *Führergewalt* (Führer power) over *Staatsgewalt* (state power) was accepted by those who served in the Nazi system as a prescriptive principle of statecraft, the result being a virtual dismantling of the legal state (*Rechtsstaat*) based on precedent and the rule of law in favor of individual power that was not bound by the norms of law and public morality.[15]

What this meant was that racial politics were dictated from the beginning by Adolf Hitler himself; and given his hatred of Jews, he immediately assumed a firm role in directing anti-Jewish policies with what has been aptly described as a combination of cold calculation and blind fury.[16] Hitler also galvanized and encouraged countless subordinates in both the state and party to organize racial policies.

In 1933, of course, Hitler did not have a definitive master plan, ready to be taken off the shelf and dictated uniformly to all party or state agencies. The Nazi seizure of power not only involved a power struggle with traditional institutions such as opposition parties, the military, the conservative bureaucracy, labor unions, and churches, but it also involved intense intramural battles between various factions and personalities in the Nazi movement itself. These internal struggles revolved around Röhm and his plans for a revolutionary army of SA brownshirts, left-wing Nazis who were intent on changing the economy to bring it into line with "real" National Socialism, *völkisch* enthusiasts who preached utopian panaceas of rustic arcadias, or psychopathic or Machiavellian opportunists who tried to build up their own empires in the new Nazi state (Goebbels, Himmler, Heydrich, Göring, Rosenberg, Hess). It took several years to sort out these struggles, although the revolutionary techniques of trying to construct the Nazi state had emerged as early as March 31, 1933, when the new government passed a law called Temporary Law for Coordination (*Gleichschaltung*) of the States with the Reich. This law introduced the term *Gleichschaltung* into the political vocabulary, which referred to the Nazi strategy of coordinating or "synchronizing" all German institutions with the goals and objectives of National Socialism.[17] Named after an electronic device called a *Gleichrichter* (synchronizer), which allows electric current to flow in only one direction, *Gleichschaltung* was designed to nazify all German institutions in order to produce the ideal of the totalitarian state in which everyone thinks the same. *Gleichschaltung* proceeded along two related paths: synchronization of all government institutions and mass mobilization of citizens for the National Socialist cause; the first involved the eradication of all political parties and the second the creation of mass organizations for mass control.

Historians have argued endlessly and needlessly whether nazification actually succeeded in breaking down all opposition and achieving its totalitarian goal. No regime, however revolutionary, can tear out the pages of one thousand years of Christian civilization in just twelve years. Added to this obvious historical obstacle to complete nazification were two other inherent limitations that prevented the Nazis from successfully carrying out their racial and imperialistic fantasies, and that was the fact that the Nazi leaders were sociopathic and that their faith was a combination of ideological delusion and murderous pseudoscience. For all these reasons, the Nazis never fully approximated their totalitarian goal of absolute control; what is surprising, given the interaction of irrational ideas and psychopathic personalities, is how close their radical policies actually came to turning reality upside down. This was especially true in the field of racial policy, where a consensus of belief, if not always a policy of coordinated action, quickly developed among the leading figures of the Third Reich and their supporters in the party, academia, big business, the military, and the population at large. Despite the loose direction from the top and the apparent confusion and competition that developed between various contending agencies — Justice, Interior, the party branches (SA, SS, Propaganda), the army, or Göring's Four-Year Plan — there was a spirit of shared belief that, on racial issues, usually transcended personal or institutional rivalry. As Raul Hilberg correctly saw it, "in the final analysis the destruction of Jews was not so much a product of law and commands as it was a matter of spirit, of shared comprehension, of consonance and synchronization."[18]

The racial beliefs of the Nazis, as Benno Müller-Hill has written, can be summarized in a few basic propositions, namely, that "there is a biological basis for the diversity of Mankind. What makes a Jew a Jew, a Gypsy a Gypsy, an asocial individual asocial, and the mentally abnormal abnormal is in their blood, that is to say in their genes."[19] Müller-Hill's work on "murderous science," along with several other recent works on the implication of German doctors in the Nazi enterprise, have documented the fact that the German medical community enthusiastically supported the Nazi racist vision of improving the racial quality of the German people. As previously shown, this racial belief had been upheld since the late nineteenth century. At that time, various racial thinkers had sounded shrill alarms that Germany, indeed all of Europe, was being biologically degraded by too many inferior breeds who were reproducing their own kind at an alarmingly higher rate than people from good racial stock. Although the early racial hygienists were not racists in the Nazi sense of the term, nor did they subscribe to a common political ideology, their political sympathies definitely leaned to the *völkisch* right. Among their ranks could be found such prominent figures as Friedrich Lehmann, the chief publisher of racial books in Germany; Alfred Ploetz, the founding father of German racial science; and well-known biologists such as Fritz Lenz, Eugen Fischer, Hermann Muckermann, and Otmar von Verschuer. Their most prominent intellectual or scientific center was the Kaiser Wilhelm Institute for Anthropology, Human Genetics, and Eugenics; it was headed by Eugen Fischer, who professed a passionate belief in racially perfecting the German people.

The Nazis grafted themselves onto already existing doctrines of racial hygiene by promoting its aims through political means. In the words of Rudolf Hess, Hitler's deputy, National Socialism was basically "applied racial science."[20] This explained why the Nazis looked to the academic world, especially the medical community, for support in translating their ideological beliefs into scientific fact. Thus, when the Nazis assumed control over the instruments of power, they immediately coordinated the medical and pharmaceutical professions and organized them hierarchically according to the leadership principle. As Führer of the League of Reich Physicians they picked Gerhard Wagner, a strong advocate of sterilization, euthanasia, and racial laws prohibiting miscegenation. Wagner mobilized the medical community into redirecting the aim of German medicine from the one-on-one relationship that had characterized the relationship between doctor and patient, to a community-oriented program based on racial hygiene. Medical journals were coordinated and expected to reflect the new ideological orientation. The journal *Ziel und Weg* (Goal and Path) became the ideological standard for all medical journals as well as the mouthpiece of Nazi racial policy.

In 1933 Dr. Walter Gross established a new racial office called Office of Public Enlightenment on Population Politics and Racial Hygiene,. renamed on May 1, 1934, as Racial-Political Office (Rassenpolitisches Amt). Headed throughout the Third Reich by Gross, the Racial-Political Office became one of the most important racial agencies because it formulated racial programs and laws, notably the Nuremberg Racial Laws, and issued the certificates of ancestry that had become mandatory for party employment. In addition, Gross's office conducted a variety of propaganda campaigns in order to heighten public awareness of the need for strict racial controls. The Racial-Political Office also published a popular magazine, *Neues Volk* (New people), and an in-house informational journal called *Informationsdienst* (Information service) designed to keep medical practitioners abreast of the latest medical developments in the area of racial hygiene. The importance of this racial office to the Third Reich may be gauged by the sheer intensity of its propagandistic activities. After only four years in existence, according to Robert Proctor, the Racial-Political Office sponsored sixty-four thousand public meetings and thousands of eight-day conferences in which some four thousand party members participated. It also tried to shape public opinion with a staff of thirty-six hundred employees and an affiliated journal that enjoyed a mass circulation of as many as three hundred thousand copies per issue.[21]

On June 28, 1933, the minister of the interior, Wilhelm Frick, established the Expert Committee for Population and Racial Policy, which was composed of the most important racists in the Third Reich, including SS chief Heinrich Himmler, the minister of agriculture Walther Darré, and Reich physician leader Wagner. The committee also contained famous academics such as Fritz Lenz and Alfred Ploetz, along with important ministerial officials such as Friedrich Burgdörfer, director of the Reich Office for Statistics, and Arthur Gütt, head of the Public Health section in the Ministry of the Interior. Although the committee did not become a major instrument for the implementation of racial policies, it acted as an important catalyst for drafting racial legislation, most notably the formulation of the sterilization law that went into effect on July 14, 1933. Entitled Law for the Prevention of Progeny with Hereditary Diseases (Gesetz zur Verhütung erbkranken Nachwuchses), the new racial law provided that individuals could be sterilized if, in the opinion of a genetic health court, they suffered from certain specified genetic diseases. The categories of genetic illnesses, however, were so sweeping and scientifically ambiguous that many people, otherwise perfectly healthy, could be sterilized. Nine types of "illnesses" were listed: congenital feeblemindedness, schizophrenia, manic-depressive insanity, hereditary epilepsy, Huntington's chorea, hereditary blindness, deafness, serious physical deformities, and, as an addendum to the list, chronic alcoholism.

Beginning with the sterilization law the German medical community was the first group to initiate that fatal step that would lead, by a series of ever more radical increments, to genocidal actions against "lives not worth living." The first victims were the "feebleminded" or anyone who had been designated by the officials of the Hereditary Health Courts to be afflicted with mental-physical disabilities that were likely to contaminate the racial health of the German people. These Hereditary Health Courts, like most of the emerging Nazi agencies, were immune from public scrutiny and staffed, for the most part, by zealous and arrogant officials who saw themselves as the gatekeepers of a new racial science aimed at perfecting the Aryan race.[22] It is estimated that close to four hundred thousand people received the "Hitler-cut" (*Hitlerschnitt*) — vasectomy for men and tubal ligation for women — between 1933 and the fall of 1939.[23] The Nazi racial fanatics, however, did not stop with such preliminary measures but pushed their radical agenda into the broad political arena by passing racial legislation against "racial pollution" and race defilement and ultimately setting in motion the annihilation of biological inferiors — Gypsies, "asocials," homosexuals, the mentally ill, Slavic subhumans, and Jews.

Unlike a liberal state, which protects the weak, the handicapped, and ethnic minorities, the Nazi racial state was dedicated to the opposite ideal of ridding itself of such social groups because they supposedly undermined the racial purity of the German people. Although a host of leading Nazis such as Goebbels, Streicher, Rosenberg, and Darré, assisted by a swarm of dedicated bureaucrats, advocacy groups, and research institutes, toiled away to implement various racial fantasies, the real instrument of racial destruction, the institution that, more than any other, was responsible for devising a clear-cut annihilatory racial policy, was the most racist institution in Nazi Germany: the SS. This is why, in Karl Schleunes's correct estimation, the "development of a clearly defined Jewish policy parallels very closely the development of the SS."[24]

The SS: Instrument of Totalitarian Control and Racial Destruction

The SS (Schutzstaffel, or Protective Squadron), founded in 1923, was originally an elite paramilitary organization of the Nazi Party whose primary function was to protect the Führer from his political enemies. From a small group of bodyguards initially subject to the much larger SA (Sturmabteilung, storm troopers), the SS developed into a party police force, a terrorist Reich police force, a regular army within the army commanding its own forces, the armed SS (Waffen-SS), a huge economic conglomerate with its tentacles reaching deeply into big business in Germany and later in the conquered territories, and a gigantic murder machine that supervised a far-flung system of concentration camps in which people were tortured and annihilated.[25] Without this instrument of terror the Nazis would have lacked the intense racial fanaticism, calculated cruelty, and organizational framework that was required for the successful annihilation of the Jews and other victims. The SS incubus, like the Nazi Party itself, had been planted in Bavaria in the 1920s, and it was a pudgy, short, unathletic, myopic, and balding Bavarian, Heinrich Himmler, who built up this initially small force into the most dreaded criminal organization of the Third Reich.

Heinrich Himmler, Reichsführer SS, was Hitler's alter ego and ruthless bloodhound, the personification, as some have claimed, of Nazism itself.[26] With meticulous skill and single-minded dedication, this cold and calculating busybody, aptly described by Albert Speer as "half school master and half crank,"[27] systematically assembled the major instruments of Nazi terror: SS, police, and concentration camp. His goal was not so much to unleash terror for its own sake but to use it for the purpose of building up a pure racial state. Heinrich Himmler was a true believer, one of those dangerous human beings who, like the Grand Inquisitors of the past, passionately believed in his religion, even if that religion was absurd. Such fanatics, as George Orwell has pointed out, might shrink from taking a single human life but murder millions for the sake of an abstraction.

With the blood of millions of lives on Himmler's hands, historians have understandably tried to find an explanation for the end of his career by examining its beginning. It was assumed that a man who had perpetrated such unspeakable horrors must have been the product of horrible circumstances; but when nothing dramatic in his upbringing was found, some historians threw up their hands in exasperation and reluctantly admitted that Himmler's youth was "depressingly normal,"[28] a judgment that has also been made about other Nazi murderers. Because Himmler came, we are told, from the most ordinary of Bavarian middle-class families, it is futile to invent some psychological explanation to explain the inexplicable.[29]

The truth is that Himmler was not the product of normal times nor of normal, healthy, or loving parents. His father, Gebhard Himmler, was an extremely rigid, pedantic, and compulsively legalistic schoolmaster who exemplified the much dreaded authoritarian type that was so common in the German school system at the time.[30] Professor Himmler's father had been a police sergeant with decidedly authoritarian habits, and it was on the same principles that the professor brought up his own children, teaching them to be meticulously clean, orderly, and obedient. Although the young man looked for relief from the heavy hand of his father by turning to his mother, who spoiled him considerably, the young man internalized the exacting, rigid, ethnocentric, and arrogant values of his father as unconditionally true, while at the same time fighting against everything soft, sensitive, spontaneous, or unstructured as unconditionally bad. There is considerable evidence that Himmler had a particularly difficult adolescence because he failed to measure up to the exacting standards his overbearing father expected him to meet. The young man's dreams, reinforced by his stern father, of becoming a heroic officer who would lead his men into battle foundered on a combination of bad timing — the war was over by the time he had finished officers' training school — and the fact that young Himmler was too unathletic and unassertive enough to be an inspiring leader.

He also disappointed his caste-conscious parents in not pursuing an academic course of study that would lead to a prestigious profession. Himmler studied agriculture at the Technical University of Munich, and he did so at a time of constant crisis in the immediate postwar period. In 1922, he received his agricultural diploma, but job prospects were abysmal. He worked for a while as a technical assistant doing research on manure; he was lonely, drifting, and insecure, looking for a sense of meaning and purpose in life. He found that meaning by joining the Nazi Party and by substituting one stern father figure and one stern value system with another. It appears that Himmler had no inner substance whatsoever because he never allowed himself to undergo a genuine process of self-discovery that would lead to self-growth. His culture had taught him that one could be good only by submitting oneself unconditionally to authority, and that even if one questioned traditional authority, that of his father or of his Roman Catholic upbringing, one had to substitute an equally absolute set of authoritarian principles in its place. Already doubting his Roman Catholic beliefs and carrying within himself little more than insubstantial ideas or habits imposed by his rigid upbringing, the anxiety-ridden young man resolved his identity crisis by attaching himself to a new authority and substitute religion: Adolf Hitler and National Socialism.

Like so many Germans at the time, certainly those who became true Nazi believers, Himmler did not choose freedom in the form of questioning authority or spontaneous experimentation; he escaped from the possibility that freedom offered in the new democratic Germany by unconditionally submitting himself to a new form of bondage. He wanted to be free from freedom because to be so promised release from the worst nightmare a conservative and security-conscious German of his class could have, and that was a life outside a constant routine of rules and regulations, of orders and directions, identity cards, admission tickets, and itemized inventories.[31] The petty bureaucrats who supervised the Holocaust, pedantically and meticulously recording the possessions of their Jewish victims, making sure that all the umbrellas, hats, shoes, and eyeglasses were neatly accounted for, were all little Himmlers with similar compulsive cultural traits. A German of Himmler's class and generation had great difficulty in doing anything freely or spontaneously, that is, on the spur of the moment. Even taking a vacation required long-range planning, obligatory letters and postcards, keeping of diaries, or hanging onto a variety of informational or photographic mementos. It should be recorded that, after disguising his identity and going under cover following the collapse of the German military in May of 1945, Himmler instinctively, without being prompted to do so, handed over his false identity papers to a British control point. The name he had chosen, Heinrich Hitzinger, was that of a former sergeant in the Geheime Feldpolizei who had been executed for defection. The escape, like everything else Himmler did, was done by the book, the wrong book as it turned out because the Geheime Feldpolizei was on the Allied black list, as were all those wearing its uniform or carrying its official identity cards.[32]

In 1929 Adolf Hitler appointed Himmler Reichsführer-SS, which at that time was still a minor position in the shadow of the SA and its swashbuckling commander Ernst Röhm. Yet Himmler envisioned his black-shirted soldiers to be more than just political foot soldiers or street brawlers; his dream was to transform them into an elite racial cadre, carefully picked from the most talented and the physically strongest segments of the population. They would serve as the vanguard of a racially purified Germany. About this time, Himmler also fell under the influence of the racial theories of Walther Darré, an agronomist and former artillery officer, whom he had met in the ranks of the Artamans, a group of racial utopians who believed in the back-to-the-soil movement that had been organized by various *völkisch* youth groups in the early 1920s. The Artamans called for new eastern settlements, the subjugation of the "inferior" Slavs, and the cultivation of a new Teutonic peasant class that would revitalize German blood and soil. Out of the ranks of the Artamans would emerge some well-known SS racists: Himmler, Darré, and Rudolf Höss, future commandant of Auschwitz.

In the years of struggle for power, the gray, colorless, emotionally flat but intensely focused Himmler built up his elite order by screening his new members according to height (at least 5'8"), pure Aryan descent back to 1750 for officers and 1800 for enlisted men, and appropriate health and hygienic specifications.[33] Being obsessed with Nordic beauty, the very things he was not, Himmler preferred tall, blond, and blue-eyed specimens. His own almost Mongoloid features, combined with his lack of physical strength, caused him no amount of neurotic anxiety and insecurity, which may explain why he constantly suffered from various illnesses, mostly psychosomatic, with attendant physical manifestations of acute headaches, colitis, stomach cramps, and sore muscles. The diary of Felix Kersten, Himmler's Swedish masseur, who tended the sore muscles of his anxiety-ridden client, bears testimony to Himmler's fantasies and obsessions. Like Hitler, Himmler was a neurotic hypochondriac who was at home in the world of crankish herbalists and health faddists.[34]

It may be true, as some have argued, that Himmler was "schizoid,"[35] an anal-retentive sado-masochist,[36] or an "obsessive-compulsive personality," but these terms do not capture the man's essential historical significance. He was, as H. R. Trevor-Roper noted long ago, the prototype of the Grand Inquisitor, the mind-numbing fanatic who, though personally kind, fastidious, austere, and incorruptible, could murder millions for the sake of some intensely held faith.[37] Himmler's ideal was a racial utopia dominated by new Aryan God-men who would redeem Germany from its suffering and evil. He stared endlessly at the photographs of prospective candidates, pried into the personal lives of his subordinates, and strictly prohibited SS personnel from marrying their prospective spouses until they had been racially screened. Each SS member had to keep a genealogical clan book (*Sippenbuch*) that contained specific family facts and relationships on the grounds that only in this way could the racial purity of future generations be safeguarded. As early as 1931 Darré joined Himmler's staff and organized the Race and Settlement Main Office (Rasse und Siedlungshauptamt) charged with setting racial norms, conducting research into European ethnicity, and developing plans for resettling German colonists in eastern territories.

What clearly emerged from these early party efforts and would later be confirmed by the frightening practices of "ethnic cleansing" on the eastern front, was Himmler's belief that the German race could be biologically improved, and that he knew the standards and techniques by which this racial purification could be accomplished. Having been, for a short time, a chicken farmer in Waldtrudering near Munich, Himmler seems to have believed that human breeding was essentially just like animal husbandry, so that "on the basis of Mendel's Law" the German people could in 120 years once more become "authentically German in appearance."[38] By weeding out undesirable features in the German gene pool through sterilization and strict racial laws prohibiting Germans from consorting with Jews and other inferior breeds, Himmler believed that it was possible to breed a superrace of fair-haired, blue-eyed, tall, and athletic Aryans. World domination, he pointed out, depended on such a racial purification: "Unless the blood of leadership in German veins, by which alone we stand or fall, can be increased by the admixture of good blood from elsewhere, we shall never achieve world mastery."[39]

In June of 1931, such an Aryan specimen, looking for a position in the SS, came to see Himmler at his farm in Waldtrudering, became his closest henchman, and helped him to perfect his evolving SS empire. This man was Reinhard Heydrich, a twenty-five-year-old ex-naval officer who had been recently dismissed from the German navy for conduct unbecoming an officer.[40] Heydrich was the son of a well-known tenor and director of a conservatory of music in Halle. The young man, who was himself musically talented and athletically gifted, grew up in a strict middle-class Catholic family in which cleanliness, order, discipline, and high achievement were the order of the day. Introspective and somewhat shy, Heydrich had difficulty in making friends, often compensating for his shortcomings through arrogant behavior and aggressive self-assertion.[41] Usually going his own way, he was frequently shunned by schoolmates and later by naval comrades, all the more so when rumors began to circulate that his father was Jewish. In school Reinhard was sometimes mocked by his schoolmates as "Isi," an allusion to his Jewishness.[42] No credible evidence has yet surfaced that Heydrich's father was in fact Jewish, but the allegations of Jewishness would follow Reinhard Heydrich throughout his murderous career and may account for the remarkable self-hatred he often demonstrated.

Out of his adolescent struggles emerged a twisted personality, deeply ambivalent about his identity, craving approval and recognition. Throughout his relatively short life, Heydrich was a torn and insecure man, trying to cover up his shallowness with arrogant assertion and suave posturing, only to encounter an empty void that was as ugly as his cultivated, aggressive exterior. Carl Burckhardt, the Swiss League of Nations Commissioner, told a story he picked up from SS men close to Heydrich to the effect that one day, after an evening of heavy drinking, Heydrich staggered into his brilliantly lit bathroom and came up against his reflection in the Great Hall mirror. He drew his revolver from his holster and fired twice at the mirror, shouting: "At last I've got you, scum!" Burckhardt said: "The man with the split personality had shot at his reflection because at last he had met his other half — but he had met him only in the mirror and could never get rid of him; that other half was to accompany him to the end."[43]

Of all the major Nazi leaders, Heydrich conformed most closely to the much touted Aryan ideal: he was tall, slender, blond, and good-looking, although his horse-like head, long nose, and brutal mouth with protruding teeth tarnished otherwise handsome features. His voice and laugh were so high pitched and bleating that his comrades nicknamed him *Ziege,* or goat. He was highly intelligent and athletically gifted, especially in fencing, swimming, and running. Such abilities, however, were not matched by strength of character. His dismissal from the navy was the result of rejecting one young lady for another, and doing it in such an ungentlemanly way as to drive the jilted woman into a nervous breakdown. The affair illustrates Heydrich's insensitive and callous treatment of others. People were means but never ends to Heydrich; he used them unscrupulously to get what he wanted. This is why historians have described him as totally amoral, comparable only to the great criminals of the Renaissance.[44] Like Hitler, he was always thinking the unthinkable, unrestrained by law or social convention. Indeed, he could well have been the Führer's favorite son were it not for the fact that even Hitler was slightly intimidated by the young man's overbearing ambition, brash arrogance, and brazen unscrupulousness. Hitler even used veiled threats of exposing his alleged Jewishness to keep him in his place. At Heydrich's funeral Hitler referred to the assassinated SS leader as the "man with the iron heart,"[45] an epithet echoed by Burckhardt, who referred to him as the "young, evil god of death."[46]

The Himmler-Heydrich partnership represented an evil convergence of the most destructive potentials in both men: Himmler's mind-numbing attention to detail and Heydrich's suave viciousness and unscrupulous aplomb. Working like moles inside the institution of party and state, the two men aimed at nothing less than the subversion of the law and complete control over the instruments of power. Their methods consisted of insinuating themselves into the regular bureaucracy, planting their own men into positions of influence, eliminating rivals through extortion and arrests, and all the while playing the role of dedicated, innocent, and unknowing public officials who were simply trying to do what was best for Germany. In reality, the racial fanatic chief and his psychopathic sidekick were systematically assembling the material for the organization of Nazi terror.

In the spring of 1933, when the two men began their grab for power, they were only thirty-three and twenty-nine years old respectively, and largely unknown to the public. On March 9, 1933, Himmler became police president of Munich; on April 1, he was promoted to the post of political police commander of Bavaria, which put him in charge of a statewide network of police agencies as well as the first major concentration camp of Dachau. The two men made sure that the key positions in their police apparatus were in the hands of the most ruthless and effective police officials, preferably proven Nazi loyalists. One of Heydrich's most capable officials, previously not affiliated with the Nazis, was Heinrich Müller, later nicknamed "Gestapo Müller," a man of driving ambition who quickly earned his new master's trust through a combination of blind obedience and unscrupulous behavior. As head of Department IV (Gestapo) in the later Reich Main Security Office (RSHA), Müller would participate in numerous crimes against humanity and became one of the most feared officials in the Nazi system. Although Müller had previously worked against the Nazis as had colleagues of his, such as Franz Josef Huber and Josef Meisinger, Heydrich recognized his own kind: control technicians willing to serve any regime that would promote them and allow sufficient scope to their talents and brutal predilections. Müller and men of his type came from middle-class parents, were brought up religiously, served and were highly decorated in World War I, joined the Free Corps, ended up in various police departments, and later served as obedient henchman to their Nazi masters. Müller and men of his stripe were amoral technicians of police terror for whom ideology served essentially as a justificatory mechanism; their primary motivation was careerism at any price.[47]

While helping Himmler gain control over the police in Bavaria and in the rest of Germany, Heydrich also solidified the apparatus that helped make it possible: the Security Service Branch (SD) of the SS which he had built up as early as 1931. At first, the personnel of the SD consisted of a small group of young and well-educated idealists who had been occupationally uprooted by hard times and, as desocialized drifters, were looking for some ideological commitment in their lives. For example, Heydrich's second-in-command, Carl Albrecht Oberg, son of a Hamburg professor of medicine, had joined the army at the age of seventeen, fought bravely in World War I, joined the Free Corps, and then drifted through much of the 1920s without steady employment until, at length, he found his way into the Nazi Party and its Security Service. Somewhat similar types were Heydrich's senior officials, many of whom were amateurs in a field that was beginning to define itself. Dr. Werner Best, Otto Ohlendorf, Professor Reinhard Höhn, Professor Franz Six, and Dr. Herbert Mehlhorn were all lawyers, while Helmut Knochen was a man with literary ambitions, Gunter d'Alquen a journalist, and Walter Schellenberg an aspiring master spy. In fact, it was the aura of adventure, the delight in spying on others, and the ingenuity required in setting up a system of surveillance and enforcement that captured the imagination of these men and attracted them to the Security Service. Walter Schellenberg, future SS spy master and espionage chief, later recalled that he joined the SS because, unlike the beerhall rowdies of the SA, one found "the better sort of people" in the SS, quite apart from the fact that the black SS uniforms were so dashing and elegant.[48] What the men who were attracted by SS glamor did not know was that, once involved in the system, they would have to work with very unsavory types and follow unethical orders; but rather than disengaging themselves from a criminal organization whose aim was to annihilate fictitious enemies, they rationalized their complicity and obediently carried out even more monstrous crimes.

In the beginning it was not entirely clear what the mission of the SD should be, that of an information service, a secret service, a party watchdog, or a quasi-police unit. At one time or another, the SD was all of these things, claiming simply to fight "oppression." By 1937, it had three thousand members and a growing army of over fifty thousand informers.[49] What were these inquisitorial fighters trying to unearth? The answer was the machination of their enemies, real or imagined. Working with but sometimes also at cross-purposes with the Gestapo, the SD sleuths turned first against political opponents or suspects such as Communists, Social Democrats, trade unionists, clergymen, recalcitrant intellectuals, and so on. After the neutralization or elimination of these domestic enemies (1933–35), came phase two of the assault on "racial enemies," primarily Jews and Gypsies but later also Slavic or "Asiatic inferiors." The SD Department on Jewish Affairs (II-112), which was headed by a number of fanatical Judeophobes in the 1930s, such as Leopold von Mildenstein, Kurt Schröder, Dieter Wislenscy, and Herbert Hagen, was divided into such branches or "desks" as assimilated Jewry (II-1121), Orthodox Jewry (II-1122), and Zionists (II-1123).

The Zionist desk was given to young Adolf Eichmann in 1935; its aim was to explore, by every possible means, the rapid emigration of German Jews, preferably to Palestine. Acquiring a smattering of Yiddish and Hebrew phrases along with a superficial overview of Jewish history, the former salesman for the Vacuum Oil Company quickly transformed himself into an expert on Jewish affairs that would make him a key figure in the Holocaust. The Department of Jewish Affairs, in fulfilling the general mission of the SD of identifying its enemies and directing the police to trace its activities, drew up a massive index card catalogue (*Judenkartei*) of all Jews living in Germany and of prominent Jews living elsewhere in the world. SD sleuths identified suspect individuals, dangerous organizations, and potential plots against Nazi Germany and its leaders. The paranoid assumption behind this massive undertaking, which required a nationwide network of reliable party members (*Vertrauensleute*), reliable informers (*Agenten*), paid informers (*Zubringer*), informers with motives (*Helfer*), and even unreliable collaborators (*Unzuverlässige*), was the belief in the existence of a unified Jewish world organization that planned to take over the whole world. The rantings of racial cultists, formerly restricted to the lunatic fringe, were now being seriously promoted by a growing state bureaucracy staffed by well-educated, zealous, and hard-working enthusiasts.

The racial fanatics of the SS and their supporters in state or party organizations fabricated an amorphous group of enemies so malignant and pervasive that no effort was too demanding, no financial sacrifice too costly to protect Germany from such evil-doers. This belief in a world of illusory malefactors who had to be unmasked and ruthlessly eliminated was reminiscent of the delusions of inquisitorial ecclesiastics in the Middle Ages who invented witches in order not only to satisfy an aberrant theology but also the proliferating bureaucracy of destruction that had developed to justify and reinforce it. From 1933 to 1938 the SD labored mightily with other organizations to eliminate the Jews from German public life by depriving them of their civil rights and undermining their means of livelihood. Enforced emigration, as will be seen, followed from 1938 to 1941, and that by the actual extermination of all the Jews of Europe. Although the precise method of solving the Jewish question was seen as yet through a glass darkly, the Judeophobes were already face to face with its annihilatory ending. It could also be seen and easily inferred from Streicher's slogan, plastered on walls, billboards, and party marquees all over Germany: "Ohne Lösung der Judenfrage keine Erlösung des deutschen Volkes" (Without a solution of the Jewish question no salvation for the German People).

In constructing their network of totalitarian control, Himmler and Heydrich not only built up the SS, especially its security service (SD), but also plotted to infiltrate and take over the whole German police system. Himmler had already amalgamated all the police forces of the German states by the end of 1933, but the Prussian police had remained under the control of Hermann Göring and the Prussian Ministry of the Interior that was under his control. The plumb in Göring's police system was the Gestapo (Geheime Staatspolizei), a department within the Prussian police force that had been set up to monitor suspect and potentially subversive activities by leading politicians, political parties, and political associations. Until the spring of 1934 the Gestapo was still under Göring's control; by that time its tentacles had spread throughout Germany, as did its terroristic practices of intimidation, extortion, and blackmail in forcing its victims to confess their political sins. Putting people in "protective custody" (*Schutzhaft*) for "their own good," forcing them to confess, consigning them to a concentration camp, and shooting them "while attempting to escape," became some of the favorite tactics of the emerging Nazi tyranny.

On April 20, 1934, Göring, who had been feuding with Wilhelm Frick and Ernst Röhm over the direction of the Gestapo, allied himself with Himmler by appointing him "Inspector of the Gestapo," sacrificing his previous Gestapo chief, Rudolf Diels. Himmler was still subordinate to Göring as minister president of Prussia, to Frick as minister of the interior for the Reich, and Röhm as chief of both the SA and SS. During the Night of the Long Knives (June 30, 1934), Himmler's black-shirted SS assassins liquidated Röhm on Hitler's orders; as a reward for their bloody contribution in ridding him of a serious political liability, Hitler transformed the SS into an autonomous elite order with complete control over the Gestapo. After a year-long conflict with Frick, who tried to bring the Gestapo under more effective supervision of the Ministry of the Interior, a new Gestapo law was passed in February of 1936 that typified the cunning mind of Hitler and his two-faced character: although the various Gestapo officers were ostensibly made responsible to the minister of the interior (Frick), the law also stipulated that the Gestapo regional officers were responsible to the head Gestapo office in Berlin, leaving open the question of which main office had the ultimate authority in jurisdictional conflicts. In the Nazi terror state, such jurisdictional disputes were eventually resolved in favor of the strongest and most determined leader, and that happened to be the tenacious Heinrich Himmler. Only four months after the Gestapo law was decreed (June 17, 1936), Hitler placed all police powers in Himmler's hands, making him chief of German police in the Ministry of the Interior. Frick was still nominally in charge, but in practice Himmler and Heydrich operated the police as they saw fit.

Shortly after his appointment as chief of German police, Himmler reorganized the German police system by forming a new "Security Police" (Sicherheitspolizei; Sipo), which consisted of the Gestapo (Geheime Staatspolizei, Secret State Police), the Criminal Police (Kriminalpolizei; Kripo), and the Gendarmerie; it was headed by Heydrich. The remainder of the German police system, consisting of the former urban constabulary and now renamed Order Police, or Orpo (Ordnungspolizei), was given to an old but ineffectual loyalist called Kurt Daluege, a pugnacious thug who was nicknamed "Dummi Dummi" (dumb-dumb) by the Berlin underworld for his limited intelligence.[50] In full possession of the instruments of terror, Himmler's loyalists steadily infiltrated the German state machinery, neutralized the efforts of honest and law-abiding officials, and constructed what Shlomo Aronson aptly termed the triangle of SS, police, and concentration camp. Himmler's new men, following their amoral chief, completely overwhelmed the legalistic and cautious members of the civil service with their unscrupulous tactics.[51] Müller was transferred from Munich to Berlin to become head of the Gestapo and later became a key figure in the Holocaust. In fact, the murderous personnel that would carry out the annihilation of millions of Jews and other innocent victims of the Nazi regime were being assembled in the mid-1930s.

Besides "Gestapo Müller," there were Bruno Streckenbach, former chief of the Hamburg police, who would set up the first ghettos in Poland and put together the infamous *Einsatzgruppen,* or special task forces, that rounded up and murdered Jews and other racial enemies; SS-Obergruppenführer Oswald Pohl, destined to build up a huge economic conglomerate of SS business enterprises based on slave labor, extortion, and murder; Dr. Walter Stahlecker, who was until his death the commander of Einsatzgruppen A, which followed Army Group North through the Baltic states to Leningrad, killing mercilessly as it went along; Arthur Nebe, head of the Criminal Police (Kripo) who was the first to volunteer enthusiastically to exterminate Jews in Poland under the cover of "employment duty to the east"; Erich von dem Bach-Zelewski, who had earned his badge of honor by exemplary brutality during the Röhm Purge and was assigned by Himmler to combat partisans on the whole eastern front, which involved him in liquidating countless opponents, including many Jews; Otto Ohlendorf, chief of Einsatzgruppe D, who was responsible for the liquidation of at least ninety thousand civilians, mostly Jews, in Southern Russia between Bessarabia and the Crimea; and Theodor Eicke, murderer of Ernst Röhm and sadistic sociopath who ran the whole system of Nazi concentration camps.

Behind the men who had blood on their hands were the lawyers and technical experts who put a shiny legalistic veneer on extortion, torture, and state killings — men like Werner Best, Reinhard Höhn, Franz Six, and Herbert Mehlhorn. Intellectuals also helped glamorize the SS. The most interesting was Gunter d'Alquen, a young journalist of outstanding ability who became the chief editor of the SS weekly journal *Das Schwarze Korps* (The Black Corps), a slick and sophisticated periodical of propaganda and investigative reporting that was widely read inside and outside the Nazi Party. Benefiting from a huge SD network of informants, the journal engaged in some biting criticism of highly placed party members. The favorite targets of *Das Schwarze Korps* were Jews, church officials, suspect intellectuals, independent-minded businessmen, and bumbling officials. Since the journal showed traces of self-criticism, which frequently annoyed major Nazi leaders, it was widely read. In 1937, it sold 189,317 copies and by the end of the war its circulation had reached close to 750,000.[52]

It is important to realize that the SS was perceived by most Germans, especially those who joined its various branches, as a noble elite order that only accepted the brightest and the best. This was part of the Nazi policy of public deception, of enshrouding aggression and immoral goals in the noblest form of idealism, and what could be more idealistic than to join an elite guard, draped from head to foot in puritanical black, whose mission consisted in defending the Führer and the institutions of state and party? The desire to become part of such a noble venture was therefore understandably strong, especially among the upper classes. In the 1920s the SS consisted largely of former Free Corps members, but after 1933 there was a steady influx from the upper classes and the old aristocratic elite. By the fall of 1933, Himmler stopped recruiting and decided to weed out people who did not fit the image of the heroic SS man — opportunists, alcoholics, homosexuals, and men of uncertain origins. Himmler wanted an elite order, rigorously trained and imbued with esprit de corps. Using the Jesuit model developed by Ignatius Loyola, Himmler aimed at remolding the whole character of his novices. Candidates were required to undergo a grueling two-year training program before they were allowed to swear the Sippeneid, or Kith and Kin Oath. The whole training was based on pseudoreligious notions that made a fetish of honor, loyalty, and unconditional obedience to authority. The motto "Meine Ehre ist Treue" (My honor is loyalty) was pounded into the heads of all SS members and was inscribed on all SS daggers.

The SS faith amounted to little more than a belief in the Führer as the savior of Germany, a distorted sense of Germanic superiority, and racial ideas under the guise of scientific truth.[53] These shallow and self-serving doctrines, however, were shrouded by the Reichsführer-SS with the trappings of perverse spirituality. Only those candidates survived in Himmler's order who had withstood the worst psychic assaults on their human dignity that a military organization could devise, but when they succeeded, they felt themselves reborn as part of a unique fraternity entrusted with a sacred mission. As members of this fraternity, they were not responsible to any court of German justice. The SS had its own court of honor, and Heinrich Himmler made it a principle that no one trained in the law would serve on it. It is therefore not surprising that the men of the SS saw themselves as the chosen ones and that they treated each other like comrades with a special bond. As Hans Buchheim has observed, however, these bonds were not based on strength of character, which respects the dignity of the individual, but rather often depended on weaknesses concealed, transgressions overlooked, and failures covered up, by superiors as well as outsiders.[54] In Wolfgang Sofsky's words, SS personnel were bound to each other by personal authority and camaraderie; they functioned as a self-protective unit that in its administrative structure often bore little resemblance to the familiar ideal type of rational bureaucracy.[55]

Although the SS was highly structured, its members were empowered with a great deal of arbitrary force, provided that they ruthlessly and successfully turned it against their enemies. The cruelties of their own training resembled the tortures they inflicted on others and made the infliction of cruelty easier because it had been experienced by themselves. The glorification of hardness (*Härte*) of character, written in the faces of robot-like SS men, expressed itself in the utter contempt and brutality with which these specimens of Aryan superiority mistreated their opponents. For the SS man the word "impossible" was not supposed to exist; his life's oxygen was struggle, unconditional obedience to authority, suppression of feelings or emotions because they implied softness, contempt for inferiors, arrogant behavior toward outsiders, and internal bonding with his own kind. As Sofsky reminds us, SS bonding was really camaraderie rather than comradeship, a distinction that involves important moral considerations:

> Comradeship means that people help each other, assuming mutual responsibility; by contrast, camaraderie means that they accommodate each other, each making concessions. Comradeship adheres to general normative rules; camaraderie is purely an internal relation. People cover for each other, hush up misdeeds and mistakes, conceal weaknesses; they cultivate a corps spirit with which the group delimits and defines itself, with which it elevates itself over outsiders. Comradeship is having a friend when in need; camaraderie is being an accomplice, but solely for the group. It eludes external control; consequently, its moral level tends to be in constant decline.[56]

It would naturally follow that the centerpiece of totalitarian terror, the concentration camp, could be entrusted only to such technicians of inhumanity. Following the Nazi seizure of power, Himmler groomed a special volunteer unit of SS men for long-term service as concentration camp guards. These units were called Death's-Head Units (*Totenkopfverbände*) because its members wore a special insignia of skull and crossbones on their black caps. The man Himmler put in charge of this system was Theodor Eicke, a brutal psychopath who standardized a set of cruel punishments in all of his camps. He insisted that each prisoner be treated with fanatical hatred as an enemy of the state. He also routinized a system of graded punishments consisting of solitary confinement of eight, fourteen, twenty-one, and forty-two days with warm "meals" served only after every fourth day. Corporal punishment (*Prügelstrafe*) was routinely administered by SS men on a rotating basis so that every guard had a chance to whip prisoners in the presence of fellow inmates. Prisoners were constantly bullied and harassed, especially while urinating or defecating. Some were thrown into the cesspool if they were too slow. In October 1937, ten prisoners suffocated in excrement at Buchenwald.[57] Every conceivable indignity was inflicted on inmates, particularly on Jews, homosexuals, and Jehovah's Witnesses. It was common for prisoners to be flogged by bullwhips, sticks, or clubs;

to be urinated upon from head to foot; to be made to roll around in the mud; to be buried alive; to be crushed under arbitrarily engineered rockfalls; to be "bathed" to death in freezing water; to be hung from tree limbs and forced to croak "cuckoo"; to squat, hours on end, in the "Saxon salute" with arms laced behind the head and in deep knee-bend; or to rot and suffocate in sadistically designed torture chambers.

The concentration camp was a moral mutation, a crossing over the boundary of civilized existence. It was a new kind of absolute control peculiar to the age of the masses, to the twentieth-century industrial world and its distinct style of organizing, exploiting, and annihilating human or natural resources. In Wolfgang Sofsky's judgment, the concentration camp was dedicated to the systematic destruction of human beings by violence, starvation, and labor — all of which it accomplished in an efficient, businesslike manner. In the span of just twelve years, the concentration camp "metamorphosed from a locus of terror into a universe of horror."[58] Its existence was well known by the German people, and it always found tens of thousands of willing accomplices; its accessories probably numbered in the millions. The torture and cruelty that was inflicted on the victims in the concentration camps cannot be explained solely by reference to ideology or motivation. In the concentration camp, terror did not have to be justified because it was an end in itself rather than a means to some end such as rehabilitation. The culture of the camp system was collective cruelty. Guards were trained and conditioned to inflict a maximum of pain and degradation on the inmates; they were initiated into a training routine that involved a high degree of specialization of labor, normalization of cruelty, and schedules of rewards and punishments for degrading the inmates. There was also considerable peer pressure to be the best torturer one could be; there were rewards in the form of commendations, extra rations, promotions, and trophies. In fact, "the more dead bodies subculture members could chalk up, the greater was their fame."[59] The guards, in other words, flogged, tormented, and killed prisoners because the culture encouraged them to do it, no holds barred.[60] It is true, of course, that many guards were sadistic and that some held strong ideological convictions, but these are not the primary reasons for their cruelty. As Wolfgang Sofsky has pointed out, "all cruelty needs is a lack of a sense of morality and brutalization by daily routines,"[61] a truth that has been well known for a long time by students of military or penal institutions.

The concentration camp made no pretense of rehabilitating anyone; its mission was to inflict punishment, to exploit inmates by working them to death under the euphemistic motto inscribed on all concentration camp gates, *Arbeit macht Frei* (Work makes one free), and ultimately to annihilate certain targeted groups: Jews, Gypsies, Jehovah's Witnesses, homosexuals. Shortly after the concentration camp of Dachau opened its gates, an SS commander gave a pep talk to his men that set the tone for the next twelve years:

Comrades of the SS! You all know what the Führer has called upon us to do. We haven't come here to treat those swine inside like human beings. In our eyes, they're not like us, they're something second-class. For years they've been able to pursue their criminal devices. But now we've got the power. If these swine had taken over, they'd make sure that our heads rolled in the dust. So we too know no sentimentality. Any man in our ranks who can't stand the sight of blood doesn't belong here, he should get out. The more of these bastards we shoot, the fewer we'll have to feed.[62]

Anyone who was committed to one of the major concentration camps quickly discovered that he or she was entering a living hell. One camp commandant made this quite clear to every new group of arrivals by barking at them: "Forget your wives, children, and families; here you will die like dogs."[63] Although at first only four specific groups were targeted for the concentration camps — political enemies, inferior races, criminals, and "asocial elements" (Bohemians, eccentrics) — every German had reasons to be apprehensive about his or her own safety. This pervasive sense of police terror, much encouraged by Himmler, constituted the essence of Nazism and was reinforced by the steady growth of camps of all sorts. It began in the spring of 1933 at Dachau, a city located about twelve miles northwest of Munich, where the Nazis converted twenty odd dreary-looking buildings belonging to an abandoned powder factory into a make-shift concentration camp that would serve as the model for other camps. Over the course of its twelve-year existence, Dachau had 206,000 registered inmates of all sorts and nationalities, of whom 31,951 were officially listed as having died.[64] It was here that prisoners were used as living guinea pigs for "scientific research," tortured for every conceivable infraction, and brutally forced to perform slave labor for the Nazi regime. Dachau was also used as a "school of force" (*Schule der Gewalt*) because every aspiring commandant was obligated to take a special training course administered by seasoned veterans of the camp.

Between 1933 and 1939 five major concentration camps had come into existence: Dachau; Buchenwald, near Weimar; Sachsenhausen, near Berlin; Flossenbürg in the upper Palatine and Mauthausen, near Linz in Austria. At the start of the war the total inmate population was roughly 24,000. The war witnessed an immediate intensification of totalitarian terror and the camp system metastasized. By 1941 the inmate population had tripled to over 60,000; in the summer of 1942 it stood at one 115,000, and two years later it had reached 524,268. By the end of the war it had swelled to 714,211, including 202,764 women.[65] New camps of all sorts were added: Neuengamme near Hamburg, Bergen-Belsen near Celle, Gross-Rosen in Lower Silesia, Stutthof near Danzig, Theresienstadt near Prague, and the major annihilation camps in Poland — Auschwitz, Belzec, Sobibor, Majdanek, and Treblinka. The scope and dimensions of the Nazi concentration camp system are staggering.

In addition to the twenty-three main camps that developed during World War II, the Nazis set up thousands of subcamps of all kinds, camps for foreign workers, "labor-education camps" (*Arbeitserziehungslager*), camps for criminals, camps for Prisoners of War (POWs), camps for civilians, camps for adults and children. There were also transit camps (*Durchgangslager*), collection camps (*Sammellager*), five hundred forced ghettos, and nine hundred forced labor camps for Jews in eastern Europe. We do not know the total numbers for all these camps; but given the ruthless methods of ethnic cleansing the Nazis used throughout Europe, methods that involved uprooting, concentrating, resettling, redeploying, and annihilating well over twenty million people, the number of camps must have been incredibly large. G. Schwarz, who examined the system of Nazi concentration camps in great detail, estimated a total of 10,006 camps, including concentration and death camps.[66]

On the eve of World War II, Himmler's SS empire was organized into four major branches: (1) the general SS, consisting largely of part-timers who combined their regular occupations with evening or weekend service in the SS on a voluntary basis; (2) the SD, or Security Service; (3) the SS Military Formations (*Verfügungstruppen*), renamed Waffen-SS in the winter of 1939–40; and (4) the concentration camp guard units called Death's-Head Units. A month after the war began, state police and Gestapo agencies were all merged under one roof, administered by Heydrich and called the Reich Main Security Office (Reichssicherheitshauptamt, or RSHA). This monstrous bureaucratic police apparatus was divided into seven main departments: (1) Personnel (under Streckenbach), (2) Legal Affairs (under Best), (3) SD and, later, Domestic Information Service (under Ohlendorf), (4) Gestapo (under Müller), (5) Criminal police, or Kripo (under Nebe), (6) Foreign News Service (under Just and later Schellenberg), and Ideological Research and Evaluation (under Drittel). In addition to the RSHA department (Hauptamt), Himmler's SS empire comprised no fewer than eight other main departments, the last four developing during the Second World War. These included Himmler's Private Office, headed by his chief of staff and liaison man with Hitler, Brigadeführer Karl Wolff, a suave, handsome but ruthless opportunist; the Race and Settlement Main Office (Rasse und Siedlungshauptamt, or RuSHA) under Walther Darré; the SS Court under Brigadeführer Paul Scharfe; the SS Main Office (SS-Hauptamt), responsible for administrative affairs and run by August Heissmeyer, husband of the Women's Führer Gertrud Scholtz-Klink; the Operational Department (Führungshauptamt), dealing with SS commandos; the Economic and Administrative Department (Wirtschafts- und Verwaltungshauptamt, or WVHA) under Obergruppenführer Oswald Pohl, which oversaw a vast conglomerate of business enterprises and also administered the financial affairs of the concentration camps; and a reorganized SS-Hauptamt, now called Duty Station, under Obergruppenführer Heissmeyer, which took over the inspection of the elite party schools called National Socialist Educational Institutions (NPEA).

Such a proliferation of SS institutions, overlapping as well as infiltrating and engaging other institutions of the Third Reich, gave the SS an aura of fear and evil, made all the more sinister by the fact that no outsiders knew anything in detail about Himmler's empire. On the other hand, despite the fact that Himmler dropped a veil of secrecy over his evil empire, his own power was not absolute because power was always shifting among Hitler's major paladins (Goebbels, Göring, Hess, Bormann, Rosenberg, Speer) and also because the army continued to exercise its privileges as Germany's major fighting unit. There was the additional factor that Himmler remained doggedly devoted to Hitler, as did his whole organization, for he joined all SS in swearing a sacred oath to unconditional obedience "unto death" to Adolf Hitler. In the new Nazi racial state everything began and ended with Adolf Hitler, who was a murderous Jew-hater from the moment we see him in the public limelight in 1919 to the very end of his life in the bunker beneath the Reich Chancellory in Berlin on April 30, 1945.

Yet, in completing the circle of racial politics and prejudice, it is necessary to go beyond Adolf Hitler and his government, because hatred and bigotry were now officially sponsored, reinforced, and rewarded. That ideas have consequences, that people act on what they believe and what they are taught, especially when such ideas are publicly disseminated by a modern industrial state, is so obvious as to need no further comment; and yet, some historians today blithely pretend that ideas are irrelevant as determinants of action and can be ignored or marginalized in favor of economic forces, institutional structures or processes, power relationships, and the like. This work assumes, on the contrary, that everything human beings do is endowed with conscious significance: a collective historical event is an act of collective consciousness, whether it is a construction of a pyramid, a cathedral, a crusade, or a system of concentration camps. Ideology explains as well as justifies. Racial ideology is no exception. It is not a mere reflection of economic conditions or functional relationships in a society's institutional agencies. In the words of SS General Erich von dem Bach-Zelewski, "I am of the opinion that, when for years, for decades, the doctrine is preached that the Slavic race is an inferior race and the Jews are not even human, then such an explosion [the Holocaust] was inevitable."[67]

Bach-Zelewski was a Holocaust perpetrator who was not just speaking for himself but for the German people as a whole. His assertion that racial ideas had momentous consequences for German society as a whole was sadly true. Although a wealth of documentation can be cited to prove this point, nothing is more poignant and disturbing than to show the impact of racial bigotry on innocent and unsuspecting children who were taught to hate Jews in the public schools in Nazi Germany. How the vile poison bore fruit may be illustrated by a story told by the Jewish journalist Bella Fromm, who wrote society columns for the Ullstein papers in Berlin. Fromm had befriended two little girls, Inge and Ursel, who belonged to a close acquaintance. One day Inge told her: "Aunt Bella, you don't really seem so — so fiendish....I told Herr Runge, that's our teacher, that you weren't like that, Aunt Bella. So he said we didn't understand how wicked you really were. Then for the rest of the lesson, he read us out of a book about the Jews...that they are evil...they look like devils...they should all be killed. He said we should spit at them whenever we see them."[68] On their way home from school one day, that is exactly what one of the girls, Ursel, proceeded to do: "Ursel and I saw an old woman. She looked very poor, and we thought she might be Jewish. Ursel said we should spit at her....She ran up to her and spat on her coat....I didn't spit, Aunt Bella. I thought it was disgusting." Bella Fromm wondered how long Inge could withstand this sort of psychic assault on her innocence; she didn't have to wait long. A week later, Inge's mother told Bella Fromm that Herr Runge continued discussing Jews in class and pointedly asked Inge whether she agreed with him that Jews were vile. No, the girl replied bravely, because "Daddy said so." One night the Gestapo paid a visit to Inge's daddy and took him away for questioning; he returned with horrible scars on his body and a severe warning not to undermine the official values of the school system.[69] When teachers are encouraged to become betrayers of children, which they automatically become when they teach hate and bigotry, a society crosses over the boundaries of humane values. It has deliberately chosen institutional indecency.

Chapter 7

The Jews in the New Nazi
Racial State, 1933-39

The Period of Wild Actions and
Uncoordinated Assaults, 1933-35

The day after Hitler was appointed chancellor by President Paul von Hindenburg, a lead editorial in the *Jüdische Rundschau* warned its Jewish readers that "we are confronted with the fact that a power hostile to us has assumed control over the reins of government in Germany."[1] Just how hostile to the Jews the Nazis would turn out to be was not clear in January of 1933. The immediate reaction by most Germans to Hitler's appointment was one of enthusiasm and hope. The country was inundated by waves of nationalistic speeches, demonstrations, and torchlight parades, celebrating the Nazi takeover and hailing the event as a new dawn in German history.

Among the rank and file of the Nazi storm troopers, feelings of empowerment and revenge against their ideological and racial enemies combined to produce a volatile atmosphere. In the ecstatic faces of marching brownshirts one could detect a sense of grim determination to change the status quo; one could also draw obvious conclusions about the fate of the Jews from the slogans they lustily shouted in unison: "Croak the Jew" (*Jude verrecke*) or "When the Jews' blood spurts from the knife good times are once more here."

The period from Hitler's appointment to the chancellorship on January 30, 1933, to the death of President Hindenburg on August 2, 1934, marked the Nazi consolidation of power. During these eighteen months Hitler orchestrated a systematic takeover of the German government, using the Reichstag fire of February 27, 1933, as an excuse to force a pliant parliament to give him broad emergency powers in order to "enable" him to rule by dictatorial decree (Enabling Law). He used this power to bring about a systematic coordination (*Gleichschaltung*) of German institutions with the political aims of National Socialism. By the summer of 1933, he was in complete control except for the still-growing power of the SA under its mercurial and independent-minded chief, Ernst Röhm, who commanded an army of almost 3 million storm troopers; the traditional German army; and the senile president and commander-in-chief of the army, Paul von Hindenburg. Allying himself for tactical reasons with the traditionalists in the army and members of the party who stood to gain from Röhm's removal (Göring, Goebbels, Himmler), Hitler eliminated his former SA chief in a bloody purge during the "Night of the Long Knives" (June 30–July 1, 1934). Only one month later, President Hindenburg died; on that same day (August 2,) Hitler merged the office of chancellor with that of the president, which made him not only the supreme political authority but also commander-in-chief of the armed forces.

This eighteen-month period was characterized by a peculiar double face: it was outwardly a time of public excitement over the national revolution but it was also for many Germans, especially the Jews, a time of pervasive fear and terror because it witnessed both spontaneous and publicly orchestrated attacks on all political opponents and "racial enemies." In the spring of 1933 Hitler had three broad aims: to seize sole control over the German government and keep it, to mobilize the German people for war and conquest, and to eliminate the Jews. The precise methods of accomplishing these goals had not been clearly formulated; they would depend on the complex interaction of competing personalities and public agencies in the new racial state and the reaction of his opponents, both at home and abroad. Throughout the 1930s, Hitler displayed the superb skills of the opportunistic politician who had outwitted his opponents on his way to power by an impressive combination of timing, flexibility, judgment of character, and single-mindedness of purpose. He now brought the same skills to the three goals he had set himself upon becoming chancellor. On the evening of his triumph, at the very moment thousands of storm troopers marched past the chancellery and hailed him as they saw him looking down on the torchlight parade, he was overheard saying: "No power on earth will ever get me out of here alive,"[2] a sentiment that had also been voiced by his propaganda chief in 1932 when he said that "once we have the power, we will never surrender it unless we are carried out of our offices as corpses."[3] Although the Nazi leaders did not know precisely how they would accomplish their dictatorial intentions, they were fanatically determined to use any means to accomplish their sinister ends. Only a few days after his appointment to the chancellorship, Hitler attended a secret meeting with his military chiefs in which he revealed his dictatorial intentions at home and his warlike aims abroad by telling the astonished military leaders that he would destroy the Versailles Treaty, revitalize the German army, and conquer territory in the east to give the Germans more living space.[4]

As to the Jews, Hitler's immediate strategy was to play-act the role of the people's advocate who acknowledged and even condoned public anger against the Jews, but at the same time pretended his personal uninvolvement on the grounds that he was focusing all his attention and energy on the nations' economic and political crisis. In reality, Hitler encouraged both party radicals and various state agencies in perpetrating all sorts of violent anti-Jewish actions. The first few years of Nazi rule alternated between rowdy street actions (*wilde Aktionen*) and bureaucratic chicaneries. Hitler's aim, however, was always the same: to drive the Jews out of Germany and, failing that, to annihilate them altogether. The subtle politician in him realized that this plan would depend on opportunity and good timing. Given the fact that he had not fully consolidated his own power, he felt obligated to give the appearance of a responsible parliamentary leader at home and an advocate of international peace abroad. This was part of an essential psychological strategy of *Schein* (illusion) and *Sein* (reality), of rhetorical idealism and ruthless realism. The Jews of Germany were caught in this deceptive reality by being constantly harassed by the mercurial policies of a Nazi leadership and the insistent strategies it inspired in different branches of the party and the government. Worse, there were intermittent respites, marked by rays of hope, that lulled sizable sections of the Jewish community into the false belief that things would get better soon, as they always had, or alternatively stabilize to a level that could be tolerated.

In retrospect, of course, we now know that things always got worse for the Jews, but this could not have been known to the majority of Germany's half million Jews in the spring of 1933. Despite Hitler's public pronouncements on the pernicious influence of the Jews, many German Jews took a wait-and-see position, hoped for the best, and decided to remain in Germany. They did so because they felt themselves genuinely German, believed in the possibility of a viable German-Jewish symbiosis, and were deeply rooted, financially and psychologically, in their German homeland.[5] Initially, only a few Jews, mostly intellectual and political opponents of the Nazis, decided reluctantly to leave the country, particularly after they lost their positions or feared for their lives. One was Albert Einstein, who had been visiting America when Hitler came to power. Einstein had come to the conviction that Nazism was a "state of psychic distemper in the masses";[6] the Nazis, for their part, regarded the physicist as the epitome of the clever Jew whose science was founded on nothing more than perversion and distortion. Thus, when Einstein journeyed back to Europe on the Belgian liner *Belgenland* at the end of March 1933 and was informed that his house on the outskirts of Berlin had been broken into by a gang of Nazi thugs looking for incriminating papers, he decided to renounce his Prussian citizenship and his membership in the Prussian Academy and never set foot on German soil again.[7]

The philosopher Ernst Cassirer, author of an impressive three-volume work, *The Logic of Symbolic Forms,* also recognized immediately what the Nazi system would mean for the Jews, confiding in his wife that "Menschen unseres Schlages haben in Deutschland nichts mehr zu suchen und nichts mehr zu hoffen, (People of our kind have nothing to search for and nothing to hope for in Germany).[8] And in a remarkably prophetic insight, Cassirer added that "I would guess that this regime will last ten years; but the evil it will instigate is likely to last a hundred and fifty years,"[9] a judgment he based on his firm conviction that the Nazi regime aimed not so much at *Judenverfolgung* (Jewish persecution) but *Judenvernichtung* (Jewish annihilation). Cassirer admitted that he had no interest or capacity to figure out how the destruction of the Jews would unfold; but given its inherent irrational and aggressive nature, the Nazi regime would stop at nothing in eliminating its enemies, real or imagined.[10] Cassirer was one of the few intellectuals who saw the nature of Nazism with complete logical clarity from the very beginning, realizing that it was irrationally destructive both in its substantial being, which was based on racial mythology, and in its dynamic form, which was based on perpetual aggression in order to validate itself. Cassirer was always of the opinion that if one grasped the essential principle of any existential condition, one did not have to busy oneself with the details to which it gave rise. Even after he had fled from Germany, he did not bother to immerse himself in the latest Nazi activities. As far as he was concerned the land of the swastika was an aberration that bore little similarity to the Germany he had known before. The new system would, he believed, eventually destroy itself by its own irrational dynamics; by constantly having to prove itself in the form of indefinite successes, it was bound to undermine its existence when successes would eventually turn into failures.[11]

Cassirer was not the only one who saw the handwriting on the wall in the spring of 1933. By the end of 1933 Nazi Germany had disgorged a host of leading Jewish intellectuals, scientists, writers, artists, and musicians. It is significant, as Saul Friedländer reminds us, that the Nazis began their attacks on the Jews by trying to expel them immediately from the cultural domain, where they had allegedly exercised their most poisonous influence.[12]

On March 13, 1933, Joseph Goebbels was appointed to head the new Ministry of Public Enlightenment and Propaganda, consisting of several major departments or chambers: painting and sculpture, literature, music, theater, film, radio, and press. German artists, writers, and musicians were compelled to join this organization if they wanted to practice their creative craft; but non-Aryans were not permitted to join and were therefore effectively deprived of both their public and their livelihood. Only three days later, the conductor Bruno Walter was forced to cancel a concert by the Leipzig Gewandhaus Orchestra because he was a "non-Aryan." The same happened subsequently to other famous musicians such as Artur Schnabel, Otto Klemperer, and Emil Feuermann.[13]

Goebbels was particularly eager to purge the Prussian Academy of Arts of Jewish and modernist elements. In February 1933, both Heinrich Mann, head of the literature section, and Käthe Kollwitz, a member of the arts section, signed and circulated a petition calling upon the communist and socialist parties to combine forces in the upcoming March election in order to prevent Germany from "sinking into barbarism." In response to this challenge the Nazi commissioner for culture, Bernhard Rust, informed the academy's president, Max von Schilling, that he would abolish the academy unless its recalcitrant members were silenced. Kollwitz and Mann promptly resigned. Gottfried Benn was then chosen to head the new literature section; he drafted a general resolution calling upon the members of the academy to abstain from all further political activities and to devote themselves fully to the task of national regeneration. Although the majority of the academy signed the Benn resolution, several outstanding talents (Alfred Döblin, Thomas Mann, Ricarda Huch) resigned rather than put their names on such an anti-intellectual document. Thomas Mann was already living as an exile writer in Switzerland when the shameful resolution was signed and his brother Heinrich Mann, resigned as well from the academy, joining his brother in exile. Alfred Döblin also fled to Switzerland right after the Reichstag fire of February 27, shaking off a Nazi official who was shadowing him on his way to the railroad station in Berlin.

Members of the Prussian Academy who still refused to be nazified were subsequently removed by ministerial decree. By the end of 1933, half the members of the 1932 literature section of the academy had been expelled. The same happened in other sections of the academy. Max Liebermann, dean of German painters and honorary president of the Prussian Academy, resigned on May 7, 1933; he died two years later, neglected and ignored in Nazi Germany. His widow committed suicide in March of 1943 rather than face deportation to the east.[14] A steady exodus of first-rate talents in all fields followed, putting an end to the symbiosis of German and Jewish contributions that had marked Weimar culture. Arnold Schönberg came to the United States in October of 1933, Arnold Zweig was denaturalized by the Nazis and went to Palestine, while his brother Stefan fled to Brazil, where he committed suicide along with his wife. Theodor Lessing fled to Czechoslovakia, where he was tracked down by Nazi assassins and murdered. Kurt Tucholsky swallowed poison in a Swedish hotel room in 1935; Ernst Toller hanged himself in a New York hotel room. Suicide took other prominent Jewish lives: Ernst Weiss, Walter Hasenclever, Walter Benjamin, Carl Einstein, and Alfred Wolfenstein, among others.[15] Erich Mühsahm and Carl Ossietzky were hideously tortured and killed in Nazi camps. Yet many others carried the Weimar spirit abroad, where it continued to live in exile.

On May 10, 1933, Goebbels encouraged a repulsive event that will forever be a stain on Germany's cultural record — the burning of politically incorrect books. The poet Heinrich Heine had once observed prophetically that it was but a small step from burning books to burning people. This particular "cleaning action" (*Säuberung*) was carried out by the German Student Union (Studentenschaft); it was aimed at eliminating un-German or foreign writings, especially Jewish, from libraries and bookstores. Convocations were held on May 10 at all German universities, during which students, professors, and party officials outdid each other in paying homage to Nazi political correctness. Goebbels marshalled the whole communications monopoly to record this shameful event for posterity. The Berlin book burning was personally staged by the propaganda chief himself, who rationalized the event by exclaiming:

> Fellow students, German men and women! The age of extreme Jewish intellectualism has now ended, and the success of the German revolution has again given the German spirit the right of way.... You are doing the proper thing in committing the evil spirit of the past to the flames at this late hour of the night. This is a strong, great, symbolic act, an act that is to bear witness before all the world to the fact that the November Republic has disappeared. From the ashes there will arise a phoenix of a new spirit.... The past is lying in flames within our hearts.... Brightened by these flames our vow shall be: The Reich and the Nation and our Führer Adolf Hitler: Heil! Heil! Heil![16]

The event was crowned by the actual burning of the books, accompanied by SS and SA bands playing marches and folk songs. Nine student representatives, who had been given works belonging to nine categories, flung the discredited books into the flames with the following accusatory words:

First Speaker:
Against class struggle and materialism for *Volk* community and idealism! I commit to the flames the works of Marx and Kautsky.

Second Speaker:
Against decadence and moral decay. For discipline and morality in family and state! I commit to the flames the works of Heinrich Mann, Ernst Glaeser and Erich Kästner.

Third Speaker:
Against political irresponsibility and political betrayal. For dedication to *Volk* and State! I commit to the flames the works of the pacifist Friedrich Wilhelm Foerster.

Fourth Speaker:
Against the exaggeration of unconscious urges based on destructive analysis of the psyche. For the nobility of the human soul! I commit to the flames the works of Sigmund Freud.

Fifth Speaker:
Against falsification of our history and denigration of its great figures. For respect of our past! I commit to the flames the writing of Emil Ludwig and Werner Hegemann.

Sixth Speaker:
Against un-German journalism of a Jewish democratic kind. For responsible cooperation in the work of national reconstruction! I commit to the flames the works of Theodor Wolff and Georg Bernhard.

Seventh Speaker:
Against literary betrayal of the soldiers of the First World War. For the education of the people in the spirit of truthfulness! I commit to the flames the works of Erich Maria Remarque.

Eighth Speaker:
Against conceited debasement of our German language. For the cultivation of our most precious property of the people! I commit to the flames the writings of Alfred Kerr.

Ninth Speaker:
Against impudence and presumptuousness. For awe and respect before our immortal German *Volk* spirit! Devour, flames, the writings of Tucholsky and Ossietzky.[17]

At the same time that Goebbels and Rosenberg orchestrated their attacks on Jewish intellectuals, scientists, artists, writers, and musicians, other Nazi leaders and agencies were also involved in curtailing the allegedly poisonous influence of the Jews on German life and culture. On the street level, these assaults on the Jews were generally incited by the leadership of the SA and then carried out by its political foot soldiers — the rowdy brownshirts who controlled the streets of most German cities. In Michael Kater's judgment, the period from January 30, 1933, to September 1935, from Hitler's appointment to the chancellorship to the enactment of the Nuremberg Racial Laws, was characterized by a pattern of interactions that fluctuated between personal initiative, semilegal wild actions, and government legislation.[18] Most of the wild actions, enacted on the streets of Germany's cities, towns, and villages, were instigated by the SA. In 1933, as Kater points out, the SA comprised about two million young Germans over the age of seventeen, or about 10 percent of the entire civilian male population. Since the SA cultivated a murderous hatred of Jews and inculcated this hatred in its members, we can draw the conclusion that by the summer of 1933 one-tenth of the adult population was strongly infected by anti-Jewish prejudices.[19] If we add to this anti-Jewish population the many other members of the Nazi Party, numbering well over a million members by the summer of 1933,[20] the number of violent Judeophobes may have been even higher. Moreover, since the German people had been traditionally predisposed toward either a religious or a popular discriminatory type of anti-Jewish prejudice, it should come as no great surprise that the population at large was rarely outraged when the SA harassed, humiliated, or physically assaulted Jews. This, of course, does not necessarily mean that bystanders were all filled with violent hatred of Jews; some may have been and some may not. Their passivity was due, in addition to anti-Semitic prejudices, to an understandable fear of being arrested in a totalitarian state that did not tolerate opposition. It undoubtedly was also due to the traditional absence of civil dissent in German public life and to the respect, even homage, that many ordinary Germans paid to anyone who wore a uniform. The actions of the uniformed brownshirts were therefore, to say the least, widely condoned by a large segment of the German people.

It is important to realize that the Nazi regime wanted to enmesh the population at large in the attack on the Jews or any other group or persons officially targeted as an enemy. The SA, the Gestapo, and the SD relied heavily on public cooperation by monitoring public opinion, soliciting information, and encouraging citizens to denounce those Germans who represented either a real or merely potential threat to the government. In Wolfgang Sofsky's judgment, "popular participation by provision of information was one of the most important factors in making the terror system work."[21] By hook or by crook, by force or persuasion, the Nazi leadership wanted to instil a fanatical hatred of Jews in the population at large, hoping to gain broad popular support for its anti-Jewish measures or, failing such popular support, at least passive acceptance or cold indifference.

The agitation against the Jews, as against other opponents of the Nazi regime, followed a recognizable pattern that Karl Dietrich Bracher has aptly described as stage-managed from above and manipulated and carried out from below.[22] Typically, the directions would come from Hitler and his henchmen and were then communicated to the local *Gau* (district) organization for implementation. This is how the regime engineered political coups against the local state governments in March of 1933. The same broad pattern developed against the Jews. Directions to orchestrate "spontaneous" actions against the Jews would be communicated to local Nazi organizations which, in turn, sent out their agents or brownshirts to set in motion violent protest and unrest. This would be followed by state mandates and decrees, giving the impression that the government was merely embodying the will of the people in legal form. In point of fact, most of the primitive Jew-baiting was carried out by cliques of Nazi fanatics who, acting on higher instructions but sometimes also spontaneously and independently, carried out violent assaults on Jewish persons or businesses. Hans Mommsen correctly labeled these radical street actions a contrived Nazi scheme that could only continue with a constant infusion of propagandistic energy, but his judgment that these wild actions were a failure because they did not solve the Jewish problem or lacked broad public support has to be seriously modified.[23] The fact is that the Nazi regime steadily accustomed the population to acts of public brutality and thereby managed to enmesh ordinary Germans into active support, tacit complicity, or passive acquiescence. The regime, of course, preferred popular support for its policies; its leaders, after all, claimed to believe in the concept of dictatorship based on popular support, but in reality they were cynical elitists who would stop at nothing to attain their broad ends, especially the removal of the Jews. At any rate, if the wild actions were a failure, it was not because they lacked widespread popular support, but because they failed to achieve the regime's desired end: the elimination of the Jews from Germany. On a smaller scale, however, they succeeded in the sense that they jump-started the process of elimination, inured average Germans to a developing process of constant radicalization, and initiated a sizable number of Nazi fanatics into normalization of anti-Jewish brutality.

Wild actions against Jews began immediately after January 30, 1933, and accelerated after the Reichstag fire of February 27. On March 9, SA men blocked the entrances to Jewish businesses and department stores in Berlin, Magdeburg, and the Rhineland. Staging economic disruptions at a time of economic misery was hardly a very effective way of resolving Germany's economic position or presenting a good image to the rest of the world. This did not matter, however, to the SA leadership or to Julius Streicher, who tried to inject his own brand of fanatical Judeophobia into the public assault on the Jews. What mattered to them was whether the Jews were hurt. In these early assaults on Jewish businesses, little was accomplished other than annoying disruptions and damage to property. SA thugs were posted in front of Jewish businesses and ordered to warn potential customers not to buy goods from the racial enemies of the German people. Leaflets were distributed and SA bands marched or drove through predominantly Jewish sections of German cities admonishing ordinary Germans not to buy from Jews. News of these disruptions abroad led to various foreign boycotts against German goods in the United States, Britain, France, Belgium, and Poland.[24] In what would become a paradigmatic pattern of the Nazi mentality, characterized by a perverse confusion of cause and effect, the Nazis branded the organizers of these foreign boycotts as Jewish and anti-German, blamed them for starting the problem, and claimed that they were merely taking preventative measures by boycotting Jewish businesses in Germany. In other words, it was not the Nazis who started harassing the Jews but foreign hatemongers who obliged them, out of self-defense, to retaliate against the Jews of Germany. This kind of perverse reasoning was behind Joseph Goebbels's announcement that the German government planned to call a nationwide boycott of Jewish goods, scheduled on April 1, as a purely defensive measure against the Jewish-inspired hate campaign that was allegedly taking place abroad.

The boycott was preceded by a vicious propaganda campaign against the Jews throughout Germany. Nazi leaders indignantly warned foreign Jews that, if they did not desist in their "atrocity propaganda" (*Greuelhetze*) against Germany, the German Jews would pay dearly for it. In certain cities, street thugs now felt doubly empowered and proceeded to carry out "spontaneous" actions against Jewish businesses, physicians, lawyers, and judges. In Berlin, physicians were widely harassed and their contracts with hospitals were canceled. The Nazis had been pining for some time to attack Jewish professionals, especially in Berlin, where the Jews were disproportionately represented in these professions. Beginning on March 11, SA storm troopers attacked Jewish judges and lawyers in Breslau. One Jewish lawyer, Ludwig Foerder, later reported that after attending synagogue on Saturday, March 11, he went to his office and

> suddenly — it was exactly 11 o'clock — the corridors resounded with animal-like roars that approached quickly. The doors of the legal office flew open. A dozen SA-men with brown shirts and caps piled in and screamed: "Juden raus" (Jews out). For a moment everyone, Jews and Christians alike, was paralyzed. Then most Jewish attorneys left the office. I noticed how the seventy-year-old state counselor, Siegmund Cohn, member of the executive committee of the judicial chamber, sat frightened as though he were nailed to his chair and could not get up. A pair of brownshirts jumped at him. At this moment, several younger Christian attorneys...stepped in and put themselves protectively in front of him, which caused the intruders to leave him alone. I did not move from my place. An SA man jumped at me and pulled me by the arm. As I shook him off, he pulled a metallic case out of his right shirt sleeve that under pressure released a spiral with a lead ball attached to it on the end. He beat me twice over the head with this instrument, causing an immediate outpouring of blood and swelling.... One could see how judges, public prosecutors, and lawyers were driven out on the street by small groups of these brown hordes. Everywhere the intruders flung open the doors of court chambers and screamed "Juden raus." A quick-thinking young assessor, who was just presiding over a case, screamed at them: "Get out of here," whereupon they disappeared at once. Two hooligans screamed at a Jewish barrister who was sitting alone in a room: "Are there Jews here?" He responded matter-of-factly, "I don't see any" — whereupon they slammed the door and moved on.[25]

Ludwig Foerder quickly discovered that, although being part of a ministerial bureaucracy, it was difficult to appeal to the police, especially when the offenses involved illegal actions by members of the Nazi Party. Turning for help and advice to the director of the county court, he was told that higher authorities had already been notified, but such slow-moving bureaucratic measures seemed totally inappropriate to Foerder, who asked the director for permission to use his telephone so that he could call the chief of police. The director had no objection and Foerder called the police. He was informed that twenty policemen were already en route to the county court. A short while later, Foerder saw twenty policeman crossing the street at a remarkably slow pace, which told him that the police president was probably personally responsible for this pogrom. Later in the afternoon, the judges of Breslau met in the provincial court and decided to call a temporary judicial strike, which, had it been maintained, might have dealt a serious blow to the Nazi radicals. The president of the provincial court, however, caved in to Nazi pressure and decreed that only seventeen Jewish attorneys could henceforth serve in the courts of Breslau; the rest were prohibited from entering the courts.

The Breslau case, which was by no means unusual because it repeated itself in somewhat similar form in other places, illustrates the utter contempt the Nazis displayed for the rule of law. Having already suspended whole sections of the Weimar Constitution, which guaranteed civil liberties, deputizing SA thugs as "auxiliary policemen," using the Orwellian neologism "Protective Custody" (*Schutzhaft*) to arrest their enemies, and developing a new legal philosophy that rested on the principle that "law must be interpreted through healthy folk emotions," the Nazis were systematically breaching the walls of a civilized legal state (*Rechtsstaat*). The conservative legal mandarins, bookish, cautious, and legalistic in their thinking, were totally unprepared for this assault on their cherished traditions and institutions. Hitler's justice minister Franz Gürtner later sadly confessed that he would have been "eternally happy" if he did not have to go into the justice building.[26] Hitler, he said, had an insurmountable preconceived opinion against justice because "his very nature is anarchy without any sense for the necessity of political order."[27]

On March 26 Hitler and Goebbels warned that the German government would increase its anti-Jewish measures if foreign protests against Germany, which were based on false rumors of anti-Semitic actions, were not terminated! Two days later, the Nazi Party released an eleven-point program for a boycott against Jewish businesses, goods, physicians, and lawyers. Julius Streicher was appointed chairman of a central committee of the NSDAP for the Prevention of Jewish Boycott and Atrocity Propaganda (Greuel- und Boycotthetze). Interestingly enough, no one bothered to consult the Ministry of Economics on the possible economic repercussions of such a boycott.[28] Although Hitler was dubious about the effectiveness of the boycott and conscious of his still unconsolidated political power, he decided to support a one-day boycott because he believed that it was a means to test the resolve of the new regime, while at the same time creating an outlet for the revolutionary fervor of the SA and the SS. He decided, however, on tactical grounds, to keep a low profile so as to appear above the fray, uninvolved and unsullied. So far, Hitler himself had no master plan for solving the Jewish question; what he had was an obsession — to cleanse Germany of Jewish influence.[29]

The boycott began on Saturday April 1, 1933, at ten o'clock and ended during the night of April 1-2, although it was never officially terminated by the Nazi Party. Boycotts, in fact, continued intermittently and in various degrees of intensity in various sections of Germany throughout the 1930s.[30] Historians have generally agreed that the boycott was a failure because it did not succeed in inflicting serious economic damage to Jewish businesses, let alone in solving the Jewish question. It is true, of course, that the boycott was self-defeating in the first place because, by attacking Jewish businesses, the Nazis were by definition damaging German businesses. Extensive economic damage was avoided because the boycott was limited to only one day and carried out to achieve primarily a propagandistic aim, namely, to impress upon the minds of the German people the threat they supposedly faced from their Jewish neighbors. Since the boycott was officially sponsored by party and state, it was hoped that the German people could be alerted to the Jewish problem. If seen from this perspective, there can be no doubt that the Nazis succeeded in bringing the Jewish problem to the attention of the majority of the German people. Germans shop on Saturday; and wherever they were shopping that day, they could not help seeing SA-men posted in front of Jewish businesses, nor could they avoid reading:

> *Deutscher, Kaufe nicht bei Juden* (Germans, Do not shop from Jews)
>
> *Die Juden sind unser Unglück* (Jews are our misfortune)
>
> *Jede Mark in Judenhand ist gestohlen dem deutschen Vaterland* (Every mark in Jewish hand is stolen from the Fatherland)

Jewish stores were marked by the Star of David and defaced by vile graffiti. The Hermann Tietz department stores were closed, but the Nazis had defaced display windows with swastikas and painted notices warning future customers not to shop there. Elsewhere, the offices of Jewish doctors, lawyers, notary publics, and dentists were also targeted in order to alert Germans that it was unpatriotic to patronize them. Wherever one went on April 1, one encountered the same picture of rowdy storm troopers — chanting, shouting, passing out leaflets, and harassing Jews. In Baden, the *Gau* leadership released a proclamation that was typical of similar party announcements and public postings in the rest of Germany:

> German Folk Comrades!
> Avoid houses marked by boycott signs!
> Against defense of Jewish atrocity and boycott incitement!
> Boycott all Jewish businesses!
> Do not buy from Jewish department stores!
> Do not go to Jewish attorneys!
> Avoid Jewish doctors!
> The Jews are our misfortune!
> Attend the mass demonstrations![31]

Given such official incitements, it should come as no great surprise that, despite party guidelines to observe street order and not to "hurt a single hair on a Jewish head" (*keinem Juden auch nur ein Haar krümmen*), excesses nevertheless occurred throughout Germany, especially in predominantly Jewish sections with east European populations (*Ostjuden*) such as the Scheunerviertel in Berlin, in Dortmund, in Duisburg, and in Saxony.[32] In Annaberg in Saxony, SS contingents positioned themselves in front of Jewish stores and rubber-stamped the faces of customers who left the store and showered them with derogatory remarks.[33] Elsewhere, the "defensive guards" snapped pictures of customers who exited or left a Jewish store, took their names, and later either posted lists of *Volksverräter* (Traitors to the people) on bulletin boards or published them in the newspaper, sometimes accompanied by photographs. Such official intimidation was bound to have devastating consequences for the Jewish population of Germany. Indeed, recollections by German Jews reveal just how this officially sponsored hatred altered their whole way of life and their perception of Germany, a country they had called their own for generations. Hertha Nathorff, who practiced medicine along with her husband in Berlin, noted in her diary that the day of the boycott was a searing event in her life; she wondered how this could have happened in the twentieth century. She was also curious why she had been overlooked: her office sign had not been marked. Later that day, however, a young man showed up and asked whether this was a "Jewish enterprise" (*Betrieb*), to which she replied that it wasn't an enterprise but a physician's practice. When she asked the young man whether he was "sick," he abandoned the idea of standing in front of her office and left.[34] Unlike some of her acquaintances, who believed that things would blow over in a few days, Hertha Nathorff knew that the Nazis were bent upon murdering the Jewish soul and she was deeply ashamed of her country. Edwin Landauer, a Jewish war veteran and member of the Reichsbund jüdischer Frontsoldaten (Reich League for Jewish Frontline Soldiers) felt the same way, referring to the boycott action as the beginning of Satanism, adding: "I am ashamed that I formerly belonged to such a people.... I was without a homeland [*Heimatland*]."[35]

A collective sense of shock, followed by outrage, shame, and alienation was typical of Jewish responses to such Nazi campaigns of hate. Victor Klemperer, a professor of Romance languages at the Technical University of Dresden, noted in his diary that he got the feeling of living in tsarist Russia or Armenia and being held hostage by an irrational regime that judged his people on purely racial rather than religious terms. He confessed: "I actually feel more shame than fear regarding Germany. I have always genuinely felt myself as a German."[36] Yet, many Jews still did not want to believe that the new Nazi government was entirely unresponsive to their needs. Leo Baeck and other prominent Jewish leaders, fearful of what the Nazis could do to the German Jewish community, even publicly endorsed the anti-Jewish boycott. They did so to rebut Nazi accusations that the German Jews were disloyal, thus hoping to forestall further attacks on German Jews. They would discover quickly, however, that no matter how much they appeased their Nazi masters, it was never enough, and that the Nazis would always dream up an ever greater number of laws, regulations, and humiliations to marginalize, isolate, and drive them from the country.

The boycott did, however, strengthen the hands of the Zionists. Robert Weltsch, in a lead editorial in the *Jüdische Rundschau* of April 4, wrote:

> The mark of the Jew was pressed upon all Jews of Germany on the first of April.... Everyone knows who is a Jew, evasion or hiding is no longer possible. The Jewish answer is clear — it is a short sentence which the prophet Jonah spoke: *Ivri anochi, Yes, a Jew!* To say "yes" to being Jewish, that is the moral meaning of current events.... We say "yes" and wear the yellow badge with pride.[37]

Robert Weltsch and the Zionists felt that the Jews were partly to blame for what had happened to them in Germany because they had pretended to be what they were not: Germans.[38] The Nazis had presented a clear-cut challenge which left them no alternative but to feel and act as Jews. Curiously enough, however, even Weltsch still believed in the spring of 1933 that Jews could maintain an economic and cultural basis in Germany. This would turn out to be an illusion that Weltsch and many other Jews were forced to abandon under a constant barrage of anti-Jewish legislation.

Only a week after the boycott, on April 7, the Law for the Restoration of the Civil Service introduced the notion of the "Aryan paragraph," stipulating that civil servants of non-Aryan background were to be forcibly "retired." Excluded from this provision were those non-Aryans who had held government employment on or before August 1, 1914, had fought on the front in World War I, or whose fathers or sons had been killed in the war. The latter concessions were reluctantly granted by Hitler after the Reich League for Jewish Frontline Soldiers sent a special plea to the aged President Hindenburg to exempt Jewish war veterans from the provisions of the proposed law. The Nazis, of course, refused to accept the claims made by Jewish war veterans that twelve thousand of their comrades had died at the front in World War I. Deluded by their stereotypes that every Jew was a coward and a shirker, they were convinced that such claims of Jewish sacrifice were pure fiction; the propaganda ministry subsequently spread lies to the effect that the "so-called" twelve thousand Jewish deaths in World War I were the result of "natural causes."[39] The law of April 7 left open the exact determination of how a Jew should be defined, which was supplied by a supplemental enactment of April 11, identifying anyone as Jewish who had Jewish grandparents on even one side of the family tree. Acrimonious debates would subsequently erupt relating to the relative degree of Jewishness in a person's background because some of the more "benign" racial fanatics wanted to "protect" in those half-Jews (*Mischlinge*) the "valuable" German blood, which, they believed, could be salvaged over time if no further racial pollution tainted their bloodstream. "Our aim is the biological separation of the Jewish and German races" editorialized the *Völkische Beobachter* on April 8, 1933.

In rapid succession came similar laws aimed at excluding Jews from other civil service positions than those already identified by the law of April 7. Jews were excluded as lay assessors, jurors, commercial judges (April 7); from serving as patent lawyers (April 22); and from being associated with state insurance institutions as panel judges (April 22), dentists, or dental technicians (June 2). A law against the overcrowding of German schools (April 5) severely limited Jewish enrollments in German public schools by setting up a quota system by which schools and universities were required to limit Jewish enrollments to 1.5 percent. On May 6, the Law of the Restoration of the Civil Service was amended to close loopholes in order to exclude honorary university professors, university lecturers, and notaries from civil service employment. Four days later, as previously mentioned, came the infamous book burnings. On that same day, Bernhard Rust, Reich minister of education, announced that all Jewish professors at German universities would be removed. Students were urged to boycott the lectures of Jewish professors who were still teaching at German universities. Professor Max Planck, Nobel laureate in physics, came to remonstrate with Hitler about the absurdity of dismissing valuable Jewish scientists, especially those who had absorbed the best of German culture, and was told: "A Jew is a Jew; all the Jews stick together like burrs....I must proceed against all of them equally."[40] And proceed equally he did, personally taking a hand in directing dismissals of Jewish professors, lawyers, and other civil servants.

In the summer and fall of 1933 additional decrees rained down on the Jews. On July 14, a spate of laws was passed that effectively ended all vestiges of German democracy. One law prohibited all political parties except for the Nazi Party and forbade the formation of new ones. What remained was a parliamentary shell in the form of a coordinated Reichstag that would obediently do the bidding of Adolf Hitler and pass any law no matter how irrational or unjust. Thus, in the series of laws ratified on July 14, the government could confiscate the property belonging to any organization (Jewish, Communist, Social Democratic, etc.) that was deemed hostile to the state. This law, entitled Law Concerning the Expropriation of Wealth Belonging to Enemies of Folk and State, would later serve as the basis for stripping Jews of their property and forcing them into emigration or deportation to the east. Another law empowered the government to revoke anyone's citizenship without having to justify it on any legal grounds. This law was directed primarily against eastern Jews (*Ostjuden*) who had come to Germany since World War I, but it was also used against scientists, writers, creative artists, and intellectuals, both Jewish and non-Jewish, who had aroused the ire of Nazi officials. Other laws controlled rural settlements and the establishment of farmsteads; the holding of plebiscites in order to ascertain public opinion regarding proposed measures; and government centralization of the structure of the Evangelical Church by subordinating the church to the control of a government appointed "Reich Bishop." Finally, as previously mentioned, the government passed a law, entitled Prevention of Progeny with Hereditary Diseases, which legalized sterilization and set in motion a series of biological measures that would involve the sterilization, concentration, and ultimately the mass gassing of such "lives not worth living" as the Jews, the mentally ill, and the Gypsies.

In late September and early October of 1933 three additional measures struck at the Jews: the first prohibited government employment of non-Aryans and persons married to them (September 28); the second excluded Jews from cultural and entertainment activities such as art, literature, theater, and film (September 29); and the third was the National Press Law, which placed all newspapers under government control and, by applying the "Aryan paragraph," effectively excluded Jews from German journalism.

The Initial Jewish Reaction

The series of anti-Jewish laws that began in April of 1933 and continued steadily until the end of the year was only the beginning of what would turn out to be some four hundred pieces of anti-Jewish legislation enacted between 1933 and 1939.[41] Each new anti-Jewish measure was worse than the previous one, each rubbed additional salt into the wound and added insult to injury. The initial Jewish reaction, particularly after the April laws, was marked by a syndrome that would repeat itself over and over again: first shock and disbelief (This couldn't happen in a civilized society), followed by shame and disgust (I am ashamed of the country I called my own), then a spreading paralysis upon recognition that few people cared (I see no way out, *Ich sehe keinen Ausweg*), a ray of misplaced hope that things would not get too bad (*es werde schon nicht so schlimm werden*), and finally the recognition that Jews had to organize and prepare for the worst.

In assessing Jewish reactions to the Nazi onslaught, we can distinguish between the responses of individual Jews, many of whom have left revealing testimonies, and those of various Jewish organizations that spoke on behalf of their beleaguered members. The first response was generally shock and disbelief, especially at the random acts of violence, the indifferent attitude of most Germans who watched them, and the stunned recognition that the German government was officially sponsoring discrimination and embodying it in legal form. Hertha Nathorff, for example, could not comprehend the insults and humiliations that were heaped on Jewish physicians in the hospitals of Berlin, where SA thugs went berserk and forcibly evicted physicians, even those who were in the middle of performing operations. "My old hospital," she wrote, "has lost some of its most talented physicians, the patients are in despair, and everything is topsy turvy. The hate speeches of Mr. Goebbels exceed anything that has yet existed in the form of incitement and mendacity, and the people listen and remain silent — and, above all, the leading physicians and prominent professors, what are they doing for their betrayed colleagues?"[42] Another cruel blow was delivered a little over a week later when she received an official letter from the magistrate of Charlottenburg informing her that she had to terminate her position as the leading physician of the Women's Advisory Agency. Hertha Nathorff was only one of thousands of Jewish professionals who were dismissed or faced impending removals from their positions. Young Inge Deutschkron, who survived the Holocaust by going underground in Berlin during World War II, recalls that her father, a public school teacher, was in total shock as he read and studied every sentence and every comma of his dismissal notice from the Prussian school system. Although he had fought as a soldier in World War I, his dismissal, he was told, was based on his political affiliation as a Social Democrat.[43] The same happened to Emil Fackenheim's father, who had been a practicing attorney prior to 1914 and a front soldier, but was dismissed nevertheless because he had allegedly defended some communists in 1918–19.[44] Inge Deutschkron's parents were consoled by Jewish friends as yet unaffected by the new laws that some solution would turn up to get them out of their misery.

Such hopes, of course, were rarely fulfilled because temporary concessions or loopholes in existing anti-Jewish measures were always removed quickly. Victor Klemperer, after going through the considerable trouble of supplying documentation that he was a World War I veteran who had seen action at the front, received what would turn out to be a temporary reprieve. He continued teaching under increasingly impossibly conditions, losing students, being shunned by colleagues, and receiving a steady stream of bad news about his Jewish friends, relatives, and acquaintances. Klemperer's feelings alternated between hurt pride and moral outrage, followed by attitudes of hopelessness and despair. "How long will this psychosis last," he asked himself on May 13, 1933.[45]

Bella Fromm, who continued writing society columns for the Ullstein papers and kept up her busy social schedule, asked herself "Is the entire nation in a trance state?"[46] Fromm, Klemperer, and other Jews who had a wide circle of acquaintances and insights into prevailing opinions were not only shocked by the indifference of ordinary Germans to what was being done to the Jews but also winced at the gullibility and sheer stupidity fellow Germans displayed in ventilating their anti-Jewish prejudices. Fromm, for example, found it hard to accept that many Germans, including Hitler, believed that Jews could be identified by a peculiar odor. While attending an official function, at which Hitler was also present, Fromm taunted Heinrich Lammers, the chief of the Führer's Reich Chancellery, by saying "Your Führer must have a cold." When asked why, she replied: "He's supposed to smell a Jew ten miles away, isn't he? Apparently his smell isn't working tonight."[47] One of

Hertha Nathorff's patients, a gullible young lady, came crying into her practice after being told at work that anyone who had sexual relations with a Jew could never again bear pure Aryan children. "I had to speak to this primitive creature at length to convince her of the idiocy of this assertion," Nathorff noted in her diary, whereupon the girl breathed a sigh of relief and replied: "Frau doctor, I already wanted to turn on the gas tap, but ran to you at the last moment."[48] Nathorff wondered how many Germans could still run to someone who could disabuse them of anti-Jewish delusions and for how long.

Even when Germans tried to be sympathetic to the plight of individual Jews because they had known them from personal experience as good and honorable people, they could rarely divest themselves of the conviction that the measures taken against the Jews, since they were government sponsored, must somehow be justifiable. Some of these attitudes, as Saul Friedländer reminds us, depended on their faith in Hitler, because sympathy for the Jews would mean distrust of the rightness of the Führer's ways, something the majority of Germans were unwilling to admit throughout the Nazi period.[49] This surrealistic attitude is well brought out by a vignette recounted by the Jewish actress Lilli Palmer, who lost a motion picture contract because she was Jewish. Her landlady, who was sympathetic to her plight, joined her for a cup of coffee to commiserate with her and said: "It's really a shame because you can't deny that Hitler is a good man. You bet your life he'll make Germany great again. Too bad he has this ... this thing about the Jews."[50]

Perhaps the more devastating impact of anti-Jewish prejudices, as previously mentioned, was on uncomprehending Jewish children, who lost their friends, were exposed to humiliations and physical attacks by their German peers, and had to suffer insults by fanatical Nazi teachers. Jews who survived Hitler have recounted stories of petty slights and humiliations, from being called *Judenlümmel* (Jewish lout) or *Judensau* (Jewish pig) to being beaten up by their German peers. Ruth Freund-Joachimsthal, who attended the Dürerschule in Dresden, recalls:

> After the vacation the school was coordinated. The new German teacher came to class with a swastika on his lapel. He had a list of students in front of him, which he studied intensively. He then posed a question, which I remember to this day. I raised my hand along with many other classmates. The new teacher pointed at me: "Put your hand down. Jews have no business in a German class!"[51]

Interestingly enough, Ruth's classmates showed solidarity by also lowering their hands and refusing to answer. The Nazi teacher interrupted class, ran to the director of the school, who was also a confirmed Nazi, and reported the incident. The director then suspended Freund-Joachimsthal from class and explained the new political situation to the other students. Ruth Freund-Joachimsthal never returned to the Dürerschule again.[52]

In the schools of Nazi Germany, Jewish children were frequently shunned, insulted, and ultimately excluded. Many Holocaust survivors have told stories about their embarrassing experiences in the German school system, particularly the *Niederträchtigkeit der deutschen Lehrer*, the vile actions of the German teachers. Max Federmann, who went to school in Frankfurt, recalls that he was frequently taunted by German bullies on his way to and from school, forcing him to devise ingenious strategies to avoid certain conspicuous places, but sometimes simply having to stand up and fight, which he did not mind since he was well trained in boxing. His encounters with Germans were generally unpleasant, and to this day he cannot remember one sympathetic comment by any German regarding the plight Jews were exposed to on a daily basis in Nazi Germany. He still chokes back tears recalling the insensitivity and brutality meted out by the Nazis, culminating in his daring escape as a young man from the clutches of Gestapo officials who were closing in to round up the remainder of his family for deportation in 1941. Although his father had managed to emigrate to England with four of the family's eight children, fifteen-year-old Max, his mother, his twin brother, Bernhard, his sister Erma, and his older brother, Herman, remained behind in Nazi Germany. Max, who escaped and joined the partisans in Yugoslavia and later in Italy, survived the Holocaust; the rest of the family, with the exception of his brother Herman, who fled to China, perished in the death camps of Poland.[53]

Helmut Hönigsberg, whose parents owned a confectionery store in Bernkastel on Main, also vividly recalls his turbulent childhood in Nazi Germany, especially incidents he refers to as *Kinderschikane* (chicaneries by children) as well as insults by teachers. The principal of his school, he recalls, routinely struck him when he refused to say, "Heil Hitler." His German schooling ended after only one year of *Volksschule;* one day the school principal gave him a letter to take to his father that was addressed to the *Saujude Isaak Hönigsberg* (to the Jew pig Isaak Hönigsberg) and directed him to remove his loutish pig of a son from school by the end of the academic year (*soll seinen Saulümmel am Ende des Schuljahres entfernen*).[54] Young Hönigsberg, like all Jewish children in the mid- to late 1930s, was then forced to attend various Jewish schools, but even then the insults and physical attacks by his German peers continued.

It goes without saying that for many young Jews daily life in Nazi Germany was marked by constant anxiety and stress, made all the more traumatic by its unpredictability. With the complicity of many Germans, the Nazis perpetuated a ruthless psychic assault on Jewish children, robbing them of their human dignity and their innocence. Two contrasting and devastating examples of how Judeophobia operated on young children, one Jewish and the other German, illustrate the depth of psychological depravity at work on that level. A Jewish father did not realize how much his son suffered from a constant barrage of degrading remarks by his teacher who, among other petty slights, prevented him from participating in swimming lessons by telling him in front of all the other students: "With your flat feet you can go into the Jordan, but you can't pollute German water." Then one day, his son confided in him: "Father, if you had continued to force me to go to school I would have thrown myself under a train."[55] Quite a different reaction was overheard by a Jewish woman who was shopping for her daughter in a confectionery store. Another woman was buying a pair of trousers for her twelve-year-old son. The proprietor stroked the boy's hair and asked him whether he enjoyed looking forward to his Christmas presents. "Yes, very much," replied the child, "but my neatest Christmas gift would be if they clubbed to death all the Jews."[56]

In order to cope with these constant anti-Jewish attacks, the Jews sought solace and comfort in their own company and in their own organizations. Leo Baeck, the leading voice of German Jewry, announced in a meeting of the Jewish *Gemeinden* on April 13, 1933: "The thousand-year history of the German Jews has come to an end."[57] He realized that what remained to be done was to salvage what one could under the circumstances, but this required that the Jews of Germany had to rise above their differences and find strength in a common organization. Beginning in the spring of 1933, Baeck and other prominent Jews tried to construct a roof under which all Jews could unite. This was the Zentralausschuss für Hilfe und Aufbau (the Central Committee for Relief and Rehabilitation), which came into being in April of 1933 and included such major Jewish organizations as the Centralverein, the Zionistic Union of Germany, the Prussian State Association of Jewish Communities (*Gemeinden*), the Jewish *Gemeinde* of Berlin, and the Jewish Jisroel. The presiding officer was Leo Baeck, but the direction and energy were provided by younger men such as Max Kreutzberger, Salomon Adler-Rudel, Friedrich Brodnitz, and Paul Eppstein. Unfortunately, none of these men, all of whom served as prominent members of the Central Committee, were permanent members in an environment of impermanence and danger. Kreutzberger emigrated to Palestine in 1935, Adler-Rudel was expelled from Germany in 1936, Brodnitz emigrated to the United States in 1937, and Eppstein was murdered in Theresienstadt in 1943.[58]

The chief function of the Central Committee was to minister to the social and economic needs of German Jews, especially those who were unemployed, such as the professionals who had been pauperized almost overnight by the Civil Service Law. In addition to economic assistance, the Central Committee also provided legal assistance by trying to reverse "illegal dismissals" in the courts, a futile procedure because the Jewish leadership painfully discovered that it was no longer dealing with a legal but a criminal state. Since German Jews were incrementally being excluded from all existing welfare agencies, which included a whole range of economic and medical benefits, the Central Committee, which was later integrated into an even larger umbrella called Reichsvertretung der deutschen Juden (Reich Representation of German Jews), was forced to take on a truly Herculean task in helping the beleaguered Jews of Germany. In this task it did not stand entirely by itself because various Jewish organizations abroad such as the American Joint Distribution Committee and the Central British Fund, contributed generously.

In addition to organizing themselves for economic survival, the Jews also tried to develop their own educational and cultural institutions. By the mid-1930s it was becoming apparent that Jews could no longer attend German public schools, which meant that they had to organize their own Jewish schools, a daunting task given the shortage of financial resources, the problem of finding qualified teachers, and the ever-present uncertainty Jews faced as hostages in a hostile country. One bright side to this otherwise gloomy picture, as Kurt and Alice Bergel pointed out, was that these Jewish schools could at least be genuinely Jewish by encouraging instruction in Hebrew and by focusing on their own traditions, many of which had been displaced by German cultural traditions.[59] During the few years they were permitted to operate, Jewish schools became the only educational islands of rationality in Germany; in the Bergels' judgment, they also became the sole custodians of progressive education.[60] Under the impact of Nazi persecution, Jewish self-consciousness was surprisingly reinvigorated and actually indirectly encouraged by the Nazis because their racial policies would not allow them to coordinate (*gleichschalten*) Jewish institutions, restricting the Nazis to only two options: either allowing the Jews to cultivate their own traditions or driving them out of the country. Until 1938, the Nazis were willing to grant the Jews a marginal economic livelihood, provided, as Joseph Goebbels put it in a speech of May 10, 1934, that they isolated themselves from the rest of the German population, kept quiet, and gracefully accepted their inferior place in the new racial order. It was obvious, however, that such mendacious pronouncements provided no security whatsoever for the Jews of Germany, for behind deceptive Nazi assurances was the ever present reality of harassment and intimidation. In their educational activities, Jewish schools therefore emphasized a future outside Germany. Young and old had to be trained and retrained along more practical lines and in marketable skills and occupations. Zionist youth leagues, for example, operated agricultural training farms in order to prepare young people for emigration to Palestine. By the end of 1933 more than six hundred students, including older people, were receiving vocational instruction; thirteen hundred were living on agricultural teaching farms called *hachshara*, a Hebrew word for "training."[61]

The Jews also organized their own cultural activities. The Kulturbund deutscher Juden (Cultural Association of German Jews), founded in the spring of 1933, had a twofold mission: to provide work for unemployed Jewish artists, writers, and musicians and to further the cause of Jewish culture. Under the leadership of Kurt Singer, a physician as well as a musician, Kurt Baumann, a young director, and Julius Bab, a music critic, the Kulturbund attracted some first-rate talent and offered a remarkably rich variety of cultural productions in the form of concerts, theater performances, poetry reading, lectures, and art exhibitions.[62]

Many of these activities, educational, cultural, social, and economic, were also organized spontaneously and in self-help form, and special gala functions were organized by individuals or professional groups to raise money for unemployed physicians or lawyers. The Jewish Artists' Relief Group, founded by middle-class women, organized lectures and artistic performances in private homes and restaurants, in addition to setting up a soup kitchen for needy artists. Small Jewish credit associations provided financial help in the form of small, interest-free loans to artisans and tradesmen.[63] The banker Max Warburg, who had always been active in supporting welfare for the impoverished and needy in the Jewish community, was actively involved in the charitable work of the overwhelmed Hilfsverein der deutschen Juden (Aid Society for German Jews), whose primary mission in the 1930s was to help German Jews emigrate abroad. The Hilfsverein provided all sorts of information on the topic of emigration, involving the latest news from abroad, professional counseling, administrative formalities, and financial support. As a major banker, who had been a friend of the kaiser, the uncrowned financial king of Hamburg, and friend of Hjalmar Schacht, who would shortly become economic minister in Hitler's government, Warburg still believed that men of his class were special and therefore immune to Nazi persecution.[64] But as M. M. Warburg & Company steadily lost clients and the firm was expelled from many securities syndicates, its founder, himself increasingly shunned by former colleagues and business partners, was rudely awakened to the nightmare that was Nazi Germany.[65] In the face of reports that the Nazis were planning to seize the assets of Jewish banks, the ongoing assaults on Jews on a daily basis, and the double-dealing Nazi bureaucrats with whom he was negotiating to ease the transfer of Jewish assets overseas to Palestine, Warburg vowed to salvage as much as possible of his own fortune and that of many of his fellow Jews. Moreover, that his own life was hanging on a thread was vividly brought home to Warburg at the end of June 1933, when his eighty-year-old uncle, Moritz Oppenheim, and his aunt committed suicide because they saw no future for themselves in Nazi Germany.

For Max Warburg and many other well-to-do German Jews it was still possible during the early years of Nazi rule to salvage their assets and emigrate abroad. Although legal restrictions had been placed on the transfer of funds from Germany to other countries, transfer experts were generally successful in helping their clients salvage their financial assets. When Jewish assets appeared to be specifically earmarked for the purpose of emigration, Nazi officials were still prepared to deal flexibly within existing laws.[66] In September of 1933 the Ministry of Economics, the Zionist Organization for Germany (ZVFG), and the Palestine Bank reached an agreement, the Haavara Agreement (*Haavara* being Hebrew for transfer) by which Jewish emigrants or investors could export capital from Germany to Palestine in the form of various commodities. The idea behind this mutually advantageous Agreement was for the Germans to increase their exports and for the Jews to salvage a significant amount of their assets and to emigrate abroad. Although there was considerable opposition to the agreement by various foreign Jewish groups, including the Jewish community of Palestine (because the agreement benefited the Nazis at the very time that foreign boycotts against them were being organized), the Haavara Agreement greatly eased the emigration of about fifty-two thousand German Jews to Palestine. German Jews who planned to emigrate to Palestine deposited their funds into a blocked account (*Sperrkonto*) that remained in Germany. Whenever Palestine bought German goods, it had to pay only 50 percent in its own foreign exchange; the remaining 50 percent was taken from the blocked assets of German Jews who had emigrated. When these Jewish emigrants arrived in Palestine they received half the value of their blocked assets in Germany from the Haavara Trust Company of Palestine, which was registered with the Anglo-Palestine Bank. On the German end of the arrangement, it was the Palestine Trusteeship Office, assisted by two private banks (Warburg and Wassermann), that oversaw the implementation of the Haavara Agreement.[67]

Although some fifty-two thousand German Jews would eventually emigrate to Palestine in the 1930s, much of the emigration made possible by the Haavara Agreement, emigration was the last resort for the majority of German Jews. Rooted as most of them were in their German homeland, they looked upon leaving the country as a desperate flight, some even as a desertion rather than a freely chosen form of emigration. One Holocaust survivor, whose father was murdered at Auschwitz, remembers his father saying: "Why should I emigrate? Not everything is eaten as hot as it is cooked. After all, we live in a legal state [*Rechtsstaat*]. What could happen to me? I am a Front Fighter, I fought four years on the western front for my fatherland, I was a noncommissioned officer and received the Iron Cross First Class."[68] Such normal reactions, which appear in retrospect naive and tragically mistaken, were not uncommon throughout the first four years of Nazi rule.

Although roughly ten thousand intellectuals, academics, left-wing politicians and journalists, and dismissed professionals working in the larger businesses left Germany in 1933, the majority of German Jews decided to wait until the storm subsided. Besides, the obstacles to emigration were many: few countries were willing to accept immigrants at the height of the depression, setting up strict quotas and limiting emigration to young people or couples who met specific occupational needs that were at a premium in the host country. The United States, Latin America, and British dominions, hard hit by the collapse in prices in agricultural products and in raw materials, set strict limits to immigration. The same was true of European countries, most of which were also anti-Jewish to one degree or another. In order to emigrate,

Jews had to be flexible, inventive, and ingenious because they had to take risks, buck the bureaucratic systems of Nazi Germany and the host countries, and quickly adjust to different languages and new cultural practices. As Walter Laqueur recalls: "No country in the world waited for the Jews."[69] The Jews, however, increasingly waited for them. Laqueur pointed out that Jews who thought of emigrating had to master a whole new vocabulary, replete with acronyms and annoying bureaucratic euphemisms and jargon: regrouping (*Umschichtung*), existence, creating existence (*Existenz schaffen*), secure existence, Certificate of good conduct (*Leumundszeugnis*), hachshara, certificate of good health (*Gesundheitsattest*), declaration of Inoffensiveness (*Unbedenklichkeitserklärung*), boarding money, certificate, affadavit, chamada, ICA, HIAS, HICEM, Alltreu Paltreu, and the like.

In addition to mastering an array of new bureaucratic terms, foreign and domestic, Jews also had to deal with indifferent and disagreeable officials, whose overbearing tone and condescending attitudes, despised and feared by most Germans, were particularly degrading when it came to Jews. Finally, Jews who contemplated emigration had to be alert to the latest information about places in the world that might accept certain categories of Jews. The Jewish Hilfsverein, with its confidential network of informants, would tell prospective emigrants, for example, that the Fiji Islands was looking for a Jewish pastry cook and a single watchmaker who had to be between the ages of twenty-five and thirty-five, or that Paraguay was looking for a candy maker, British Bechuanaland a perfect furrier, Central Africa an unmarried kosher butcher specializing in saveloy sausage, San Salvador an unmarried Jewish engineer for the construction of electrical machinery. One's best chances were in Manchukuo, where a cabaret was looking for a Jewish director who also had to be a ballet master and was expected to perform with the first ballerina; they were also looking for six to eight ballerinas who also had to be capable of being solo performers. Moreover, Manchukuo was also seeking a Jewish women's choir and a woman pianist who could also play the accordion.[70]

With such obstacles it is no wonder that Jews bowed to emigration only in extreme circumstances, usually following major Nazi assaults on them. The first coordinated attack came in 1933, followed by a lull in 1934, a renewed assault in legal form in 1935, a lull in 1936 (the year of the Olympic Games), and a gathering storm that culminated in the pogrom of 1938 and the ensuing flood of government-sponsored measures that turned Jews into nonpersons. Despite the flood of legislation that was unleashed against the Jews in 1933, depriving them of many civil rights, they still harbored hopes of being left alone in the economic domain. In August of 1934 Hitler appointed Hjalmar Schacht to head the Ministry of Economics. Before accepting the post, Schacht had a personal meeting with Hitler in which he asked him about the role of the Jews and was told that in "economics the Jews can carry on exactly as they have up to now."[71] Schacht envisioned a different role for the Jews that involved curtailing their civil or political but not their economic rights, and Hitler initially seemed to side with him against party radicals who wanted to exclude Jews from economic life. Schacht later claimed that he protected the Jews on the economic front as long as he was minister of economics (1934–37), a claim that does not completely conform to the historical record. It is true that he protected some leading Jewish banks and opposed what he called "lawless riotous actions against the Jews," but the legend he subsequently spread about sheltering the Jews with a protective hand is little more than a self-serving apology.[72]

As early as 1933, in fact, Jews came under intense pressure to sell their businesses, a form of pressure, intimidation, and blackmail that would later be called Aryanization. Between 1933 and 1938 this practice was euphemistically called "voluntary Aryanization," and involved the transfer of Jewish-owned firms to Aryan buyers. Schacht's "protective hand" was nowhere to be seen when the first party attacks on Jewish firms began, nor could it be since Schacht's powers were limited in relationship to other Nazi leaders who had closer access to Hitler: Goebbels, Himmler, and Göring. In 1934, for example, following a lengthy period of harassment, Goebbels and Max Amann, Hitler's president of the Reich Press Chamber and publisher of the party's chief publishing house, compelled several famous Jewish publishing firms to sell out to Aryan firms. The Ullstein publishing empire, estimated to be worth between fifty and sixty million marks, was sold under pressure to the Nazi-owned Eher Verlag for a mere ten million marks.[73] The Mosse chain sold out for five million marks, and its holdings were transferred to an Aryan firm. The *Frankfurter Zeiting,* owned by the Sonnemann-Simon families, which had distinguished itself in its opposition to the Nazis prior to 1933, was transferred to I. G. Farben, and the Sonnemann heirs gave up direction of the paper.[74]

These and other as yet "voluntary" Aryanizations represented the vanguard of the Nazi economic assault on the Jews, which proceeded incrementally and simultaneously with "voluntary" emigration, rowdy street actions, and anti-Jewish decrees. Just as the lawless actions appeared to subside in 1934, giving the Jews the illusion that their tormentors were satisfied with their accomplishment and allowing them a window of opportunity, the Nazis accelerated the pace in the spring of 1935 and consummated their renewed rage by disenfranchising the Jews as German citizens and stigmatizing them as racial enemies.

The Delusion Picks Up Speed: The Nuremberg Racial Laws

For eighteen months, following his appointment as chancellor, Hitler had treated Germans to a breathless display of fireworks, speeches, appeals, coups, and histrionics. He had also unleashed an unprecedented assault on Germany's alleged enemies, especially the Jews. By the beginning of 1935, if not much earlier, both the dictator and his audience were tired of revolutionary upheavals.[75] To forestall further public unrest, the Führer announced that the revolutionary phase was over and that the emphasis from now on would be on evolution rather than revolution. This, or course, did not happen — not even after the Röhm purge and Hitler's attainment of complete dictatorial power in the summer of 1934. Although Hitler had eliminated Röhm and reduced the SA to a mere propagandistic tool of the Nazi Party, making the army rather than the SA the nation's only bearer of arms, the fact remained that the SA continued to be actively involved in stirring up anti-Jewish agitation and violence.

The year 1935 saw an increase of anti-Jewish agitation, sponsored largely by the SA and by members of the party who, for various reasons, believed that they could profit from spreading hate against the Jews. Streicher's gutter Judeophobia was on view in the pages of *Der Stürmer,* which were prominently posted in public display cases (*Stürmer-Kästen*) all over Germany. Streicher's tabloid treated Germans to hair-raising stories about alleged Jewish evil in the form of ritual child murder and race defilement. In the summer of 1935 Streicher staged mass demonstrations in Berlin and Hamburg, warning gullible Germans that the Jew was neither a man nor an animal, but the devil's handiwork, and that Germany's salvation depended on the solution to the Jewish question. In a meeting with students Streicher was quite explicit about what should be done to the Jews: "All our struggles," he told them, "are in vain if the battle against the Jew is not fought to the finish. It is not enough to get the Jews out of Germany. No, they must be killed [*totgeschlagen*] in the entire world, so that humanity will be free of them."[76] While Streicher was worrying about German race defilement by Jews, Goebbels was obsessively preoccupied with Jewish influence on German culture and excluded the Jews from the Reich Chamber of Writers (April 12) and from the Reich Press Chamber (April 24), thus effectively eliminating Jews from making a living as writers in any branch of their trade.

One Judeophobic activity or decree spawned another, but overall coordination was still lacking because no single German agency had been able to assume sole control over the direction of the anti-Jewish campaign. In what would become paradigmatic of Nazi rule on many issues, the process of decision-making and implementation would cut across a bewildering number of competing agencies and personalities, making it difficult to resolve complex issues. Since the Jewish question was one of the regime's primary obsessions, its resolution depended on clear policies and interagency coordination. By 1935 this was only loosely accomplished. There were Jewish experts (*Referenten*) in the Ministries of the Interior, Propaganda, Economics, Justice, Education, in the Foreign Office, and in Himmler's growing police empire, not to speak of the branches of the party and various research institutes or think tanks, each of them delivering weighty pronouncements and regulations. Yet, in a state that still pretended to work within the framework of legality, policies, to be efficacious, required legal formulation and legal justification. This is why the Ministries of Justice and the Interior, responsible for formulation and implementation of laws respectively, would play their part in the anti-Jewish campaign of 1935.

The question the Nazis had never conclusively resolved was: Who is a Jew and how can he or she be identified? Was it by religious convictions or by racial characteristics? Although the Nazis had reached what they thought was a definitive conclusion based on race, it was by no means clear how racial characteristics could be of much help in identifying who was a Jew in any crowd. Racial taxonomies and physiognomic criteria were notoriously vague and unreliable in making a determination as to whether a person was or was not Jewish. There were many blond and blue-eyed German Jews; some of them, notably Sally Perel, even joined the Hitler Youth and survived the Holocaust by serving in the German army.[77] Primitive Judeophobes, including Streicher and Hitler, of course, claimed that they could tell a Jew by body odor, crooked nose, or earlobes. Inge Deutschkron recounts an embarrassing incident while posing for a picture for a photographer who told her to pull her hair behind her left ear so that the form of the ear could be clearly visible. Presumably, this would prove that she was Jewish because Jewish earlobes were different from Aryan earlobes.[78] Inspecting herself a hundred times afterward in the mirror, she could find no difference between her earlobes and those of any other German. Yet the earlobe obsession continued to surface periodically in Nazi circles. Jewish passports had to reveal ears and Adolf Hitler even instructed his emissaries who negotiated the Nazi-Soviet Non-Aggression Pact in August of 1939 to make sure to inspect Stalin's ears to settle, once and for all, his curiosity whether the Soviet dictator was Jewish.[79] Julius Streicher claimed that in addition to peculiar eyes, noses, ears, or smells, he could also tell Jews by their behinds. When Doctor Gilbert, the American psychiatrist at Nuremberg, asked him what was peculiar about the Jewish behind, Streicher smirked wisely and said, "The Jewish behind is so feminine — so soft and feminine," virtually drooling as he shaped the Jewish behind with his lascivious hands. He added: "And you can tell from the way it wobbles when they walk . . . and another thing is the way they talk with their hands . . . but even if you cannot tell by these physical gestures, their behavior always gives them away."[80]

Yet, physical, behavioral, or even psychological methods of detecting Jews were of dubious help and scientifically worthless. This did not, however, deter Nazi radicals from clinging to their ideological delusion that Jews were racially different and dangerous. It was the hope of some Nazi racists in the medical profession that, sooner or later, Jewishness could be scientifically demonstrated. Dr. Eugen Stähle, head of the medical profession of Württemberg, claimed to offer new scientific evidence in a popular medical magazine, *The People's Health Watch*, that different races might also have different kinds of blood. He had reached this conclusion, he indicated, on the basis of certain blood diseases that affected only specific races: sickle-cell anemia in blacks and certain unspecified "accumulated diseases" among Jews, which he called an "irony of biology," presumably because these accumulated diseases affected only Jews.[81] These blood differences, he argued, proved beyond a shadow of a doubt that blood had not only symbolic but also physical meaning that was grounded in scientific fact. He also cited the work of Professor E. O. Maniloff of Leningrad, who claimed that he was able to distinguish with 90 percent accuracy between Jewish and Russian blood. Stähle could not disguise his excitement by pointing out to his readers: "Think what it might mean, if we could identify non-Aryans in the test tube! Then neither deception, nor baptism, nor name change, nor citizenship, and not even nasal surgery could help.... One cannot change one's blood."[82]

In the absence of scientific proof as to who was a Jew, the Nazis proceeded to rely on various traditional standbys, including baptismal birth registries obtained from the Jewish *Gemeinden,* and the less reliable methods that involved facial features, names, and various so-called Jewish cultural or behavioral traits. Following a rash of anti-Jewish outbreaks in the summer of 1935, during which signs of "Jews not wanted here" (*Juden unerwünscht*) proliferated all over Germany, the Nazi regime decided that the only way to control popular anti-Semitism was to legalize it.[83] This political strategy forms the background to the Nuremberg racial laws that came out of the 1935 annual party congress.

On September 15, 1935, Adolf Hitler called a special session of the German Reichstag at the Hall of the Nuremberg Cultural Association in order to ratify three crucial laws: the Reich Flag Law, the Citizenship Law, and the Law for the Protection of German Blood and German Honor. Convening the Reichstag at the end of the annual Nuremberg Party Congress, the first time the congress met outside Berlin, had a special political and symbolic significance. In the first place, Hitler was beginning to rearm on a massive scale, and he wanted the new German army to be a National Socialist army. Having already made major concessions to the conservative officers' corps by eliminating the threat of the SA, he now asked them to help him shape a new National Socialist army. The first step in this direction was a purely symbolic one: retiring the old imperial black-white-red flag in favor of the swastika. This explains the first Nuremberg Law, which proclaimed that henceforth black, white, and red were the national colors and the swastika was the national flag.

The flag issue was also connected to the two Nuremberg racial laws. On July 26, American protesters boarded the steamship liner *Bremen,* anchored in New York harbor, and tore off the swastika flag that had been draped on the bow of the ship. Hitler believed that this provocation had been incited by the Jewish-controlled press in America, and he was itching to send them a message in kind by further discrimination against German Jews. In his distorted racist thinking, there was only one successful way of responding to the international Jewish conspiracy, and that was to rearm Germany and use its Jews as hostages and bargaining chips. Thus, if foreign powers did not accede to his demands, he would blame foreign Jews for being responsible and mete out further punishment to the Jews under his control. In addressing the assembled delegates at Nuremberg, Hitler insisted that the recent desecration of the German flag in New York was only the latest of many hate campaigns against Germany, all of them stemming from the one source that always incited people against each other and decomposed whole nations: world Jewry.[84] Since another boycott against Germany was being organized, the time had come, Hitler said, to channel the justifiable anger the German people were publicly expressing into appropriate legislation. Perhaps in this way a legal basis could be created that would permanently regulate German-Jewish relations. The reality was that Hitler had no intention of regularizing German-Jewish relations; what he wanted to do was to appear to distance himself from the anti-Jewish violence by placing himself on the side of legality.[85] This was the real reason why Hitler asked for legal decrees against the Jews; it was not a last-minute decision on his part to include something dramatic in the Nuremberg Party Congress because the existing program was too unexciting, as some German insiders later claimed.[86]

On September 13, 1935, Bernhard Lösener, head of the Jewish Office in the Ministry of the Interior, was ordered to take a plane to Nuremberg to help formulate a law on mixed marriages. Upon arrival, Lösener and two colleagues from the Ministry of the Interior, Hans Pfundtner and Wilhelm Stuckart, hammered out a preliminary draft, which was rejected. On September 14, the drafters met at Wilhelm Frick's residence, where they crowded into the music room, Pfundtner working on the grand piano and Stuckart on the sofa, and eventually they came up with several optional drafts, differing in toughness. Just as the exhausted team had finished its work at midnight, they were asked for another law dealing with citizenship, which they produced quickly on the back of a menu. At 2:30 a.m., September 15, Hitler accepted the milder version of the law on mixed marriages along with the Reich Citizenship Law.

The law on mixed marriages, entitled Law for the Protection of German Blood and German Honor (Gesetz zum Schutze des deutschen Blutes und der deutschen Ehre), prohibited marriages and sexual relations between Germans and Jews, forbade Jews from employing female citizens of German or kindred blood under forty-five years of age, declared null and void marriages contracted despite this law inside or outside Germany, prohibited Jews from hoisting the German flag, and prescribed various penalties varying from hard labor to imprisonment with a fine. The Reich citizenship law (Reichsbürgergesetz) distinguished between citizens and subjects (*Reichsbürger* and *Staatsangehörige*), the former being of German or kindred blood with full political rights and the latter belonging (*angehörig*) to the state but enjoying only protection rather than political rights.

In justifying the distinction between Germans with superior rights and Jews with inferior ones, Wilhelm Stuckart and his legal advisor Hans Globke, who would later resurface as one of Konrad Adenauer's chief aides in the Bonn Chancellery, provided the following official commentary:

> National Socialism opposes to the theories of the equality of all men and of the fundamentally unlimited freedom of the individual vis-à-vis the State the harsh but necessary recognition of the inequality of men and of the differences between them based on the laws of nature. Inevitably, differences in the rights and duties of the individual derive from the differences in character between races, nations, and people.[87]

The citizenship law still left unclear the legal issue of who was a "full" Jew, a question that caused intense debates among racial and legal experts in the wake of the Nuremberg decrees and ultimately resulted in an addendum to the law that tried to specify who was a Jew. The legal experts defined a "full Jew" as someone who had three Jewish grandparents. Those who had smaller fractions of Jewishness were labeled as *Mischlinge,* or mixed breeds, divided, in turn, into mixed breeds first degree (two Jewish grandparents) and second degree (one Jewish grandparent). Those who had been classified as mixed breeds first degree could still be considered full Jews if they (1) belonged to a Jewish religious community, (2) were married to a Jew, (3) were offspring of marriages contracted with Jews after June 15, 1935, or were born out of wedlock to Jews. The legal experts believed that they were being humane in separating "mixed blood" from completely polluted Jewish blood. Stuckart and Lösener wanted to "protect" the good blood in such people, estimated in 1935 to number about 750,000 but actually numbering between 200,000 and 250,000.[88] The Nazi racial experts in essence had created a third race, an absurd category but one that would have serious consequences because anyone being categorized a *Mischling* stood an excellent chance in 1941 of escaping the Holocaust. The whole notion of racial half-breeds who had supposedly inherited either good or bad racial traits was a biological delusion that, in turn, rested on an ideological delusion about racial superiority and racial defilement.

It goes without saying that the exact determination of who was a Jew, subject also to religious criteria according to the Nuremberg Laws, a clear-cut admission that biological criteria were inadequate, produced a bureaucratic nightmare because it involved scores of "family researchers" hunting down uncertain records. Requests for reclassification became frequent and urgent, especially by those who wanted to escape official harassment because their livelihood was directly threatened. In-dividuals moved heaven and earth to be "liberated" from the appellation "Jewish" or *Mischling*. Such liberations required inspections, reviews, and ministerial approval. There were two kinds of liberation: artificial (*unecht*) and genuine (*echt*), the first involving reclassification based on a fact of law because it was revealed, for example, that an alleged Jew-ish grandfather was not Jewish after all, and the second pertaining to an applicant's meritorious contributions to the Reich.[89] The genuine lib-eration had to be routed through the Ministry of the Interior and the Reich chancellery for civilians and the Army High Command for sol-diers. Recipients of genuine liberations were often influential officials, such as ministerial secretary Leo Killy, who was a *Mischling* second degree and his wife a *Mischling* first degree. For meritorious work ren-dered to the Reich Chancellery, a grateful Killy received a Christmas gift in 1936 in the form of a liberation and later performed significant func-tions in destroying the Jews to prove that he was worthy of it.[90] Hitler would sign scores of documents called "declarations of German blood" to keep valuable officers with Jewish ancestors in the Wehrmacht, one being Field Marshal Erhard Milch, who was Aryanized with the help of his chief, Hermann Göring.

On September 25, 1935, the man whose office of racial policy issued "certification of ancestry," Dr. Walter Gross, assembled the regional leaders of his department and briefed them on a personal meeting with Hitler he had attended on the application of the Nuremberg Racial Laws.[91] The Führer had told him, Gross reported, that his intention was still to expunge Jewish influence on German life and culture. He criticized Streicher's actions, which had forced him to side against the extreme attitudes of the party, especially on the issue of the role of mixed breeds. Of the three options available to him on the *Mischling* question — expulsion, sterilization, assimilation — Hitler had decided in favor of assimilation on the grounds that his future plans (military preparedness and imperial expansion) required a unified and loyal popu-lation, which would be difficult if one suddenly created a caste of people of uncertain allegiance. He added that he also opposed further boy-cotts on the same grounds because they threatened to disrupt Germany's economic activities. More vigorous emigration, followed by additional economic measures, would be needed to rid the country of the Jews alto-gether, but one had to be careful not to impoverish the Jews to the point where they would become a burden to the Reich. In case of war on all fronts, Hitler ominously remarked, he was prepared for all the conse-quences, implying that he would resort to the most extreme measures in getting rid of the Jews.

Only four days later, addressing high party officials, Hitler pointed out that only a few points in the Nuremberg Laws required further clarification, which he said he would leave up to the party and the Ministry of the Interior to settle.[92] A fight between the two institutions promptly ensued, illustrating not only Hitler's mercurial leadership style but also the fact that the Jewish question was still open-ended and subject to manipulation by agencies and personalities loosely and simultaneously assigned to pursue various actions, which still included wild actions, discriminatory decrees, economic strangulation, and accelerated emigration.

Public reaction to the Nuremberg racial laws was generally supportive because most Germans assumed that these laws, having placed Jewish identity and Jewish existence on a firm legal foundation, would bring about a restoration of domestic tranquility and good order. Situation reports by the SD and by various Gestapo offices throughout Germany, intended to gauge public opinion, indicate that the laws elicited great satisfaction and enthusiasm throughout the population (*Die Gesetze haben überall grosse Befriedigung und Begeisterung im Volke ausgelöst*).[93] A report from Koblenz claimed that people were engaged in a lively discussion about the amount of Jewish blood that had to be purged from the folkish body. At the same time, these reports also stressed that Streicher's violent Judeophobia, accompanied by wild actions and excesses, were widely condemned by the majority of the population. In predominantly Catholic regions, especially in the countryside, anti-Semitic actions did not resonate with the same intensity that they did in other parts of the country. In these areas the Nazis found it difficult to break the ties between the Jews and their non-Jewish customers. Popular *Judenkoller* (choleric Jew-hatred) was largely absent from many Catholic regions until 1938.[94] The socialist left also took a negative view of the Nuremberg racial laws, distributing illegal leaflets that proclaimed: "We do not hate any race except the class of capitalists"; "Whether Jew or Christian — our enemy's name is capitalist"; or "Workers! Open your eyes! The Jewish hate is designed to divert from the broken promises of the Nazis."[95]

In general, however, the population was pleased that the Nazis seemed to have resolved the three major issues that had preoccupied the public during the first two years of Nazi rule: boycott, citizenship, and race defilement. On the other hand, the evidence also indicates that people did not approve of violent actions and persecutions. To what extent the rejection of such excesses rested on purely utilitarian or opportunistic grounds, involving fear of economic disruptions or hostile reactions from abroad, cannot be established with any degree of accuracy. Although there was some opposition to the regime's anti-Jewish activities, it was marginal and ineffective because it never rose to the level of open protest. In the absence of a civil rights movement, it would be futile to expect organized public protest or resistance on behalf of a disliked minority, especially at a time when the Nazis were scoring one success after another in both domestic and foreign affairs.

Jewish reaction to the Nuremberg racial laws reflected the various ideological positions that still divided the Jewish community. Leo Baeck and the Reichsvertretung, speaking on behalf of most German Jews, continued to pursue a conciliatory attitude and counseled acceptance of the laws on the grounds that they provided a legal framework by which the Jews could remain in Germany under restrictive conditions.[96] The notion of appeasing the oppressor by behaving as meekly as possible was offensive to the Zionists, who argued that the Nuremberg Laws had completely changed the situation for the Jews of Germany and that their only choice was emigration to Palestine. Given the fact that the Nazis were always perfidious in their dealings with the Jews and used every conciliatory Jewish gesture as encouragement to inflict further oppression, it was difficult for the liberals within the Jewish community to retain the moral high ground. Victor Klemperer was outraged by the fact that so many Jews were behaving in what he regarded as a meek and groveling manner. By stoically accepting their new legalized inequality, these Jews, he felt, were already psychologically readjusting themselves to their old ghetto mentality.[97] Klemperer had received his dismissal notice from the Saxon Ministry of Education at the end of April 1935. He lost his university post and subsisted on a meager pension, which was subsequently cut to the barest of bare bones, marginalizing the former teacher of Romance languages and exposing him to unremitting assaults on his dignity that few can imagine until they read his poignant and remarkable diary.

Whether liberal, orthodox, or Zionist, the Jews saw no alternative but that of temporizing with the Nazis and salvaging what they could by any means conceivable. Resistance was regarded as futile for several reasons: in the first place, few Jews had insight into the demonic mentality of the Nazi criminals who ran the German government; second, the Jews of Germany were too diverse — occupationally, geographically and doctrinally — to act as a cohesive unit; third, emigration deprived the Jewish population of its youngest and most energetic leaders, leaving an increasingly ageing population; fourth, the Jewish community was paralyzed by a pervasive fear that told them that opposition would be accompanied by terrible reprisals; and finally, the Jews of Germany were a peaceful people who opposed open rebellion or violence as a matter of religious conscience.[98] For all these reasons, they made perfect victims, a point brought out by Leonard Baker in his characterization of Leo Baeck, a man of quiet courage but also of gentle disposition and accommodating nature. Without an army to fight for him, the man of peace and goodwill was powerless when confronted by a racial fanatic who commanded the most powerful army in Europe. Two worlds clashed in implacable hostility, as they had when Jesus was brought in front of Pontius Pilate. In contrasting the two men, Hitler and Baeck, Baker wrote:

> While he [Hitler] preached the superiority of a group of people whose ancestors had lived in a particular geographic region for a long period of

time, the Jews preached the brotherhood of man — your neighbor is as thou, said Baeck. While Hitler tried to create a concept of racial purity, the Jews taught that all men are created in the image of God and are therefore equal before God. While Hitler spoke of the ignorance of man, Jews like Leo Baeck spoke of the decency of man; even in the years to come, as Leo Baeck watched his world destroyed in the hands of his German neighbors, he demanded that each man be judged as an individual. While Hitler preached that government and law were to be used for the advancement of a particular state,...the Jews taught that basically the ultimate law is God's law.[99]

The years 1936–37, following a period of political consolidation, witnessed the first major breakthrough in foreign policy with the reoccupation of the Rhineland, a repositioning of Germany's economic objectives with the introduction of the Four-Year Plan, rapid rearmament, and the successful weathering of the Great Depression. The Nazis had "slipped through the risky zone" in international relations by whittling away at the Versailles Treaty, undermining the western security system, especially the French, and solidifying their relationship with fascist powers, chiefly the Italian. The Nazi regime also won international recognition and good will by superbly staging the Olympic Games in the summer of 1936. But while the eyes of the world were focused on the Olympic Games, Hitler composed a top memorandum in his eyrie at Obersalzberg on economic strategy and rearmament. This document, which was greatly at odds with the Olympic spirit of peace and international goodwill, reflected Hitler's impatience with the slow pace of rearmament and his insistence that "the German economy must be fit for war within four years."[100] In case of war, the Four-Year Plan envisioned the expropriation of all Jewish property in Germany.

Hitler appointed Hermann Göring as director of the new Four-Year Plan, empowering him with sweeping authority to issue legal decrees and regulations, binding for all government or party agencies, in order to achieve the goal of economic self-sufficiency (autarky) and preparation for war. In pursuing economic self-sufficiency, Göring used neo-mercantile policies of sharply curtailing imports, fixing wages and prices, restricting dividends, and alternately cajoling and bullying big business into expanding factories geared toward the production of synthetic rubber, textiles, fuels, and other scarce raw material necessary for waging war. The culmination of this policy was the establishment of the Hermann Göring Werke — industrial plants set up to exploit low-grade iron ore in central Germany, a project that some have labeled a gigantic gangster organization designed to rob big business and enrich Hermann Göring.

Göring's accession to the pinnacle of economic power implied a basic shift in the German economy — away from Schacht's more flexible free market approach toward Göring's notion of a highly state-regulated war economy in peacetime that could deliver both guns and butter. For about a year Göring and Schacht governed "both together and at cross purposes" (*Neben und Gegeneinanderregieren*).[101] In November of 1937 Schacht resigned his post as minister of economics and plenipotentiary general for war economy, leaving Göring as the chief economic tsar and the man who enjoyed the confidence of Hitler. As head of the Four-Year Plan, Göring would also become intimately involved in stripping the Jews of their personal assets and property. Starting in the fall of 1936, Göring took charge of the Aryanization process and, working closely with the SS (Himmler and Heydrich), in overseeing the economic plunder of the Jews in the wake of Kristallnacht. It was also Göring who ordered Heydrich to carry out all the preparations needed with regard to the Final Solution of the Jewish question on July 31, 1941.

From the fall of 1936 to the fall of 1938 the Nazis set the stage for the complete exclusion of the Jews from the economic domain by a combination of restrictive decrees and stage-managed expropriations. Although the bigger Jewish firms were able to liquidate their properties for relatively fair prices until 1937, the same was not true for small or medium-sized businesses, which were harassed and intimidated into selling out far below market price. The result of these tactics was to pauperize an ever increasing number of Jews, many of whom took to peddling for a living. Since peddling was a state-registered activity, the German government falsely assumed that Jewish economic activity was actually increasing.[102] The reality, as Robert Weltsch pointed out in 1936, was that the Jewish people were threatened with destruction: "The moral, material, and intellectual basis of our life has been shattered."[103] Yet, despite the unrelenting pressures on the very life and soul of the Jewish community, the Jews still had not decided to leave Germany. On September 29, 1936, a conference was convened by Wilhelm Stuckart, a state secretary in the Ministry of Interior, which included high-ranking officials in his own agency, the Ministry of the Economy, and the Office of the Deputy Führer; its objective was to discuss strategies of dealing with the Jews in the wake of the Nuremberg Laws. The participants were unanimous in supporting a policy of complete emigration, preferably to Palestine but also to any other country that was willing to admit German Jews. Since ever tighter restrictions were being placed on Jews, limiting their ability to earn a livelihood in Germany, the conferees wondered what occupations should be left to the Jews so they would not become an economic burden to the Reich. This question was left unresolved by the conference and by the Nazi leadership as a whole.

The fact was that other countries were still unwilling to take larger numbers of Jews, partly because of economic problems stemming from the worldwide depression and partly because of prevailing anti-Jewish prejudices.[104] Although a large number of Jews were able to emigrate to Palestine, the British feared increased tensions between the growing number of Jewish settlers who were streaming into Palestine from Germany and the indigenous population of Arabs. A British royal commission had been sent to Palestine in late 1936 and issued a report in July of 1937 in which it recommended that Palestine be partitioned into separate Jewish and Arab states, but when the plan met with violent demonstrations in Palestine, the commission postponed the project and recommended limits on Jewish immigration.

By the mid-1930s it was becoming increasingly clear that Jewish emigration, along with the whole Jewish question, was passing into the hands of Himmler and the SS. As early as 1934 the SS drew up a situation report on the Jewish question that looked at the problem in cold clinical detail, assessed the nature of the German Jewish community, and recommended that a major effort should be made, by force or persuasion, to compel the Jews to leave Germany for Palestine. The SS subsequently encouraged those Jewish institutions and leaders who had committed themselves to emigration. It was hoped that Zionist and other proemigration leaders in the Jewish community could be enlisted in this project, which turned out to be disappointing to the Nazis because the basic obstacle to Jewish emigration was the loyalty the Jews still had for Germany.

The department in Heydrich's SD that dealt with Zionist affairs and Jewish emigration was called Section II-112 (Jewish Affairs). It was headed by Adolf Eichmann, a faceless and fastidious bureaucrat with a fanatical disdain for Jews. Since this small office would become one of the major instruments of the Nazi destruction machine against the Jews, it would propel Eichmann, despite his mediocre talents and total lack of affect, into becoming a key figure in the Holocaust. Eichmann went to Palestine in 1937, and two months later submitted a report, entitled "Comprehensive Report on the Jewish Problem," in which he endorsed emigration but also warned that scattering Jews in a few concentrated places might lead to hostile forces that could work against the interest of the Reich.[105] Eichmann already expressed doubts that emigration could really solve the Jewish problem, giving hints of a possible annihilatory solution. Since the SS was the spearhead of Nazi racial philosophy, in addition to controlling the machinery of force and terror, it was inevitable that, sooner or later, it would be entrusted with the annihilation process.

In the meantime, despite the apparent lull brought about by the Olympic Games, which forced the Nazis to remove anti-Jewish signs throughout Germany, party-sponsored "spontaneous" actions, followed by additional anti-Jewish decrees, continued unabated in 1936 and 1937. Impatient with the pace of Jewish emigration, which they blamed on the recalcitrant and obstructionist behavior of some Jewish organizations, chiefly the Reichvertretung, the Gestapo issued warnings and then arrested Leo Baeck and members of the B'nai B'rith on April 19, 1937. Baeck was held for two days and then asked to sign a document by which he agreed to cede all the B'nai B'rith property, valued in the millions, to the Nazi government. Baeck refused to sign, later saying "thus their act stood as the theft which it was."[106] Yet, Baeck still believed that the Jews would somehow survive the Nazi onslaught, telling a friend: "Hitler and his like cannot turn back history. We Jews will suffer, some of us may die, but we will survive. We Jews have old eyes."[107] In the summer of 1937 Baeck expressed the belief that as many as 80 percent of the German people opposed the persecution of the Jews, a statement that seemed remarkably off the mark in view of the fact that 1937 was a year of renewed Judeophobic propaganda, accelerated Aryanization, and better coordinated efforts to force the Jews into emigration. Baeck's perception, however, based as it was on his own experiences as a leading rabbi in a cosmopolitan world, was not entirely mistaken, and certainly not deluded. Baeck was familiar enough with the German population to realize that most of the Germans with whom he came in contact showed relatively little interest in the regime's extreme Judeophobic activities, but he underestimated the power of Nazi propaganda in swaying millions of Germans to believe in the regime's anti-Jewish lies. Baeck's natural inclination was to look for the best in people. The reason why he believed that the Germans did not speak up against Nazi mistreatment of Jews was that they feared reprisals by the Gestapo. This was certainly true to some extent, but the majority of the German people also preferred to be passive and uninvolved in regard to the Jews because they believed that the government's discriminatory measures against the Jews were entirely justified. What most Germans disapproved of was violent and unlawful street actions and public displays of cruelty. The Nazi regime had sufficiently indoctrinated Germans in Judeophobia to persuade them of the need for discriminatory laws, but it had not succeeded in raising the Jewish issues to the top of their priority list of social problems. Unlike their leaders, most Germans were not fanatical Judeophobes, a recognition that periodically worried party fanatics and spurred them on to greater propagandistic efforts. As David Bankier put it, "whereas antisemitism played an integrating role for the party and its followers, it did not have the same function in spurring the general population to action."[108]

Hence the constant government infusions of hateful energy, evident again in the fall of 1937. Coinciding with celebrations always scheduled in connection with the anniversary of the beerhall putsch of 1923, the Nazis staged an anti-Jewish exhibition in Munich's German Museum in which the public was invited to view various displays entitled "Jews in politics, Jews in culture, Jews in business," which repeated all the stock-in-trade of anti-Jewish stereotypes and lies that the organizers could mine from a thousand-year tradition of Judeophobia. This was followed by a great Christmas boycott initiated by Streicher in Nuremberg and accompanied by renewed waves of Jew-baiting.

The dark events foreshadowing the future, however, were taking place behind the scenes. On November 5, 1937, Hitler called a secret conference with his military and diplomatic chiefs, later called the Hossbach conference after the man who kept the minutes, in which he unburdened himself by saying openly that his goal was to bolster the German racial community and expand its territories into eastern Europe. He would start with the destruction of Czechoslovakia and the annexation of Austria in order to secure Germany's eastern and southern flanks. The Führer also indicated that the only successful method of attaining these aims was war because the acquisition of living space could not be achieved by peaceful means.[109] The Hossbach conference was designed to clear the air and test the waters with his military chiefs, who were expected to be the sort of generals who acted like mad dogs held on a leash by their Führer, obediently doing his bidding when the time came that he decided to unleash them against his victims. But judging from the downright alarmed responses of Defense Minister Werner von Blomberg and Commander-in-Chief of the Army Werner von Fritsch, Hitler decided to shake up his military command, using secret dossiers and information to discredit Blomberg and Fritsch, the former for having married a prostitute and the latter for allegedly having engaged in a homosexual affair. Hitler then replaced the old army command with the Oberkommando der Wehrmacht (High Command of the Armed Forces, or OKW), putting himself in overall charge and delegating the routine management of the new High Command to a pliant yes-man named Keitel, later renamed by cynical Germans as "Lakeitel," a play on the German word Lackei (lackey).

Hitler's public speeches had already sounded a far more belligerent tone in 1937, culminating in the aggressive rhetoric that had marked Mussolini's state visit in September. With an obedient army behind him, Hitler would shortly embark on a series of risky adventures in foreign politics. The first was the crisis over Austria, and it was surely no accident that it occurred only one week after Hitler shook up his military command and replaced his mild-mannered foreign minister, Neurath, with the aggressive and unprincipled Joachim von Ribbentrop.

Foreign Aggression, Appeasement, Pogrom, and War, 1938–39

Having pulled Germany out of the depression through government deficit spending, extensive public works projects, and massive rearmament, Hitler was now determined to make Germany the greatest power in the world. He promoted the idea that the Aryan race had a special mission to conquer and govern the Eurasian landmass; but to do so, it had to undergo internal racial purification, involving sterilization of the unfit, euthanasia of "lives not worth living," and elimination of inferior races, chiefly the Jews. In Hitler's mind, the concept of race was clearly tied to the concept of space because a people's greatness depended upon sufficient living space (Lebensraum).[110] As long as 65 million Germans remained confined to a small space, they would remain small and insignificant. Hitler promised to change this situation by rearming the German people, imbuing them with pride and imperial desire, and providing living space for them in eastern Europe. In order to achieve this mission, however, it was necessary to mobilize Germany's entire resources and to promote in its people, especially in its young people, aggressive and warlike qualities. In the Hitler Youth, where members would soon mature into hardened soldiers, he foresaw a new generation of imperial warriors who would carry out Germany's racial mission.

Between 1933 and 1939, Hitler's volatile, unstable, and sociopathic personality dominated European diplomacy, as he manipulated the war-weary western democracies into making one concession after another. By 1938, he had abandoned speaking as a man of peace, although he still successfully deluded western statesmen into believing that his aim was not war but national self-determination and justice for a nation that had been so tragically wronged at Versailles in 1919. Secretly, however, he was preparing the way for war. Beginning in 1936, one brilliant success was followed by another in foreign policy: the reoccupation of the Rhineland (March 7, 1936); the annexation (*Anschluss*) of Austria (March 13, 1938); the appeasement at Munich (September 29–30, 1939), followed by the annexation of the Sudetenland; the destruction of the rest of Czechoslovakia and its conversion into a German Protectorate (March 15, 1939); the incorporation of Memel into the Reich (March 23, 1939); and the Nazi-Soviet Non-Aggression Pact (August 21, 1939).

Each of these successes bolstered the popularity of Hitler with the German people, who were swept away with such excitement that they were more than willing to overlook the fact that with each success, the totalitarian state was also strengthened. Hitler's territorial gains involved, on each occasion, a widening of the totalitarian net and a corresponding radicalization of police terror, especially against the Jews. With Hitler's annexation of Austria, an additional 250,000 Jews fell under his control, and 357,000 Jews were added with the final destruction of Czechoslovakia. The new territories included a greater number of Jews than those residing in the old Reich. A wave of police terror swept over these acquired territories. The Gestapo and other security forces rounded up political enemies, set up concentration camps, and persecuted the Jews. Some of the new radical experiments that the Nazis practiced in these new territories, especially in Austria, were subsequently applied to the old Reich as well. After each success Hitler discovered that the western powers did not lift a finger against him, giving him the impression that he could continue his aggression with impunity. This being the case in foreign affairs, there was every reason to assume that the same would hold true for the Jews. Western appeasement in diplomacy entailed an even greater appeasement over the Jewish question because no western power considered the Jews a vital interest.

The stage was set for the tragic abandonment of the Jewish people by every single power in the world.

The annexation of Austria on March 13, 1938, unleashed an orgy of violence against the Jews of Austria, both by the Nazi officials who moved in to extend their totalitarian police system and by Austrian mobs who vented their pent-up aggression against the Jews. Austrian Nazis looted Jewish businesses and apartments at will, and howling mobs turned against conspicuous eastern Jews with their broad-brimmed hats, earlocks, and flowing beards. Despicable street scenes showed vulgar mobs forcing Jewish youngsters, old men, and women down on their knees to scrub the street with toothbrushes and sometimes with bare knuckles. The assault on Austria's Jews was often worse and better organized than the attacks that had been staged incrementally on the German Jews; in fact, Austrian Jews were not only victimized by the release of years of pent-up anti-Semitic rage but they were also more quickly pauperized, forced into emigration, or consigned to concentration camps. The sheer lust for revenge on the part of fanatical Austrian Nazis was reflected in astonishingly high suicide rates; in March 1938 alone, 1,700 Austrian Jews committed suicide. One was the famous cultural historian and actor Egon Friedell, who committed suicide by jumping out of the fourth floor of his apartment house rather than face arrest by the Gestapo. Franz Rothenberg, chairman of the board of the Kreditanstalt, Austria's leading bank, was "arrested" by Nazi thugs, thrown out of a moving car, and killed. Isidor Pollack, head of a chemical firm, was beaten up so badly by Austrian Nazis that he died. Similar treatment was meted out to countless other and lesser known Jews.

Freud was spared in the initial outburst, but his daughter Anna was briefly taken away for interrogation by the Gestapo. Some of Freud's closest followers, particularly Ernest Jones, urged the world-renowned psychoanalyst to leave Austria immediately, only to have Freud at first reply that emigration would be like a soldier deserting his post. Jones's riposte, which convinced Freud to leave, was to tell him the story of Lightoller, the second officer of the *Titanic* who had been blown to the surface when the boiler of the ship exploded as it was sinking. When asked later by an official interrogation why he had left the ship, he responded, "I never left the ship, sir; she left me."[111] With the help of his international connections, Freud was able to secure the necessary exit papers from the authorities in order to take his family out of Austria, though not before having to jump over various annoying and humiliating hurdles that the Nazis reserved for Jewish emigrants in the form of certificates of good conduct, passports, visas, and special Reich flight taxes (*Reichsfluchtsteuer*). Freud's cash and bank account were confiscated; the stock of his collected works, which had been sent to Switzerland, was to be returned so that the books could be burned. As a final act of humiliation, Freud was compelled by the Gestapo to sign a declaration that he had not been ill treated. Freud's sardonic note, fortunately exceeding the limited intelligence of his Gestapo interrogators, said: "I can most highly recommend the Gestapo to everyone," *Ich kann die Gestapo jedermann auf das beste empfehlen.*[112] On June 4, 1938, Freud left Austria with his family and emigrated to England. There was nothing more he could do in a country suffering from a collective death wish.

Within a year about a hundred thousand other Austrian Jews followed Freud's example and left the country. Several developments helped accelerate the process of emigration. One was the establishment by Adolf Eichmann of a Central Agency for Jewish Emigration (Zentralstelle für jüdische Auswanderung), which was located in the former Rothschild palace in Vienna and administered an assembly-line process of issuing the necessary exit papers Jews needed to leave Austria. According to Eichmann, the operation worked like a conveyor-belt: "The initial application and all the rest of the required papers are put on at one end, and the passport falls off at the other end."[113] An important feature of this method of enforced mass emigration was extorting as much money out of the richest Jews and using it to finance the emigration of the poorest Jews. Eichmann's operation worked so well that he subsequently replicated it also in Germany.

Another development that helped speed up the process of Jewish emigration was a model worked out by Nazi economic planners in the summer of 1938 that combined a ruthless modernization of a backward Austrian economy with the liquidation of Jewish businesses. This task of rationalizing the Austrian economy and integrating it with the German was assigned to Gauleiter Josef Bürckel, who had already distinguished himself by integrating the Saar economy with the German economy between 1935 and 1938.[114] The plans that Bürckel had used in the Saar had been prepared by Dr. Rudolf Gater, a young economist with a keen interest in human resource management who was eager to apply his expertise in Austria. Since Bürckel also valued the advice of Hamburg *Gauleiter* Karl Kaufmann, he was able to enlist the service of several Hamburg economists as well, notably Dr. Walter Emmerich, who had already won his spurs in Hamburg as an expert for excluding Jews from the German economy. Bürckel was assembling a team of eager young human resources planners in Vienna that would later be transferred to Poland, where its mandate was to rationalize the Polish economy through a combination of ethnic cleansing and economic expropriations. The team's experiences in Austria were an important stepping stone to the Holocaust.

Within just a few months, the number of Jewish businesses in Vienna was reduced by half. Even Bürckel was shocked by the downright criminal methods by which Austrians who were well connected to the Nazis plundered Jewish businesses and assets. In assessing the ruthless expropriation of Jewish businesses in the wake of the *Anschluss,* Bürckel observed that Austria presented a picture of one gigantic treasure hunt

(*Bild eines riesigen Beutezuges*).[115] Not even the Rothschilds, who had exercised so much financial influence over the affairs of Austria, were immune from rapacious Nazi gangsters. Two days after the *Anschluss,* the Viennese Rothschilds were arrested and held as bargaining chips in an elaborate cat-and-mouse game to strip the family of its German fortunes; but since the Rothschild family and its empire were international, with their fortune obscured in a maze of holding companies and financial intricacies, it proved difficult to strip them of their assets all at once. The Rothschilds controlled businesses in several different countries: in Vienna, the head of the family was Baron Louis; in Prague it was Baron Eugen, in Paris Dr. Alphons Rothschild. Their businesses were all intertwined. The Nazis tried to untangle the maze and buy out the Rothschild assets at the lowest price, using the detained Baron Louis Rothschild as a hostage chip. They especially turned their greedy eyes on the Rothschild-owned Witkowitz mines and iron-works in Czechoslovakia, whose shares and ownership had been transferred to the Alliance and Insurance Company of London. After protracted negotiations, the Nazis finally received the Witkowitz firm and its Swedish subsidiary Freja for 3,600,000 pounds. In order to ransom Baron Louis, the transfer had to be made before his release.[116]

Göring, as head of the Four-Year Plan, supported by the Ministry of the Interior, the Foreign Office, the Ministry of Economics, and the machinery of Nazi terror, orchestrated a systematic assault on Jewish businesses in the wake of the Austrian *Anschluss.* On March 28, Göring announced in a speech in Vienna that the Aryanization of business and commercial activity had begun. A month later, on April 22, a decree was released by the Ministry of the Interior prohibiting the practice of disguising Jewish ownership of businesses under Aryan names or management. Four days later, on April 26, the Ministry of the Interior announced that Jews were required to register property valued in excess of five thousand marks. The registration of Jewish property, in turn, made it possible to identify potentially lucrative businesses and target them for spoliation. German banks quickly discovered that they could reap handsome profits from such expropriations; they offered themselves as middlemen, bringing together buyers and sellers, and reaped double profits: first, from the loans they had extended to the buyers, and second, from the subsequent business transactions they conducted with the Aryanized firms. The banks also eliminated their Jewish competitors, the Bleichröders, Warburgs, and Wassermanns. From April of 1938 to November of that year over four thousand Jewish businesses were Aryanized, which amounted to a "business plunder of huge proportions."[117] The little thieves plundered on a small scale but the big thieves plundered on a gigantic one. The big sharks, headed by Hermann Göring, who disguised his own venal motives under the cover of national interest, included some of the major German industrial giants such as Krupp, Thyssen, Kirdorf, Flick, and I. G. Farben. What this meant was that wealth was being concentrated in fewer and fewer hands, disproportionately benefiting the rich and contributing nothing at all to the standard of living for most Germans.

The summer of 1938 saw another wave of officially orchestrated anti-Jewish activities. On June 9, Munich's chief synagogue was torn down on Hitler's orders. Party officials incited mobs into committing street violence against Jews in Vienna, Berlin, and other cities, proceeded to arrest thousands, and then threw them into concentration camps. This was part of the regime's June-actions, culminating on June 15 with the arrest of fifteen hundred "previously convicted" (*vorbestrafte*) Jews who were thrown into concentration camps. Some party radicals, notably Gauleiter Odilo Globocnik of Vienna, who would later distinguish himself as a key figure in the Holocaust, announced the coming of radical steps that would lead to the "solution of the Jewish question," warning that dire consequences would befall Germans who still did business with Jews. Bella Fromm, who would shortly leave Germany, was shattered by what she saw in Berlin: vicious acts of violence, especially against small Jewish retail stores, whose windows were smashed and their contents strewn all over the street. "We were just about to enter a tiny jewelry shop when a gang of ten youngsters in Hitler Youth uniforms smashed the shop, brandishing butcher knives and yelling: "To hell with the Jewish rabble! Room for the Sudeten Germans." Inside the shop, she saw other boys breaking glass shelves and counters, hurling alarm clocks, cheap silverware, and other trifles to their accomplices outside. A little shrimp of a boy put rings on his fingers and stuffed his pockets with loot; he then turned around and spat squarely into the shopkeepers face and dashed off. The shopkeeper told Fromm that he was glad his wife, who had recently died, was spared this ordeal.[118] Another store, run by two friends of hers, was also smashed. Upon returning next day with some food for the couple, she discovered two coffins in the smashed-up store: the couple had committed suicide during the night.[119]

The Jews were caught in a crossfire of Nazi agencies and street mobs. Nazi bureaucrats dreamed up more and more strategies by which Jews could be identified, registered, plundered, harassed, and compelled to leave the country. Jews were forbidden to change their names in order to "disguise" their Jewish origin; they had to carry identification papers indicating Jewishness; and, adding insult to injury, Nazi officials specified that Jews were required to bear only those first names that they had officially designated as Jewish, and that all male Jews must in addition assume the given name of Israel, while all female Jews had to take the given name of Sarah. Passport restrictions had been in force since the fall of 1937; new passports were rarely issued except for purposes of emigration. In October of 1937, all Jewish passports were recalled by the government and reissued with a printed J (*Jude*) for only one allowable purpose — emigration.[120]

It is important to realize that these accelerated anti-Jewish measures did not take place in a vacuum; they must be seen in the context of the larger actions that took place on the international stage. In the summer of 1938, Hitler whipped up a constant atmosphere of crisis over the Sudetenland. German newspapers and radio broadcasts talked in hysterical terms about the terrible outrages committed by the Czechs against the poor Sudeten Germans. Secretly, Hitler had already decided to smash the Czechs, not because he wanted the Sudeten Germans, whose grievances ranked relatively low on his political agenda, but because he wanted Czechoslovakia as a springboard to the east. The frenzied diplomatic actions that would lead to the appeasement in Munich reveal a close relationship between western appeasement of Hitler on the Sudeten issue and western appeasement on the Jewish question. Just as the western powers negotiated over the heads of the Czechs, ignoring and selling out their vital national interests, so they negotiated over the heads of the Jews by ignoring the deadly threat they faced from the Nazis.

A perfect example of this diplomatic betrayal was the conference that convened July 6–14 in the French resort of Evian, on the shore of Lake Geneva, to discuss the Jewish refugee problem. Although the conference had been set in motion by President Roosevelt in a sincere effort to address the worldwide refugee crisis that the Nazis had caused by their anti-Jewish policies, the 140 representatives from 32 nations arrived at Evian with predetermined agendas that were less designed to help the Jews than to prevent them from emigrating into their respective countries. The Jewish delegation from Germany at Evian, which included representatives from the Reichsvertretung, quickly discovered that neither the British nor the Americans, let alone any of the other nations, were willing to relax their immigration laws. Neville Chamberlain, in fact, had urged the Americans to keep Palestine off the agenda at Evian because he did not want to place his representative in the embarrassing position of publicly having to reject proposals aimed at further Jewish immigration to Palestine or the rest of the British dominions.[121] Chamberlain was well on his way to appeasing Hitler, and that meant that the British did not want to expose the real cause of Jewish immigration — the relentless persecution by an out-of-control Nazi regime.

Since neither the British nor the Americans were willing to admit more Jews into their territories, the other thirty nations quietly followed on cue and closed their doors. Helen Fein wrote that observers at the time saw the Evian conference as "an exercise in Anglo-American collaborative hypocrisy,"[122] and several other commentators pointed out that Evian is "naive" spelled backward. A subsequent memorandum drafted by the Evian conference and sent to the German Foreign Office in October of 1938 gave further support to Hitler by stating that none of the nations represented at Evian challenged the right of the German government to handle its own internal affairs, which included matters of emigration. Behind the sanctimonious phrases uttered at Evian and elsewhere in the world one could periodically detect explicit anti-Jewish prejudices, whether by officials in the U.S. Department of State, the British Foreign Office, or the world's press. The chief U.S. delegate at Evian, Myron C. Taylor, undoubtedly believed that his warning against "dumping" Jewish refugees on American shores merely reflected American public opinion, which, according to a recent opinion poll, indicated that 67.4 percent wanted to keep refugees out.[123]

If Evian proved to be an excuse in western collaborative hypocrisy, reinforcing Hitler's mental image of democratic weakness, it accomplished at least one practical purpose, and that was to establish the Intergovernmental Committee for Refugees (ICR) whose task consisted of coordinating international efforts to aid Jewish refugees from Nazi Germany. Heading the committee was Roosevelt's personal friend George Rublee, a seventy-year-old international lawyer, who was given the thankless task of negotiating with the Nazis on behalf of the Jews. Rublee's negotiations with the Nazis generally bogged down because the two sides could not agree on how much money the Jews should surrender in return for their freedom and because of the difficulty of finding countries that were willing to take them in. Hitler, who had been taunting the democratic nations for some time because they refused to relieve him of his Jewish population, subsequently heaped scorn on their feeble efforts at Evian. In his closing speech at the Nuremberg Party Congress on September 12, 1938, in which his primary object was to whip up war hysteria over Czechoslovakia, he did not miss another opportunity to point out the connection between Jewish capitalism and Jewish-inspired anti-capitalist communism, which reflected his belief that the Jews were conspiring to destroy the nations of the world by planting opposing ideological beliefs into the fabric of their societies, manipulating the inevitable confrontations, and waiting to take over the world as soon as their enemies had destroyed themselves. Hitler believed that the ruling elites of the major nations, insofar as they had not already been contaminated by Jewish subversion, instinctively despised the Jews, and that their own people shared with them a deep revulsion of the Jews. In his mind, this explained why nations refused to accept additional Jewish "parasites." Germany at least was honest about its own Jews; as far as he was concerned he was tired of western hypocrisy, for when the democracies had an opportunity to act, all they offered the Jews was morality.[124]

Moral support was about the best the Jews could hope for, and there was precious little of it at home or abroad, especially among the leading spokesmen of Germany's two Christian churches. A great deal has been written, both apologetic and condemnatory, on the passive, if not complicit, role of both the Protestant and the Catholic churches in Nazi Germany.[125] It is true, of course, that the major leaders of both churches, with very few exceptions, watched the relentless persecution of the Jews in silence. Few public protests by leading church leaders or theologians can be found; and when the church authorities did protest, it was primarily over Nazi encroachments on their own institutions. It is also true that the Christian churches had absorbed a thousand-year tradition of Christian prejudices against the Jews, which prevented them at this critical juncture from displaying a true and compassionate Christian heart and therefore from coming to the aid of their Jewish neighbors. The German Christian churches, as all other churches in the western world, belonged to the same circulatory cultural system, and that system, unfortunately, had been susceptible for some time to strong secular pressures such as nationalism, socialism, and even anti-Semitic and racist ideologies. The *völkisch* movement, for example, had made inroads among German Protestantism in the form of a "German Christianity" that rejected "Jewish" elements and even insisted that Jesus was a stout-hearted Aryan who wielded the sword rather than wore a crown of thorns. The Nazis, of course, welcomed such views and tried to use the German Christians in order to drive a stake into the heart of Christianity. Their general position was to wedge divisive issues into both churches in order to undermine their strength and solidarity and therefore their will to resist Nazi domination.

The Nazis succeeded in cowing the leadership of both churches into passive submission, but they did not succeed in destroying the churches, a goal that Hitler postponed until after the war had been won. Throughout the Nazi period the churches were enmeshed in a deadly conflict with their Nazi masters. They had known from the beginning what a Hitler victory would mean; they did not welcome but feared a Nazi seizure of power, and for good reason. Although some church leaders may initially have made highly flattering comments about the Nazis, which many deeply regretted later, they quickly discovered the evil they confronted in Adolf Hitler. By the mid-1930s they knew that the Nazis were intent upon destroying the institutional foundation of the churches themselves, including their political organizations, youth associations, unions, and communication systems. Klaus Scholder has reminded us that retroactive indictments are always morally easy, and that it is perhaps unrealistic to expect the churches to have come to the aid of the Jews at the very time when they themselves were deeply embroiled in a conflict with the state in the sphere of church politics. None of the church leaders wanted to be exposed on two fronts at the same time, hardly an inspired moral example worthy of Christian martyrs, but not necessarily an act of craven cowardice or an expression of willful indifference to other sufferers. In fact, thousands of clerics and theologians, including Martin Niemöller, Dietrich Bonhoeffer, Heinrich Grüber, Bernhard Lichtenberg, Max Josef Metzger, Albert Riesteler, Augustine Rüsch, Joseph Rossaint, Paul Schneider, Katharina Staritz, Franz Weimann, Theophil Wurm, and countless others, known and unknown, were persecuted, thrown into concentration camps, and killed for defying the Nazi regime.

That the top leadership of the church did not speak up publicly on behalf of the Jews will forever be a blemish on their record. This was particularly true of the leadership of the Catholic Church, which was initially lulled by Hitler's conciliatory phrases and by his pious declarations about the inviolability of church doctrines and institutions. It was in this spirit that the church negotiated a concordat with Hitler in July of 1933, only to discover shortly afterward that the Nazi regime was actively subverting religious freedom. This prompted Pope Pius XI to issue an encyclical, entitled *With Deep Anxiety* (1937), in which he accused the Nazis of violating the terms of the concordat and condemned them for undermining the foundation of natural law and justice. In the summer of 1938 Pius asked an American Jesuit, John LaFarge, who had written a book entitled *Interracial Justice,* in which he condemned American racial segregation and bigotry, to prepare a text for an encyclical condemning racism and anti-Semitism.[126] The encyclical, entitled *Unity of Mankind,* boldly declared that "it is impossible for Christians to participate in anti-Semitism. We recognize that everyone has the right to self-defense.... But anti-Semitism is inadmissible. Spiritually, we are all Jews."[127] Unfortunately, the encyclical was transmitted to the general of the Jesuit order, Wladimir Ledochowski, a Polish clergymen with strong anti-communist and anti-Semitic convictions, who delayed sending the draft to the pope, rerouting it first to the anti-Semitic editor of *Civiltà Cattolica,* the official Jesuit organ. By the time the draft reached Pius XI, the pope was too ill to deal with it. The document was on the pope's desk when he died on February 10, 1939, was shelved by his pro-German successor, Pius XII, and disappeared for three decades. Pius XII, who saw his church threatened throughout the world by evil secular powers, put aside morality in favor of Machiavellian diplomacy and chose to remain silent when the persecution and annihilation of the Jews was brought to his attention.[128]

Although many acts of heroism by individual clergymen, theologians, monks, and nuns can be documented, the institutions of the church failed tragically in mustering the sort of Christian love, compassion, and courage it would have required to stop the Nazis from committing their unspeakable crimes against both Christians and Jews. Offering prayers and feeble protests were tragically ineffective against the Nazi machinery of terror and little solace to the beleaguered Jews who needed actions rather than words.

By the fall of 1938 the Jews had been practically excluded from most economic activities; they were harassed when they tried to go to cinemas, theaters, public swimming pools, hotels, or resorts. Villages and towns competed for the honor of being "Jew free," proudly advertising this claim and posting signs reading "Jews are not wanted here" (*Juden sind hier unerwünscht*). Park benches were also clearly marked "Aryan" and "Jew." German Jews were being pushed into a frightening and shadowy "no-man's-land" of great danger; they could be arrested without due process and imprisoned in concentration camps. Their property could be seized and confiscated for the flimsiest of reasons. They had no legal recourse. Many Jews got the message and tried to rush for the exits. In late August of 1938 Max Warburg sailed to New York and never returned to Germany again. Bella Fromm left in early September; at the Belgian border a German custom officer, after discovering her jewelry, called her a "Jewish whore," seized her valuables, and made her sign a confession before letting her cross into freedom. Robert Weltsch left shortly thereafter for Warsaw and then Palestine. Of the six German Jews whose lives are described in John Dippel's book *Bound upon a Wheel of Fire,* five escaped Nazi Germany. Only Leo Baeck, who survived, remained behind: "I will go," he later said, "when I am the last Jew alive in Germany."[129] For thousands of other Jews the time for escape was running out. The trap had already been set.

In November 1938 came an unexpected opportunity for the Nazis to tighten the screws on the Jews. On November 7, 1938, a secretary in the German embassy in Paris, Ernst vom Rath, was assassinated by a seventeen-year-old Polish refugee named Herschel Grynszpan in response to the mistreatment of his parents and seventeen thousand others by the German government. In March of 1938, Poland had passed a law that proposed to denaturalize Polish nationals who had been living outside Poland for a period of five years. The law was specifically aimed at about fifty thousand Polish Jews who had been residing in Germany and whom the Polish government did not want to return to Poland. The Polish government throughout the 1930s was semifascist and strongly anti-Semitic; its Jewish population was over three million, or 10 percent of the population. Unlike the German Jews, who had defined themselves as Germans as well as Jews, the Polish Jews saw themselves as a separate nationality within the Polish national community.[130] Given the fact that the Poles had been struggling for centuries to define themselves in national terms, a struggle that was always difficult because it took place in a historical context of foreign domination and internal divisiveness, it was inevitable that a strong need for national self-identity would be accompanied by intense frictions with a large Jewish minority that defined itself as a separate nation. This political friction was exacerbated by additional religious and economic frictions that divided Roman Catholic Poles from their Jewish neighbors. Poland was a predominantly agrarian and overpopulated country of some 34 million people undergoing wrenching economic pressures stemming from the Great Depression and also from a lack of investment capital, technological development, and purchasing power. The Polish Jews, who could have been the agents of modernization, lived in a time warp of earlier ages as separate communities in the larger cities of Cracow, Lodz, Warsaw, and Lublin, where they followed various economic professions limited largely to small businesses, retailing, handicrafts, money lending, and other commercial activities associated with a bygone age. Prevented from owning agricultural land and increasingly excluded from certain markets through the enactment of state monopolies, the Jewish population was slowly pauperized. It was also subject to periodic pogroms and government legislation aimed at reducing the number of Polish Jews, hopefully through emigration.

Yet, the emigration of Polish Jews, just as that of German Jews, foundered on the anti-Jewish discrimination policies that were being pursued simultaneously by most European governments, so that the Jews were treated like hot potatoes thrown back and forth between various states, all practicing restriction and expulsion games that offset each other and caught their Jewish victims in a bureaucratic nightmare.

Herschel Grynszpan's parents, who had emigrated from Poland and had lived in Hannover since 1914, automatically became stateless as a result both of the new Polish law and of the restrictive German citizenship rules that made it practically impossible for any Polish Jew to ever become a German citizen. The German government regarded the Polish law as a provocation designed to dump their Jews permanently in Germany. Accordingly, the Gestapo rounded up some seventeen thousand Polish Jews and transported them to the Polish border; but since the Polish authorities refused to accept them, they were herded into camps where, in a kind of no-man's-land, they were kept in protective custody under deplorable conditions. Young Grynszpan wanted to send a message of protest to the world through his desperate deed.[131]

The Nazis were quick to retaliate against the assassination of Rath. On November 8, the day the Nazi leadership celebrated the anniversary of the beerhall putsch in Munich, Ernst vom Rath died in Paris. News of Rath's death was conveyed to Hitler while he was eating dinner with his old fighters in the old town hall in Munich. The Führer then engaged Goebbels, who was sitting next to him, in a lengthy discussion regarding the appropriate action that should be taken in response to Rath's assassination. The evidence indicates that Hitler authorized a proposal by Goebbels to set in motion spontaneous demonstrations against the Jews throughout Germany, slyly suggesting that the "SA should be allowed to have a fling."[132] He then play-acted his typical script of fading into the background in order to immunize himself in case the pogrom should backfire. The propaganda minister, who had been out of favor for his sexual peccadillos, was eager to rehabilitate himself with the Führer and to prove that, in addition to being a man of words, he could also be a man of independent action, subsequently discovering that his hate-inspired program was widely condemned as ineffectual by other Hitler paladins such as Himmler and Heydrich.

The result was an orchestrated nationwide pogrom later referred to as the Night of Crystals (Kristallnacht) after the shattered glass of Jewish businesses that littered the streets of Germany.[133] The pattern of this collective hate crime was a repetition of earlier anti-Jewish actions, except on a far larger scale. After a demagogic speech by Goebbels against the Jews at City Hall, which left no doubt in the minds of the assembled leaders of the party and the SA as to what was expected of them, orders were relayed to local party functionaries to incite violent actions against the Jews. The result was an orgy of violence throughout Germany. The interaction between fanatical party functionaries, vulgar storm troopers, and inflamed citizens with brutal predilections and loose morals produced a veritable lust for destruction. There was nothing spontaneous about this shameful event, except the improvised individual actions that exploded here and there after the green light had been given by the party. The people, in Hermann Graml's judgment, had reacted to Grynszpan's deed before the hate campaign was instigated no differently than they would have to an earthquake in Japan;[134] but now that the government was unleashing an officially sponsored campaign of hate, it should not be surprising that many ordinary people, who would have otherwise been restrained by the fear of law or by the actions of their neighbors, felt empowered to vent their hatreds and frustration in an uninhibited and public manner.

The actions of party functionaries, storm troopers, and incited mobs produced widespread devastation of property and many injuries and deaths. It is estimated that 276 synagogues were burned to the ground and their contents looted or defiled. Over 7,500 businesses were vandalized, and 91 Jews were killed, while others, despairing, committed suicide. These crimes were committed openly and blatantly because they were sponsored by the government. The police were helpless because orders had been given that the Führer did not want them to interfere except when German lives or properties were directly involved. This explains, among other things, why fire departments sprang into action only when synagogue fires threatened to spread to neighboring German buildings. As to Jewish lives, they were not worth a dime, as Goebbels revealed when he responded to a report from the field warning of more casualties after the first death by saying that one shouldn't get "upset because of a dead Jew."[135]

A great deal has been written about the November pogrom, particularly the lustful destructiveness and the desire to kill that turned ordinary people into raging beasts, but this has sometimes created the impression that Kristallnacht represented the deepest wishes of the German people. Such a blanket indictment, however, is far too sweeping. It is true that Goebbels and the branches of the party he tried to enlist in the program, chiefly the SA, wanted to enmesh as many ordinary Germans as possible in what was hoped would be a collective action; but when this failed, the clever propaganda minister quickly claimed that the party was really speaking for the people and representing their wishes. To what extent is this claim true? Did the events of November 9–10 really represent the wishes of the German people? In the absence of opinion polls, it is, of course, impossible to answer this question objectively, but the available evidence, drawn from Gestapo and SD reports, Deutschland-Berichte of the SPD (SOPADE), reports by state governors, and eyewitness accounts, indicates that the pogrom was widely criticized and condemned by large sections of the public.[136] The truth is that most people were deeply ashamed and condemned the violence and destruction of property. An SD report comments that:

> The actions against the Jews in November were very badly received.... Business circles pointed to the damage which had arisen through the actions, others criticized the legal measures, and the bourgeoisie, just freed from anxiety about war, pointed to the dangerous effects which would arise abroad. When then the reaction from abroad expressed itself in vile inflammatory campaigns and boycott measures, these liberal-pacifist circles agreed with foreign opinion and labeled the measures taken as "barbaric" and "uncivilized" [*Kulturlos*]. From a basic liberal attitude, many believed they had openly to stand up for the Jews.[137]

The same reactions were relayed to the Social Democratic leadership in exile. Condemnation of the pogrom was strongest among the Catholic population in the south, the Marxist left, the liberal intelligentsia, and the business community. Strong outrage was also recorded by foreign diplomats who were stationed in Germany. One British diplomat said: "Inarticulate as the mass of people may have been, I have not met a single German of whatever class who in varying measure does not...disapprove of what has occurred."[138] United States Ambassador Hugh R. Wilson reported that the reaction on the part of the German people was "one of utter shame at the actions of the Government and of their fellow Germans."[139] President Roosevelt immediately recalled his ambassador, saying: "I myself could scarcely believe that such things could occur in a twentieth-century civilization."[140]

Ian Kershaw has written that the pogrom of November 1938 "was the only occasion during the Third Reich when the German public was confronted directly, on a nationwide scale, with the full savagery of the attack on the Jews."[141] If it is true, as the evidence seems to indicate, that most Germans disapproved of these violent measures, some on economic and some on humanitarian grounds, why was there no concerted effort to oppose it? In the first place, by 1938 Himmler had successfully instituted a nationwide network of police terror, which made public opposition difficult, if not impossible. In the second place, the Nazi regime had just scored spectacular victories in foreign policy with the annexation of Austria and the Sudetenland with the full complicity of the western powers. Hitler's popularity was largely unaffected by the pogrom. As Ian Kershaw has shown, the unpopularity of the pogrom was incurred by Goebbels and the militant sections of the party, not by Hitler, who did not even mention the death of Rath in his speech on the evening of November 9 and subsequently faded into the background to let Goebbels take the credit if the pogrom succeeded or the blame if it failed.[142] There is, however, a third factor that must be mentioned if we are to account fully for the inactivity that was displayed by most

Germans during and after the pogrom. Five years of intense anti-Jewish propaganda had made itself felt on the collective mentality, rendering most Germans receptive to the discriminatory measures that had been taken against the Jews; what they did not support was the wild outburst of brutality that the pogrom of November 9 had unleashed.

The Nazi leadership recognized these realities; it was secure enough in its power and popularity to press on with additional anti-Jewish actions. At the same time, it was determined to conceal any public outbursts of violence from the public in the future. Never again were the SA or the party allowed full rein in launching an independent anti-Jewish action without the approval of the one institution that now put itself clearly at the helm of the anti-Jewish campaign: the SS and its affiliated branches (Gestapo, SD, etc.).[143] Indeed, the round-ups of some thirty thousand Jews and their incarceration in the concentration camps of Dachau, Buchenwald, and Sachsenhausen was carried out by the Gestapo during and after the pogrom.

Two days after Kristallnacht a meeting was held on "the Jewish question" which was under the chairmanship of Hermann Göring and was attended by high ministerial officials that included Goebbels, Funk, von Krosigk, Heydrich, Daluege, and a representative of the German insurance companies (Hilgard).[144] Göring opened the conference by informing the participants that he had received a letter written on the Führer's orders by Bormann "requesting that the Jewish question be now, once and for all, coordinated and solved one way or another."[145] The immediate objection, Göring said, was to proceed along the main line of attack, which, in his view, was chiefly economic. The immediate problem was to take care of the damage that had resulted from the destruction of property during the night of November 9–10, and to do it in such a way that the Jews would carry the full cost incurred. Beyond that, Göring and the participants agreed to accelerate the process of Aryanization and to afflict the Jews with a whole array of new chicaneries so that they could "kick the Jew out of Germany."[146] In an act of brazen insolence, Göring and his henchmen then blamed the Jews for having caused all the damage by their very presence and agreed that the government was to impound the money the insurance companies were obligated to pay out to the Jewish owners whose properties had been destroyed. As to complete Aryanization, Göring made it clear that the main goal was to eject the Jews from the economy by forcing them to transfer their properties to the state. They would be compensated in the form of interest derived from the sale of their assets, but they would have no claim to the assets themselves. The transfer of Jewish property was to be mediated by a state trustee who would estimate what amount Jews were to receive. This amount was to be set as low as possible. The state trustees would then sell a Jewish business to the new Aryan owner at its real value. During the course of Göring's remarks on how one could best plunder Jewish assets, the discussion then turned to related strategies of harassing Jews. Goebbels proposed a decree prohibiting Jews from entering German theaters, cinemas, and circuses. On further reflection, he added that he also wanted Jews eliminated from "all positions in public life in which they may prove to be provocative" — for example, from compartments in sleeping cars with Germans.[147] If there is no more room, Goebbels said, Jews would simply have to stand in the corridor, a remark that prompted an interjection by Göring:

Göring: In that case, I think it would make more sense to give them separate compartments.

Goebbels: Not if the train is overcrowded!

Göring: Just a moment. There'll be only one Jewish coach. If that is filled up, the other Jews will have to stay home.

Goebbels: Suppose, though, there won't be many Jews going on the express to Munich, suppose there will be two Jews in the train and the other compartment would be overcrowded. These two Jews would then have a compartment all themselves. Therefore, Jews may claim a seat only after all Germans have secured a seat.

Göring: I'd give the Jews one coach or one compartment. And should a case like you mention arise and the train be overcrowded, believe me, we won't need a law. We'll kick him out and he'll have to sit alone in the toilet all the way.

Goebbels: I don't agree, I don't believe in this. There ought to be a law. Furthermore, there ought to be a decree barring Jews from German beaches and resorts.

Why stop with prohibiting Jews from gaining access to theaters, cinemas, circuses, train compartments, beaches, or resorts? Goebbels also wondered whether it might not become necessary to forbid the Jews to enter German forests because "whole herds" of them were already running around the Grunewald. In order to stop this provocation Göring suggested that Jews be given a certain part of the forest, and "the Alpers shall take care of it that various animals that looked damned much like Jews — the Elk has such a crooked nose — get there also and become acclimated."[148] The discussion then moved on to parks and park benches. These could pose a real danger because Jews might engage German women or children in gossip and incite them. "Furthermore," Goebbels said, "Jewish children are still allowed in German schools. That's impossible. It is out of the question that a German boy should sit beside a Jewish boy in a German Gymnasium and receive lessons in German history."[149]

After further agreeing to force the Jews to pay an "atonement" penalty (*Sühneleistung*) of one billion Reichmarks, accelerating the process of both Aryanization and emigration through the application of the

Vienna model, it did occur to Göring that this might completely pauperize Jews. In that case, wouldn't those pauperized Jews have to be
segregated from the normal mainstream and to be placed in huge ghettos? Heydrich thought it best to avoid such ghettos because "the control
of the Jew through the watchful eye of the whole population" is better
than controlling him by the thousands in districts that cannot be properly controlled by Gestapo agents.[150] After dreaming up some additional
chicaneries such as suspending Jewish driver's licenses and exclusion-
ary measures relating to health spas, hospitals, and public conveyances,
the meeting broke up on a gratifying note of accomplishment. Göring
summed it up by saying:

> I shall close the wording this way; that German Jewry shall, as punish-
> ment for their abominable crimes, etc., etc., have to make a contribution
> of one billion. That'll work. The pigs won't commit another murder.
> Incidentally, I'd like to say again that I would not like to be a Jew
> in Germany.[151]

Between November of 1938 and January 1939 the Nazi regime sealed
the fate of the Jewish community in Germany. The measures proposed
by Göring and his henchmen on November 12 were formally embodied
in various government decrees, notably the Atonement Payment of one
billion Reichsmark, the requirement that all Jewish proprietors must pay
for the damage of November 9–10 out of their own pockets and relin-
quish insurance claims to the German state, and the sweeping ordinance
that mandated that, effective January 1, 1939, Jews would be excluded
from the economic life of the German nation as owners of businesses,
mail-order houses, artisan or craftsman's enterprises, commercial activities relating to trade markets, fairs, and exhibitions, and as managers of
factories or workshops. Corresponding cultural, educational, and social
restrictions also followed: Jews were prohibited from attending theaters,
cinemas, concerts, and cultural exhibits of any kind, except those specifically organized by authorized Jewish groups. On November 14, Jews
were prohibited from attending any public school. In addition to these
economic and cultural restrictions, the Nazis also instituted measures
aimed at concentrating Jews in the larger cities, where they were separated from the German population in their own districts or apartment
houses. The purpose of this policy was to sever their contact with fellow Germans, which could only be accomplished if they were racially
stigmatized, isolated, concentrated, and subject to severe restrictions on
their movements. On November 23, for example, a police ordinance,
entitled Appearance of Jews in Public (Auftretung der Juden in der
Öffentlichkeit) proposed spatial and temporal restrictions that prohibited Jews from entering certain districts and specified when they were
allowed to appear in public. Restrictions concerning communications
and transportation followed. On November 29, Jews were prohibited
from keeping carrier pigeons; in early December Jews were no longer al-

lowed to keep automobiles and motor bikes, and they had to surrender their driver's licenses.

On December 13, 1938 a decree declared all Jewish economic assets in the form of business, landed property and all other valuables (jewelry, art objects, etc.) at the disposal of the nation. The sale of any Jewish asset had to go through a state purchasing agency. The German government estimated the total wealth of the Jews at 7,538,500 marks and was determined to seize every penny of it by every confiscatory means conceivable.[152] The reality was that the Germans, deluded by the mythology of legendary Jewish wealth and power, vastly overestimated Jewish wealth. Thus, despite these predatory measures, there was no great economic windfall at all. It is true that a few corporate giants such as the Hermann Göring Werke, Mannesmann, Flick, and Otto Wolff were able to engorge the most powerful Jewish firms, including the Czech firms of Weimann and Petschek. Through the use of such state-sponsored gangster methods these firms reaped handsome benefits, but the same advantages did not benefit the German consumer, the party, or the country as a whole. What these seizures did was to benefit the corporate few and convince the Judeophobes that justice was being done to the Jews because all Jewish capital belonged to Germany; its confiscation was only fair since the Jews had stolen it from the German people.

But now that the delusion had done its work by stripping the Jews of their financial resources, what was to be done with this pauperized minority? The regime still toyed with emigration and half-heartedly pursued a number of possibilities, including the idea of sending the Jews to the island of Madagascar off the coast of East Africa in the Indian Ocean and at that time under French colonial control. The plan had come up first in the mid-1930s in negotiations between Poland and France regarding the feasibility of transferring Polish Jews to Madagascar.[153] Nothing tangible had been accomplished by these discussions, but on December 7, 1938, the topic figured prominently in the Bonnet Ribbentrop talks, and it continued to be entertained for over a year by the German Foreign Office. On January 5, 1939. Hitler told the Polish foreign minister, Josef Beck, that he would send the Jews to some faraway country. On January 21, 1939, however, he told the Czech foreign minister that he was planning to annihilate the Jews, saying that he would not let the Jews get away again with what they had done on November 9, 1918, a reference to the German political collapse, which he had always attributed to the Jews.[154] Only a little over a week later, on January 30, 1939 speaking to the Reichstag on the anniversary of his appointment to the chancellorship, Hitler publicly issued the following threat to the Jews:

> In the course of my life I have very often been a prophet, and have usually been ridiculed for it. During the time of my struggle for power it

was in the first instance only the Jewish race that received my prophecies with laughter when I said that I would one day take over the leadership of the state, and with it that of the whole nation, and that I would then among other things settle the Jewish question. Their laughter was uproarious, but I think that for some time now they have been laughing on the other side of their face. Today I will once more be a prophet: if the international Jewish financiers in and outside Europe should succeed in plunging the nation once more into a world war, then the result will not be the Bolshevizing of the earth, and thus the victory of Jewry, but the annihilation of the Jewish race in Europe.[155]

Such annihilatory talk, now publicly revealed by Hitler himself, was creating an atmosphere of eminent danger for those Jews who were still living in Germany. Emigration was still officially one of the main goals of the Nazis, and on January 24, Heydrich had been authorized to solve the Jewish question either through emigration or through evacuation, depending upon favorable political circumstances. Although between 100,000 and 150,000 left Germany during the ten months following Kristallnacht,[156] it was becoming extremely difficult to find countries that welcomed Jews. This terrible dilemma was brought home to the world in the summer of 1939 when the *St. Louis,* carrying 1128 German refugees on board, was anchored off the coast of Cuba; neither the United States nor Cuba was willing to take these refugees because their emigration permits were not valid until 1942. Only 22 of the refugees were allowed to land in Havana, while the rest were forced to journey back to Europe. Few survived the Holocaust.[157] Before long, most countries slammed their doors on the Jews. One of the few remaining escape routes was Shanghai, where Herman Federmann and 14,000 other German Jews found a haven during the war.

By the summer of 1939 the Jewish community in Germany had been reduced and degraded to about 250,000 entrapped Jews. Leo Baeck presided over this remnant as head of a reconstituted Reichsverband der Juden in Deutschland (National Association of Jews in Germany), an emasculated shell of the former Reichsverband that took its orders from the Gestapo. By this time, as Dippel has shown, the Nazis looked upon Baeck as "just another old, groveling Jew taking up their valuable time, delivering only more abuse, another butt for their jokes."[158] The final brutal onslaught was about to begin, and the nature of that impending brutality can be gauged by Hitler's warmongering remarks, private and public, in the summer of 1939, particularly the bloodthirsty comments he made to his generals on August 2, in which he revealed to them just what kind of war he was going to unleash on the world.

In 1934, a novel about the life of Genghis Khan, entitled *Genghis Khan: The Storm Out of Asia,* was released by the well-known German publishing house Deutsche Verlags-Anstalt. One year later, a sequel appeared under the title *The Legacy of Genghis Khan.* The author of both books, which combine historical facts with a considerable degree of poetic license, was a Russian emigré, Michael Charol, who wrote under the pen name Michael Prawdin. The books so impressed Heinrich Himmler that he made arrangements with the SS Training Office to print a special one-volume version of both books, commending it to SS personnel because it could teach valuable lessons for the task that lay ahead. There is also some evidence that Adolf Hitler might have read Prawdin's books.[159]

Genghis Khan was one of the world's greatest conquerors, combining extraordinary bravery with superb military tactics and shrewd diplomacy. His Mongol hordes covered incredible distances and cut a huge swath through the Eurasian landmass, sweeping like a scourge through Russia, China, Korea, Prussia, Asia Minor, and eastern Europe between 1206 and 1227. What both Himmler and Hitler admired about the great Khan was not so much his charismatic leadership, but his utter ruthlessness, his disregard for the value of human life, and his tribal ethos of loyalty to leader and kinsmen. They also liked the conqueror's apparent delight in smashing his enemies, killing their men, women, and children if military necessity or vengeance dictated it, and grabbing their possessions — not so much to enrich or gorge himself, but to prove his superiority. Conquest and combat ennoble a people and strengthen its character. Another quality that the Führer and his SS chief liked about Genghis Khan was the belief in and practice of "blood cement" (*Blutkitt*).[160] According to this practice, shared participation in spilling blood bonds the perpetrators with blood cement, strengthens their brutal impulses, and ties them more closely to the leader and to each other. With blood on their hands, the killers will also be less prone to defect to the enemy because they know they can expect no mercy. Complicity in shared crimes became an important principle of Nazi conduct on the eastern front and was also used as a motivational principle in the annihilation of the Jews.

Himmler believed that Genghis Khan's empire declined because the conqueror weakened the racial purity of his people by permitting racial intermingling with inferior groups. In the coming racial conflict with inferior Slavic groups, the Nazis were determined only to conquer and enslave, not to be biologically weakened by the inferior blood of the conquered. The confrontation with the Slavic hordes would test the mettle of the German people and produce a cruel and hard race that the Nazis always wanted to nourish.

On August 22, 1939, while Joachim von Ribbentrop was winging his way to Moscow to sign the Nazi-Soviet Non-Aggression Pact, a euphoric Hitler decided to entertain the senior commanders of the armed forces at the Berghof. There had been frank meetings between Hitler and his generals before, but this one exceeded all the others in the blatant manner in which Hitler ventilated his warlike feelings. He spoke of his own genius and mocked his western opponents as little worms who would not lift a finger against him, as the events of the past few years had conclusively shown. He was at the height of his political author-ity, commanding the absolute and undisputed confidence of the German people. Germany's military superiority, the weaknesses of the western powers, the support of the Duce — all of these factors dictated a conflict now rather than later. Militarily, Hitler pointed out, neither France nor Britain was prepared for war; they were in no position to come to the aid of Poland. Being psychologically war-weary, they would be unlikely to strike first, and certainly not through neutral countries like Belgium, Holland, or Switzerland. Furthermore, Germany did not have to fear ei-ther a two-front war or an economic blockade because the Soviet Union was its ally and would provide the raw material needed to wage war and maintain the home front. The only thing he feared, said the Führer, was "that at the last moment some *Schweinehund* will present me with a mediation plan."[161]

The generals were stunned by this warlike and histrionic perfor-mance; their mood was not as upbeat as Hitler expected it to be. This is why, after lunch, he gave them another pep talk, telling them that victory was inevitable, provided that the German people closed ranks behind the war effort, showed no pity to its enemies, and proceeded brutally with a good conscience. He would find a convenient pretext to ignite war, regardless of whether it was convincing or not; in the end, the victor is never asked whether he had spoken the truth. Judgments about the ori-gins and conduct of war always depend upon the end results — victory or defeat — not right or wrong:

> Act brutally, 80 million people must obtain what is their right.... Genghis Khan has sent millions of women and children into death willingly and with a light heart... for the goal to be obtained in the war is not that of reaching certain lines but of physically demolishing the opponent. And so for the present only in the east I have put my Death's Head formations in place with the command relentlessly and without compassion to send into death many women and children of Polish origin and language. Poland will be depopulated and settled with Germans.... As for the rest... the fate of Russia will be exactly the same... after Stalin's death — he is a very sick man — we will break the Soviet Union. Then will begin the dawn of the German rule of the earth.[162]

One participant who sat through this incendiary address recounts that after Hitler had explained that he would kill without pity all men, women, and children of Polish origin and language, Hermann Göring allegedly jumped on the table and offered "bloodthirsty thanks and bloody promises and proceeded to dance around like a savage."[163] In-stead of taking determined actions to prevent the unleashing of war, the generals took notes and clicked heels, disregarding Hitler's lunatic comments about wiping out millions of men, women, and children as a pardonable overexpression of the Führer's rhetorical enthusiasm. Yet, everything Hitler said came to pass. Only eight days later, Hitler found his "propagandistic reason" for waging war of aggression. On

August 31, 1939, Heydrich ordered SD attachments dressed as Polish soldiers, to "engineer border incidents"; in one of these incidents the fake Polish soldiers seized a German radio station at Gleiwitz, shouted some anti-German slogans into the microphone, and then withdrew. To lend realism to this provocation the SD men littered the area with actual bodies dressed in Polish uniforms. The dead bodies were those of concentration camp inmates who had been murdered by lethal injections to play their part in the drama. On September 1, 1939, Hitler announced that he had struck back at the Poles without a declaration of war. Hitler now had the war he always wanted, a war aimed at the domination of the earth and the destruction of the Jews.

Chapter 8

Prologue to the Holocaust: From Euthanasia to Ethnic Cleansing

The Great Racial Purification Begins: Euthanasia

In 1938 a severely deformed and handicapped baby was born to a family called Knauer. The baby had a leg and half of an arm missing, appeared to be blind, suffered from convulsions, and was dismissively labeled an "idiot" by the attending physicians.[1] After placing the baby in the care of the Children's Clinic at the University of Leipzig, the baby's father asked Dr. Werner Catel, director of the clinic, to kill the baby. When this request was denied, the father appealed directly to Adolf Hitler. All requests of such a nature were routinely routed through the Führer's private chancellery, the Kanzlei des Führers, or KdF, headed by Philipp Bouhler, who briefed Hitler on the Knauer petition. Hitler then instructed one of his personal physicians, Dr. Karl Brandt, to investigate the case. Brandt was told that if the diagnosis, concerning the Knauer baby was medically correct, the child should be given a merciful death. Brandt consulted with Dr. Catel, confirmed the diagnosis and recommended death. The baby was then killed. This action set in motion the infamous euthanasia program, which Hitler authorized in writing in October of 1939 but symbolically backdated to September 1, 1939, the outbreak of World War II.[2]

Strictly speaking, Hitler's written authorization to kill people who did not conform to Nazi racial norms, the only murderous document he ever personally signed himself, did not have the force of law; but such was his personal power that few physicians either seriously questioned Hitler's authorization or openly defied it.[3] In Nazi Germany one man could decide who should live or die and why. The physicians, as it would turn out, were particularly susceptible to Nazi racial ideals, and they would also play a major role in the Holocaust.

The euthanasia program's racial ideology, personnel, and machinery of destruction served as a prototype for the much larger annihilation program we call the Holocaust. Both the euthanasia program and the Holocaust involved Hitler, his personal chancellery, and a host of related agencies. The euthanasia program, like the "Final Solution" to the Jewish question, was also a top secret program that involved an elaborate game of deception by Hitler's personal chancellery as well as a panoply of governmental agencies such as the Ministry of the Interior, the Ministry of Justice, state health departments, numerous scientific institutes, and Himmler's SS. At one time or another, Germany's premier universities were involved in the program: of the forty physicians who had a leading role in the killings, nine were university professors.

The ideology behind euthanasia was a racial or biomedical vision of cleansing the German gene pool of imperfections. Anything that defiled the blood had to be removed from the people's body (*Volkskörper*). As previously shown, the defilers of the German blood fell into several vague ethnic, social, or medical categories: Gypsies, "Rhineland bastards" (children born to German mothers and fathered by French colonial occupation troops after World War I), criminals or "asocial" elements, homosexuals, the mentally ill or severely handicapped, and the Jews. The outbreak of the war removed any restraints that had previously existed regarding these unwanted people. All-out war was now being waged on them. Since war entailed enormous material sacrifice on the part of the German people, the Nazi killers justified their crimes on economic as well as on ideological grounds by arguing that they were killing the handicapped or mentally ill because they were simply eliminating "useless eaters."[4]

The nerve center of the euthanasia program was right in the Führer's personal chancellery, or KdF. The chancellery's primary purpose was to serve as Hitler's personal link to party affairs; it operated side by side with two other state agencies: the Presidential Chancellery, headed by Otto Meisner, and the Reich Chancellery, headed by Hans Lammers. Since the KdF was not a government agency, limiting itself to clemency issues, petitions, and personnel matters, it was ideally suited to serve as the nerve center for what was manifestly an illegal and criminal program. The agency's five central offices oversaw the following areas: Personal Affairs, State and Party Affairs, Pardon Office, Social and Economic Affairs, and Internal Affairs and Personnel. The office that took charge of the euthanasia program, working out its logistical details, was Central Office II (State and Party Affairs), headed by Viktor Brack, Philipp Bouhler's chief of staff and close friend of Heinrich Himmler. Central Office II had four subdivisions, and it was to Office IIb, which served as a liaison to the Reich government, that Brack assigned the euthanasia program. Section IIb was headed by Hans Hefelmann and his deputy Richard von Hegener: the former held a Ph.D. in agriculture and the latter had a background in banking and business. Since department IIb needed the cooperation of the Ministry of the Interior, especially Department IV dealing with public health and the supervision of all health facilities in Germany, Office IIb quickly established a close working relationship with Dr. Herbert Linden, who was a state counselor in the Ministry of the Interior responsible for state hospitals and nursing homes.

These key officials in the KdF and the Ministry of the Interior brought in a select group of physicians, including Karl Brandt, Werner Catel, Hans Heinze, Hellmuth Unger, and Ernst Wentzler. Brandt was one of Hitler's personal physicians; Catel, as previously mentioned, was head of the children's clinic at the University of Leipzig; Heinze was a psychiatrist who managed the Prussian state hospital of Brandenburg-Görden; Unger was an ophthalmologist who had written an influential novel called *Sendung und Gewissen* (mission and conscience), which recommended mercy deaths as the most humane treatment of dealing with hopelessly ill people;[5] and Wentzel was a Berlin pediatrician who had been recommended to serve in the euthanasia program by the Reich physician leader, Dr. Leonardo Conti.

Given the project's top secret nature, it became necessary to disguise the program under a fictitious name: the Reich Committee for the Scientific Registry of Severe Hereditary Ailments. The euthanasia team used a post office box as a mailing address, assigned code names to its officials, and took up residence in a confiscated Jewish mansion on Tiergartenstrasse 4, hence the acronym T-4 to describe the program. Working in close partnership with the Ministry of the Interior, the T-4 team sent out forms to health facilities asking them to report all deformed infants. Catel, Heinze, and Wentzler served as the ultimate arbiters of life and death of such deformed infants, but their decisions were based on the recommendations of physicians or health care experts in the field who had forwarded the forms, marking them with either a + (death) or a − (life).

Since hundreds of thousands of children were potential targets for euthanasia, the T-4 team tried to enmesh other bureaucrats or physicians, some of whom would give enthusiastic support to the killing program. One was Dr. Hermann Pfannmüller, director of Bavaria's Eglfing-Haar Hospital near Munich, whom Robert J. Lifton has called "the epitome of the brutalized physician-turned-killer."[6] Pfannmüller proudly conducted tours of his facility and had no qualms in showing visitors those infants who were targeted for death. On one occasion, he told a group of visitors that the creatures he was pointing to represented a burden on the health of the nation. As he spoke, a nurse pulled a baby out of a crib and displayed it like a dead rabbit. The doctor's contemptuous remarks were: "with this one, for example, it will take two or three days,"[7] by which he meant the starvation time needed for the baby to die. Another of the many eager participants of the program, whom we have already encountered as an expert on blood, was Dr. Eugen Stähle, who managed the health care system in the state of Württemberg.

The T-4 killers proceeded ruthlessly and methodically; some starved their victims, others killed them through lethal overdoses of barbiturates, sleeping tablets, or morphine. As the program grew, so did the demand for lethal medication and a supplier who was beyond the scrutiny of the law. One major Nazi institution that was beyond the law was its law-enforcing agency — the SS. The Reich Main Security Office of the SS (RSHA) was only too willing to oblige in supplying the necessary poison through its criminal division (Kripo), headed by Arthur Nebe, who gave the job to the Technical Institute for the Detection of Crime. The latter agency was a division of the Central Office of the Reich Detective Office (RKPA). Within this office, the relevant department for the euthanasia program was the one that dealt with chemical analysis. It was headed by Dr. Albert Widmann, an SS officer with a Ph.D. in chemical engineering. The program thus had its organizational structure, personnel, and killing agents.

The first phase of the euthanasia program involved the murder of infants; it began in October of 1939 and continued right to the end of the war. Child euthanasia, however, was quickly overshadowed by the adult euthanasia program, which was far more extensive and included a greater number of victims, many of whom, by today's standards, were capable of leading normal lives with appropriate help: epileptics, blind and deaf people, chronic alcoholics, severely handicapped individuals, manic-depressives, and the like. The adult program, like the child program, had been formulated before the war began, but once more it involved the KdF's top leadership of Bouhler, Brack, and many prominent medical authorities. The physicians and other members of the adult program all joined completely voluntarily. Recruitment procedures were based on connections, nepotism, and confidential recommendations. The bureaucrats who administered the program from Berlin financed the salaries of the killers, ordered the poison, handled routine personnel matters, and supervised a host of related activities. When the Final Solution was instigated in 1941, the KdF also paid the salaries of the T-4 team that had been transferred to the killing fields in the east.[8]

There was one important feature of the adult euthanasia program that distinguished it from the child program, and that was the method of killing. Since a far greater number of people were targeted for death in the adult program, it became necessary to find a more efficient method of dispatching the victims. Dr. Brandt remembered that he once lost consciousness by breathing in the fumes of a malfunctioning stove. This recollection may just possibly have been the idea behind using stationary gas chambers in the adult euthanasia program and the Holocaust.[9] The T-4 team chose several killing centers in Germany and Austria, most of them attached to converted hospitals and nursing homes. There were six major killing sites: Brandenburg on Havel, Hadamar near Limburg, Bernburg on Saale, Grafeneck near Stuttgart, Sonnenstein near Pirna, and Hartheim near Linz.

It began at Brandenburg on the Havel in a converted jail building that had been empty since 1932. The T-4 team constructed a gas chamber in the old jail building and disguised it as an ordinary shower. In either December of 1939 or January of 1940, the top leaders of the T-4 program assembled at Brandenburg to watch the first experimental gassings. Among the dignitaries present were Phillip Bouhler, Karl Brandt, Leonardo Conti, Herbert Linden of the Ministry of the Interior, the T-4 physicians, the chemists of the Technical Institute for the Detection of Crime, and a Stuttgart police officer named Christian Wirth, one of the most brutal perpetrators of the Holocaust. The dignitaries were first treated to witness several lethal injections before observing the pièce de résistance — the actual gassing of eight patients. The naked victims were taken into the fake "shower room" and reassured that they were going to take a shower. Instead of water, carbon monoxide was pumped into the shower room through water pipes that had holes in them so that the gas could escape. The director of the Brandenburg institution, Dr. Irmfried Eberl, was highly pleased by the successful demonstration, as were all the other dignitaries present on that momentous occasion of industrial killing. As Henry Friedlander rightly put it, the gas chamber was a unique invention of Nazi Germany, and so was the way in which the naked victims were processed after they had been exterminated.[10] The gas chamber at Brandenburg became, with certain variations, the prototype for other stationary gas chambers. They outwardly looked like shower rooms with tiled floors, wooden benches along the walls, and showerheads on the ceiling. Once gassed, the dead bodies were hauled away by stokers (*Heizer*) for further waste processing. Bodies marked with an "X" on their backs were given additional treatment because they had gold teeth fillings that could be extracted to benefit the Reich. Once the corpses had been stripped in this manner, they were thrown on a metal plate that was shoved into a clay grill in the crematorium oven and then incinerated. Everyone concerned rationalized the gassings as the quickest and most humane method of delivering patients from suffering.

To keep these killings secret, the T-4 team perfected an elaborate shell game to disguise them from the public and from the relatives of the victims. Various ruses were designed to mislead loved ones from ever finding out why, how, or where the victims actually died. Fraudulent death certificates were fabricated, showing that the victims died of normal causes such as heart attacks, pneumonia, or stroke. Letters of condolence were sent out with stock phrases that began "we are truly sorry to inform you" or "one can understand the death as deliverance" (*Erlösung*). Yet despite these precautions, the killings on such a scale became widely known to the public and caused considerable opposition. The activities at Hadamar, the most brutal killing site, leaked out almost immediately, and they were rarely exaggerated. It was at Hadamar that the whole killing staff held a special ceremony upon reaching the ten thousandth victim. As number 10,000 lay naked on a stretcher, surrounded by flowers, the supervisor gave a speech and rewarded the staff with bottles of beer.[11]

Contrary to past historical accounts, the euthanasia program was never completely terminated because children continued to be killed, and so did handicapped inmates in concentration camps. Hitler stopped only the adult euthanasia program and only inside Germany. Some accounts hold that he did so because there was widespread opposition to the euthanasia program in Germany. Local authorities were alerted by parents and relatives of the victims to what was going on at the killing sites. Ugly scenes also occurred at some of the asylums where the regular staff often desperately tried to protect their patients from the clutches of the murderers.[12] Relatives of the victims notified clergymen and judicial authorities, demanding that immediate action be taken against the perpetrators. One judge even initiated criminal charges against Buhler and paid for it by being prematurely "retired." Both Catholic and Protestant clergymen, notably Bishop Clemens von Gehlen of Münster, Bishop Adolf Bertram of Breslau, State Bishop Theophil Wurm of Württemberg, and the provost of St. Hedwig's Cathedral in Berlin, Bernhard Lichtenberg, all publicly protested the euthanasia program. These protests, however, were not the reason why Hitler terminated the adult euthanasia program in August of 1941. It is far more likely that the program was terminated because it had met its original target figure.[13] By the summer of 1941, 70,273 people had been exterminated. Yet, as Henry Friedlander has shown, the killing of children continued. In fact, the program seems to have become so routine and "normal" that hospitals continued murdering helpless children even after the war ended and under the very noses of the occupying forces. The last victim of the euthanasia program, a four-year-old child named Richard Jenne, was murdered at Kaufbeuern in the American zone of occupation on May 29, 1945.[14]

There are four features of the euthanasia program that made it an important model and training ground for the Holocaust:

1. A pseudoscientific racial ideology that justified killing as healing.

2. The gas chamber as the most "humane" method of killing.

3. Euthanasia killing sites as training schools for genocide.

4. Insight into the nature of the killers.

In regard to the first of these features, the euthanasia program represented the deepest wishes of the Nazi racial state and its supporters. It illustrated the Nazi compulsion to breed a superior race of Aryans, perfect and flawless, by eliminating all impurities from the national gene pool. As Robert J. Lifton put it, "Scientific racism and mental hygiene were the medical-material principles by which the Nazis murdered in the name of purification."[15] Lifton cites the celebrated Austrian biologist Konrad Lorenz, who was hailed in the postwar era as a major authority on "aggression," as saying in 1940:

It must be the duty of racial hygiene to be attentive to a more severe elimination of morally inferior human beings than is the case today.... We should literally replace all factors responsible for selection in a natural and free life.... In prehistoric times of humanity, selection for endurance, heroism, social usefulness, etc., was made solely by *hostile* outside factors. This role must be assumed by a human organization; otherwise, humanity will, for lack of selective factors, be annihilated by the degenerative phenomena that accompany domestication.[16]

It would follow for the Nazis that the traditional role of the doctor as a healer and caretaker of the sick had to be radically revamped. Physicians and other health care professionals had to become, in addition to being caretakers, "cultivators of genes" and "biological soldiers."[17] Above all, they also had to become annihilators if it benefited the health of the nation. Such attitudes served not only as a motivational and justificatory basis for killing, but they also made the psychological process of destruction much easier because what one was destroying was, after all, considered life not worth living.

In the second place, the euthanasia program made a unique contribution to genocide by making use of the stationary gas chamber. The killing centers at Brandenburg, Hadamar, Grafeneck, Bernburg, Sonnenstein, and Hartheim served as a model for the Final Solution. This was also true of the way in which the murderers selected and processed the corpses — that is, how they branded the victims, degraded them as human beings, gassed them, stripped their bodies of remaining valuables, and incinerated them in crematoriums. Furthermore, the success of the T-4 program convinced Hitler and Himmler that mass murder was technically feasible and could therefore be replicated on an even larger scale in the east, where the killings would be out of sight and out of mind for most Germans.

In the third place, the killing sites in the euthanasia program served as training schools for genocide. Almost a hundred supervisors and staff members of T-4 were transferred to the concentration camps of Operation Reinhard: Belzec, Sobibor, and Treblinka. Among those who were involved in running the euthanasia centers, many would later play prominent roles in the Holocaust. The most important was Christian Wirth, who was personally selected by Himmler to embark on a "special mission for the Führer"[18] to the east, where he was instrumental in launching the first mass gassings of Jews at a place called Chelmo (Kulmhof) and then supervising mass killings at Belzec, Sobibor, and Treblinka. Wirth's activities in the east were conducted in close cooperation with other brutal euthanasia veterans. One was Franz Stangl, an Austrian policeman, who was chief superintendent at the Hartheim killing site near Linz and later became camp commandant at Sobibor and Treblinka. Another euthanasia veteran transferred to the east was Dr. Irmfried Eberl, who went from being head of the Bernburg killing center to becoming, for a short period of time, the commandant of

Treblinka. The euthanasia gas specialists with doctoral degrees such as Albert Widmann, August Becker, and Helmut Kallmeyer also played a key role in the gassing of Jews and Gypsies. Even lesser skilled euthanasia functionaries were later transferred to the gassing sites in Poland. Willi Mentz, who took care of cows and swine at both Grafeneck and Hadamar, turned up at Treblinka, where he sadistically killed many prisoners and earned the title of "Frankenstein."[19] Robert Jührs, who had drifted from one unskilled job to another in the 1930s, moved from Hadamar to Belzec and then to Sobibor. Two T-4 cooks, Gustav Münzberger and Kurt Franz, turned up at Treblinka, the latter becoming the last commandant of Treblinka. Karl Frenzel, a stoker at Hadamar, was posted to Sobibor; another stoker at Hadamar, August Miete, was sent to Treblinka. Several male nurses also ended up following their superiors and colleagues to the east.

Finally, the euthanasia program yields some important clues about the nature and character of the killers and why they committed such unspeakable crimes. It is important at the outset to clarify certain issues relating to motivation. Since the euthanasia program, and later the annihilation of the Jews, involved a large number of different types of killers who killed for different reasons, it is, of course, impossible on principle to find a covering law that reduces the motivation of the killers to one basic cause. Historical description by itself, recounting what actually happened, also does not fully explain the whole range of factors involved in mass genocide. For an understanding of genocide and the genocidal mentality, it is necessary to ask the larger philosophical questions about the nature of human social programs, their ideological underpinnings, the degree of faith exhibited by participating members, and the nature and scope of their implementation. The Nazi racial state committed itself, as we have seen, to what Robert J. Lifton has called a biological vision, a biocracy,[20] which involved racial purification for the sake of racial perfection. In order to accomplish this divine mission, the Nazis set in motion a five-step program: coercive sterilization; killing handicapped children in hospitals; gassing handicapped adults in state-administered hospitals; bringing euthanasia programs to the concentration camps and annihilating "handicapped" foreigners, Gypsies, and Jews (Operation 14f13); and murdering "inferior" racial groups, chiefly Gypsies and Jews in extermination camps.

What inspired these mass murderers was the ideological belief system of the planning elite: Hitler, Himmler, Streicher, Rosenberg, Goebbels, Bormann, Heydrich, and a sizable number of fanatical Nazi bureaucrats who were directly involved in the crime. It is true that many perpetrators were motivated by conformism, careerism, blind obedience to authority, or sadistic impulses. Many killed because they had become incrementally brutalized to the point where the lives they took meant nothing more than shooting animals or exterminating vermin. These reasons, however, are not primary determinants of the collective crime itself because they explain only individual actions but not the overall deed itself. The many thousands of killers in the field who, in one degree or another, had blood on their hands — the murderous physicians and their helpers in the euthanasia program and the men of the Einsatzgruppen or concentration camp guards in the east — were all carrying out a task that embodied the ideological mind-set of the ruling Nazi elite.

It follows that the crime of mass murder was ideologically inspired; the reasons why individuals were willing to carry it out depended on a number of complex ideological, psychological, and sociological factors, including their relative commitment to Nazi ideology, strength or weakness of moral character, and social conditioning. In the case of the euthanasia program, which involved a large number of physicians, nurses, and health care workers, there was a very strong commitment to the eugenic ideals of Nazism, although many perpetrators took thousands of lives for reasons other than ideology. Henry Friedlander has shown that the euthanasia physicians were generally young men who were just starting their careers and looked upon their new assignments as means of advancement and personal profit, rationalizing their underlying economic motives in either racial or utilitarian terms.[21] Some, like Hermann Pfannmüller or Friedrich Mennecke, were unsavory characters without any moral scruples whatsoever.

Participation in mass murder for these men was the result of a mixture of ideology, careerism, and greed. The same can be said of the less influential perpetrators who occupied the bottom rung of the murder hierarchy: the nurses, technicians, and clerical and custodial personnel. All of these perpetrators, high or low level, performed their duties voluntarily and without any significant duress. Their claim afterward that they were forced to participate in mass crimes does not hold up because, as Henry Friedlander correctly points out, "after almost fifty years of postwar proceedings, proof has not been provided in a single case that someone who refused to participate in killing operations was shot, incarcerated, or penalized in any way, except perhaps transferred to the front, which was, after all, the destiny of most German soldiers."[22] This being the case, are we entitled to dismiss the claims of the perpetrators that they did what they did because they followed orders on the grounds that had they not done so, they would have been shot or incarcerated? Blind obedience to higher authority was a German cultural trait and cannot be completely dismissed as a factor in genocide. Reared in a society with long-standing traditions of authoritarianism, now elevated to a national fetish by the Nazis, many Germans sincerely believed that defying orders was not only morally wrong but bound to have devastating consequences. That this was not true in the case of mass murder is known to us today; but it was not widely known by the perpetrators at the time. Moreover, disobeying orders in the Third Reich was a capital offense.

The majority of the Nazi killers did indeed follow orders, but this is not the primary reason why most of them killed innocent people. They killed out of a combination of reasons, including ideology, careerism, personal gain, the lust for domination, lack of moral and civic virtue, and sheer sadism. Yet even these factors do not wholly explain why the killers did what they did, day in and day out. This missing element can only be supplied by entering the nightmare world of the mass killers, which pushes the historical imagination beyond the conventional protocols or explanatory strategies, limited as these have been largely to a sanitized world of academic discourse. Historians in general, and German historians in particular, have usually shied away from descending into the bowels of the beast; trained in the neutral terminology of the social sciences or the elevated style of historicism, they have generally refused to descend into the hell of mass shootings, tortures, or gas chambers. And yet, it is in this charnel house that the missing element resides, as some researchers, taking their cue from the relevant documentation, are gradually discovering.

It appears that this missing element involved a process of incremental brutalization that was sanctioned and reinforced, every step along the way, by higher authority until, at length, the population of killers was enmeshed in a culture of brutality held together by a synchronization of purpose, complicity, and technique. One can already see the shape of things to come at Auschwitz by looking at the day-to-day operation of the euthanasia program and how it brutalized its members and schooled them for the even harder tasks that lay ahead. At Hadamar, as we have seen, the whole staff celebrated when the number of patients they had killed reached ten thousand. As Henry Friedlander reminds us, in a factory of death that produces only corpses, people are quickly desensitized and lose any humane connection to either their victims or to each other. At Hadamar "an attitude of licentiousness rapidly developed, an attitude that 'anything goes.' One constantly used stimulus was alcohol, which was freely distributed by the supervisors.... Reports abounded of drunken orgies, numerous sexual liaisons, brawling and bullying, and stealing the property of victims."[23] The brutalizing effects of war, especially on the eastern front, only heightened these attitudes.

The Theory and Practice of Ethnic Cleansing in the East

On September 1, 1939, Hitler attacked Poland without a declaration of war, unleashing a massive force that consisted of a million infantrymen, fifteen hundred fighter planes, and close to a thousand tanks. The assault on Poland was a calculated act of terrorism that combined three elements Genghis Khan would have admired: surprise, superb tactical strategy, and shrewd insights into the strengths and weaknesses of the opponent. Hitler needed a quick tactical victory against the Poles before the western powers could mobilize their forces and threaten Germany's

western frontier. As long as he did not directly challenge France and
Britain, he calculated that they would not attack him. He still believed
that their commitment to Poland was lukewarm and that they would
leave him alone in dealing with the Poles. In the meantime, he flung
most of his forces against the outnumbered, surprised, and unprepared
Poles. The military tactics Hitler used in Poland and later in France
have been labeled *blitzkrieg,* or lightning wars. These tactics involved
the use of swiftly moving mechanized spearheads slashing through enemy lines, the employment of assault teams of infantry, sophisticated
air-to-ground coordination of fighter planes, and a campaign of lies and
subversion waged by the ideological troops who followed in the wake
of the invading Wehrmacht.

Hitler's reliance on blitzkrieg tactics was both a reflection of his
terroristic mentality, which preferred smashing his opponent through
surprise and superior power, and certain geopolitical considerations that
dictated a quick victory because Germany lacked the resources to wage
all-out war for long. The use of terror and force as exclusive means
of waging war, however, brought only short-range successes that were
eventually followed by long-range failures. Hitler did not seem to understand that if the threat of terror has only terror as its objective, the
enemy's will to resist will not break but strengthen; he also did not seem
to realize that quick "smash-and-grab" tactics, unaccompanied by long-
range planning and humane treatment of the conquered people, might
contain the seeds of defeat, particularly if the war turned into a long
drawn-out war of attrition. At first, Hitler's blitzkrieg tactics worked
well against powers of Germany's own size or smaller — Poland, Denmark, Norway, Belgium, Holland, and France — fostering the illusion
that war could be waged relatively painlessly with an economy geared
to both "guns and butter"; but when the war expanded in 1941 and involved Germany at one and the same time with the three great powers
in the world — the United States, the Soviet Union, and the British empire — Hitler's military strategy revealed its essential bankruptcy. Even
so, Hitler thought that he could still win the war by enlarging Germany's
resource base in the east and by making up the deficiency in resources
with ideological fanaticism.

Hitler's military strategies and their underlying assumptions had a
direct bearing on the treatment of conquered people. Whenever the German army conquered new territory, it was accompanied in the rear by
ideological or racial troops of SS men who rounded up racial or political enemies, instituted a network of police terror, herded opponents into
camps, secured the country's economic assets, and ruled in the officially
proclaimed motto of "dominate, administer, and exploit." The degree
of inhumanity inflicted on conquered people varied according to Nazi
racial perceptions of the value of different ethnic groups. Eastern European countries, which contained "inferior" Slavs, Gypsies, and Jews,
were treated with unprecedented brutality, whereas the people of Scandi-

navia and those of the western countries received a far milder treatment. It was after all against the east that Hitler launched his campaign for *Lebensraum,* and it was here that the Nazi racial delusion reached its greatest pitch of intensity, for this was to be a biological-racial war to secure Germany's greatness for the next thousand years.

Poland is basically a vast open plain, ideally suited for tank warfare, and it was across this wide-open plain that the Nazis swept to a quick victory within less than three weeks. Between the German forces that invaded Poland from the west and the Russian troops that moved in from the east, Poland was crushed, as one American journalist put it, like "a soft-boiled egg."[24] Warsaw was captured, the Polish government fled to London, and the victors divided the spoils. Hitler annexed the Polish corridor outright, merged Polish Silesia into German Silesia, and incorporated other parts of Polish territory into East Prussia. The rump of Poland, called the General Government (General Gouvernement), was ruled by one of Hitler's old paladins, Hans Frank, who took to calling himself "King of Poland" and exploited the country with such brutality that he was later hanged at Nuremberg. The annexed Polish territories were divided into two new provinces (*Reichsgaue*): West Prussia, later renamed Danzig-Westpreussen, including Danzig, Marienwerder, and Bromberg; and Posen, later called Wartheland, including Posen, Hohensalza, and Kalisch. The Nazis also annexed the two Polish districts of Kattowitz and Zichenau, incorporating the former into Silesia and the latter into East Prussia. In all of these areas the Nazis extended the whole panoply of German law, administration, police, and education, depriving non-German groups of their civil rights and severely curtailing their economic and cultural activities. Recalcitrant Poles who resisted the new master race (*Herrenvolk*) were imprisoned, dumped into the General Government, or killed.

Behind the invading forces of the regular Wehrmacht came special SS task forces (*Einsatzgruppen*) that had been put together by Heydrich under the code name of Tannenberg.[25] Their task was to liquidate important sections of the Polish intelligentsia. Five *Einsatzgruppen* of SD men and police officials, consisting of about twenty-six hundred men, followed the regular five armies, to whom they were ostensibly subordinate, and carried out rearguard actions against real or presumed enemies of the Reich. Under the cover of this vague mandate, however, these ideological troops carried out a far more sinister plan aimed at decapitating the whole political and intellectual leadership of Poland. In practice, this meant the actual extermination of the Polish elite, including its prominent doctors, lawyers, professors, priests, and landowners. The little people, Heydrich had said, should be left alone, but aristocrats, professionals, ecclesiastics, and Jews had to be murdered (*müssen umgebracht werden*).[26]

What remained of Poland was subjected to a policy of spoliation and terror that Hitler himself called the devil's work (*Teufelswerk*).[27] It is important to realize that Hitler's devil's work, which involved extensive. ethnic resettlements, organized expropriations, and mass liquidations, involved a coordinated effort between the Wehrmacht that secured the conquered space, the SS formation that carried out the police functions, and a host of eager economic planners and logistical experts who provided the expertise required to reorganize the new territories. Although the army at first pretended to be shocked by the excesses that were being committed in the rear areas, there was never any serious opposition to the work of the Nazi racial fanatics. In fact, as the eastern war expanded, the millenarian racial thinking of the Nazi elite began to spread among the rank-and-file of the armed forces, from the commanding officers at the top to the ordinary *Landser* (GI) at the bottom.

In examining the shape of things to come, it is important to spell out, if only briefly, the racial dimensions of the ethnic cleansing that began in Poland in the fall of 1939. This ethnic purification was based, first and foremost, on preconceived ethnic stereotypes about Poland and its people, the malignant Jews who allegedly were polluting the country, the primitive economy and way of life that prevailed there, and Germany's God-given right to "restore order" and transform the country in its own image.

German perceptions of Poland and its people had always been negative and condescending. The Poles, it was said, were a gifted but basically unruly and slovenly sort of people who had been wallowing for centuries in a morass of economic backwardness and political instability. The German phrase *Polnische Wirtschaft* (Polish management of affairs) was a byword for a slovenly, backward, and run-down way of life, and German militarists had generally rationalized their eastern expansionism under the guise of cleaning up the Polish pigsty and bringing Germanic civilization to that unfortunate part of the world. German academics, far from correcting these negative stereotypes, deliberately reified them and strengthened them through selective empirical evidence.[28] There was a whole group of academic *Ostforscher* (eastern researchers), most of them with strong *völkisch* and conservative leanings, who had made it their personal mission to explore every aspect of the eastern territories as a prerequisite to their actual acquisition by Germany. These scholars did their work in a number of key research institutes, of which one of the most important was the Publikationsstelle Dahlem (Publication Department Dahlem), a branch of the secret Prussian State Archive. The agency's scholars, which included the well-known social historian Werner Conze, specialized in all aspects of eastern Europe; they collected statistics and reports about Polish and Russian territories and translated important studies by Polish and Russians writers.[29] The agency worked closely with the SD and the Reich Commissioner for the Strengthening of Germandom (Himmler). Moreover, the Publikationsstelle housed and maintained the infamous Zentralkartei (central card-index) of all Jews in Germany.[30]

Another research department was the Institut für Osteuropäische Wirtschaft (Institute for East European Economics), located in Königsberg and headed by Dr. Theodor Oberländer, an apostle of eastern expansionism, German resettlements, forced evacuations of Poles, and exclusion of Jews from the economies of eastern Europe.[31] Oberländer's deputy, Peter-Heinz Seraphim, was a particularly prolific author and advocate of reclaiming eastern European territories for Germany. In 1938, Seraphim published a highly influential work of scholarly advocacy, *Das Judentum im Osteuropäischen Raum* (Jewry in east European space), in which he depicted the Jews as economic parasites who had grafted themselves onto the Polish economy and exploited it for their own good, creating a veritable *Judenreich,* or Jewish empire. Throughout the book Seraphim used a series of malicious Judeophobic metaphors and phrases to warn his readers of the Jewish peril in Poland, a country that was in a state of ferment and decomposition (*Gärung und Zersetzung*) a as consequence of Jewish piling up (*Judenballung*), or Jewish thickening (*Judendichte*). Seraphim attributed the Polish malaise, indeed the whole east European problem, to the unholy alliance of Jews and Bolsheviks, a view that conformed exactly to what Hitler had been saying throughout his political career. Both Seraphim and Oberländer went to Poland as German officers, set up residence in Krakow, and went to work on what they regarded as the major problem afflicting the Polish economy, and that was the problem of overpopulation, which, in turn, was directly related to the Jewish question.[32] The work of these *Ostforscher* (eastern planners) received an important boost with the founding of the Institut für deutsche Ostarbeit (Institute for German Research on the East) in Krakow on April 20, 1940, the Führer's birthday, under the leadership of Hans Frank.[33] Its task was to research the fundamental questions relating to the eastern territories, particularly as they impinged on the General Government.

Behind such innocuous phrases always lurked a sinister political agenda that went far beyond scientific exploration of population density or economic resources to the raison d'être of Germany's intentions in eastern Europe: domination, exploitation, and extermination. In fact most of the environmental planners (*Raumplanner*), economists, statisticians, population experts, historians, sociologists, and the like were not particularly squeamish in openly revealing their unethical assumptions. In their estimate, Poles and Jews, and later Russians, were not humans but negative factors in the socioeconomic equation; it made no difference to them whether the Polish or Jewish population starved or not. What counted was the expansion of the German resource base, for that was the key to eastern Europe, the continent, and the successful conclusion to the war itself. The mental world of these technicians of power was entirely rigid and one-dimensional. It assumed, as a starting point, two fundamental axioms, namely, that there is only a fixed amount of wealth in the world (zero sum game) and that too many people were competing for it. From these axioms two Darwinian corollaries followed: there is a struggle for existence in which only the fittest survive. The German planners, of course, did not want this process to play itself out in a natural way, which would have made them redundant as planners. They saw themselves as scientific auxiliaries to the men on the battlefield, with slide rule and calculator in hand they would provide the logistical and organizational directions necessary to secure the conquered space for the German people. They were, in short, a new species of political "scientists," emboldened by both their misunderstanding of science and their racial agenda of disregarding even minimal standards of ethical thinking and conduct.[34]

This can be illustrated by their callous disregard for the rights of other people, including their inherent right to live. Oberländer, for example, admired Soviet starvation policies in the 1930s, especially in the Ukraine, because it was a most effective solution to the problem of rural overpopulation, quite apart from the fact the it led to enforced urbanization and industrial growth. That this calculated form of mass murder resulted in the deaths of nine million human beings was for Oberländer and the Soviet perpetrators a tolerable side effect of modernization. In other words, expropriation, starvation, and mass murder are necessary and legitimate methods of providing for the greater good over the long run. By that logic, even the Black Plague, though a natural disaster, was a fine thing, as historians remind us, because a far smaller population in 1450 enjoyed a much higher standard of living than the population did in 1300. The Black Plague was a naturally induced phenomenon and therefore beyond human manipulation at the time. The German planning elite, however, was quite willing and eager to use artificially induced disasters if that benefited German power. For these Nazi planners, "the resettlement or evacuation of whole ethnic groups or great numbers of population groups had already become second nature." Likewise was the "reduction of population" an integral part of their concept of greater space (*Grossraum*), either by sucking off excess population into empty space (*Meinhard*) or deporting it as slave labor to Germany.[35]

This sort of inhumane and unethical thinking meshed perfectly with that of Hitler and the Nazi political leadership — so well, in fact, that some historians have suspected that the decision-making leading to the Final Solution was actually made by planners in the field rather than the strategists in Berlin.[36] Although it is true that the planners insisted that the Polish and Jewish population needed to be reduced and that the ghetto dwellers had to be murdered because the ghetto was not cost effective, the political orders to proceed came not from the field but from Berlin. Nor was the Final Solution dictated primarily by economic factors or resettlement schemes, which only provided additional support to what had been an ongoing Nazi project all along: the racial exclusion of Jews by whatever means, from all German-controlled territories. The prime mover throughout this process was Adolf Hitler and the institution he had chosen to carry out this mission of annihilation — the SS. As the SS went about its business of rounding up Poles, Russians, and Jews, it needed the support of a host of German institutions, including the army, the Foreign Office, state ministries and planning agencies, and perpetrators in the killing fields. This need for a symbiotic relationship became apparent during the course of the Polish campaign. On September 19, 1939, Heydrich briefed the army quartermaster general, Eduard Wagner, on the mission and purpose of the special SS task forces (*Einsatzgruppen*), pointing out that these forces received their instructions directly from him but were otherwise subordinate to the army. Wagner apparently had no objections to Heydrich's proposals and passed on the details of Heydrich's instructions to his superior, General Halder, who made a a few marginal remarks in his diary about the meeting saying that the mission of the SD must be known to the army and, more vaguely, that there would be a "cleaning out" of Jews, intelligentsia, clergy, and nobility.[37] The army chiefs learned quickly what "cleaning out" really meant, but they did nothing to stop it because the process of destruction proceeded slowly and incrementally, did not directly involve them personally or administratively, and happened to a group of people against whom they harbored deep-seated prejudices.

The fate of Poland's 2.5 million Jews rested very much in Hitler's hands. Having toured parts of Poland, Hitler found his worst stereotypes about the Jews empirically confirmed, reportedly telling Rosenberg that "the Jews are the most gruesome thing one can imagine."[38] It was undoubtedly Hitler, in cooperation with Himmler and Heydrich, who identified the various steps that should be taken against the Jews; deportation, concentration, expropriation. In pursuance of these broad aims, Heydrich issued a major directive to his *Einsatzgruppen* on September 21 in which he outlined the tasks that still lay ahead for them in Poland. Entitled "The Jewish Question in the Occupied Territories,"[39] it directed the chiefs of the *Einsatzgruppen* to draw up lists of major Polish leaders and targeted them for liquidation. In addition, Heydrich ordered the SS leaders to move Jews into the major cities still under nominal Polish control. This was aimed at driving the Jews who were living in the new German territories into what would become the General Government. An important section (II) of Heydrich's directive dealt with the establishment of councils of Jewish elders (*Judenräte*), which was to be created in every Jewish community from the leading persons or rabbis. Heydrich stated that "the concentration of the Jews in the cities will probably necessitate... regulations banning the Jews from certain parts of the city, forbidding them to leave the ghetto."[40]

At this stage, the German strategy was aimed primarily at ethnically cleansing German territories of Poles as well as Jews. In the fall of 1939 the Nazis had not moved beyond their policies of stripping Jews of their civil rights, "Aryanizing" their property, and trying to force them into emigration. What was true of the old Reich was also true of Poland, but there was a major difference: what was Adolf Hitler going to do with over two million Jews who were now under his control? The war made emigration increasingly difficult, if not impossible, because frontiers closed down, trapping the Jews inside Hitler's growing empire. Before the invasion of Poland, less than half a million Jews lived under Nazi control. The invasion meant that four times the number of Jews who lived under German control in 1933 were now caught in Hitler's trap. Although about 250,000 Jews fled to the Soviet zone of occupation, those who remained behind were caught in a brutal and chaotic resettlement scheme that forced them to migrate from their small communities into the larger Polish cities and the specific ghetto sections of those cities that had been reserved for them.

Once the border lines between German- and Soviet-occupied Poland had been finalized, the Nazis recognized the daunting task that confronted them. In the newly annexed German territories, which were to be made Jew free (*Judenfrei*) and predominantly German, statistics revealed that the German element was in the small minority. For example, the new Wartheland was 85 percent Polish, 8 percent Jewish, and 7 percent German. This picture was to be changed by deporting both Poles and Jews into the General Government and replacing them with ethnic Germans from other parts of eastern Europe. The task of accomplishing these massive resettlement schemes fell to Heinrich Himmler, the SS, and the many affiliated institutions that now began to proliferate in order to process, concentrate, resettle, and, eventually annihilate such vast numbers of people. By 1939 Himmler had successfully brought most Nazi racial offices under his control.[41] These included the Race and Settlement Main Office (Rasse und Siedlungshauptamt, or RuSHA), responsible for ethnic settlement; the Ancestral Heritage Society (Ahnenerbe),[42] responsible, among other things, for investigating the racial credentials of potential settlers; the Life Springs Society (Lebensborn)[43] of SS orphanages and stud farms for racially valuable children; and the Ethnic German Coordinating Agency (Volksdeutsche Mittelstelle, or VOMI), a liaison agency dealing with ethnic Germans abroad.

After the defeat of Poland, Himmler persuaded Hitler to set up a supreme advisory office for racial questions — the Reich Commission for the Strengthening of Germandom (Reichskommissariat für die Festigung des deutschen Volkstums, or RKFDV).[44] Within the RKFDV there was an important office, headed by SS-Obergruppenführer Ulrich Greifelt, that dealt with immigration and repatriation (Leitstelle für Ein- und Rückwanderung), assessing Jewish and Polish property, confiscating it, and making the resources available to incoming ethnic Germans. The RKFDV spawned a number of associated agencies dealing with ethnic cleansing, such as the Central Immigration Agency, responsible for processing repatriates; the German Resettlement Trusteeship Society (Deutsche Umsiedlungs-Treuhand-Gesellschaft), which handled the accounts of repatriates and compensated them for their past possessions or assets with the equivalent in expropriated (stolen) Polish or Jewish property; the Central Evacuation Agency (Umwanderungszentrale), a department responsible for deporting Poles and Jews; the East German Agrarian Company (Ostdeutsche Landwirtschaftung Gmbh), entrusted with "managing" confiscated Jewish or Polish property; the Resettlement Staff (Ansiedlungsstab), to coordinate resettlement of ethnic Germans in the Old Reich and Austria; and the Guidance Office for German People (Germanische Leitstelle), dealing with the resettlement of people from the Germanic countries of western Europe.

The purpose behind this growing octopus of racial offices, with its tentacles reaching into every aspect of ethnic cleansing, resettlements, expropriations, deportations, and ghettoization, was to bring about a gigantic social and racial transformation of eastern Europe. If this utopian project had been carried out successfully, it would have dwarfed the forced urban migration set in motion by the Soviets in the 1930s. The problem with Himmler's monstrous project, apart from its insane racial motivation, was that it was being carried out in time of war and within territories that had not been secured by military victory. Yet, this made no difference to the lunatic racists who forged ahead without regard of consequences, shifting around masses of peasants, their livestock and supplies, from one part of Europe to another. It goes without saying that the vagaries of war, with its shifting fronts and logistical requirements, disrupted the Reichführer's blueprints at every turn. For example, peasants who had been invited to settle in the former Polish or Russian territories had to spend months and even years in resettlement camps until the racial officials had completed their work of reviewing the racial backgrounds of the new settlers, compiling ethnic charts and surveys, supervising the political indoctrination of new arrivals, allocating new farmsteads, and the like.

Over two hundred thousand ethnic Germans (*Volksdeutsche*) who had been living in various parts of eastern and southeastern Europe were invited to settle in Poland, ostensibly at the expense of the German government but actually at the expense of the stolen assets of Poles and Jews. Degraded and pauperized, Poles and Jews were driven into the General Government. By the time Germany invaded the Soviet Union (June 22, 1941), over a million Poles had been driven from their homes. By the end of 1942, they had been replaced by an equal number of German settlers.

What kind of future did the new master race envision for the territories of eastern Europe? In May of 1940, at a time when the war against the western powers was as good as won, Heinrich Himmler submitted a top secret document to Hitler about the future of the occupied territories in the east. Entitled "Some Thoughts on the Treatment of Foreign Populations in the East," Himmler's paper recommended a thoroughgoing racial cleansing by splintering non-Aryan populations into innumerable particles and thereby preventing them from ever regaining any distinct

form of national consciousness.[45] While decomposing substandard nationalities, special care should be taken, Himmler advised, in salvaging
valuable racial elements from this brew and integrating them with the
newly formed Aryan elite. The non-Aryan population, Himmler stated,
should exist for the sole purpose of serving the Germanic elite; its educational and cultural level must therefore be kept artificially primitive.
Polish children, for example, should be taught to count only up to 500,
learn to write only their names, and memorize the precept "to obey Germans and to be honest, industrious, and trustworthy."[46] Reading was
not considered necessary for a people destined to be mere servants; but
if Polish parents wanted something better for their children, they would
have to ask for special permission, which would be granted or withheld
strictly on racial criteria.

Himmler regarded his proposal as a humane one, certainly far more
humane that the communist method of physical annihilation, which he
called "un-Germanic." What he was proposing was not mass liquidation but the elimination of only a small ruling elite. Having eliminated
the Polish upper class, he proposed to segregate the racial wheat from
the chaff and to take for Germany "racially valuable blood." What this
meant in practice (and much of it was already a fait accompli) was that
thousands of Polish intellectuals had been murdered and racial selections
were underway separating Polish children with Germanic features from
their parents and raising them as Germans. Parents with good blood
would be given a choice of either surrendering their children or moving to Germany. Himmler stressed that such parents and their children
should not be treated as lepers because "we believe they are really our
blood, which has found its way into a foreign nationality through the
mistakes of German history."[47]

As to the Jews, Himmler also wanted to make sure that history did
not make another mistake in their favor. In his brief reference about
depriving people of their national consciousness, Himmler briefly mentioned that the Jews should be driven out of Europe to Africa or some
other place. Neither Himmler nor Hitler had yet decided on a radical
solution to the Jewish question and in the summer of 1940 were still
alternately toying with the idea of shipping them out of Europe, preferably to Madagascar, or deporting them to a reservation in the area of
Lublin. The Führer judged the Himmler document to be "very good
and right," and argued that it should be shared with the relevant authorities, notably Hans Frank and the *Gauleiter* of the newly annexed
Polish territories.[48]

The tragedy of ethnic cleansing now unfolded relentlessly, eliminating
one victim after another. Himmler's *Einsatzgruppen* implemented their
policy of decimating the ranks of the upper classes and screening for
racial elements considered valuable. In the initial stages of this genocidal policy, the *Einsatzgruppen* encountered opposition from the regular
army (Wehrmacht) because the army had been given the responsibility

for maintaining order in the occupied territories. It did not take long before members of the armed forces realized what Hitler's assassins were really up to, namely, murdering Polish teachers, doctors, aristocrats, priests, and businessmen. Yet few dared to stand up to these organized massacres. One who did was General Johannes Blaskowitz, commander in chief in the east, who, "in language unparalleled in German military history,"[49] condemned the acts of the SS murderers and called for a full-scale investigation into the atrocities. Since the murders were instigated as a result of policies that had originated at the top of the Nazi hierarchy, there could be no official investigation. Blaskowitz's protest, therefore, did not go very far; Hitler simply reassigned him to the west and replaced army control with party and SS control. As Heinz Höhne observed, although the generals shuddered at the ghastly atrocities, they were "only too glad for the dictator to relieve them of responsibility for murder."[50] At any rate, the army, far from becoming an obstacle to genocide, was quickly evolving into a reliable partner by allowing the murderers to operate freely in its occupied space and lending them active support. Indeed, once the campaign against the Soviet Union began, the Wehrmacht became ever more enmeshed with genocide. By that time it had become a highly political army whose members were also undergoing a process of unprecedented brutalization.[51]

For Himmler and his racial enthusiasts, however, there was another and just as important war going on, and that was a war of missionizing the vast eastern territories with Germanic blood. As "Reich Commissioner for the Strengthening of Germandom," he was intent on settling the new living space with robust Aryan peasants who would become modern Teutonic Knights on Germany's new frontier; they would turn the eastern territories into an everlasting fountain of youth that would perpetually replenish the lifeblood of Germany. Now that additional new territories were being added to the Reich, Himmler redoubled his efforts and scoured the Baltic regions, eastern Poland, Romania, Yugoslavia, Slovakia, and Russia for Germanic material. Not deterred by the conflicts that were raging on the eastern battlefields, Himmler involved all of the racial offices and experts in the great racial purification. For example, he enlisted the Life Springs (Lebensborn) organization in a bizarre project of kidnapping racially valuable children. As previously mentioned, the Life Springs organization was an SS mating or stud farm that also functioned as an SS maternity home and orphanage. The Lebensborn homes now took Polish and Russian children of Nordic appearance, some orphaned but many brutally taken from their parents. Under the code name "Haymaking," thousands of children were kidnapped and sent to Germany; most of these children were never returned to their parents.[52]

The Russian campaign removed whatever constraints the Nazi racial fanatics may have had up to this time. From Hitler at the top to midlevel planners and low-level executioners at the bottom, there was a ired sense of unlimited possibilities about the conquest and exploitation of Russia's vast resources. The Führer set the tone. In a series of brilliant campaigns, his armies had overrun Poland and Norway in four and eight weeks, respectively; Holland and Belgium in five days; France in six weeks; Yugoslavia in eleven days; and Greece, including the island of Crete, in three weeks. Why should the conquest of the Soviet Union be any different? So persistent was the Führer's need to justify his impending sneak attack on Russia that it amounted to a kind of auto-intoxication, manifesting itself in grandiose and sweeping judgments about the "clay colossus without a head; the Bolshevized wasteland."[53] He decided it would all be over in a matter of weeks, and he expostulated to Jodl: "We have only to kick in the door and the whole rotten structure will come crashing down."[54] The rewards of such a conquest, he had convinced himself, would be colossal, as immense riches would flow into the fatherland from the inexhaustible resources of Russia's wheat fields in the Ukraine. Eventually, all of Russia would become Germany's breadbasket, the new frontier of proud Aryan colonists who would reenact in the east what the American pioneers had achieved in the west. Naturally, there would be obstacles in the way, just as there had been unfamiliar terrain and native Indians in the American West, but these barriers would be ruthlessly brushed aside by the conquering master race (*Herrenvolk*).

The Führer's daydreams were not unique nor did they float in empty space. On the contrary, these fantasies, as previously shown, had seized a whole generation of racial experts who enthusiastically embraced the Führer's delusions and tried to translate them into action in the field. It is, in fact, in this lethal interaction between the lofty policy guidelines dreamed up at the top and the practical implementation, sometimes idiosyncratic and spontaneous, at the bottom that the key to the Holocaust resides. The leadership conceptualized bold racial fantasies in often nothing more than vague guidelines and expectations, and then left it up to SS racial planners to translate them into action. For example, what was one to make of Hitler's pet project of annexing the Crimea, as though that were the most natural thing in the world, settling it with Germans, and linking it to the west by a thousand-mile Autobahn? For the Führer, this presented no real problem because all the new settlers, preferably south Tyrolians, had to do was to "sail down just one waterway, the Danube, and there they are."[55] How did the Nazis realistically plan to settle the vast Russian steppes?

The blueprint for this fantasy, which was worked out by the Nazi planning elite, was called "Master Plan East" (Generalplan Ost).[56] This plan was worked out in great haste before the invasion of Russia by a group of SS racial planners who operated on the assumption that Russia would be quickly conquered in a four-month blitzkrieg, followed by a general military and political collapse. Given such grandiose expectations, it is not surprising that Himmler's planners went into overdrive and hastily produced equally confident proposals about the future of Russia under German occupation. Coming together in Group III/B of the Race and Settlement Main Office (RuSHA), the SS planners worked out a model of ethnic cleansing and resettlement that was projected to encompass the fate of over two hundred million people. Their starting point was the assumption that thirty million Slavs had to be killed in order to settle what would eventually become an equal number of ethnic Germans. In other words, the built-in promise of this, as of all the other racial blueprints of Nazi officialdom, was the forced evacuation or displacement of people in the conquered areas through either enslavement or annihilation.

That this was to be done on a grand scale can be illustrated by the territorial dimensions the new German empire was supposed to entail: all of Western Russia, from Leningrad in the north to the bend of the Dnieper in the south. And this projection was made before the invasion of Russia. When the Wehrmacht slashed deeply into Western Russia in the summer of 1941, the planning visions became even bolder. Yet, even with the eventual elimination of thirty million Slavs, how could the numerically much smaller German settlers assert themselves in a sea of "substandard ethnicities"? Professor Konrad Meyer, responsible for planning in the Reich Commission for the Strengthening of Germandom (RKFDV), had an astonishing solution: the new territories, he proposed, should be divided into settlement provinces (*Marks*), under the overall authority of the SS, because "the east belongs to the Protective Squadron" (*Der Osten gehört der Schutzstaffel*).[57] According to this fantasy, Himmler would assign fiefs of various types (life fiefs, hereditary fiefs) to the new settlers in the manner of past feudal lords. The new settlements, constructed like medieval fortifications, were to be defended by twenty-six strong points in the form of small towns situated at the intersections of German communications arteries.

In practice, most of these grandiose plans had to be postponed by the exigencies of the war, but they reflect the lunatic racial mentality of a sizable section of the Nazi leadership before and during World War II. The inhumane and unethical nature of the German drive for empire was not only unprecedented, but it was also carried out by millions of willing participants who had been persuaded that this enterprise was noble and just. The countless death notices of the fallen soldiers ring out with the same refrain as the following: "In remembrance of Alfons Heizer, born on January 10, 1920, and fell as a gunlayer for Führer and Reich, September 28, 1939, at Lemberg. I have fought a good fight. I have finished my course, I have kept the faith; Henceforth there is laid up for me a crown of righteousness ... (II Timothy 4:7)." That Hitler, Himmler, the SS racialists, the troops of the Ostheer (Eastern Army), the population at large believed in the righteousness of their cause — a cause that was bereft of a single humane or Christian principle of conduct — constitutes one of the most appalling acts of collective self-delusions in history. It illustrated the demonic power of evil in its modern incarnation of insinuating itself behind a façade of leadership charisma and lofty nationalistic goals, mobilizing a technology of mass persuasion to delude millions of people into thinking that inflicting death and annihilation on other people constitutes redemption for the perpetrators.

Indeed, the Nazi leadership proclaimed a holy crusade on the eastern front, a battle of Armageddon that would pit two hostile worldviews against each other — National Socialism and communism. Hitler's eastern war, especially against the Soviet Union, was more than just a conventional military war; it was a racial-biological war whose ultimate goal was the extermination of the "Jewish-Bolshevik intelligentsia." In a key military conference, held three months before the invasion of Russia began, Hitler spelled out graphically how he expected the senior commanders to conduct the war:

> The war against Russia will be such that it cannot be conducted in a chivalrous manner. This struggle is one of ideologies and racial differences and will have to be conducted with unprecedented, merciless and unrelenting harshness. All officers will have to rid themselves of obsolete ideologies.... The [Russian] communists are the bearers of ideology directly opposed to National Socialism. Therefore the commissars will be liquidated.[58]

The Nazi leadership regarded the Russians as subhuman and the Soviet territories as a Bolshevized wasteland. Hitler believed that the Russian people were fit only to be slaves. "Nothing would be a worse mistake," he asserted, than to seek to educate the masses there. It is in our interest that the people should know just enough to recognize the signs on the roads. At present they can't read, and they ought to stay like that.[59] As early as the spring of 1941, three months before the invasion of Russia, Hitler issued the infamous Commissar Order, which gave a unit commander carte blanche to liquidate Soviet commissars; and shortly before the attack, Hitler made the military immune to prosecution for crimes committed against civilians. Himmler and Heydrich, as will be seen, gave the leader of the eastern task forces (*Einsatzgruppen*) their blessing to murder Jews, Asiatic inferiors, communist functionaries, and Gypsies. The Nazi racial war was about to be radicalized on the killing fields of eastern Europe, and with it came a quantum leap in the war against the Jews.

Waiting Rooms to Destruction: Jewish Concentration in Ghettos

By 1942, eleven million Jews were caught in the quagmire of Nazi racial programs. The pace of these schemes had been greatly accelerated by the euthanasia program and its extermination of "lives not worth living," chaotic resettlements, and the brutalizing effects of the eastern war. The invasion of Poland, followed by the ruthless reorganization of Polish territories, had already set in motion a chain reaction of indiscriminate pogroms, ranging from petty humiliations in which Jews were publicly forced to scrub toilets or streets, submit to having their beards shorn, or perform "gymnastic exercises," to the more violent acts involving the rape of Jewish women, mock executions, and actual shootings.[60] Under the cover of "necessary reprisals" against political enemies or partisans, SS security forces, following upon the heels of the Wehrmacht, took Jewish hostages, tortured them, and on the slightest pretext often murdered them in cold blood. The Nazi racial fanatics also incited anti-Jewish elements in the population to commit pogroms against the Jews.

Before the invasion of Russia, however, the Nazis had only vague and shifting objectives about the final goal (*Endziel*) for the growing number of Jews under their control. As previously shown, Heydrich had informed the leaders of his special task forces on September 21, 1939, that Polish Jews were to be concentrated in ghettos in the larger cities, that Jewish councils (*Judenräte*) were to be established, and that eventually all Jews, including those living in the Reich, were to be deported to the area east of Krakow. The final goal (*Endziel*) at this time meant deporting the Jews from all German territories (West Prussia, the Warthegau, East Upper Silesia) and concentrating them in ghettos in the General Government, particularly in the area of Lublin, where SS police commander Odilo Globocnik, a psychopath, had been directed by Himmler to set up a new German resettlement province and also to clear part of the area for a large Jewish reservation (*Judenreservat*). For about a month, starting in October 1939, tens of thousands of Jews were transported to the Lublin district, but the plan to construct a Jewish reservation was eventually abandoned as impractical. The plan had been originated by Heinrich Müller of the Gestapo, who had authorized Eichmann to handle the deportation of Jews from Upper Silesia. Eichmann, however, exceeded this authorization by including Jews from the Protectorate and from Vienna. The destination of these Jews was to be the transit camp near Lublin called Nisko, but as soon as the first transport arrived there, Himmler stopped the program because it interfered with German resettlements of Baltic Germans who were just then being relocated in West Prussia and the Wartheland.[61]

What was happening was that one resettlement plan clashed with another, forcing Himmler to assign a racial priority to the German resettlement project. The Nisko experiment clearly illustrated how closely the Jewish problem was connected to the problem of ethnic cleansing in general. The racially intoxicated Himmler and his planners were trying to pursue the Jewish question side by side with complicated resettlement schemes, creating monumental confusion and offsetting policies that made the task of finding a space for the Jewish people impossible, which left them with a solution they had subconsciously desired all along — namely, to annihilate the whole Jewish race. In fact, the notion of a Jewish reservation completely clashed with Nazi racial and territorial fantasies, which precluded the presence of a prolonged Jewish existence in *any* Nazi-controlled area.[62] This is why the Madagascar project, which was pursued intermittently by the department of Jewish Affairs (Judenreferat, DII) in the German Foreign Office between 1938 and 1940, never gained serious consideration by the Nazi racial elite. Although the plan was drawn up by Franz Rademacher, who headed section DIII (Jewish Question), a subsection of Abteilung Deutschland (Section Germany) under the leadership of Hans Luther, it quickly became apparent that the implementation of the project would depend on the SS. In fact, the SS delivered its own version of the plan, which would have given the SS a clear-cut mandate to run the Madagascar reservation as a *Polizei-Staat* (police state). As Christopher Browning has shown, the plan "was born and died of military circumstances"; it showed promise after the defeat of France, which controlled the island, but died quickly because Britain, controlling the seas, remained unconquered and the Russian campaign pointed toward a more promising Final Solution.[63]

Browning's skillful analysis of the involvement of the Foreign Office in the Final Solution also shows conclusively how the Foreign Office, originally kept in the dark on the Jewish question, was increasingly enmeshed in the annihilation process by Himmler's SS and allowed itself to become a pliant and dominated agency. In tracing the correspondence or following the interaction between members of the Foreign Office and the SS one can also glimpse the shifting direction of the annihilation process. For example, beginning in the fall of 1940 Foreign Office requests for emigration were rejected by the Reich Main Security Office (RSHA) with the excuse that "in view of the doubtless imminent Final Solution of the Jewish question" (im Hinblick auf die zweifelslos kommende Endlösung der Judenfrage) emigration was no longer a viable option. This phrase, which turned up verbatim in the correspondence between various high-ranking officials, did not mean that the Jews would be annihilated in the gas chambers in eastern Europe, but it did mean that some final annihilatory solution was imminent. As early as June 24, 1940, Heydrich had written to Ribbentrop that the whole Jewish problem, now involving 3.5 million Jews residing in German controlled territories, "can no longer be solved through emigration" (*kann aber durch Auswanderung nicht mehr gelöst werden* (Heydrich's underlining).[64]

Having dropped plans for emigration and Jewish reservations in Europe or overseas, the Nazis concentrated their efforts on cleansing Germany and Europe of as many Jews as they could, deporting them eastward into the General Government, concentrating them in ghettos, and then finding a permanent solution that would get rid of them for good. Deportations from the Protectorate and Austria, followed by deportations from the annexed territories, began in October of 1940 and continued into the spring of 1941. This first wave of deportation involved, besides Polish Jews, a sizable number of German Jews, many of whom ended up in the Lodz ghetto in the Warthegau, now a German territory. Since these Jews were still considered German citizens with definite legal rights, the legalists in the Ministry of the Interior quickly covered the criminal deportations and seizures of Jewish assets by issuing another addendum to the Reich Citizenship law which automatically stripped German Jews of both their citizenship and their property if they took up residence in a foreign country or territory occupied by the Wehrmacht.

At first, Hans Frank, the governor of Poland, did not object to all these population movements in and out of his General Government, but once it had become clear that the SS wanted to dump every Jew into his overcrowded territory, reducing it to a social and economic wasteland, he became alarmed.[65] As one of Hitler's oldest paladins, he did not want to preside over a depressed wasteland, but a viable economic country that would make an important contribution to the Reich. This would be made impossible, however, by the influx of millions of pauperized Jews and Poles who would permanently cripple the economy and turn the country into a social and hygienic sewer. Frank even showed traces of humanity by pointing out that brutality was not only inconsistent with the rule of law but also self-defeating as a means of trying to secure a country's economic prosperity. A prolonged and ugly conflict between Frank and Himmler began to unfold, revealing not only the inherent instability of the Nazi system but also the growing power of Himmler's police state, which began to infiltrate and engulf every institution that blocked its way.[66] Without a power base of his own, other than a close tie to Hitler, Frank operated from a position of weakness in his power struggle with Himmler. While Frank publicly denounced the brutality of the SS police state, the Reichsführer SS built up a case against his adversary involving corruption and malfeasance in office and persuaded Hitler, who took his side, to deprive Frank of his power. Although Hitler sided with Himmler and stripped Frank of his party offices and his ministerial rank, he respected his past services and kept him on as governor of Poland without any significant power to influence the process of destruction that was about to unfold under the direction of Himmler and the SS.

The physical destruction process of the Jews began with their deportations into the ghettos of eastern Europe. The ghettos were not permanent places of settlement, as the murderous SS made the Jews believe, but mere roundup centers that would make it more convenient either to let them die in overcrowded and unsanitary conditions or to annihilate them by other means. The Jewish ghettos in Poland were generally located in the poorest or dirtiest sections of a city or on the outskirts of cities that lacked the facilities associated with urban living: paved streets, electricity, adequate sewage, and water supply.[67] With the constant influx of Jews first from all over Poland and then from other countries, the ghettos became overcrowded death traps, where people died in droves from a combination of scourges that raged simultaneously: dysentery, typhoid, tuberculosis, diseases of the digestive tract, and mass hunger.[68] Although the first ghetto was established in the city of Lodz in the Warthegau, most of the ghettos were located in the General Government.[69] The Warsaw ghetto, established on October 12, 1940, became the largest ghetto in the Nazi system, eventually holding 350,000 people. The Lublin ghetto formed in April 1941; Radom formed in May, and so did Czestochowa and Kielce, which were also located in the Radom district. In August of 1941, two months after the invasion of Russia, Galicia was conquered and incorporated into the Nazi slave empire, and Galicia's capital city of Lwów (Lemberg) became the site of the third largest ghetto. In November of 1941 the Nazis turned the Bohemian town of Theresienstadt into a "showcase" ghetto for privileged Jews in order to disguise what was going on elsewhere, so that whenever the Red Cross or foreign critics might ask uncomfortable questions about the fate of the Jews they could always hold up this Potemkin village as a typical Jewish ghetto.

The Jewish ghetto administration, usually consisting of twenty-four members for the larger ghettos, was drawn from prominent prewar leaders with professional or religious backgrounds.[70] The head of the Warsaw ghetto, Adam Czerniakow, was a chemical engineer;[71] Mordechai Chaim Rumkowski, chairman of the Lodz ghetto, was a businessman and director of a Jewish council in Upper Silesia; Moshe Merin, head of the Jewish council in Upper Silesia, had been a businessman and active Zionist before the war; Solomon Ullmann, head of the Belgian Jewish council, was a rabbi; and Ephraim Barash, who chaired the Jewish council in Bialystok, was an engineer. Since the councils were a pliant tool of the Nazis, they were caught in an impossible situation. Their primary purpose was to furnish slave labor for the Nazis, to keep accurate records about the Jewish population, to vacate homes and surrender them to the Germans, to pay periodic contributions, and to confiscate Jewish valuables. Above all, when the time came, the councils were required to select people for deportation to the death camps. In most cases, the councils performed their assigned duties by rubber-stamping Nazi demands, though a number of councils performed virtuoso acts in delaying the inevitable. There is no reason to challenge Raul Hilberg's judgment that the Jewish councils constituted an integral part in the destruction process by lulling their own people into a sense of false security and then handing them over to the perpetrators without any serious opposition. In this sense, as Hilberg put it, the "Jewish leadership both saved and destroyed its people, saving some Jews and destroying others, saving the Jews at one moment and destroying them at the next. Some leaders refused to keep this power, others became intoxicated with it."[72]

One Jewish council leader who became intoxicated by power was the elder of Lodz, Rumkowski, who became an obedient collaborator with the Germans and a dictator to his own people. Referring to the Lodz ghetto inmates as "my Jews," Rumkowski began printing banknotes with his own likeness on it. His bizarre rule illustrates, as Primo Levi reminds us, what a degrading game the Nazis were playing with their victims by touching them with their own corruption. Rumkowski was a good-looking man with snow-white hair and blue eyes, and he managed to radiate a certain amount of hope and confidence. He even simulated the oratorical style of Mussolini and Hitler, thus paying perverse homage to evil. An unwholesome relationship between Rumkowski and his Nazi superiors quickly developed, from which both profited. The fact that Rumkowski garnered a few scraps from his business dealings with the Nazis confirmed the Judeophobic stereotype that all Jews were profit-hungry jackals who turned on their own people, if given the opportunity. Nothing, of course, excuses Rumkowski's conduct, but as Primo Levi points out, there are extenuating circumstances because "an infernal order such as National Socialism exercises a frightful power of corruption against which it is difficult to guard oneself. It degrades its victims and makes them similar to itself, because it needs both great and small complicities."[73]

It was a mark of radical evil that the Nazis succeeded in degrading the ghetto Jews to the point where they actually began to resemble the subhuman types they believed them to be all along. In this way their stereotype was empirically confirmed. Ghetto Jews were dirty, disease ridden, and driven by sheer hunger to do anything, no matter how humiliating, in order to stay alive. Thus, it was easy for criminal inspector Brack to say that all of the 250,000 Jews living in the Lodz ghetto had more or less criminal tendencies.[74] After visiting the Warsaw ghetto, Alfred Rosenberg reported that "seeing this race en masse, which is decaying, decomposing, and rotten to the core, will banish any sentimental humanitarianism."[75] Propaganda Minister Goebbels, who visited the Vilna ghetto, carried away identical impressions of horror, saying that Jews are piled on top of each other, ugly figures to look at, let alone touch....The Jews are the lice of civilized humanity. One has to exterminate them somehow, otherwise they will continue to play their torturous and annoying role."[76] The Nazi doctors, propagating such images of disease-ridden Jews, became the most vocal spokesmen for ghettoization.[77] They advocated declaring the Jewish ghettos a *Seuchengebiet* (quarantine area) and demanded that they be fenced in by high walls (*Seuchenmauer*). As Isaiah Trunk put it, the Germans "deliberately created unsanitary conditions which could not but spread diseases.[78]

These conditions in turn served as a justification for the Nazis to wipe out the ghetto dwellers as the correct way of dealing with diseases and epidemics. During a meeting of a hundred public health officials at the Polish resort of Krynica on October 13–16, 1941, Dr. Jost Walbaum, who hosted the meeting, said that the German authorities had only two choices when it came to the ghetto dwellers: they could sentence the Jews to death by hunger or they could shoot them. Given the fact that the ghetto could not be sufficiently supplied during times of war, he saw no alternative to these two harsh choices. A Doctor Hagen, who recommended a more lenient policy of giving the Jews sufficient food and opportunity for work, received a cool response from the participating physicians, who had been clapping and applauding Dr. Walbaum's presentation. As Christopher Browning summed it up, "having decided to treat the Jews not as victims to be cured but as carriers to be avoided, the doctors were only a short psychological step from Hitler's belief that the Jews were no better than bacilli and vermin.[79] Two accounts, one from a German army field report and the other from a Polish visitor to the Warsaw ghetto, reveal the state of degradation to which the Germans had reduced the ghetto dwellers in 1941. The army field report refers to the situation in the ghetto as "catastrophic" and adds:

> Dead bodies of those who collapsed from lack of strength are lying in the streets, Mortality...had tripled since February. The only thing allotted to the Jews is 1.5 pounds of bread a week. Potatoes, for which the Jewish council has paid in advance of several million, have not yet been delivered. The larger number of welfare agencies created by the Jewish council are in no position to arrest the frightful misery. The ghetto is growing into a social scandal, a breeder of illnesses and of the worst subhumanity.[80]

The diary of a visitor to the Warsaw ghetto, Stanislav Rozycki, is even more graphic:

> The majority are nightmare figures, ghosts of former human beings, miserable destitutes, pathetic remnants of former humanity. One is most affected by the characteristic change one sees in their faces: as a result of misery, poor nourishment, the lack of vitamins, fresh air and exercise, the numerous cares, worries, anticipated misfortunes, suffering and sickness, their faces have taken on a skeletal appearance. The prominent bones around the eye sockets, the yellow facial colour, the slack pendulous skin, the alarming emaciation and sickliness. And, in addition, this miserable, frightened, restless, apathetic and resigned expression like that of a hunted animal....
>
> On the streets children are crying in vain, children who are dying of hunger. They howl, beg, sing, moan, shiver with cold, without underwear, without clothing, without shoes, in rags, sacks, flannel which are bound in strips round the emaciated skeleton, children swollen with hunger, disfigured, half-conscious, already completely grown up at the age of five, gloomy and weary of life....
>
> There are not only children. Young and old people, men and women, intelligentsia and business people are all being declassed and degraded....
>
> For various reasons standards of hygiene are terribly poor. Above all the fearful population density in the streets with which nowhere in Europe can be remotely compared....Having said all this, one can easily

draw one's own conclusion as to the consequences: stomach typhus and typhus, dysentery, tuberculosis, pneumonia, influenza, metabolic disturbances, the most common digestive illnesses.... There are victims in every family. On average up to a thousand people are dying every month. In the early morning the corpses of beggars, children, old people, young people and women are lying in every street — the victims of the hunger and the cold....

While this cruel struggle for a little bit or bread, for a few meters of living space, for the maintenance of health, energy and life is going on, people are incapable of devoting much energy and strength to intellectual matters. In any case, there are German restrictions and bans. Nothing can be printed, taught or learnt.... Nothing reaches us, no products of the human spirit reach us. We have to smuggle in not only foodstuffs and manufactured goods, but also cultural products. For that reason everything which we achieve... is worthy of recognition.[81]

The majority of the Nazi officials who were directly involved with Jewish affairs admitted that the ghetto was only a transitional solution. Friedrich Übelhör, the chief of the Lodz district, for example, made this quite clear when he wrote to Gauleiter Arthur Greiser that "the creation of the ghetto, is of course, only a transition measure. I shall determine at what time and by what means the ghetto... will be cleansed of Jews. In the end,... we must burn out this bubonic plague."[82] At first, the aim had been to isolate, segregate, and control the Jews so that they could be either sent overseas or evacuated further east. The Madagascar plan had died because of military circumstances; the same would be true of all the plans that proposed evacuation of the Jews eastward. The ghetto, as a transitional measure, had a three-year window of opportunity (1939–42), and it was during these three years that the entrapped Jewish population confronted an ever shrinking number of choices that were entirely in the hands of their Nazi tormentors.

Once the ghettos had been established, the Berlin authorities essentially left the day-to-day operation to the local authorities: the *Gauleiter*, Hans Frank and his civilian staff at Krakow, and the relevant SS police chiefs. The decision to seal the ghettos from the surrounding communities, for example, was made by local authorities, but once the overcrowded Jewish community was isolated from all contact with the outside world, the inhabitants quickly exhausted all their resources and faced mass starvation. This problem developed almost immediately at Lodz, which had been sealed on April 30, 1940. As more and more pauperized Jews from Germany, Austria, and the Protectorate were squeezed into the small ghetto, driving up the population to 204,800 people, imminent disaster threatened its existence. The head of the Jewish council, Rumkowski, told the German officials that the community had exhausted its assets and was unable to purchase any additional food or supplies from the outside. This confronted the Nazi leaders in Lodz, and elsewhere, with several choices: they could strangle the ghetto dwellers through starvation, force the able-bodied Jews to perform slave labor, or turn the ghetto into a viable and self-sustaining economy, perhaps even reopening its gates and allowing Jews to reestablish ties with their neighbors.

The debate relating to these issues was set off at Lodz, where Hans Biebow, who was responsible for the administration of the ghetto, expressed himself in favor of turning the ghetto into a viable economy by allowing the Jews to work and to be productive in various trades and commercial enterprises. Biebow's deputy, Alexander Palfinger, on the other hand, believed that the Jews were still hoarding enough wealth, should not be made to work, and ought to be allowed to die en masse. Both Biebow and Palfinger were committed Nazis, but Biebow, who had been a former Bremen coffee importer, had enough economic sense to overrule his colleague's ideological passion for destruction by managing to secure a loan of three million Reichsmark at 4.5 percent interest for the maintenance of the Jewish ghetto, the source of the loan being confiscated Jewish assets. Thus, money previously robbed from the Jews by the German government was being made available, at a tiny fraction of the original and with interest, to sustain the ghetto for the time being until another solution to the Jewish problem could be found.[83]

Did the Lodz decision set a precedent in the sense that it signaled a change from ghetto starvation to ghetto maintenance? A shift in policy can definitely be identified, but it was inconsistently applied, frequently sabotaged by Nazi fanatics, and eventually terminated when the great deportation to the death camps began in the spring of 1942. Biebow's deputy, Palfinger, subsequently went to the Warsaw ghetto, where he was appointed head of the Transfer Agency (Transferstelle), a department of the ghetto administration that served as an intermediary between the ghetto and the outside world by providing food and raw material to the ghetto and negotiating contracts with various suppliers. Palfinger used this position to strangle the ghetto economy, forcibly extracting as much wealth as he could lay his hands on and letting those who were too weak — children, the sick, or the elderly — simply to die by the thousands. Supported by other like-minded officials, notably Karl Neumann, who supervised the Warsaw Division of Food and Agriculture, Palfinger even withheld food allocations for a whole month in December of 1940 in order to force the Jews to use up their last food supplies and to surrender their valuables in order to buy food. The result of this policy of deliberate starvation was that the Warsaw ghetto faced impending collapse in the spring of 1941, prompting Hans Frank to dispatch his economic chief for the General Government, Walter Emmerich, to Warsaw to give him a report on what could be done to turn the ghetto into a viable economic entity.

Emmerich's report was extremely blunt in outlining the few options available once the ghetto had been completely drained of its assets: one could either treat the ghetto as a means of liquidating the Jews or one could use it as a source of labor, in which case it had to be made economically productive. It was a repetition of the Lodz dilemma, except that this time the lines between what Christopher Browning calls the attritionists and the productionists were more sharply defined and passionately debated. This came out clearly in a meeting held on April 3 in Warsaw, in which the Krakow productionists (Walter Emmerich, Rudolf Gater, Max Biebow) debated the Warsaw attritionists (Alexander Palfinger, Ludwig Fischer, Waldemar Schön). Emmerich rejected Ludwig Fischer's optimistic position that the ghetto population was in no danger of famine or starvation. The ghetto, Emmerich pointed out, was clearly at a crossroad, either facing starvation or receiving strong support in order to become a viable entity. The starting point for all economic measures, he stated, "has to be the idea of maintaining the capacity of the Jews to live,"[84] a view that Palfinger rejected out of hand in a subsequent exposé of Emmerich's report of April 3. Hans Frank, however, sided with Emmerich and gave his support to the idea of turning the Warsaw ghetto into a productive entity. Palfinger was replaced by Max Bischof, a Viennese bank director who was assigned the task of trying a limited experiment (*befristetes Experiment*) in order to prove that a free enterprise economy could be established in the Warsaw ghetto. This, of course, was ludicrous because free enterprise is impossible in a slave empire.

The fact was that Emmerich and those who advocated a viable ghetto economy had scored a Pyrrhic victory. The majority of Nazi officials who were involved in Jewish affairs, inside the Reich and in the eastern territories, were already moving beyond the notion of maintaining Jewish lives to the conviction that they had to be destroyed. This explains why the work of the productionists was undermined at every turn by Nazi predators who believed that supporting the Jews was a waste of time and money. Bischof for example, was actively sabotaged in his effort to provision the ghetto. Many Nazi functionaries believed that it was wasteful to feed people who would be exterminated sooner or later. As it turned out, the total amount of foodstuffs supplied to the Warsaw ghetto never increased at all, but was simply reallocated so that the "productive" element would not get more food than the "nonproductive" one. As Aly and Heim indicate, the death figures jumped incrementally higher under the productive ghetto phase than before: 818 deaths in January of 1941, 1023 in February, 1608 in March, 2061 in April, 3821 in May, 4290 in June, 5550 in July, and 5560 in August.[85]

The change in policy from ghetto maintenance to liquidation coincided with the implementation of the "Final Solution to the Jewish Question" in the spring of 1942. This decision was not made by the ghetto authorities or by other planners in the field but by Adolf Hitler. Until the invasion of Russia on June 22, 1941, Nazi policies relating to the Jews had gone through three phases since the war had begun: the first phase began with the invasion of Poland on September 1, 1939, and ended by June of 1940. The Jewish question was closely tied to Nazi resettlement plans and it involved extensive border changes, population transfers, and the formation of ghettos. Hans Frank and his Krakow planners played an important part in these initial planning stages because the General Government was the location of over two million Jews. At this point neither Frank, his Krakow planners, nor Berlin knew exactly how to dispose of these Jews. In his diary, Frank later admitted that the Jews represented "extraordinary malignant gluttons," but he confessed that "we cannot shoot or poison those 3,500,000 Jews."[86] In some way, he added, measures had to be taken that would lead "somehow" to their annihilation. This would be done, Frank surmised, by the planners in Berlin. These discussions, in fact, took place largely in Berlin during phase two, starting with the defeat of France in June of 1940 and extending to March of 1941. Frank and the Krakow planners faded into the background as Himmler and his SS utopians began to assume firm control over both the ideological planning process and its implementation. Himmler submitted his Memorandum on the Treatment of Foreign Populations in the east, the Madagascar plan was effectively shelved, and Jewish resettlement plans to a reservation were also abandoned in favor of an interim policy of ghettoization and attrition. Phase three began with Hitler's decision to set in motion the necessary steps required for the invasion of the Soviet Union. The Nazi racial fanatics, drunk with visions of even greater conquests and resettlement, joined their Führer in conceptualizing not only a greater German racial empire but also the annihilation of Jews and millions of Slavs. The techniques of annihilation were developed between June 22, 1941, when Germany attacked the Soviet Union, and June 1942, when the annihilation camps had been constructed and were fully operational.

The End of German Jewry

On the eve of the first great deportations in October of 1941 there were still 164,000 Jews living a marginal existence in the Old Reich.[87] By that time, German Jewry was a pale remnant of its former self, consisting largely of disenfranchised, pauperized, and elderly souls who had been concentrated in overcrowded commercial apartments (*Judenhäuser*) in Germany's major cities. Those who could work were forced to perform menial labor under degrading conditions, while those who could not work lived isolated and frightened lives behind doors that had to be well marked by the Star of David.

Yet the Nazi fanatics could never leave bad enough alone; they always dreamed up new regulations by which they could hound the Jews a little more. In September of 1939, coinciding with Yom Kippur, the Jews were required to give up their radio sets. Shortly afterward, they were prohibited from using telephones. This was followed by a directive to surrender all their wool and fur clothes, leaving them, for the most part, with their shabbiest clothes — the very thing their tormentors intended. As we have already seen, an important part of Nazi persecution involved a steady process of destroying the human dignity of their victims, to degrade them to the point where they looked less than human, which also made them more susceptible to ill treatment because it is easier to beat or torture "subhumans." Jews were routinely forced to perform the dirtiest, most distasteful tasks, such as cleaning toilets or latrines. The chief inspector of the Lehrter railroad station enjoyed detailing his Jewish workers to latrine work, barking at them: "You Jews are used to wallow in dirt, so go to the shit."[88] This same man once shadowed one of his Jewish workers on his cleaning rounds and physically forced him to putter around with his hands in human vomit.

Despite such individual acts of sadism, the German degradation process was generally orderly and impersonal. In fact, the degrading was done, every step of the way, by the book of officialdom; it was a publicly administered process of incremental degradation and destruction. This made it more acceptable to a people who had always needed the sanction of government rules and regulations or the blessings of officials with degrees or titles when they did anything out of the ordinary. Thus, even the destruction process had to proceed in a smooth and orderly fashion. When this did not happen, even dyed-in-the-wool Nazis became perturbed. The editor of the SS journal *Das schwarze Korps*, for example, wrote an irate letter to one of Himmler's staff members complaining that Jews were being publicly lashed right next to his editorial office, where one of the Jewish deportation halls was located. He pointed out that his employees and those of the Eher publishing house, including men, women, and foreigners, were being exposed to this degrading and shameful spectacle. The author of the letter hastened to add that his complaint had nothing to do with humanitarian or sentimental feelings, but things just had to be done in a proper German manner, that is, in a methodical and cold-blooded way that at the same time maintained and reinforced discipline.[89] And this was indeed how the destruction process unfolded. The Ministry of Justice stripped the Jews of their citizenship, the Employment Exchange took away their work permits, the municipal welfare offices confiscated food rationing books, and the housing office closed the book on them by noting: "unknown, moved to the East."[90]

The officials could always count upon the public to do its share as well. Many Germans, for example, participated freely and eagerly in seizing Jewish homes and valuables. This was done shamelessly and under a great deal of intimidation. In some parts of Germany, especially Streicher's Franconia, many Jews were simply overwhelmed by corrupt party officials and forced to "donate" their assets or else. Many Germans appeared to be well enough informed about what would happen to the Jews that they wrote letters to the Gestapo requesting apartments that would become vacant with the deportation of their Jewish tenants.[91]

In the fall of 1941, the Jews were forced to wear the Star of David on their clothes. The purpose was to brand them publicly as *Volksverräter* and *Volksfeinde* (traitors and enemies of the people). A moving force behind this legislation was Propaganda Minister Joseph Goebbels, who considered this to be a humane hygienic and prophylactic measure that would prevent the Jews from infecting the German people. Public reaction, however, was not at all what the propaganda minister expected. From the accounts of Jewish survivors as well as objective observers such as foreigners, the Jews received more sympathy than insults from ordinary Germans. Leo Baeck recalled being treated more courteously than usual. In fact, a number of remarkable statements could be overheard in public, such as: "Your sign is our shame"; or "It takes more courage to wear the yellow star than to sign up for the Wehrmacht."[92] Speer recalls that during a boring luncheon at the Reich chancellery Goebbels began complaining to Hitler about the Berliners, admitting that "the introduction of the Jewish star has had the very opposite effect from what we intended, mein Führer. Our idea was to exclude the Jews from the Community. But the man in the street doesn't avoid them. On the contrary, people everywhere are showing sympathy for them. This nation is simply not yet mature; it's full of all kinds of idiotic sentimentality."[93]

To make sure that the Germans showed more "maturity" on the Jewish question, the propaganda chief inspired a new decree, released by the Reich Main Security Office, that made it a punishable offense to display sympathy or to engage in any friendly relationship with Jews. And just to make doubly sure that those sentimental Germans got the message, Goebbels had a special anti-Jewish leaflet printed and sent to German families along with their ration cards. The leaflet, printed with a yellow star on the cover that said: "German, this is your mortal enemy," warned that the Jews had inspired the war against Germany and must therefore be destroyed.[94] Goebbels followed this up by a remarkable revelation in the journal *Das Reich* on November 16, entitled "The Jews Are Guilty," by telling the public that the Jews, being guilty of treason, were now being justly annihilated.[95]

German Jews were now on the verge of being deported and annihilated. The atmosphere for many of them was surrealistic. Victor Klemperer gave testimony to the strange temper of the time, living as he did in a kind of twilight zone as a Jew married to an Aryan woman. Klemperer noted how sympathy curiously alternated with steady humiliations and degradations. Side by side with acts of small kindnesses by ordinary people there came the unexpected and degrading house searches during which both Klemperer and his wife were cursed, beaten, and spat upon. "Why do you people get so old? Why don't you just open the gas tap?" one official sneered; while another beat up his wife and screamed: "You Jewish whore! Why did you marry a Jew? In the Talmud it says that each non-Jewish woman is for us a whore."[96] And, despite it all, Klemperer had to confess that "I think German, I am German, I did not choose it and I cannot tear it out."[97] In response to a friend's urgent plea that he had to become Jewish and teach Jews in Jerusalem, the only place for a Jew, Klemperer said, "I am German; I can't be anything else. The National Socialists are not the German people; today's Germans are not the whole of Germany."[98]

In June of 1942, Klemperer made a list of thirty-one anti-Jewish ordinances he could think of that had been making life a living hell for him and other victims in Nazi Germany. These included, among others, prohibitions against being out at night after eight o'clock; against owning one's own house; against possessing radios or making telephone calls; against buying or subscribing to newspapers; against attending theaters, cinemas, concerts, or museums; against operating vehicles or riding buses; against buying cigars or cigarettes; against purchasing flowers; against going to the barber; against owning typewriters; against keeping dogs, cats, or birds; against entering parks; against borrowing books from public libraries.[99]

It should not be surprising that in light of such oppressive conditions many Jews gave up and committed suicide; a favorite method was taking an overdose of Veronal sleeping tablets. One survivor noted how strange it was for so many people to take their lives because they feared for their lives. Many still could not believe that this was happening to them; they could not grasp the reason behind the great German cultural contradiction that involved the question of why a people who produced Bach, Beethoven, and Goethe were now worshiping Hitler, Himmler, and Goebbels.[100] It is estimated that about ten thousand Jews committed suicide because they saw no future and expected to be exterminated by the Nazis.[101]

Having gone through a kind of ghettoization of their own that concentrated them in urban communal apartments, the Jews of Germany faced imminent deportations to the east. The first wave of deportations began in November of 1941. The end of German Jewry was clearly in sight. Historians looking back on these deportations still marvel at how smoothly they were executed. No major hitches or disruptions have been recorded. Neither the Jews nor the German public caused any fuss over what was, after all, the beginning of an unspeakable crime. Here, as elsewhere, historians have to pause and remind themselves that the lemming-like behavior of the victims must be attributed to the fact that the vast majority of Jews did not know the fate that awaited them. Clever dissimulation by the Nazis was an integral part of the destruction process, as was the reliance on Jewish leaders and organizations to support it unwittingly. This accounts for the fact that the Reichsvereinigung obediently carried out the bidding of the Nazis, naively thinking that the Jews would find it easier to be processed by their own people because they would display greater sensitivity and kindness than the Nazis. One survivor later marvelled at the stoic acceptance and smooth operation that characterized the deportation proceedings:

> It appears astonishing to me with what self-possession and stoical calm the highest administrative body of Jewish autonomy let themselves be forced into deportation work by the National Socialist authorities! I recall very clearly the evening in which a hundred of the employees of the Jewish community and Jewish institutions were called together in the meeting room and given the job of bringing together an orderly list by profession and age from the material the Germans gave them.[102]

The assumption that it was more humane if the Jews organized the details of the deportation proceedings themselves was a tragic miscalculation because it only lulled the Jews into a false sense of security. The Nazis understood only force, nothing else. A dramatic and collective act of resistance might just possibly have made some difference. A friend of Leo Baeck's had a discussion with Mahatma Gandhi in which the question was raised what the German Jews should do in order to counter Nazi tyranny. Gandhi advised collective suicide, which would have shocked the conscience of the civilized world and exposed the evils of Nazism with dramatic force.[103] Such ideas, however, ran completely counter to Leo Baeck's convictions about saving lives rather than destroying them. Baeck also opposed active resistance as futile and self-defeating. This came up in May of 1942 when a Jewish resistance group, led by Herbert Baum and Marianne Cohn, tried to burn down a Nazi hate exhibition called the "Soviet Paradise" in Berlin. The group set fire to the exhibition, but only inflicted minor damage. Shortly afterward, the Gestapo arrested the ringleaders, including Baum, who was horribly tortured, and also rounded up hundreds of innocent Jews, including Leo Baeck and other leading members of the *Reichsvereinigung*. Baeck subsequently sent out word to the dissidents who had not been arrested that they should stop their self-defeating acts of resistance because they were jeopardizing the Jewish community.[104] Baeck's plea was, of course, entirely futile because the Nazis wanted to break up the Jewish community anyway, so that neither Baeck's passive methods nor Baum's active resistance made any difference whatsoever. On January 27, 1943, the Gestapo came for Baeck and took him to Theresienstadt. On that day, German Jewry had come to a formal end.

A few Jews survived, some by finding a will to live in the concentration camps and cheating death by accident, while others went into hiding in Germany and elsewhere. Most of those who survived were single, though a number of families also managed to survive as a unit by living an underground existence. Inge Deutschkron and her mother survived through a combination of sheer luck and help by courageous Germans who jeopardized their own lives in providing shelter and assistance. Other survivors were Ludwig Collm, a former teacher, who went through years of harrowing experiences with his wife, Steffy, and their small child, Susi, and managed to survive, thanks to many courageous Germans who braved the omnipresent Gestapo police terror. Many of the fifteen thousand Jewish spouses who lived in mixed marriages, as did Victor Klemperer, also survived. On February 27, 1943, hundreds of Jews who lived in such mixed marriages were taken from their homes and workplaces and sent to collection points for imminent deportation. This "Factory Aktion" prompted the only determined public protest of its kind when about three hundred spouses of the arrested victims staged a public demonstration on Rosenstrasse in Berlin and actually succeeded in forcing the stunned Gestapo to release their spouses.[105]

For the most part, however, Jews had to fend for themselves and rely upon the kindness and courage of individual Germans who were willing to stand up to Nazi tyranny. In general terms, it can be said that Germany's major institutions that could have made a difference — the churches, big business, the leadership of the armed forces — failed completely in mustering the courage and conviction it would have required to stop the Nazis from committing their heinous crimes. In the absence of such opposition, resistance was left up to small and clandestine networks that took the risk and either sheltered individual Jews or helped them escape certain arrest by the Nazis. Although the number of people who helped Jews was relatively small, it was not entirely insignificant. The couple Max and Ines Krakauer put together a list of helpers after their liberation that included many church parishes in Berlin, Pomerania, and Württemberg, which illustrates that while the institutional leadership of Germany's two major churches may have failed, some individual clergymen did not.[106] Quite a number of clergymen openly defied the Nazis and showed solidarity with their Jewish neighbors. One was Heinrich Grüber, a Protestant clergyman in Berlin, who publicly identified himself with Leo Baeck. The two men became good friends and, at one time, were arrested together by the Gestapo. When the Gestapo officer offered a chair only to Grüber, he refused by saying that "if Leo Baeck cannot sit, then I will not sit."[107] Grüber was only one of a number of clergymen who spoke up for the Jews and, in Leonard Baker's words, "organized against the Nazis, hid Jews in their churches, publicly prayed for them, went to the concentration camps with them, stood with them before the threatening Nazi officials."[108]

These efforts, of course, were too ineffectual and too late. By 1941–42 the Nazi terror system was too extensive to be easily breached. The population was also preoccupied with the war and paid scant attention to what was happening to a small minority in its midst or to rumors about what was happening to the Jews in the east. The Gestapo, well-entrenched in every nook and cranny of German society, could always count upon thousands of informers who were willing to denounce Germans and Jews for the slightest profit. Thus, those Jews who lived on the run not only had to fear the Gestapo, but also the thousands of eager informants. There were even informants within their own midst: so-called

Jewish *Greifer* (snatchers) who worked for the Gestapo and denounced their own people, the most notorious being Stella Goldschlag, who saved her own miserable skin by turning in hundreds of Jews.[109]

Given the fact that institutional opposition to the evils of Nazism had largely collapsed, it should not be surprising that individuals who tried to combat it were quickly silenced. Klaus Bonhoeffer's wife tells the story of how she came home from the market feeling rather proud of herself for having spoken to her skeptical neighbors of the reports she heard about the atrocities that were being committed against the Jews in the east. Far from praising her, Klaus Bonhoeffer sternly rebuked his wife by telling her that a dictatorship was like a snake: "If you put your foot on its tail, which is what you are doing, it will just bite you. It doesn't help anybody. You have to meet the head. And that's what you cannot do, and that's what I cannot do."[110]

Klaus Bonhoeffer felt that the only chance to get the head of the Nazi hydra was to persuade the generals that they had to get rid of Hitler in a coup d'état because nothing could function in Germany if it did not come from above. Yet, the generals were no more courageous in resisting tyranny than the prelates of the church, the big industrialists, prominent academics, or higher civil servants. By the time Hitler came for the Jews the German people had effectively abdicated standing up for any group. As pastor Martin Niemöller so poignantly put it, no one was really left to resist:

> First the Nazis went after the Jews, but I was not a Jew, so I did not object. Then they went after the Catholics, but I was not a Catholic, so I did not object. Then they went after the trade unionists, but I was not a trade unionist, so I did not object. Then they came after me, and there was no one left to object.[111]

Chapter 9

The Harvest of Judeophobic Hatred: The Holocaust

Planning for Mass Murder

In 1977 the journalist Gitta Sereny interviewed Hitler's second senior secretary, Christa Schröder, and mentioned to her that one of Bormann's former adjutants, Heinrich Heim, had told Sereny that he did not believe that Hitler knew about the extermination of the Jews. According to Sereny, Schröder laughed, saying "Oh, Heimchen, ... he's too good for this life. Of course Hitler knew! Not only knew, it was *all* his ideas, his orders."[1] Schröder then mentioned a remarkable incident: "I clearly remember a day in 1941, I think it was in early spring. . . . I don't think I will ever forget Himmler's face when he came out of one of his long, "under four eyes" conferences with Hitler. He sat down heavily in the chair on the other side of my desk and buried his face in his hands, his elbows on the desk. "My God, my God," he said. "What am I expected to do?" Schröder added: "Later, much later, ... when we found out what had been done, I was sure that that was the day Hitler told him the Jews had to be killed."[2]

No one knows exactly when Hitler gave the order to annihilate the Jews. No written document has ever been discovered that bears Hitler's signature and indicates, beyond a shadow of a doubt, that he ordered the extermination of the Jews. It was a mark of his evil cunning that he stayed in the shadow and limited all discussions relating to the Final Solution to a handful of henchmen, chiefly Himmler, Heydrich, Bormann, and Goebbels. Moreover, he played an elusive charade telling different people different things, partly to test their reactions and partly to allow himself the flexibility he needed to play-act both the role of charismatic leader for the benefit of decent Germans and the role of evil genius to his party henchmen.[3] After the victory over France, the apotheosis of Adolf Hitler was well in place, and in the eyes of party members as well as ordinary people the Führer's wish (*der Wunsch des Führers*) was everyone's command. Given his unstable personality, cursed by insecurities and deep mistrusts, it was not always clear what was really on the

Führer's mind or on his dark soul because he never shared with anyone the process he had gone through to reach a certain decision. His evil ruminations on the extermination of the Jews took place in the silence of his twisted mind or in the company of like-minded henchmen. Nothing in detail will ever be known about it.

On the other hand, no one can ever keep a secret for very long, especially a dark secret of this magnitude. Freud once brushed aside the objection to his conviction that people, sooner or later, always disclose their innermost feelings by saying that what is hidden becomes manifest, openly or obliquely, to anyone who has eyes and ears; and even if a person's lips are silent, "he chatters with his fingertips and betrayal oozes out of him at every pore."[4] Hitler may have tried to keep the decision-making process that led to the Final Solution a carefully guarded secret, but his irrational Judeophobia compelled him, again and again, to disclose both privately and publicly what he intended to do with the Jews. Although we have only indirect evidence from insiders such as Gerda Schröder and others as to when and how the dictator made his decisions about the Jews, there is a long trail of documentation going back to 1919 that reveals Hitler's intention to exterminate the Jews. What was pure bluster and hyperbole in the 1920s became a deadly reality in 1941; the question now was not whether the Jews would be annihilated but how soon and by what means.

As will be recalled, Hitler issued a public threat to the Jews on January 30, 1939, warning them that he would annihilate them in case of war. This was no idle threat or rhetorical grandstanding; Hitler really believed in the existence of an international Jewish world government, and he twisted every scrap of alleged Jewish influence to buttress his stereotype. Just shortly after the war began, for example, Hitler learned that Chaim Weizmann, head of the World Zionist movement, had written a letter to Prime Minister Chamberlain, published in the *Jewish Chronicle* of September 8, 1939, in which he declared that the Jews would be fighting on the side of Britain and the democracies. Hitler regarded this statement not only as a declaration of war by the Jews on Germany but as a rationale for interning the Jews as prisoners of war, using them, whenever needed, as a bargaining chip with his enemies. Such was the nature of his delusion or stupidity or both that he actually believed that his enemies were dominated by or in league with "international Jewry." As late as July 1942, when Jews were already being gassed in the death camps, Hitler personally referred to Weizmann's letter in reminding his dinner guests that in World War II, "one should never forget that world Jewry, after its declaration of war by the Zionist Congress and its leader Chaim Weizmann, was National Socialism's enemy number one."[5] After the war, the Führer continued, he would threaten to destroy every city unless it disgorged its Jews so that he could pack them off to Madagascar or some other location.[6] These remarks illustrate not only Hitler's conviction that the war he had unleashed had actually been forced on him by world Jewry but also his cunning double-dealing in not disclosing what was actually being done to the Jews and giving his evening guests the impression that he had not made a final decision.

Apparently some concern for possible public reaction, combined with a mania for secrecy and perhaps some psychological need to maintain this atrocity at a distance, kept Hitler from revealing the awful secret and his role in it to anyone but trusted henchmen such as Himmler, Heydrich, Bormann, and Goebbels. But the fact is that Hitler had been step-by-step the guiding spirit of what happened to the Jews since he gained power in 1933. And just as he orchestrated the various efforts aimed at stripping the Jews of their rights, properties, and livelihood, he now spearheaded the drive to exterminate them. His role in the decision-making leading to that final goal, though not entirely known in detail, can be reconstructed by examining the planning process that led to the invasion of Russia. The documentary trail leaves no doubt that Hitler decided to use the coming campaign against Russia as a cover for killing the Jews of Europe. Planning for what would be called Operation Barbarossa began in December of 1940 and continued until the actual invasion on June 22, 1941.

Hitler had convinced himself that the war with the Soviet Union would be over in a few months, that the rotten Bolshevik "colossus with clay feet" would collapse under its own rotten weight, and that immense territories would then open up for German exploitation and settlements. European Russia from the Volga river to Archangel would be detached from Asiatic Russia and brought under German control. A bureaucratic feeding frenzy then developed relating to the actual conquest, control, and administration of territories yet unconquered. Himmler had already drawn up his memorandum on the treatment of alien population in the east; its policy objectives had been approved by Hitler and so had the authorization to set in motion the technical means of implementing them. In January of 1941 Heydrich began negotiations with the commander in chief of the army about the role of the *Einsatzgruppen* in the coming war with Russia, making it clear that their role was to be vastly expanded from what it had been in Poland. Heydrich was also working on a short-term plan (*Nahplan*) of "resettling" more Jews from the west to the east, particularly after the Madagascar plan had been abandoned.[7]

On January 30, 1941, Hitler publicly repeated the threat he had made against the Jews two years earlier to the date and prophesied that the coming months and years would prove that he meant what he said.[8] A few days later, Hitler remarked to a number of military chiefs that his goal was to eliminate Jewish influence throughout the axis sphere of power.[9] According to Major Gerhard Engel's account, Hitler seems to have ruminated extensively on how the Jewish problem could be resolved once and for all. Originally, he said, he only wanted to drive the Jews out of Germany, but now it was clear that he also had to drive them out of the whole axis sphere of domination. Although the war was speeding up the solution regarding the Jews, it had also created new problems. A Madagascar-like plan was still on his mind, but he was also "thinking of many things in a different way that was not exactly friendly."[10] What these unfriendly things were about is not so difficult to imagine. By the time of these Führer ruminations, the gassing of mental patients had been going on for over a year. Himmler had several discussions with various technical experts involved in the gassings, exploring the feasibility of disposing of people in the concentration camps through the methods that were proving so successful in the euthanasia program. The idea of an assembly-line method of mass gassing was definitely germinating in both Himmler's and Hitler's mind. Although Hitler was probably telling the truth when he said that he was thinking different unfriendly things about what he planned to do with the Jews, it is highly likely that gassing them was one of the unfriendly things he had in mind. Poison gas, after all, was not unfamiliar to him. He had been subjected to poison gas himself near the end of the First World War, and the trauma he experienced, as we have seen, triggered a number of insights that never left him. References to poisoning abound in his overwrought rhetoric and invariably include the Jews, who represented the most deadly poison of all. Thus, when it came to the solution of the Jewish problem "you can fight one poison only with another"; you must poison Germany's poisoners.[11] In *Mein Kampf*, he had written that many German lives would have been saved in World War I "if these Hebrew corruptors of the people had been subjected to poison gas."[12]

During the three months preceding the invasion of Russia, Hitler and his planners were preoccupied with three major projects: military preparations for the attack on the Soviet Union, assembly of civilian organizations to administer the conquered territories, and training special task forces to exterminate political and racial enemies on Soviet soil. In the beginning of March Alfred Jodl, head of the Operational Staff of the High Command of the Armed Forces (OKW), issued general guidelines to the relevant military authorities in which he spelled out what Hitler had told him about the military administration of Soviet territories. The army was expected to secure the conquered territories, but it was also commanded to provide support to Himmler, who had been entrusted by Hitler with "special tasks" for the political administration of the areas under occupation. Himmler was authorized to seal off these areas and cleanse them of all opposition; while doing so, he was empowered to act under his own responsibility and was not to be interfered with — not even by "the highest personalities of government or party."[13] On March 30, Hitler addressed the senior commanders of the armed forces at the Reich chancellery and briefed them on the upcoming conflict with the Soviet Union. Interestingly enough, a crisis had broken out only a few days before in Yugoslavia, which would divert German military resources in the Balkans for the next two months, but Hitler was so obsessed with Russia that he did not seem to think much about the impending campaign in the Balkans.

What was on Hitler's mind was the military and political destruction of the Soviet Union, which would require, as he told his generals, the most brutal measures against the Bolshevik commissars and the communist leadership in general. The guidelines he revealed to the generals, as we have seen, were subsequently translated into the infamous Commissar Order, authorizing army commanders to round up and kill captured Soviet commissars or to turn them over to the security service of the SS for "special treatment," a euphemism for torture and extermination. These orders were clearly designed to enmesh the army in the coming atrocities against both Russians and Jews.[14] Hitler's concerns that the generals might develop moral scruples in executing his brutal order turned out to be misplaced, because the German High Command saw basically eye to eye with the Führer on the communist menace and the association of Bolshevism with Jewry.[15]

Nazi planning for the civilian administration of the eastern territories turned out to be haphazard and unrealistic. These preparations have been brilliantly analyzed by Alexander Dallin in his classic work *German Rule in Russia 1941–1945* and do not have to be spelled out in great detail here. Dallin correctly showed that German policy was neither uniform nor efficiently coordinated, because it reflected a continued tug-of-war between feuding blocs and coalitions of various elements within the Nazi constellation of power.[16] There were at least eight major foci of power: Hitler, Martin Bormann and the Nazi Party machinery, Alfred Rosenberg and the Ministry for the Occupied Eastern Territories, Joseph Goebbels and the Propaganda Ministry, Joachim Ribbentrop and the Foreign Office, Hermann Göring and the Office of the Four-Year Plan, Heinrich Himmler and the SS, and the armed forces. The least effective of these power blocs was Alfred Rosenberg, the Nazi racial philosopher whom Hitler basically took out of mothballs because of his presumed expertise on the Soviet Union. Appointed to his post on April 20, 1941, Rosenberg quickly proved that he had no leadership abilities whatsoever and simply could not assert himself against the likes of Bormann, Göring, Goebbels, or Himmler. When Hitler told him in a private meeting before his appointment what lay ahead in Russia and what he expected Rosenberg to do, the muddled philosopher was so stunned that he confided to his diary: "what I do not write down today, I will nevertheless never forget."[17] Although the Reich Commissariats Ostland (the Baltic States and White Russia) and the Ukraine were ostensibly under his jurisdiction, the Reich commissioners ignored his orders and rejected his pragmatic approach to working with various ethnic groups, especially the Ukrainians. They favored, and Himmler insisted upon, repression and annihilation. Rosenberg had no gift for political infighting and never gained access to Hitler's inner circle. Like Himmler, he was a racial utopian, but unlike Himmler he believed that extermination was counterproductive. In the coming power struggles, it was Himmler who had the greatest staying power and therefore the greatest influence on the annihilation process.

Christopher Browning has rightly pointed out that if one wanted to know what Hitler was thinking one had to look at what Himmler was doing,[18] and the most important thing the Reichsführer and his staff were doing in the three months leading up to the invasion of Russia was putting together the SS murder squads and working out an arrangement with the armed forces so that they could operate freely and without interference. The negotiations proceeded by fits and starts because Heydrich had mistakenly selected Heinrich Müller of the Gestapo to represent the SS side in the discussions. Müller was a blunt Bavarian wholly lacking in diplomatic aplomb, and it was not until the more suave Walter Schellenberg, head of the secret service of the SS, took over the negotiations that a satisfactory agreement between the SS and the Wehrmacht was worked out.[19]

In the meantime, Heydrich pressed on with the task of putting together the *Einsatzgruppen*, the special task forces that were to accompany the German army into Russia and carry out "security measures" in the rear of the fighting units. The key personnel for these killer units was put together in May 1941 at a border police school in Pretzsch, northeast of Leipzig.[20] Four major *Einsatzgruppen*, consisting of some three thousand men who had been recruited from all over Germany, were formed; they were labeled A, B, C, and D, corresponding to the army groups that were scheduled to invade Russia. Einsatzgruppe A, led by Brigadeführer Dr. Walter Stahlecker, was to follow Army Group North through the Baltic states to Leningrad; Einsatzgruppe B, led by Arthur Nebe, head of the SS criminal police (Kripo), was attached to Army Group Center operating between the Baltic and the Ukraine; Einsatzgruppe C, headed by SS Brigadeführer Dr. Otto Rasch, operated in the western areas (Lwów, Rowne, Zhitomir, Kiev, Kursk, Poltava, Kharkow); and Einsatzgruppe D, commanded by Dr. Otto Ohlendorf, head of the inland SD, was to follow the Eleventh Army in the area of Bessarabia and the Crimea (Nikolayev, Odessa, Taganrog, Rostov, Krasnodar). The leaders of these units and the commanders of the *Sonderkommandos* (special details) and *Einsatzkommandos* (individual detachments) into which these forces were subdivided, consisted of educated men who were both professionally and ideologically committed to their murderous assignment. Three of the four *Einsatzgruppen* leaders (Stahlecker, Rasch, Ohlendorf) held doctoral degrees. Nebe, head of the criminal police in the Reich Main Security Office, was an enthusiastic volunteer until he learned what the exciting assignment really entailed: killing men, women, and children. Nebe then asked to be relieved, went into opposition, and was executed shortly before the end of the war.

Dr. Stahlecker had been chief of the Württemberg police and advanced rapidly through the ranks of the SD, holding a variety of important posts in Vienna, Bohemia-Moravia, and Norway, and in Berlin as ministerial secretary. Dr. Otto Rasch, with two doctoral degrees, had been the former lord mayor (*Oberbürgermeister*) of Wittenberg, the city where Luther had ushered in the Protestant Reformation. Dr. Otto Ohlendorf was an economist and legal scholar. All of them were true believers and fanatical Judeophobes. The same was true of other *Einsatzgruppen* leaders: the SS *Sturmbannführer* and *Obersturmbannführer* who came from the ranks of academics, ministerial officials, and lawyers. There was even an opera singer, Waldemar Klingelhöfer, among them.[21] An analysis of Einsatzgruppe A reveals that its leadership consisted of highly motivated young men, most of them under forty years of age, who came from middle-class backgrounds, were well educated, had served in the Free Corps or various paramilitary groups, experienced unemployment some time before 1933, and generally rejected religious beliefs in favor of Nazi ideology.[22]

Most of the enlisted personnel had to be drawn from the Order Police (Ordnungspolizei), the regular, uniformed police of the Third Reich. When the available manpower pool of SS security police, SD, and regular Order Police forces proved to be inadequate in dispatching hundreds of thousands of victims, Himmler augmented the original pool with Reserve Police Battalions and foreign units of Lithuanians, Estonians, Latvians, and Ukrainians. The question whether these killer troops, officers and enlisted men, represented a good cross-sample of ordinary Germans has been much debated in recent years and will be taken up in a later section, as will the question why these men killed so obediently and efficiently.

Considerable controversy still exists about the instructions that were given to the *Einsatzgruppen* chiefs and the major officers under their command. What were they told to do in Russia? Where were they briefed and by whom? The only written document that has survived was a directive by Heydrich of July 2, 1941, to the four *Einsatzgruppen* leaders spelling out who should be executed, including communist commissars, party functionaries, "Jews in the service of the party or the state," and other extremist elements.[23] The document says nothing about exterminating all Jews, but refers only to "Jews in the service of the party or the state." Before the invasion began, however, the available evidence indicates that the leaders of the task forces were given several oral orders that left no doubt in their minds that all Jews on Soviet soil should be exterminated. Ohlendorf testified at Nuremberg that a few days before the invasion Bruno Streckenbach, head of the Personnel Office (Amt I) of the Reich Main Security Office, informed the *Einsatzgruppen* leaders that Himmler and Heydrich had selected him to relay orders stating that all Jews in Soviet territories should be exterminated.[24] At the time of Ohlendorf's testimony (1946 and 1948), Streckenbach was assumed to have died in Russia, but he subsequently turned up in the mid-1950s and promptly denied ever having relayed or issued such an order. Other perpetrators, including Dr. Walter Blume and Karl Jäger, among others, insist that they heard Heydrich issue unmistakably murderous orders. On June 17, for example, Heydrich invited the leaders of the *Einsatzgruppen* to his headquarters at Prinz Albrechtstrasse in Berlin and gave them a briefing in which he said that east European Jewry was the intellectual reservoir of Bolshevism, and that the Führer had decided to destroy it.[25]

The perpetrators who later recalled their preinvasion instructions claimed that they had received a summary order to exterminate the Jews in Russia. They also remembered that Heydrich asked them to take an oath to the Führer, which could have left no doubt in their minds that everything they were about to do was in compliance with Hitler's wishes.[26] The research to date indicates that even if the *Einsatzgruppen* leaders did not receive specific orders to shoot every single Jew — man, woman, or child — they felt that they had been given such broad authorization that they could get rid of the Jews in any way they pleased — the more radical and inhumane the better.

This was indeed the shared mentality of the Nazi leadership before the invasion of Russia. On all levels of the Nazi power elite the atmosphere was ripe for murder. The tone was set by the Führer in public statements and policy meetings, producing a ripple effect through the system. In Jerusalem, Eichmann provided an insight into how this happened:

> No sooner had Hitler made a speech — and he invariably touched on the Jewish question — than every party or government department felt that it was up to them to do something. And then Himmler authorized the order on to Heydrich, head of the Security Police and the SD, who would pass it on to Müller, and then it came to me.[27]

What Eichmann described here was the direct line by which the Jewish destruction process traveled through the Nazi chain of command. It began with Hitler, moved to Himmler, to Heydrich's Reich Main Security Office, to Department IV of the Security Service (Heinrich Müller of the Gestapo), to Department IV-B-4 (Eichmann and Jewish Affairs), and finally to the *Einsatzgruppen* and Death's-Head Units in the concentration camps. From this center of the destruction process, where the planning and policy-making decisions were made, links were quickly established with all sorts of agencies whose expertise was essential for the practical implementation of mass murder. Both Himmler and Eichmann eagerly traveled the length and breadth of the Greater German Reich to see to it that Jews were properly rounded up, deported, put into ghettos, and ultimately shipped to the death camps. Before the Russian invasion, for example, Himmler talked to technical experts about "crematorium-delousing units" and the feasibility of converting them into gas chambers and human waste disposal plants.[28] He traveled to a place called Auschwitz, where a former Polish artillery camp was being converted into a larger concentration camp, and told the German commandant, Rudolf Höss, that the new facility would have a multipurpose use as both a concentration camp and a gigantic industrial plant for the production of synthetic oil and rubber. Himmler also established contact with professor Carl Clauberg, a gynecologist who had been experimenting with new fertility methods, but had lately focused his research on finding "better" methods of sterilization. The Professor was an ugly and unbalanced "mad scientist," which may have commended him to Himmler, who subsequently gave him a whole block at Auschwitz so that he could conduct experiments on human guinea pigs.

By carefully noting the nature of Hitler's rhetoric and by tracing what Himmler was up to during the months preceding the invasion of Russia, one cannot avoid the overwhelming impression that mass murder was in the air. Even those who were not directly or only peripherally involved in Jewish affairs had a strong sense that something new and dramatic was about to occur. In fact, a number of agencies had been alerted to expect an imminent solution to the Jewish question. The phrase that surfaced repeatedly in the correspondence of Nazi officials was "im Hinblick auf die zweifelslos kommende Endlösung der Judenfrage" (in view of the doubtless imminent Final Solution of the Jewish question). The phrase was used to justify the cancellation of any further approvals for Jewish emigration and to alert German officials that another and Final Solution was near.[29]

Within the framework of Nazi ideology the term "final" could only mean death; in other words, when it came to the Jews a total solution — one that takes care of the problem once and for all — logically excluded anything that fell short of extinction. For purposes of concealment, of course, Hitler and other Nazi leaders kept on using euphemistic words to the very end.[30] Yet betrayal oozed out of their every pore. For example, on March 17, 1941, Hitler made a pledge to Hans Frank that the General Government would be the first area to be *Judenrein* (cleansed of Jews),[31] a pledge, incidentally, that he had made to other Nazi governors who fiercely competed with each other in clearing their areas of all Jews. As Richard Breitman points out, this is a particularly interesting promise because it referred to the former Poland, where most of the Jews were then concentrated. How is it possible, Breitman asks, to deport all the European Jews to Poland and at the same time to clear Poland of all its Jews? The only possible answer is to annihilate them in Poland.[32] One could, of course, object to this interpretation by arguing, as some historians have done, that Hitler looked to Russia as a place of settlement for the Jews, thus making Poland *judenrein* by driving the Jews eastward into Siberia.[33] Indeed, "evacuation to the east" was one of those stock phrases along with "resettlement" (*Aussiedlung*), "cleansing" (*Säuberung*), and "special treatment" (*Sonderbehandlung*). In my judgment, the talk of driving all the Jews eastward into Siberia was never anything but an act of concealment. It is extremely unlikely that

Hitler ever entertained this project because it would have fallen short of the "final" solution he sought, which was not to give them a land of their own but to exterminate them. The conquest of Russia would have been a failure, in his view, if it did not provide the conditions he needed for a military victory over his political enemies and a biological victory over his racial enemies. In short, he did not believe that there was a territorial solution to the Jewish question, but only a biological solution.

Before his armies marched into Russia, Hitler gave unmistakable signals that he wanted all the Jews eliminated as soon as possible, but neither he nor Himmler had formulated a consistent method by which the millions of Jews under their control could be annihilated. One gains the impression that Hitler had crossed the point of no return as soon as his killer troops piled up mountains of Jewish corpses in Russia, for this, surely, was the right path to a "final" solution; all the others (deportation, ghettoization, expropriation, emigration) had been nothing but failed improvisation that deferred the inevitable. The Final Solution to the Jewish problem thus began with the mass shootings of Russian Jews and then escalated into a mass murder of all the Jews that the Germans could lay their hands on. It is a linguistic snare to talk about the "incremental radicalization" of the Final Solution; once the decision to exterminate the Jews had been made, probably in the late spring or in the summer of 1941, there could be no further radicalization except in the means or techniques of destruction. The question as to when Hitler gave the final order, written or oral, cannot be answered definitely. What can be established conclusively, however, is that the Germans invaded Russia with mass murder on their minds, carried out immediate atrocities, and shared the apocalyptic mood of their leadership. A *Blutkitt* (blood cement) quickly developed between Hitler, the Nazi power elite, and the killers in the field. The war on the Jews had evolved in the form of an interplay between the leadership's annihilatory Judeophobia, often expressed in sweeping pronouncements or guidelines, and the interpretation and implementation of these intentions by the bureaucratic machinery. By the summer of 1941 a critical mass had gathered on all sides in favor of annihilation. The point of no return had been reached.

State Mandated Murder:
Mass Shootings and Gassings

On June 22, 1941, the Germans attacked the Soviet Union with the most awesome arsenal of arms ever assembled in human warfare: 153 divisions (over 3,000,000 million men), 600,000 motorized vehicles, 3,580 tanks, 7,184 artillery pieces, and 2,740 airplanes.[34] The German force was buttressed by twelve Romanian divisions, eighteen Finnish divisions, three Hungarian divisions, two and a half Slovak divisions, and later also by three Italian divisions and a Spanish "blue division." This massive force had been assembled in great secrecy and when the flash of over seven thousand artillery pieces lit the sky in the early morning hour of June 22, raining fire and destruction on the thinly manned and totally unprepared Russian line, the Russians fled in utter panic and tried to get out of the way of the German juggernaut.

Hitler's sneak attack on the Soviet Union was a larger reenactment of his earlier blitzkrieg campaigns. After a swift surprise assault of the Luftwaffe, which resulted in a stunning loss of over four thousand Russian airplanes, mostly on the ground, armored columns carved up the Soviet army in pincerlike encirclement. Three major army groups, supported by four independent tank forces, converged on three strategic Soviet centers of power: Leningrad in the north, Moscow in the center, and the Ukraine in the south. The German objective was to bring about the destruction of the Soviet political system. The end goal was the enslavement of inferior Slavs, the annihilation of racial subhumans, and the transformation of Russia into a new German frontier.

The first three months of Operation Barbarossa, as the campaign against Russia was called, seemed to bear out all of Hitler's optimistic predictions. In early July, Army Group North reached Riga on the Baltic; a month later Army Group Center conquered White Russia and captured Smolensk, thus drawing within two hundred miles of Moscow; finally, in the south the Germans captured the Ukrainian capital of Kiev, taking 665,000 prisoners and enormous materiel.

In retrospect, we now know that these were inconclusive victories, because Hitler's campaign was tactically flawed and strategically self-defeating. It was based on self-serving assumptions about Russian weaknesses and overestimation of German strengths. Both Hitler and his military chiefs based their decisions on faulty intelligence, biased views about the inferiority of the Russians, and anti-communist wishful thinking about the ineffectiveness of the Soviet government and its armed forces.[35] German expectations of inferior Russian military performance had been nurtured by the poor showing of the Russian army in World War I, Stalin's purge of the Soviet officer corps in the 1930s, the lackluster Soviet campaign against the Finns in the winter of 1939–40, and the Soviets' inability to withstand the initial German onslaught in the summer of 1941. The Russian strategy, on the other hand, was to withdraw into the vast interior, trading space and men for time, wearing the invader down, and at the same time fighting furious rearguard actions. German lack of strategic coordination, combined with an inability to force a successful conclusion to the fighting on any of the three fronts, is a classic example of imperial overstretch. By the fall of 1941 Hitler had switched his objectives repeatedly, overextended himself on a thousand-mile front stretching from the Baltic to the Black Sea, and failed to deliver a knockout blow in any single sector. Without knowing it at the time, Hitler was about to be drawn into a lengthy war of attrition, which made blitzkrieg tactics obsolete, and squandered one army after another in battles and conditions that increasingly resembled those of World War I.[36]

With all eyes focused on the spectacular advance of the German army, few foreign observers or uninformed Germans realized what was happening in the rear areas behind the advancing Wehrmacht. Two grand designs were being carried out immediately: an ambitious scheme of occupation was assembled and the occupied areas and its people were exposed to an unprecedented campaign of persecution, enslavement, and annihilation. In the halcyon days of military victories, German ambitions had swelled into grand illusions. All of European Russia was to be divided into four Reich commissariats: Ostland, the Ukraine, Moscovy, and the Caucasus. But due to military circumstances only two of these were actually established.[37] The Reichcommissariat Ostland, administered by Hinrich Lohse, *Gauleiter* of Schleswig-Holstein, included the Baltic states of Lithuania, Latvia, and Estonia as well as White Russia. Given its immense geographical dimensions the area was divided into four general commissariats, each named after its major territory: Lithuania was placed under the control of Dr. Adrian von Ranteln, Latvia under Dr. Otto Drechsler, Estonia under SS-Obergruppenführer Karl Sigismund von Litzmann, and White Russia under Wilhelm Kube. The least organized of these areas, as it would turn out, was White Russia, where Kube constantly battled powerful Nazi functionaries and made himself so hated that if a Russian partisan had not blown him up by planting a bomb under his bed, he would have been fired or executed by the Nazis. The Ukraine, which was also subdivided into general commissariats, was expected to become the breadbasket of the Greater German Reich (Das Grossdeutsche Reich), as Nazi propaganda now began to refer to the German empire. Rosenberg, as Reich commissioner for the occupied eastern territories, urged an alliance with the Ukrainians, but he was overruled by Hitler, Himmler, and Erich Koch, the civilian head of the Ukraine. Koch was indisputably the most venal and incompetent administrator the Nazis could have put in charge of the area, "monumentally stupid" and brutal.[38] His brutalization and exploitation of the population alienated the Ukrainians, whose hostility to Russia made them likely German allies. This policy gave rise to a widely told joke that "Stalin, in awarding a medal for supreme service to the Soviet State, regretted that the man who deserved it most (Koch) was not yet in a position to receive it personally."[39]

This could be said of German rule in Russia as a whole, which was almost universally grim and ill advised. Although the Germans were greeted by the people as liberators, especially in the Ukraine, their brutal treatment of the population invariably elicited fierce reactions in the form of partisan activities and terroristic reprisals. Refusing to enlist the despised Slavic people in the campaign against Bolshevism as well as adamantly refusing to arm them, the Germans deprived themselves of important support that very possibly might have made the difference between victory and defeat. Furthermore, starving prisoners of war or ruthlessly working them to death served no useful purpose, quite apart from the fact that it was criminal as well as immoral.[40] Germany almost certainly lost the war when Hitler made Himmler his executive officer in Russia and assigned him a twofold task — to settle ethnic Germans in the conquered territories and enslave subhuman Slavs. Himmler went about his task so ruthlessly, ignoring moral, military, and even economic considerations, that the Germans earned the utter hatred of the Russians and could look forward to the same treatment from them when the tide of war turned in 1942.

Even more gruesome events were initiated when the Germans set in motion their other grand design in Russia: the extermination of the Jews, which began from the first day of the invasion of the Soviet Union. Following upon the heels of the Wehrmacht, Himmler's *Einsatzgruppen* systematically rounded up communist functionaries, Jews, intellectuals, and other "subversives," herded them into makeshift camps, tortured them, or shot them on the spot. The advance of the German forces was so rapid that tens of thousands of Jews, unable to outrun it, found themselves trapped behind the lines, where they were rounded up, tortured, and killed, not only by the Germans but also by the local population of Lithuanians or Ukrainians who had been incited by German proclamations and pamphlets into launching pogroms against the Jews.[41] In Martin Gilbert's view, "the invasion of Russia had provided the Germans with an opportunity hitherto lacking: a remote region, the cover of an advancing army, vast distances, local collaborators, and an intensified will to destroy."[42] The "will to destroy" was so strong because it was largely based on ideological-racial hatred, was officially sanctioned by the highest authority, and was made easier by a breakdown in civilized conduct by Himmler's racial warriors. The men of the *Einsatzgruppen* began increasingly to conform to Nietzsche's blond beasts of prey, who

> in their relations with one another show themselves so resourceful in consideration, self-control, delicacy, loyalty, pride, and friendship — once they go outside, where the strange, the *stranger* is found, they are not much better than uncaged beasts of prey. There they savor a freedom from all social constraints, they compensate themselves in the wilderness for the tensions engendered by enclosure within the peace of society, they go *back* to the innocent conscience of the beast of prey, as triumphant monsters who perhaps emerge from a disgusting [*schleusslichen*] procession of murder, arson, rape, torture, exhilarated and undisturbed of soul, as if it were no more than a student's prank.[43]

Between June 22, 1941, and the end of the year the *Einsatzgruppen* went on a bloody rampage, hunting down Jews wherever they could find them. Instructions to shoot only specifically targeted groups quickly broke down when individual units and their commanders killed at will while in the grip of homicidal frenzy. A few days after the invasion, for example, Major Weiss of Police Battalion 309 initiated mass murder in Bialystok because he correctly interpreted the Führer's wish to mean that *all* Jews, regardless of age or sex, should be exterminated. His men combed the city for Jews and then went berserk, beating, humiliating, and shooting at will. The Jewish leaders of the city went to the head-quarters of the 221st Security Division and knelt at the feet of General Pflugbeil, pleading for army protection. At that moment, a member of Police Battalion 309 undid his fly and urinated on the Jewish delegation while the general turned his back.[44] The onslaught was on its way.

All over the conquered areas, from the Baltic provinces to White Russia and the Ukraine, the *Einsatzgruppen* conducted mass shootings on an unimaginable scale. Typically, the killers would round up Jews in towns and villages, march them outside the town, and shoot them along-side ditches or antitank trenches where they would be buried. In most cases, the Jews had to dig their own graves before they were shot:

> The condemned people were not only brought in trucks but also on foot in groups of seventy and eighty and beaten mercilessly along the way. The twenty to twenty-five who were to be shot were taken to a spot fifty meters from the execution site, where they were guarded until they were ready to be shot. They undressed near the graves.... Completely undressed, they were driven into the graves and forced to lie face down. The Germans shot them with rifles and machine pistols. In this way, one party after another was driven to lie face down on the corpses of those who had already been shot.[45]

There was fierce competition among the leaders of the various *Einsatzkommandos* to repeat the highest body counts, and some commandos proudly reported back that their areas were free of Jews:

> I can now state that the aim of solving the Jewish problem for Lithuania has been achieved by Einsatzkommando 3. There are no more Jews in Lithuania apart from work-Jews and their families.... I wanted to bump off these work Jews and their families but this brought me smack up against the civil administration and the Wehrmacht and prompted a ban on the shooting of these Jews and their families.[46]

This report comes from Karl Jäger, head of *Einsatzkommando* 3, which operated in Lithuania; his men murdered 133,346 in Lithuania and White Russia between July and the end of October 1941. Jäger's troops were also one of the first to shoot women, infants, and children. Although the army occasionally voiced feeble objections to anti-Jewish atrocities, the *Einsatzgruppen* commanders often praised the army for its cooperation: "From the first day onward," one report declared, "the *Einsatzgruppe* has succeeded in establishing an excellent understanding with all sections of the Wehrmacht."[47] One report even claimed that the relationship that had been forged between the genocidal killers and the regular army was *recht herzlich,* almost in the nature of an emotional bond. While this goes too far, there is no denying the fact that the Eastern Army (Ostheer) was increasingly brutalized by the savage conflict it had unleashed. Officers as well as enlisted men were enmeshed with the genocidal killers from the moment the conflict began. Although some officers were morally outraged by what they saw or heard and warned their men to stay away from the killings, the vast majority quickly disassociated themselves from the atrocities or else rationalized mass murder by accepting the party line that these killings were necessary reprisals against partisan attacks on the German army. Since the anti-partisan campaign officially sanctioned the slaughter of noncombatants, the line between partisans, civilians, and Jews quickly became blurred.

The army that marched into Russia, and this included the *Einsatzgruppen* which formed an integral part of the fighting force, was a nazified army that saw itself waging a racial as well as a military war. Hitler was right when he said that the world would hold its breath when he unleashed his forces against Russia; he was also correct when he confessed before the invasion that he was kicking open a door leading into a dark void. What the Führer imagined, his troops experienced. Pushing into an unfamiliar landscape that might as well have been on another planet, the troops encountered conditions that simply did not fit into their familiar western framework. The immense territory, the unfavorable weather, the great cultural differences evoked perceptions of an alien and hostile universe. The Nazi soldiers came flushed with great victories and ideological blinders, confidently expecting a quick end to the war. When that victory became ever more elusive and the casualties mounted, the atmosphere, already highly charged with apocalyptical expectations in 1941, became more and more hysterical, and so did the collective determination to wipe out as many alleged subhumans as possible.

The Eastern Army, in other words, shared the ideological world picture of the Nazi leadership, including belief in German racial superiority, commitment to a homogenous *Volk* community, obedience to the Führer, and conquest of *Lebensraum* in the east.[48] A substantial majority of the commanding officers and enlisted men also equated communism and Jewry, an equation that justified annihilating them both. Field Marshal Walter von Reichenau, commander of Army Group South, was particularly insistent in reminding his troops that the Russian campaign was aimed at wiping out the "Jewish-Bolshevist" system and that therefore "soldiers must show full understanding for the necessity for the severe but just atonement [*Sühne*] being required of the Jewish subhumans."[49] Reichnau was an unconditional follower of Hitler, but his views were shared by many generals, even those who later conspired against their Führer. General Karl Heinrich Stülpnagel, for example, who joined the military opposition to Hitler in 1944, issued a number of Judeophobic directives as head of the Seventeenth Army in Russia. On August 17, 1941, Stülpnagel wrote to the army propaganda department that more intensive anti-Jewish propaganda was needed to enlighten the troops.[50]

The troops did not have to be "enlightened" about the culpability of the Jews; they already believed it. Moreover, they acted on their beliefs by giving support to the killer troops, volunteering for execution squads, showing up at mass shootings, and snapping pictures of the gruesome events. Since mass executions were a common occurrence, German soldiers frequently observed these atrocities and carried the news back home in word and picture. A British interrogation officer later deduced that there was widespread awareness of atrocities against civilians, Jews, and prisoners of war from the type of photographs found in the wallets of hundreds of captured German soldiers. These photographs fell into a recurring pattern — pictures of *Mutti* (mom), wife, or sweetheart, obscene pictures, and photos of floggings, hangings, or mass executions.[51] The observance and participation in atrocities against the Jews thus involved, besides the killer troops themselves, a sizable number of people. Anti-Jewish elements in the local population were especially encouraged to initiate pogroms and to involve as many people in them as possible. In many towns the locals eagerly participated in pogroms against helpless Jews, as they did in Kaunas, Lithuania, where local thugs clubbed Jews to death with crowbars in plain sight of cheering crowds, with mothers holding up their children to enjoy the spectacle and soldiers milling around to watch the fun like a football match.[52] These were indeed gratifying scenes to the men of the *Einsatzgruppen;* as one of their leaders reported, "it is difficult to imagine the joy, gratitude and delight our measures awoke in . . . the local population. We often had to use sharp words to cool the enthusiasm of women, children and men who with tears in their eyes tried to kiss our hands and feet."[53] Such reactions undoubtedly emboldened the genocidal killers in pursuing their prey without pity, conscience, or regard for unsuspecting bystanders. One of the most shocking accounts of such mass killings was reported by a German engineer, Hermann Friedrich Graebe, who along with his foreman stumbled on a ghastly mass execution of Jewish men, women, and children.

> Moenikes and I directly went to the pits. Nobody bothered us. Now I heard rifle shots in quick succession, from behind one of the earth mounds. The people who got off the trucks — men, women, and children of all ages — had to undress upon the order of an SS man, who carried a riding or dog whip. They had to put down their clothes in fixed places. . . . I saw a heap of shoes of about 800 to 1000 pairs, great piles of underlinen and clothing. Without screaming and weeping these people undressed, stood around in family groups, kissed each other, said farewells, and waited. . . . I heard no complaint or plea for mercy. . . . An old woman with snow-white hair was holding a one-year-old child in her arms singing to it, and tickling it. The child was cooing with delight. The couple were looking on with tears in their eyes. The father was holding the hand of a boy about 10 years old and speaking to him softly; the boy was fighting his tears. The father pointed to the sky, stroked his head, and

seemed to explain something to him. At that moment the SS man at the pit shouted something to his comrade. The latter counted off about 20 persons and instructed them to go behind the earth mound. Among them was the family which I have mentioned. I well remember a girl, slim and with black hair, who, as she passed close to me, pointed to herself, and said "23." I walked around the mound, and found myself confronted by a tremendous grave. People were closely wedged together and lying on top of each other so that only their heads were visible. Nearly all had blood running over their shoulders from their heads. Some of the people shot were still moving.... I looked for the man who did the shooting. He was an SS man, who sat at the edge of the narrow end of the pit, his feet dangling into the pit. He had a tommy gun on his knees and was smoking a cigarette. The people, completely naked, went down ... the pit and clambered over the heads of the people lying there.... Then I heard a series of shots. I looked into the pit and saw that the bodies were twitching.... Blood was running from their necks.[54]

Only the most sadistic or hardened executioners could stomach such horrors indefinitely. Some SS men, it is true, enjoyed killing Jews for fun, and many incidents of such bloodlust have been recorded. A few examples may suffice. Major Rössler, commanding the 528th Infantry Regiment, came upon a mass execution near Zhitomir and was horrified by the scene of an execution pit in which bodies were still twitching; he ordered a policeman to kill an old man with a white beard clutching a cane in his left hand who was still twitching in agony. The policeman laughed and said: "I have already shot him seven times in the stomach. He can die on his own now."[55] In one town the Jews had gone into hiding, and when the SS killers combed the town they discovered a woman with a baby in her arms. When the woman refused to tell them where the Jews were hiding, one SS man grabbed the baby by its legs and smashed its head against a door. Another SS man recalled: "It went off with a bang like a bursting motor tire. I shall never forget that sound as long as I live."[56] In Riga, an SS man saw two Jews carrying a log; he shot one of them, saying, "One's enough for that job."[57] Jews were often shot for sport or recreation. Some SS men believed that they made great targets for marksmanship.[58]

The culmination of mass shootings came at Babi Yar on the outskirts of Kiev, where 33,771 Jews were murdered at the end of September 1941. Afterward, the men of the *Einsatzgruppen* were physically and psychologically drained. Some sought refuge in alcohol, some became physically ill, a few committed suicide. In August Himmler himself witnessed a mass shooting at Minsk. His chief of staff, Karl Wolff, later recalled that the Reichsführer went soft in the knees, and that his face turned almost green after a piece of brain had squirted on his cheek, causing him to vomit. One of Himmler's minions, Erich Bach-Zelewski allegedly used this occasion to take advantage of Himmler's momentary weakness to plead mercy, not for the victims but for their executioners:

"Look at the eyes of the men in this *Kommando,* how deeply shaken they are! These men are finished [*fertig*] for the rest of their lives. What kind of followers are we training here? Either neurotics or savages [*Entweder Nervenkranke oder Rohlinge*]."[59] Several months later, Bach-Zelewski himself had a nervous breakdown that, in turn, triggered hallucinations about the murdered Jews, keeping him screaming uncontrollably at night. When the doctor asked him why he was so afraid, Bach-Zelewski told him about the extermination of the whole Jewish people. Although solicitous of his health, Himmler adamantly rejected his plea to stop the genocide by telling him bluntly to keep his nose out of the business and not to interfere with a Führer order.[60]

Indeed, the Führer was keenly interested in how much progress the *Einsatzgruppen* were making in wiping out the Jews. Only a month after the invasion of Russia, Heinrich Müller of the Gestapo wired coded instructions to the commanders of the *Einsatzgruppen* that "the Führer is to be kept informed continually from here about the work of the *Einsatzgruppen.*"[61] As a result of these reports and Himmler's personal observations from the killing fields, Hitler realized that if the destruction of the Jews was to be successfully carried out, it was necessary to use more effective methods of extermination than the messy shootings currently employed. The Führer's bean counters undoubtedly pointed out that by the current methods of mass shootings, which were embarrassingly public, wasteful, and psychologically debilitating to the executioners, it would probably take ten years to accomplish the goal of eradicating Europe's eleven million Jews. In short, a better method of mass murder had to be employed, one that was out of the limelight and more lethal, efficient, and cost effective. It so happened that shortly after Himmler's brief spell of nausea at Minsk, the gassing specialists from the euthanasia program, which Hitler terminated near the end of August, were now available for more challenging duties in the east.

In the summer of 1941 Himmler consulted with Dr. Ernst Grawitz, chief SS physician and president of the German Red Cross, and asked him how the mass extermination of Europe's Jews could be accomplished. Grawitz recommended the use of gas chambers.[62] At about the same time, Wirth and his euthanasia experts were being transferred to the Lublin area, where Himmler had ordered SS *Obergruppenführer* Odilo Globocnik to construct a system of extermination camps. Coincidentally, Rudolf Höss, the commandant of Auschwitz, was summoned to Himmler and told:

> The Führer has ordered that the Jewish question be solved once and for all and that we, the SS, are to implement that order. The existing extermination centers in the East are not in a position to carry out the large actions which are anticipated. I have therefore earmarked Auschwitz for this purpose, both because of its good position as regards communications and because the area can easily be isolated and camouflaged.... You will treat this order as absolutely secret, even from

your superiors. After you talk with Eichmann you will immediately forward to me the plans of the projected installations.... The Jews are the sworn enemies of the German people and must be eradicated. Every Jew that we can lay our hands on is to be destroyed now during the war, without exception.[63]

Eichmann later said at his trial in Jerusalem that he was informed of the Final Solution by Heydrich two or three months after the invasion of Russia — that is, in late August or September 1941. Heydrich told him: "The Führer, well, emigration is.... The Führer has ordered the physical extermination."[64] Eichmann claimed that Heydrich seemed to test his reaction, pausing between words, which was not his customary style. Heydrich concluded his interview by telling Eichmann to go to Lublin and get further details of the annihilation process from Globocnik.[65]

Such briefings, accompanied by clear-cut annihilatory statements, indicate that the Nazi machinery of mass destruction was being assembled step by step. Statements by Hitler, Himmler, Heydrich, and Goebbels throughout the summer and fall of 1941 are replete with exterminatory images in which Jews are depicted in parasitical terms as carriers of infectious physical as well as spiritual diseases. On July 10, Hitler described himself as a political-biological pioneer: "I feel myself like Robert Koch in politics. He discovered the bacillus and opened up new paths for medical science. I discovered the Jew as the bacillus and ferment of social decomposition."[66] The Führer at that time still endorsed mass shootings, exhorting his troops "to shoot anyone who even has a cross look,"[67] but as the reference to Koch clearly indicates, he was beginning to move to a biological solution by ordering a feasibility study on the most effective way of murdering all the Jews of Europe.[68] This was behind Heydrich's visit to Göring and the letter that Göring sent to Heydrich on July 30, 1941, giving him a special commission, stating: "I herewith commission you to carry out all necessary preparations with regard to organizational, substantive, and financial viewpoints for a total solution of the Jewish question in the German sphere of action."[69] At Nuremberg, Göring, of course, downplayed the significance of this letter, as have some historians, as being nothing more than a routine administrative directive assigning the SS leader expanded power to solve the Jewish problem through emigration or evacuation, and that the term "Final Solution" certainly did not refer to annihilation. The truth is that Göring's directive, which was "on the Führer's instructions,"[70] marked the formal beginning of a broad government involvement in the biological extermination of the Jews. It illustrates, once again, the cunning of the killers to enmesh not only each other but to involve a whole network of bureaucratic agencies so that as many people as possible would have to share in the guilt. Göring's directive set the stage for broad interagency cooperation that led to the Wannsee Conference of January 20, 1942.

In the meantime, plans were afoot to set up extermination sites and to work out the technical details required for the gassing of human beings. In early September 1941 Karl Fritsch, deputy commander of Auschwitz, experimented with a pesticide called Zyklon-B and used the poison to murder 600 Soviet prisoners and 250 other inmates. On October 25, Dr. Wetzel, who served as an adviser on Jewish affairs in Rosenberg's Ministry for the Occupied Eastern Territories, drafted a letter, on Rosenberg's orders, intended for Reichcommissioner Lohse, in which Rosenberg pointed out that Brack from the Führer's private chancellery (KdF) was ready to assist with gassing equipment. Brack promised to send Dr. Kallmeyer, his euthanasia gas expert, to Riga to assist in the gassing of Jews who were not fit for work.[71] On that same day, Himmler and Heydrich were guests at Führer headquarters and were told that disseminating terror stories about the extermination of the Jews was an excellent means of waging war.

And spreading the word of annihilating Jews is exactly what the Nazi leadership did. On November 8, 1941, Hitler branded the Jews as the world's greatest arsonists and proclaimed that the German goal in the east was to fulfill the goals of Nazi racial programs. A week later Himmler confided in his Swedish masseur, Felix Kersten, that the destruction of the Jews was being planned, justifying the impending action as a measure of self-defense against a foe who dominated the entire world and constantly sought to overturn every system of government through war and revolution. "Only when the last Jew has disappeared from the world will there also be an end to the destruction of nations,"[72] Himmler told Kersten while receiving a rubdown for his sore muscles. Kersten's appeal to his client's conscience elicited only a glimmer of ethical insight with the remark that it was, indeed, "un-Germanic" to exterminate whole peoples, but this was a price that had to be paid for historical greatness: "It is the curse of greatness that it must step over dead bodies to create new life. Yet we must create new life, we must cleanse the soil or it will never bear fruit. It will be a great burden for me to bear. . . . It's the old tragic conflict between will and obligation."[73] Such sentimental and insincere twaddle was Himmler's way of distancing himself from the horrors that he helped to unleash. A few days after Himmler's confession to Kersten, Goebbels informed the German people in the journal *Das Reich* that the Jews were guilty and were now being exterminated. The propaganda minister was particularly prone to diarrhea of the mouth, both in public and in private, and he simply could not relax his Judeophobic obsession. His diary entries provide a running account of anti-Jewish measures that leave no doubt about the spreading delusion and its institutionalization by a murderous state.[74] Two days after Goebbels's article in *Das Reich*, Himmler announced to a group of German journalists on November 18 that "the biological extermination of all Jews in Europe had begun."[75]

Indeed, on the evening of December 7, 1941, Pearl Harbor Day, seven hundred Jews were taken to the remote Polish village of Chelmo, thirty-five miles northwest of Lodz. The prisoners were told that they would be taken to the east to work; instead, on the morning of December 8, long transportation vans, which had been converted into gas trucks that channelled exhaust fumes back into the van, arrived and took away one load of Jews after another and gassed them on its journey to the burial ground in a nearby forest. All the Jews, men, women, and children, were gassed. As this drama unfolded, the Japanese attacked Pearl Harbor. The connection of these two events, as Martin Gilbert has pointed out, was that the day that lived in infamy was also the day on which the Final Solution began.[76] There is another and more significant connection: Hitler's declaration of war on the United States, which was irrational and militarily self-defeating, was a defiant gesture by which the Führer flung down the gauntlet to Roosevelt, whom he regarded as a stooge for world Jewry. Hitler now saw himself confronted by two interrelated foes: the United States and the Soviet Union, and the link between them was the Jew. He made this quite clear in his speech of December 11 when he pointed out that Germany was now facing a common front between the Anglo-Saxon Jewish capitalist world and the Jewish Bolshevist world. If he could not defeat this formidable coalition, he swore to annihilate the Jews who once more had conspired to use foreign powers to exterminate Germany. This explains the urgency that underlay the execution of Hitler's greatest crime and the fact that the project was given the same priority as military operations.

Since gas vans could exterminate only a limited number of victims, they were never regarded as anything but makeshift killing machines. Near the end of 1941 a new camp, the first annihilation camp, was set up at Belzec near Lublin and became operational in the spring of 1942. It was here that the first gassings using stationary gas chambers took place. The architect and chief exterminator of Belzec was Christian Wirth, who had previously served in the euthanasia program and was one of about a hundred people who were transferred from the euthanasia program to the extermination camps in Poland. Wirth pumped exhaust fumes into the death chambers by using diesel engines; his first gas chambers became operational in March 1942 and could dispose of twenty thousand Jews a week. A second death camp opened in the same month at Sobibor in eastern Poland, a third one a little later in Treblinka (seventy-five miles northeast of Warsaw), and a fourth one at Majdanek, located just a mile from Lublin. The fifth and arguably the most gruesome camp was Auschwitz in Upper East Silesia, formerly Oswiciem, Poland. Wirth administered the exterminations of Jews at Belzec, Sobibor, and Treblinka, coordinating the activities with Odilo Globocnik and the SS police office in Lublin. At Auschwitz, as will be seen, a new and more effective chemical agent, Zyklon-B, was introduced.

The continuation of mass shootings and the emergence of new death camps, along with technical problems relating to transportation, the confiscation of Jewish property, and liaison work with foreign powers who were asked to surrender their Jewish population, necessitated a more coordinated strategy for the Final Solution. For this purpose, Heydrich called a meeting at a villa in a posh Berlin suburb located on Lake Grosser Wannsee. On January 20, 1942, major representatives of various agencies involved in the Final Solution came together to discuss the technical details of murdering the remaining Jews of Europe. The meeting was hosted in a very genial atmosphere by Heydrich; the minutes were kept by Eichmann, who had also sent out the invitations.[77] Besides Heydrich and Eichmann, the other major SS representatives were Gestapo Chief Heinrich Müller; Dr. Otto Hoffmann of the Race and Settlement Main Office; Karl Eberhard Schöngarth, SD chief of the General Government; and Dr. Rudolf Lange, commander of the Security Police in Riga. Representing various important government agencies were several state secretaries, ministerial directors, and party functionaries: Dr. Wilhelm Stuckart from the Ministry of the Interior, who had coauthored the Nuremberg racial laws; Dr. Josef Bühler from the Office of the Governor-General; Erich Neumann representing Göring's Office of the Four-Year Plan; Dr. Roland Freisler from the Ministry of Justice; Dr. Martin Luther from the Foreign Office; Dr. Friedrich Wilhelm Kritzinger from the Reich chancellery; Oberführer Dr. Gerhard Klopfer from the party chancellery; Gauleiter Dr. Alfred Meyer representing Rosenberg's Ministry of the Occupied Eastern Territories; and Dr. Georg Leibbrandt, chief Reich administration officer.[78] Of the fifteen participants, eight held doctoral degrees from major German universities. The final minutes of the Wannsee Conference are written in bureaucratic double-talk that the regime had adopted to conceal mass murder: it was replete with euphemistic terms such as "evacuation to the east" (*Evakuierung nach dem Osten*), "natural diminution" *(natürliche Verminderung)*, "appropriately treated" (*entsprechend behandelt*), "Final Solution (*Endlösung*), "pushing back" (*Zurückdrängung*), "legal means of cleansing German Lebensraum" (*legale Weise den deutschen Lebensraum zu säubern*), etc.

The Wannsee conferees all agreed that war had to be waged against the Jews because they represented a hazard to the Reich. Heydrich unfolded a monstrous demographic chart listing over eleven million Jews living in the various European nations. Lively discussion then ensued as to how these Jews could be rounded up, stripped of their possessions, transferred eastward, and annihilated. The minutes, couched in revolting bureaucratic euphemisms, reveal little of these gruesome realities. According to Eichmann's testimony at Jerusalem, however, the participants at the Wannsee Conference discussed "the subject quite bluntly: quite differently from the language which I had to use later in the record. During the conversation they minced no words about it at all."[79]

The overall plan outlined at Wannsee was to conduct sweeps of Jews throughout the whole of Europe, starting with Germany and the Protectorate. Jews were to be rounded up to "transit ghettos" in the east and then transported "farther eastward," a euphemism for the death camps. Jews over sixty-five or highly decorated Jewish war veterans, rather than being killed, were to be interned at the showcase ghetto of Theresienstadt in Bohemia, where prominent Jews like Leo Baeck were sent. No conclusive decision was reached about half-Jews (*Mischlinge*), especially whether exceptions should be made to the general rule that first-degree half-Jews should be treated as full Jews and therefore exterminated. The decision was postponed for the next meeting, though the general consensus was to sterilize such Jews in order to prevent further racial pollution of the German people.

The Wannsee Conference lasted for only an hour and a half. After the formal session the members broke into groups for further discussion of technical details. Everyone endorsed the general policy of exterminating the Jews of Europe, although no complete consensus had been reached about one single method of accomplishing this goal — mass shootings, gassings, or death through slave labor. This decision was out of the hands of the participants: it would define itself outside the conference rooms in the killing fields of eastern Europe. The significance of the Wannsee Conference was not the initiation of the Final Solution — that had already begin with the mass shootings of Jews seven months ago — but the fact that a broad segment of the German government (not just Hitler and the SS) had endorsed the Final Solution and worked out common procedures and methods for its implementation. The systematic roundup of Jews began almost immediately all over the Nazi empire. This involved extensive bureaucratic complicity on the part of German as well as foreign officials. Working through satellite governments or German-controlled administrations, the German authorities sequestered Jewish property and liquid assets in these countries. Legislation was drawn up to turn the Jews into stateless persons because then it became impossible or irrelevant for any country to enquire into the fate of its former Jewish inhabitants.[80]

Moreover, any state that had transformed its Jews into stateless persons could then lay claim to their property. Stripped of their nationality and relieved of their assets, the Jews were allowed to keep only a hundred Reichsmark and fifty kilograms of personal possessions. Before being removed (*abgeschoben*) to the east, the Jews also had to turn over an itemized list of their assets, which the Gestapo graciously accepted as payment rendered for the services about to be provided.

The trains of the German Reichsbahn now went into action, regardless of bad weather, Allied bombings, or the need of the Wehrmacht. Jews were herded like cattle into sealed freight cars and dispatched to the five eastern extermination camps of Auschwitz, Belzec, Sobibor, Treblinka, and Majdanek. By the spring of 1942 these camps had installed stationary gas chambers that could annihilate up to twenty-five thousand people a day. Early methods of using exhaust gases from diesel engines gave way to hydrocyanide (prussic acid) that had been marketed under the trade name of Zyklon-B by a firm called Degesch, an acronym that stood for Deutsche Gesellschaft für Schädligungsbekämpfung (German Vermin-Combating Corporation).[81] We know a great deal about this company and the use of its chemical agents in exterminating human beings from the testimony of Kurt Gerstein, the chief disinfection officer in the Department of Hygiene in the Waffen SS.[82] Gerstein has left us with a graphic account of how he was ordered by Eichmann's office to accompany Rolf Günther, Eichmann's right-hand man, to transport prussic acid to a secret place.[83] When they arrived at the secret place, Belzec concentration camp, they witnessed an extermination under the direction of Wirth. During this particular operation, the diesel engine refused to fire. Wirth was beside himself — not because seven hundred men, women, and children had to suffer two hours and forty minutes of agony stuffed into a small gas chamber (Gerstein had a stopwatch) — but because of the embarrassment such a malfunction had caused in the presence of visitors. Gerstein was so horrified by what he saw that he told Wirth that the gas he had brought with him was no longer usable and had to be buried.[84] Gerstein stayed on in his post, he later said, in order to bear witness to mass murder and to inform the world — unsuccessfully as it would turn out — about the extermination of the Jews.

At Auschwitz, Rudolf Höss decided to use Zyklon-B, strongly convinced that he could attain a better kill-ratio with this gas than Wirth could with his diesel method. Zyklon-B consisted of bluish pellets that could be carried in a small canister. The operator, wearing a mask, only had to drop the pellets into the gas chamber through a hole, whereupon they turned into deadly gas that killed people within twenty to thirty minutes. Auschwitz became the most monstrous death factory of the whole Nazi annihilation system.[85]

Auschwitz started out as a camp for political prisoners, mostly Polish, but it was rapidly expanded as a work camp and then as a major site for exterminating Jews, Gypsies, and "racial subhumans." By the middle of 1942 the camp was divided into three sites: Auschwitz 1 with its brick barracks was the original camp; Auschwitz 2 at nearby Birkenau, built to accommodate two hundred thousand victims, was the annihilation camp; and Auschwitz 3 was the industrial center at Monowitz. Auschwitz had its own soccer stadium, library, photographic laboratory, symphony orchestra, medical facility of sixty doctors and more than three hundred nurses, a large bakery, a tannery, and a tin-smithy. There were also thirty barracks, nicknamed "Canada" by the Polish prisoners, which stored the loot taken from the prisoners. These barracks were chock-full of clothing, shoes, spectacles, jewelry, watches, silk underwear, gold and diamond rings, and the finest liquors. Auschwitz was the greatest necropolis the world has ever seen, the "asshole of the world," as its inmates called it. Everything the Germans did there seemed to expunge the finest things they had contributed to western civilization. Auschwitz was a bestial city where men who were once members of a civilized community degraded helpless victims and themselves to the lowest level human beings could ever sink.

Whether at Auschwitz or Belzec, Sobibor, Treblinka, or Majdanek, arriving Jewish prisoners encountered the same reality. Upon arrival, they were driven out of their freight cars, often leaving behind them human excrement and trampled infants, and assembled on the ramp for the "welcome" (*Begrüssung*). A selection officer, with the simple wave of a hand, directed each new prisoner into one of two lines: on the right, those who were sentenced to hard labor and on the left those who were condemned to death. Old men, women, and children were usually exterminated immediately. Those marked for death were ordered to undress and told that they would have to take a shower. A number of psychological ploys, varying from camp to camp, were used to conceal the horrible reality that awaited the condemned. At Auschwitz, people were told to tie their shoes together and hang their clothes on numbered hooks so that they could easily find them after they had taken their showers. They were even given soap to take to the gas chambers. Women were shorn of all their hair. Prodded and hurried along like a herd of cattle by special commandos wielding whips, sticks, or rifle butts, the victims were then driven into the gas chambers. The special commandos included Ukrainian and even Jewish helpers, a particularly horrible practice that had Jews serving as executioners of their own people. "I have never known," Höss wrote later,

> of any of its members giving these people who were about to be gassed the slightest hint of what lay ahead of them. On the contrary, they did everything in their power to deceive them.... Though they might refuse to believe the SS man, they had complete faith in these members of their own race.[86]

Yet even such fiendish deceptions did not fool everybody, and there were anguished cries and heartrending scenes of indescribable horror. Once the victims had been shoved into a gas chamber, which could hold close to eight hundred people when tightly packed, the doors were sealed and the gas was released through vents in the ceiling:

> It could be observed through the peephole in the door that those who were standing nearest to the induction vents were killed at once.... The remainder staggered about and began to scream and struggle for air. The screaming, however, soon changed to the death rattle and in a few minutes all lay still. After twenty minutes at the latest no movement could be discerned.[87]

It took at least half an hour to extract the mass of bodies, which were glued together "like pillars of basalt, still erect, not having any space to fall"; legs were covered with feces and menstrual blood.[88] Another special crew, the "tooth commando," sprang into action and extracted the fillings from the victims. Such valuables were collected by Globocnik, one of the chief agents of "Aktion Reinhard," as the gassings of the Jews were now called after the assassination of Reinhard Heydrich; Globocnik was responsible for rounding up the loot (money, gold, diamonds, watches, etc.) and sending it to the Deutsche Reichsbank, which, in turn, deposited some of the loot, especially gold bars of melted down gold fillings, into Swiss bank vaults.

After the gold fillings had been extracted, the bodies were cremated, either in the open air or in gigantic crematoria. The stench could be smelled for miles around. German manufacturers competed for government contracts to build the most automated and efficient incinerators. The top contract went to I. A. Topff and Sons of Erfurt, which eventually perfected a unit that contained an underground gas chamber together with electric elevators for hauling up the bodies.[89] Given time, the technicians of mass murder would undoubtedly have perfected a completely self-contained unit in which people entered as living human beings and were processed, efficiently and cleanly, so that they could exit as smoke through the belching chimneys.

For those who were not marked immediately for extermination, life in the death camps was hell on earth. Many survivors have borne witness to the inhumane conditions that beggar description. These range from the sophisticated voices of Elie Wiesel, Primo Levi, Tadeusz Borowski, Viktor Frankl, and Jean Améry to hundreds of heartrending stories by ordinary men and women. Their experiences cannot be re-created by scholarly discourse; they must be allowed to speak for themselves without analysis.

The gassings at the five major extermination camps, which began in the spring of 1942, continued until the fall of 1944. By the summer of 1944, most of the Jews in eastern Europe had been annihilated, as was true of the Jews from the rest of Europe, except for countries that had obstructed Hitler's genocidal mania. One such country was Hungary, where Jews had been protected until Hitler deposed the government of Miklós Horthy in October 1944 and set up a puppet regime he could control. Himmler's bloodhounds then immediately descended on Hungary and rounded up as many Jews as they could find. Eichmann and his agents personally supervised the operation, sending trainloads of the country's Jews to Auschwitz.[90] The Nazis also half-heartedly experimented with a new technique: selling Jews to the western world, a plan, unfortunately, that never worked because of Nazi duplicity and western indifference.[91] Denmark, Norway, and Sweden did much to save their Jews. Sweden sent Raoul Wallenberg to Hungary as a special envoy to assist Hungarian Jews in emigrating to Sweden; he later disappeared into the bowels of the Soviet police state. Wallenberg's efforts, like other similar gestures of help, hardly made a dent in the mass deportations. Himmler and his murderous agents, now working under the cloud of impending military defeat, intensified their efforts to make Europe "Jew free." Driven by an insatiable appetite for destruction, the killers combed areas and camps previously overlooked or off-limits. It was in this way that thousands of Jews who had been interned at Theresienstadt were gassed at Auschwitz. Leo Baeck, who miraculously survived, accidentally ran into Eichmann in the Gestapo office. Baeck recalled: "He was visibly taken aback at seeing me. 'Herr Baeck, are you still alive?' He looked me over carefully, as if he did not trust his eyes, and added coldly, 'I thought you were dead.' " Baeck's reply was: "Herr Eichmann, you are apparently announcing a future occurrence."[92]

By November 1, 1944, the gassings stopped, but the killing and dying continued until the liberation in May 1945. As the Nazi slave empire reeled from one military defeat to another, the Judeophobic killers drew upon every strength and malice they still possessed and continued to hound the Jews under their control. This explains the death marches that took place during the last six months of the war. As the Allied forces closed in on various camps, the Nazis expended every effort to prevent prisoners from falling into the hands of the advancing Allied armies. Many starving and emaciated prisoners were evacuated by rail to camps inside Germany, but equally as many were forced to march over incredible distances and under terrible climatic conditions, harassed, abused, and shot as they went along.[93] Nearly sixty thousand were forced on death marches from Auschwitz, twenty-five thousand from Stutthof, thousands from Gross-Rosen, Buchenwald and Dachau. These death marches were not ordered by Hitler or Himmler, but by commanders in the field whose malignant Judeophobia held to the end. Their need for pure vengeance, combined with motives of covering up the crime, proved to be far stronger than their hatred of the Allied Powers. In fact, with defeat and retribution staring them in the face, the perpetrators did their best to hide every trace of their evil deed, blowing up the gas chambers and destroying as much incriminating evidence as they could. A special detachment called Commando 1005, headed by Paul Blobel of the SS, was assigned to reopen mass graves and burn the corpses on stacks of oil-soaked railroad ties and grind up the bones in special machines.[94] The team started in Russia in the spring of 1943, moved to Poland, and ended up combing the killing fields as far as southeastern Europe. Blobel assigned the job of digging up the decomposed bodies to Jews and to locals. Once the grave diggers had performed their gruesome tasks, they were murdered. The murderers believed that they would have the last laugh, and that the world would never find out or would reject the testimony of the few survivors as simply unbelievable. As the SS guards had always told their victims:

> However this war may end, we have won the war against you; none of
> you will be left to bear witness, but even if someone were to survive, the

world will not believe him. There will perhaps be suspicions, discussions, research by historians, but there will be no certainties, because we will destroy the evidence together with you. And even if some proof should remain and some of you survive, people will say that the events you describe are too monstrous to be believed: they will say that they are the exaggerations of Allied propaganda and will believe us, who will deny everything, and not you. We will be the ones to dictate the history of the Lagers.[95]

The SS militiamen who used these cruel words were wrong in their self-confident expectations that the world would not believe the unbelievable or that the lies of the killers would be given more credence than the honest testimonies of the survivors. The killers were right in one respect: what they had done was truly monstrous — so much so, that we ask less about how many people they murdered — five or six million — but what motivated them to carry out such an unspeakable crime. Beyond that, historians are still asking themselves what causes could have produced the Holocaust and how many Germans and non-Germans actually knew that genocide was being committed on such a massive scale.

The Perpetrators: Ordinary Germans?

Since the Holocaust required a massive bureaucracy with a high degree of specialization and division of labor, it is useful to distinguish from the outset between remote-control bureaucratic killers who planned and supervised genocide and the professional killers in the field or in the annihilation camps who shot Jews or exterminated them in the gas chambers. It is also important to remember that the genocide itself may have been motivated by fanatical Judeophobia but that individual killers were not necessarily motivated by a uniform and internally consistent Judeophobic frame of reference. This is why historians have rightly distinguished between different types of perpetrators: fanatical Judeophobes, amoral technicians of power, careerists, conformists, moral cowards, or sadists. There can be no doubt, however, that the intellectual frame of reference that inspired the crime itself was, first and foremost, the mental aberration that characterized the thinking of the Nazi leadership, particularly the hatred that fueled the mentality of Adolf Hitler.

What type of human being, it has often been asked, could commit such crimes? In answering this question, the focus must always be on the interaction of both psychological and cultural factors because the killing was sanctioned by a death culture that glamorized violence and destruction. At the same time, recognition of this fact should not tempt us to identify as a major factor the one reason that many people mistakenly identify as the most important, and that is sheer, unadulterated

sadism. The evidence shows that only a small percentage of the perpetrators were actually sadistic killers. Even among the Nazi doctors
who dispatched thousand of victims with dispassionate efficiency, few
were sadistic in any clinical sense. As Dr. Ella Lingens-Reiner, a survivor physician of Auschwitz, observed: "There were few sadists. Not
more than five or 10 percent were pathological criminals in the clinical
sense. The others were all perfectly normal men who knew the difference between right and wrong. They all knew what was going on."[96]
The same was true of most camp commandants and their associates who
rarely murdered for sadistic reasons and led apparently "normal" lives
outside the charnel houses they supervised.[97] It is, of course, true that
the concentration camp guards and their associates were often recruited
from the dregs of society, so that statistically speaking, one would expect a fair number of sadistic psychopaths to show up in such settings.
These men and women constituted what Eugen Kogon has called the
"negative elite" of the Nazi system. The number of sadists among this
negative elite, however, was no more than ten percent; and in many
cases of sadistic degradation, it is not always possible to distinguish between degradation by pleasure and degradation by "alleviation of guilt,"
the former being a sheer delight in cruelty and the latter a means of
escaping guilt.

   If sadism played only a minor role in genocide, the focus must be
shifted to certain larger cultural patterns in German society that furnished the motives and institutional mechanisms that made it possible
to kill millions of people by state mandate. The perpetrators killed,
directly or indirectly, because they believed in a shared ideology of violent Judeophobia that had conditioned them to perceive Jews as a
malignant cancer on German life and culture. This group consisted of
true believers who deluded themselves into thinking that extermination
was a form of national redemption. It is this form of consciousness
that characterized the top leadership of the Nazi state and provided
the energy that fueled the genocidal machinery. There were many other
perpetrators, however, who lent a willing hand because they had been
acculturated to obey orders without questioning. There were still others who participated in mass murder because it benefited their careers
or economic circumstances. Often, a combination of all these factors
motivated the perpetrators.

   In general terms, there were two types of murderers: those who
administered the destruction process from their desks and issued various orders (the "desk murderers" such as Hitler, Himmler, Heydrich,
Müller, Eichmann) and the men who carried out the actual executions
or gassings (Höss, Wirth, Mengele, the men of the *Einsatzgruppen,* the
guards in the concentration camps). Here again, there were few sadists.
Men like Himmler and Eichmann saw themselves as decent men who
were doing important work in the service of a noble cause. Himmler's infamous address to his SS leaders on October 4, 1943, at Posen,

in which he lionized the murderers for their strength and courage in carrying out their appalling assignment is a perfect illustration of this self-deceptive attitude. Himmler praised the men who had piled up mountains of corpses while still remaining decent fellows: "To have stuck it out — and apart from a few exceptions due to human weakness — to have remained decent, that is what has made us tough. This is a glorious page in our history and one that has never been written and can never be written."[98]

If it was so glorious but could never be written, the architect of genocide was implicitly admitting that the deed, since it defied all canons of civilized existence, was so ignoble that it had to be permanently covered up. References to glory or decency, of course, were defense mechanisms by which the murderers justified the deed and kept it at arm's length so that it would not disturb their emotional equilibrium. Eichmann was a master at such self-justifying tactics. Although he was a murderous Jew-hater, once telling an associate that knowledge of having done his part in killing millions of Jews gave him such great satisfaction that he would jump into his grave laughing,[99] Eichmann fabricated a completely different persona during his trial at Jerusalem. He repeated, again and again, that he was just a tiny cog in the Nazi bureaucracy carrying out minor functions relating to Jewish emigration and deportation. The monumental ignorance he feigned at Jerusalem, which misled Hannah Arendt into referring to his activities as the "banality of evil," was really a combination of self-deception and deliberate lying. Eichmann was stupid in the sense that he moved entirely within the confines of his narrow ideology, but he was also a cunning and shrewd liar. He killed out of ideological convictions as well as dogged devotion to career and authority. Eichmann represents the inauthentic little German at his worst; he acted on a flimsy ideology because he was told to believe it and because he was commanded to carry out its doctrines without questioning.

When afterward confronted by his accusers, Eichmann and many like him tried to use inauthenticity to their advantage. He described himself as belonging to that category of people who had no opinion of their own, merely carried out orders, and never killed a single Jew. He even claimed that he had never been an anti-Semite.[100] All of these were lying evasions that Eichmann and his type had perfected to a fine art. When ignorance did not work, he would unfold the "tiny cog in the machine," followed by the "orders are orders" defense:

> Herr Hauptmann, if they said to me: "Your father is a traitor," if they had told me that my own father was a traitor and I had to kill him, I'd have done it. At that time I obeyed my orders without thinking, I just did what I was told."[101]

In Jerusalem Eichmann adamantly rejected the notion that he believed that the salvation of the German people depended on the extermination of the Jews; the Jews were killed because it was a Führer order, which made it good and valid. The commandant of Auschwitz, Rudolf Höss, said exactly the same thing: "I must emphasize that I have never personally hated the Jews. It is true that I looked upon them as the enemies of our people. But just because of this I saw no difference between them and the other prisoners, and I treated them all in the same way."[102] No, he did not treat them all the same: he gassed the Jews. Well, that was not his choice, Höss claimed, because he was given a Führer order to kill the Jews. The same moral evasion was echoed by Eichmann when he told the court: "Who is a little man like me to trouble his head about it? I get orders from my superiors and I look neither right nor left.... Little by little, we were taught all these things. We grew into them, all we knew was obedience to orders. We were chained to our oath."[103]

The assumption behind such statements is that the perpetrators were totally determined by "higher forces" beyond their control. Franz Stangl, camp commandant of Sobibor and later Treblinka, told Gitta Sereny that "he had done nothing wrong; there had always been others above him; he had never done anything but obey orders; he had never hurt a single human being."[104] It was the "system" that made him do it, a system that was irreversible and could not be changed by any single person.[105] Thus, if the system could not be changed, it was best to adapt oneself to its will and purpose, to force oneself to "appear cold and indifferent," to "see everything," to "maintain iron discipline," to "bury all human considerations."[106] After all, "There is only one thing that is valid — orders," a maxim that adorned the letterhead of Theodor Eicke.[107]

Had these perpetrators internalized a set of German cultural traits, best expressed by the proverb *Nicht sein kann, was nicht sein darf* (what may not be cannot be), or were they willfully lying and deceiving themselves? Are their actions a textbook case of bad faith, of lying self-deception, and of outrageous stupidity, as Hannah Arendt asked herself after listening to Eichmann?[108] Mendacity was indeed common to all the perpetrators, so that it is often impossible to sort out the real motives that inspired these men to participate in mass murder. Himmler, Eichmann, Höss, Stangl, and many others thought exclusively in Nazi jargons, clichés, and bureaucratic circumlocutions; they were unable or unwilling to look at any position outside their narrow ideology or to show any empathy for their racial enemies. To what extent and to what degree pure conviction, lying self-deception, or obedience to authority predominated in the thinking and actions of these men is impossible to determine. They certainly knew the difference between right and wrong and, on certain occasions, were definitely aware of the conflict between higher morality and worldly power. Eichmann, for example, admitted that he had tried all of his life to live up to the Kantian categorical imperative. When the dubious defense asked him to elaborate on this claim, Eichmann managed to provide a fairly decent formulation of the principle that one should act in such a way that the principle of one's action could become by one's will and duty a general law of human conduct.

Eichmann admitted that as soon as he had decided to participate in the Final Solution he could no longer claim to live by Kant's imperative. Since his faculty of judgment was no longer free, he felt compelled to bow to superior orders. His new imperative now held: act in such a way that the principles of your actions are the same as those of Adolf Hitler. We are apt to dismiss these explanations as contemptible efforts to evade personal responsibility, which, of course, they were. But many Germans believed such ideas and acted on them. Hans Frank, for example, had proposed the following as the Categorical Imperative of the Third Reich: "Act in such a way that the Führer, if he knew your action, would approve it."[109] And Hermann Göring once confessed, "I have no conscience; my conscience is Adolf Hitler."[110] Thus, if the conscience of Adolf Hitler substitutes as the collective super ego and sanctions mass murder, individual Germans are automatically absolved of responsibility. The escape from freedom is apparently assured.

An important psychological factor that made participation in genocide possible by so many people was remoteness from the crime itself. The bureaucrats who labored over railroad timetables, collected statistics, drew up anti-Jewish regulations, or busied themselves in processing Jews for deportation did not actually see the shootings and gassings. They were merely doing the work of specialists in a large organization and therefore rarely witnessed the end product — mountains of corpses. Their compartmentalized existence isolated them from the hideous consequences of their actions and made it possible for them to pretend that they were merely carrying out the routine functions of their profession. For many of these bureaucrats, career objectives were just as important as ideological commitment. The head of Abteilung Deutschland in the German Foreign Office, Martin Luther, who represented the Foreign Office at the Wannsee Conference, was one such careerist of genocide. Luther was a talented, ambitious, and hard-working administrator whose primary goal was power rather than ideological zeal; he was not a doctrinaire racist but an amoral technician of power.

The same was true of his subordinate Franz Rademacher, who was in charge of the Jewish section in Abteilung Deutschland. Rademacher came from a middle-class family, studied law, and served as an assistant judge before joining the Foreign Office in 1937. After serving as chargé d'affaires at the German embassy in Montevideo, Uruguay, he assumed control over Jewish affairs in the Foreign Office and became involved in the decision-making process that would lead to the Final Solution. Rademacher worked on the abortive Madagascar Project and later became enmeshed in the government's anti-Jewish measures relating to foreign Jews, especially in southeastern Europe. In October of 1941 Rademacher went to Serbia to deal with Jewish "deportation problems" that had become complicated by a strong partisan campaign against German occupation forces. The local military authorities wanted to shoot partisans on a 100 to 1 ratio and proposed to shoot Jews instead of the communists they could not find. The subsequent murder of thousands of Jews implicated Rademacher and his office and earned him the title of Jewish butcher (*Judenschlächter*).[111] Rademacher himself never saw any of these atrocities. In fact, after the fall of his superior, Martin Luther, he left the Foreign Office and volunteered for the navy. Although Rademacher was strongly anti-Semitic, he did not make his prejudice the key to his activities but used it instead as a means to advance his career. One gets the definite impression that he bolted the Foreign Office when it appeared that his career had been damaged. His raison d'être was his career, which depended on doing everything the state demanded he do: "My entire education from childhood," he later said, "aimed at serving the state, irrespective of the political opinion of the state leadership of the moment."[112]

There were thousands of Rademachers in the German bureaucracy; they could be found in every agency. Placing careers and personal ambitions over ethical considerations, these men quickly adapted themselves to the new racial state and eagerly tried to prove their merit by carrying out any assignment, no matter how immoral. A few showed a twinge of conscience; most did not. And why should they? Having been brought up to carry out orders and to perform their duties with meticulous attention to detail, while at the same time being discouraged from asking the larger moral questions, these men had no ethical foundation to draw on in times of moral crisis; they were hollow and inauthentic men of modern bureaucratic culture, not significantly different from corporate technicians today who labor on projects of mass destruction without bothering to ask why they are dedicating their lives and careers to the destruction of life on this planet. Such men are moral mutants no different, perhaps worse, from those who have blood on their hands, because these little cogs add up to a lethal collective machinery.

The bureaucratic technicians of power could use their remoteness from the crime as an excuse for being either ignorant or innocent of any wrongdoing. Those who knew what was going on either split themselves or dodged behind various rationalizations such as "I was only doing my job," "I just follow orders," "If I had not obeyed, I would have been shot," or "Others were worse." What about those who were directly involved in mass murder: the gassing experts, *Einsatzgruppen* killers, concentration camp personnel, murderous doctors?

In attempting to understand these technicians of mass murder, Robert J. Lifton has drawn attention to a key psychological principle called splitting or doubling.[113] This involves a process by which the self divides into two functioning wholes so that either one (the cold-blooded killer) or the other (the good doctor, family man, or conscientious employee) can function separately within its proper domain. A certain dialectic based on autonomy and connection regulates the relationship between the two selves. The Auschwitz self has to be autonomous to be able to function in all its brutality, but at the same time a connection must be maintained to the former self because the murderer must still see himself as a decent human being, a good father, or a good colleague. In the situation in which the genocidal killers operated on a daily basis, it was not unusual for the Auschwitz self to become a usurper and displacer of whatever remained of the civilized self. In order to maintain the illusion of normality that one really had not become, as Eichmann put it, "a dirty bastard in the depth of one's heart" (*ein innerer Schweinehund*),[114] the murderous self pretends to be in a life-and-death struggle and justifies killing as a means of self-defense, survival, and even national self-purification. Guilt is avoided by transferring conscience to the Auschwitz self, which justifies murder as self-defense or racial healing.

Such forms of behavior and the justifications by which they are accompanied have been observed many times in connection with Mafia or terrorist organizations. Lifton points out that doubling is a choice (rather than a character disorder) that may have been prompted by entrapment in a criminal situation or lifestyle.[115] One could extend this point by arguing that all of us, at one time or another, chose doubling as a defense mechanism to protect the self from the voice of a higher moral consciousness. In other words, doubling operates not only in criminal settings but in any organization that expects its member to internalize an ethics of aggression, greed, competition, and amoral expertise. No entrapment in a criminal situation is needed in any modern corporation; all that is required of its members is that they internalize its values and leave their love and compassion at home.

The internalization of the ethics of mass murder as a redemptive activity of national self-purification was particularly strong in the medical profession. The Nazi physicians who were implicated in genocide justified killing as a healing process, insisting that in order for Germany to live another group had to die. Within the delusional system of Nazi racial ideology, this argument made perfect sense to those who believed in it. Moreover, this delusional system had deep roots in various German traditions of a neo-romantic, *völkisch,* Judeophobic, and pseudoscientific nature. The Nazis, in Lifton's view, made use of a culture that had a tendency toward death-haunted, apocalyptic historical visions and for that reason seized upon the relationship between killing and healing.[116]

The concentration camp doctors exemplified this killing-healing syndrome more than most other Nazis. They believed that by killing they were actually healing, as did those who burned heretics in the Middle Ages. A Jewish physician who survived the Holocaust once asked a Nazi physician, Dr. Fritz Klein, how he could reconcile his murderous activity with his Hippocratic Oath as a doctor. His answer was: "Of course, I am a doctor and want to preserve life, and out of respect for human life, I would remove a gangrenous appendix from a diseased body. The Jew is the gangrenous appendix in the body of mankind."[117] Many SS doctors who served as selection officers in the death camps, deciding who should live or die, or conducted gruesome medical experiments on innocent victims saw themselves as the vanguard of a new racial elite that would improve the biological quality of the German people. Having been indoctrinated to regard Jews, Gypsies, or Slavs as subhumans, they had no qualms in using them as guinea pigs in a variety of medical experiments. In the words of one SS physician, such people were the cheapest experimental animals, cheaper than rats.

Not all of these experiments were conducted to improve the racial quality of the German people; many were carried out to save German lives during wartime conditions. Dr. Sigmund Rascher and his team, for example, performed freezing experiments at Dachau on hundreds of Jews, Gypsies, Poles, or Russians, dumping their subjects, naked or dressed in aviator's uniforms, into icy tanks to observe how long their bodies would withstand the cold, and then searching for methods of reviving near frozen bodies. The doctors carefully recorded every detail of the prisoners' reactions, noting that they foamed at the mouth, writhed in pain, went into death rattles, or faded into semiconsciousness. These experiments on hypothermia were sponsored by Himmler and the armed forces in an effort to find better means of dealing with exposure to extreme cold. Rascher and his colleagues also conducted experiments for the Luftwaffe on human reactions to high altitude flight. Prisoners were thrown into a decompression chamber and exposed to extreme pressure or vacuum conditions; and as they screamed or writhed in agony, the physicians dispassionately observed how these subjects reacted until their lungs ruptured. Rascher was only one of many medical experimenters; he worked closely with two professors at the University of Kiel, Dr. Holtzlöhner and Dr. Finke, who produced a lengthy research report on "Freezing Experiments with Human Beings" that they shared with hundreds of colleagues at a medical conference at Nuremberg in October 1941.

Other experiments involved using "subhuman" Gypsies. At Sachsenhausen concentration camp Gypsies were forced to drink seawater, be shot with poison bullets, and be injected with contagious jaundice; at Ravensbrück they were inflicted with gangrenous wounds. Polish female prisoners, laughingly referred to as "rabbit girls," were given bone grafts. One of the most extensive experiments involved sterilization. One approach, pursued by Dr. Maudas, was to inject or administer liquid doses of the juice of the plant *Caladium sequinium;* another was X-ray sterilization. The most notorious program for mass sterilization and castration was conducted in Block 10 in Auschwitz, where hundreds of human guinea pigs were injected with various caustic substances by Professor Carl Clauberg, an expert on fertility whose preparations are still used today. Dr. Horst Schumann, a key figure in the euthanasia program, tried to sterilize hundreds of subjects at Auschwitz by inventing a kind of assembly-line method that was quick and seemingly innocuous: prisoners were told to fill out a form at a counter, and while they did so they were irradiated by a hidden X-ray device. In this way Schumann hoped to sterilize four thousand persons a day. Mutilations and over-doses were common, causing acute swelling and genital deterioration. These regrettable side effects paled by comparison to the great benefits that would be reaped: "the thought alone that the 3 million Bolshe-viks now in German captivity could be sterilized so that they would be available for work but precluded from propagation, open up the most far-reaching perspectives."[118]

One of Dr. Schumann's colleagues at Auschwitz, Dr. Johann Paul Kremer, was avidly conducting research on the problems of starvation. Since there was a never-ending supply of starving patients at Auschwitz, Dr. Kremer could pursue his hobbyhorse with uninhibited abandon: he would select "the proper specimens," kill them with a lethal injection of phenol into the heart, and then harvest various organs for detailed analysis. His ghastly experiments did not seem to have upset his normal routine at all; in fact, his infamous diary shows us just how grotesquely humans can split themselves by killing people on the one hand and simultaneously maintaining a "normal" way of life on the other:

> September 4, 1942...present at a special action (selection) in the women's camp....The most horrible of horrors....
>
> September 6...Today, Sunday, an excellent dinner: tomato soup, half a chicken with potatoes and red cabbage (20g. of fat), sweet pudding and magnificent vanilla ice cream....
>
> October 10...I took and preserved material from quite fresh corpses, namely, liver, spleen, and pancreas....
>
> October 11...Today, Sunday, we got for dinner quite a big piece of roast hare with dumplings and red cabbage for 1.25 RM.[119]

A brisk trade also occurred in the collection of human body parts, especially well-preserved heads of racial subhumans, for the purpose of racial research. A professor at the University of Strasbourg, Dr. August Hirt, conducted research on subhuman heads and prevailed on Himm-ler to send him well-preserved heads of Jewish-Bolshevik commissars. The delighted Reichsführer turned over the task of selecting good can-didates to Wolfram Sievers, head of the SS Ahnenerbe, or Ancestral Heritage Society. Also nicknamed "bluebird," Sievers scoured Auschwitz for good candidates, ordered them killed, and sent the bodies to Profes-sor Hirt, later claiming that he "simply carried through a function of a postman."[120] Hirt's research was entirely in line with Himmler's racial obsession to discover traces of pure Aryan origins and to perfect pure Aryan blood.

Such perverted racial science found its highest expression in the infamous Dr. Josef Mengele, the "Angel of Death" at Auschwitz. Most Auschwitz survivors remembered Mengele as a dapper, immaculately dressed German officer, frigid and ruthless, who met new arrivals as they stepped down from the squalid boxcar to meet their fate. Like an operatic stage director, sometimes whistling tunes from Wagner's operas, he would point his cane at each person and order them to the right or the left.[121] He immensely enjoyed these selections, and in his various medical experiments he killed many patients, especially children, without blinking an eye — "willfully and with blood lust."[122] As in Himmler's case, his upbringing did not seem to predict his murderous activities at Auschwitz. He came from an upper-middle-class Bavarian family that owned a business selling farm equipment in Günzburg. His youth followed a pattern we have previously encountered with sons of middle-class parents: rigidly pedantic education in the Gymnasia, those breeding grounds of authoritarianism and arrogant elitism, rejection of religion in favor of *völkisch* racial ideology, and a fondness for nationalistic and military values. Mengele joined the paramilitary Stahlhelm in 1931 and the SA in 1934, though it was not until 1938 that he joined the Nazi Party. After receiving his *Abitur* (secondary school-leaving examination), he studied physical biology and genetics at the Universities of Munich, Bonn, Vienna, and Frankfurt. In 1935 he completed his Ph.D. at the University of Munich with a dissertation that focused on the lower jaw sections of four racial groups and claimed that it was possible to identify racial groups by studying their jaws. In 1936 he passed his state medical examination and took up his first position at the University of Leipzig medical clinic.

What changed Mengele's life, however, was his appointment as a research assistant at the Third Reich Institute for Hereditary Biology and Racial Purity at the University of Frankfurt, where he worked under the direction of Otmar von Verschuer, one of Germany's premier geneticists. Mengele became Verschuer's favorite understudy. The eminent professor encouraged the young man's career, secured his appointment as chief medical researcher at Auschwitz, and used his political power as director of the Kaiser Wilhelm Institute for Anthropology, Human Genetics, and Eugenics in marshalling funds for Mengele's research in the concentration camp. The grateful Mengele repaid the professor's services by periodically sending him perfectly preserved body parts from Auschwitz.[123]

When war broke out, Mengele joined the medical corps of the Waffen-SS and served with great distinction on the eastern front, receiving the Iron Cross first- and second-class. In May 1943, at the height of the gassings, he arrived at Auschwitz to take advantage of the rare opportunity offered there to experiment on human beings, especially twins. Mengele was convinced that by experimenting on twins, abnormal genetic transmissions could be identified and controlled. He collected about 250 sets of twins and treated them as any laboratory researcher might treat frogs, mice, or rats. According to Lifton, Mengele brought a "murderous scientific fanaticism" to Auschwitz;[124] its aim was to breed a higher form of Aryan being. In the words of one of his coerced Polish assistants, Dr. Martin Puzyna:

> I found Mengele a picture of what can only be described as a maniac. He turned the truth on its head. He believed you could create a new super-race as though you were breeding horses. . . . He was a racist and a Nazi. He was ambitious up to the point of being completely inhuman. He was mad about genetic engineering. I believe that when he'd finished with the Jewish race, he'd start on the Poles, and when he finished with them, he'd start on someone else. Above all, I believe that he was doing this . . . for his career. In the end I believed that he would have killed his own mother if it would have helped him.[125]

For the sake of his utopian dream and his career, Mengele tortured and murdered with a good conscience. Yet to his co-workers he was one of the most decent colleagues (*anständigste Kollegen*): correct, congenial, and "cultured." This, of course, is the Auschwitz syndrome of doubling with attendant justifications of noble research and removing poisonous abscesses from the German people's body (*Volkskörper*). Mengele was the fanatical true believer, the mad professor with a vision of human perfection. Auschwitz was his ideal world, his dream come true. Here he could live out his racial fantasy and justify dissecting twins, injecting methylene blue dye directly into his victim's eyes, collecting body parts, and giving vent to his explosive anger by shooting, injecting (*abspritzen*), or sending his victims to the death chambers. If in ordinary times he would probably have been a slightly sadistic German professor, as one colleague speculated, Auschwitz transformed him into the archetype of Nazi evil. In the eyes of his Jewish victims, he became the embodiment of their deepest collective fears — the key to their "sense of fear of everything that is German."[126]

But how "ordinary" a German was Mengele? How ordinary were Himmler, Eichmann, Höss, or other Nazi racial fanatics just like them? Were these men representative of the German population as a whole and, beyond that, were they "just like us," which the term is often meant to suggest? Since it would be difficult on both statistical and psychological grounds to answer these questions in any other than the most speculative sense, Holocaust researchers have moved from idiographic to nomothetic approaches by looking at a far larger and cohesive group of killers and asking themselves: are these men more representative of the general population of Germans than the leaders of the Nazi racial elite? If this could be established, one could then perhaps hold all Germans equally responsible for mass murder because it would presumably prove that every single ordinary German, had he or she been in the shoes of the genocidal killers, would have murdered in the same way. Alternatively, and less provocatively, one could conclude that, although

given certain cultural conditions, ordinary Germans became mass murderers, so have many other ordinary people, past or present. This line
of research has focused on the genocidal killers of the *Einsatzgruppen,*
particularly the auxiliary police battalions that were used in Russia
to augment the originally small numbers of special task forces. The
Einsatzgruppen and its special units consisted of highly trained and
ideologically indoctrinated commandos whose men carried a violent
Judeophobic hatred into their killing operation. One would be hard put
to refer to their members as "ordinary" Germans.

The same was not true, however, of the men of the Reserve Police
Battalions who were sent into Poland and Russia to lend support to a
rapidly expanding program of mass murder. So far, we have only two
major studies which deal with these units whose members, we are told,
consisted of "ordinary" Germans, middle-aged men who were recruited
from a cross-section of the German population. The first study is by
Christopher Browning, who focused his research on Reserve Police Battalion 101 and its five reserve policemen, many of whom came from the
city of Hamburg.[127] Most of Browning's information comes from the
interrogation of 210 men conducted by the Office of the State Prosecu-
tor of Hamburg between 1962 and 1972, which yielded a good sample
about this police battalion, including the age, education, and occupational background of its members. Browning shows that most of the
men of Police Battalion 101 were middle-aged family men who came
from the lower order of society, possessed a broad range of vocational
skills, and acquired little formal education beyond elementary school
(*Volksschule*). Their transformation from average policemen into mass
killers represents one of the most remarkable stories of the Holocaust,
a story Browning recounts in minute details as he follows their killing
and policing actions in Russia between the summer of 1941 and the
collapse of the Third Reich in 1944–45. Since forty similar police battalions operated in Poland and Russia at about the same time, more
research would be required on these other units to gauge the representative value of Reserve Police Battalion 101. Daniel Jonah Goldhagen, in
his controversial book *Hitler's Willing Executioners,*[128] examined nine
police battalions, in addition to focusing on a broad range of killing
activities by what he, too, calls "ordinary" Germans.

Both scholars agree on two major points: a sizeable number of ordinary Germans participated in mass murder, their numbers reaching
well beyond a hundred thousand, and their involvement was, for the
most part, voluntary rather than coerced. Although both researchers
studied the same documentary evidence, they came away with vastly different interpretations about the motives of the murderers. Goldhagen,
as previously mentioned, identifies one common motive that compelled
the perpetrators to exterminate the Jews: "eliminationist anti-Semitism."
It operated almost like an unmoved mover by grafting itself, without
significant exceptions, on all Germans, forcing them to hate and ex-

terminate Jews. Such demonization explains a part but not the whole story. Goldhagen has a vivid sense of Judeophobic evil and traces its horrors with consummate skill, providing a thick narrative of murderous frenzy that Browning's meticulous and cautious empiricism simply cannot equal. On the other hand, the dark logic of cruelty is not illuminated by a monocausal explanation that rejects all other cultural or psychological reasons. It is in this sense that Goldhagen reveals himself as one of Jakob Burckhardt's terrible *simplificateurs* by attributing "eliminationist anti-Semitism" to the average German citizen, thus draining the real meaning out of both "anti-Semitism" and "ordinary German." Browning proceeds far more cautiously and avoids overarching explanations of a reductionist nature. His ordinary Germans killed not only out of ideological convictions but also out of "situational" factors that involved group pressure, obedience to authority, brutalization and breakdown of civilized values, bitterness over their own casualties, and the like.

Reserve Police Battalion 101 was initiated into mass murder in the summer of 1942 as it followed the *Einsatzgruppen* into the killing fields. Its baptism of blood was quick and terrible. The place was Józefów, a small village south of Chelm in the Lublin district. The battalion's commander, fifty-three-year-old major Wilhelm Trapp, who was affectionately referred to by his men as "Papa Trapp," received an order to round up eighteen hundred Jews. Trapp was told to separate male Jews who were capable of work from the rest of the Jews and to transport them to a labor camp; the remainder — old men, women, and children — were to be shot on the spot. He informed the officers first; only one of them, reserve lieutenant Heinz Buchmann, refused to participate on the grounds that a German soldier should not be expected to shoot women and children. Trapp gave the older noncommissioned men, who might feel that they were not up to such a heavy task, the choice of opting out. Ten to twelve men did so after watching one of their comrades break ranks. Trapp was emotionally distraught. One of his men later recalled him saying, "Oh God, why did I have to be given these orders";[129] another saw him weeping bitterly. Yet Trapp composed himself because, as he told another man, "orders are orders."[130] He confided to his driver, however, that "if this Jewish business is ever avenged on earth, then have mercy on us Germans."[131] The battalion performed unevenly but accomplished its mission of shooting most of the Jews of Józefów. Although the men seemed to have experienced considerable emotional distress in having to shoot innocent people, they quickly developed suitable defense mechanisms to keep the atrocity at arm's length. Some men showered their squeamish comrades with derogatory remarks like "weakling" or "shithead."[132] The men also tried to alleviate the terrible stress by drinking heavily and taking frequent cigarette breaks. Still, returning from the woods covered with blood and pieces of brain, the men arrived at their barracks "depressed, angered, embittered and shaken."[133] One gains the impression that killing became increasingly easier on subsequent occasions because civilized taboos had been smashed, blood cement helped bond the killers, and defense mechanisms such as doubling and numbing relegated the killing to the domain of "situational" violence over which one had no real control.

Afterward, the men of Reserve Police Battalion 101 justified their murderous activities by claiming that they had no choice, merely followed orders, felt the pressure of their peers, retaliated for fallen comrades or innocent German civilians killed by Allied bombing. Curiously, the men said little about hating Jews, a significant and glaring omission that could only point to repression or willful self-deception.

Browning points out, and Goldhagen strongly confirms, that these men had been exposed to years of anti-Jewish propaganda, and that this had also become an integral part of their professional training and indoctrination. If they had been only mildly anti-Jewish before their experiences in the east, most of the men eventually learned to look at Jews as being less than human. One of the perpetrators confirmed this view by saying that "the Jew was not acknowledged by us to be a human being."[134] Their later excuse that they merely followed orders or had no choice is invalidated by the fact that some men, perhaps amounting to 10 percent, refused to participate in mass murder and suffered no serious consequences. Expressions of horror, reported, of course, after the fact, are also unpersuasive. The killers were proud of their achievements, as evidenced by the photographs they snapped, letters they wrote, or mementos they kept. The photos they snapped of themselves and their victims reveal the dark underside not just of Germans but of all humans. As Goldhagen points out, the men of the police battalions led thick lives in which normality and abnormality alternated in the course of a single day marked by mass shootings of women and children followed by jolly amusements and other social diversions. Their wives and sweethearts were never too far away; in fact, one officer, Captain Wohlauf, let his wife attend a day-long killing operation, which the men considered inappropriate not because they were ashamed of what they were doing but because they considered it unchivalrous for a German woman to be present during such killings.[135]

The men also considered it inappropriate to mistreat animals, and they showed great sensitivity to their dogs, protecting them from epidemics and rushing them to the veterinarian on the slightest symptom of illness, behavior that prompted Goldhagen to ask whether the killers upon reading proclamations concerning dog care did not "reflect on the difference in treatment they were meting out to dogs and Jews."[136] It never occurred to Goldhagen that this is what brutalization of human life and doubling can do. Their indifference to the suffering of Jews was not merely the result of violent Judeophobia but of the brutalizing effects of the killings themselves. To extend the dog analogy to the human level: just as dogs who taste blood become tainted by its effects, human beings also become avid killers if given the authority and occasion for it.

Hatred by itself, ideological or otherwise, does not suffice in explaining the genocidal murderers, many of whom inflicted entirely gratuitous cruelty on their victims that had little to do with ideology or even sadism. Torture, cruelty, degradation are necessary elements in destroying human beings because they make it easier for the perpetrators to kill. In Franz Stangl's shocking remark, gratuitous cruelty conditions those who have to carry out mass killings; it makes it possible for them to do what they did.[137]

These considerations raise the larger philosophical and psychological questions about unspeakable human cruelties and why they seem to be a permanent feature of human and not only of German history. Each time we are confronted with mass atrocities, whether by Nazi killers, Khmer Rouge Cambodians, or communist Chinese or Russian apparatchiks, we want to know the dimensions involved to be able to understand and to prevent the same horror from happening again. Little is served by reducing such multilayered horrors to a singular idea, an "immanent structure of cognition," or national character. Browning rightly made the point that the full understanding of the men of Police Battalion 101 requires knowledge of those universal aspects of human nature that transcend the cognition and culture of ordinary Germans. He shows, for example, that the actions and behaviors of the men of Police Battalion 101 conform closely to certain psychological experiments that have been conducted in clinical settings, notably the famous Milgram and Zimbardo experiments at Yale and Stanford. The assumption behind both experiments is that inhumanity is a function of social relationships rather than of characterological disorders.

In the Zimbardo experiment, conducted at Stanford University in 1971, a normal test group of college students was divided into guards and prisoners in a mock experimental prison.[138] The test subjects consisted of two dozen young men from middle-class homes in California and other American states who were judged to be normal, mature, and emotionally stable college students. By the flip of a coin one group was told to play prisoners and the other guards. During their eight-hour, three-men shifts the guards were free to make up their own formal rules for maintaining order and respect. After only six days the experiment got so completely and disturbingly out of hand that it had to be canceled. What happened was that the prison environment threatened to suspend a lifetime of learning and values, creating an atmosphere in which the participants began to confuse role-playing with reality. The guards began to display some marked pathological tendencies, treating prisoners like animals and humiliating them with obvious pleasure. Conversely, the prisoners became meek and servile and acted like dehumanized robots. One-third of the guards became tyrannical and enjoyed the arbitrary use of their power over the prisoners. Some of the guards just did their jobs, while still others were perceived to be "good guards" by the prisoners. Not a single guard, however, sided with the prisoners in a dispute with other guards, never interfered with the commands of another guard, and never complained to the superintendent. The experiment confirmed what practitioners in the field and criminologists had been familiar with all along, namely, that the roles we play influence our social behavior, and that authorization to wield power over "lesser beings" tends to release callous, cruel, and brutal impulses.

Hurting others when commanded to do so by lawful and respected authority was also the subject of the famous Milgram experiments at Yale University between 1960 and 1963.[139] Stanley Milgram conducted a series of experiments to test people's willingness to obey authority. He picked his subjects at random by placing advertisements in the newspapers and then told the subjects that they were going to participate in experiments designed to test the effects of punishment on learning. When the volunteers arrived at the laboratory, they were briefed by a stern-looking experimenter in a technician's coat. What they did not know was that the experiment was rigged, and that they were about to become unwitting "teachers" who had to test whether the "learners," other volunteers who had been initiated beforehand, had correctly memorized a list of word-pairs. The teacher was led to a fake electric "Shock Generator" with an instrument panel that had a row of thirty switches, calibrated from a low point of 15 volts, labeled "slight shock," to increasingly higher points, called moderate shocks, to severe shocks of 450 volts. The learner was led into an adjoining room, strapped into a fake electric chair, and began to play his part in the drama, which consisted in simply answering a prepared script. Every time the learner in the other room failed to recall a word-pair correctly, the teacher was to give him an electric shock of increasing voltage. To Milgram's astonishment, the teachers all applied shocks right up to the maximum level. He then varied the experiments by introducing tape-recorded protests by which the learner called out "I can't stand the pain" at 125 volts, complained of heart trouble at 195, screamed at 270 volts, and was completely and ominously silent at 450 volts. Amazingly, 65 percent of the teachers continued to administer maximum doses despite the protestations and the ominous silence in the next room. Milgram then varied the experiment again. He put the learner in the same room with the teacher and told the learner to put his hand on a "shock plate" in order to receive the punishment. Even under these gruesome conditions, with the learner screaming and complaining about his heart, 30 percent of the teachers still continued to administer maximum levels of electric shock.

The Milgram experiment came as a stunning surprise to both the public and the academic world because it revealed what five thousand years of recorded history, the *real* laboratory of human nature, could have taught anyone who bothered to examine its record: an astonishingly large number of people will inflict pain and cruelty on other people when they are ordered to do so by lawful or trusted authority. Remoteness from the victim made it easier to obey and to administer pain.

Milgram's experiment, like Zimbardo's, does not exactly parallel historical circumstances; no experiment in a laboratory setting can do that. On
the other hand, as Milgram points out, "the laboratory problem is vivid,
intense, and real. It is not something apart from life, but carries to an extreme and very logical conclusion certain trends inherent in the ordinary
functioning of the social world."[140] Moreover, these experiments are directly relevant to what happened in Nazi Germany and have happened
throughout history. Christopher Browning found a remarkable similarity in the behavior of Zimbardo's subjects and the members of Reserve
Police Battalion 101.[141] There was a nucleus of enthusiastic killers who
volunteered for firing squad duties or "Jew-hunts," a large group of
"good" policemen who performed executions because they were ordered
to do so, and a small group of refusers or evaders. Browning also argues
that "many of Milgram's insights find graphic confirmation in the behavior and testimony of the men of Reserve Police Battalion 101."[142]
Obedience to authority was a common psychological process in both
the test subjects and the Nazi killers, the difference being, of course,
one of magnitude. Milgram put this point in the form of an analogy,
saying that his laboratory subjects are to the Nazi killers what a match
flame is to the Chicago fire of 1898.[143] His experiment showed how
ordinary Americans, through simple manipulation, no longer perceived
themselves a responsible part of the causal chain that led to the violation
of a person's right to life, liberty, or human dignity. Such human flaws,
as he reminds us, are more common than we believe:

> One can find evidence of its occurrence time and again as one reads the
> transcripts of the war criminals at Nuremberg, the American killers at
> My Lai, and the commander of Andersonville. What we find in com-
> mon among soldier, party functionary, and obedient subject is the same
> limitless capacity to yield to authority and the use of identical mental
> mechanisms to reduce the strain of acting against the helpless victim.[144]

It is important to raise the debate about the Holocaust killers from
the level of "ordinary" Germans to ordinary humans because Germans
are both. The term "ordinary German" cannot have exact scientific
specification. We cannot "measure" the whole of German society by its
policemen because they are not a representative cross-section of the population at large. The men of the Order Police were representative only in
a loose sense of German policemen, but not of German teachers, professors, physicians, lawyers, nurses, or businessmen. The core of German
policemen, particularly Hamburg policemen, was recruited from right-
wing Free Corps units whose militaristic and extremely Judeophobic
convictions do not statistically correlate with the majority of the population. We do not know enough about how these men were recruited
and trained, how many of them were policemen in long standing, and
how many were just called to duty between 1941 and 1945 to be able
to formulate anything but ad hoc statistical statements attesting to their

"ordinariness." The search for a statistical "ordinary" German or ordinary anything else is, to my mind, nothing more than a useful stepping stone to the real moral rather than scientific answer we all seek: as members of the human race could all of us but for the grace of God become killers? The Holocaust was both a German crime and a modern crime against humanity; it was both a crime against the Jewish people and a crime against humanity. It had to be both because Jews and Germans are part of humanity so that any crime perpetrated by either one against the other is a crime in both senses of the word.

The Converging Paths to Radical Evil

Emil Fackenheim tells the story that he once asked Raul Hilberg, who is generally considered the greatest living Holocaust scholar, the following question: "Raul, you have thought as long and as hard about how they did it. Now tell me, why did they do it?"[145] Hilberg heaved a sigh and replied: "They did it because they wanted to do it."[146] Fackenheim, an important philosopher and theologian, reported this incident to a meeting of the American Philosophical Association where someone, during the course of the ensuing discussion, substituted "They did it because they *decided* to do it." As Fackenheim rightly pointed out, neither of these answers is sufficient or satisfactory, because if one limits oneself to small questions out of fear that one might give too small an answer to the big question, one has effectively forestalled the possibility of ever getting close to the big question. No one can improve on Raul Hilberg's account on how the Nazis planned and executed the Holocaust, but Fackenheim was surely right in arguing that a great deal still needs to be done about the big question, the global human implications of this event in the stream of both German and human history. Fackenheim himself has opened up several suggestive paths by which the bigger questions might be illuminated, proposing the thesis that the Nazi racial Weltanschauung provided the genocidal perpetrators with a comprehensive cosmic principle by which they structured their experiences. Fackenheim also makes the point that an understanding of the importance of all-embracing worldviews in German history is an essential prerequisite for an understanding of the acceptance of the Nazi Weltanschauung.[147] The following analysis and summary of the reasons why the Holocaust happened in Nazi Germany affirms this argument by Fackenheim and uses it as a point of departure in spelling out all the additional reasons that must be explored in order to comprehend its occurrence. There are seven broad reasons that account for the occurrence of the Holocaust:

1. The biological-racial Weltanschauung of the Nazi power elite

2. The effects of propaganda in a totalitarian police state

3. The complicity of an authoritarian bureaucracy

4. The breakdown of civilized restraints

5. The cover of wartime conditions and the brutalizing effects of the Russian campaign

6. The cooperation of conquered countries and satellite nations

7. The passivity of the victims within an indifferent world

1. The Biological-Racial Weltanschauung of the Nazi Power Elite

Any crime, large or small, other than a crime of passion, presupposes motive or rational intention. The Holocaust is no exception; it happened by a conscious design and by a logic that was peculiar to the Nazi mindset. One could argue that the Holocaust was caused by a special kind of thinking that compelled the perpetrators to exterminate what they genuinely believed to be subhuman and guilty people. We have already examined the content of this sort of thinking by exploring its intellectual origins and the claims it made about the power of general structural principles by which human communities both define and radically separate themselves from each other. Such thinking moves in patterns of exclusive associations and polarizations; it defines individuals by reference to some general and exclusive good that resides outside themselves in class, gender, nation, and race. The major political and social movements of the twentieth century, abandoning the universal human ideals of the Enlightenment, have all, in one way or another, conditioned people into thinking in polarized and antagonistic terms. The great "isms" of the modern age have all insisted upon categorizing and differentiating individuals as exclusive members of a larger group that is allegedly economically, politically, or morally chosen as all good, while others are deemed as either unworthy or inherently evil, to be converted or to be annihilated. It is this ideological thinking, rooted in the psychology of group identification and some existential need for absolute answers, that furnished the annihilatory rage inherent in Nazism and communism, the two greatest pseudoreligious movements of the twentieth century. Both Nazism and communism were internally self-contained worldviews; their intellectual leaders were motivated by a deep psychological need for certainty that demanded the strictest dichotomization of reality into absolute good and absolute evil.

Although aspects of this kind of thinking are embodied in some of the world's greatest religions, it would be incorrect and unfair to hold traditional religion responsible for a mental disease that is distinctly modern. Nazi racial consciousness or communist class consciousness is not a simple reversion to primitive or mythical thinking; rather, it made use (or misuse) of the conceptual principles of modern scientific consciousness. These modern movements appealed to science for validation of their political or social prejudices: they claimed certainty not by reference to God but to putative laws of economic or biological necessity. Both Nazism and communism defined individuals by reference to either race or economic affiliation and threatened extermination or revolution against their opponents. The Nazis carried this sort of thinking to its most radical conclusions because, unlike the communists, they rejected conversion as impossible for certain targeted groups they considered "alien in type" (*artfremdig*). For such people — Jews, Gypsies, Slavs, homosexuals, mentally disabled — there was no hope of salvation in a Nazi dominated world. The communists were at least willing to admit former members of the bourgeoisie into their ranks, provided that they had "seen the light" and converted to an ideology that, admittedly one-dimensional and psychologically fallacious, was based on an ideal of human brotherhood rather than, in the case of the Nazis, on inhuman and depraved principles.[148] Behind both ideologies, however, one can identify a clear-cut perversion of scientific reasoning, either deliberately or by a mistaken overextension of scientific principles into the area of human behavior.

As soon as scientific methodology moved from the analysis of nature to human nature, with "social scientists" claiming to work with the same apodictic principles that allegedly existed in the natural sciences, the modern mind embarked upon several dangerous missions that were marked by monumental blind spots, dead ends, and self-serving ideologies. Some have labeled this intellectual passion as "scientism,"[149] which consists in elevating a particular technique to the level of the absolute and then claiming magical, therapeutic, or salvational results from it. On one level, it surfaces as the latest self-help method that promises instant happiness, marital bliss, sexual fulfillment, or financial success. On the educational level, it promises instant proficiency in reading, writing, or arithmetic for children. On the global level, it promises national salvation through revolution, war, or ethnic cleansing. Scientism is a perversion of science because it assumes the predictability of human behavior on the analogy of natural behavior, overextends the boundaries of scientific analysis beyond their inherent limitations, and fills in the gaps between the unknown and the ultimate certainty it seeks with magic tissue. One can see these pitfalls in every major ideological passion of our century; nor is there any end in sight because we are currently inundated by scientific magicality in advertising, commerce, and politics. The sort of thinking that characterized the Nazis is also alive and well in racist prejudices, ethnic forms of self-identity, and millenarian mumbo jumbo.[150]

There is beyond content and form a certain quality about the Nazi mentality that must also be mentioned, and that is its fascination with and love of death. This is the core element of all life-denying ideologies; it is their participation in evil. In a recent book by John Weiss, entitled *Ideology of Death: Why the Holocaust Happened in Germany*, reference is made to certain life-denying traditions in German culture that, directly or indirectly, encouraged the sort of malignant thinking that defined the Judeophobic elite of the Nazi movement. Weiss's analysis is shrewd and far-ranging, entirely correct in most of its judgments about the peculiarities of German history, but the author is so concerned with establishing a special path (*Sonderweg*) for Germany that he does not pose the larger questions about the lust for destruction in human nature itself. Ideologies of death have been endemic in history, and Lewis Mumford was surely right in labeling western culture in our own times as a death-oriented culture because it worships technologies that are calculated to destroy life.[151] By contrast with the Egyptian cult of the dead, with its grandiose pyramids, magical rituals, and elaborate techniques of mummification, the modern dance with death is far more sinister because it involves atomic weapons, missiles, and ecocidal destruction.

The need to dominate and to extend one's power over others, singly or in groups, constitutes a recurring theme in human history. As Lewis Mumford reminds us, the "Pentagons of Power" with their power elites, destructive technologies, and ideological underpinnings have grown exponentially over time and at the expense of the needs and purposes of life.[152] If technology is placed in the hands of amoral technicians of power, the dangers multiply because, in the words of the mathematician John von Neumann, "technological possibilities are irresistible in man. If man can go to the moon, he will."[153] More ominously, would it not therefore also follow that if man has the power to destroy life, he will?

I leave indefinite the question whether the urge to dominate and to destroy those who block its path is rooted in human nature or in the organization of social life. Its reality is beyond dispute. The love of power entails the fascination with death; in fact, death has often been used to serve a perverted sense of life and power.[154] People have spilled blood with delight because it invigorates the power drive, urging it on to further control and domination. Such appetites for destruction have been embodied in elaborate ideologies of a warlike nature that celebrate struggle, combat, heroism, and self-sacrifice. The German people stand out in singing paeans to such martial beliefs during the course of their two-thousand-year history. In Norbert Elias's words, "few people had in their national mystique, in their poetry and in their songs so many allusions to death and self-sacrifice as the Germans.... Few other nations were as inclined as the Germans to give place in their national pantheon to heroes who died in defeat."[155] The Nazis, of course, represented the culmination of this enchantment with *thanatos;* they had a ready-made ideology of blood and soil that glamorized death as life-enhancing. Leo Alexander has called this attitude "thanatolatry," or the delight in death, arguing that those who acted it out, especially the men of the SS, believed that the infliction of death on others strengthened their own vital powers and validated their racial superiority.[156]

Conversely, they saw their own death as a noble sacrifice that would strengthen the Nazi movement.

Hitler and the Nazi power elite made a fetish of death and celebrated it in pseudoreligious rituals. Goebbels, in his speech on "Total War," said that "we go into war as we would into high mass." His Führer believed that the destruction of his enemies, especially the Jews, validated his own omnipotence; he looked at success in war as a sign that he was favored by higher powers, to the point of believing that the amount of favor bestowed on him by higher power was directly proportional to the number of enemies he killed — the more corpses the greater the favor from above. Some have argued that this irrational belief may have motivated Hitler to give the green light to genocide in 1941, particularly after the tide of war seemed no longer propitious. In Hitler's demented mind, the awareness of his own death could only be assuaged by piling up ever more heaps of corpses.

There is in all such death fascinations and death-defying urges a deep-seated anxiety that cries out to be assuaged. In Lifton's judgment, Nazi ideology dealt with this death anxiety by glorifying and even worshiping death itself, thus mistakenly assuming that anxiety and the guilt associated with it have been exorcised:

> While one's death as a warrior is idealized, the self mostly escapes death — achieves the death of death — by killing others. There can readily follow a vicious circle in which one kills, needs to go on killing in order to maintain one's cure, and seeks a continuous process of murderous, deathless, therapeutic survival. One can then reach the state of requiring a sense of perpetual survival through the killing of others in order to reexperience endlessly what Elias Canetti has called "The moment of power" — that is, the moment of cure.[157]

The Nazi killing elite believed it had death-defying skills that would redeem not just themselves but the German people as well. For them, death was a means of national self-purification; by inflicting it on the Jews, they would cleanse the German soil of a malignant disease. In short, for the Nazis death was a means of national self-transcendence. In reality, their love of death served a different purpose: an invocation of and participation in evil.

2. The Effects of Propaganda in a Totalitarian Police State

When the Nazis gained control over the German government in 1933, they assembled an extensive machinery of power that aimed at both persuasion and terror, the former relying on propaganda and the latter on the Gestapo and the concentration camp. The racial worldview the Nazis attempted to disseminate contained an inherent genocidal logic; with the help of Nazi propaganda and power behind it, that logic began to unfold in accordance with its genocidal premises. Only historians who dissect the Nazi period microscopically and blur the distinction between the short-term objectives (legal discrimination, expropriation, emigration) and the longer-term goals (extermination) the Nazis were pursuing simultaneously can speak of a "twisted road to Auschwitz." On the contrary, there were no bends or detours in that road: it ran broad and direct. This is clear from the growth of annihilatory Judeophobia after World War I, the rise of biological nationalism, the convergence of xenophobic movements and psychopathic Jew-haters, and the takeover of a modern technological state, suffering from the illusion of a world power complex, by fanatical and murderous Jew-haters. Given these facts, the possibility of genocide was a clear and present danger as soon as the Nazis controlled the machinery of government and started implementing their grand design. The most important part of that grand design included preparation for a world war that Hitler believed had never ended and had to be waged for purposes of both revenge and racial regeneration. Steady preoccupation with the one-dimensional and demented minds of the Nazi elite for over thirty years has disabused me of the notion, still propounded by some historians, that somewhere and somehow, at some point during the course of the Third Reich, events could have gone in a different direction than they actually did. Any argument of this sort, for whatever reason, is a hypothesis contrary to fact.

The role of propaganda and brainwashing in this development is crucial because propaganda made and destroyed the Third Reich. One of the major goals of Nazi propaganda was to project a racial Weltanschauung that would provide all Germans with a comprehensive and internally consistent view of the world. As previously shown, the Germans have prided themselves historically for being a nation of *Dichter und Denker,* poets and thinkers; in few other nations has the preoccupation with philosophizing on a grand scale been taken so seriously as in Germany. For all its shabby inhumanity and deliberate distortion of reality, Nazi Weltanschauung was just one more German grand design. The Nazi power elite had every intention of brainwashing the German people into accepting their racial views as the sole compass to reality.

Ideological indoctrination, like everything else in the new racial state, was designed to be total: every German, young or old, male or female, was to be initiated into the new pseudoreligion. All this, of course, is well known, but what is less well known, perhaps unmeasurable, is the degree to which years of indoctrination actually altered or modified the thinking of millions of ordinary Germans. The impact of racial beliefs in the Nazi elite, however, is known from the documents they left and the deeds they committed. Ideological training on all levels was quite extensive in the Hitler Youth, the armed forces, and all party and state agencies. Enough training manuals, pamphlets, and informational handouts have survived the Third Reich to reveal how extensive the propagandistic onslaught really was on millions of German. These documents leave absolutely no doubt about what the Nazis intended to do with the Jews. Christopher Browning briefly explored the ideological training received by Reserve Police Battalion 101, which included such provocative subjects as "Maintaining the Purity of Blood," "The Question of Blood," "The Politics of Race," "The Blood Community of the Germans Peoples."[158] This is just the tip of the iceberg, for similar training courses were being conducted on all levels for physicians, lawyers, civil servants, teachers, etc. As Browning rightly put it, "the men of Reserve Battalion 101, like the rest of German society, were immersed in a deluge of racist and anti-Semitic propaganda."[159]

The research that has been conducted on the effects of Nazi propaganda indicates that there was considerable public resistance to frequent, obsessive, and mind-numbing propaganda, a fact Goebbels himself appreciated because he realized that unrelenting propaganda, unrelieved by entertainment, quickly produced counterproductive reactions on the part of the recipients. Many Germans, in fact, learned to tune out much of the regime's overheated rhetorical claims, becoming increasingly numb and desensitized. On the other hand, support for the regime, especially for Hitler, remained remarkably solid despite the devastating setbacks and casualties that the public had to accept after victories turned into constant defeats. If this is not a living testimonial to the power of Nazi propaganda, what is?

3. The Complicity of an Authoritarian Bureaucracy

Besides being an outcome of racial fanaticism, the Holocaust was also the product of modern bureaucratic culture because it involved the cooperation of many governmental and party agencies, each playing a unique role in the destruction process.[160] The German bureaucracy was an authoritarian institution that had survived the Kaiserreich unreformed and undemocratized. It was, like many German institutions, a curious blend of tradition and modernity. In the process of modernization, all the industrial nations of the western world had developed a set of bureaucratic institutions that were still strongly tied to feudal and authoritarian traditions. This explains their adherence to organizational principles that reflected the nature of predemocratic models of hierarchical (vertical) order in which authority began at the top and extended, by way of carefully defined positions, to the lowest position at the bottom. Respect for authority, loyalty, and obedience were the chief institutional values that defined the relationships among the members of an institution. The rise of commercial capitalism added the values of thrift, frugality, and hard work. In societies that were undergoing a considerable degree of democratization, the axis of both political and bureaucratic power began to shift away from concentration of power at the top to either shared or redistributed power at the middle or lower end of the system. Germany was a notable exception because its bureaucracy remained rigidly Mandarin and authoritarian in nature. At the same time, it absorbed a new ethos of rational efficiency that was divorced from larger ethical or political considerations. German bureaucrats were technically and legalistically trained officials who prided themselves on their technical expertise and their value-neutral approach to routine administrative procedures. Adherence to the letter of the law, fastidious work habits, and obedience to superiors were the values they cherished. If a directive or assignment was endorsed by higher authority, it had to be carried out in the same spirit in which a soldier carried out orders from his commanding officers. The allusion to the military ethos is obvious: militarism is the state of mind of the civil servant.

Adolf Hitler bent the authoritarian bureaucracy to his will by simply being the ultimate source of authority in Nazi Germany. Civil servants obeyed because he was their commanding officer. Yet there was something more involved. The German civil servants, despite their pretended neutrality, were authoritarian conservatives and saw in National Socialism a reflection of their own authoritarian longings; they also saw something else that resonated with their neo-feudal political traditions: the romantic charisma that characterized the leadership style in the Third Reich. Although trained to perform their duties in accordance with the highest standards of technical expertise, the German civil servants had also assimilated neo-feudal and romantic traditions that glamorized hero worship and militaristic values such as loyalty, obedience, duty (*Pflicht*), and honor. One should not be surprised, therefore, that such men carried out orders without questioning their moral validity. Bureaucrats in general, and German bureaucrats in particular, were "organization men" who had to conform to a set of institutional values that rarely transcended purely prudential or conventional moral rules. They were not expected to exercise individual conscience or even individual initiative without the approval of higher authority. The personality and moral structure of German bureaucrats reflected the authoritarian nature of German society with all its strengths and weaknesses. One of the greatest weaknesses of German bureaucracy and the culture it reflected was its intolerance of weakness. Its organizational ideal reflected what Norbert Elias has identified as a general German failing: the inability to make concessions to human imperfections and frailties; "its demands were absolute and uncompromising. Nothing less than total compliance with its norms provided satisfaction."[161]

The compulsion with perfection was and is a German cultural trait that has made the German people admired, envied, and despised. Whatever the Germans do as individuals or as a people, they do it with great seriousness and with a singleminded purpose that aims at perfection, success, and validation of superiority. We know about the positive side of this cultural obsession. The Germans have historically demonstrated an extraordinary capacity for organizing convictions on many different levels, and they have often found innovative means of translating them into successful practice. Their capacity for creative accomplishment is in many ways the product of a way of thinking peculiar to themselves and characterized by unusual consequentiality. They have put convictions into practice with impressive energy and consistency that were also wrong-headed and destructive and could not be corrected because German institutions lacked the means of self-correction.

When Hitler bent the German bureaucracy to his will and purpose, the German bureaucracy made its Faustian bargain by providing the best talents it could muster in support of the best machinery of destruction it could produce. The perfection of mass destruction was the negative side of the German bureaucratic equation. If that bureaucracy had been commanded to organize the best life possible for the Jews, it would probably have carried out the best plan to do so. Such amoral efficiency raises a larger and equally disturbing question about bureaucracies in general. Officials or workers in large corporations must work hard, obey, and do the very best they can for their organizations. Morality in the highest sense plays no major part in their corporate existence; they are not expected to question whether it is moral to produce napalm, missiles, or weapons of destruction. Their government absolves them of moral responsibility and implicitly clears them of all legal complicity in potential mass destruction. As Zygmunt Bauman bluntly put it, "the result is the irrelevance of moral standards for the technical success of the bureaucratic operation."[162] The German bureaucracy should serve as the worst example of bureaucratic complicity in modern industrial mass murder, but judging from the behavior of present-day power elites and their bureaucratic helpers, who continue to divorce force from morality, the world seems to have learned little about the amoral abuse of power and its evil consequences.

4. The Breakdown of Civilized Restraints

The German bureaucratic machinery of destruction was an "orderly" machinery, but for that very reason it was also more destructive because that destruction was authorized by the highest source of authority. Herbert C. Kelman has argued that moral inhibitions against violent atrocities are broken by three factors, singly or together: (1) the violence is authorized by duly constituted legal sources; (2) it is routinized by established practices and assigned functions; and (3) the victims are dehumanized by ideological brainwashing and indoctrination.[163]

Authorized violence means bureaucratically sanctioned and administered violence, which distinguishes it from the rage and frenzy that is characteristic of mob violence. The Holocaust was a carefully planned and executed form of mass destruction that was carried out, for the most part, in a detached and cold-blooded manner. It also had an official purpose, as Zygmunt Bauman reminds us, because it aimed at "a good vision of a better, and radically different society. Modern genocide is an element of social engineering, meant to bring about a social order conforming to the design of the perfect society."[164] In the Nazi context, this perfect society was a racially pure Aryan society from which all inferior races had been eliminated. Killing was really a form of healing and therefore entirely justified.

A great deal has already been said about the routinizing of violence, particularly in the concentration camps, where the annihilation of human beings by forced labor, starvation, and violence was carefully supervised in a businesslike manner. The men who administered this violence were, for the most part, brutal but not sociopathic functionaries. As Rappoport and Kren show:

> All the available evidence shows that the psychology of the vast majority of SS men was not characterized by any symptoms of gross pathology. It was apparently based instead upon a personality structure emphasizing obedience in service to heroic ideals and intense loyalty to the group and group leaders embodying these ideals.... Our judgment is that the overwhelming majority of SS men, leaders as well as rank and file, would have easily passed all the psychiatric tests ordinarily given to American army recruits or Kansas City policemen.[165]

Dehumanization of the victim makes violence more acceptable and easier to inflict. This is the function of torture and degradation. In Jean Améry's judgment, torture was the paradigmatic style of the Third Reich, its essential being.[166] Its victims were automatically degraded by the very act of torture. The preferred style of degradation was to subject the victims to filth and excrement. The barracks reeked with the smell of urine and feces. Sickness made matters worse. Typhus caused diarrhea, which "flooded the bottoms of the cages into the faces of the women lying in the cages below, and mixed with blood, pus and urine, formed a slimy, fetid mud in the floor of the barracks."[167] Latrines were inadequate and unsanitary. Over thirty thousand women had to use one latrine at Auschwitz; they had to stand in line to get into the tiny building where it was located, knee deep in human excrement. Alexander Donat said that dysentery "melted people down like candles, relieving themselves in their clothes, and swiftly turned into stinking repulsive skeletons who died in their own excrement."[168] Reducing people to a whimpering half-human state made it easier for the killers to dispatch their victims because they were, after all, only pieces of shit. Primo Levi recounts an incident during his deportation to Auschwitz when the convoy of freight cars stopped in an Austrian railroad station:

> The SS escort did not hide their amusement at the sight of men and women squatting wherever they could, on the platform and in the middle of the tracks, and the German passengers openly expressed their disgust: people like this deserve their fate, just look how they behave.... They are not *Menschen*, human beings, but animals; it's clear as the light of day.[169]

5. The Cover of Wartime Conditions and the Brutalizing Effects of the Russian Campaign

It is generally agreed that the brutal wartime conditions on the eastern front made it more manageable to annihilate millions of people without greatly alerting the rest of the world. Postwar German attempts to separate the SS killer troops from the rest of the Eastern Army, aimed at maintaining the legend of a "clean Wehrmacht" (*saubere Wehrmacht*), have obscured the fact that the army and the genocidal killers were an integral part of a genocidal whole whose mission consisted in annihilating both Jews and Slavs for the sake of a new German racial frontier. The conditions encountered in Russia by these biological warriors transformed previously victory-flushed soldiers into brutal killers who devastated the land and pitilessly terrorized and killed millions of people, soldiers and civilians alike. What kept group cohesion during these four years of savage fighting was a combination of intense political indoctrination and brutal discipline unheard of in the history of warfare. The troops were exposed to a barrage of propaganda that on the one hand demonized the Jewish-Bolshevik enemy and on the other deified the Führer. The soldiers were told that they were fighting subhumans (*Untermenschen*) and were therefore entitled to treat them with the utmost cruelty. When the supposedly inferior subhumans retaliated with great bravery and excellent machinery, the Nazi power elite, far from correcting the stereotypical image of inferior subhumans, cranked up the propaganda machine to an even higher pitch of hysterical intensity and urged greater ruthlessness against the satanic foe.

In describing the mindset of the Eastern Army, Omer Bartov referred to it as a "distortion of reality,"[170] the same distortion of reality we might add that defined the Judeophobic thinking of the Holocaust perpetrators. In fact, as Bartov convincingly showed, the Judeophobic mindset of ordinary soldiers on the eastern front did not significantly differ from that of the genocidal murderers. In order to gain a clearer insight into this distorted thinking, one should read the many letters that still survive of German soldiers who described to their loved ones what they experienced and learned while fighting on the eastern front. Two themes are particularly jarring: the demonization of the enemy, particularly the Jews, and the deification of Hitler.[171] Communists were seen as Jews in disguise and vice versa; the whole social system was viewed as a Jew-ridden wasteland. Preconceived stereotypes about horrible looking subhumans were confirmed ex post facto by reducing the local population to wretched replicas of the dreaded *Untermenschen*. Killing such aliens was just like killing animals. Karl Fuchs wrote home to report about the glaring contrast he discovered between a world of civilization and a world of barbarism by saying: "No matter where you look, there is nothing but filthy block houses. You can't find a trace of culture anywhere. Now we realize what our great German Fatherland has given its children. There exists only one Germany in the entire world."[172]

From such deliberately fostered ethnocentric stereotypes of a barbaric land and its people, it was only a short step to greater delusions. Even Streicher's hysterical visions were being confirmed by average soldiers. In the words of one NCO, "I have received the *Stürmer* now for the third time. It makes me happy with all my heart.... What the Jewish-regime has done in Russia, we see every day, and even the last doubters are cured here in view of the facts."[173] Another soldier wrote that "the *Stürmer* has, thank God, still remained true to its old position."[174] A corporal observed that the Jews he encountered near Lublin were worse than the *Stürmer* described them. Jews were overwhelmingly described as "unappetizing and unclean...and their homes are more like holes. No, such conditions cannot be found in Germany."[175] A corporal entering the Polish city of Siedlce was disgusted to find "Jews lying in the streets like pigs," while another soldier was offended by their filthy beards and caftans. The consensus was that such a filthy people (*verdrecktes Volk*) deserved to be ghettoized. Many soldiers were of the opinion that such a people did not even deserve to live. As one soldier put it, "if one looks at them one gains the impression that they have no right to live on God's earth."[176]

If the troops had had their way, they would have gladly wiped out the Jewish plague root and branch. Many soldiers projected their own fears and failures onto the Jews, holding them responsible for military failures or for the miserable conditions they were experiencing in a hostile and alien world. Nazi propaganda encouraged these attitudes. A lieutenant wrote that "it is simply impossible to describe what we have experienced. The most satanic system of all times is the Jewish system in the "Soviet Paradise," which is a paradise for Jews.... My men are thankful for the *Stürmer*."[177] Germany's salvation, the men believed, was Adolf Hitler, who would protect them against the Jewish scourge. One lance corporal blamed the endless fighting on the Jews, writing that "these swine of human creatures" had "brought us this outrage of a war."[178] Many soldiers claimed that once having seen what the Jews had done in Russia, one could then understand why the Führer had made it his life's mission to combat them. "What sorrows would have come to our homeland," one NCO wrote in July 1942, "had this beast of a man had the upper hand?"[179] Another wrote:

> The Führer has grown into the greatest figure of the century, in his hand lies the destiny of the world and of culturally perceptive humanity. May his pure sword strike down the satanic monster. Yes, the blows are still hard, but the horror will be forced into the shadows through the inexorable need, through the command which derives from our National Socialist idea. This [battle] is for a new ideology, a new belief, a new life; I am glad that I can participate, even if as a tiny cog, in this war of light against darkness.[180]

The men of the Ostheer, including the genocidal murderers, actually believed that the salvation of Germany depended upon the destruction of both communism and Jewry, which in their minds were really one and the same. They saw themselves waging what one of them called a *Glaubenskrieg,* a holy war that pitted two great and contrasting world-views against each other: National Socialism and Jewish-Bolshevism.[181]

The nazification of the Eastern Army and its transformation into Hitler's soldiers does not in itself prove that ordinary soldiers were all potential genocidal killers. What their ideological delusions and their experiences show, however, is that these soldiers were thoroughly brutalized and dehumanized, which made it easy for them to create the psychological distance they needed to turn the Jews into subhuman creatures that deserved to be exterminated.[182] Their distorted view of reality also accounts for the fact that the Wehrmacht closely cooperated with the genocidal killers and therefore enabled the murderers to perform their crimes without serious opposition. Genocidal killers and Wehrmacht soldiers were comrades-in-arms (*Waffenbrüder*) supporting each other because they saw themselves as part of the same mission.[183]

The mission of the German GI (*Landser*), of course, was to destroy his Russian counterpart, but the war in Russia was waged against all of its inhabitants. The army waged, besides a conventional military conflict, an increasingly powerful anti-partisan campaign in which there were no rules whatsoever. As previously seen, Hitler had given the military broad authorization to slaughter noncombatants. The result was that the distinction between Bolshevik, partisan, Jew, and civilian became completely blurred, making it possible to declare open season on everybody and kill people for the flimsiest of reasons. Without the active support of the Wehrmacht, the genocidal killers would have never been able to carry out the Holocaust. In other words, if the Wehrmacht had been a clean Wehrmacht (*saubere Wehrmacht*), even observing the traditional ethos of the Prussian Army, the Holocaust would not have been possible. The truth is that the Eastern Army, and to some extent the German army in general, had been transformed into a nazified army and its soldiers significantly corrupted by Judeophobic prejudices.

6. The Cooperation of Conquered Countries and Satellite Nations

The Nazi machinery of destruction could not have functioned as lethally as it did without the collaboration of occupied countries and satellite nations. In their relentless compulsion to extend the killings, the genocidal murderers demonstrated a Promethean quality of frightening proportions by vowing to consume every single Jew throughout Europe in a fiery inferno. The demographic and technological dimensions of such an undertaking, especially in wartime, were truly staggering. With a population of less than eighty million people the Germans had enough trouble on their hands in controlling a conquered continent of more than five hundred million people, let alone launch a machinery of destruction that required the identification, expropriation, denaturalization, and deportation of millions of Jews who were residing in over twenty different nations.

In order to annihilate eleven million Jews, which was the goal set at the Wannsee Conference, the genocidal killers not only had to augment their relatively small number of professional killers with foreign auxiliaries, but also required the active collaboration of foreign governments. Reference has been made to the involvement of anti-Semitic auxiliaries in the east as concentration camp guards. Globocnik, for example, used special service (*Sonderdienst*) units of ethnic Germans to staff the civil administration in each county of the Lublin district; he also persuaded Himmler to allow him to recruit non-Polish auxiliaries from the border areas. These units were the so-called Trawnikis, named after the forced labor camp southeast of Lublin where the SS trained Ukrainians, Latvians, and Lithuanians as "volunteers" (*Hilfswillige*, or *Hiwi*) in a former sugar factory. The men were trained to augment the skeleton crew in the annihilation camps and to provide support to the Order Police in rounding up and guarding Jews as well as in fighting partisans. They were picked on the basis of their anti-communist and anti-Semitic convictions, which they often displayed with such ferocity that even the Germans were astonished.

A great deal has been written about the role of eastern anti-Semitism in aiding the extermination process. It is generally admitted that eastern anti-Semitism was primarily nationalistic rather than racial, expressing itself differently depending on the degree to which nations had succeeded in gaining a strong sense of national self-identity and assimilating their Jewish populations. Eastern European governments reacted differently, with some willing to discriminate or persecute their Jews, even turning a blind eye to periodic pogroms, but none advocating or endorsing the cold-blooded extermination of all the Jews that the Germans favored. In the judgment of Vago and Mosse, "the bureaucratic cold-blooded 'Final Solution' was a German and not an eastern European invention."[184] The fact that anti-Semitism was endemic in eastern Europe, however, meant that the Germans were always able to find enough supporters, inside or outside the government, who were only too glad to help them get rid of their Jews. As one Holocaust survivor pointed out, "For years the Poles have been dreaming of getting rid of the Jews and now at last Hitler does it for them.... At bottom they are delighted, however horrified by the inhuman cruelty. The Krauts devouring the Kikes: what could be sweeter."[185] Although Polish anti-Semitism was not of the annihilatory kind, it was sufficiently strong in a nationalistic and religious sense to help the German killers. Even the Polish underground was strongly anti-Jewish, which accounts for the fact that few resistance groups came to the aid of the Jews and sometimes killed Jews who had escaped from the ghettos.

After the Germans invaded and occupied the Baltic countries, European Russia, the Ukraine, Caucasus, and Crimea, they always found willing collaborators in these areas who did not mind becoming close partners in crime.[186] The SS routinely employed Baltic, White Russian, and Ukrainian personnel in rounding up Jews, guarding them in the concentration camps, and then exterminating them in the gas chambers. Finding partners in crime served a triple purpose: it made killing more efficient, enmeshed non-Germans in mass murder, and relieved the primary perpetrators from bearing sole responsibility.

In general terms, the Germans were most successful in flushing out the Jewish population in countries they directly controlled and that had strong authoritarian, fascistic, and anti-Semitic traditions. This was particularly true of Poland and most southeastern European countries such as Slovakia, Croatia, Hungary, Romania, and Bulgaria. The latter were satellite nations that responded differently to German pressures regarding the Jews. All of them, however, issued various anti-Semitic types of legislation between 1939 and 1941. Slovakia and Croatia were puppet states set up by the Nazis in 1939 and in 1941 respectively. The Slovakian government, headed by Jozef Tiso in Bratislava, was a clerical-fascist regime that curried favor with the Nazis and willingly let the Germans deport most of the country's Jews.[187] Slovakia also had an extremely pro-German ultranationalistic and anti-Semitic movement, the Hlinka Guard, that favored the elimination of Slovakian Jews and actively participated in the deportation procedures of the country's ninety-two thousand Jews. Tisa's deputy prime minister and foreign minister, Vojtech Tuka, became the spokesman for radical anti-Jewish measures and the instigator of denaturalization, expropriation, and deportation procedures against Slovakian Jews in 1942. The former Yugoslavia had been divided into three puppet regimes; Croatia, led by the Fascist Ante Pavelić; Serbia, ruled by a military collaborator, General Milan Nedić; and Montenegro, governed by a council of local profascists under Italian control.[188] Ante Pavelić and his ultranationalist and secessionist party, called Ustaša, plunged Croatia into a bloodbath by murdering countless Serbs, Muslims, Jews, and Gypsies. Croatian Jews were subjected to Nuremberg-like racial laws, expropriated, denaturalized, driven into concentration camps, and eventually exterminated. In Serbia, ruled by German military occupation forces, the Jewish population came under direct control of the German authorities, which meant that they were caught in a maelstrom of accelerated persecution and extermination. Few Serbian Jews received any help from the Serbs or escaped to join the partisans. Of Serbia's Jewish population of 145,000, over 90 percent were exterminated.

In Hungary, where Miklós Horthy governed in an old-fashioned dictatorial but not a totalitarian manner, the Jews were subjected to discrimination rather than persecution.[189] Cooperation with Germany was lukewarm, although Hungary had committed itself to specific economic and military obligations. As in most southeastern European nations, there were strong fascistic and anti-Semitic groups in Hungary, notably the Arrow Cross Party led by Ferenc Szálasi. When Hungary tried to bolt Hitler's Axis coalition, the Germans helped job the Arrow Cross Party into power and accelerated the anti-Jewish campaign, eventually eliminating over 70 percent of Hungarian Jewry. Although the majority of Hungary's Jews had been spared until the summer of 1944, the onslaught came quickly and with devastating consequences between the spring and fall of 1944.[190] Eichmann's henchmen, supported by Hungarian fascists, quickly rounded up as many Jews as they could lay their hands on, deported some 437,000 Jews directly to Auschwitz, and gassed them quickly. Out of Hungary's total population of 825,000 Jews 600,000 were exterminated.

Marshal Antonescu of Romania, who succeeded the discredited government of King Carol in September 1940, originally governed the country in cooperation with the fascistic Iron Guard, a rabidly anti-Jewish right-wing party, and instituted various anti-Jewish measures, including forced labor service.[191] Raul Hilberg has shown that, next to Germany, no other country was involved in massacres of Jews on such a massive scale as Romania.[192] The Romanians eagerly cooperated with the *Einsatzgruppen* in the Crimea and southern Ukraine, massacring twenty-six thousand Jews in Odessa alone. When the Romanians joined the Germans in the war against Russia, Antonescu deployed Romanian police and army units to help the Germans annihilate the Jews of Bessarabia, the Bukovina, and southern Russia, but he refused to cooperate with the Germans in handing over Romania's own Jews. Most of the three hundred thousand assimilated Romanian Jews survived the Holocaust. Romania's refusal to surrender most of its own assimilated Jews was by no means unique; similar refusals, hesitations, and deliberate obstructions could be seen in other countries that resented Nazi encroachment on their sovereignty. During the high tide of Nazi military successes most satellite governments or local administrations serving their occupied German masters tried to curry favor with the Nazis by passing their own anti-Semitic laws and expelling foreign Jews under their control. Most of them, however, distanced themselves from the Final Solution, and when the tide of war changed in favor of the Allied Powers, they were determined not to burn their bridges to the west and decided to resist Nazi pressures to deport their Jews.

This was certainly true in Bulgaria, where King Boris pursued a very clever and opportunistic strategy of joining the Axis without, however, following Hungary and Romania into the war with Russia.[193] Although Bulgaria enacted anti-Jewish legislation in January 1941, which declared the Jews to be a destructive foreign element within the Bulgarian nation, even the German observers in Bulgaria admitted that anti-Semitism lacked broad popular support. Bulgarian cooperation with Germany on Jewish deportation was limited to the territories Bulgaria had occupied in Macedonia and Thrace. The Bulgarians evacuated about eleven thousand Jews from these areas, but they refused to deport their own Jews when the Germans approached them in 1943. By that time the fortunes of war had shifted, making it easier for the Bulgarians to turn down the SS killers.

In the end, the fate of the European Jews resided not so much in the various Judeophobic traditions of individual nations but in the degree of control the Germans were able to exert in persuading or forcing foreign or occupied governments to surrender their Jewish populations. The Germans made most headway in Poland, occupied Russia, and southeastern Europe — in short, in those areas where German military power provided the greatest protective umbrella under which the genocidal killers could operate most effectively against their victims. It was this coercive factor rather than local anti-Semitism, geographic dispersion or concentration of Jews, or political-ideological commitment to fascism that proved to be the decisive factor.

As long as the Italian army protected the Jews from the Final Solution in areas under its control (Albania, Montenegro, Greece, etc.), the Jews in these areas did not have to fear imminent deportation; as soon as Mussolini fell from power, however, the Germans pounced on the Jews in all of these countries and dispatched most of them to the death camps.[194] Local fascist collaborators throughout Europe such as Quisling's Nasjonal Samling's Party in Norway, Rexists in Belgium, and similar pro-Nazi groups in Denmark, Holland, and France played an important role, as did local prejudices against the Jews, but the real impetus to destruction resided in German power and the degree to which countries succumbed to it. The reason why the Jews of Denmark were saved was due to the absence of most of the previously mentioned obstacles to German control.[195] Although Denmark was an occupied country, the Germans exercised only loose control; they permitted the Danes to retain the monarchy, which became a rallying point in their opposition to Nazi demands. Denmark had neither a tradition of Judeophobia nor a sizeable Jewish community. Nor did Denmark have any refugee Jews because the Danish government had imposed very tight limitations on immigration in the 1930s. When the Nazis tried to round up the Danish Jews, the Danish government, having been forewarned, acted quickly and saved its Jewish citizens by evacuating them to nearby neutral Sweden. Belgium and Holland did not have such leeway, for both countries were directly governed and occupied by meddlesome military and civilian administrations with intrusive political and ideological agendas.[196]

France was in many ways a unique case because its role in the Jewish destruction process was roughly intermediate between the individual satellite nations and the states that the Germans directly occupied and administered.[197] France's dual position was the result of the defeat of 1940, which had resulted in the military occupation of its northern territories, including Paris, and the establishment of a dependent state in the south called Vichy France, named after the southern health resort where Marshal Pétain tried to form the nucleus of a future regenerated France. The collapse of France, the bulwark of civilized western values, had been a traumatic experience for the western world. The ensuing shock of defeat, the internal scapegoating, and the humiliations that occupation brought over the next four years caused lasting scars in France, not least of which was the distorted historical perception of a whole generation of survivors, collaborators, and resisters. The legend that Vichy France tried its best to protect the Jews is just that — a legend. Michael Marrus and Robert Paxton have exploded the myth that Vichy France was run by a clique of reactionary Frenchmen who had been coerced by the Germans into doing their nefarious bidding. The same has been shown visually by the brilliant documentary work of Marcel Ophul, entitled *The Sorrow and the Pity,* which chronicles the agony of defeat, collaboration, and resistance. Ophul's documentary shows that few people had clean hands and a good conscience in occupied France, a point that has also been made in a recent book on occupied France by Philippe Burrin.[198]

France had a prewar heritage of ugly Judeophobia, especially in right-wing and clerical circles, that stretched over centuries and included a host of brilliant literary anti-Semites with a flair for demagoguery.[199] Paxton and Marrus show that the anti-Jewish measures sponsored by Xavier Vallat, the commissioner-general for Jewish affairs, especially the infamous Statut des Juifs of October 1940, were initiated without any pressure by the Germans and reflected entirely indigenous French prejudices against the Jews.[200] Although these anti-Jewish measures must be seen in a larger context that takes into account France's economic problems and an upsurge of xenophobic, not just anti-Semitic, sentiments, they expressed the feelings and beliefs of important sections of French society. Both the Vichy government and the civilian authorities of occupied France actively cooperated in the Final Solution. In defense of most French authorities one could say that French Judeophobes were not pro-Nazi and rarely advocates of the sort of biological racism advocated by Nazi fanatics.[201] French Judeophobes for the most part were spokesmen for a homogeneous France, one in which all ethnic minorities had assimilated and become culturally French. Politically, it was incorrect to be a believer in pluralism in the 1930s or 1940s; it was "not a happy time to be different in France,"[202] certainly not if one was a foreigner, especially a Jewish foreigner.

In fact, the French authorities in occupied France insisted upon making a big distinction between a French and a foreign Jew, and they had no qualms about deporting most of the fifty-five thousand foreign Jews who had sought refuge in France. Vichy France did not do much for French Jews either, probably out of two primary motives: fear of German power and indifference to the fate of the Jews. The Vichy authorities had no qualms in deporting foreign Jews wholesale, first by herding many into internment camps and then by handing them over to the Germans. The most scandalous deportations, in 1942, concerned those of thousands of foreign Jewish children, ranging in age from three to seventeen years. All of these children were gassed at Auschwitz. By that time Vichy officials were beginning to suspect what the Final Solution really meant, prompting them to drag their feet and obstruct the German death machine. The evidence, however, clearly shows that the Germans could have never carried out their murderous designs if they had not received active support from the French administration and public services, especially police and railroad officials who rounded up Jews and made sure that the trains promptly left for their eastern destinations.[203] By the end of 1944 almost seventy-five thousand Jews had been deported from France, a catastrophe of the greatest magnitude because it involved a great civilized nation in active complicity with evil.

7. The Passivity of the Victims within an Indifferent World

The Jews, it has often been pointed out, made perfect victims because they had been conditioned to play the victimhood role for over two thousand years. Too much can be made of this point, but there is no doubt that Jewish experiences with oppression predisposed the Jews to be submissive in their relations with other people, thus considerably enhancing the advantage of the oppressor. Resistance, if attempted at all, was thereby quickly overcome. What had made the Jews historical victims has already been explained at length: it resided in a combination of religious beliefs and historical experiences that taught the Jews that violence was wrong and that resistance to organized oppression was futile for people who lived as foreigners in other nations and had no state or army of their own to defend them.

This does not mean that the Jews have always been lambs waiting for the slaughter, for they developed an arsenal of strategies in order to survive in a world dominated by others. Raul Hilberg has described this Jewish coping mechanism with its unique strategies of alleviation, evasion, paralysis, and compliance.[204] Alleviation is a response to danger or an attempt to diminish the violence that has already been initiated; it involved petition, protection payment, ransom arrangement, anticipatory compliance, relief, rescue, salvage, and reconstruction. Evasion, for most Jews over the ages, typically meant flight, while compliance meant accepting anti-Jewish measures in hopes that they might be mitigated in severity, greatly relaxed, or removed altogether. What is distinctly absent in these strategies is armed resistance. Submission to constituted authority, good or bad, has been the Jewish norm until the creation of the state of Israel. Compared to the warlike traditions of the western world, the Jews have not glamorized violence as a cultural or spiritual ideal. Their poets did not reach great lyrical epiphanies glorifying combat as a noble enterprise. The Germans, on the other hand, had made a cultural fetish of martial values, institutionalizing them in family, school, and everyday life. Was there ever a better lock and key, a more perfect fit, than this negative German-Jewish relationship? Could the perfect Nazi oppressor have found a more perfect victim than the Jew? Being confronted by murderous Nazis, the Jews fell back in vain on their traditional strategies of coping with the oppressor; they did not realize that they were not dealing with a traditional oppressor but with an exterminator pure and simple. There could be no alleviation, compliance, and ultimately no evasion or flight.

There could only be resistance, but that was foreclosed by the psychological frame of reference by which most Jews, especially their leaders, had structured their experiences. Those experiences had been flawed by a faulty psychological assessment of the oppressor's state of mind. Jews had assumed that the real problem resided in the oppressor's faulty thinking, which they believed could be corrected or modified by the victim's appeal to reason and justice. Appeals to assumed universal norms of reason and justice, however, failed to convince the oppressors and did not change their behavior. Speaking truth to the powerful did not force them to change their violent ways until confronted with an equal or stronger amount of power. This is the fallacy of victimology: it fails to see its own blindspots. Kren and Rappoport rightly point out that victims were also at fault because they mistakenly believed that they could guard their psychic innocence while at the same time trying to convince the oppressors that they were wrong and should therefore desist in oppressing them. Moreover, since a violent act of resistance would spoil the victim's innocence, it could not be considered as a viable response to oppression. In other words, "the fact that one is innocent, in the sense of not being guilty of the oppressor's accusations, clearly works against adoption of effective action because of fear that such action may contaminate or discredit one's primary claim to innocence."[205] Ironically, then, innocence became an obstacle that blocked the Jews from perceiving the mortal danger they faced from the Nazis, and changing their mode of response accordingly. In the words of one Jewish survivor, "this feeling of being innocent and yet having to suffer all this misery aroused self-pity and weakened the energy that was essential for survival."[206]

These general observations about Jewish behavior in relation to Nazi oppression are not meant to discount the fact that far more Jews than is commonly supposed actually resisted Nazi persecution.[207] The Jews resisted in the Warsaw ghetto and in well over twenty camps throughout Poland. More than fifty thousand Jews escaped into the forests of Poland and Russia, where they either linked with partisan groups or tried to fight back as well as they could under the circumstances. Revolts broke out in several extermination camps such as Sobibor, Treblinka, and Auschwitz. Unfortunately, these revolts or acts of resistance were staged by a few desperate individuals or groups lacking the material resources and support that would have been necessary to make a major difference. The Jews were poorly organized, internally divided by religious and cultural differences, and faced with overwhelming Nazi force. The Nazi killers had close to absolute power over the Jews, so that resistance was extremely difficult, if not futile; and when it was attempted at all, the Nazis retaliated massively and killed hundreds of Jewish hostages under their control. German reprisals against any act of resistance was governed by the principle of "collective responsibility," which meant that the Jewish community was automatically blamed for every act of resistance and had to surrender whatever number of hostages the Germans specified for immediate punishment, usually execution. The practice of massive retaliation persuaded Jewish leaders and councils (*Judenräte*) to oppose active resistance because it threatened the Jewish community as a whole. The example of Leo Baeck, who warned the Baum group to stop its violent activities against the Germans in May 1942, has already been mentioned. Many similar objections to active resistance were voiced by Jewish councils and their leaders all over Europe. Resisters were sometimes even labeled traitors by their own communities. Recognition of the fact that the Nazis planned to kill the whole Jewish community was blocked from conscious awareness until it was too late.

Meaningful resistance against Nazi tyranny meant more than just keeping body and soul together, taking evasive maneuvers, or even escaping the oppressor. As Raul Hilberg rightly put it, the Jews were "caught in the straitjacket of their history," precluding them from active armed resistance, and plunging them physically and psychologically into catastrophe.[208] And what made this destruction all the more horrible was the fact that the rest of the world either did nothing or was indifferent to the plight of the Jews.

We now know that the world learned about the Holocaust almost as soon as it began. There was, of course, some initial skepticism, particularly since similar atrocity stories relating to World War I had turned out afterward to be hoaxes. The real truth of the terrible secret, as Walter Laqueur rightly called the Nazi genocide, was known by more people than is commonly supposed.[209] Both Churchill and Roosevelt knew the truth. Since the British had cracked Germany's top secret military codes, enabling them to decipher Hitler's secrets, Churchill had impeccable sources that told him what the Germans were doing to the Jews. In a public broadcast to the British people on August 24, 1941, he revealed in general terms, without specifically mentioning the Jews, that "since the Mongol invasions of Europe in the sixteenth century, there has never been methodical merciless butchering on such a scale, or approaching such a scale," and he added "we are in the presence of a crime without a name."[210] Yet neither Churchill nor Roosevelt went beyond providing moral or symbolic support to the Jews. Although the War Refugee Board was established by Roosevelt in January 1944 in order to do everything possible to rescue the victims of Nazism, the board came up against massive institutional indifference and entrenched anti-Jewish prejudices, especially in the State Department. David Wyman, in his book *The Abandonment of the Jews: America and the Holocaust* (1984), mentions that America's abandonment of the Jews was the result of a complicated interplay between the political expediency of its leaders, especially Roosevelt, the obstructionist nature of some U.S. institutions, and a population that was strongly apposed to further immigration and favored tight quotas to keep foreigners out. The same, of course, could be said of all nations at the time; their borders never opened to the Jews, and any rescue efforts were mired in governmental restrictions. Recent revelations about the role of Switzerland not only in restricting immigration but also in laundering Nazi gold and swindling countless Jews out of their savings and deposits throws a particularly sinister light on the activities of the Swiss government and the nations it implicated in such immoral financial transactions.[211]

In fairness to the bystanders, few at the time could have known about the magnitude of suffering the Nazis were inflicting on the Jews. Many countries, Britain and the United States included, assumed that the German government was not much different from that of the Kaiserreich, and that its institutions were still essentially decent and civilized, Hitler and his Nazi regime notwithstanding. It was inconceivable to western statesmen that a modern state like Germany could murder six million people by assembly-line methods. As Walter Laqueur rightly pointed out, "the whole scheme was beyond human imagination."[212] Hitler's enemies not only misjudged the Nazi regime, they also showed only marginal concern for the plight of the Jews. In Raul Hilberg's judgment, the rescue of Jewry was not a priority but only a by-product of the war.[213] The rest is tragedy: with no single country behind them and no army to fight directly on their behalf, the Jews were utterly helpless to withstand the onslaught of a racist state that believed its mission was to destroy them and that was indirectly assisted in this mission by Judeophobic governments and an indifferent world.

Chapter 10

The Germans and the Holocaust in War and Peace

The "We Did Not Know and Could Not Do Anything" Legend

As the tanks of the liberating Allied Powers overran a war-torn Germany, they encountered two sharply contrasting Germanies: first, a façade of many picture postcard towns and smiling fräuleins, and then the gruesome legacy of the Nazi death camps. Almost every major camp harbored heaps of mangled and foul-smelling corpses, which presented such a revolting sight that soldiers sometimes vented their moral outrage on the Nazi guards by either shooting them or letting the inmates tear them limb from limb. The commander of the U.S. Fourth Armored Division, who liberated the slave labor camp at Ohrdruf near Gotha, rounded up the local mayor and his wife and gave them a guided tour of the camp. Given the fact that the Nazis had operated this charnel house in plain sight of the mayor's town, the U.S. commander was incredulous when the mayor told him that he knew nothing about the stench of decomposing bodies. After promising to return to the camp on the next day with all the adult villagers, the mayor and his wife, unable to face another confrontation with the truth, committed suicide. Ohrdruf was one of many death camps liberated by Allied troops in April and May 1945 that revealed the horrors of Nazi tyranny. The refrain by many Germans, then and later, was that they knew nothing of the crimes committed in their name. Ohrdruf also played a brief role in the world's press. When the supreme commander of the Allied Expeditionary Force, General Dwight D. Eisenhower, flanked by two of his major commanders, Omar Bradley and George Patton, toured the camp, he addressed his men in cold fury by saying, "I want every American unit not actually in the front lines to see this place. We are told that the American soldier does not know what he is fighting for. Now, at least, he will know what he is fighting *against*."[1]

Eisenhower and other Allied leaders had already pledged themselves to prosecute Nazi war criminals, and they made good on that promise by convening the War Crimes Tribunal at Nuremberg. The victorious powers were determined to try not only the major Nazi leaders who were still alive but also to hold the German people responsible for all the crimes committed in their name by Hitler and his henchmen. The Nuremberg trials presumed the guilt rather than the innocence of the German people. How morally or legally proper was this presumption of guilt? One could reasonably argue that in a moral sense we are all co-responsible for what our rulers do in our name and for our collective good. Citizens, however, are not criminally responsible for the crimes of their leaders. As Karl Jaspers pointed out long ago, there are degrees of guilt, just as there are degrees of responsibility that are entailed by it.[2] Guilt and responsibility presuppose knowledge of and complicity in criminal activity. What did the German people know about the Holocaust and how many of them participated in the crime?

Once the war was over, most Germans claimed widespread ignorance. No one, it seemed, knew anything directly; they only heard rumors and unconfirmed reports of atrocities in the east. In any case, what could one do, Germans later said, with reports of mass atrocities? Report them to the police? Milton Mayer, who interviewed former Nazis after the war, heard the same rhetorical self-excuse over and over again: "Who will be the first to undertake...to track down the suspicion of governmental wrongdoing under a governmental dictatorship, to occupy himself, in times of turmoil and in wartime with evils, real or rumored, that are wholly outside his own life,...outside his own power? After all, what if one found out?"[3] Hiding behind the excuse of being tiny cogs in a vicious system that forced them to do its bidding, the common refrain by ordinary Germans was: there was *Nichts dagegen zu machen* (There was nothing that could be done against it).[4] When confronted with direct complicity in criminal wrongdoing, however, many Germans claimed that they were just following orders. First came lies or denials, then the appeal to the tiny cog in the machine argument, followed by *Befehlsnotstand,* or order from higher authority. What was the real story behind these claims, and can it be unearthed beneath layers of lies, denials, evasions, repressions, deflections, and rationalizations? Is this a hopeless academic endeavor, especially if one accepts Hannah Arendt's judgment that mendacity had become an integral part of the German national character?[5] Since it is impossible to "fix" the past retroactively, and little is served by tendentious moral judgments about dead perpetrators or cowardly bystanders, we might perhaps be best served by focusing on what we do know with some degree of certainty about the reliability of public information during World War II and the likelihood that Germans were aware of this information and could assess it properly.

In order to answer the question of how many Germans knew about the Holocaust, we must begin with a series of deductions that relate to the number of people who were, directly and indirectly, involved in the crime itself. Broadly speaking, this would involve Hitler, most of the top Nazi leadership, the *Einsatzgruppen* and its auxiliaries, the SS concentration camp personnel, and the majority of the officials in various state or party agencies who handled matters relating to Jewish expropriation, legal discrimination, emigration, forced labor, ghettoization, and deportation.

Conservatively, this would include about a hundred thousand people and perhaps as many as a quarter of a million. Whatever the figure, and no one will ever know for sure, it stands to reason that so many people could not keep quiet about a crime of this magnitude. Indeed, as previously shown, countless soldiers on leave from the east, many of whom carried photographs of atrocities in their wallets, talked to loved ones who talked to others. Information about mass executions in the east leaked out quickly and was widely known by 1942.[6] Nazi propaganda, if properly decoded and assessed, left no doubt in the public mind that terrible vengeance was being visited on the Jews. The war, of course, cut off the Germans from most foreign sources of information and made them even more dependent on Nazi propaganda. Moreover, the Holocaust took place in the east and was therefore out of sight and out of mind for most Germans. Yet, Germans knew exactly how cruelly the Jews had been treated by their government, and they could not have been oblivious to the deportations that were being conducted in broad daylight and in plain sight of hundred of thousands of Germans all over the country. According to Lawrence Stokes's assessment, it seems undeniable that most of the anti-Jewish terror was widely known by the German people. After all, the endless line of trains from every part of the Reich and all over Europe, packed with hungry, thirsty, and dying Jews and heading eastward, was scarcely concealable.[7]

Although a shroud of strict secrecy had been pulled over the mass shootings and gassings, confirming that the Nazi leaders did not believe that their people were ready to accept the crime, it proved impossible to conceal the crime and its horrors for very long. The leaders of the German opposition to Hitler knew about the atrocities by the summer of 1941 and they received information about the gassings almost as soon as they began.[8] The same was true of the leaders of the Polish underground, one of whom, Jan Karski, went to Britain and then the United States to alert the western leaders, including Anthony Eden and Franklin D. Roosevelt. When Karski told them that millions of Jews were being gassed by the Germans, no one believed him; in fact, Supreme Court Justice Felix Frankfurter, who listened to Karski's story in disbelief, frankly told him: "Mr. Karski, a man like me talking to a man like you must be totally frank. So I say I am unable to believe you."[9] Karski was only one of many eyewitness observers of the Holocaust who tried desperately to alert the rest of the world to what he had seen.[10] Kurt Gerstein, as previously mentioned, was another messenger bringing the ghastly news of Jewish annihilation, as were the escapees of the death camps who informed the Polish underground, the Vatican, and the western powers.

How much of this information, however, reached the German public? According to Ian Kershaw's detailed analysis of German public opinion during World War II, the Jewish question "was of no more than minimal interest to the vast majority of Germans."[11] It appears that only when rumors circulated that the terror bombings by air were really in reprisal for German atrocities against the Jews in the east did the German people take notice of the Jewish problem. Many feared that the Jews, supported by Allied governments, might wreak terrible vengeance for what was being done to their people in eastern Europe. One German clergyman said that government reports about Soviet atrocities at Katyn, where the communists massacred over ten thousand Polish officers, should not gloss over the fact that the SS was committing similar atrocities against the Jews. The priest warned that "the terrible and inhumane treatment meted out to the Jews by the SS demands nothing short of God's punishment of our people. If these murderers do not bring bitter revenge upon us, then there is no longer any divine justice. The German people has taken such blood guilt upon itself that it cannot reckon with mercy and pardon."[12] These comments about German atrocities against the Jews, as Kershaw pointed out, referred entirely to mass shootings by the *Einsatzgruppen.* Sifting through a mass of contemporary sources, Kershaw could not find any mention of the gassings, nor any reference to the extermination camps in Poland.[13]

In order to counter rumors about Jewish exterminations, the Nazi leadership sent out ambiguous and often conflicting messages. On the one hand, Nazi propaganda justified persecution of Jews on the grounds that Jews were waging guerrilla war against German soldiers, practicing widespread sabotage and fighting shoulder to shoulder with Germany's enemies. On the other hand, Jews were declared guilty simply because they were Jews. During the war, however, a popular propaganda theme depicted the Jews as instigators of war and as deadly military opponents. This theme of Jewish warmongers surfaced periodically in the German press and illustrates the regime's ongoing need to deflect attention from its military failures as well as to justify, if only obliquely, what was being done to the Jews. Caught in its own web of mendacity, the regime never came clean publicly on what was really done to the Jews, except on one occasion when Joseph Goebbels published his infamous article in the journal *Das Reich* (November 16, 1941), entitled "The Jews Are Guilty," in which he announced that the Jews were responsible for having started the war and were now "suffering a gradual annihilation process," as foretold by the Führer's prophecy of January 30, 1939.[14] There was no need, the propaganda minister insisted, to show any sympathy for the Jews, because they were undermining the Reich. Every soldier who dies in this war, he said, would be automatically registered on the "Jewish Guilt Account." Germans who showed the slightest degree of pity were remiss in their duty and effectively committing a crime against the state. *Das Reich* had a circulation of half a million copies and appealed to an educated readership. Goebbels's message, however, fell largely on stony ground and was completely ignored at the time. In fact, the propaganda minister's remarkable admission was also ignored by postwar historians, including Gerald Reitlinger and Raul Hilberg, the first historians to write accounts of the Nazi genocide.

How do we account for this widespread indifference to the Jewish problem on this as well as on other occasions? In the first place, the German public had become satiated by the rhetorical exaggerations of Nazi propaganda to the point of tuning them out or downplaying their significance. This may have happened on the occasion of Goebbels's article as well.[15] In the second place, it is impossible to expect people at the time to have been endowed with such insights and powers of imagination that they could have extrapolated from what they knew to be overblown Nazi propaganda the actual truth of Jewish mass extermination. The first president of the German Federal Republic, Theodor Heuss, a staff member of *Das Reich,* later explained that most educated Germans simply could not comprehend the dimensions of this genocide because their imagination did not exceed the boundaries set by their conventional middle-class and Christian presuppositions.[16] A similar view was expressed by West Germany's former chancellor Helmut Schmidt, who served in the German army on the eastern front and angrily rejected the accusation by some historians that the German army took an active role in the genocide against the Jews. Having served on the eastern front, he said, he would have heard about atrocities that were allegedly committed either under the protective umbrella of the Wehrmacht or by Wehrmacht personnel themselves. Schmidt claimed that ordinary German soldiers were essentially leading segregated, even ghettoized, lives that separated them from the Jewish victims and kept them limited strictly to their own military sphere of action.[17]

In retrospect, the validity of this argument must be rejected, but its psychological import is clear: Schmidt and a generation of Germans were and still are in denial about their own role in the Third Reich as active participants or passive onlookers. They saw and heard enough of the truth but subsequently disassociated themselves from what they saw and heard. This defensive maneuver permeated both the war and postwar period; its successive stages have recently been characterized by a German historian as *Nichtgenauwissenwollen* (not wanting to know exactly), *Nichtertragenwollen* (not wanting to stomach it), and *Nichtwahrhabenwollen* (not wanting it to be true).[18] Germans did not want to know; but when confronted with the truth, they either willfully denied the truth or deflected it psychologically by making use of such mental defenses as projection, scapegoating, repression, or comparative trivialization. Thus, the Jews just "disappeared," many claimed; they were "just being resettled in the east" to do some honest work. In any case why worry about a few Jews when millions of Germans died in faraway places or when hundreds of thousands of civilians perished as a result of Allied terror bombings from the air? In short, the German people did not concern themselves with the fate of the Jews. Except for a few sympathetic bystanders, whose diaries or memoirs represent a small oasis of insight and courage, there is little evidence of public concern, shame, or anger about the way in which Jews were being treated. For those who deeply cared, there was little to do but to record their own impotence and their own shame for future generations. One Berliner who helped Jews and knew how they were exterminated wrote:

> The horror is so indescribable, that the imagination refuses to accept its reality. Something fails to click. Some conclusion is simply not drawn. Between knowledge in theory and practical application to individual cases...there is an unbridgeable gulf....We don't permit our power of imagination to connect the two, even remotely. Could we continue to live if we realized that our mother, our brother, our friend, our lover, enduring inconceivable suffering, was being tortured to death?...Is it cowardice that lets us think that way? Maybe! But then such cowardice belongs to the primeval instincts of man. If we could visualize death, life as it exists would be impossible. One can imagine torture, horror, and suffering as little as death....Such indifference alone makes continued existence possible. Realizations such as these are bitter, shameful and bitter. They admit that we also do not belong to the strong and proud who arise to begin a great crusade against injustice. Who in the world stood up to revenge the agony of a hundred thousand murdered Armenians? Who rebelled against the tortures of the Inquisition? The news of the massacre of Jews spread around the world. Did breakfast agree less with a single person as a result? Did living become impossible for anyone because the plight of the martyred shocked them and tore at their conscience?[19]

This pained reaction explains, but, of course, does not excuse, passivity or indifference. It also seems to reveal that in most historical crises societies, like individuals, rarely recognize the depth of the crisis because they seek refuge in self-protective psychological attitudes.[20] If the few courageous Germans withdrew into despair and engaged, at best, in small acts of opposition and the majority took a moral sleeping pill, who was left to commit mass murder? The answer is the hardcore of the Nazi movement and all those who were persuaded to condone the murderous project. Their numbers cannot be exactly ascertained, nor is it possible to measure the degree of Judeophobic intensity involved in individual cases. It is also difficult, if not impossible, to distinguish in most cases whether the motives that drove the killers were the result of violent Judeophobia, obedience to authority, careerism, or sadism.

In trying to measure what is probably immeasurable and working with scraps of evidence, deductions, and plain hunches, it should not surprise us that historians have been unable to agree on how strong Judeophobia was among the general population. One emerging consensus, however, indicates that the German people did not subscribe to the biological-racial Jew-hatred of the Nazi leadership. Even under Nazi rule Judeophobia was not made out of whole cloth. One still has to distinguish between traditional Judeophobia that aimed at discriminatory measures and Hitler's biological Judeophobia that aimed at annihilation.[21] Nor can one neglect, even during wartime, the continued persistence of Christian Judeophobia, for that explains, at least in part, the failure of religious institutions during the Holocaust. Nazi propaganda had succeeded in indoctrinating a far greater number of Germans in Judeophobic prejudices than ever before but failed in fanaticizing the majority to participate in the annihilatory Jew-hatred of the sort that had infected the Nazi ruling elite. Goebbels, Himmler, and other top Nazi leaders constantly complained about the lack of fanaticism on the part of ordinary Germans when it came to the Jews. We have already cited Goebbels's frustrations on this issue, especially his exasperation when he heard that Berliners showed sympathy with the Jews when they had to wear the yellow star. On October 4, 1944, Himmler complained to his SS *Gruppenführer* that many people, party members included, "send their precious plea for clemency to me or some other authority; they invariably say that all Jews are, of course, swine but that Mr. So-and-so is the exception, a decent Jew who should not be touched."[22] Two days later, in his infamous address to a convention of *Reichsleiter* and *Gauleiter* at Posen, he referred to the extermination of the Jews as a glorious page in German history, but at the same time expressed frustration over "all the 80 million Germans, every one of whom had his decent Jew."[23] The best judgment on the nature of public Judeophobia in Nazi Germany and its effects is that of Norman Cohn, who argued that "the majority was conditioned not so much to fanatical hatred as to utter indifference."[24] This was no small achievement, for it was all that the murderers needed by way of public support to carry out their crime.

Throughout World War II, the majority of Germans continued to hold strong anti-Jewish prejudices of a discriminatory but not an exterminatory nature. Such popular discriminatory Judeophobia had little to do with causing the Holocaust. The German people did not collectively decide to launch the Holocaust; their fanatical leaders initiated the crime in great secrecy, indicating clearly that they were unsure of widespread popular support. Hitler and his genocidal henchmen invested in the prevailing public prejudices against the Jews, not because they expected a full return in the form of popular approval, which could not be harvested from discriminatory Judeophobia in any case, but because it allowed them to intensify their own radical measures, knowing that the public would probably not make much of a fuss about what was being done to the Jews. Ian Kershaw saw this quite clearly when he said that "the latent anti-Semitism and apathy of the German people sufficed to allow the increasingly criminal 'dynamic' hatred of the Nazi regime the autonomy it needed to set in motion the Holocaust."[25]

From Collective Guilt to Collective Repression

In the summer of 1945, posters appeared in many German towns and villages proclaiming: "You are guilty!"[26] These posters showed pictures and stories from Belsen concentration camp, causing widespread horror and anxiety among the general public for several reasons. The pictures were horrible and shocking, the accusation "You are guilty" made people uneasy because it was directed against all Germans, and the fact that the displays were not signed by any authority prompted feelings of uncertainty about who was passing such sweeping judgments. Germans quickly found out that the victorious Allied Powers, claiming to speak on behalf of the victims of Nazism, were not only making these judgments but planned to hold the Germans accountable for the crimes they committed. The Germans themselves were in no position to judge themselves because their country had been occupied and divided up by their enemies. Whether they liked it or not, they would have to get used to being judged by the Americans, Russians, British, and French, either acting in concert or following their own legal, political, or moral codes of justice. What followed, as is commonly known, was a period of about four years (1945–49) during which concerted efforts were made to punish those Germans who had been responsible for plunging the world into war and for having perpetrated unspeakable crimes against the people who fell under their control.

Since the scope of Nazi crimes was so extensive, involving millions of victims who were dead, unaccounted for, or difficult to enlist as witnesses, it was not easy to identify and punish the guilty. This task was made even more difficult by the fact that Germany's defeat had caused utter devastation and a complete breakdown of all its institutions. In the wake of this breakdown, there was widespread confusion by everyone concerned, by dazed Germans and befuddled military authorities alike. The country was beset by staggering socioeconomic problems, not least of which were the millions of bombed-out families and the well over twenty million "displaced persons" of many different nationalities. It was in this chaotic atmosphere that the victorious powers convened the War Crimes Tribunal at Nuremberg to judge those Nazi leaders who had been responsible for committing war crimes and crimes against humanity. A great deal has been written about the Nuremberg proceedings against the well-known twenty-one Nazi leaders, countless lesser-known henchmen, and the criminal institutions with which they were affiliated, chiefly the SS. It is commonly agreed that the trials served a useful purpose in highlighting the inhumanity of the Nazi regime and in trying to mete out justified punishment.[27]

The trials, however, were a failure on two important counts: they did not persuade the German people that justice had been dispensed and they prosecuted only a very small number of perpetrators. Although the crimes against the Jews were prominently featured for a short period of time, the Nuremberg Tribunal and related trials were conducted by victorious governments that did not represent the interests of the Jews but their own national interests. At Nuremberg the Holocaust was a peripheral issue; its significance was not recognized by anyone outside the Jewish community, least of all by the Germans themselves.

As previously mentioned, the Germans were in no position to judge themselves, and many did their best to evade judgment altogether. Their former leaders presented a pathetic spectacle at Nuremberg, denouncing the trial as victor's justice and dodging behind a series of defensive postures that included *Befehlsnotstand* (forced to take orders), comparative trivialization, and the plea of general ignorance about alleged crimes. When not engaged in deflecting personal responsibility, they attacked each other for having lost battles or having failed to perform duties as administrative or military leaders. Some of the major leaders appeared to show twinges of conscience and a recognition that they had been willing participants in the crimes of Nazism. Hans Frank rededicated himself to Roman Catholicism and confessed openly, much to the consternation of his fellow defendants, that "a thousand years will pass and this guilt of Germany will not be erased."[28] Albert Speer accepted full responsibility for his own role in Nazi Germany, a position that prompted disgust on the part of his fellow defendants and suspicion on the part of his accusers.[29] The Allied judges or attorneys could be forgiven for showing skepticism when confronted by belated pleas or confessions, suspecting that these might be prompted by self-serving motives on the part of the perpetrators to enhance their self-importance or to please the accusers and persuade them to be more lenient.

If the Nazi leaders did not come clean in the immediate postwar world, neither did the majority of the German people. Except for a few religious and intellectual figures who called for a period of atonement and deep moral reflection, the majority was too preoccupied with sheer survival to spend much time on what had happened during the past twelve years. Traumatized by war and economic ruin, ordinary people acted defensively and often defiantly, particularly when their new masters unfolded various conflicting strategies to punish and reeducate them. One British official stated in 1945 that the German people lacked "the moral acceptance of defeat,"[30] which he found quite shocking given the fact that the Germans had caused so much suffering and devastation. In the eyes of many occupation officials, the German people were easily controllable but proved defiant when confronted with past crimes. The Germans showed little understanding of what they had done; they showed little humility and sloughed off the pain and suffering they had caused to others by wallowing in their own self-pity. It dawned on the more perspicacious Allied officials that Nazism had had a far greater support among the German people than they suspected; in fact, most Germans had found the Nazi regime quite tolerable and beneficial. After all, Hitler had taken Germany out of the Great Depression and restored the country's prestige at home and abroad; even during the war, Germans lived much better than most Europeans. They had plenty of food, raw materials, industrial goods, and slave labor — making them better off than their enemies, except the Americans.[31] There was, of course, a great deal of whining and self-pity afterward by ordinary Germans who claimed that they had been caught in a totalitarian web and had suffered much at the hands of both their own government and their enemies. The notion of "victim Germany" was born not in the 1990s but at the very moment of Germany's defeat in 1945. Having suffered so much at the hands of their own criminal regime and that of their enemies, many Germans, then and now, believed that the suffering already inflicted on them ought to remove the stigma of collective responsibility or guilt.

In the immediate postwar period questions of punishment, responsibility, and guilt resided squarely in the hands of the victors, who pursued five broad goals in dealing with the Germans: punishing the guilty, denazifying the German people, imposing reparations as a means of restitution, reconstructing the German political system, and reeducating the Germans to a different way of life. Punishment and denazification proceeded by fits and starts because the victorious powers were divided by different ideological and cultural traditions. German intransigence added to the difficulties. The Soviets, who had occupied much of eastern Germany, had their own ideas about how they could bring *their* Germans into the communist sphere of control; the Americans, the British, and the French, though loosely agreeing to democratize *their* Germans, had different conceptions about how this could be accomplished. All of them agreed to punish and to "denazify" Germany by identifying the guilty, punishing them, and excluding them permanently from public office. This was done by dividing the whole population into five categories: (1) major offenders, punishable by death or life imprisonment; (2) offenders, sentenced to a maximum of ten years; (3) lesser offenders, to be placed on probation; (4) followers who went along with the Nazi regime; and (5) exonerated persons. Although denazification was placed in the hands of German tribunals (*Spruchkammer*), the Allied Powers supervised the overall process. Germans quickly learned to manipulate the proceedings; they gave evasive answers and mocked the elaborate questionnaires they had to fill out. Many later admitted that the process had often been an elaborate whitewash. Too many people, it was said, had received *Persilscheine*, testimonials named after the detergent Persil, that allowed perpetrators to take their brown shirts to the laundry and get them back clean and white. All they had to do was to ask priests, former anti-Nazis, or Jewish survivors to write them testimonials attesting to their sterling character.

Although many heavy offenders were punished and imprisoned, equally as many, if not more, got off scot free. A thorough denazification never took place because the pollution was simply too extensive. Many Allied officials openly quipped that if the victorious powers had actually tried to convict every Nazi most Germans would have to be thrown in prison. Some also wondered whether a national purge might not destabilize the country, plunging it into a prolonged period of internecine recrimination and social conflict and thus making it impossible either to govern it or to move it toward self-government. Among the British and the French, who were not as ideologically committed to a single worldview as the Americans and the Soviets, there was also considerable soul-searching about converting the Germans to a correct way of life. As one British official, who represented the British Education Branch in Germany, admitted "it would be the height of arrogance to assume that victory somehow gave us the moral right to impose our way of life.... In any case how could one educate an already civilized nation that had produced some of the greatest geniuses and benefactors of mankind."[32]

If the British and the French were less inclined to launch far-reaching plans of political or cultural reorientation in Germany, the Soviets and the Americans increasingly saw Germany as a proving ground for the superiority of their own way of life. In 1949 two separate Germanies came into being: a Soviet-dominated German Democratic Republic (GDR) and an American-dominated Federal Republic of Germany (FRG). The Soviets despoiled the economic infrastructure of their zone, while the Americans invested in it as part of a broad European project of economic reconstruction. The Marshall Plan, which pumped close to thirteen billion dollars into war-torn Europe, not only laid the foundation of European economic recovery but ultimately helped win the Cold War against the short-sighted and flawed economic policies of the Soviet Union. The impact of the Marshall plan on West Germany was nothing less than spectacular. The massive infusion of American money, combined with sound economic management (*soziale Marktwirtschaft*) and the energy and hard work of the German people, produced over a decade of sustained growth and material affluence. In addition to financial aid and German know-how, the economic "miracle" of the 1950s and '60s was also the result of a collective displacement of psychological guilt into economic reconstruction. It seemed as though the Germans could not move fast enough to clear away the rubble of their pulverized cities and industries because they represented visible reminders of defeat and shame. Putting their shoulders to the economic wheel was one way of repressing the Nazi past. Another means of escaping the past was offered by the Cold War. Germans on both sides were being courted as allies, which made it easier and more convenient to gloss over past misdeeds or crimes. For the Americans the new Nazis were the communists, but in fact the real Nazis worked with the Americans against the communists. Most Germans also welcomed the opportunity of using the Cold War as an escape into forgetful silence. In short, the Cold War and the division of Germany into a communist east and a capitalist-democratic west put an end to any real soul-searching about what would later be called the unmastered past. The question of German guilt, revolving around the Holocaust, remained in a kind of suspended animation until a new generation, educated in freedom, began to chip away at the wall of silence their parents had raised to repress the past.

Even during the years of silence, however, the governments of West and East Germany acknowledged the crimes that had been committed against the Jews. Both sides provided various reasons for why it had happened and stated their official policies regarding the Jews. The Bonn Republic, headed by its wily, prowestern, and Catholic chancellor Konrad Adenauer, assumed complete responsibility for what had been done during the Third Reich because it considered itself as the only legitimate heir to the German Reich. Adenauer and subsequent West German leaders adopted a pro-Jewish (philo-Semitic) position and pledged to make amends by paying reparations to the victims of Nazism. This policy of reparation was referred to as *Wiedergutmachung* (making amends). It was formulated by Adenauer in a famous speech to the Bundestag in September 1951 and was subsequently embodied in treaty form between West Germany and the state of Israel. By the terms of the final settlement (September 1952), the West German government agreed to pay 3 billion marks to the state of Israel and 450 million to Jewish organizations representing Jews inside and outside Israel.[33] The whole concept of making amends, which was strongly criticized by many German and Jewish leaders as "blood money" that no self-respecting nation should either pay out or accept, was actually a brilliant strategy on Adenauer's part because it served two vital purposes: legitimizing the Bonn government and handling the problem of German guilt by government decree. By accepting responsibility for the crimes of Nazism, the Bonn government and its conservative Christian leaders captured both the moral and nationalistic high ground, tacitly saying that as the legitimate heir to the German nation they were willing to make amends for the terrible wrongs that had been committed by a Nazi government that represented an aberrant exception in German history.

But the strategy of making amends had another and perhaps more far-ranging implication that has been neglected by historians: its peculiar German approach to the problem of guilt. Whether Adenauer consciously intended it or not, he was trying to solve the problem of guilt by authoritarian means, for it was the state that took the responsibility rather than its individual citizens. The old wily chancellor and good Catholic took the institutional way out of a dilemma that should perhaps have been placed on the shoulders of individual Germans themselves. If the state accepted responsibility for the crimes of Nazism, was there any reason why individual Germans should make amends? Would ordinary Germans interpret this state-sponsored act of atonement as implying that there was very little for them to do since the state was already doing it for them? What institutional mechanisms did Adenauer put in place to make it possible so that individual Germans, singly and collectively, could work through their guilt rather than repress it? The answer is that, apart from strong anti-discriminatory laws that put limits on free speech when it threatened democracy, very little was done by West Germans to work through and publicly express the kind of amends that transcended state regulations or reparations and resulted in a change of heart and mind.

In fairness to the Bonn government, it must be said that the East German government was far more remiss in honestly coming to terms with the Nazi past. The communist leaders, also relying on authoritarian solutions, tried to obviate guilt through ideological sleight of hand by arguing that National Socialism was an extreme form of capitalist imperialism and a plot against the working people. The communist left, they argued, had nothing to do with Nazi crimes against the Jews and was therefore automatically absolved from responsibility by the communist government of East Germany. For that reason, East Germany refused to pay any reparations to the victims of Nazism.

The resolution of the Jewish problem in both cases was by government fiat, and so was the predictable consequence: the past was inadequately dealt with either by ideological evasion or by what Anson Rabinbach called "moral amnesia."[34] Both East and West Germans refused to grapple with the Nazi legacy. Important research on Hitler and National Socialism took place in Britain, France, and the United States rather than in Germany, where historians were reluctant to reopen old wounds and where the relevant documents were difficult to obtain because they had been taken away by the victorious powers and stored in faraway places. Until the late 1960s German schools continued past practices of neglecting the importance of contemporary history in favor of more remote historical periods, thereby making it conveniently difficult to confront the recent Nazi past. My own Gymnasium history text contained one short paragraph on "fanatical Jew hatred" (*Fanatischer Judenhass*) between 1933 and 1939 and three sentences on the "Final Solution to the Jewish Question" in a paragraph on National Socialist domination of Europe, which read: "During these years Hitler decided the Final Solution of the Jewish Question. Millions of Jews came to a terrible end in the concentration camps. These brutal murders were carried out in the strictest secrecy."[35] It goes without saying that the class never got around to discussing this issue.

The fact that the Holocaust played no significant role in German historical circles was not surprising because most academically trained historians in the postwar period were tied in one way or another to the Nazi regime. They were also trained in the elevated style of historicism that taught its practitioners to strive toward rhetorical elegance and scientific precision and focus for its subject matter on *Geistesgeschichte* (history of ideas) or diplomatic history rather than on the hell of tortures, mass shootings, or gassings. There was also widespread suspicion that the evidence controlled by the victors might be tainted, unreliable, and propagandistic. More time was needed, it was argued, to gain a critical perspective; in the meantime, it might be academically and pedagogically wiser to limit scholarship to the non-judgmental level of documentary collection and leave moral judgments to future generations.

Either by default or by design, German historians let the outside world control the scholarly debate on Hitler and the Third Reich well into the 1960s. One bright light was the establishment of the Institut für Zeitgeschichte in Munich, a research and archival center that specializes in topics and material dealing with National Socialism and publishes a scholarly journal called *Vierteljahreshefte für Zeitgeschichte.* One of the institute's original pioneers, Hans Rothfels, provided the impetus for a series of fine articles on the Final Solution with the publication of the Gerstein Report. This was followed by a number of excellent contributions on Nazi crimes by Martin Broszat, Helmut Krausnick, and Helmut Heiber. On the public level, however, Germans were unable to read a single Holocaust book in German. One of the earliest, and still most comprehensive, works on the Holocaust, by Raul Hilberg, published originally in English in 1962, was not translated into German until 1982 — twenty years later and thirty-seven years after the Holocaust.[36] If any book on the Holocaust made an impression on the German public at large, it was the *Diary of Anne Frank* and the subsequent motion picture that was based on her tragic short life under Nazi control. Fleetingly, at least, Germans were forced to associate a young innocent face with the evils perpetrated by their former Nazi masters, an association too close for comfort for many of them. This is why German victims always received top billing whenever the topic of collective suffering was raised in the public forum. There was also undue emphasis on the conservative resistance to Hitler, which was minimal and ineffective. Finally, there was a concerted effort to project all the blame for Nazi crimes onto the SS.

By demonizing the SS as the sole perpetrator of the Holocaust, German apologists could absolve other institutions from being criminally responsible. This is how the myth of the clean Wehrmacht came into being in the immediate postwar period. Ordinary soldiers and their commanding officers, the legend claimed, kept their distance from Adolf Hitler and the Nazi regime and merely did their duty as German soldiers. They fought bravely and heroically against overwhelming odds and were completely unaware of any atrocities that were being committed by the SS behind the fighting front.[37] For well over a quarter of a century after World War II the German mass media manufactured a popular image of the Wehrmacht that bore little resemblance to the actual reality. In illustrated magazines, cheap war novels, and films the war was always portrayed as an exciting adventure in which millions of courageous Germans manned the Stukas, tanks, and fighting ships and battled against an enemy who won only because he had ten times as many men and an infinite industrial resource base on which he could draw. The poor German GI was therefore doomed from the start, yet he fought on bravely and always kept faith with his comrades. Not a word in all of this about the annihilation of Jews and other racially inferior "subhumans." Instead, the perpetrators were actually perceived as victims. But victims of what? Presumably of a mad Führer and his fanatical helpers, but anyone looking for clear-cut confrontation with Nazism will be sadly disappointed because the tragedy of military defeat was usually shrouded in the mass media in purposeful ambiguity. In fact, the impression one gains from this mass of popular and often sentimental *kitsch* is an entirely apologetic message: despite the horrors of war and the ensuing ruin of the country, a positive legacy can be identified in the form of comradeship to the death and the noble campaign against communism.

The Cold War reinforced some of these popular attitudes because it gave the Hitler Youth generation an opportunity to transform itself into self-righteous cold warriors, reminding their children that they had been anti-communists all along. No such argument, of course, could be made in East Germany, where everybody had been victimized (the government maintained) by fascism and was duty-bound to wall out western capitalism. On both sides of the wall the repression was complete. The Cold War furnished the convenient objectives of repression and the energy was expended in either walling out western capitalism or in walling in communism through "containment." What this did, however, was to delay the process of denazification, restitution, and justice.

Given these historical circumstances, it should not surprise us that the beliefs and values that had shaped the Third Reich were not swept away in 1945 but lingered on into the postwar period and continued, also in transmuted form, to influence a new generation. In order to understand the German-Jewish problem in the post-Holocaust period, it is of great importance to realize that Nazi Germany has not passed into history but is alive in the political debates and the historical consciousness of the present.[38] The ghost of Hitler and National Socialism has not been laid to rest, and that includes the racial hatred and bigotry Nazism spewed forth for over twenty-five years. The utter defeat and discredit of Nazism in 1945 entailed the defeat of biological racism of the sort that Hitler propounded. But this did not mean that Judeophobia was also rooted out once and for all in Germany. Biological-racial Judeophobia may have been discredited and legally prohibited in Germany, but other forms of Judeophobia have survived and even flourished in the postwar period. The attitudes of many Germans about the Jews changed only slowly, and in some cases remained intractable to correction.

Since the German defeat of 1945, numerous surveys of public opinion, first by the western powers and then by various German research institutes, have been conducted to gauge the nature and extent of Judeophobic prejudices among the general population. The original opinion polls, conducted by the Office of the Military Government for Germany, United States (OMGUS), presented a curious mixture of past prejudices and apparent changes of beliefs and attitudes. Since they were conducted by a military occupation force that wielded absolute power over a conquered and disoriented population, questions have naturally been raised about their scientific validity.[39] It may have been in order to please the authorities that there were no respondents who agreed with the statement that "Hitler was right in his treatment of Jews." In the same sample of Hitler's racial policies toward the Jews, 77 percent of the respondents agreed with the statement that "the actions against the Jews were in no way justified"; only 19 percent agreed with the statement that "Hitler went too far in his treatment of the Jews, but something had to be done to keep them in bounds."[40] A subsequent poll, indicating a shifting mood of denial, disbelief, and confusion, showed that 37 percent of the respondents disagreed with the statement "Extermination of the Jews and Poles and other non-Aryans was not necessary for the security of the Germans." The disparity between the two polls is obvious because zero percent disapproved of the actions taken against the Jews on the one hand and 37 percent, or over one-third, of the respondents favored extermination to preserve German security. The disparity could be explained by arguing that the sample was poorly written. As Sarah Gordon points out, the implicit double negative (no I don't agree) may have meant for some respondents that yes they did agree that extermination was not necessary.[41] The OMGUS surveys were generally encouraging because they seemed to indicate that Germans were relatively free of Judeophobia. Even on the question of racial intermarriage, a key indicator of racial prejudice, 91 percent of the respondents answered that a German should not be condemned if he married a non-Aryan. Another survey showed that 94 percent of respondents believed that all those who had committed or participated in the murder of civilians should be tried, and 72 percent felt that Hitler should have been tried and was wrong to shoot himself.[42]

Subsequent surveys, conducted over the past fifty years by the Institut für Demoskopie in Allensbach, give us a more pessimistic picture about the persistence of anti-Jewish prejudices among the general population in West Germany. In 1947 three-quarters of Germans considered the Jews to belong to a different race, a figure that stayed remarkably stable over the next twenty years. In 1961, 73 percent still agreed that the Jews were a different race than the Germans.[43] On the question of interracial marriages, a similar pattern of prejudice emerged: in 1949, a strong majority of German men and women, 67 percent and 73 percent respectively, answered no to the question "would you marry a man (woman) of Jewish origin." Twelve years later the figures had dropped only to 47 and 60 percent respectively.[44] For all his destructive legacy, Hitler was rated positively by a third of the respondents in 1952; in the same year, a hefty 88 percent of Germans claimed that they had no personal responsibility for mass exterminations. As late as 1978 over a third held that Nazi Germany had not been all that bad.[45]

In tracing the public mood over two decades, several encouraging features could also be identified. In the first place, it became clear that strong anti-Jewish prejudices were linked to the older generation, particularly those who could be categorized as the Hitler Youth generation, which includes those who were born between 1919 and 1931 and received most of their essential values under the influence of National Socialism.[46] Germans who were socialized after World War II have shown increasingly fewer anti-Jewish prejudices. The process of democratization, which proceeded steadily in West Germany in the postwar period, together with the availability of greater educational opportunities, also worked against anti-Jewish and illiberal tendencies. Even in the quiet 1950s, popular Judeophobia played little role in German society. Nazism had collapsed, and with it had any anti-Semitic political movement. Since there were hardly any Jews left, the old hatred of Jews existed in a vacuum. Frederick Weil has argued that "it is only a slight exaggeration to say that anti-Jewish prejudice in Germany since 1945 is a paradox; for it exists without anti-Semites and without Jews."[47] This paradox becomes all the more startling when we realize that despite the physical absence of a significant Jewish presence in postwar Germany old anti-Jewish stereotypes continued to operate among the older generation. More importantly, the problems associated with the Nazi past remained unresolved, buried under layers of repression and displaced by other concerns such as the Cold War or material affluence.

In 1959 Theodor Adorno wrote an important essay entitled "Was bedeutet: Aufarbeitung der Vergangenheit"(What does it mean to complete the work of the past?)[48] What Adorno meant by this question was how one could genuinely come to terms with the past. He answered by arguing that the past could be mastered only when its causes had been overcome in the present. He clearly believed that Germans had failed to accomplish this task and were therefore living with a time-bomb in the form of an unmastered past. In his view, the Germans had repressed the past and betrayed the future by doing so.

The Return of the Repressed

The fact that Adorno was remarkably prescient was proved by subsequent events in West Germany that brought the repressed past back into the light of day. In the winter of 1959/60 numerous desecrations of Jewish synagogues and cemeteries were recorded throughout West Germany. The past reared its ugly head again, reminding Germans that evasion was no longer possible. As the tranquil Adenauer years began to fade by the early 1960s, giving way to a decade of social conflict, Germans were once more confronted with the specter of Auschwitz. The younger generation of Germans who were not personally involved in World War II demanded better answers from their parents about the Third Reich and their participation in it. In West Germany the younger generation was increasingly Americanized and radicalized, which caused acute generational conflicts and led to widespread criticism of government institutions, particularly the universities where conservatism and authoritarian ways were still strongly entrenched. For better or worse, the social tension of the 1960s prepared the way for a more open forum of ideas, which unfortunately also erupted into violence and sorely tested West Germany's democratic institutions.

The young radical Germans of the 1960s, resembling their youthful counterparts in other western industrial nations such as France, Britain, and the United States, represented the vanguard of a general countercultural movement that opposed the conventional and authoritarian values of their elders. They demanded greater personal freedoms, social justice, and international peace; their sympathies, especially in Germany, were toward the political left. Walter Laqueur argued that many radical young Germans were anti-authoritarian with an admixture of anarchist and Marxist elements.[49] They had no memory of Nazism, which made their protest against the "rotten" West German system sound peculiarly strange and startling. As one German-Jewish observer put it, they were brought up between repression and economic affluence, never had to win freedom by struggling for it, and embraced lofty causes for which they had no strong spiritual affinity. Their political activism struck him as "just so much eyewash."[50] This judgment, however, was not shared by the majority of Germans, who overreacted to youthful protests by calling for severe repression. It was one thing to question the mores of one's parents or grandparents from a moral high-horse, but quite another to challenge the very structure of postwar German society. When some of the 1968ers, so-called because 1968 was the stormiest year of the protest movement, resorted to terrorism, the majority of Germans became alarmed and retaliated with vengeful repression that would have done the Nazis proud. The overwhelming majority of German students opposed the terrorism of the Bader-Meinhof Red Army Faction, just as they were equally shocked to encounter so much pent-up aggression by the establishment, which made some wonder just how many illiberal and fascistic tendencies were still active in German society.

The generational upheavals of the 1960s brought with them renewed preoccupation with the repressed past. In 1961 Eichmann was tried in Jerusalem; from December 1963 to August 1965 Germans followed the Auschwitz proceedings of twenty major offenders who were tried for war crimes at Frankfurt. The international spotlight was again directly shining on past German crimes, highlighting the institutional procedures that had led to the mass murder of Jews during World War II. Young Germans were shocked to learn just how deeply hundreds of thousands of their parents and grandparents had been implicated in mass murder. Intense public debates occurred over extending the statute of limitations on Nazi crimes. Scheduled to expire in 1960, the statute of limitation for first degree murder was extended to 1965 and then to 1979. The country's moral conscience was also being pricked by a number of controversial plays and novels about the Holocaust and the personal and institutional failures that had made it possible. The most important literary contributions that fueled the debate were Rolf Hochhuth, *The Deputy* (1963), Peter Weiss, *The Investigator* (1965), and Heiner Kipphardt, *Jöel Brandt* (1965). Historians also joined the debate, notably Martin Broszat, Hans Buchheim, Hermann Graml, Helmut Heiber, Helmut Krausnick, Hans Mommsen, Joachim Fest, and Karl Dietrich Bracher — all of whom wrote or edited incisive and comprehensive studies on Hitler and National Socialism. Except for Eberhard Kolb's work *Bergen Belsen* (1962), Heinz Höhne's splendid book on the SS (1966), Uwe Adam's *Study on Jewish Politics under the Nazis* (1972), and Karl Dietrich Bracher's synthesis on the nature of the Nazi dictatorship (1969), very little was done by German scholars on questions relating directly to the Holocaust. Even Bracher's comprehensive work on Nazism devoted only 13 out of 580 pages to the Final Solution.[51]

Although a great deal more information about Nazi Germany was becoming available in the 1960s and 1970s, many Germans chose to ignore it and turned instead to the half-truths and lies that were being disseminated by Holocaust deniers. Even in 1969, the author of the first comprehensive work on National Socialism, Karl Dietrich Bracher, had to admit that old National Socialist ideas, now camouflaged under the guise of "National Opposition," were again gaining wide currency in elite journals, newspapers, pamphlets, and exculpatory memoirs or sanitized biographies of fallen idols of World War II.[52] The bulk of the revisionist literature pointed to the existence of influential circles in German society nourishing a strong fondness for right-wing ideologies of the sort that had characterized the Nazis only two decades earlier. In fact, many former Nazis had weathered the storms of war and postwar denazification extremely well and were eager to transplant their ideas into the new German society. For those who had traced the lives and careers of the former Nazi elite, it was shocking, if not downright alarming, to discover how many Nazis, formerly in high positions, reemerged unscathed and unrepentant in the Federal Republic. Among them were many perpetrators of the Holocaust who had been overlooked by a lax system of justice.

In examining the role of the Holocaust in postwar Germany, it is instructive to take a closer look at the way in which the Germans tried to deal with Holocaust perpetrators who slipped through the initial scrutiny of the victorious powers. The task involved in bringing well over 150,000 people to justice was a daunting and, given the shifting nature of postwar conditions, probably an impossible undertaking. Of the approximately 150,000 Germans involved directly in Nazi murders, 1,814 were convicted by the Americans, 1,085 by the British, 2,107 by the French, and the rest by eight other nations, including 75 by Belgium, 10 by Denmark, 197 by the Netherlands, 92 by Norway, 5,452 by Poland, and an estimated 25,000 by Yugoslavia, Russia, and East Germany. This makes a total of roughly 35,000 convictions.[53] What about the remaining 115,000 perpetrators?

The answer is that most of these perpetrators slipped through the porous net of denazification proceedings and easily reintegrated themselves into the postwar societies of both East and West Germany. In the west, elite institutions such as the civil service, public schools and universities, courts, and police forces were only superficially denazified. A number of "high profile" Nazis were removed or retired from their posts, but the majority, sooner or later, resumed their professional activities after the war. Members of the legal profession, with a few notable exceptions, remained in their offices and mentored a new generation of Germans in the conservative and authoritarian principles of the past that always upheld the claims of state authority at the expense of individual rights.[54] Some government agencies employed more Nazi Party members in the late 1940s than they did during the Third Reich.[55] In 1951 the West German government passed "the 131 Law" which sanctioned the reemployment of all former Nazi civil servants except Gestapo officials and those who had been identified as "major offenders" by the denazification proceedings. The vast majority of the professors who had shaped the National Socialist legal system returned to their university chairs and continued to instruct their students. The same was true in most other academic fields as well. One of the first acts of the new West German parliament (*Bundestag*) was to grant a general amnesty for all crimes committed during the Third Reich with a maximum prison sentence of one year or less. In order to expedite the reintegration of many former Nazis who were living in West Germany under assumed names, the Bundestag also granted amnesty to those who had disguised their identity or given false information to the authorities.[56] On the assumption that vigorous justice had already been meted out to Nazi criminals, the German authorities showed little urgency in prosecuting any but the most blatant types of offenses. The Allied Powers, now urgently requiring the support of West Germany in the Cold War, played into the mood of "forgetting and forgiving" by catching what Robert Kempner, one of the prosecuting lawyers at Nuremberg, called "pardon fever." General Lucius D. Clay, the U.S. High Commissioner, supported by a special clemency board, either reduced the prison sentences of many Nazi criminals or granted outright pardons. Fritz Ter Meer, manager of the I. G. Farben plant at Auschwitz, walked out of prison and reportedly told his entourage, "Now that they have Korea on their hands, the Americans are a lot more friendly."[57] The British followed the Americans in opening the prison doors to former Nazi criminals.

Given that the political mood had shifted fundamentally during the Cold War and that the Allied Powers had turned over jurisdiction to the West German government, the sense of urgency in convicting Nazi criminals dissipated quickly. Legal proceedings ground down to a snail's pace. In 1958, the state governments of West Germany established a Zentralstelle (Central Place) in Ludwigsburg near Stuttgart for the purpose of investigating individuals who might have committed crimes during the Third Reich. The findings of the Ludwigsburg agency were to be communicated to the relevant state prosecuting attorneys in whose jurisdiction the alleged Nazi criminal lived. Since the statute of limitation on all crimes except manslaughter and murder had already expired in 1955, Ludwigsburg could no longer focus its investigation on crimes relating to property (Aryanization) and ghettoization. Manslaughter was dropped in 1965, which left murder. Under German law, revised in 1941, a murderer was defined as "someone who kills...a person for the pleasure of killing...or otherwise from base motives, with malicious intent or by means dangerous to the public at large."[58] Judges who were motivated by political agendas had no trouble in twisting these words to their own purpose.

Moreover, questions immediately arose whether a "desk murderer" (*Schreibtisch Mörder*) was actually a hands-on murderer or merely an unwitting accomplice. For example, after a lengthy series of investigations into the activities of the Reich Main Security Office of the SS (RSHA), preparations were made to try three hundred major offenders. The Federal Supreme Court, however, ruled in the first trial of an official in the Krakow Police Department that the defendant had been an accomplice who had not acted out of "base motives" (racial hatred) and had merely obeyed orders as a police officer and member of the SS. Furthermore, the court ruled that according to paragraph 50, section 2, of the Criminal Code, passed by the Bundestag in 1968, an accomplice to murder with no ascertainable personal motives could be punished by a maximum of only fifteen years. By 1969 such maximum sentences had already exceeded the statute of limitations. By one stroke of the pen, the court had effectively stopped prosecution against the three hundred perpetrators who had been scheduled for trial.

This decision by the Federal Supreme Court in 1969 sent a message that was not lost on most lower courts throughout Germany. Charges against high-ranking Nazis were dropped by many courts because the defendants were just "unwitting tools," "mere accomplices" acting on duty but not from base motives or malicious intent to harm the public at large. Alois Häfele, a former SS man who had participated in the killing of eighty-nine thousand people at Chelmo, where the first mass gassings of Jews took place, was classified by a Bonn County Court as a mere "accomplice without the intentions of a perpetrator."[59] The Federal Supreme Court also classified Karl Wolff, Himmler's personal chief of staff, as a perpetrator who "merely wanted to help Himmler carry out his task" and "lent his occasional support to Himmler's criminal motives from his subordinate position."[60]

If Wolff, who "merely" requisitioned and scheduled the trains that sent millions of Jews to their deaths, was not a murderer, who was? Clearly, the courts assumed that only Hitler, Himmler, Heydrich, Müller, Eichmann, and others in this direct chain of Holocaust perpetrators could be considered unconditional murderers. Most of the others were accomplices who acted on motives other than those mentioned as prosecutable by the criminal code. They were motivated by a sense of duty, by obedience to orders (*Befehlsnotstand*) or, alternatively, they acted out of fear or even out of noble idealistic beliefs. A Frankfurt County Court cleared Dr. Kurt Borm, a euthanasia physician who sent 6,652 people to the gas chambers, because he had not killed his victims "with malicious intent" but believed he had released them from suffering.[61] Probably the most common reason for dismissing charges against Nazi perpetrators or to mitigate them was the defendants' plea that their lives would have been in jeopardy if they had not followed orders. Only one member on the staff of the Belzec administration was sent to prison for aiding and abetting the extermination of six hundred thousand people.[62] The man received only four years as an accomplice to murder; all the others, in the judgment of the court, had "acted believing they were in a totally hopeless situation of constraint [*Zwangslage*], unable to do anything except obey the orders given to them."[63] In 1966 a Darmstadt district court dismissed charges of mass murder against former members of Police Battalion 322, many of whom had been reinstated after the war and advanced steadily through the ranks, on the same grounds of "putative constraint to obey orders" (*Putativnotstand*).

If constraint to obey orders was not a feasible tactic, defendants tried another successful ploy by claiming to be too ill or too old to stand trial. The chief defendant of the Auschwitz trial, Robert Mulka, was given a fourteen-year sentence but was almost immediately freed for medical reasons. Bruno Streckenbach, who had been one of the chief organizers of the mass shootings by the *Einsatzgruppen,* was never tried because of "poor health." Similarly, SS *Sturmbannführer* Helmut Bischoff could not be tried because, in the view of Hamm Court of Appeals, "the charge that the accused was guilty of murder would of necessity be presented in a form likely to cause... excessively high blood pressure."[64]

Although the Zentralstelle in Ludwigsburg investigated well over 100,000 cases of former Nazi perpetrators, as of 1993 only 6,487 Nazi criminals were tried and 6,197 convicted by various German courts on charges of murder or accomplice to murder. Only 163 received life sentences.[65] One former director of the Ludwigsburg Zentralstelle, Adalbert Rückerl, claimed in an official report, entitled the *Investigation of Nazi War Crimes 1945–1978,* that few Nazi criminals escaped justice but then, as Tom Bower points out, Rückerl went out of his way to explain why the German government was not responsible for the few that did.[66]

One of Rückerl's major excuses for why the wheels of justice did not move faster was that the Allies shipped vital documents after the war to the United States or elsewhere and therefore out of reach of German prosecutors. The real reason, however, was German obstructionism and defiance, made all the easier by the Cold War, the economic miracle, and the reemergence of the old elites.

For Germans who genuinely tried to come to terms with their Nazi past it was particularly galling to watch the reemergence of former Nazis in high positions in West German institutions. Dr. Hans Globke, who helped draft the Nuremberg Laws and dreamed up the middle names of "Israel" and "Sarah" that all German Jews were forced to adopt, became a state secretary in the Adenauer government until his retirement in 1963. Friedrich Flick, the wealthy industrialist who had enriched himself by impoverishing Jews and using them as slave labor, had to sell his coal mines but got quickly back on his financial feet by acquiring Daimler Benz instead and becoming one of the wealthiest men in the Federal Republic. Flick, like other fellow industrialists such as Alfried Krupp, had been sentenced to substantial prison terms, which were subsequently reduced or commuted. The I. G. Farben directors involved in the Auschwitz (Monowitz camp) project all went on to lucrative positions in German industry: Fritz Ter Meer became chairman of Bayer Chemicals and Heinrich Bütefisch board member of Ruhrchemie A. G.; Walter Dürrfeld, who had managed the Monowitz concentration camp at Auschwitz, became a member of the board of directors of Scholven-Chemie; Otto Ambros was appointed to several boards of directors and served as an adviser to the Bonn government; August Heissmeyer, SS general, associate to Himmler, and husband of Reich Women's Führer Gertrud Scholtz-Klink, got a slap on the wrist for falsifying his name and spent the rest of his postwar years as the director of a Coca-Cola subsidiary. The list could be extended by the thousands. According to Tom Bower, more than sixty West German ambassadors and foreign service officials in the early 1960s had been prominent members of the Nazi Party who had helped Fritz Rademacher organize the Final Solution.[67] One young Foreign Office official who worked with Rademacher and, of course, claimed to know nothing, was Kurt Georg Kiesinger, who became chancellor of West Germany in 1966.

The controversy around the Kiesinger appointment to the chancellorship, perhaps even more than the early Globke case, focused public attention on the burden of the past, previously repressed but always erupting into public consciousness. Kiesinger's Nazi past, which had been the subject of some public debate, became big news when a young woman, Beate Klarsfeld, slapped the chancellor's face in public because she thought he was a Nazi criminal. Though denounced by many, Klarsfeld also had her supporters, notably the writer Heinrich Böll, who sent her a bouquet of roses after she had received a prison sentence.[68] Kiesinger's case illustrated just how pervasive the Nazi past still was, poisoning the atmosphere and paralyzing the country's collective self-confidence. It became clear, at least, that until the older generation had turned power over to the postwar generation there would be no end to exposés of Nazis operating unrecognized in sensitive public posts. Even the director of the Ludwigsburg Zentralstelle for the investigation of Nazi war crimes, Erwin Schüle, was under suspicion (wrongly as it would turn out) for having been personally implicated in war crimes on the eastern front; rather than compromise the mission of his office, he resigned from his position.

The unmastered past, of course, was not the only wall that separated the Germans from a healthier future. Since August 13, 1961 a physical wall had also divided East and West Germany from each other, solidifying the apparent drift into two separate nations that were pursuing different ideological, social, and cultural goals. In West Germany two other walls went up in the 1960s and 1970s that reinforced the others. In addition to the generational conflict already mentioned, West German society also faced acute social problems in the form of "guest workers" (*Gastarbeiter*), who had been invited to Germany from various Mediterranean countries, especially Yugoslavia and Turkey, to fill the gap caused by a severe labor shortage. German industry relied heavily on such foreign workers to fill low-paying, unskilled, temporary positions — the sort of jobs that unionized German workers refused to accept. Neither the German government nor the employers who hired these foreign workers gave any thought to what would happen if these workers chose to stay, brought their families with them, and had their children born and raised in Germany. These *Gastarbeiter* were less welcome when the German economic miracle ended in the 1970s and gave way to a series of setbacks in the form of recession and rising unemployment. The unification of Germany in 1989–90 would bring this social problem into sharp relief, as it did all the other obstacles that continued to divide the German people from each other and therefore from the world at large.

By the late 1970s the two Germanies, separated from each other by both a physical and a psychological wall, were settling down to accept their separate status, opening up better lines of communications but otherwise seeing no possibility of bridging the growing divide. As far as the Jews were concerned, especially those living in Israel, there was only one Germany, and that was the Federal Republic, because East Germany had neither participated in the reparations agreements negotiated by the Adenauer government nor established diplomatic relations with the state of Israel. It was developments in the Federal Republic that the Jewish community in and outside Israel was following very carefully, paying particular attention to German-Israeli relations and the way in which Germans were handling their anti-Jewish past. The Federal Republic had always been a close friend and ally of Israel, and both of its major parties — the Social Democratic Party (SPD) and the Christian Democratic Union (CDU) — took a pro-Israeli position throughout the 1960s and

'70s. When the Israelis took a more aggressive line against the Palestinians, the solid wall of support for Israel began to form cracks. The intellectuals on the left, despite their anti-fascist and anti-racist rhetoric, discovered in the Palestinians a new victim and took to demonizing Israel as a copy of the Third Reich, thus perhaps projecting their own German guilt feelings in displaced form on the Jews.[69] In fact, extremists on the left referred to the Palestinians as the new Jews of the Near East and demonized what they called the "Zionist genocide."

Some have argued that this attitude about Israeli imperialism is a thinly disguised form of anti-Semitism, equally at home on both the political left and the right. Its left-wing version has been called left-fascism, and it can crop up in unfamiliar form; for example, one was an apparently innocuous play written but never produced by the late Rainer Fassbinder, entitled the *Garbage, the City and Death,* in which one character excoriates a rich Jew, whose financial greed has helped in turning the city into a foul dump, by exclaiming "they forgot to gas him. . . . I rub my hands when I think of the air going out of him in the gas chamber."[70] The Fassbinder controversy was a *cause célèbre* for years for exposing latent Judeophobic prejudices. The play provoked sharp differences of public opinion. Some found it obscene and defamatory to Jews, while others found it powerful and worthy to be performed in an open democratic society.[71] Ignatz Bubis, who later disrupted a planned performance of the play in Frankfurt, found the play insulting and unacceptable. Others felt that the time had come to be less oversensitive and to normalize the German-Jewish relationship so that things could be openly stated on both sides, for better or worse. There seemed to be a growing feeling on the part of many Germans that an artificially cultivated policy of pro-Jewishness could be a liability, in this case undermining artistic freedom.

Such an attitude was also behind a new orientation toward Israel in German foreign policy. The government of Helmut Schmidt and later that of Kohl abandoned the symbolism of guilt in dealing with Israel in favor of normalization. On his return flight from Israel in April 1981 Schmidt reportedly said that "German foreign policy can and will no longer be overshadowed by Auschwitz."[72] But when the German chancellor criticized Menachem Begin's settlement programs in the occupied territories, the Israeli prime minister publicly insulted Schmidt by insinuating that, maybe as an officer on the eastern front, Schmidt had himself participated in atrocities against Jews, which should not be surprising since he represented a nation that had tried to exterminate Jews and that was now showing the Arab countries how to complete the job.[73] The Germans tried to ignore Begin's overheated rhetoric, which they found insulting, but they could not fail to notice that the specter of Auschwitz was difficult to exorcise, let alone normalize. Schmidt's successor, Helmut Kohl, found this out in February 1984 on a trip to Israel. The chancellor's first visit was a public relations disaster, marked by embarrassing remarks, not least of which was his reference to his own unblemished past, which he ascribed in false modesty to the "grace of a later birth" (*Gnade der späteren Geburt*). He made it clear, however, that the younger generation of Germans, though prepared to accept the past, refused to acknowledge a collective guilt for the deeds of their fathers. The German chancellor, who had a Ph.D. in history, wanted to take the lead in shaping a more normal and balanced account of the German past than the one he believed was being cultivated by guilt-ridden liberals who insisted upon treating Germany as a patient in need of endless therapy.

But for all his supposed sensitivity to history, Kohl has not always been the best in recreating the right kind of history. This became evident in the spring of 1985, when he prevailed on President Reagan to combine his state visit to Germany with attending a reconciliation ceremony at a military cemetery in Bitburg, where both Allied and German soldiers were buried. Since the cemetery also contained forty-nine SS graves, the possibility existed that Reagan might symbolically give his blessing to both the victims and the killers of World War II. Having unconditionally supported the Reagan administration on its defense policy, Kohl was undeterred by the possible political and moral repercussion of such a visit or by what it might do to the reputation of the American president. In the end, Reagan did give his version of "Ich bin ein Bitburger" speech to an audience of dead Wehrmacht soldiers, but critics rightly pointed out that it contrasted poorly with John F. Kennedy's "Ich bin ein Berliner" speech to hundreds of thousands of Berliners yearning to be free from communist oppression.

The political atmosphere in the mid-1980s was ripe with resurgent nationalistic and apologetic tendencies. Many Germans, especially on the political right, were becoming uncomfortable with having to wear what they regarded as a permanent political hair shirt. They became resentful that their past forced them to operate from a position of moral weakness rather than of strength, and that any strong nationalistic position or statement might be misinterpreted variously as xenophobic, authoritarian, or fascistic. Those who advocated strong nationalistic positions, for whatever ideological reason, exposed themselves to highly charged counterattacks by opponents who were not afraid to wield the Auschwitz club (*Auschwitz-Keule*).

In the summer of 1986 a red-hot controversy erupted in the press after Ernst Nolte, a conservative historian, had written a provocative article in the *Frankfurter Allgemeine Zeitung* (June 6), entitled "Die Vergangenheit die nicht vergehen will" (The past that will not pass away), in which he argued that the Third Reich, particularly the Holocaust, had made it impossible to treat the recent German past as a normal series of events that should have passed from present memory.[74] Nolte suggested that there were certain interest groups that artificially inflated the significance of the Third Reich for their own ulterior ends.

They had succeeded in treating the Holocaust as *sui generis,* as a unique event without parallel in history; by doing so, Nolte claimed, they had lifted the Holocaust out of time and place, relegating it to the unhistorical level of absolute evil, while at the same time wielding it as a pedagogical threat over the German people in order to reinforce their guilt and squash their nationalistic pride. Nolte, of course, did not say it as directly as I have put it here, but this is what emerged from his contorted language. His style, with its provocative questions and clever insinuations, was intentionally evasive, which served a double purpose: it allowed him the luxury to escape possible entrapment in what is clearly indefensible while at the same time playing into the hands of right-wing radicals who are not afraid to draw unsavory conclusions from his bold musings.[75]

On a historiographical level, Nolte's complaint was well taken. The historiographic effect of Hitler's twelve-year Reich has produced a series of optical illusions in the eyes of many historians who have plotted Hitler's rise and fall. The evil that Hitler unleashed was so great that it had the effect of magnifying the Third Reich within the stream of history and made it appear that Nazism was absolutely unique and without precedent or parallel in history. The net effect of internalizing such a paradigm is that it removed the Third Reich from the realm of history and relegated it to the field of ethics, theology, or journalistic punditry. This, in turn, has resulted in misleading theories of political causation and psychological motivation. For some historians the Nazi experience still serves as *the* pivot around which explanations about German history are formulated. At its most extreme, this has resulted in the practice of twisting many personalities or events in German history into a prefiguration of Hitler and Auschwitz. And what has been perpetrated on the past has also been extended into the future, for Hitler's shadow is still stretching beyond the present.

Nolte's approach, however, moved in the opposite direction, which is called exculpatory. Nolte rejected the theory of the unique evil of the Holocaust on the grounds that the Nazi genocide was only one of many genocidal occurrences in the twentieth century. In the 1960s Nolte had written a well-received book, *Three Faces of Fascism,* in which he compared the worldviews of various European types of fascism, including National Socialism, pointing out that their broad aim was to usurp the radicalization of the left and usher in a homogenized community of the people. Nolte's work had been a sound comparative study of fascistic ideologies and their clash with equally fanaticized opponents on the political left. Nolte subsequently broadened his comparative approach by examining the genocidal activities of both right- and left-wing totalitarian regimes; but by so doing, he stirred up a hornet's nest because it was his contention that Hitler's extermination of the Jews was not a unique act but was to be expected from a political religion that presupposed extermination as a necessary element of its worldview.

It was at this point that Nolte began stretching both the comparison between Nazism and communism and historical truth in general. The Russian Bolsheviks, it is true, wanted to eliminate their class enemy: the bourgeoisie. They believed that class membership determined whether individuals were either saved or damned. Some fanatical Bolsheviks undoubtedly believed that it was their ideological duty to exterminate the whole bourgeoisie as a class, but this overheated rhetoric never included exterminating middle-class women or children. Nolte's point was that the Nazis were no different except that they aimed at exterminating races rather than classes. If Nolte had stopped at this point, we could credit him with having uncovered a grain of truth. Both communism and Nazism were metaphysical systems that claimed to hold a monopoly on political truth and considered their opponents to be living in a state of sin, to be either saved by conversion or damned by physical annihilation. Yet the Nazis went far beyond the communists in their radical aims. Expropriation of expropriators, according to Karl Marx, did not mean physical annihilation of the whole bourgeoisie; by contrast, Hitler's slogans about racial subhumans did mean the extermination of whole races.

Overextending a comparison is one thing, but using it as a point of departure to draw causal connections is quite another matter. Nolte claimed that the class murder committed by the Bolsheviks, which he called an "Asiatic deed," motivated the Nazis to respond in kind and out of self-defense because they saw themselves threatened by the communists who wanted to exterminate them. According to this view, for which Nolte provided little factual support, Hitler saw himself fighting a purely defensive conflict with an enemy who believed in genocidal activities and had already exterminated close to ten million people. And since Hitler linked communism and Jewry, he saw no other way of saving Germany than by exterminating them both. This way of thinking was mad, and by stepping into its irrational mentality, if perhaps only to understand it, Nolte created some unfortunate impressions, including the thesis that Hitler's genocidal policies against the Jews were not unique at all but merely one aspect of the historical hatreds that have erupted with particular virulence in the twentieth century.

Nolte was not a racist or an anti-Semite but a historical revisionist who deliberately set out to undermine the "singularity postulate" around which postwar political issues had been centered. Nolte and his conservative defenders, wittingly or unwittingly, wanted to diminish the uniqueness of the Holocaust, thereby hoping to minimize the guilt and responsibility of the generation of Germans who had shaped the Third Reich. Nolte was entitled to draw comparisons between the exterminatory practices of two totalitarian systems, but he was wrong to derive one genocide from an allegedly prior one (post hoc, ergo propter hoc), which manages to make the first one — the "Asiatic deed" — appear to be far more significant than the second one that the author does *not* call the "Germanic deed." Very little is served by arguing that the biological extermination of the Jews was a copy of the class extermination practiced by the communists and that "Auschwitz did not result in the first place from inherited anti-Semitism and was at its core not a mere genocide [*Völkermord*], but was really a reaction born out of the anxiety of the annihilatory occurrences of the Russian Revolution."[76] Such speculations not only trivialize the Holocaust but also play into the hands of racist revisionists who argue that German treatment of Jews was no different than Stalin's treatment of Kulaks, and that societies have a perfect right to preserve their ethnic purity and are therefore justified in removing alien or recalcitrant minorities.

Nolte's revisionist writings coincided with other revisionist works, notably Andreas Hillgruber's book *Two Kinds of Collapse: The Destruction of the German Reich and the End of European Jewry*. The book, as the title indicates, consisted of two essays: the first dealt with the collapse of the German army on the eastern front and the second with the Final Solution. The ambiguous juxtaposition of the two titles raised serious questions because the author, unwilling to put his nationalistic cards on the table, did not make it clear why the collapse of the German army was a catastrophe comparable to the extermination of six million Jews. The ambiguous comparison was compounded by the qualitatively different approach the author pursued in discussing the two collapses; his account of the collapse of the German army, as he openly admitted, was written with great empathy, whereas the events leading to the Final Solution were written in cold clinical detail. Having himself been a German soldier on the eastern Front, Hillgruber admitted that he could not help but identify himself with the plight of the Wehrmacht and the terrible treatment of Germans civilians by out-of-control Soviet troops. That he could not show an equal, if not greater, amount of empathy for the fate of six million Jews says a great deal about the author as both a historian and a human being.

The little book, which has been given far too much attention, was a thinly disguised work of conservative revisionism because it contained an unstated and undeveloped nationalistic agenda. One of the main unstated assumptions of the book, as critics charged, was the accusation that the western powers actively promoted the destruction of Germany as a continental power and were therefore responsible for causing the postwar crisis with the Soviet Union. The western powers, Hillgruber was saying, capitulated to Stalin by giving him the dismembered eastern territories on a silver platter. For Hillgruber and a growing number of nationalistically minded German historians, the "German catastrophe" was the end of Germany as a great power. The German philosopher Jürgen Habermas saw this quite clearly and accused Hillgruber, Nolte, and other historians of propounding false nationalistic and apologetic principles that were undermining the West German commitment to liberalism, constitutionalism, and western democracy.[77] He also believed that these revisionist views could serve as convenient rationales for evading the hard truths that Germans should confront after Auschwitz. The escape from historical truth, for whatever reason, is an evasion of the collective responsibility all Germans should still accept for the Holocaust. Such a collective responsibility (*kollektive Mithaftung*), Habermas suggested, does not mean personal guilt, but rather an admission by the German community that it failed to prevent Auschwitz and still collectively atones for this failure by institutionalizing the truth in the form of honest historical knowing for the benefit of future generations.

The *Historikerstreit* (historians' quarrel) was over the question of German guilt and German self-identity, and it revealed a host of contending claims that remain unresolved. The controversy illustrates how sensitive the issue of Nazism still is after more than half a century after its ignominious demise. Even the assertion of minimal national pride evoked paranoia outside Germany, especially in Israel, where alarms were raised about the rise of a "Fourth Reich." German historians were accused of whitewashing the past and promoting, as one author put it, an ominous political agenda aimed at political unification and teaching Germans to assert themselves again as a great power. These fears became even more acute when Germany did achieve unification in 1990. As long as Germany was divided, questions relating to German national identity were relegated to the periphery of political concerns; but now that East and West Germany have been reunited, the question of national identity, which also involves the Jewish question and a host of other related questions, has been moved from the periphery to the very center of German politics. How have the Germans responded to this challenge since unification?

The Walls in the New Unified Germany

If any metaphor or symbol describes modern Germany, it would not be the imperial eagle or the swastika but the image of walls, visible or invisible, that Germans have erected to insulate themselves from the outside world or to divide themselves from each other. During the euphoric days leading up to and following the unification of Germany (1989–90), Germans experienced a rare moment of national solidarity, rediscovering, as the popular slogan expressed it, that "We are one People." Since that time, the euphoria has given way to a more sober, if not somber, mood of impatience, frustration, and even pessimism about the nation's uncertain future. The political and cultural absorption of the former Communist East Germany into the democratic Republic of West Germany has proved to be far more difficult than most people had assumed. This should have been expected in light of the fact that a wall and two wholly different ways of life had separated the two Germanies for forty-five years. The economic integration of the former Communist

East Germany, with its decaying industrial infrastructure, has turned out to be extraordinarily difficult, particularly at a time of major structural changes in the global economy and its interdependent markets, financial mobility, and new technologies. Profound fissures quickly developed between "Ossies" and "Wessies," characterized by mutual distrust and feelings of resentment.

As unemployment has steadily risen, now standing above 12 percent, higher than at any other time since the Great Depression, social tranquility has given way to mutual recrimination and scapegoating. A subculture of economic and political malcontents, expressing itself in right-wing xenophobic terms, has given cause for concern, particularly since politicians have jumped on the xenophobic bandwagon. In Germany, as in other parts of Europe, the objects of scapegoating are the immigrants who are blamed for the complex socioeconomic problems that currently beset Germany. Violence against foreign immigrants has become endemic in Germany since the unification, and anti-Semitism followed on the heels of xenophobia.[78] Jews were blamed for encouraging immigration of foreigners in order to dilute the national substance.

Scapegoating foreigners, in turn, has drawn dramatic attention to an age-old German problem that always arose in the past in connection with the German-Jewish question. What is it that makes somebody a German? Is it socialization as a German or is it ancestral blood ties to the German ethnic group? The decisive factor, today as it was in the past, is racial rather than social. It is still blood rather than place of birth or cultural assimilation that determines whether an individual is a German or a foreigner. Despite the horrors caused by this conception of national identity, the Germans have refused to change their citizenship laws. The problem has surfaced repeatedly over the last thirty-five years because West Germany invited millions of foreign workers to reconstruct the country's industrial infrastructure. Since the mid 1950s the country has experienced a steady influx of foreign workers from Turkey, Yugoslavia, Italy, and other Mediterranean and Near Eastern countries. Many of these "guest workers" (*Gastarbeiter*) returned, but many decided to stay in Germany by starting families or arranging for loved ones to join them. There are many young Turkish children in Germany today who are completely assimilated, speak only German, and have never traveled anywhere else. Yet, according to current German citizenship laws, they can never become Germans and are thus permanently stigmatized as "foreigners." According to current figures, there are well over six million such foreigners, which is 8 percent of the population. Many foreigners live isolated lives and suffer discrimination at the hands of their German hosts.

The German reply to the immigration problem has been evasive and vacillating. The message seems to be: "We appreciate your work but we don't appreciate you permanently in Germany." The official government position is to say that "we are not an immigration country, but we are friendly to foreigners." This ambiguity, which does not solve the problem, is the outcome of a purely opportunistic strategy of importing cheap labor in times of labor shortages and exporting that labor force when it had fulfilled its short-range purpose. What was not but should have been foreseen was that millions of foreign workers would stay in Germany. So far, the German government has no long-term policy of integrating its foreign minority, nor has it any intention of adopting the American model of a multiethnic society. In the meantime, the German government is stuck, unable either to expel its unwanted foreigners or assimilate them into the German mainstream. Both solutions, I would contend, are dictated by Germany's unmastered Nazi past. Assimilation is impossible because Germans are still believers in ethnic self-identification; expulsion is impossible because resorting to perceived Nazi-like tactics would arouse indignation and opposition.

Around the question of foreigners another wall has developed: a generational, indeed intergenerational one between the 1968ers and the 1989ers. Four out of five Germans today belong to the postwar generation, but that generation is showing deep political splits over the question of German national self-identification. Since the late 1980s a noticeable shift to the political right has taken place that challenges the previous West German national image of a cosmopolitan, democratic, and western-oriented Germany and threatens to replace it with a nationalistic Germany seeking "great power" status. So far, the shift is essentially intellectual and in search of a broad political power base. The name "New Right" comes from the French *Nouvelle Droit* associated with Alain de Benoist, a French thinker who tried to refurbish traditional right-wing and neo-fascist ideas by grafting them onto the fashionable rhetoric of the left, Gramscian ideas of cultural hegemony, and Jacques Derrida's ideas of cultural differences.[79] There are at least four different shadings of the New Right, including ethnopluralists who support the notion that ethnicities must preserve their purity in order to retain their unique identity and cultural creativity; *Etatisten,* who follow the conservative philosopher Carl Schmitt in advocating a strong nationalistic state; spiritual reactionaries, who denounce the "cultural imperialism" of America and its influence on German life and culture; and neo-nationalistic historians (Nolte, Stürmer, Hillgruber, Zitelmann, Weissmann, and Nipperdey), who want to restore German national pride and power so that the nation can take its place once more among the great powers.

Among the more influential and energetic New Right advocates are Rainer Zitelmann, one of the editors of the conservative newspaper *Die Welt;* Karlheinz Weissmann, a high school teacher in Göttingen who published a highly controversial history of Nazi Germany in which the Holocaust is marginalized and relativized in favor of the minutiae of everyday life in the Third Reich; Dieter Stein, editor of the slick New Right organ *Neue Freiheit* (New Freedom); and Botho Strauss, a leading poet and recent convert to the New Right who stirred up a mighty furor in the periodical *Der Spiegel* (1993) with a provocative essay called "The Swelling Song of the Billy Goat," in which he attacked the 1968ers as a deformed generation that had exchanged a sense of nationhood and spiritual depth for rampant consumerism. More often than not the New Right targets the decadent values of American culture as a corrosive agent in undermining traditional German values. As Karlheinz Weissmann pointedly told Jacob Heilbrunn in an interview for an article in *Foreign Affairs,* Germans would no longer be tyrannized into putting up with the American version of a multicultural society. Germans would instead return to their traditional values.[80]

Upon closer inspection of what the New Right holds to be traditional German values, one encounters the contour of a familiar landscape: *völkisch* beliefs about the soul of the people and its deep instincts, moods, and dreams, deeper than the rationalistic abstractions spun out by deracinated liberal minds. The young supporters of Junge Freiheit, for example, appear to be a reincarnation of the Bündische Jugend of the 1920s. The neo-romantic notions of blood and soil are remarkably similar in both cases, except that the 1990s version contains curious admixtures of modern rock music and technological gadgetry. The underlying message of these extreme right-wing groups is calculated to set up roadblocks to interracial and ethnic harmony because it celebrates ethnocentrism and nationalism as useful tribal cult rituals that allegedly preserve the purity of the national group by means of sacred rituals and customary observances. Hatred of foreigners, in this view, is not to be condemned, since it serves the cathartic and therapeutic purpose of externalizing pent-up hostilities and aggression.

At present, the New Right is not a menace to democracy, and its intellectual spokespersons are relatively marginalized in academia or the mass media. At the same time, their provocative and belligerent revisionism has created new divisions. According to Ignatz Bubis, the current chairman of the Jewish Zentralrat, these rebellious young conservatives are well-connected to wealthy conservative circles and deserve to be monitored because of their potential harm to minority rights in Germany. The New Right understands that the "battle for Germany is waged for the most part not in the streets but on the field of collective memory and the self-image of the nation."[81]

In the final analysis the conflicts between Ossies and Wessies, Germans and foreigners, and generations 1968 and 1989 all come down to the unmastered past and how it should be handled. As Jürgen Habermas pointed out in connection with the historians quarrel, the real point of the debate was not a quarrel over epistemological differences but over different conceptions of how history is to be publicly used.[82] Is is to be used in the service of reinforcing group cohesion through nationalistic ideologies or is it used as a moral reference point by which the past becomes a learning experience for the present generation? In Germany, the politics of collective memory, of who interprets the past, has been particularly intense over the last ten years. At the center of this debate is still the Third Reich and the Holocaust. Except for a lunatic minority of Holocaust deniers, most Germans do not deny that the Holocaust occurred. According to international surveys, Germans have a good basic knowledge of the Final Solution. The revisionist claim that it did not happen has no mass support.[83] The arguments over the Holocaust have focused on the meaning and importance that should be ascribed to the event — that is, how it should be remembered and how that memory is to be institutionalized in the new unified Germany.

Although the majority of Germans prefer to draw a final line on the Holocaust, a *Schlusstrich,* the uniqueness of the crime and the widespread horror it still evokes all over the world make it impossible to ignore or repress it for very long. The burden of Auschwitz is a permanent cross the Germans as a nation will have to bear, and no amount of denial, repression, or relativization will alter that fact. For Jews, too, Auschwitz symbolizes a radical caesura in their history and collective existence, a theological crisis of the greatest magnitude because it raises the unavoidable question, for Jews as well as Christians, "Where was God at Auschwitz?" Auschwitz ties Germans and Jews in a perpetual and troublesome relationship as perpetrators and victims, fixated in time, and unable to extricate themselves from a historical morass. Time has not healed all wounds. Whether it can depends on how the perpetrators and the victims come to terms with tragedy, how they cope with the past. Repression implies failure and inauthenticity; the same is true of denial, trivialization, marginalization, and relativization. The authentic approach is honest memory and moral growth in the direction of the universal human values of the Enlightenment.

What progress have the Germans made in coping with their recent tragic past, and what is the nature of the German-Jewish relationship today? Four methods of coping with the past have been instituted since 1945, first by the Allied Powers and then by the Germans: denazification, which included legal proceedings against Nazi criminals; financial restitution to the victims in the form of reparations (*Wiedergutmachung*); postwar political and constitutional measures aimed at protecting democratic and human rights and at combatting Judeophobia; and educational and moral efforts to reeducate a younger generation in the blessings of democracy. The least successful has been denazification and punishment of perpetrators, most of whom are now dead or dying. Restitution to the survivors of the Holocaust, which has been well-meaning but inadequate, at least accelerated the process of integrating the Federal Republic into the western world and raised the reputation of the German people in the international community. For almost fifty years Germany has been a stable democracy based on the rule of law (*Rechtsstaat*); its economy has been, until recently, equally impressive in per capita output, income levels, and distributive social justice. Extremist movements and parties have been marginalized and periodic outbreaks of xenophobic and Judeophobic violence have been matched by numerous grassroots organizations dedicated to tolerance, protection of refugees, and opposition to racism. Anyone who incites racial hatred or denies the Holocaust faces stiff fines and prison sentences. In 1985 the Bundestag passed a law (*Gesetz gegen die Auschwitz Lüge*) that made the distribution of political hate material and the denial of the Holocaust punishable offenses. The West German Constitution, now binding on the former East German territories, puts limits on free speech when it threatens democracy, thus automatically restricting the sort of hate material and political activities that destroyed the Weimar Republic.

It could be argued that the Germans have paid far more public attention to the dark underside of their recent history than have the Japanese, Russians, or Americans. Public debates in recent years have been intense, and Germans of good will have agonized a great deal over the national divisions and economic setbacks that have fueled xenophobic violence and right-wing activities. The wave of xenophobic violence that erupted during the early 1990s, though magnified in the world press, did not represent a reversal of trends in the direction of an open, tolerant, and democratic country.[84] The fact that Germany and other European countries have spawned a subculture of rebellious adolescents, countercultural outsiders, and social malcontents does not mean that these social groups constitute a significant threat to the mainstream. Germans frequently complain that foreign observers magnify isolated incidents of neo-Nazi activities and generalize them as implying "attitudinal changes in the population at large."[85] According to one study of ethnic intolerance and extremism in the new unified Germany, "the public and the press accurately perceive the extremist incidents but mistakenly take them as an indicator of public opinion, which they are not."[86] The bizarre and violent behavior of skinheads, alcoholic thugs, hooligans, and rabble-rousers seems to make a deeper impression on the public psyche than the peaceful marches and vigils of hundreds of thousands of decent Germans, which is itself a commentary on our global media culture and its fascination with sensationalism, deviant behavior, and vulgarity. Thus, the torching of a shelter for foreigners in Lübeck in January 1996 overshadowed another important event that took place on the same day: the state visit of Israeli's President Ezer Weizman and his address to the Bundestag on the occasion of a new Holocaust Remembrance Day, which had been inaugurated by Germany's Roman Herzog in order to demonstrate that Germany would continue to mark the liberation of Auschwitz even though its fiftieth anniversary had passed.

Roman Herzog and the presidents before him (Weizäcker, Heinemann, Heuss) who spoke for the nation in a symbolic or cultural sense all agreed that after Auschwitz German national consciousness could only be derived from Germany's best humanistic traditions rather than from the polluted stream of *völkisch* and extreme ethnocentric ideologies. The better minds of the nation, spanning a political spectrum from Social Democrats on the left to Christian conservatives on the right, have endorsed this position throughout the history of the Federal Republic, although Jürgen Habermas's warning that the current threat to this consensus comes from the extreme right is well taken. The German mass media and educational institutions have taken a similar position. In the last ten years, in fact, issues relating to Jews and the Holocaust have been prominently featured in the media, especially television. Marc Fisher, in his perceptive snapshots on Germans *After the Wall* (1995), shows that the liberal German media may have overcompensated for past neglect by a surfeit of attention. In Germany today, he wrote, "Jews are history. They are forced down the Germans' throats like bitter medicine: Hardly a week passes without a TV documentary on one or another aspect of the Holocaust; publishers never tire of recording the cultural legacy of German Jews. Jews are embraced as a tragic loss."[87]

Such liberal overcompensation, concealing latent guilt feelings, has raised critical eyebrows because it is belated, oversentimentalized, and artificial. False solicitude may be no better than neglect or denial. Gordon Craig drew reference some time ago to two forms of unhealthy German attitudes about the Jews and the state of Israel: bad conscience and its expiation in horribly artificial friendships for the Jews or the state of Israel.[88] Every "progressive" middle-class family in Germany, Craig pointed out, wanted at some time or other to travel to Israel and to meet with Israelis. Although Israeli military successes somewhat dampened this oversolicitude for Jews, it is still quite strong in Germany. According to Marc Fisher, "there are Germans who 'collect' Jews like an exciting hostess adds potential party guests to the card file. There are Germans who study Jewish history and religion as a form of reparation. There are Germans who have built careers out of mourning the loss of the Jews."[89]

Since the late 1980s there has been a debate in Germany about how the tragic loss of the Jewish community should be approached. Since the institutional approach is second-nature to Germans, many looked to government rather than to private enterprise to handle the problem of collective memory. The Kohl government obliged by giving the Germans two major museums: the House of History in Bonn and the German Historical Museum in Berlin. A great deal has been written about these museums and the contentious debates over the representation of the nation's past, particularly the two German World Wars, the destruction of the Jews, and the deaths of fifty million people.[90]

The conflict over Kohl's pet projects, particularly the Berlin Museum, was only a warm-up for a squabble about a projected Holocaust memorial proposed by Lea Rosh, a television talk-show hostess and media celebrity, who has been the moving force behind the construction of a memorial in Berlin that would commemorate the Holocaust victims. Since the project, though privately funded, requires the support of both the Bonn government and the Berlin Senate, not to mention a string of planners, architects, and artists, it has bogged down and probably will never be built, certainly not in the grandiose form envisioned by Rosh. Jane Kramer has described the controversy surrounding Rosh's Holocaust-memorial as having turned into "a ghoulish public entertainment."[91] She depicted Rosh, who gave herself the Jewish name, as a histrionic media grande dame who has gone into the "Shoa Business" out of a combination of reasons ranging from genuine empathy for the victims of the Holocaust to self-promotion and externalization of guilt. If it is up to her, Germans will have a massive tombstone in the middle of Berlin that is the size of a football field, shaped in the form of a tilted concrete slab on which the names of four million Jewish victims would be engraved. Scattered among the names would be eighteen stones from Masada, one for each death camp. The project has been condemned as too costly, impractical, and pretentious. Developers who are planning to erect apartment houses in the area earmarked for the memorial objected because they wanted their prospective tenants to look down on a statue of Goethe, not a five-acre concrete slab with Jewish names engraved on it.[92]

Chancellor Kohl and the conservative historians and politicians who share his sentiments are willing to accommodate the evils of the German past in collective remembrance, but they want to marginalize it in favor of the more glorious parts of the past, which includes Goethe, Schiller, Herder, Bach, Mozart, and Beethoven. To them, confessional memory, aiming at contrition and atonement, is not the only, let alone the most important, form of collective remembrance. The chancellor and historian Kohl wants to finish the circle of the Roman Catholic chancellor Adenauer and deliver the Germans from their bondage to history. This is to be done by reinventing a more heroic German past; its accomplishments are to be proudly displayed in public museums where people can see a nobler and more heroic image of German greatness. It is hoped that by displaying a thousand years of German history, the twelve-year Reich will shrink in importance by comparison. The evil that Hitler had unleashed would then have been banished into history.

This act of historical exorcism, which requires the creation of a new mythical history, has its supporters among many Germans today. Kohl knows his people; he knows that they are looking to the government to draw the final line, to relieve them of their remaining guilt feelings. Too much memory, as Nietzsche noted long ago, can be debilitating to the living because the past sits too heavily upon them. Creative achievement, either under the halo of past greatness or the pall of past evil, is very difficult.[93] Germans, like Jews, have periodically suffered from a malignant historical fever, a morbid obsession with the heavy past that has spread paralysis in the lives of the living. Chancellor Kohl and many conservative historians seem to prefer escaping from the dark past by employing what Nietzsche called the "monumental" approach that emphasizes the great shining moments of the past at the expense of the darker episodes. There are other German historians and philosophers, however, who would want to employ the "critical" mode of looking at the past, which consists in bringing it to the bar of judgment, interrogating it remorselessly, and finally condemning it so that something new can be born.[94] The debate over history, no matter on which side one stands, is a healthy one because it is only in this way that the unmastered past can be retrieved from the dark morass of repression and examined by the light of reason. In this way future generations may breathe easier and suffer less from the pains of the unmastered past.

A very important and related question, frequently asked inside and outside Germany, is whether Jews can live and breathe freely in Germany today. In the wake of World War II and the Holocaust, Jews understandably felt that they had no business living in Germany. Holocaust survivors could not forgive or forget; for them, the Germans were eternally guilty. Less than ten thousand German Jews had survived the Final Solution, and many of them planned to leave the murderous country they had come to fear and despise. Leo Baeck did not return nor did most of the intellectuals who had been driven from the land by Adolf Hitler. A few, like Alfred Döblin, Arnold Zweig, Ernst Bloch, and Hans Joachim Schoeps, returned to help in reconstructing a war-torn and spiritually impoverished country. Despite the persecutions they suffered in Nazi Germany, still others like Viktor Klemperer decided to stay because there was nowhere else to go; their ties, it appears, may have been stronger than the damage the Nazis had inflicted upon them.

Fifty years later, there are now well over fifty thousand Jews living in Germany, most of them, as before, in the larger cities such as Berlin, Frankfurt, Düsseldorf, Cologne, and Munich. Today, a third generation of German Jews still lives in Germany, and a fourth will soon be born. During his visit to Germany a few years ago, the Israeli president, Ezer Weizman, told a group of German Jews that he could not understand why they were living in Germany, when their real home was in Israel. This not too gentle reproach elicited a number of strong objections by German Jews who responded to the Israeli president that they felt at home in Germany and had no intention to live in Israel. The fact that well over fifty thousand Jews apparently prefer to live in Germany, where they are a legally recognized and protected minority, does not mean that all of them feel at home in Germany in the sense of feeling themselves Germans. Far too many Germans still regard the Jews as non-German. Ignatz Bubis, the head of the Jewish Zentralrat, recounts a very telling episode of what it means to be a Jew in Germany today. On the occasion of the Israeli president's visit to Germany, Bubis was invited to a gathering of government officials who were hosting the Israeli president. After the formal ceremonies were over and everyone relaxed, cocktail glasses in hand, the head of the Federal Agency for Political Education approached Bubis and cheerfully remarked: "Your state president really gave a good speech." Bubis's reply was, "Of course, Roman

Herzog always gives good speeches." The German official's reply was: "No, No, I mean your state president, Mr. Weizman!"[95] Bubis took it with good humor, but sadly recognized that Jews were still not seen as full Germans, but as Jews living in Germany. Too many Germans, as several polls indicate, assume that Germans and Jews belong to different ethnic groups, and that the center of Jewishness resides outside Germany in Israel. The majority of Germans, however, do not feel like the bigoted women who sent Bubis a signed telegram that told him to take his millions and go to Israel.[96] Clichés of rich Jews persist; they are part of everyday Judeophobic prejudices.

Although social-discriminatory Judeophobia continues in the new Germany, it is largely latent and marginalized. Contrary to the impressions created by the press, neither Judeophobia nor xenophobia increased greatly in Germany since reunification.[97] A comparison of poll findings from 1989, 1991, and 1994 reveals the continuation of a trend that started well before 1990 toward more tolerance and a greater willingness to come to terms with the Nazi past.[98] Two surveys conducted in 1990 on anti-Jewish prejudices in the former East Germany, where no surveys had been held before, revealed that East Germans were even less prejudiced against the Jews. These and other polls do not imply that Judeophobia, xenophobia, or nationalistic arrogance are unimportant or do not contain a danger to the democratic process in Germany.[99] The many xenophobic and anti-Jewish acts of violence that have marked Germany since unification in 1990 cannot be ignored, but they should not detract from the progress the Germans have made since 1945. To use a medical analogy, the Judeophobic obsession is in remission in Germany today, but it is far from being eradicated. It continues as an underground stream of floating resentments and deep-seated prejudices; it is tied to resentments of having to pay reparations, having one's peace and prosperity disturbed by annoying reminders of Nazi atrocities and of constant reminders, especially by the outside world, that one's parents or grandparents may have been mass murderers. How many Germans feel this way is difficult to determine. There is undoubtedly a small hard core of Jew-haters that will never forgive the Jews for Auschwitz. Such perverse views, however, are part of the underground stream, which is unlikely to swell into another Nazi torrent, certainly not in the form it did sixty-five years ago.

The Nazi racial obsession has not survived the fall of the Third Reich, but what did survive the twelve-year Reich and proved stronger than Hitler, denazification, Sovietization, and Americanization was the German national character with all its strengths and weaknesses. Underneath the façade of a communist east and a capitalist west, Germans continued to be Germans; an intractable, immutable core of Germanness persisted and refused to be altered or significantly shaped by the dictates of outside powers. Moreover, it is likely to shape the future of Germany by its own inner logic. This enduring core of a German national character is not Hitlerean nor is it incompatible with democracy, but it is not the sort of pluralistic spirit that is at the heart of the American experience. The Germans will not accept the American model of an immigrant society: multiethnic, multireligious, or multicultural. This would run against their German identity, their spinal beliefs. Germans still endorse the cultural model of homogeneous wholes by which Germany is to be for the Germans, France for the French, and Italy for the Italians. The mixing of groups, according to this model, dilutes the national substance; conversely, it also deprives ethnic groups of their distinct identity by forcing them into a liberal and multicultural (meaning minimal cultural) pan-European or American society. Many Germans, especially on the political right, seem to feel that there can be no collective whole if national groups are not allowed to be objectively different from each other. Having just regained national unification, the Germans are once more searching for national unity and they seem to feel that the solution resides in rebuilding a strong national self-identity. They are ambiguous, however, about the range of permissible differences they will grant minorities because they are unsure, as before, what it means to be German. The recent shift to the right promises to keep these issues alive.

On the positive side, however, is the fact that the majority of Germans have been conditioned by fifty-five years of democratic practice to be tolerant, to respect individual and group differences, and to safeguard basic human rights. They have become tolerant by law but not by the heart, which remains defiantly and often self-righteously ethnocentric. Yet the rule of reason and the blessings of democracy have accomplished a great deal in weaning the younger generation of Germans away from the polluted stream of their parents and grandparents. Although young Germans continue to live under the dark shadow of the Nazi past, they have been given sufficient support to confront their nation's past and turn it to their advantage rather than their detriment. It is hoped that they will do so wisely by linking with the best of their traditions and by learning from their worst.

The Holocaust perpetrators and victims will be dead within the next fifteen years. This means that the German-Jewish relationship will have devolved on the following generations. How post-Holocaust generations of Jews and Germans interact and explain the meaning of the Shoa, how they integrate it into their national life, will have a profound impact on their future self-identity. At this moment both German and Jews, especially German Jews, bear the marks of a broken identity that can be mended only by turning to humane traditions and opening up a civilized dialogue so that reciprocal prejudices and resentments can be overcome. The hatreds of past generations should not be allowed to infect the new generations, as is happening around the world and in places where ancient cruelties are passed on by older generations who cannot let go of inherited prejudices. Nothing except violence is gained by endlessly turning the wheel of ethnocentric, racial, and religious hatred, by indulging in reciprocal demonization, tabulation of wrongdoing, and prejudicial beliefs.

The Final Solution to the Jewish question, which has been at the heart of the German obsessional neurosis for the past five hundred years, was really about the Final Solution to the German question. Germans have been shadowboxing with delusions all along, sparring with imaginary demons (Jews) that were really projections of their own darker nature. This darker nature was spawned by hoary traditions that celebrated war and the martial virtues associated with it: glory, honor, loyalty, courage. Germans tried to define themselves not as individual citizens endowed with inherent rights vis-à-vis the state but as an ancestral blood community whose members were tied to each other by ethnic bonds and a shared mythic history of legends and heroic exploits.

The Jews had committed themselves to a different social reality and their presence in a divided and deeply ethnocentric German culture was perceived as a deadly threat. As the agents of modernization, the Jews promoted a set of secular, commercial, and cosmopolitan values that threatened what many Germans had come to accept as their essential national character. When liberalism and social democracy failed and Germans turned their backs on their humane traditions, all that remained was the dark shadow of a split nation, whose defeat in war and reduction in great power status caused seething resentments and cries for scapegoats. Hitler organized these resentments and, linking with the worst traditions in the nation's past, promised national redemption through war and conquest. Germany, he insisted, would either be a world power or there would be no Germany, a false dilemma that led to Germany's destruction.

The Final Solution to the German question consists in permanently giving up the quest for great power status and in setting realizable goals that are consonant with the nation's resources, manpower, and abilities. Germany's grab for world power has brought nothing but pain, suffering, and destruction. When Germany was reunified in 1990, many Jews feared a possible return of the Germanocentric mythology, a fear that seemed reinforced by the country's shift to the political right, the increase in xenophobic and Judeophobic violence, and the projected transfer of the nation's capital from provincial Bonn to the former imperial Berlin.

The Jews, however, do not have to fear the possibility of a rising "Fourth Reich," because an insurmountable wall has already formed to block its path. It is a solid and impenetrable shield forged by the blood and sacrifice of the innocent victims of Nazism. Its name is Auschwitz, and it will protect both Jews and Germans, and hopefully the rest of the world, from ever having to relive the same hell again. By some inexplicable force of history, the symbolic wall of Auschwitz may well serve as a deterrent to future evil, for it is unthinkable that what has happened there can ever be allowed to repeat itself. Evil may have caused an inferno that fed on Nazi gas and consumed millions, winning a battle but quite possibly losing the long-range war to goodness. In this sense, the Holocaust was indeed a burnt offering, for the victims did not die in vain; they may have given future generations the precious gift of life.

Notes

Introduction

1. This thesis, recently revived by Daniel Jonah Goldhagen in his widely discussed and controversial book *Hitler's Willing Executioners: Ordinary Germans and the Holocaust* (New York: Knopf, 1996), holds that the Holocaust was not perpetrated by a few elite Nazi killers but by many "ordinary" Germans who were motivated by what he calls "eliminationist anti-Semitism." His line of argument holds that that this kind of lethal anti-Semitism was deeply embedded in German culture for well over 150 years before Hitler took power and therefore represents a necessary and sufficient reason for the Holocaust (23, 31, 48, 417, 447). Putting it more bluntly, he indicts the German people as a whole by saying that for many Germans fanatical and murderous Jew-hatred had been a main staple of their lives; it was like "mother's milk" (89), for how else do we explain why so many of them voluntarily and with great pleasure contributed to the mass murder of the Jews? Since in the author's view the killings cannot be explained by appeal to universal human traits (389), the implication seems to be that the sort of eliminationist thinking and practice that led to the Holocaust is an exclusively German trait, which is really not an ordinary human trait ("transhistorical" or "acculturated"), but something peculiar (408). With single-minded purpose the author then proceeds to portray every German, even Nazi victims and resisters, as anti-Semitic, and he widens the circle of responsibility for the Holocaust to prove his central conviction that the mass murder was a German national project. In order to make his indictment that "ordinary" Germans carried out this murderous project by lending a willing bloody hand, he concentrates, in part, on "ordinary" perpetrators who were running the work camps, staged mass killings in the east, and conducted the death marches near the end of the war. These perpetrators, he tries to show, were not coerced into committing their heinous deeds, nor were they mindless robots following orders or subject to psychological pressures or disorders. They acted entirely in conformity with their "eliminationist" convictions. As to how many "ordinary" Germans were involved directly in the Holocaust, Goldhagen suggests rather vaguely a hundred thousand to five hundred thousand (167). The road to Auschwitz was therefore straight rather than twisted; it was a German national project that reflected the deepest wishes of the German people.

Given the book's provocative nature and its condemnatory moral tone, it is not surprising that it quickly engendered a storm of controversy, especially in Germany. Of the responses to Goldhagen's work, many of them critical in one way or another, the following are fairly representative: Gordon Craig, "How Hell Worked," *New York Review of Books,* April 18, 1996; John Elson, "What Did They Know?" *Time Magazine,* April 1, 1996; George F. Will, "There Is Nothing Uniquely Evil about the Germans," *Los Angeles Times,* April 14, 1996; Hans-Ulrich Wehler, "Wie ein Stachel im Fleisch," *Die Zeit,* April 1996; Volker Ulrich, "Hitlers willige Mordgesellen," *Die Zeit,* April 19, 1996; Christopher R. Browning, "Dämonisierung erklärt nichts," *Die Zeit,* April 26, 1996; Steven E. Aschheim, "Reconceiving the Holocaust," *Tikun,* July–August 1996; Richard John Neuhaus, "Daniel Goldhagen's Holocaust," *First Things,* August–September 1996; Hans Mommsen, "Die dünne Patina der Zivilisation," *Die Zeit,* September 6, 1996; and Fritz Stern, "The Goldhagen Controversy: One Nation, One People, One Theory? *Foreign Affairs* (November–December 1996), 128–38.

2. A good survey of such revisionist views, especially as they pertain to the Holocaust, can be found in Deborah Lipstadt, *Denying the Holocaust: The Growing Assault on Truth and Memory* (New York: Penguin, 1994).

3. Besides the book by Goldhagen already mentioned, the most notable work that revives the concept of a German national character is Paul Lawrence Rose, *German Question/Jewish Question: Revolutionary Anti-Semitism from Kant to Wagner* (Princeton, N.J.: Princeton University Press, 1990), a penetrating study of Judeophobic ideas in German intellectual life, but one that also suffers from the author's misconceived intellectual scaffolding by which, so it seems, every single German thinker, liberal, conservative, socialist, nationalist, is tarred with the same brush of "revolutionary anti-Semitism."

4. John Weiss, *Why the Holocaust Happened in Germany* (Chicago: Ivan R. Deer, 1996), 24.

5. The quote comes from Martin Himmelfarb in *Commentary* (March 14, 1984): 37–43.

6. See Robert Lifton and Eric Markusen, *The Genocidal Mentality: Nazi Holocaust and Nuclear Threat* (New York: Basic Books, 1990); Robert Lifton, *The Nazi Doctors: Medical Killing and the Psychology of Genocide* (New York: Basic Books, 1986); Florence R. Miale and Michael Selzer, *The Nuremberg Mind: The Psychology of the Nazi Leaders* (New York: Quadrangle, 1976); Leon Rappoport and George Kren, *The Holocaust and the Crisis of Human Behavior* (New York: Holmes and Meier, 1980); and H. V. Dicks, *Licensed Mass Murder: A Socio-Psychological Study of Some SS Killers* (New York: Basic Books, 1972).

7. Isaac Deutscher, *The Non-Jewish Jew and other Essays* (New York: Oxford University Press, 1986), 163.

8. See Ernst Nolte, "Zwischen Geschichtslegende und Revisionismus?" in Rudolf Augstein et al., *Historikerstreit: Die Dokumentation der Kontroverse um die Einzigartigkeit der nationalsozialistischen Judenvernichtung* (Munich: Piper, 1987), and Nolte's *Der Europäische Bürgerkrieg, 1917–1945* (Frankfurt: Ullstein, 1987).

9. Immanuel Kant, *On History* (New York: Bobbs-Merrill, 1963), 17–18.

10. Jeffrey Burton Russell, *Mephistopheles: The Devil in the Modern World* (Ithaca, N.Y.: Cornell University Press, 1986), 276.

11. Max Domarus, ed., *Hitler: Reden und Proklamationen, 1932–1945* (Wiesbaden: R. Löwit, 1973), 4:1713.

Chapter 1: The Rise of Judeophobia

1. Quoted in Saul Friedländer, *Memory, History and the Extermination of the Jews of Europe* (Bloomington: Indiana University Press, 1993), 58.

2. Ibid., 107.

3. For Globocnik's testimony at Nuremberg, see International Military Tribunal, *Trial of the Major War Criminals before the International Tribunal: Proceedings and Documents* (Nuremberg, 1947–49), case no. 9, 4:356–58.

4. For an excellent reconstruction of the year 1096, see Robert Chazan, *In the Year 1096: First Crusade and the Jews* (Philadelphia: Jewish Publication Society, 1996).

5. Ibid., 31.

6. Ibid., 23.

7. Ibid., 53.

8. Quoted in ibid., 132.

9. Jeffrey B. Russell, *A History of Witchcraft* (London: Thames and Hudson, 1982), 69.

10. Ibid., 172. The literature on witchcraft is quite extensive. In addition to Russell's work on the history of witchcraft, there is also his comprehensive *Witchcraft in the Middle Ages* (Ithaca, N.Y.: Cornell University Press, 1972). Other excellent studies are Norman Cohn, *Europe's Inner Demons: An Enquiry Inspired by the Great Witchhunt* (London: Sussex University Press, 1975); Henry C. Lea, *Materials towards a History of Witchcraft*, 3 vols. (New York: ANS Press, 1986); Joseph Hansen, *Zauberwahn, Inquisition und Hexenprozess im Mittelalter, und die Entstehung der grossen Hexenverfolgung* (Munich: Oldenbourg, 1900; reprinted Aalen: Scientia, 1983); and H. R. Trevor-Roper, *The European Witch Craze of the Sixteenth and Seventeenth Centuries and Other Essays* (New York: Harper and Row, 1967).

11. Norman Cohn, *Warrant for Genocide: The Myth of the Jewish World Conspiracy* (Chico, Calif.: Judaic Studies, 1981), 13.

12. Quoted by Eliot B. Wheaton *The Nazi Revolution, 1933–35: Prelude to Catastrophe* (New York: Doubleday, 1969), 123.

13. Benedict de Spinoza, *The Works of Spinoza* (New York: Dover Publications, 1955), 1:229.

14. Arno J. Mayer, *Why Did the Heavens Not Darken? The Final Solution in History* (New York: Pantheon Books, 1988), chapter 1.

15. Social and historical psychologists have investigated this phenomenon of mass delusion and its connection to various belief systems at some length. One of the earliest, and still useful, studies is Charles Mackay, *Extraordinary Popular Delusions and the Madness of Crowds* (London: Office of the National Illustrated Library, 1852); other relevant studies are Michael Barkun, *Disaster and the Millennium* (New Haven: Yale University Press, 1974); Norman Cohn, *In Pursuit of the Millennium* (New York: Harper & Row, 1961); Whitney Cross, *The Burned Over District* (Ithaca, N.Y.: Cornell University Press, 1951); Leon Festinger et al., *When Prophecy Fails* (Minneapolis: University of Minnesota Press, 1956); Otto Friedrich, *The End of the World: A History* (New York: Coward, McCann & Geoghegan, 1982); Eric Hoffer, *The True Believer* (New York: Harper & Row, 1966); Vittorio Lanternari, *The Religion of the Oppressed: A Study of Modern Messianic Cults* (New York: Alfred

Knopf, 1963); James M. Rhodes, *The Hitler Movement: A Modern Millenarian Movement* (Stanford, Calif.: Stanford University Press, 1980).

16. Georg Wilhelm Friedrich Hegel, *The Philosophy of History*, trans. J. Sibree (New York: Dover, 1956), 21.

17. Rhodes, *The Hitler Movement*, 31–32.

18. Nathan Adler, *The Underground Stream: New Life Styles and the Antinomian Personality* (New York: Harper & Row, 1972), 21.

19. Ibid.

20. Rhodes, *The Hitler Movement*, 30.

21. Eric Hoffer, *The True Believer* (New York: Harper & Row, 1966), 18.

22. Rhodes, *The Hitler Movement*, 16.

23. See Cohn, *In Pursuit of the Millennium*.

24. Cohn, *Warrant for Genocide*, 14.

25. H. R. Trevor-Roper, *Men and Events: Historical Essays* (New York: Harper & Brothers, 1957), 146.

26. Gavin I. Langmuir, *Toward a Definition of Antisemitism* (Berkeley: University of California Press, 1996), 313.

27. Gordon Allport, *The Nature of Prejudice* (New York: Doubleday, 1958), 19.

28. Ibid., 38.

29. See T. W. Adorno et al., *The Authoritarian Personality* (New York: W. W. Norton, 1959); and Milton Rokeach, *The Open and Closed Mind* (New York: Basic Books, 1960).

30. Peter Schäfer referred to this ancient anti-Jewish position as Judeo-phobia, to distinguish it from the virulent and obsessional form of anti-Semitism found in some Christian and in all racial-biological types of Jew-hatred (*Judeophobia: Attitudes towards the Jews in the Ancient World* [Cambridge, Mass.: Harvard University Press, 1997], especially 197–211). The ancient people, he argued, felt threatened by the Jews; their attitude toward Jews was an ambivalent combination of fear and hatred. In this sense, of course, it is quite true to say that anti-Semitism predated Christianity. It is not clear from his analysis, however, whether Judeophobia is a strain of anti-Semitism or something separate from it, another good reason to scrap the term "anti-Semitism" altogether and replace it by "Judeophobia." "Anti-Semitism" is linguistically confusing and lacks the strong psychological connotation we associate with Judeophobia. The various forms of Judeophobia are xenopho-bic, religious, racial, and what Langmuir calls chimerical (delusional). In many cases, a combination of these can be identified, attesting to the protean nature of this evolving human obsession.

31. Leon Poliakov, *The History of Anti-Semitism* (New York: Schocken, 1974), 21.

32. Quoted by Poliakov, *History of Anti-Semitism*, 23.

33. Ibid., 25.

34. Robert Wistrich, *Anti-Semitism: The Longest Hatred* (New York: Schocken, 1994), 18–19.

35. St. Augustine, *The City of God* (London: J. M. Dent & Sons, 1931), especially books 18 and 20.

36. St. Augustine, *The City of God*, book 20, chap. 30; see also Poliakov, *History of Anti-Semitism*, 160–61.

37. Steven T. Katz, *The Holocaust in Historical Context* (New York: Oxford University Press, 1994), 1:250.

38. Chazan, *In the Year 1096*, 134.

39. Langmuir, *Toward a Definition of Antisemitism*, 17.

40. Ibid., 303.

41. Ibid., 308.

42. Quoted in Poliakov, *History of Anti-Semitism*, 160–61.

43. For the history of this legend, see George K. Anderson, *The Legend of the Wandering Jew* (Providence: Brown University Press, 1965) and G. Hasan-Roken and A. Dundes, eds., *The Wandering Jew: Essays in the Interpretation of a Christian Legend* (Bloomington: Indiana University Press, 1986).

44. Paul Lawrence Rose, *German Question/Jewish Question: Revolutionary Antisemitism from Kant to Wagner* (Princeton, N.J.: Princeton University Press, 1990), 24.

45. Joshua Trachtenberg, *The Devil and the Jews: The Medieval Conception of the Jew and Its Relation to Modern Antisemitism* (New Haven: Yale University Press, 1943), 32.

46. Wistrich, *Anti-Semitism: The Longest Hatred*, 30.

47. Ibid., 17.

48. Trachtenberg, *The Devil and the Jews*, 47.

49. Jeffrey B. Russell, *Mephistopheles: The Devil in the Modern World* (Ithaca, N.Y.: Cornell University Press, 1986), 61.

50. Poliakov, *History of Anti-Semitism*, 142–43.

51. Edward J. Tejirian, *Sexuality and the Devil* (New York: Routledge, 1990), 169.

52. Wayland Young, *Eros Denied: Sex in Western Society* (New York: Grove Press, 1966), 170–71.

53. Trachtenberg, *The Devil and the Jews*, 50.

54. For an excellent reconstruction of this case, see Langmuir, *Toward a Definition of Antisemitism*, 209–36.

55. Ernst Kantorowicz, *Frederick the Second, 1194–1250* (New York: Frederick Ungar, 1967), 413–15.

56. Poliakov, *History of Anti-Semitism*, 61.

57. Langmuir, *Toward a Definition of Antisemitism*, 225.

58. Poliakov, *History of Anti-Semitism*, 104–5.

59. Ibid., 110.

60. John Weiss, *Ideology of Death: Why the Holocaust Happened in Germany* (Chicago: Ivan R. Dee, 1996), 4.

61. Quoted in Fritz Stern, *Gold and Iron: Bismarck, Bleichröder and the Building of the German Empire* (New York: Knopf, 1977), 5.

62. Katz, *Holocaust in Historical Context*, 1:278.

63. Poliakov, *History of Anti-Semitism*, 66.

64. Katz, *Holocaust in Historical Context*, 1:259.

65. Ibid., 1:375–76.

66. Franz Boas, "Racial Purity," *Asia* 40 (May 1940), 231.

67. Heinrich Heine, *Religion and Philosophy in Germany*, trans. John Snodgrass (Boston: Beacon Press, 1959), 46.

68. I. Brandt, ed., *Luther's Works* (Philadelphia: Muhlenberg Press, 1930–43), 45:200–201; see also Wistrich, *Anti-Semitism: The Longest Hatred*, 39.

69. Quoted by Robert G. L. Waite, *The Psychopathic God Adolf Hitler* (New York: Basic Books, 1979), 288.

70. Ibid., 289

71. Rose, *German Question/Jewish Question*, 7.

72. Weiss, *Ideology of Death*, 20.

73. Paul Johnson, *A History of the Jews* (New York: Harper & Row, 1987), 242.

74. On linking Luther and Hitler, the following are samples of contrasting views: Karlheinz Deschner, *Abermals krähte der Hahn: Eine Demaskierung des Christentums von den Evangelisten bis zu den Faschisten* (Düsseldorf: Econ Verlag, 1986); William M. McGovern, *From Luther to Hitler* (London: Houghton Mifflin, 1941); Peter Matheson, "Luther and Hitler: A Controversy Revisited," *Journal of Ecumenical Studies* 17 (Summer 1980): 445–53; and Kurt Meier, "Zur Interpretation von Luthers Judenschriften," in *Vierhundertfünfzig Jahre lutherische Reformation, 1517–1967* (Göttingen: Vandenhoeck & Ruprecht, 1967).

75. Poliakov, *History of Anti-Semitism*, 249.

76. Quoted by Peter Pulzer, *Jews and the German State: The Political History of a Minority, 1848–1933* (Oxford: Blackwell, 1992), 72.

77. Jacob Katz, *From Prejudice to Destruction: Anti-Semitism, 1700–1933* (Cambridge, Mass.: Harvard University Press, 1980), 52.

78. Stern, *Gold and Iron*, 7.

79. Hannah Arendt, *The Origins of Totalitarianism* (New York: Meridian, 1958), 27.

80. Stern, *Gold and Iron*, 11.

81. Quoted in David Philipson, *The Reform Movement in Judaism* (New York: Macmillan, 1931), 122.

82. Katz, *From Prejudice to Destruction*, 108.

83. Ibid., 13–22.

84. For the convergence of Judeophobia and nationalism, see Shmuel Almog, *Nationalism and Antisemitism in Modern Europe, 1815–1945* (New York: Pergamon Press, 1990); Salo W. Baron, *Modern Nationalism and Religion* (New York: Meridian Books, 1960); and Eleonore Sterling, *Judenhass: Die Anfänge des politischen Antisemitismus in Deutschland* (Frankfurt: Europäische Verlagsanstalt, 1971).

85. On racism and racial thinking, see Jacques Barzun, *Race: A Study in Superstition* (New York: Harper & Row, 1965); George Mosse, *Toward the Final Solution: A History of European Racism* (New York: Harper & Row, 1978); Leon Poliakov, *The Aryan Myth* (New York: New American Library, 1977); and Paul Weindling, *Health, Race, and German Politics between National Unification and Nazism, 1870–1945* (New York: Cambridge University Press, 1989).

86. Gerhard Masur, *Prophets of Yesterday: Studies in European Culture, 1890–1914* (New York: Harper & Row, 1961), 13–14

87. On Chamberlain, see Geoffrey G. Field, *Evangelist of Race: The Germanic Vision of Houston Stewart Chamberlain* (New York: Columbia University Press, 1981).

88. Fritz Stern, *The Politics of Cultural Despair: A Study in the Rise of the German Ideology* (New York: Doubleday, 1965).

89. See George Mosse, *The Crisis of German Ideology: Intellectual Origins of the Third Reich* (New York: Grosset & Dunlap, 1964).

90. Quoted in H. Stuart Hughes, *Consciousness and Society: The Reorientation of European Social Thought, 1890–1930* (New York: Vintage, 1958), 56–57.

91. For the origin and impact of the *Protocols*, see Cohn, *Warrant for Genocide*.

92. Quoted in Karl Schleunes, *The Twisted Road to Auschwitz* (Chicago: University of Illinois Press, 1990), 7.

Chapter 2: German and Jew, 1700–1871

1. Gordon Craig, *The Germans* (New York: New American Library, 1982), 9–10.

2. Henry V. Dickes, *Licensed Mass Murder: A Socio-Psychological Study of Some SS killers* (New York: Basic Books, 1972), 108.

3. Wolfgang Scheffler, *Judenverfolgung im Dritten Reich* (Berlin: Colloquium Verlag, 1964), 14; see also Hermann Graml, *Antisemitism in the Third Reich* (Oxford: Blackwell, 1992), 39; and Sarah Gordon, *Hitler, Germans, and the Jewish Question* (Princeton, N.J.: Princeton University Press, 1984), 7–23.

4. An excellent recent reevaluation of the German problem of national self-identity is Otto Dann, *Nation und Nationalismus in Deutschland, 1770–1990* (Munich: Verlag C. H. Beck, 1996).

5. Craig, *The Germans,* 20

6. Karl Biedermann, *Deutschland im Achtzehnten Jahrhundert* (Leipzig: Verlagsbuchhandlung von J. J. Weber, 1854–80), 1:162.

7. On the German Enlightenment, see Hans M. Wolff, *Die Weltanschauung der deutschen Aufklärung in Gesellschaftlicher Entwicklung* (Bern: Francke Verlag, 1963); Herbert Schöffler, *Deutscher Geist im 18. Jahrhundert* (Göttingen: Vandenhoeck & Ruprecht, 1956); W. H. Bruford, *Germany in the Eighteenth Century: The Social Background of the Literary Revival* (Cambridge: Cambridge University Press, 1965); Leonard Krieger, *The German Idea of Freedom* (Chicago: University of Chicago Press, 1972); and Wilhelm Dilthey, "Studien zur Geschichte des Deutschen Geistes," in *Gesammelte Schriften,* vol. 3 (Göttingen: B. G. Teubner, 1959).

8. On Mendelssohn's philosophical contributions, see David Sorkin, *Moses Mendelssohn and the Religious Enlightenment* (Berkeley: University of California Press, 1996); on his life, see Heinz Knobloch, *Herr Moses Mendelssohn in Berlin* (Frankfurt: Fischer, 1996).

9. Craig, *The Germans,* 130.

10. Leon Poliakov, *A History of Anti-Semitism: From Voltaire to Wagner* (New York: Vanguard, 1975), 189.

11. Quoted in ibid., 164–65.

12. Erich Schmidt, *Lessing, Geschichte seines Lebens und seiner Schriften* (Berlin: Weidmannsche Buchhandlung, 1909), 1:148.

13. Poliakov, *History of Anti-Semitism,* 195.

14. Ibid., 197; see also Knobloch, *Herr Moses Mendelssohn,* 315–16.

15. On Rahel Varnhagen, see Hannah Arendt's sympathetic portrait, *Rahel Varnhagen: The Life of a Jewess* (London: Leo Baeck Institute Publications, 1957).

16. On the German idea of freedom, see Leonard Krieger, *The German Idea of Freedom* (Chicago: University of Chicago Press, 1957).

17. Quoted by Albert Köster, *Die deutsche Literatur der Aufklärungszeit* (Heidelberg: Karl Winters Universitätsbuchhandlung, 1925), 10.

18. Quoted by Peter Gay, *The Enlightenment: An Interpretation* (New York: Alfred Knopf, 1969), 2:273.

19. On the German reaction to the French Revolution, the following are samples of different interpretations: G. P. Gooch, *Germany and the French Revolution* (London: Longmans, Green, 1920); Jacques Droz, *L'Allemagne et la Revolution Francaise* (Paris: Presses universitaires de France, 1949); Eugene N. Anderson, *Nationalism and the Cultural Crisis in Prussia, 1806–15* (New York: Farrar & Rinehart, 1939); Friedrich Meinecke, *Weltbürgertum und Nationalstaat* (Munich: R. Oldenbourg, 1962).

20. Jacques Barzun, *Classic, Romantic and Modern* (New York: Doubleday, 1961). Other useful works include H. G. Schenk, *The Mind of the European Romantics* (New York: Doubleday, 1969); Oskar Walzel, *German Romanticism,* trans. Alma Elise Lussky (New York: Capricorn Books, 1966); Robert F. Gleckner and Gerald E. Enscoe, eds., *Romanticism: Points of View* (Englewood Cliffs, N.J.: Prentice-Hall, 1970); Gerhart Hoffmeister, *Deutsche und europäische Romantik* (Stuttgart: Metzler, 1978)

21. See Hans Kohn, *The Mind of Germany: The Education of a Nation* (New York: Harper & Row, 1960).

22. On Herder see Isaiah Berlin, *Herder and Vico: Two Studies in the History of Ideas* (New York: Viking, 1976); Robert T. Clark, *Herder: His Life and Thought* (Berkeley: University of California Press, 1969); Robert R. Ergang, *Herder and the Foundations of German Nationalism* (New York: Columbia University Press, 1931); and Rudolf Stadelmann, *Der historische Sinn bei Herder* (Halle: Niemeyer, 1928).

23. Quoted by Kohn, *The Mind of Germany,* 76.

24. Ibid., 78.

25. Carl Euler, ed., *Friedrich Ludwig Jahns Werke* (Hof: G. A. Grau, 1884–87), 1:419.

26. Quoted in John Hermann Randall, *The Career of Philosophy* (New York: Columbia University Press, 1965), 2:244.

27. Some of the problematical aspects of German historiographic theory and practice are discussed brilliantly by Georg G. Iggers, *The German Conception of History* (Middletown, Conn.: Wesleyan University Press, 1968; rev. ed., 1983).

28. There are two excellent studies on the Jewish response to emancipation by Michael A. Meyer: *The Origins of the Modern Jew: Jewish Identity and European Culture in Germany, 1749–1824* (Detroit: Wayne State University Press, 1967), and *Response to Modernity: A History of the Reform Movement in Judaism* (New York: Oxford University Press, 1988).

29. Ruth Gay, *The Jews of Germany: A Historical Portrait* (New Haven: Yale University Press, 1992), 132–34.

30. See Walter Laqueur, *A History of Zionism* (New York: Schocken, 1972), 14–15; also Gay, *The Jews of Germany,* 139.

31. Gershom Scholem, "Jews and Germans," in *On Jews and Judaism in Crisis: Selected Essays* (New York: Schocken, 1976), 75.

32. Craig, *The Germans,* 126. There is also an excellent chapter (chapter 1), in Frederic V. Grunfeld's *Prophets without Honor: Freud, Kafka, Einstein, and Their World* (New York: Kodansha International, 1996), which explores this German-Jewish "family resemblance."

33. Paul Johnson, *A History of the Jews* (New York: Harper & Row, 1987), 470.

34. Erich Kahler, *The Jews among the Nations* (New York: Ungar, 1967), 99.

35. Quoted in Horst von Maltitz, *The Evolution of Hitler's Germany: The Ideology, the Personality, the Moment* (New York: McGraw-Hill, 1973), 86–87.

36. Quoted in Peter Gay, *Freud, Jews and Other Germans: Masters and Victims in Modernist Culture* (New York: Oxford University Press, 1978), 4.

37. Walter Laqueur, *Out of the Ruins of Europe* (New York: Library Press, 1971), 479.

38. Quoted in Maltitz, *Evolution of Hitler's Germany,* 85.

39. Scholem, "Jews and Germans," 79.

40. Shmuel Almog, *Nationalism and Antisemitism in Modern Europe 1815–1945* (New York: Pergamon Press, 1990), 9.

41. Quoted in Katz, *From Prejudice to Destruction,* 77.

42. Graml, *Antisemitism in the Third Reich,* 43–44.

43. Johann Gottlieb Fichte, *Beitrag zur Berichtung der Urteile des Publikums über die französische Revolution* (Jena, 1793), 101.

44. Graml, *Antisemitism in the Third Reich,* 44–45.

45. Gay, *The Jews of Germany,* 139.

46. Ludwig Börne, *Gesammelte Schriften* (Milwaukee, 1858), 5:31–32.

47. Franz Mehring, *Karl Marx,* trans. Edward Fitzgerald (Ann Arbor: University of Michigan Press, 1962), 78–79.

48. Boris Nikolaievsky and Otto Maenchen Helfen, *Karl Marx, Man and Fighter,* trans. Gwenda David and Eric Mosbacher (London: J. B. Lippincott, 1936), 5.

49. Quoted by Mehring, *Karl Marx,* 5.

50. Siegfried Landshut, ed., *Karl Marx: Die Frühschriften* (Stuttgart: Alfred Köhler, 1964), 201.

51. Karl Marx and Friedrich Engels, *Werke* (Berlin: Dietz Verlag, 1961), 27:415.

52. Quoted by Koppel S. Pinson, *Modern Germany: Its History and Civilization* (New York: Macmillan, 1966), 104.

53. A point eloquently stated by Edmund Wilson, *To the Finland Station: A Study in the Writing and Acting of History* (New York: Doubleday, 1940), 306–7.

Chapter 3: German and Jew in the Second Reich

1. Quoted in Otto Pflanze, *Bismarck and the Development of Germany: The Period of Unification, 1815–1871* (Princeton, N.J.: Princeton University Press, 1963), 177.

2. A. J. P. Taylor, *Bismarck: The Man and the Statesman* (New York: Vintage Books, 1967), 49.

3. Ruth Gay, *The Jews of Germany: A Historical Portrait* (New Haven: Yale University Press, 1992), 160–65.

4. Jack Wertheimer, in his book *Unwelcome Strangers: East European Jews in Imperial Germany* (New York: Oxford University Press, 1987), 55 ff., has shown that citizenship for Jews, especially eastern Jews, was made nearly impossible by pettifogging civil servants and jurists who often acted under strict orders to deny citizenships to Jews. The merit of his book lies not only in reminding us of how German officials treated Jews in the nineteenth century, but also in showing that even today Germans still maintain attitudes and laws that discriminate against foreigners.

5. Uriel Tal, *Christians and Jews in Germany: Religion, Politics and Ideology in the Second Reich, 1870–1914* (Ithaca, N.Y.: Cornell University Press, 1975), 290.

6. Friedrich Meinecke, *The German Catastrophe*, trans. Sidney Fay (Boston: Beacon Press, 1963), 10.

7. Alfred Vagts, *A History of Militarism* (reprint, Westport, Conn.: Greenwood Press, 1981), 14.

8. J. W. Wheeler-Bennett, *The Nemesis of Power: The German Army in Politics* (London: Macmillan, 1964), 9.

9. Gordon Craig, *Germany, 1866–1945* (New York: Oxford University Press, 1978), 39–40.

10. Ibid., 45.

11. Ralf Dahrendorf, *Society and Democracy in Germany* (New York: Doubleday, 1969), 33.

12. Ibid., 37.

13. Oswald Spengler, *Selected Essays,* trans. Donald O. White (Chicago: Henry Regnery, 1967), 47–48.

14. Fritz Stern, *The Failure of Illiberalism: Essays on the Political Culture of Modern Germany* (New York: Knopf, 1972), xxiii.

15. For an excellent study of the German intellectual elite, see Fritz Ringer, *The Decline of the German Mandarins* (Cambridge, Mass.: Harvard University Press, 1969).

16. Quoted in Robert G. L. Waite, *The Psychopathic God Adolf Hitler* (New York: Basic Books, 1977), 341.

17. Walter Kaufmann, ed. *The Portable Nietzsche Reader* (New York: Viking, 1968), 570–71; see also the relevant passages in *Thus Spoke Zarathustra* (part 1, no. 3; part 2, no. 3) and *The Will to Power* (especially the section entitled "The Masters of the Earth").

18. On Treitschke's belligerent nationalism, see Hans Kohn, *Prophets and Peoples: Studies in Nineteenth Century Nationalism* (New York: Collier, 1966), 100–121.

19. See Klemens von Klemperer, *Germany's New Conservatism: Its History and Dilemma in the Twentieth Century* (Princeton, N.J.: Princeton University Press, 1957), 47–69.

20. For the most astute account of Germany's imperial aims during the Second Reich, see Fritz Fischer, *Germany's Aims in the First World War* (New York: Norton, 1967).

21. For an excellent study of the jingoistic Pan-German League, see Roger Chickering, *We Men Who Feel Most German: A Cultural Study of the Pan-German League, 1886–1914* (London: Allen & Unwin, 1984).

22. Hans Kohn, *The Mind of Germany: The Education of a Nation* (New York: Harper & Row, 1960), 11.

23. Hermann Glaser, *The Cultural Roots of National Socialism* (Austin: University of Texas Press, 1978), 174.

24. Friedrich Nietzsche, *Beyond Good and Evil*, no. 244.

25. A point well made by Stanley Edgar Hyman in his work *The Tangled Bank: Darwin, Marx, Frazier and Freud as Imaginative Writers* (New York: Atheneum, 1974), 133–50.

26. Quoted in ibid., 134.

27. Karl Marx, *Capital* (New York: Modern Library, n.d.), preface, 15.

28. Gay, *The Jews of Germany*, 169.

29. Fritz Stern, *Dreams and Delusions: National Socialism in the Drama of the German Past* (New York: Vintage Books, 1989), 64.

30. Fritz Stern, *Gold and Iron: Bismarck, Bleichröder and the Building of the German Empire* (New York: Knopf, 1977), especially chapters 17 and 18.

31. Gay, *The Jews of Germany*, 176.

32. For the rise of the Mosse chain, see Werner Mosse, "Rudolf Mosse and the House of Mosse, 1867–1920," in *Yearbook of the Leo Baeck Institute* 4 (1958).

33. Monika Richarz, ed., *Jüdisches Leben in Deutschland: Selbstzeugnisse zur Sozialgeschichte im Kaiserreich* (Stuttgart: Deutsche Verlags-Anstalt, 1979), 26–27.

34. Quoted in Peter Gay, *Freud, Jews and Other Germans: Masters and Victims in Modernist Culture* (New York: Oxford University Press, 1978), 101.

35. Ibid., 105.

36. Quoted in E. Werner, *Mendelssohn* (New York: Free Press, 1963), 100; also Paul Johnson, *The Birth of the Modern: World Society, 1815–1830* (New York: Harper Perennial, 1991), 817–18.

37. Gay, *Freud, Jews and Other Germans*, 116.

38. Ibid., 117.

39. Stern, *Dreams and Delusions*, 108.

40. Quoted in Peter Pulzer, *Jews and the German State: The Political History of a Minority, 1848–1933* (Oxford: Blackwell, 1992), 81.

41. Peter Pulzer, *The Rise of Political Anti-Semitism in Germany and Austria* (New York: Wiley, 1964), 71.

42. Quoted in John Weiss, *Ideology of Death: Why the Holocaust Happened in Germany* (Chicago: Ivan R. Dee, 1996), 85–86.

43. Pulzer, *Jews and the German State*, 56.

44. Paul Lawrence Rose, *German Question/Jewish Question: Revolutionary Anti-Semitism from Kant to Wagner* (Princeton, N.J.: Princeton University Press, 1990) 33.

45. Quoted in Fritz Stern, *The Politics of Cultural Despair: A Study in the Rise of the German Ideology* (New York: Doubleday, 1965), 93.

46. Ibid.

47. Rose, *German Question/Jewish Question*, 34.

48. George Mosse, *The Crisis of German Ideology* (New York: Grosset and Dunlap, 1964).

49. Ibid., 66.

50. Besides the studies of Fritz Stern, Peter Gay, and George Mosse already mentioned, the antimodernist prejudices among important sections of German society are also the subject of two other important works: Thomas Nipperdey, *Wie das Bürgertum die Moderne fand* (Berlin: W. J. Siedler, 1988) and Peter Paret, *The Berlin Secession: Modernism and Its Enemies in Imperial Germany* (Cambridge, Mass.: Harvard University Press, 1980).

51. Mosse, *The Crisis of German Ideology,* 153. The nature of reactionary conservatism among the German professoriat and its students has been the subject of several studies, notably Fritz Ringer, *The Decline of the German Mandarins: The German Academic Community, 1890–1933* (Cambridge, Mass.: Harvard University Press, 1969); Walter Laqueur, *Young Germany: A History of the German Youth Movement* (London: Routledge & Kegan Paul, 1962); H. P. Bleuel and A. Klinert, *Deutsche Studenten auf dem Weg ins Dritte Reich* (Gütersloh: Mohn, 1967); Howard Becker, *German Youth: Bond or Free* (London: Kegan Paul, Trench, Trubner & Co., 1946).

52. Quoted in Joachim Remak, ed., *The Nazi Years: A Documentary History* (Englewood Cliffs, N.J.: Prentice-Hall, 1969), 13–14.

53. Leon Poliakov, *A History of Anti-Semitism: From Voltaire to Wagner* (New York: Vanguard, 1975), 444. For an interesting portrait of the Jewish Wagnerites, see Elaine Brody, "The Jewish Wagnerites," *Opera Quarterly* (Autumn 1983): 1:66–80, and the penetrating chapter "Hermann Levi: A Study in Service and Self-Hatred" in Peter Gay's *Freud, Jews and Other Germans,* 189–230.

54. Gordon Craig, *The Germans* (New York: New American Library, 1982), 139.

55. Stern, *Gold and Iron,* 182.

56. Pulzer, *The Rise of Political Anti-Semitism in Germany and Austria,* 92.

57. Shulamit Volkov, "Kontinuität und Diskontinuität im deutschen Antisemitismus, 1878–1945," *Vierteljahreshefte für Zeitgeschichte* 33 (1985): 230.

58. Craig, *Germany: 1866–1945,* 204–5.

59. Quoted in Kohn, *Prophets and Peoples,* 115.

60. Stern, *Gold and Iron,* 495.

61. Paul W. Massing, *Rehearsal for Destruction: A Study of Political Anti-Semitism in Imperial Germany* (New York: Harper & Brothers, 1949), 12.

62. Weiss, *Ideology of Death,* 80.

63. Pulzer, *The Rise of Political Anti-Semitism in Germany and Austria,* 119.

64. There are two excellent cultural and intellectual portraits of Vienna in the late nineteenth and early twentieth centuries: Allan Janik and Stephen Toulmin, *Wittgenstein's Vienna* (New York: Touchstone, 1973), and Carl E. Schorschke, *Fin-de-Siècle Vienna: Politics and Culture* (New York: Knopf, 1980).

65. Quoted in Wertheimer, *Unwelcome Strangers,* 50–51.

66. Ibid., 148.

67. Quoted in Horst von Maltitz, *The Evolution of Hitler's Germany: Ideology, the Personality, the Moment* (New York: McGraw-Hill, 1973), 115.

68. Adolf Hitler, *Mein Kampf* (New York: Reynal & Hitchcock, 1941), 73–75.

69. Wertheimer, *Unwelcome Strangers,* 178.

70. Ibid., 179.

71. For Hitler's indebtedness to Liebenfels, see Wilfried Daim, *Der Mann der Hitler die Ideen gab* (Munich: Isar Verlag, 1958).

72. Ibid., 20–21.

73. Leon Poliakov, *The Aryan Myth: A History of Racist and Nationalist Ideas in Europe* (New York: Meridian, 1971), 296. For just how these racist ideas turned into "racial hygiene" under the Nazis, see Robert N. Proctor, *Racial Hygiene: Medicine under the Nazis* (Cambridge, Mass.: Harvard University Press, 1988).

74. Proctor, *Racial Hygiene,* 20–21.

75. Poliakov, *Aryan Myth,* 296.

76. Pulzer, *Jews and the German State,* 26.

Chapter 4: The Rise of Pathological Judeophobia, 1918–33

1. Richard Hanser, *Putsch: How Hitler Made Revolution* (New York: Pyramid, 1971), 81.

2. Adolf Hitler, *Mein Kampf* (New York: Reynal & Hitchcock, 1941), 210.

3. Quoted in Alan Palmer, *The Kaiser: Warlord of the Second Reich* (New York: Scribner's, 1978), 175.

4. Quoted in James M. Rhodes, *The Hitler Movement: A Modern Millenarian Movement* (Stanford, Calif.: Stanford University Press, 1980), 86.

5. Leonard Baker, *Days of Sorrow and Pain: Leo Baeck and the Berlin Jews* (New York: Macmillan, 1978), 68.

6. Much has been written about Jewish participation and sacrifices in World War I. The most reliable material in English, from which these figures were taken, comes from two excellent studies: Marvin Lowenthal, *The Jews of Germany* (Philadelphia: Jewish Publication Society of America, 1939), 285, and Sidney Osborne, *Germany and Her Jews* (London: Soncino Press, 1939), 71–72. The most indispensable German studies which challenged anti-Jewish lies in the early 1920s are Franz Oppenheimer, *Die Judenstatistik des Preussischen Kriegsministeriums* (Munich: Verlag für Kulturpolitik, 1922), and Jakob Segall, *Die deutschen Juden als Soldaten im Kriege 1914–18* (Munich: M. Hueber, 1922). These two German studies were in reply to a slanderous work by Alfred Roth, written under the pseudonym Otto Armin, entitled *Die Juden im Heer* (Munich: Deutscher Volks-Verlag, 1919).

7. Baker, *Days of Sorrow and Pain,* 69.

8. See Werner E. Mosse, ed., *Deutsches Judentum in Krieg und Revolution* (Tübingen: J. C. B. Mohr, 1971), 30, n. 7.

9. Quoted in Koppel S. Pinson, *Modern Germany: Its History and Civilization* (New York: Macmillan, 1966), 315.

10. Ernest Jones, *The Life and Work of Sigmund Freud* (New York: Doubleday, 1963), 327.

11. Peter Gay, *Freud: A Life for Our Time* (New York: W. W. Norton, 1988), 350.

12. Martin Gilbert, *The First World War: A Complete History* (New York: Henry Holt Company, 1994), 38.

13. For the origins of the "stab-in-the-back" legend (*Dolchstosslegende*), see John Wheeler-Bennett, *Wooden Titan: Hindenburg* (New York: W. Morrow, 1938), 238.

14. Robert G. L. Waite, *The Psychopathic God Adolf Hitler* (New York: Basic Books, 1979), 352–53.

15. Werner E. Mosse, "Die Krise der europäischen Bourgeoisie und das deutsche Judentum," in Mosse, ed., *Deutsches Judentum in Krieg und Revolution*, 16.

16. Ernst Jünger, *Kampf als inneres Erlebnis* (Berlin: E. S. Mittler, 1925), 2, 3, 76–77.

17. Omer Bartov, *Murder in Our Midst: The Holocaust, Industrial Killing, and Representation* (Princeton, N.J.: Princeton University Press, 1996), 5.

18. Hitler, *Mein Kampf*, 25–51.

19. Jürgen Kocka, *Facing Total War: German Society, 1914–1918*, trans. Barbara Weinberger (Cambridge, Mass.: Harvard University Press, 1984), 123.

20. See John Wheeler-Bennett, *The Nemesis of Power: The German Army in Politics* (London: Macmillan, 1964), 21.

21. Werner E. Mosse, "Die Krise der europäischen Bourgeoisie und das deutsche Judentum," in Mosse, ed., in *Deutsches Judentum in Krieg und Revolution*, 19–20.

22. Konrad Heiden, *Der Fuehrer: Hitler's Rise to Power* (Boston: Houghton Mifflin, 1944), chap. 7.

23. Bayerisches Hauptstaatsarchiv München, Staatsministerium des Innern, 66 282; also Werner Jochmann, "Die Ausbreitung des Antisemitismus," in Mosse, ed., *Deutsches Judentum in Krieg und Revolution*, 471–72.

24. Richard M. Watt, *The Kings Depart: The Tragedy of Germany, Versailles, and the German Revolution* (New York: Simon & Schuster, 1968), 248.

25. See Robert G. L. Waite, *The Vanguard of Nazism: The Free Corps Movement in Germany, 1918–23* (Cambridge, Mass.: Harvard University Press, 1952).

26. Ibid., 131.

27. Jochmann, "Die Ausbreitung des Antisemitismus," in Mosse, ed., *Deutsches Judentum in Krieg und Revolution*, 440.

28. Waite, *Vanguard of Nazism*, 206.

29. Ibid.

30. Jochmann, "Die Ausbreitung des Antisemitismus," in Mosse, ed., *Deutsches Judentum in Krieg und Revolution*, 448.

31. Quoted in Jochmann, "Die Ausbreitung des Antisemitismus," in Mosse, ed., *Deutsches Judentum in Krieg und Revolution*, 445.

32. On the rise of the Nazi Party, see Werner Maser, *Der Sturm auf die Republik: Frühzeit der NSDAP* (Stuttgart: Deutsche Verlags-Anstalt, 1973); Georg Franz-Willing, *Ursprung der Hitlerbewegung, 1919–22* (Preussisch-Oldendorf: Schütz, 1974); Reginald Phelps, "Before Hitler Came: Thule Society and Germanen Orden," *Journal of Modern History* 35 (1963): 245–61; and Dietrich Orlow, *The History of the Nazi Party*, 2 vols. (Pittsburgh: University of Pittsburgh Press, 1969).

33. Quoted in Richard Grunberger, *Red Rising in Bavaria* (London: Arthur Barker, 1973), 153.

34. Richard Hofstadter, *The Paranoid Style in American Politics* (New York: Vintage Books, 1967).

35. Robert Cecil, *The Myth of the Master Race: Alfred Rosenberg and Nazi Ideology* (New York: Dodd Mead, 1972), 45.

36. Joachim Fest, *Das Gesicht des dritten Reiches* (Munich: R. Piper, 1980), 230.

37. Roger Parkinson, *Tormented Warrior: Ludendorff and the Supreme Command* (New York: Stein and Day, 1979), 197.

38. Ibid., 203.

39. Ibid.

40. Ibid., 207.

41. On the exiles from Bolshevism, see Robert C. Williams, *Culture in Exile: Russian Emigres in Germany, 1881-1941* (Ithaca, N.Y.: Cornell University Press, 1972).

42. Otto Friedrich, *Before the Deluge: A Portrait of Berlin in the 1920s* (New York: Avon Books, 1972), 120.

43. On the *Protocols of the Elders of Zion*, Jochmann, "Ausbreitung des Antisemitismus," in Mosse, ed., *Deutsches Judentum in Krieg und Revolution,* 460–61; Norman Cohn, *Warrant for Genocide: The Myth of the Jewish World Conspiracy* (Chico, Calif.: Judaic Studies, 1981), 136; and Christian Zentner and Friedemann Bedürftig, eds., *Das Grosse Lexikon des dritten Reiches* (Munich: Südwest Verlag, 1985), 461.

44. Saul Friedländer, "Die politischen Veränderungen der Kriegszeit und ihre Auswirkungen auf das Judentum," in Mosse, ed., *Deutsches Judentum in Krieg und Revolution,* 60.

45. Quoted in Cohn, *Warrant for Genocide,* 136–37.

46. Randall L. Bytwerk, *Julius Streicher* (New York: Dorset Press, 1983), 1.

47. Ibid., 15.

48. Gordon Craig, *The Germans* (New York: New American Library, 1982), 8.

49. Bytwerk, *Julius Streicher,* 105.

50. Joseph Goebbels, *Michael: Ein deutsches Schicksal in Tagebuchblättern* (Munich: Franz Eher Nachfolger, 1935), 57, 82; also Rhodes, *The Hitler Movement,* 46.

51. I owe this reference to Bry to an excellent article on the transformation of sacred history into secularized religion by Manfred P. Fleischer, entitled "Die Religionsphänomenologie als Hilfswissenschaft der Zeitgeschichte," in *Zeitschrift für Religions- und Geistesgeschichte* 27 (1975): 218–20.

52. Rhodes, *The Hitler Movement,* 29–30.

53. Ibid., 77.

54. See Saul Friedländer, "Die politischen Veränderungen der Kriegszeit," in Mosse, ed., *Deutsches Judentum in Krieg und Revolution,* 63–64.

55. Ibid., 64.

56. Hans Zöberlein, *Der Befehl des Gewissens* (Munich: Franz Eher Nachfolger, 1937), 295–97.

57. Hans Frank, *Im Angesicht des Galgens* (Munich: A. Beck, 1953), especially 320–21, 330; also Franz Jetzinger, *Hitler's Youth,* trans. Lawrence Wilson (Westport, Conn.: Greenwood Press, 1976), 19–24.

58. On Hitler's belief that he might have been "infected" by Jewish blood, see Waite, *The Psychopathic God Adolf Hitler,* 146–52; Joachim Fest, *Hitler*

(New York: Harcourt, Brace, Jovanovich, 1974), 15; Norbert Bromberg and Verna Volz Small, *Hitler's Psychopathology* (New York: International Universities Press, 1983), 280–81; and Gertrud M. Kurth, "The Jew and Adolf Hitler, *The Psychoanalytical Quarterly* 16 (1947): 11–32

59. On the question of Döllersheim, see Waite, *The Psychopathic God Adolf Hitler*, 150–51; and Jetzinger, *Hitler's Youth*, 24

60. Waite, *The Psychopathic God Adolf Hitler*, 421.

61. Hitler, *Mein Kampf*, 73.

62. The belief that Jews had a different body odor, as previously mentioned, dated back to the Middle Ages. Hitler strongly subscribed to this belief and held that, next to their long noses, Jews stood out by their distinct (foul) body odor. See Waite, *The Psychopathic God Adolf Hitler*, 151.

63. Hitler, *Mein Kampf*, 75,

64. Rudolph Binion, *Hitler among the Germans* (New York: Elsevier, 1979), 14–25.

65. Ibid., 34.

66. Ibid., 19.

67. Hitler, *Mein Kampf*, 950.

68. Quoted in Henry Picker, ed., *Hitlers Tischgespräche im Führerhauptquartier* (Stuttgart: Goldmann Verlag, 1981), 365.

69. Hermann Rauschning, *Gespräche mit Hitler* (New York: Europa Verlag, 1940), 22.

70. Hitler, *Mein Kampf*, 469.

71. Ibid., 389.

72. Ibid., 398.

73. Ibid., 419–20.

74. Ibid., 421.

75. Eberhard Jäckel, ed., *Hitler Sämtliche Aufzeichnungen, 1905–1924* (Stuttgart: Deutsche Verlagsanstalt, 1980), 89.

76. For the whole speech, see ibid., 607–25.

77. Ibid., 89.

78. Ibid., 622.

79. Ibid., 620.

80. Eberhard Jäckel, *Hitlers Weltanschauung* (Stuttgart: Deutsche Verlags-Anstalt, 1983), 108–11.

81. Hitler, *Mein Kampf*, 447.

82. Ibid., 448.

83. Ibid., 313ff.

84. Ibid., 448.

85. Ibid., 452.

86. Ibid., 609.

87. Ibid., 906.

88. Adolf Hitler, *Hitler's Secret Book*, trans. Salvator Attanasio (New York: Grove Press, 1961), 213.

89. Hitler, *Mein Kampf*, 984.

Chapter 5: German and Jew in the Weimar Period

1. On the psychological dimension of German films, the most astute study is still by Siegfried Kracauer, *From Caligari to Hitler: A Psychological History of the German Film* (Princeton, N.J.: Princeton University Press, 1947; repr., 1974). For his discussion of *The Student of Prague* and similar forerunners of future split personality films, see chapter 2.

2. Ibid., 32.

3. Ibid., 5–6.

4. Voltaire, *A Treatise on Toleration and Other Essays* (New York: Prometheus Books, 1994), chapter 18.

5. On the nature and shortcomings of the Weimar Republic, the following books are especially revealing: Karl Dietrich Bracher, *Die Auflösung der Weimarer Republik: Eine Studie zum Problem des Machtverfalls in der Demokratie* (Villingen, Schwarzwald: Ringer Verlag, 1960); Gordon Craig, *Germany, 1866–1945* (New York: Oxford, 1978); Erich Eyck, *A History of the Weimar Republic*, trans. Harlan P. Hanson, 2 vols. (Cambridge, Mass.: Harvard University Press, 1962); Otto Friedrich, *Before the Deluge: A Portrait of Berlin in the 1920s* (New York: Avon Books, 1973); Peter Gay, *Weimar Culture: The Outsider as Insider* (New York: Harper & Row, 1968); William S. Halperin, *Germany Tried Democracy: A Political History of the Reich from 1918–1933* (New York: Norton, 1965); Walter Laqueur, *Weimar: A Cultural History* (New York: Putnam, 1974); Hans Mommsen, *Die Verspielte Freiheit: Der Weg der Republik von Weimar in den Untergang 1918 bis 1933* (Berlin: Propyläen, 1993); and Detlev J. K. Peukert, *The Weimar Republic: The Crisis of Classical Modernity*, trans. Richard Deveson (New York: Hill & Wang, 1992).

6. Quoted by Eyck, *History of the Weimar Republic*, 1:66.

7. Richard Grunberger, *The Twelve-Year Reich: A Social History of Nazi Germany, 1933–1945* (New York: Holt, Rinehart and Winston, 1979), 3.

8. Wolfgang J. Mommsen, *Imperial Germany, 1867–1918*, trans. Richard Deveson (New York: Arnold, 1995), 120–23.

9. Quoted by Laqueur, *Weimar: A Cultural History*, 115.

10. Ibid.

11. Ibid., 225.

12. John Weiss, *Ideology of Death: Why the Holocaust Happened in Germany* (Chicago: Ivan R. Dee, 1996), 246.

13. For a vivid reconstruction of this controversy over Schnitzler's *Reigen*, see Ludwig Marcuse, *Obszön: Geschichte einer Entrüstung* (Munich: Paul List Verlag, 1962), 209–63.

14. Ibid., 219.

15. Laqueur, *Weimar: A Cultural History*, 225.

16. Ludwig Marcuse, *Mein Zwanzigstes Jahrhundert: Auf dem Weg zu einer Autobiographie* (Munich: Paul List Verlag, 1960), 120.

17. Thomas Childers, *The Nazi Voter: The Social Foundations of Fascism in Germany, 1919–1933* (Chapel Hill: University of North Carolina Press, 1983), 266.

18. On the youth movement, see Howard Becker, *German Youth: Bond or Free?* (London: Kegan Paul, Trench, Trubner & Company, 1946); H. P. Bleuel and A. Klinert, *Deutsche Studenten auf dem Weg ins Dritte Reich* (Gütersloh:

Mohn, 1967); and Walter Laqueur, *Young Germany: A History of the German Youth Movement* (London: Routledge & Kegan Paul, 1962).

19. Peukert, *Weimar Republic,* 149–50.

20. Ibid., 150.

21. Christopher Isherwood, *The Berlin Stories* (New York: New Directions, 1954), 86.

22. Alan Bullock, *Hitler: A Study in Tyranny* (New York: Harper & Row, 1962), 257.

23. Craig, *Germany, 1866–1945,* 484.

24. Friedrich, *Before the Deluge,* chapter 15.

25. Quoted in ibid., 383.

26. Robert G. L. Waite, *The Psychopathic God Adolf Hitler* (New York: Basic Books, 1979), 303–4.

27. Ralf Dahrendorf, *Society and Democracy in Germany* (New York: Doubleday, 1969), 331.

28. Quoted by Friedrich, *Before the Deluge,* 396.

29. Walter Laqueur even goes so far as to say that "what made Weimar culture *sui generis* is unthinkable without the Jews" (*Weimar: A Cultural History,* 77).

30. Werner Mosse, *The German-Jewish Economic Elite, 1820–1935* (Oxford: Clarendon Press, 1989), 344.

31. Ibid., 334.

32. Eva G. Reichmann, *Hostages of Civilization: The Social Sources of National Socialist Anti-Semitism* (London: Gollancz, 1950), 1–39.

33. Karl A. Schleunes, *The Twisted Road to Auschwitz: Nazi Policy toward German Jews, 1933–1939* (Urbana: University of Illinois Press, 1990), 38.

34. John V. H. Dippel, *Bound upon a Wheel of Fire: Why So Many German Jews Made the Tragic Decision to Remain in Nazi Germany* (New York: Basic Books, 1996).

35. Ibid., xxiii.

36. See Franz Rosenzweig, "Draft of the Address at the Opening of the Freies Jüdisches Lehrhaus in Frankfurt," in Nahum N. Glatzer, ed., *The Judaic Tradition* (Boston: Beacon Press, 1969), 573–79.

37. Leonard Baker, *Days of Sorrow and Pain: Leo Baeck and the Berlin Jews* (New York: Macmillan, 1978), 93.

38. Ibid., 117.

39. Ibid., 119.

40. Quoted by Baker, *Days of Sorrow and Pain,* 134.

41. *Statistik des Deutschen Reiches* 451, no. 5 (Berlin: Statistisches Amt, 1936): 7; also Schleunes, *Twisted Road to Auschwitz,* 38.

42. Wolfgang Minaty, ed., *Das Alfred Döblin Lesebuch* (Freiburg im Breisgau: Walter-Verlag Olten, 1985), 150.

43. Alfred Döblin, *Flucht und Sammlung des Judenvolks* (Amsterdam: Querido Verlag, 1935), 37.

44. Ibid., 42.

45. Baker, *Days of Sorrow and Pain,* 93.

46. Peter Gay, *Freud, Jews and Other Germans: Masters and Victims in Modernist Culture* (New York: Oxford University Press, 1978), 149–50.

47. Jakob Wassermann, *Deutscher und Jude: Reden und Schriften 1904–1933* (Heidelberg: Verlag Lambert Schneider, 1984), 60.

48. Ibid., 124.

49. Ibid., 96.

50. Ibid.

51. Ibid., 65–73.

52. Ibid., 276.

53. Gay, *Freud, Jews and Other Germans,* 195.

54. For a biographical account of Weininger, see David Abrahamsen, *The Mind and Death of a Genius* (New York: Columbia University Press, 1946).

55. Henry Picker, ed., *Hitler's Tischgespräche im Führerhauptquartier* (Stuttgart: Goldmann Verlag, 1981), 79.

56. Gay, *Freud, Jews and Other Germans,* 197.

57. Ibid., 192–93.

58. Walter Laqueur, *Weimar: A Cultural History,* 72.

59. Ibid., 73.

60. Quoted in Horst Maltitz, *The Evolution of Hitler's Germany: The Ideology, the Personality, the Moment* (New York: McGraw-Hill, 1973), 148.

61. Ibid.

62. Laqueur, *Weimar: A Cultural History,* 47.

63. Gay, *Freud, Jews and Other Germans,* 176.

64. Laqueur, *Weimar Culture,* 74.

65. Friedrich, *Before the Deluge,* 251.

66. Ibid., 251.

67. Frederic Grunfeld, *Prophets without Honor: Freud, Kafka, Einstein, and Their World* (New York: Kodansha International, 1996), 151.

68. Ibid., 153.

69. Quoted in Weiss, *Ideology of Death,* 241.

70. Quoted in Andrew Samuels, *The Political Psyche* (London: Routledge, 1993), 292–93.

71. Baker, *Days of Sorrow and Pain,* 119.

72. Ernest Jones, *The Life and Work of Sigmund Freud* (New York: Doubleday, 1963), p.212.

73. Gay, *Freud, Jews and Other Germans,* 162.

74. Quoted in Peter Gay, *Freud: A Life for Our Time* (New York: W. W. Norton, 1988), 448.

75. On Vienna and Austria during Freud's life, see Alan Janik and Stephen Toulmin, *Wittgenstein's Vienna* (New York: Touchstone, 1973); W. A. Jenks, *Vienna and the Young Hitler* (New York: Columbia University Press, 1962); William M. Johnson, *The Austrian Mind: An Intellectual and Social History, 1848–1938* (Berkeley: University of California Press, 1972); Sydney Jones, *Hitler in Vienna, 1907–13* (London: Blond & Briggs, 1983); Hans Kohn, *Karl Kraus, Arthur Schnitzler, Otto Weininger: aus dem Jüdischen Wien der Jahrhundertwende* (Tübingen: Mohr, 1962); Arthur J. May, *The Habsburg Monarchy 1867–1914* (New York: W. W. Norton, 1968); Marsha L. Rozenblit, *The Jews of Vienna: 1867–1914: Assimilation and Identity* (Albany: State University of New York Press, 1983); Carl E. Schorschke, *Fin-de-Siècle Vienna: Politics and Culture* (New York: Knopf, 1980); A. J. P. Taylor, *The Habsburg Monarchy, 1809–1918* (New York: Harper & Row, 1965).

76. Taylor, *The Habsburg Monarchy,* 78.

77. Ibid., 12.

78. Quoted in Jonathan Miller, ed., *Freud: The Man, His World, His Influence* (Boston: Little, Brown and Company, 1972), 17.

79. Ibid., 16.

80. Philip Rieff, "The Meaning of History and Religion in Freud's Thought," in Bruce Mazlish, ed., *Psychoanalysis and History* (Englewood Cliffs, N.J.: Prentice-Hall, 1963), 23-44.

81. Sigmund Freud, *Civilization and Its Discontents* (New York: W. W. Norton, 1963), 69.

82. Quoted in Donald L. Niewyk, *The Jews in Weimar Germany* (Baton Rouge: Louisiana State University Press, 1980), 82-83.

83. Point 4 of the Nazi Party program reads: "Only members of the nation may be citizens of the State. Only those of German blood, whatever their creed, may be members of the nation. Accordingly, no Jew may be a member of the nation" (Jeremy Noakes and Geoffrey Pridham, eds., *Nazism: A History in Documents and Eyewitness Accounts, 1919-1945* [New York: Schocken, 1984], 1:14).

84. Quoted in Niewyk, *The Jews in Weimar Germany,* 83.

85. Arnold Paucker, "Der Jüdische Abwehrkampf," in Werner E. Mosse, ed., *Entscheidungsjahr 1932: Zur Judenfrage in der Endphase der Weimarer Republik* (Tübingen: J. C. B. Mohr, 1965), 412.

86. Ibid., 437.

87. Ibid., 446.

88. Ingo Müller, *Hitler's Justice: The Courts in the Third Reich,* trans. Deborah Lucas Schneider (Cambridge, Mass.: Harvard University Press, 1991), 18.

89. Niewyk, *The Jews in Weimar Germany,* 90.

90. Eberhard Jäckel et al., eds., *Enzyklopädie des Holocaust: Die Verfolgung und Ermordung der europäischen Juden* (Berlin: Argon, 1993), 2:1201.

91. Dippel, *Bound upon a Wheel of Fire,* 39.

92. Ibid., 36.

93. Ibid., 39.

94. Ibid.

95. Ibid., 142.

96. Quoted in Baker, *Days of Sorrow and Pain,* 146.

97. Ibid., 124.

98. Dippel, *Bound upon a Wheel of Fire,* 32.

99. Niewyk, *The Jews in Weimar Germany,* 141.

100. Ibid., 51.

101. Ibid., 68.

102. Sarah Gordon, *Hitler, Germans, and the Jewish Question* (Princeton, N.J.: Princeton University Press, 1984), 27.

103. Eugene Davidson, *The Making of Adolf Hitler* (New York: Macmillan, 1977), 374.

104. For the *Sonderweg* historians with strong Germanophobic overtones, see Peter Viereck, *Metapolitics: The Roots of the Nazi Mind* (New York: Capricorn Books, 1961); Edmond Vermeil, *L'Allemagne contemporaine: sociale, politique et culturelle, 1890-1930,* 2 vols. (Paris: Aubier, 1953), translated in a one-volume English edition entitled *Germany in the Twentieth Century* (New York: Praeger, 1956); Rohan Butler, *The Roots of National Socialism* (London: Faber and Faber, 1941); A. J. P. Taylor, *The Course of German History* (New

York: Capricorn Books, 1962); and William L. Shirer, *The Rise and Fall of the Third Reich* (New York: Simon and Schuster, 1960).

105. Shirer, *The Rise and Fall of the Third Reich*, 90.

106. Taylor, *The Course of German History*, 213.

107. Daniel Jonah Goldhagen, *Hitler's Willing Executioners: Ordinary Germans and the Holocaust* (New York: Knopf, 1996), 89.

108. Ibid., 11.

109. Niewyk, *The Jews in Weimar Germany*, 78.

110. Werner Jochmann, "Die Ausbreitung des Antisemitismus," in Werner E. Mosse, ed., *Deutsches Judentum in Krieg und Revolution* (Tübingen: J. C. B. Mohr, 1971), 473.

111. Hsi-Huey Liang, *The Berlin Police Force in the Weimar Republic* (Berkeley: University of California Press, 1970), 71, 84–85.

112. George L. Mosse, "Die Deutsche Rechte und die Juden," in Mosse, ed., *Entscheidungsjahr 1932*, 187.

113. Friedrich, *Before the Deluge*, 258.

114. George L. Mosse, *The Crisis of German Ideology: Intellectual Origins of the Third Reich* (New York: Grosset & Dunlap, 1964) 271.

115. Richard Willstätter, *From My Life: The Memoirs of Richard Willstätter*, trans. Lilli S. Horning (New York: W. A. Benjamin, 1965), 360.

116. Arnold Paucker, "Der Jüdische Abwehrkampf," in Mosse, ed., *Entscheidungsjahr 1932*, 483–84.

117. Willstätter, *From My Life*, 360ff.

118. George L. Mosse, "Die Deutsche Rechte und die Juden," in Mosse, ed., *Entscheidungsjahr 1932*, 192–93.

119. Robert N. Proctor, *Racial Hygiene under the Nazis* (Cambridge, Mass.: Harvard University Press, 1988), 38.

120. Niewyk, *The Jews in the Weimar Republic*, 65.

121. Centralverein deutscher Staatsbürger jüdischen Glaubens, *Friedhofsschändungen in Deutschland, 1923–1932: Dokumente der politischen und kulturellen Verwilderung unserer Zeit* (Berlin: Centralverein, 1932).

122. *Vossische Zeitung*, November 6, 1923.

123. John Dornberger, *Munich 1923: The Story of Hitler's First Grab for Power* (New York: Harper & Row, 1982), 180–88.

124. Arnold Paucker, "Der jüdische Abwehrkampf," in Mosse, ed., *Entscheidungsjahr 1932*, 478.

125. Ibid., 478–79.

126. Dippel, *Bound upon a Wheel of Fire*, 54.

127. Hans-Joachim Kraus, "Die evangelische Kirche," in Mosse, ed., *Entscheidungsjahr 1932*, 256, 269.

128. Richard Hamilton, *Who Voted for Hitler?* (Princeton, N.J.: Princeton University Press, 1983), 72, 110–12.

129. The thesis that the Nazi Party was a "lower-middle-class" party of small shopkeepers, teachers, preachers, lawyers, doctors, farmers, and skilled craftsmen has had a long history, starting with its original formulation by Harold Lasswell ("The Psychology of Hitlerism," *Political Quarterly* 4 [1933], 337–84) and subsequently repeated as historical orthodoxy by historians who were trained to explain social change in terms of class affiliation or economic status. Although the thesis has some merit, it is inadequate as an explanatory model. Several studies (Hamilton, Childers, Merkl) have shown that the ap-

peal of the Nazi Party was far broader than has been previously assumed. The
NSDAP was a populist party that appealed to diverse social groups — from
Lasswell's Kleinbürger to young people, urban workers, upper-class elites, and
military men.

Chapter 6: The Nazi Racial State

1. Hermann Rauschning, *Gespräche mit Hitler* (New York: Europa Verlag,
1940), 223.

2. Ibid.

3. Ibid.

4. Ibid.

5. Ibid., 227–28.

6. Ibid., 231–33.

7. In recent years, historians have refocused attention on the importance
of racial doctrines and practices in Nazi Germany, pointing out that the essence
of Nazism was to transform Germany biologically and replace race with class.
Some of the more important studies in this field are Robert N. Proctor, *Racial
Hygiene: Medicine under the Nazis* (Cambridge, Mass.: Harvard University
Press, 1988); Michael Burleigh and Wolfgang Wippermann, *The Racial State:
Germany 1933–1945* (Cambridge: Cambridge University Press, 1991); Benno
Müller-Hill, *Murderous Science: Elimination by Scientific Selection of Jews,
Gypsies, and Others: Germany, 1933–1945,* trans. George R. Fraser (New
York: Oxford University Press, 1988); Ute Deichmann, *Biologists under Hit-
ler,* trans. Thomas Dunlap (Cambridge, Mass.: Harvard University Press, 1996);
Michael Kater, *Doctors under Hitler* (Chapel Hill: University of North Carolina
Press, 1989); Paul Weindling, *Health, Race and German Politics between Na-
tional Unification and Nazism, 1870–1945* (New York: Cambridge University
Press, 1989); and Henry Friedlander, *The Origins of Nazi Genocide: From Euthanasia to the Final Solution* (Chapel Hill: University of North Carolina Press,
1995).

8. Karl Dietrich Bracher, *The German Dictatorship: The Origins, Structure, and Effects of National Socialism* (New York: Praeger, 1970), 10.

9. On the antidemocratic views of the German conservatives, especially
during the Weimar period, see Kurt Sontheimer, *Anti-Demokratisches Denken
in der Weimarer Republik* (Munich: Nymphenburger, 1962); Klemens von
Klemperer, *Germany's New Conservatism: Its History and Dilemma in the
Twentieth Century* (Princeton, N.J.: Princeton University Press, 1957); Jeffrey
Herf, *Reactionary Modernism: Technology, Culture and Politics in the Third
Reich* (Cambridge: Cambridge University Press, 1984); and Martin Greiffen-
hagen, *Das Dilemma des Konservatismus in Deutschland* (Munich: R. Piper,
1971).

10. The most penetrating studies of Hitler, concentrating on various aspects
of his life, beliefs, and personality are Rudolph Binion, *Hitler among the Germans* (New York: Elsevier, 1979); Allan Bullock, *Hitler: A Study in Tyranny*
(New York: Harper & Row, 1962); Joachim Fest, *Hitler* (New York: Harcourt, Brace & Jovanovich, 1973); Eberhard Jäckel, *Hitler's Weltanschauung*
(Stuttgart: Deutsche Verlags-Anstalt, 1983); Ian Kershaw, *The "Hitler Myth":*

Image and Reality in the Third Reich (New York: Oxford University Press, 1987); Walter C. Langer, *The Mind of Adolf Hitler* (New York: Basic Books, 1982); Werner Maser, *Hitler,* trans. Peter and Betty Ross (London: Allen Lane, 1973); Hermann Rauschning, *Gespräche mit Hitler* (New York: Europa Verlag, 1940); J. P. Stern, *Der Führer and the People* (Glasgow: William Collins' Sons, 1975); Helm Stierlin, *Adolf Hitler: A Family Perspective* (New York: Psychohistory Press, 1976); John Toland, *Hitler,* 2 vols. (New York: Doubleday, 1976); Robert G. L. Waite, *The Psychopathic God Adolf Hitler* (New York: Basic Books, 1977); and Rainer Zitelmann, *Hitler: Selbstverständnis eines Revolutionärs* (Stuttgart: Klett-Cotta 1987).

11. Carl J. Friedrich and Zbigniew K. Brzezinski, *Totalitarian Dictatorship and Autocracy* (New York: Praeger, 1962), 3–13.

12. A vast scholarly literature has grown up in defining the essence of the Nazi state. In the 1930s and 1940s the term "fascist" was in fashion, followed in the 1950s and 1960s by the term "totalitarian," and lately by such designations as the "racial" or "polyocratic" state. Academic historians have also categorized themselves as intentionalist or functionalist, depending on their commitment to either formal behaviorist approaches that describe historical events through the impersonal and underlying functions of society or that see events being shaped by the decisions and beliefs of individuals. The latter debate, which appears to be a needless conflict over the nature of historical reality and is reminiscent of the narrow historiographic conflicts between positivists and idealists, has caused a great deal of turbulence and confusion in the profession and, we might add, has also made an understanding of the Holocaust more difficult. It is a false dilemma to separate function and intention in historical explanation; both are equally necessary elements in reconstructing any event that was made by human beings. For a sampling of various interpretive studies of the Nazi state: the dual state argument, now largely abandoned, was first proposed by Ernst Fraenkel in *The Dual State* (New York: Oxford University Press, 1941). Among the better studies of fascism and totalitarianism, besides the work of Friedrich and Brzezinski already cited, are Hannah Arendt, *The Origins of Totalitarianism* (New York: Meridian, 1958); Karl Dietrich Bracher, *Zeitgeschichtliche Kontroversen: Um Faschismus, Totalitarismus, Demokratie* (Munich: Piper, 1976); Franz Neumann, *Behemoth: The Structure and Practice of National Socialism* (New York: Harper & Row, 1966); Ernst Nolte, *Three Faces of Fascism* (New York: Holt, Rinehart and Winston, 1966); Walter Laqueur and George L. Mosse, eds., *International Fascism, 1920–1945* (New York: Harper & Row, 1966); Walter Laqueur, *Fascism: A Reader's Guide* (Berkeley: University of California Press, 1976); F. L. Carsten, *The Rise of Fascism* (Berkeley: University of California Press, 1967). The theory of Nazi polyocracy was formulated by Martin Broszat, notably in *The Hitler State* (London: Longman, 1981). The most refreshing statement that Nazi Germany was not really a modern state but more like an oriental court was made by H. R. Trevor-Roper in *The Last Days of Hitler* (New York: Macmillan, 1947).

13. See Edward Peterson, *The Limits of Hitler's Powers* (Princeton, N.J.: Princeton University Press, 1969), 4.

14. Norman Rich, *Hitler's War Aims: Ideology, the Nazi State, and the Course of Expansion* (New York: Norton, 1973), 11.

15. Hans Buchheim et al., *Anatomie des SS Staates* (Freiburg: Walter-Verlag, 1965), 1:20–21.

16. Saul Friedländer, *Nazi Germany and the Jews: The Years of Persecution, 1933–1939* (New York: HarperCollins, 1997), 111.

17. Helmut Krausnick, "Stages of Coordination," in *The Path to Dictatorship, 1918–1933* (New York: Doubleday, 1966), 140.

18. Raul Hilberg, *The Destruction of the European Jews* (New York: Holmes & Meier, 1985), 1:55.

19. Müller-Hill, *Murderous Science*, 22.

20. Quoted in Proctor, *Racial Hygiene*, 64.

21. Ibid., 89.

22. See Burleigh and Wippermann, *The Racial State*, 100.

23. Proctor, *Racial Hygiene*, 101–2, 108.

24. Karl A. Schleunes, *The Twisted Road to Auschwitz* (Chicago: University of Illinois Press, 1990), 173.

25. On the SS, see Shlomo Aronson, *Reinhard Heydrich und die Frühgeschichte von Gestapo und SD* (Stuttgart: Deutsche Verlags-Anstalt, 1971); Buchheim et al., *Anatomie des SS-Staates;* William L. Combs, *The Voice of the SS: A History of the SS Journal Das Schwarze Korps* (New York: Peter Lang, 1986); Edward Crankshaw, *Gestapo* (New York: Jove, 1956); Henry V. Dickes, *Licensed Mass Murder: A Socio-Psychological Study of Some SS Killers* (New York: Basic Books, 1972); Robert Gellately, *The Gestapo and German Society: Enforcing Racial Policy, 1933–1945* (Oxford: Clarendon Press, 1990); G. S. Graber, *The History of the SS* (New York: David McKay, 1978); Heinz Höhne, *The Order of the Death's Head* (New York: Ballantine, 1971); Robert Lewis Koehl, *The Black Corps: The Structure and Power Struggles of the Nazi SS* (Madison: University of Wisconsin Press, 1983); Gerald Reitlinger, *The SS: Alibi of a Nation* (Englewood Cliffs, N.J.: Prentice-Hall, 1981); Charles W. Snydor, *Soldiers of Destruction: The SS Death's Head Division, 1933–1945* (Princeton, N.J.: Princeton University Press, 1977); George H. Stein, *The Waffen SS* (Ithaca, N.Y.: Cornell University Press, 1966).

26. On Himmler, see Richard Breitman, *The Architect of Genocide: Heinrich Himmler and the Final Solution* (New York: Knopf, 1991); Peter Loewenberg, "The Unsuccessful Adolescence of Heinrich Himmler," in *American Historical Review* 76 (1971–72): 612–41; Roger Manvell and H. Fraenkel, *Himmler* (New York: Paperback Library, 1968); Peter Padfield, *Himmler: Reichsführer SS* (New York: Henry Holt, 1990); B. F. Smith, *Heinrich Himmler: A Nazi in the Making, 1900–1926* (Stanford, Calif.: Hoover Institution Press, 1971); R. Vogelsang, *Der Freundeskreis Himmler* (Göttingen: Musterschmidt, 1972); Josef Wulf, *Heinrich Himmler: Eine Biographische Studie* (Berlin: Arani, 1960)

27. Joachim Fest, *Gesicht des dritten Reiches* (Munich: Piper, 1980), 157.

28. Reitlinger, *The SS: Alibi of a Nation*, 16.

29. Höhne, *The Order of the Death's Head*, 35.

30. The profession of schoolmaster, especially on the Gymnasium level, seems to have attracted its share of authoritarian personalities with definite sadistic tendencies. In the case of Himmler's father the terms "vindictive" and "sadistic" may not be inappropriate. There is a telling episode, recounted by Padfield (*Himmler*, 16–17), in which a former student in Professor Himmler's school recalls a particularly nasty form of mental torture he had to endure at the hand of the sadistic professor in front of his class at the Wittelsbacher Gymnasium in Munich in 1928. Bullying, mocking, belittling, and humiliat-

ing students in front of the whole class, all done with a supercilious and authoritarian air, was common practice in the German school system.

31. Manvell and Fraenkel (*Himmler,* 20ff) write that his "exactness of habit" amounted to a mania, that he never ceased to record everything he did, even when he shaved, had his hair cut, bathed. Many of his receipts, lists, drafts, ticket-stubs, and so on survived the Holocaust.

32. Padfield, *Himmler,* 608–9.

33. Breitman, *The Architect of Genocide,* 34–35.

34. Felix Kersten, *The Kersten Memoirs, 1940–45* (New York: Macmillan, 1957).

35. Loewenberg, "The Unsuccessful Adolescence of Heinrich Himmler," 612–41.

36. Erich Fromm, *Anatomy of Human Destructiveness* (New York: Holt, Rinehart and Winston, 1973), 301.

37. Trevor-Roper, *The Last Days of Hitler,* 18–20.

38. Fest, *Gesicht des dritten Reiches,* 160.

39. Quoted in Höhne, *The Order of the Death's Head,* 370.

40. So far, Heydrich has not found a good biographer. The most reliable study is by G. Deschner, *Reinhard Heydrich* (New York: Stein & Day, 1981).

41. Aronson, *Reinhard Heydrich,* 17.

42. Ibid., 19.

43. Quoted in Höhne, *The Order of the Death's Head,* 184.

44. Fest, *Gesicht des dritten Reiches,* 139.

45. Ibid.

46. Ibid., 142.

47. Aronson, *Reinhard Heydrich,* 97–98.

48. Walter Schellenberg, *Hitler's Secret Service: Memoirs of Walter Schellenberg,* trans. Louis Hagen (New York: Pyramid Books, 1974), 21.

49. Höhne, *The Order of the Death's Head,* 246.

50. Ibid., 69.

51. Aronson, *Reinhard Heydrich,* 225.

52. Höhne, *The Order of the Death's Head,* 249–50.

53. As a typical example, see "SS-Hauptamt: Die SS, Geschichte und Aufgabe," in Hans-Adolf Jacobsen and Werner Jochmann, eds., *Ausgewählte Dokumente zur Geschichte des Nationalsozialismus* (Bielefeld: Verlag Neue Gesellschaft, 1961), Dokument 1943/44. This document, one of many informational pamphlets issued by the SS, addresses itself to all SS men, but especially new members, by reminding them of the history and tasks of the black corps. It recapitulates the history of the SS and reminds members of their privileged position and their responsibilities, to display "unconditional obedience, total commitment of personality, and iron discipline" (bedingungslose Treue, totaler Einsatz der Persönlichkeit, eiserner Disziplin). It postulates a three musketeer ethics of "All for one and one for all" and sets up four guidelines and corresponding virtues: (1) Race and Tribe (*Rasse und Sippe*), (2) Independent Spirit and Aggressive Mentality (*Freiheitswille und Kampfgeist*), (3) Loyalty and Honor (*Treue und Ehre*), and (4) Unconditional Obedience (*Bedingungsloser Gehorsam*). Its chief task is to wage unconditional warfare against Bolshevism and Jewish plutocracy.

54. Buchheim et al., *Anatomie des SS Staates,* 2:308.

55. Wolfgang Sofsky, *The Order of Terror: The Concentration Camp,* trans. William Templer (Princeton, N.J.: Princeton University Press, 1997), 103.

56. Ibid., 103–4.

57. Eugen Kogon, *The Theory and Practice of Hell: The German Concentration Camps and the System behind Them* (New York: Berkley Books, 1968), 59.

58. Sofsky, *The Order of Terror,* 5.

59. Ibid., 229.

60. Ibid., 115.

61. Ibid.

62. Ibid., 3–4.

63. Höhne, *The Order of the Death's Head,* 227.

64. Christian Zentner and Friedemann Bedürftig, eds., *Das Grosse Lexikon des dritten Reiches* (Munich: Südwest Verlag, 1985), 106.

65. Sofsky, *The Order of Terror,* 38.

66. Gudrun Schwarz, *Die Nationalsozialistischen Lager* (Frankfurt: Campus, 1990), 221–22.

67. International Military Tribunal, *Trial of the Major War Criminals,* 1:129.

68. Bella Fromm, *Blood and Banquets: A Berlin Diary* (New York: Harper & Brothers, 1942), 207–8.

69. Ibid., 208.

Chapter 7: The Jews in the New Nazi Racial State, 1933–39

1. "Regierung Hitler," *Jüdische Rundschau,* January 31, 1933.

2. Eliot B. Wheaton, *The Nazi Revolution, 1933–1935: Prelude to Calamity* (New York: Doubleday, 1969), 224.

3. Joseph Goebbels, *Vom Kaiserhof zur Reichskanzlei* (Munich: Eher Verlag, 1937), 139.

4. Hans-Adolf Jacobsen and Werner Jochmann, *Ausgewählte Dokumente zur Geschichte des Nationalsozialismus* (Bielefeld: Verlag Neue Gesellschaft, 1961), doc. no. 4; also Gerhard Weinberg, *The Foreign Policy of Hitler's Germany: Diplomatic Revolution in Europe, 1933–36* (Chicago: University of Chicago Press, 1981), 26–27.

5. Wolfgang Benz, ed., *Die Juden in Deutschland, 1933–1945: Leben unter nationalsozialistischer Herrschaft* (Munich: C. H. Beck, 1993), 31.

6. Frederic V. Grunfeld, *Prophets without Honor: Freud, Kafka, Einstein, and Their World* (New York: Kodansha International, 1996), 149.

7. Ibid., 147–48.

8. Toni Cassirer, *Mein Leben mit Ernst Cassirer* (Hildesheim: Gerstenberg Verlag, 1981), 189.

9. Ibid., 190.

10. Ibid., 233.

11. Ibid., 260.

12. Saul Friedländer, *Nazi Germany and the Jews: The Years of Persecution, 1933–1939* (New York: HarperCollins, 1997), 12.

13. Wheaton, *The Nazi Revolution,* 286.

14. Friedländer, *Nazi Germany and the Jews,* 12.

15. Peter Gay, *Freud, Jews and Other Germans: Masters and Victims in Modernist Culture* (New York: Oxford University Press, 1978), 163.

16. Quoted in J. M Ritchie, *German Literature under National Socialism* (Totowa, N.J.: Barnes & Noble, 1983), 70.

17. Ibid., 68–69.

18. Michael H. Kater, "Everyday Anti-Semitism in Prewar Nazi Germany: The Popular Bases," *Yad Vashem Studies* 14 (1984): 138.

19. Ibid., 142.

20. Michael M. Kater, *The Nazi Party: A Social Profile of Members and Leaders, 1919–1945* (Cambridge, Mass.: Harvard University Press, 1983), 263.

21. Wolfgang Sofsky, *The Order of Terror: The Concentration Camp,* trans. William Templer (Princeton, N.J.: Princeton University Press, 1997), 136.

22. Karl Dietrich Bracher, *The German Dictatorship: The Origins, Structure, and Effects of National Socialism* (New York: Praeger, 1970), 206.

23. Hans Mommsen, "Der Nationalsozialistische Polizeistaat und die Judenverfolgung vor 1938," *Vierteljahreshefte für Zeitgeschichte* 10 (January 1962): 69, 74.

24. Helmut Genschel, *Die Verdrängung der Juden aus der Wirtschaft im Dritten Reich* (Göttingen: Musterschmidt, 1966), 46.

25. Quoted in Benz, ed., *Die Juden in Deutschland,* 284–85.

26. Quoted in Edward Peterson, *The Limits of Hitler's Power* (Princeton, N.J.: Princeton University Press, 1969), 67.

27. Ibid.

28. Genschel, *Verdrängung der Juden aus der Wirtschaft,* 55.

29. Philippe Burrin, *Hitler and the Jews: The Genesis of the Holocaust* (London: Edward Arnold, 1994), 19.

30. Benz, ed., *Die Juden in Deutschland,* 280.

31. Ibid., 278.

32. Avraham Barkai, *From Boycott to Annihilation: The Economic Struggle of German Jews, 1933–1943* (Hanover, N.H.: Brandeis University Press, 1989), 19.

33. Ibid., 18.

34. Hertha Nathorff, *Das Tagebuch der Hertha Nathorff: Berlin–New York, Aufzeichnungen 1933 bis 1945* (Frankfurt: Fischer, 1989), 38.

35. Margarete Limberg and Hubert Rübsaat, eds., *Sie durften nicht mehr Deutsche sein: Jüdischer Alltag in Selbstzeugnissen, 1933–1938* (Frankfurt: Campus Verlag, 1990), 31–33.

36. Victor Klemperer, *Ich will Zeugnis ablegen bis zum letzten: Tagebücher, 1933–1945* (Berlin: Aufbau Verlag, 1996), 1:15.

37. *Jüdische Rundschau,* April 4, 1933.

38. John V. H. Dippel, *Bound upon a Wheel of Fire: Why So Many German Jews Made the Tragic Decision to Remain in Nazi Germany* (New York: Basic Books, 1996) 94.

39. Bella Fromm, *Blood and Banquets: A Berlin Diary* (New York: Harper & Brothers, 1942), 133.

40. Quoted in Benno Müller-Hill, *Murderous Science: Elimination by Scientific Selection of Jews, Gypsies, and Others: Germany, 1933–1945,* trans. George R. Fraser (New York: Oxford University Press, 1988) 26.

41. For a compendium of all the anti-Jewish laws and guidelines passed in Nazi Germany, see Joseph Walk, ed., *Das Sonderrecht für die Juden im NS-Staat: Eine Sammlung der gesetzlichen Massnahmen und Richtlinien — Inhalt und Bedeutung* (Heidelberg: C. F. Müller Juristischer Verlag, 1981).

42. Nathorff, *Das Tagebuch der Hertha Nathorff*, 39.

43. Inge Deutschkron, *Ich trug den gelben Stern* (Munich: Deutscher Taschenbuch Verlag, 1985), 17.

44. Leonard Baker, *Days of Sorrow and Pain: Leo Baeck and the Berlin Jews* (New York: Macmillan, 1978), 200.

45. Klemperer, *Ich will Zeugnis ablegen*, 106.

46. Fromm, *Blood and Banquets*, 100.

47. Ibid., 96.

48. Nathorff, *Das Tagebuch der Hertha Nathorff*, 46.

49. Friedländer, *Nazi Germany and the Jews*, 116.

50. Quoted in Baker, *Days of Sorrow and Pain*, 150.

51. Benz, ed., *Die Juden in Deutschland*, 332-33.

52. Ibid.

53. Personal interview, June 2, 6, 1997.

54. Personal interview, March 21, 1997.

55. Limberg and Rübsaat, eds., *Sie durften nicht mehr deutsche sein*, 211.

56. Ibid., 153.

57. Quoted in Lucy Dawidowicz, *The War against the Jews* (New York: Bantam, 1976), 227. There is some difference about the time and the occasion of Baeck's well-known remark. See also Dippel, *Bound upon a Wheel of Fire*, 98, and Baker, *Days of Sorrow and Pain*, 145, 152.

58. Wolfgang Benz, *Der Holocaust* (Munich: C. H. Beck, 1995), 19-20.

59. Interview with Alice and Kurt Bergel, Santa Barbara, August 7, 1997.

60. Ibid. Kurt Bergel spelled out the task that lay ahead for Jewish education in Germany in two articles on "Unsere Rationale Erziehungsaufgabe," in the periodical *Der Morgen* (1933). On the contribution of the Jewish Lehrhaus, see Michael Brenner, *The Renaissance of Jewish Culture in Weimar Germany* (New Haven: Yale University Press, 1996).

61. Barkai, *From Boycott to Annihilation*, 46.

62. For an excellent account of Jewish cultural activities in the Third Reich, see "Kulturelles und geistiges Leben," in Wolfgang Benz, ed., *Die Juden in Deutschland*, 75-267.

63. Barkai, *From Boycott to Annihilation*, 43-45.

64. David Farrer, *The Warburgs: The Story of a Family* (New York: Stein and Day, 1975), 112-13.

65. Ron Chernow, *The Warburgs* (New York: Vintage, 1994), 375-76.

66. Barkai, *From Boycott to Annihilation*, 51.

67. On the Haavara arrangement, see E. Black, *The Transfer-Agreement* (New York: Macmillan, 1984); W. Feilchenfeld et al., *Haavara-Transfer nach Pälestina und Einwanderung deutscher Juden, 1933-1939* (Tübingen: Mohr, 1972); and D. Yisraeli, "The Third Reich and the Transfer Agreement," *Journal of Contemporary History* 6 (1971): 129-48.

68. Quoted in Benz, ed., *Die Juden in Deutschland*, 414.

69. Walter Laqueur, *Heimkehr: Reisen in die Vergangenheit* (Berlin: Propylaen, 1964), 53.

70. Ibid., 58.

71. Hjalmar Schacht, *My First Seventy-Six Years: The Autobiography of Hjalmar Schacht* (London: Wingate, 1955), 320

72. Barkai, *From Boycott to Annihilation*, 63.

73. Oron J. Hale, *The Captive Press in the Third Reich* (Princeton, N.J.: Princeton University Press, 1973), 133.

74. Ibid., 289-90.

75. Joachim Fest, *Hitler* (New York: Harcourt, Brace, Jovanovich, 1974), 512.

76. Randall L. Bytwerk, *Julius Streicher* (New York: Dorset, 1983), 169, 221.

77. See Sally Perel, *Ich war Hitlerjunge Salomon* (Munich: Wilhelm Heyne Verlag, 1993).

78. Deutschkron, *Ich trug den gelben Stern*, 28-29.

79. Robert N. Proctor, *Racial Hygiene under the Nazis* (Cambridge, Mass.: Harvard University Press, 1988), 150.

80. G. M. Gilbert, *Nuremberg Diary* (New York: Signet, 1961), 376.

81. Proctor, *Racial Hygiene*, 78-79.

82. Ibid.

83. David Bankier, *The Germans and the Final Solution: Public Opinion under the Nazis* (Oxford: Blackwell, 1996), 41.

84. Max Domarus, ed., *Hitler: Reden und Proklamationen, 1932-1945* (Wiesbaden: R. Löwit, 1973), 1:536.

85. Ian Kershaw, *The Hitler Myth: Image and Reality in the Third Reich* (New York: Oxford University Press, 1989), 236.

86. This was the claim of Bernhard Lösener, one of the legal experts from the Ministry of the Interior who was called to Nuremberg to help draft the anti-Jewish measures ("Das Reichsministerium des Inneren und die Judengesetzgebung," *Vierteljahreshefte für Zeitgeschichte* 9 (1961): 273). For a correction of the record and the impact of the Nuremberg Laws on the population at large, see Otto Dov Kulka, "Die Nürnberger Rassengesetze und die Deutsche Bevölkerung im Lichte geheimer NS-Lage und Stimmungsberichte," *Vierteljahreshefte für Zeitgeschichte* 32 (1984): 582-624.

87. Jeremy Noakes and Geoffrey Pridham, eds., *Nazism: A History in Documents and Eyewitness Accounts, 1919-1945* (New York: Schocken, 1988), 1:537.

88. Friedländer, *Nazi Germany and the Jews*, 151.

89. Raul Hilberg, *The Destruction of the European Jews* (New York: Holmes & Meier, 1985), 1:78.

90. Ibid., 1:79.

91. Bundesarchiv Koblenz, NS2/143; also Burrin, *Hitler and the Jews*, 48-49.

92. Burrin, *Hitler and the Jews*, 50ff.

93. Kulka, "Die Nürnberger Rassengesetze," 602.

94. Ian Kershaw, "The Persecution of the Jews and German Popular Opinion in the Third Reich," *Yearbook of the Leo Baeck Institute* 26 (1981): 270.

95. Kulka, "Die Nürnberger Rassengesetze," 604.

96. Dippel, *Bound upon a Wheel of Fire*, 165.

97. Klemperer, *Ich will Zeugnis ablegen*, 1:58.

98. Baker, *Days of Sorrow and Pain*, 197-98.

99. Ibid., 140.

100. Noakes and Pridham, eds., *Nazism*, 1:286-87.

101. Genschel, *Verdrängung der Juden aus der Wirtschaft*, 141.

102. Friedländer, *Nazi Germany and the Jews*, 235.

103. Quoted in Dippel, *Bound upon a Wheel of Fire*, 178.

104. On the problems involved with emigration, see Hermann Graml, "Die Auswanderung der Juden aus Deutschland zwischen 1933 und 1939," *Gutachten des Instituts für Zeitgeschichte* (Munich: Selbstverlag, 1958), 79-85.

105. Karl A. Schleunes, *The Twisted Road to Auschwitz* (Chicago: University of Illinois Press, 1990), 206-7.

106. Quoted in Baker, *Days of Sorrow and Pain*, 208.

107. Quoted in Dippel, *Bound upon a Wheel of Fire*, 198.

108. Bankier, *The Germans and the Final Solution*, 70.

109. For the text, see Domarus, ed., *Hitler: Reden und Proklamationen*, 1:571.

110. On Hitler's foreign policy, the most sensible and the most comprehensive account is by Gerhard Weinberg, *The Foreign Policy of Hitler's Germany*, 2 vols. (Chicago: University of Chicago Press, 1971).

111. Peter Gay, *Freud: A Life for Our Time* (New York: W. W. Norton, 1988), 624.

112. Ibid., 628.

113. Jochen von Lang, ed., *Eichmann Interrogated: Transcripts from the Archives of the Israeli Police*, trans. Ralph Manheim (New York: Farrar, Straus & Giroux, 1983), 52.

114. Götz Aly and Susanne Heim, *Vordenker der Vernichtung: Auschwitz und die deutschen Pläne für eine neue europäische Ordnung* (Frankfurt: Fischer, 1993), 34.

115. Genschel, *Die Verdrängung der Juden aus der Wirtschaft*, 165.

116. Hilberg, *The Destruction of the European Jews*, 1:106.

117. Genschel, *Die Verdrängung der Juden aus der Wirtschaft*, 176-78.

118. Fromm, *Blood and Banquets*, 273-74.

119. Ibid., 275.

120. The practice of marking Jewish passports with a J (*Jude*) was, in part, at the behest of Swiss authorities, who wanted Jews to be officially identified so that they could be excluded from Switzerland.

121. Dippel, *Bound upon a Wheel of Fire*, 230-31.

122. Helen Fein, *Accounting for Genocide* (New York: Free Press, 1979), 167.

123. Dippel, *Bound upon a Wheel of Fire*, 231.

124. Domarus, *Hitler: Reden und Proklamationen*, 2:899.

125. The most sensible accounts are by Victoria Barnet, *For the Soul of the People: Protestant Protest against Hitler* (New York: Oxford University Press, 1992); John S. Conway, *The Nazi Persecution of the Churches, 1933-1945* (London: Weidenfeld & Nicolson, 1968); Günter Löwy, *The Catholic Church in Nazi Germany* (London: Weidenfeld & Nicolson, 1966); and Klaus Scholder, *Die Kirchen und das Dritte Reich* (Berlin: Ullstein, 1972).

126. The details on the background of Pope Pius XI's encyclical on anti-Semitism have only recently been brought to light by the research of Georges Passelecq, a Benedictine monk, and Bernard Suchecky, a Jewish historian, in their book *The Hidden Encyclical of Pius XI*, trans. Steven Rendall (New York: Harcourt Brace, 1997).

127. Quoted in Friedländer, *Nazi Germany and the Jews,* 251.

128. On the role of Pope Pius XII in the Holocaust, see Saul Friedländer, *Pius XII and the Third Reich* (New York: Knopf, 1966).

129. Baker, *Days of Sorrow and Pain,* 230.

130. Friedländer, *Nazi Germany and the Jews,* 212.

131. On Herschel Grynszpan, see Helmut Heiber, "Der Fall Grünspan, *Vierteljahreshefte für Zeitgeschichte* 5 (1957): 134–72.

132. Dawidowicz, *The War against the Jews,* 134–35.

133. On Kristallnacht, see Hermann Graml, *Reichskristallnacht: Antisemitismus und Judenverfolgung im Dritten Reich* (Munich: Deutscher Taschenbuch Verlag, 1988); Walter H. Pehle, ed., *November 1938: From Kristallnacht to Genocide,* trans. William Templer (New York: Berg, 1991); Peter Freimark and Wolfgang Kopitsch, eds., *Der 9./10. November 1938 in Deutschland: Dokumente zur Kristallnacht* (Hamburg: Landeszentrale für politische Bildung, 1978); Herbert Rosenkranz, *Reichskristallnacht 9. November 1938 in Österreich* (Vienna: Europa Verlag, 1968); and Herbert Schultheis, *Die Reichskristallnacht in Deutschland: Nach Augenzeugenberichten* (Bad Neustadt: Rotter Druck und Verlag, 1985).

134. Graml, *Reichskristallnacht,* 23.

135. Friedländer, *Nazi Germany and the Jews,* 276.

136. Kershaw, "The Persecution of the Jews and German Popular Opinion," 275–81; also Bankier, *The Germans and the Final Solution,* 86.

137. *Bundesarchiv Koblenz,* R 581 1094, fol. 109; also Kershaw, "The Persecution of the Jews and German Popular Opinion," 279.

138. *Documents on British Foreign Policy, 1938–39,* series 3, vol. 3 (London: HMSO), 277.

139. *United States Department of State, Foreign Relations* (1938), 2:400.

140. Quoted in Leonard Baker, *Roosevelt and Pearl Harbor* (New York: Macmillan, 1970), 120.

141. Kershaw, "The Persecution of the Jews and German Popular Opinion," 275.

142. Kershaw, *The Hitler Myth,* 238.

143. Robert Gellately, *The Gestapo and German Society: Enforcing Racial Policy, 1933–1945* (Oxford: Clarendon Press, 1990), 121.

144. For the full transcript of this conference, see *Nazi Conspiracy and Aggression* (Washington, D.C.: U.S. Government Publishing Office, 1946), vol. 4, doc. 1816–PS.

145. Ibid., 425.

146. Ibid., 450.

147. Ibid., 432.

148. Ibid., 433.

149. Ibid.

150. Ibid., 452.

151. Ibid., 455.

152. Hilberg, *The Destruction of the European Jews,* 1:138.

153. On this phantom solution, see Leni Yahil, "Madagaskar: Phantom of a Solution for the Jewish Question," in Bela Vago and George L. Mosse, eds., *Jews and Non-Jews in Eastern Europe, 1918–1945* (New York: Wiley, 1974), 315–34; and Christopher Browning, *The Final Solution and the German Foreign Office* (New York: Holmes & Meier, 1978).

154. Helmut Krausnick, in Hans Buchheim et al., *Anatomie des SS Staates* (Freiburg: Walter-Verlag, 1965), 2:340.

155. Noakes and Pridham, eds., *Nazism*, 2:1049.

156. Dippel, *Bound upon a Wheel of Fire*, 247.

157. Martin Gilbert, *The Holocaust: A History of the Jews of Europe during the Second World War* (New York: Holt, Rinehart and Winston, 1985), 80.

158. Dippel, *Bound upon a Wheel of Fire*, 248.

159. For this peculiar but highly revealing episode on Genghis Khan, see Richard Breitman, *The Architect of Genocide: Himmler and the Final Solution* (New York: Knopf, 1991), 39–43.

160. Ibid., 43.

161. International Military Tribunal, *Trial of the Major War Criminals before the International Tribunal: Proceedings and Documents* (Nuremberg, 1947–49), 26:798–PS; also Fest, *Hitler*, 594.

162. Ibid., 26:1014–PS.

163. There are several accounts of this bizarre military pep-talk or blood ritual, whatever one wants to call it. The most reliable is the one by Admiral Canaris, *Documents on German Foreign Policy*, series D, 7: 200–206, which is reprinted in Noakes and Pridham, eds., *Nazism*, 2:739–43. See also Domarus, *Hitler: Reden und Proklamationen*, 3:1233–38, and Alan Bullock, *Hitler: A Study in Tyranny* (New York: Harper & Row, 1962), 525–27.

Chapter 8: Prologue to the Holocaust

1. Henry Friedlander, *The Origins of Nazi Genocide: From Euthanasia to the Final Solution* (Chapel Hill: University of North Carolina Press, 1995), 39.

2. On the euthanasia program, see besides the work of Friedlander already cited, Michael Burleigh, *Death and Deliverance: Euthanasia in Germany, 1914–1945* (Cambridge, England: Cambridge University Press, 1994; Ernst Klee, *Euthanasie im NS-Staat: Die Vernichtung lebensunwerten Lebens* (Frankfurt: Fischer, 1983); Kurt Nowak, *Euthanasie und Sterilisierung im Dritten Reich* (Weimar: Hermann Böhlaus Nachfolger, 1980); and Hans-Walter Schmuhl, *Rassenhygiene, Nationalsozialismus: Von der Verhütung lebensunwerten Lebens, 1890–1945* (Göttingen: Vandenhoeck & Ruprecht, 1987).

3. Friedlander, *Origins of Nazi Genocide*, 67.

4. Popular medical and racial hygiene journals ran numerous charts showing how expensive it was to maintain the sick at the expense of the healthy. School textbooks, too, featured mathematical problems in which inordinate health costs for the mentally ill were used for pedagogic purposes. Robert Proctor cites the following math problem: The construction of an insane asylum requires 6 million RM. How many housing units at 15,000 RM each could be built for the amount spent on an insane asylums? (Robert N. Proctor, *Racial Hygiene: Medicine under the Nazis* [Cambridge, Mass.: Harvard University Press, 1988], 183–84).

5. This book, subsequently made into a motion picture under the title *I Accuse (Ich klage an)*, was probably the single most important work to pave the way toward the euthanasia program. See Proctor, *Racial Hygiene*, 183.

6. Robert J. Lifton, *The Nazi Doctors: Medical Killing and the Psychology of Genocide* (New York: Basic Books, 1986), 120.

7. Lehner testimony, Nuremberg Document NO-863.

8. Friedlander, *Origins of Nazi Genocide,* 72.

9. Ibid., 86; Lifton attributes the idea to Hitler, who accepted it on the medical advice of Dr. Werner Heyde (*The Nazi Doctors,* 71).

10. Friedlander, *Origins of Nazi Genocide,* 93.

11. Ibid., 110.

12. Michael Burleigh and Wolfgang Wippermann, *The Racial State: Germany, 1933–1945* (Cambridge: Cambridge University Press, 1988), 152.

13. Ibid., 153.

14. Friedlander, *Origins of Nazi Genocide,* 162–63.

15. Lifton, *The Nazi Doctors,* 483.

16. Ibid., 134.

17. Ibid., 30.

18. Gerald Fleming, *Hitler and the Final Solution* (Berkeley: University of California Press, 1987), 25.

19. Friedlander, *Origins of Nazi Genocide,* 238.

20. Lifton, *The Nazi Doctors,* 17.

21. Friedlander, *Origins of Nazi Genocide,* especially chapter 11.

22. Ibid., 236–37.

23. Ibid., 237.

24. Quoted in Gordon Wright, *The Ordeal of Total War, 1939–1945* (New York: Harper & Row, 1968), 44.

25. On the *Einsatzgruppen* see the definitive work is by Helmut Krausnick and Hans-Heinrich Wilhelm, *Die Truppe des Weltanschauungskrieges: Die Einsatzgruppen der Sicherheitspolizei und des SD, 1938–1942* (Stuttgart: Deutsche Verlags-Anstalt, 1981).

26. Ibid., 63. "Die kleinen Leute wollen wir schonen, der Adel, die Popen und Juden müssen aber umgebracht werden." Such murderous sentiments were communicated almost immediately to important leaders of the German high command such as Wilhelm Canaris, Walther von Brauchitsch, and Franz Halder.

27. Ibid., 86.

28. Michael Burleigh, *Germany Turns Eastward: A Study of Ostforschung in the Third Reich* (Cambridge: Cambridge University Press, 1988), 9.

29. Burleigh, *Germany Turns Eastward,* 46–59; for a profile of the staff, 90–91; also Götz Aly and Susanne Heim, *Vordenker der Vernichtung: Auschwitz und die deutschen Pläne für eine neue europäische Ordnung* (Frankfurt: Fischer, 1993), 402.

30. Aly and Heim, *Vordenker der Vernichtung,* 402.

31. Ibid., 92.

32. Ibid., 101.

33. See Hans Frank's entry regarding this event in his *Diensttagebuch des deutschen Generalgouverneurs in Polen, 1939–1945,* ed. Werner Präg and Wolfgang Jacobmeyer (Stuttgart: Deutsche Verlags-Anstalt, 1975), 172–77.

34. Götz Aly and Susanne Heim, "The Holocaust and Population Policy: Remarks on the Decision on the Final Solution," *Yad Vashem Studies* 24 (1994): 46.

35. Aly and Heim, *Vordenker der Vernichtung,* 120

36. This is the major theme in Aly and Heim's recent works on the planning elite in Nazi Germany, especially in their work, *Vordenker der Vernichtung,* which has aroused a great deal of controversy. For a critical evaluation of their argument, see Dan Diner, "Rationalization and Method: Critique of a New Approach in Understanding the Final Solution," *Yad Vashem* 24 (1994): 71–108. Diner's critique, to my mind, is excessively harsh. For a more balanced assessment, see Christopher Browning, "German Technocrats, Jewish Labor, and the Final Solution: A Reply to Götz Aly and Susanne Heim," in *Paths to Genocide* (New York: Cambridge University Press, 1995), 59–76.

37. Lucy Dawidowicz, *The War against the Jews* (New York: Bantam, 1976), 153.

38. See Dieter Pohl, *Von der Judenpolitik zum Judenmord: Der Distrikt Lublin des Generalgouvernement, 1939–1945* (Frankfurt: Peter Lang, 1993), 26. The quote comes from Rosenberg's diary of September 29, 1939 ("Die Juden, das Grauenhafteste, was man sich überhaupt vorstellen könne").

39. For an English version of these instructions, see Jeremy Noakes and Geoffrey Pridham, eds., *Nazism: A History in Documents and Eyewitness Accounts, 1919–1945* (New York: Schocken, 1988), 2:1051–52.

40. Ibid., 2:1052.

41. For an excellent brief summary of Nazi racial institutions, on which I have relied, see Norman Rich, *Hitler's War Aims: Ideology, the Nazi State, and the Course of Expansion* (New York: W. W. Norton, 1973), 55–58.

42. For a detailed account of the Ahnenerbe, see Michael Kater, *Das "Ahnenerbe" der SS 1935–1945* (Stuttgart: Deutsche Verlags-Anstalt, 1974).

43. For the Lebensborn organization, see Georg Lilienthal, *Der Lebensborn e.V.: Ein Instrument Nationalsozialistischer Rassenpolitik* (Mainz: Akademie der Wissenschaften und der Literatur, 1985); and Marc Hillel and Clarissa Henry, *Of Pure Blood* (New York: McGraw-Hill, 1976).

44. For the RKFDV, see Robert Koehl, *RKFDV: German Resettlement and Population Policy* (Cambridge, Mass.: Harvard University Press, 1957).

45. On the document and its significance, see Helmut Krausnick, "Denkschrift Himmlers über die Behandlung der Fremdvölkischen im Osten," *Vierteljahreshefte für Zeitgeschichte* 5 (1957): 194–98; also Peter Padfield, *Himmler: Reichsführer SS* (New York: Henry Holt, 1990) 301–2.

46. Padfield, *Himmler,* 301–2.

47. Ibid., 302.

48. Philippe Burrin, *Hitler and the Jews: The Genesis of the Holocaust* (London: Edward Arnold, 1994), 76.

49. Helmut Krausnick, "Hitler und die Morde in Polen," *Vierteljahreshefte für Zeitgeschichte* 4 (1963): 204.

50. Heinz Höhne, *The Order of the Death's Head* (New York: Ballantine, 1971) 344.

51. This point is brought out strikingly in Omer Bartov's study, *Hitler's Army: Soldiers, Nazis, and War in the Third Reich* (New York: Oxford University Press, 1992).

52. Hillel and Henry, *Of Pure Blood,* 236–43.

53. Joachim Fest, *Hitler* (New York: Harcourt, Brace, Jovanovich, 1974), 646.

54. Alan Bullock, *Hitler: A Study in Tyranny* (New York: Harper & Row, 1962) 652.

55. *Hitler's Secret Conversations, 1941–44* (1953; repr., New York: Octagon Books, 1972), 513.

56. For the documentation of this plan, see Helmut Heiber, "Der Generalplan Ost," *Vierteljahreshefte für Zeitgeschichte* 3 (1958): 281–325.

57. Ibid., 284.

58. Quoted in Bullock, *Hitler: A Study in Tyranny,* 640–41.

59. *Hitler's Secret Conversations,* 13.

60. Pohl, *Von der Judenpolitik zum Judenmord,* 23.

61. On the Nisko project, Jonny Moser, "Nisko: The First Experiment in Deportation," *Simon Wiesenthal Center Annual* 2 (1985): 1–30; also Christopher R. Browning, *The Path to Genocide: Essays on Launching the Final Solution* (Cambridge: Cambridge University Press, 1992), 9–11.

62. Dawidowicz, *The War against the Jews,* 158.

63. Christopher Browning, *The Final Solution and the German Foreign Office* (New York: Holmes & Meier, 1978), 40–42.

64. *Eichmann Prozess, Beweis Dokument, NR 464,* Institut für Zeitgeschichte.

65. Raul Hilberg, *The Destruction of the European Jews* (New York: Holmes & Meier, 1985), 1:206–8.

66. On this conflict between Frank and Himmler, see Höhne, *The Order of the Death's Head,* 361–66.

67. Dawidowicz, *The War against the Jews,* 280.

68. Ibid., 289.

69. On the Jewish ghettos, see Christopher Browning, "Nazi Ghettoization Policy in Poland, 1939–1941," in *Paths to Genocide,* 28–56; Yitzak Arad, *Ghetto in Flames* (New York: Ktav, 1982); H. G. Adler, *Theresienstadt, 1941–1945* (Tübingen: J. C. B. Mohr 1960); Lucian Dobroszycki, ed., *The Chronicle of the Lodz Ghetto* (New Haven: Yale University Press, 1984); Isaiah Trunk, *Judenrat: The Jewish Councils in Eastern Europe under Nazi Occupation* (New York: Macmillan, 1972); Ysrael Gutman, *The Jews of Warsaw 1939–1943: Ghetto, Underground Revolt* (Bloomington: Indiana University Press, 1982).

70. On the Jewish councils, the definitive work is Trunk, *Judenrat.* For a select bibliography of books dealing with Jewish Council, see V. Wahlen, "Select Bibliography on Judenräte under Nazi Rule," *Yad Vashem Studies* 10 (1974): 277–94.

71. Czerniakow left a moving and valuable diary of his experiences before committing suicide in July of 1941. The book has been translated into several languages. For the English version, see Raul Hilberg et al., eds., *The Warsaw Diary of Adam Czerniakow* (New York: Stein and Day, 1979).

72. Hilberg, *Destruction of the European Jews,* 1:218.

73. Primo Levi, *The Drowned and the Saved* (New York: Vintage, 1989), 68.

74. Hilberg, *Destruction of the European Jews,* 1:223.

75. Quoted in Noakes and Pridham, *Nazism,* 2:1069.

76. Quoted in Martin Broszat, "Hitler und die Genesis der Endlösung: Aus Anlass der Thesen von David Irving," *Vierteljahreshefte für Zeitgeschichte* 25, no. 4 (October 1977): 755.

77. Browning, *The Path to Genocide,* 152.

78. Trunk, *Judenrat,* 143.

79. Browning, *The Path to Genocide,* 161.

80. Quoted in Ronnie S. Landau, *The Nazi Holocaust* (Chicago: Ivan R. Dee, 1992), 158.

81. Quoted in Noakes and Pridham, *Nazism,* 2:1067–69.

82. Hilberg, *Destruction of the European Jews,* 1:222.

83. For an account of these discussions, see Browning, *The Path to Genocide,* 34–42; also Aly and Heim, *Vordenker der Vernichtung,* 300–330.

84. Quoted in Browning, *The Path to Genocide,* 39.

85. Aly and Heim, *Vordenker der Vernichtung,* 330.

86. *The Trial of German Major War Criminals* (London: HMSO, 1946), 2:386.

87. Konrad Kwiet, "Nach dem Pogrom: Stufen der Ausgrenzung," in Wolfgang Benz, ed., *Die Juden in Deutschland, 1933–1945: Leben unter nationalsozialistischer Herrschaft* (Munich: C. H. Beck, 1993) 545.

88. Ibid., 581.

89. David Bankier, *The Germans and the Final Solution: Public Opinion under the Nazis* (Oxford: Blackwell, 1996), 135.

90. Kwiet, "Nach dem Pogrom," in Benz, ed., *Die Juden in Deutschland,* 569.

91. Otto Dov Kulka, "Public Opinion in National Socialist Germany and the Jewish Question," *Zion, Quarterly for Research in Jewish History* 40 (1975): 287–88.

92. Kwiet, "Nach dem Pogrom," in Benz, ed., *Die Juden in Deutschland,* 622.

93. Albert Speer, *Spandau,* trans. Richard and Clara Winston (New York: Pocket Books, 1977), 287.

94. Bankier, *The Germans and the Final Solution,* 127.

95. *Das Reich,* no. 46 (November 16, 1941).

96. Victor Klemperer, *Ich will Zeugnis ablegen bis zum letzten: Tagebücher, 1933–1945.* (Berlin: Aufbau Verlag, 1996), 2:92.

97. Ibid., 2:56.

98. Ibid., 2:147.

99. Ibid., 2:107–8.

100. Kwiet, "Nach dem Pogrom," in Benz, ed., *Die Juden in Deutschland,* 652.

101. Konrad Kwiet, "To Leave or Not to Leave: The German Jews at the Crossroads," in Walter Pehle, ed., *November 1938: From Kristallnacht to Genocide* (New York: Berg, 1991), 149.

102. Quoted in Leonard Baker, *Days of Sorrow and Pain: Leo Baeck and the Berlin Jews* (New York: Macmillan, 1978), 270.

103. Ibid., 246.

104. Ibid., 274.

105. For a splendid oral history of this episode, see Nathan Stoltzfus, *Resistance of the Heart: Intermarriage and the Rosenstrasse Protest un Nazi Germany* (New York: W. W. Norton, 1996).

106. Wolfgand Benz, "Überleben im Untergrund, 1943–45," in Benz, ed., *Die Juden in Deutschland,* 672.

107. Baker, *Days of Sorrow and Pain,* 266.

108. Ibid.

109. For a vivid account of this sordid chapter of Jewish betrayal of their own people, see Peter Wyden, *Stella* (New York: Doubleday, 1992).

110. *Dietrich Bonhoeffer: Memories and Perspectives,* Trinity Films, Inc., 1983.

111. Quoted in Klemens von Klemperer, *German Resistance against Hitler: The Search for Allies Abroad, 1938–1945* (Oxford: Clarendon Press, 1992), 39.

Chapter 9: The Harvest of Judeophobic Hatred

1. Gitta Sereny, *Albert Speer: His Battle with Truth* (New York: Alfred A. Knopf, 1995), 248.

2. Ibid., 248–49.

3. See the excellent chapter in Gerald Fleming's book *Hitler and the Final Solution* (Berkeley: University of California Press, 1987), entitled "The Art of Dissembling" (17–31).

4. Quoted in Stanley Edgar Hyman, *The Tangled Bank: Darwin, Marx, Freud and Frazer as Imaginative Writers* (New York: Atheneum, 1974), 343.

5. Henry Picker, *Hitlers Tischgespräche im Führerhauptquartier* (Stuttgart: Goldmann Verlag, 1981), 456.

6. Ibid.

7. Richard Breitman, *The Architect of Genocide: Heinrich Himmler and the Final Solution* (New York: Knopf, 1991), 152.

8. See Max Domarus, ed., *Hitler: Reden und Proklamationen, 1932–1945* (Wiesbaden: R. Löwit, 1973), 4:1657–64.

9. Notation by Engel: "Ziel muss sein den jüdischen Einfluss in gesammten Machtbereich der Achse auszuschalten." Institut für Zeitgeschichte, *Sammelakte Judenfrage* (Akz 5750/77 Best FA 246/1).

10. Quoted in Hildegard Kotze, ed., *Heeresadjutant bei Hitler 1938–1943: Aufzeichnungen des Majors Engel* (Stuttgart: Deutsche Verlags-Anstalt, 1974), 94–95.

11. Rudolph Binion, *Hitler among the Germans* (New York: Elsevier, 1979), 26.

12. Adolf Hitler, *Mein Kampf* (New York: Reynal & Hitchcock, 1941), 984.

13. International Military Tribunal, *Trial of the Major War Criminals before the International Tribunal: Proceedings and Documents* (Nuremberg, 1947–49), 447–PS

14. Breitman, *Architect of Genocide,* 150.

15. Helmut Krausnick and Hans-Heinrich Wilhelm, *Die Truppe des Weltanschauungskrieges: Die Einsatzgruppen der Sicherheitspolizei und des SD, 1938–1942* (Stuttgart: Deutsche Verlags-Anstalt, 1981), 122–23.

16. Alexander Dallin, *German Rule in Russia, 1841–1945* (London: Macmillan, 1957), 20.

17. Quoted in Breitman, *Architect of Genocide,* 147.

18. Christopher R. Browning, *The Path to Genocide: Essays on Launching the Final Solution* (Cambridge: Cambridge University Press, 1992), 121.

19. See Schellenberg's account in his memoirs, *Hitler's Secret Service,* trans. Louis Hagen (New York: Pyramid Books, 1958), 198–201.

20. See Krausnick and Wilhelm, *Die Truppe des Weltanschauungskrieges,* 141ff.

21. Raul Hilberg, *The Destruction of the European Jews* (New York: Holmes & Meier, 1985), 1:288.

22. Krausnick and Wilhelm, *Die Truppe des Weltanschauungskrieges,* 281–85.

23. The document is reproduced in Jeremy Noakes and Geoffrey Pridham, eds., *Nazism: A History in Documents and Eyewitness Accounts, 1919–1945* (New York: Schocken, 1984), 2:1090–91.

24. International Military Tribunal, *Trial of the Major War Criminals,* 4:350.

25. U.S. *National Archives,* RG 238 M-1019/R71841; also Breitman, *Architect of Genocide,* 164.

26. Krausnick and Wilhelm, *Die Truppe des Weltanschauungskrieges,* 159–62.

27. Jochen von Lang, ed., *Eichmann Interrogated: Transcripts from the Archives of the Israeli Police,* trans. Ralph Manheim (New York: Farrar, Straus & Giroux, 1983), 59.

28. Breitman, *Architect of Genocide,* 87–88.

29. Institut für Zeitgeschichte, *Eichmann-Prozess,* doc. no. 441. ("Im Hinblick auf die zweifelos kommende Endlösung der Judenfrage ist daher die Auswanderung von Juden aus Frankreich und Belgien zu verhindern," signed Schellenberg.)

30. For a list of the various euphemisms the Nazis used to disguise their crime against the Jews, see Hilberg, *The Destruction of the European Jews,* 1:328.

31. Hans Frank, *Das Diensttagebuch des deutschen Generalgouverneurs in Polen, 1939–1945,* ed. Werner Präg and Wolfgang Jacobmeyer (Stuttgart: Deutsche Verlags-Anstalt, 1975), 332–33, 336–37.

32. Richard Breitman, "Himmler, the Architect of Genocide," in David Cesarini, ed., *The Final Solution: Origin and Implementation* (New York: Routledge, 1996), 81.

33. See Christian Streit, "Wehrmacht, Einsatzgruppen and Anti-Bolshevism," in Cesarini, ed., *The Final Solution,* 106–7.

34. Joachim Fest, *Hitler* (New York: Harcourt, Brace, Jovanovich, 1974), 648.

35. Andreas Hillgruber, *Germany and the Two World Wars,* trans. William C. Kirby (Cambridge, Mass.: Harvard University Press, 1981), 80–81.

36. See the excellent chapter in Omer Bartov's book *Hitler's Army: Soldiers, Nazis, and War in the Third Reich* (New York: Oxford University Press, 1992), entitled "The Demodernization of the Front" (12–28), in which the author shows convincingly that the Third Reich was able to win a European blitzkrieg but not a total war with the three major industrial powers of the world and experienced conditions in Russia of the utmost primitiveness. The Nazi leadership responded to these conditions by regressing to racial fantasies of the worst and most self-defeating kind, substituting a ruthless and amoral view of war for material strength and rational planning.

37. The best study of Nazi rule in Russia is still Alexander Dallin's *German Rule in Russia, 1941–1945* (London: Macmillan, 1957).

38. Norman Rich, *Hitler's War Aims: Ideology, the Nazi State, and the Course of Expansion* (New York: Norton, 1973), 376.

39. Ibid., 377.

40. For the treatment of Soviet prisoners of war, see Christian Streit, *Keine Kameraden: Die Wehrmacht und die sowjetischen Kriegsgefangenen* (Stuttgart: Deutsche Verlags-Anstalt, 1978). Between June 22, 1941, and the end of the war, 5,700,000 Soviet soldiers fell into German captivity. By the end of the war only 930,000 remained in German camps, a million probably were released or worked as "volunteers" for the Germans, and 500,000 fled or were released. The rest, 3,300,000 (57.5 percent), died.

41. Martin Gilbert, *The Holocaust: A History of the Jews of Europe during the Second World War* (New York: Holt, Rinehart and Winston, 1985), 170.

42. Ibid., 175.

43. Friedrich Nietzsche, *On the Genealogy of Morals,* trans. Walter Kaufmann (New York: Vintage Books, 1969), 40.

44. Christopher Browning, *Ordinary Men: Reserve Police Battalion 101 and the Final Solution in Poland* (New York: HarperCollins, 1992), 11–12.

45. Krausnick and Wilhelm, *Die Truppe des Weltanschauungskrieges,* 579.

46. Noakes and Pridham, *Nazism,* 2:1094; also Krausnick and Wilhelm, *Die Truppe des Weltanschauungskrieges,* 536–37.

47. Noakes and Pridham, *Nazism,* 2:1095.

48. Bartov, *Hitler's Army,* especially chapter 4.

49. Noakes and Pridham, *Nazism,* 2:1069.

50. Krausnick and Wilhelm, *Die Truppe des Weltanschauungskrieges,* 220.

51. Richard Brett Smith, *Berlin 1945: The Great City* (London: Macmillan, 1966), 31.

52. This and similar atrocities are recorded in a book of chilling documents collected by Ernst Klee, Willi Dressen, and Volker Riess, *The Good Old Days: The Holocaust as Seen by Its Perpetrators and Bystanders,* trans. Deborah Burnstone (New York: Free Press, 1991). The term "good old days" (*schöne Zeiten*) was taken from a photo album left behind by one of the perpetrators. For more gruesome documents, see Yitzak Arad, ed., *The Pictorial History of the Holocaust* (New York: Macmillan, 1990).

53. Klee et al., *The Good Old Days,* 58.

54. *Nazi Conspiracy and Aggression* (Washington, D.C.: U.S. Government Publishing Office, 1946), vol. 5, doc. 696–98, 2992–PS.

55. Heinz Höhne, *The Order of the Death's Head* (New York: Ballantine, 1971) 409.

56. Ibid.

57. Ibid.

58. Leni Yahil, *The Holocaust: The Fate of European Jewry* (New York: Oxford University Press, 1990), 325.

59. Hilberg, *The Destruction of the European Jews,* 3:1008.

60. Höhne, *The Order of the Death's Head,* 411.

61. Institut für Zeitgeschichte, Fa, 213/3; also Fleming, *Hitler and the Final Solution,* 45.

62. Hilberg, *The Destruction of the European Jews,* 3:873.

63. Rudolf Höss, *Commandant of Auschwitz: The Autobiography of Rudolf Höss* (New York: Popular Library, 1959), 173; also International Military Tribunal, *Trial of the Major War Criminals,* 2:398, 416.

64. Lang, ed., *Eichmann Interrogated,* 75.

65. Ibid.

66. Institut für Zeitgeschichte, *Sammlung Irving;* also Martin Broszat, "Hitler und die Genesis der Endlösung, *Vierteljahreshefte für Zeitgeschichte* 25 (October 1977): 749.

67. Quoted in Breitman, *Architect of Genocide,* 183.

68. Christopher Browning, "Hitler and the Euphoria of Victory," in Cesarini, ed., *The Final Solution,* 143.

69. International Military Tribunal, *Trial of the Major War Criminals,* 26:266–67, doc. 710–PS.

70. Fleming, *Hitler and the Final Solution,* 67.

71. *National Archives,* NO-365; also Fleming, *Hitler and the Final Solution,* 70–71.

72. Felix Kersten, *The Kersten Memoirs, 1940–45* (New York: Macmillan, 1957), 120.

73. Ibid.

74. See for example, the entries for February 14, 1942, March 6, 7, 27, December 14; April 18, May 13, 1943 (Louis P. Lochner, ed., *The Goebbels Diaries* [New York: Popular Library, 1948]).

75. Breitman, *Architect of Genocide,* 219.

76. Gilbert, *The Holocaust,* 239–40.

77. For a copy of the German document, see Jacobsen and Jochmann, *Ausgewählte Dokumente,* DH Dokument, Wannsee Protokoll, January 20, 1942; for a partial English translation, see Noakes and Pridham, *Nazism,* 2:1127–34.

78. See Fleming, *Hitler and the Final Solution,* 91–94.

79. Raul Hilberg, ed., *Documents of Destruction: Germany and Jewry, 1933–1945* (Chicago: Quadrangle Books, 1971), 102–3.

80. Hannah Arendt, *Eichmann in Jerusalem: A Report on the Banality of Evil* (New York; Viking Press, 1965), 115.

81. On the use of Zyklon-B, see Hilberg, *Documents of Destruction,* 102–3.

82. On Gerstein and his role in the Holocaust, especially his futile efforts to inform the world about what he knew, see Saul Friedländer, *Kurt Gerstein: The Ambiguity of Good* (New York: Knopf, 1969).

83. Statement by Gerstein, April 26, 1945, in International Military Tribunal, *Trial of the Major War Criminals,* PS-1553.

84. Ibid.

85. The literature on Auschwitz has been mounting steadily. The reader is best served by turning to the personal accounts of the survivors, particularly the works by Elie Wiesel, Primo Levi, Jean Améry, Tadeusz Borowski, Victor Frankl, Rudolf Vrba, Miklos Nyiszli, and Filip Müller. A good insight into the Nazi perpetrators can be gained by reading the memoirs of Rudolf Höss, the camp commandant, the collection of documents entitled *KZ Auschwitz as Seen by the SS* (Warsaw: Interpress, 1992), and the court testimonies of survivors, collected by Bernd Naumann, entitled *A Report on the Proceedings against Robert Karl Mulka and Others before the Court at Frankfurt,* trans. Jean Seinberg (New York: Praeger, 1966). The most poignant general account of Auschwitz in English is by Otto Friedrich, "The Kingdom of Auschwitz," the last chapter in his *The End of the World: A History* (New York: Coward, McCann & Geoghegan, 1982).

86. Höss, *Commandant of Auschwitz,* 139.

87. Ibid., 187–88.

88. Lucy Dawidowicz, *The War against the Jews* (New York: Bantam, 1976), 199.

89. Hilberg, *The Destruction of the European Jews*, 3:883–85.

90. There is an excellent chapter in Hans Safrian's book *Eichmann und seine Gehilfen*, entitled "Menschenjagden in Ungarn und der Slowakei," which chronicles the details of this last frantic operation (Frankfurt: Fischer, 1995), 293–319.

91. On these Nazi-Jewish negotiations, see Yehuda Bauer, *Jews for Sale?* (New Haven: Yale University Press, 1994).

92. Quoted in Leonard Baker, *Days of Sorrow and Pain: Leo Baeck and the Berlin Jews* (New York: Macmillan, 1978) 315.

93. There is a vivid and moving reconstruction of these marches in David Jonah Goldhagen, *Hitler's Willing Executioners: Ordinary Germans and the Holocaust* (New York: Knopf, 1996), 328–71.

94. See Heinz Artzt, *Mörder in Uniform* (Munich: Kindler, 1979), 70–72; also Höhne, *The Order of the Death's Head*, 422.

95. Primo Levi, *The Drowned and the Saved* (New York: Vintage, 1989), 11.

96. Quoted in Friedrich, *The End of the World*, 292.

97. As Wolfgang Sofsky put it, "The perpetrators behind their desks and many junior-level, whip-wielding associates were neither perverse nor sadistic — they were frighteningly normal" (*Order of Terror: The Concentration Camp*, trans. William Templer [Princeton, N.J.: Princeton University Press, 1997], 224).

98. Noakes and Pridham, *Nazism*, 2:1199.

99. Lang, ed., *Eichmann Interrogated*, 169.

100. Ibid., 57.

101. Ibid., 157.

102. Höss, *Commandant of Auschwitz*, 122.

103. Lang, ed., *Eichmann Interrogated*, 158.

104. Gitta Sereny, *Into That Darkness: From Mercy Killing to Mass Murder* (New York: McGraw Hill, 1974), 22.

105. Ibid., 201–2.

106. Höss, *Commandant of Auschwitz*, 144–45.

107. Ibid., 77.

108. Arendt, *Eichmann in Jerusalem*, 51–52.

109. Ibid., 136.

110. Joachim Fest, *Das Gesicht des dritten Reiches* (Munich: R. Piper, 1980) 108.

111. Christopher Browning, *The Final Solution and the German Foreign Office* (New York: Holmes & Meier, 1978), 63.

112. Ibid., 180.

113. Robert J. Lifton, *The Nazi Doctors: Medical Killing and the Psychology of Genocide* (New York: Basic Books, 1986), chapter 19.

114. Arendt, *Eichmann in Jerusalem*, 25.

115. Lifton, *The Nazi Doctors*, 423.

116. Ibid., 481.

117. Ibid., 15–16.

118. *The Trial of German Major War Criminals* (London: HMSO, 1946), 21:11.

119. Quoted in Lifton, *The Nazi Doctors,* 292.

120. International Military Tribunal, *Trial of the Major War Criminals,* pt. 20, 402.

121. Gerald L. Posner and John Ware, *Mengele* (New York: Dell, 1986), 27–28.

122. Lifton, *The Nazi Doctors,* 341.

123. Posner and Ware, *Mengele,* 12.

124. Lifton, *The Nazi Doctors,* 351.

125. Quoted in Posner and Ware, *Mengele,* 46.

126. Lifton, *The Nazi Doctors,* 381.

127. Browning, *Ordinary Men.*

128. Daniel Jonah Goldhagen, *Hitler's Willing Executioners: Ordinary Germans and the Holocaust* (New York: Knopf, 1996).

129. Browning, *Ordinary Men,* 58.

130. Ibid.

131. Ibid.

132. Ibid., 66.

133. Ibid., 69.

134. Goldhagen, *Hitler's Willing Executioners,* 286.

135. Ibid., 241.

136. Ibid., 268.

137. Sereny, *Into That Darkness,* 101.

138. For the Zimbardo experiment, see Philip Zimbardo, *The Psychological Power and Pathology of Imprisonment,* statement prepared for the U.S. House of Representatives Committee on the Judiciary, Subcommittee No. 3: Hearings on Prison Reform, San Francisco (October 25, 1971); Philip Zimbardo, "Pathology of Imprisonment," *Society* 9 (April 1972), 4–8; and the more comprehensive study by Craig Haney, Curtis Banks, and Philip Zimbardo, "Interpersonal Dynamics in a Simulated Prison," *International Journal for Criminology and Penology* (1983): 69–97.

139. For a summary of the Milgram experiments and their implications, see Stanley Milgram, *Obedience to Authority* (New York: Harper & Row, 1974).

140. Ibid., xii.

141. Browning, *Ordinary Men,* 168.

142. Ibid., 174.

143. Milgram, *Obedience to Authority,* 175

144. Ibid., 176.

145. Emil L. Fackenheim, "Holocaust and Weltanschauung: Philosophical Reflections on Why They Did It," *Holocaust and Genocide Studies* 3, no. 2 (1988): 197.

146. Ibid.

147. Ibid., 203–6.

148. Jean Amery, "Torture," in John K. Roth and Michael Berenbaum, eds., *Holocaust: Religious and Philosophical Implications* (New York: Paragon House, 1989), 170.

149. For an excellent appraisal of the pretensions of such misapplied science, see Malachi Martin, "The Scientist as Shaman," *Harper's Magazine* (March 1972): 54–61.

150. On current millennial mumbo jumbo, see Elaine Showalter, *Hysterical Epidemics and Modern Media* (New York: Columbia University Press, 1997),

and Michael Shermer, *Why People Believe Weird Things: Other Confusions of Our Times* (New York: W. H. Freeman & Co., 1997).

151. Lewis Mumford, *The Myth of the Machine: The Pentagon of Power* (New York: Harcourt Brace, Jovanovich, 1964).

152. Ibid., 260.

153. Quoted in Mumford, *Myth of the Machine,* 186.

154. Ernest Becker, *Escape from Evil* (New York: Free Press, 1975), 96–127.

155. Norbert Elias, *The Germans* (New York: Columbia University Press, 1996), 331–32.

156. Leo Alexander, "Socio-Psychologic Structure of the SS," *Archives of Neurology and Psychiatry* 58 (1948): 626.

157. Lifton, *The Nazi Doctors,* 494.

158. Browning, *Ordinary Men,* 184.

159. Ibid.

160. Zygmunt Bauman, *Modernity and the Holocaust* (Ithaca, N.Y.: Cornell University Press, 1989), 15.

161. Elias, *The Germans,* 325.

162. Bauman, *Modernity and the Holocaust,* 101.

163. Herbert C. Kelman, "Violence without Moral Restraint," *Journal of Social Issues* 29 (1973): 29–61.

164. Bauman, *Modernity and the Holocaust,* 91.

165. Leon Rappoport and George Kren, *The Holocaust and the Crisis of Human Behavior* (New York: Holmes and Meier, 1980) 70.

166. Jean Amery, "Torture," in Roth and Berenbaum, eds., *Holocaust,* 173.

167. Gisella Perl, *I Was a Doctor in Auschwitz* (New York: International Universities Press, 1948), 171.

168. Alexander Donat, *The Holocaust Kingdom* (New York: Holocaust Library, 1978), 269.

169. Levi, *The Drowned and the Saved,* 111.

170. Bartov, *Hitler's Army,* chapter 4.

171. Ibid., 152.

172. Quoted in Bartov, *Hitler's Army,* 157.

173. Ibid., 163.

174. Ibid.

175. Walter Manoschek, ed., *Es gibt nur eines für das Judentum: Vernichtung. Das Judenbild in deutschen Soldatenbriefen 1939–1944* (Hamburg: HIS Verlages, mbH, 1995), 15.

176. Ibid., 18.

177. Ibid., 51.

178. Bartov, *Hitler's Army,* 162.

179. Ibid.

180. Ibid., 166.

181. Manoschek, ed., *Es gibt nur eines für das Judentum: Vernichtung,* 52.

182. Wolfram Wette, "Rassenfeind," in Walter Manoschek, ed., *Die Wehrmacht im Rassenkrieg* (Vienna: Picus, 1996), 69.

183. Hannes Heer, "Bittere Pflicht," in Manoschek, ed., *Die Wehrmacht im Rassenkrieg,* 124.

184. Bela Vago and George Mosse, eds., *Jews and Non-Jews in Eastern Europe* (New York: Wiley, 1974), xvi.

185. Quoted in Rappoport and Kren, *The Holocaust and the Crisis of Human Behavior*, 91.

186. For the most comprehensive account of different national responses to the Holocaust, see Helen Fein, *Accounting for Genocide: National Responses and Jewish Victimization during the Holocaust* (New York: Free Press, 1979). For a briefer version, there is a good comparative study by Yeshayahu Jelinek, "The Holocaust and the Internal Policies of the Nazi Satellites in Eastern Europe," in *Proceedings of the Eighth World Congress of Jewish Studies* (Jerusalem: Magnes Press, 1985), 173–78.

187. For Slovakia, see Yeshayahu Jelinek, *The Lust for Power: Nationalism, Slovakia, and the Communists, 1918–1948* (Boulder, Colo.: East European Monographs, 1976), and the same author's "The Final Solution: The Slovak Version," *East European Quarterly* 4 (1970): 431–44; L. Lipscher, *Die Juden im Slowakischen Staat, 1939–1945* (Munich: Oldenbourg, 1980).

188. On Yugoslavia's role in the Holocaust, see Z. Löwenthal, ed., *The Crimes of the Fascist Occupants and their Collaborators against Jews in Yugoslavia* (Belgrade, 1957); Walter Manoschek, ed., *Serbien ist judenrein: Militärische Besatzungspolitik und Judenvernichtung in Serbien* (Munich: Oldenbourg, 1995), and Jasa Romano, *Jews of Yugoslavia, 1941–1945: Victims of Genocide and Freedom Fighters* (Belgrade: Savez jevrejskih Opstina Jugoslavije, 1982).

189. On the Jews in Hungary, see Randolph L. Braham, *The Politics of Genocide: The Holocaust in Hungary*, 2 vols. (New York: Columbia University Press, 1981).

190. This story has been skillfully retold recently by Hans Safrian, *Eichmann und seine Gehilfen* (Frankfurt: Fischer, 1995), 293–311.

191. On the Jews in Romania, see the works of A. Ancel, particularly the twelve-volume documentary collection entitled *Documents concerning the Fate of Romanian Jewry during the Holocaust* (Jerusalem: Beale Klarsfeld Foundation, 1986); Martin Broszat, "Das Dritte Reich und die Rumänische Judenpolitik," in *Gutachten des Instituts für Zeitgeschichte* (Munich: Institut für Zeitgeschichte, 1958), 102–83; A. Cohen, "Pétain, Horthy, Antonescu and the Jews, 1942–44," *Yad Vashem Studies* 18 (1987); S. Fischer-Galati, "Fascism, Communism, and the Jewish Question in Rumania," in Vago and Mosse, eds., *Jews and Non-Jews in Eastern Europe*.

192. Hilberg, *The Destruction of the European Jews*, 2:759.

193. On Bulgaria's Jewish policies, see Frederick Chary, *The Bulgarian Jews and the Final Solution, 1940–1944* (Pittsburgh: University of Pittsburgh Press, 1972); Nisan Oren, "The Bulgarian Exception: A Reassessment of the Salvation of the Jewish Community," *Yad Vashem Studies* 7 (1968): 83–106; and Vicki Tamir, *Bulgaria and Her Jews: The History of a Dubious Symbiosis* (New Haven: Yale University Press, 1979).

194. On Italian policies relating to the Jews there are two important studies: Meir Michaelis, *Mussolini and the Jews: German-Italian Relations and the Jewish Question in Italy, 1922–1945* (Oxford: Oxford University Press, 1978); and Susan Zuccotti, *The Italians and the Holocaust: Persecution, Rescue, and Survival* (New York: Basic Books, 1987).

195. On Denmark and the Jews, see Harold Flender, *Rescue in Denmark* (New York: Holocaust Library, 1963); and Leni Yahil, *The Rescue of Dan-*

ish Jewry: Test of a Democracy (Philadelphia: Jewish Publication Society of America, 1969).

196. On the Jews of Belgium and Holland, see H. D. Arntz, *Judenverfolgung im deutsch-belgischen Grenzgebiet* (Euskirchen: Kumpel, Volksblatt-Druckerei & Verlag, 1989); Michael R. Marrus and Robert O. Paxton, "The Nazis and the Jews in Occupied Western Europe: A Comparative Study," *Journal of Modern History* 54 (1982): 687–714; and Jacob Presser, *The Destruction of the Dutch Jews* (New York: Dutton, 1969).

197. The definitive work on France and the Jewish question is by Michael R. Marrus and Robert O. Paxton, *Vichy France and the Jews* (Stanford, Calif.: Stanford University Press, 1995; originally published in English by Basic Books in 1981).

198. Philippe Burrin, *France under the Germans* (New York: New Press, 1996).

199. Marrus and Paxton, *Vichy France and the Jews*, 33.

200. Ibid., 366.

201. Ibid., 368.

202. Ibid., 366.

203. Ibid., 228, 370–71.

204. Hilberg, *The Destruction of the European Jews*, 1:22ff.

205. Rappoport and Kren, *The Holocaust and the Crisis of Human Behavior*, 75.

206. Ibid., 76.

207. The literature on Jewish resistance has been growing steadily, but all the books, articles, memoirs, and diaries dedicated to acts of resistance against the Nazis by either Jews or Germans do not alter the fact that resistance, no matter how noble or brave, made no difference in the outcome. Of the many books on Jewish resistance, the following are especially important: Reuben Ainsztein, *Jewish Resistance in Nazi-Occupied Eastern Europe* (New York: Barnes and Noble, 1974); Yehuda Bauer, *They Chose Life: Jewish Resistance in the Holocaust* (New York: American Jewish Committee, 1973); H. Eschwege, "Resistance of German Jews against the Nazi Regime," *Yearbook of the Leo Baeck Institute* 15 (1970): 143–80; I. Gutman, *Fighters among Ruins: The Story of Jewish Heroism during World War II* (Washington: B'nai B'rith, 1988); M. M. Kohn, ed., *Jewish Resistance during the Holocaust* (Jerusalem: Yad Vashem, 1971) .

208. Hilberg, *The Destruction of the European Jews*, 3:330–44.

209. See Walter Laqueur, *The Terrible Secret: Suppression of the Truth about Hitler's Final Solution* (New York: Penguin, 1982).

210. Gilbert, *The Holocaust*, 186. See also the same author's *Auschwitz and the Allies* (New York: Henry Holt, 1981).

211. On what we know so far of Swiss complicity in the Holocaust, especially on Swiss financial transactions with the Nazis, see Adam Le Bor, *Hitler's Secret Bankers: The Myth of Swiss Neutrality* (Secaucus, N.J.: Birch Lane Press, 1997), and Tom Bower, *Nazi Gold* (New York: HarperCollins, 1997).

212. Laqueur, *The Terrible Secret*, 198.

213. Raul Hilberg, *Perpetrators, Victims, Bystanders: The Jewish Catastrophe* (New York: HarperCollins, 1993), 249–55.

Chapter 10: The Germans and the Holocaust in War and Peace

1. Quoted in Robert Leckie, *Delivered from Evil: The Saga of World War II* (New York: Harper & Row, 1978), 904. For Eisenhower's own account, see Dwight D. Eisenhower, *Crusade in Europe* (New York: Doubleday, 1948), 408–9.

2. Karl Jaspers, *The Question of German Guilt* (New York: Capricorn Books, 1961), 31–46.

3. Milton Mayer, *They Thought They Were Free* (Chicago: University of Chicago Press, 1955), 74.

4. Ibid., 75.

5. Hannah Arendt, *Eichmann in Jerusalem: A Report on the Banality of Evil* (New York; Viking Press, 1965), 52.

6. See David Bankier, *The Germans and the Final Solution: Public Opinion under the Nazis* (Oxford: Blackwell, 1996), 104–15.

7. Lawrence D. Stokes, "The German People and the Destruction of the European Jews," *Central European History* 6, no. 2 (1973): 190.

8. Peter Hoffmann, *Stauffenberg: A Family History, 1905–1944* (New York: Cambridge University Press, 1995), 133–34, 151.

9. Quoted in John K. Roth and Michael Berenbaum, eds., *Holocaust: Religious and Philosophical Implications* (New York: Paragon House, 1989), 101.

10. For Karski's own account, see his work *The Story of a Secret State* (London: Hodder, 1945). There is also a good snapshot of Karski's role as a messenger reporting on the evils of the Holocaust in Raul Hilberg, *Perpetrators, Victims, Bystanders: The Jewish Catastrophe* (New York: HarperCollins, 1993), 221–24.

11. Ian Kershaw, "The Persecution of the Jews and German Popular Opinion in the Third Reich," *Yearbook of the Leo Baeck Institute* 26 (1981): 281.

12. Quoted in ibid., 285.

13. Ibid.

14. *Das Reich,* November 16, 1941.

15. See Siegfried Maruhn, "Das Deutsche Volk war eingeweiht, *Die Zeit,* no. 22 (June 2, 1995).

16. Ibid.

17. See *Die Zeit* (January 1995); also Hannes Heer, "Bittere Pflicht: Der Rassenkrieg der Wehrmacht und seine Vorraussetzungen," in Walter Manoschek, ed., *Die Wehrmacht im Rassenkrieg* (Vienna: Picus, 1996), 116–17.

18. Norbert Frei quoted in Bernhard Moltmann et al., eds., *Erinnerung: Zur Gegenwart des Holocausts in Deutschland-West und Deutschland-Ost* (Frankfurt: Haag & Herchen, 1993), 34.

19. Quoted in Marlis Steinert, *Hitler's War and the Germans* (Athens, Ohio: Ohio University Press, 1977), 146.

20. Leon Rappoport and George Kren, *The Holocaust and the Crisis of Human Behavior* (New York: Holmes and Meier, 1980), 14.

21. See Shulamit Volkov, "Kontinuität und Diskontinuität im Deutschen Antisemitismus, 1878–1945," *Vierteljahreshefte für Zeitgeschichte,* 221–43.

22. Quoted in Heinz Höhne, *The Order of the Death's Head* (New York: Ballantine, 1971), 413.

23. International Military Tribunal, *Trial of the Major War Criminals before the International Tribunal: Proceedings and Documents* (Nuremberg, 1947–49), document PS-1919.

24. Norman Cohn, *Warrant for Genocide: The Myth of the Jewish World Conspiracy* (Chico, Calif.: Judaic Studies, 1981), 212.

25. Kershaw, "The Persecution of the Jews and German Popular Opinion in the Third Reich," 289.

26. Jaspers, *The Question of German Guilt*, 47.

27. For the most balanced account of the Nuremberg trials, see Telford Taylor, *The Anatomy of the Nuremberg Trials* (New York: Knopf, 1992).

28. International Military Tribunal, *Trial of the Major War Criminals,* 12:7–8.

29. We might add that Speer's account of his involvement in the crimes of the Third Reich has been questioned by a number of historians, notably by Mathias Schmidt, *Albert Speer: The End of a Myth* (New York: St. Martin's Press, 1984).

30. Quoted in Tom Bower, *Blind Eye to Murder: Britain, America and the Purging of Nazi Germany — A Pledge Betrayed* (London: Andre Deutsch, 1981), 157.

31. Ibid.

32. Ibid., 185.

33. George Lavy, *Germany and Israel: Moral Debt and National Interest* (London: Frank Cass, 1996), 11.

34. Anson Rabinbach, "The Jewish Question in the German Question," in Peter Baldwin, ed., *Reworking the Past: Hitler, the Holocaust, and the Historian's Debate* (Boston: Beacon Press, 1990), 48.

35. Josef Habisreutinger and Walter Krick, *Geschichte der Neuesten Zeit* (Bamberg: C. C. Buchners Verlag, 1955), 163–64, 173.

36. Ulrich Herbert, "Der Holocaust in der Geschichtsschreibung der Bundesrepublik Deutschland," in Moltmann, ed., *Erinnerung*, 41.

37. For an excellent treatment of this legend of the *saubere Wehrmacht*, see the disturbing visual material and commentary put together by the Hamburger Institut für Sozialforschung entitled *Vernichtungskrieg, Verbrechen der Wehrmacht 1941 to 1945* (Hamburg: HIS Verlags.mbH., 1996).

38. For a comprehensive history of how the Nazi past has shaped the postwar world, see Jeffrey Herf, *Divided Memory: The Nazi Past in the Two Germanys* (Cambridge, Mass.: Harvard University Press, 1997), especially chapter 9.

39. Werner Bergmann and Rainer Erb, *Antisemitismus in der Bundesrepublik: Ergebnisse der empirischen Forschung von 1946–1989* (Opladen: Leske & Budrich, 1991), 57–58.

40. Sarah Gordon, *Hitler, Germans, and the Jewish Question* (Princeton, N.J.: Princeton University Press, 1984). 198–99.

41. Ibid., 199–200.

42. Ibid., 202.

43. Elizabeth Noelle and Erich Peter Neumann, eds., *Jahrbuch der öffentlichen Meinung, 1959–1964* (Allensbach: Verlag für Demoskopie, 1965), 214.

44. Ibid., 215.

45. Robert Wistrich, *Antisemitism: The Longest Hatred* (New York: Schocken, 1994), 79.

46. Bergmann and Erb, *Antisemitismus in der Bundesrepublik Deutschland*, 71

47. Frederick Weil, "The Imperfectly Mastered Past: Anti-Semitism in West Germany since the Holocaust, *New German Critique*, no. 20 (Spring–Summer 1980), 141.

48. Theodor W. Adorno, "Was bedeutet: Aufarbeitung der Vergangenheit," in *Erziehung zur Mündigkeit*, ed. Gerd Kadelbach (Frankfurt: Suhrkamp, 1970), 10–28.

49. Walter Laqueur, *Germany Today* (London: Weidenfeld and Nicolson, 1985), 54.

50. Richard C. Schneider, "Germany — Home Sweet Home?" in Susan Stern, ed., *Speaking Out: Jewish Voices from Germany* (Chicago: Atlantik Brücke, 1995), 95

51. Karl Dietrich Bracher, *The German Dictatorship: The Origins, Structure, and Effects of National Socialism* (New York: Praeger, 1970), 420–31. By contrast, the topic of German resistance is given twenty-nine pages (431–60).

52. Ibid., 476.

53. Bower, *Blind Eye to Murder*, 385.

54. Ingo Müller, *Hitler's Justice: The Courts of the Third Reich*, trans. Deborah Lucas Schneider (Cambridge, Mass.: Harvard University Press, 1991), 203.

55. Ibid., 205.

56. Ibid., 242.

57. Quoted in Raul Hilberg, *The Destruction of the European Jews* (New York: Holmes & Meier, 1985), 3:1079.

58. Paragraph 211 of the Criminal Code.

59. Müller, *Hitler's Justice*, 254.

60. Ibid.

61. Ibid., 255.

62. Willi Dressen, "The Role of the Wehrmacht and the Police in the Annihilation of the Jews: The Prosecution and Postwar Careers of Perpetrators in the Police Force of the Federal Republic of Germany, *Yad Vashem Studies* 22 (1993): 305–6.

63. Ibid., 306.

64. Müller, *Hitler's Justice*, 260.

65. Dressen, "The Role of the Wehrmacht and the Police in the Annihilation of the Jews," 309.

66. Ibid., 385.

67. Bower, *Blind Eye to Murder*, 382.

68. Alfred Grosser, *Germany in Our Time: A Political History of the Postwar Years* (New York: Praeger, 1970), 220–21.

69. Wistrich, *Antisemitism: The Longest Hatred*, 82.

70. Quoted in Gordon Craig, *The Germans* (New York: New American Library, 1982), 144.

71. On the Fassbinder controversy and the various conflicting views it stirred up, see Heiner Lichtenstein, *Die Fassbinder-Kontroverse oder das Ende der Schonzeit* (Königstein: Athenäum, 1986).

72. Michael Wolffsohn, *Ewige Schuld: 40 Jahre Deutsch-Jüdisch-Israelische Beziehungen* (Munich: Piper, 1988), 42.

73. Lavy, *Germany and Israel,* 199–200.

74. Nolte's essay and his replies to his critics are contained in a collection of essays entitled *Das Vergehen der Vergangenheit: Antwort an meine Kritiker im sogenannten Historikerstreit* (Berlin: Ullstein, 1987). A good collection of historical replies to Nolte, positive and negative, is Rudolf Augstein et al., *Historikerstreit: Die Dokumentation der Kontroverse um die Einzigartigkeit der nationalsozialistischen Judenvernichtung* (Munich: Piper, 1987). A critical assessment in English of the German historical quarrel is by Richard J. Evans, *In Hitler's Shadows* (New York: Pantheon Books, 1989), who faulted Nolte and the neoconservative historians with the sort of revisionism that has made it much easier for political extremism to flourish in Germany (138).

75. For an excellent brief critique of Nolte's style, see Peter Gay, *Freud, Jews and Other Germans: Masters and Victims in Modernist Culture* (New York: Oxford University Press, 1978), xi–xiv.

76. Ernst Nolte, "Zwischen Geschichtslegende und Revisionismus?" in Augstein et al., *Historikerstreit,* 32.

77. For Habermas's critique, see *Eine Art Schadensabwicklung* (Frankfurt: Suhrkamp, 1987) and the excellent chapter "Habermas among the Historians," in Charles S. Maier, *The Unmasterable Past: History, Holocaust, and German National Identity* (Cambridge, Mass.: Harvard University Press, 1988), 34–65.

78. Hermann Kurthen et al., eds. *Antisemitism and Xenophobia in Germany after Unification* (New York: Oxford University Press, 1997), 32–35.

79. Ibid., 193.

80. Jacob Heilbrunn, "Germany's Past and Future," *Foreign Affairs* (November–December 1996), 89.

81. Kurthen et al., eds. *Antisemitism and Xenophobia in Germany,* 197.

82. Augstein et al., *Historikerstreit,* 251–52.

83. Kurthen et al., eds., *Antisemitism and Xenophobia in Germany,* 46.

84. Ibid., 128.

85. Ibid., 13.

86. Ibid., 118.

87. Marc Fisher, *After the Wall: Germany, the Germans and the Burdens of History* (New York: Simon & Schuster, 1995), 205

88. Craig, *The Germans,* 144.

89. Fisher, *After the Wall,* 207.

90. For the most sensible and sensitive account of this debate, see Maier, *The Unmasterable Past,* 121–59.

91. Jane Kramer, "The Politics of Memory," *The New Yorker* (August 14, 1995): 49.

92. Ibid., 61.

93. Friedrich Nietzsche, *The Use and Abuse of History,* trans. Adrian Collins (Indianapolis: Bobbs-Merrill, 1981), 3–4.

94. Ibid., 21.

95. Ignatz Bubis, *Juden in Deutschland* (Berlin: Aufbau Verlag, 1996), 20.

96. Ibid., 17.

97. Kurthen et al., eds., *Antisemitism and Xenophobia in Germany,* 119.

98. Ibid., 58.

99. Ibid., 60.

Select Bibliography

This bibliography makes no pretense toward completeness. It is safe to say that the Holocaust will rank as one of the defining events of the twentieth century. Since quantrophilia (love of the colossal) has been another tendency, and the literature of the Shoa is already incapable of being digested by any single mind, it is safe to say that the century's greatest tragedy may be buried in the mass knowledge industry of the future. Setting limits to intrusive academic excesses is an obligation Holocaust writers owe to their readers. The following selection is primarily limited to the German-Jewish relationship and to certain larger themes that impinged on it. It serves two purposes: as a guide to those who want to explore the resources that seem to me important and to pay my debt to the many authors without whom this book could not have been written.

Original Sources

Archives

Berlin Document Center (BDC)
Bundesarchiv Freiburg (BA Freiburg)
Centre de Documentation Juive Contemporaine (Paris)
Hoover Institution on War, Revolution and Peace (HI, Stanford, California)
Institut für Geschichte der deutschen Juden (Hamburg)
Institut für Zeitgeschichte (Munich)
Institute of Jewish Affairs (London)
Jewish Historical Institute (Zydowska Instytut Historyczny w Polce, Warsaw)
Leo Baeck Institute (New York, London, Jerusalem)
National Archives (Washington, D.C.)
Simon Wiesenthal Center (Los Angeles)
United States Holocaust Memorial Museum (Washington D.C.)
Yad Vashem (Jerusalem)
Yiddish Scientific Institute (YIVO, New York)
Zentrale Stelle der Landesjustizverwaltungen zur Aufklärung nationalsozialistischer Verbrechen (Ludwigsburg, Germany)

Published Documents and Collections

Archives of the Holocaust: An International Collection of Selected Documents. 22 vols. Ed. Henry Friedlander and Sybil Milton. New York: Garland, 1990–93.

Boberach, H., ed. *Meldungen aus dem Reich: Auswahl aus dem geheimen Lageberichten des Sicherheitsdienstes der SS, 1933 bis 1944.* Berlin: Luchterhand, 1965.

Broszat, Martin et al. *Bayern in der NS-Zeit.* 6 vols. Munich: R. Oldenbourg, 1977–83).

Dawidowicz, Lucy S. *A Holocaust Reader.* New York: Behrman House, 1976.

Deutschland-Berichte der Sozialdemokratischen Partei Deutschlands (Sopade), 1934–1940. 8 vols. Frankfurt: Verlag Petra Nettelbeck, 1980.

Documents on German Foreign Policy, 1918–1945. Washington D.C.: U.S. Department of State, 1949–83.

Dokumentation zur Geschichte der jüdischen Bevölkerung in Rheinland-Pfalz und im Saarland von 1800 bis 1945. Edited by Landesarchivsverwaltung Rheinland-Pfalz in Verbindung mit dem Landesarchiv Saarbrücken. Koblenz: Selbstarchiv der Landesarchivsverwaltung Rheinland-Pfalz, 1974.

Dokumente zur Geschichte der Frankfurter Juden. Edited by Kommission zur Erforschung der Geschichte der Frankfurter Juden. Frankfurt: W. Kramer, 1963.

Ein Stempel hat gefehlt: Dokumentation zur Emigration deutscher Juden. Ed. Rolf Vogel. Munich: Droemer Knauer, 1977.

Gedenkbuch: Opfer der Verfolgung der Juden unter der Nationalsozialistischen Gewaltherrschaft in Deutschland, 1933–1945. 2 vols. Koblenz: J. Weisbecker, 1986.

Hilberg, Raul, ed. *Documents of Destruction: Germany and Jewry, 1933–1945.* Chicago: Quadrangle Books, 1971.

Holocaust: Selected Documents. Ed. John Mendelsohn. 18 vols. New York: Garland, 1982.

International Military Tribunal. *Trial of the Major War Criminals before the International Tribunal: Proceedings and Documents.* 42 vols. Nuremberg, 1947–49.

Jacobsen, Hans-Adolf and Werner Jochmann, eds. *Ausgewählte Dokumente zur Geschichte des Nazionalsozialismus.* Bielefeld: Verlag Neue Gesellschaft, 1961.

Kennzeichen J. Bilder, Dokumente, Berichte zur Geschichte der Verbrechen des Hitlerfaschismus an den deutschen Juden 1933–1945. Ed. Helmut Eschwege. Berlin: VEB Deutscher Verlag der Wissenschaften, 1981.

Meldungen aus dem Reich: Die geheimen Lageberichte des Sicherheitsdienstes der SS 1938–1945. Ed. Heinz Boberach. 17 vols. Herrsching: Pawlak, 1984.

Michaelis, Herbert, and Ernst Schraepler, eds. *Ursachen und Folgen: Vom deutschen Zusammenbruch 1918 und 1945 bis zur staatlichen Neuordnung Deutschlands in der Gegenwart.* 21 vols. Berlin: Wandler, 1958.

Nazi Conspiracy and Aggression. 8 vols. Washington, D.C.: U.S. Government Printing Office, 1946.

Noakes, Jeremy, and Geoffrey Pridham, eds. *Nazism: A History in Documents and Eyewitness Accounts, 1919–1945.* 2 vols. New York: Schocken, 1988.

Schramm, Percy E., et al., eds. *Kriegstagebuch des Oberkommandos der Wehrmacht, 1940–1945.* 4 vols. Frankfurt: Bernard Graefe, 1961–65.

Bibliographic Aids

Charny, Israel W., et al., eds. *Genocide: A Critical Bibliographic Review.* London: Mansell, 1988.

Edelheit, Abraham J., and Hershel Edelheit. *History of the Holocaust: A Handbook and Dictionary.* Boulder, Colo.: Westview Press, 1994.

Freeman, Michael. *Atlas of Nazi Germany.* New York: Macmillan, 1987.

Friedmann, Saul S. *Holocaust Literature: A Handbook of Critical, Historical, and Literary Writings.* Westport, Conn.: Greenwood Press, 1993.

Gilbert, Martin. *Atlas of the Holocaust.* New York: Morrow, 1993.

Hüttenberger, Peter. *Bibliographie zum Nazionalsozialismus.* Göttingen: Vandenhoeck & Ruprecht, 1980.

Jäckel, Eberhard, et al., eds. *Enzyklopädie des Holocaust: Die Verfolgung und Ermordung der europäischen Juden.* 3 vols. Berlin: Argon, 1993.

Shermis, Michael. *Jewish-Christian Relations: An Annotated Bibliography and Resource Guide.* Bloomington: Indiana University Press, 1988.

Shimoni, Gideon, ed. *The Holocaust in University Teaching.* New York: Pergamon Press, 1991.

Snyder, Louis L. *Encyclopedia of the Third Reich.* New York: Paragon, 1973.

Szonyi, David M., ed. *The Holocaust: An Annotated Bibliography and Resource Guide.* New York: Ktav, 1985.

United States Holocaust Memorial Museum. *Historical Atlas of the Holocaust.* New York: Simon & Schuster Macmillan, 1996.

Wistrich, Robert S. *Who's Who in Nazi Germany.* London: Routledge, 1995.

Zentner, Christian, and Friedemann Bedürftig, eds. *Das Grosse Lexikon des Dritten Reiches.* Munich: Südwest, 1985.

Autobiographies, Diaries, Memoirs

Amery, Jean. *At the Mind's Limits: Contemplations by a Survivor on Auschwitz and Its Realities.* Trans. Sidney and Stella Rosenfeld. New York: Schocken, 1986.

Andreas Friedrich, Ruth. *Schauplatz Berlin: Ein deutsches Tagebuch.* Munich: Rheinsberg, 1962.

Baynes, Norman H., ed. *The Speeches of Adolf Hitler: April 1922–August 1939.* London: Oxford University Press, 1942.

Benz, Wolfgang, ed. *Das Tagebuch der Hertha Nathorff.* Frankfurt: Fischer, 1989.

Boehm, Eric H. *We Survived: The Stories of Fourteen of the Hidden and Hunted of Nazi Germany.* New Haven: Yale University Press, 1949.

Boor, Lisa de. *Tagebuchblätter aus den Jahren 1935–1945.* Munich: Biederstein, 1963.

Borowski, Tadeusz. *This Way for the Gas, Ladies and Gentlemen.* New York: Penguin, 1979.

Braun-Vogelstein, Julie. *Was niemals stirbt; Gestalten und Erinnerungen.* Stuttgart: Deutsche Verlags-Anstalt, 1966.

Cassirer, Toni. *Aus meinen Leben mit Ernst Cassirer.* Hildesheim: Gerstenberg Verlag, 1981.

Czerniakow, Adam. *Im Warschauer Getto: Das Tagebuch des Adam Czerniakow, 1939–1942.* Munich: Beck, 1986.

Des Pres, Terrence. *The Survivor: An Anatomy of Life in the Death Camps.* New York: Oxford University Press, 1976.

Deutschkron, Inge. *Ich trug den gelben Stern.* Munich: DTV, 1990.

Domarus, Max, ed. *Hitler: Reden und Proklamationen, 1932–1945.* 4 vols. in 2. Wiesbaden: R. Löwit, 1973.

Donat, Alexander. *The Holocaust Kingdom: A Memoir.* New York: Schocken, 1978.

Eichmann, Adolf. *Ich, Adolf Eichmann.* Leoni am Starnberger See: Druffel, 1980.

Frank, Anne. *The Diary of a Young Girl.* New York: Doubleday, 1952.

Frank, Hans. *Im Angesicht des Galgens.* Munich: A. Beck, 1953.

———. *Das Diensttagebuch des deutschen Generalgouverneurs in Polen, 1939–1945.* Ed. Werner Präg and Wolfgang Jacobmeyer. Stuttgart: Deutsche Verlags-Anstalt, 1975.

Fredborg, Advin. *Behind the Steel Wall: A Swedish Journalist in Berlin, 1941–43.* New York: Viking, 1944.

Fröhlich, Elke, ed. *Die Tagebücher von Joseph Goebbels: Sämtliche Fragmente.* 4 vols. Munich: Saur, 1987.

Fromm, Bella. *Blood and Banquets: A Berlin Social Diary.* New York: Harper & Brothers, 1942.

Goebbels, Joseph. *Vom Kaiserhof zur Reichskanzlei.* Munich: Eher Verlag, 1937.

Groscurth, Helmuth. *Tagebuch eines Abwehroffiziers.* Stuttgart: Deutsche Verlags-Anstalt, 1970.

Haag, Anna. *Das Glück zu Leben.* Stuttgart: Bonz, 1968.

Hahn, Lilli. *Bis alles in Scherben fällt. Tagebuchblätter, 1933–1945.* Cologne: Braun, 1979.

Halder, Franz. *Kriegstagebuch: Tägliche Aufzeichnungen des Chefs des Generalstabs des Heeres, 1939–1945.* 3 vols. Stuttgart: Kohlhammer, 1962–64.

Hassel, Ulrich von. *Vom anderen Deutschland: Aus dem nachgelassenen Tagebüchern, 1939–44.* Frankfurt: Fischer, 1962.

Haydn, Ludwig. *Meter immer nur Metter. Das Tagebuch eines Daheimgebliebenen.* Vienna: Scholle, 1946.

Heid, Ludger, and Julius H. Schoeps. *Juden in Deutschland: Von der Aufklärung bis zur Gegenwart: Ein Lesebuch.* Munich: Piper, 1994.

Höss, Rudolf. *Commandant at Auschwitz.* New York: Popular Library, n.d.

Hecht, Ingeborg. *Als unsichtbare Mauern wuchsen: Eine deutsche Familie unter den Nürnberger Rassengesetze.* Munich: DTV, 1987.

Hitler, Adolf. *Mein Kampf.* New York: Reynal & Hitchcock, 1941.

Jäckel, Eberhard, ed. *Sämtliche Aufzeichnungen, 1905–1924.* Stuttgart: Deutsche Verlags-Anstalt, 1980.

Jünger, Ernst. *Der Kampf als inneres Erlebnis.* Berlin: Mittler, 1925.

Kardorf, Ursula von. *Berliner Aufzeichnungen aus den Jahren 1942–45.* Munich: Biederstein, 1962.

Kersten, Felix. *The Kersten Memoirs, 1940–45.* New York: Macmillan, 1957.

Klemperer, Victor. *Ich will Zeugnis ablegen bis zum letzten: Tagebücher, 1933–1945.* 2 vols. Berlin: Aufbau-Verlag, 1995.

Kotze, Hildegard von. *Heeresadjutant bei Hitler 1938–1943: Aufzeichnungen des Majors Engel.* Stuttgart: Deutsche Verlags-Anstalt, 1974.

Laqueur, Walter. *Heimkehr: Reisen in die Vergangenheit.* Berlin: Propylaen Verlag, 1964.

Levi, Primo. *Survival in Auschwitz.* New York: Collier, 1961.

Limberg, Margarete, and Hubert Rübsaat, eds. *Sie durften nicht mehr Deutsche sein.* Frankfurt: Campe Verlag, 1990.

Lochner, Louis, ed. *The Goebbels Diaries.* New York: Doubleday, 1948.

Mann, Thomas. *Diaries, 1918–1939.* Trans. Richard and Clara Winston. New York: Abrams, 1982.

Manoschek, Walter, ed. *Es gibt nur eines für das Judentum: Vernichtung. Das Judenbild in deutschen Soldatenbriefen 1939–1944.* Hamburg: HIS Verlages. mbH, 1996.

Marcuse, Ludwig. *Mein Zwanzigstes Jahrhundert: Auf dem Weg zu einer Autobiographie.* Munich: Paul List, 1960.

Obenaus, Herbert and Sibylle, eds. *"Schreiben wie es wirklich war!" Aufzeichnungen aus den Jahren 1933–1945.* Hannover: Fackelträger, 1985.

Picker, Henry. *Hitlers Tischgespräche im Führerhauptquartier.* Stuttgart: Goldmann Verlag, 1981.

Richarz, Monika, ed. *Jüdisches Leben in Deutschland: Selbstzeugnisse zur Sozialgeschichte 1918–1945.* Stuttgart: DVA, 1982.

Ringelblum, Emmanuel. *Notes from the Warsaw Ghetto.* New York: McGraw-Hill, 1958.

Rosenthal, Hans. *Zwei Leben in Deutschland.* Bergisch Gladbach: Luebbe, 1980.

Schoenaich, Paul Freiherr von. *Ich will leben: Ein autobiographischer Bericht.* Berlin: Oberbaum, 1982.

Schoeps, Hans-Joachim. *Die letzten dreissig Jahre: Rückblicke.* Stuttgart: Ernst Klett Verlag, 1956.

Seraphim, Hans-Günther, ed. *Das Politische Tagebuch Alfred Rosenbergs, 1934–5 und 1939–40.* Munich: DTV, 1956.

Shirer, William. *Berlin Diary: The Journal of a Foreign Correspondent, 1934–41.* New York: Alfred A. Knopf, 1941.

Speer, Albert. *Memoirs.* Trans. Richard and Clara Winston. New York: Macmillan, 1970.

Wassermann, Jakob. *Deutscher und Jude: Reden und Schriften, 1904–1933.* Heidelberg: Verlag Lambert Schneider, 1984.

Weil, Bruno. *Durch drei Kontinente.* Buenos Aires: Cosmopolita, 1948.

Weitzmann, Chaim. *Trial and Error: The Autobiography of Chaim Weitzmann.* New York: Harper, 1949.

Wiesel, Elie. *Night.* Trans. Stella Rodway. New York: Bantam, 1986.

Willstätter, Richard. *From My Life: The Memoirs of Richard Willstätter.* Trans. Lilli S. Horning. New York: W. A. Benjamin, 1965.

Major Judeophobic Works

Luther, Martin. "On the Jews and Their Lies" (1543) in Jaroslav Pelikan, ed., *Luther's Works.* Vol. 47 (St. Louis: Concordia Publishing House, 1955–86).

Kurze Beschreybung und Erzählung von einem Juden mit Namen Ahasverus. Leiden: Christoff Creutzer, 1602.

Hell, François. *Observation d'un Alsacien sur l'affair presente des juifs d'Alsace.* Frankfurt, 1779.

Dohm, Christian Wilhelm. *Über die bürgerlicher Verbesserung der Juden.* Berlin: Friedrich Nicolai, 1781.

Grattenauer, Karl Friedrich. *Über die physische und moralische Verfassung der heutigen Juden.* Leipzig, 1791.

Paalzow, Christian Ludwig. *Die Juden nebst einigen Bemerkungen überdas Sendschreiben an Herrn Probst Teller zu Berlin.* Berlin, 1799.

———. *Der Jude und der Christ — eine Unterhaltung auf dem Postwagen.* Berlin, 1803.

———. *Über das Bürgerrecht der Juden.* Berlin, 1803.

Schleuring, Theodor A. *Das Staatsbürgerrecht der Juden.* Würzburg, 1819.

Holst, Ludolf. *Judenthum in allen dessen Theilen aus einem staatswissenschaftlichen Standpunkte betrachtet.* Mainz: Florian Kupferberg, 1821.

Chiarini, Luigi A. *Theorie du judaisme.* Paris: J. Barbezat, 1830.

Toussenel, Alphonse. *Les Juifs rois de l'epoque, histoire de la féodalité financière.* Paris: de Gonet, 1845.

Gobineau, Arthur de. *The Inequality of Human Races.* Trans. Adrian Collins. New York: Putnam, 1915. Originally published 1853–54.

Rupert, Louis. *L'Eglise et la Synagogue.* Paris, 1859.

Stöcker, Adolf. *Das Moderne Judenthum in Deutschland, besonders in Berlin.* Berlin, 1880.

Treitschke, Heinrich von. *Ein Wort über unseres Judenthum.* Berlin: G. Reimer, 1880.

Dühring, Eugen. *Die Judenfrage als Rassen-und-Sitten-und Culturfrage.* Karlsruhe: H. Reuther, 1881.

Renan, Ernest. *Histoire du peuple d'Israel.* 5 vols. Paris: Calmann Levy, 1887.

———. *Vie de Jésus.* Paris: Nelson, 1963.

Chamberlain, Houston Stewart. *Die Grundlagen des neunzehnten Jahrhunderts.* Munich: F. Bruckmann, 1900.

———, ed. *Die Protokolle der Weisen von Zion und die jüdische Weltpolitik.* Munich: Deutscher Volksverlag, 1923.

Eckart, Dietrich. *Der Bolshevismus von Moses bis Lenin.* Munich: Hoheneichen, 1924.

Retcliff, Sir John (Hermann Goedsche.) *Biarritz*. Munich: Hoheneichen, 1929; originally published in 1868.

Rosenberg, Alfred. *Der Mythos des 20. Jahrhunderts*. Munich: Hoheneichen, 1930.

Fritsch, Theodor. *Handbuch der Judenfrage: Die wichtigsten Tatsachen zur Beurteilung des jüdischen Volkes*. 41st ed. Leipzig: Hammer Verlag, 1933.

Secondary Sources

Christian and Western Judeophobia

Almog, S. *Nationalism and Antisemitism in Modern Europe 1815–1945*. Oxford: Pergamon Press, 1990.

———, ed. *Antisemitism through the Ages*. New York: Pergamon Press, 1988.

Anderson, George K. *The Legend of the Wandering Jew*. Providence: Brown University Press, 1965.

Baron, Salo W. *Social and Religious History of the Jews*. 8 vols. 2d ed. New York: Columbia University Press, 1952.

———. *Modern Nationalism and Religion*. New York: Meridian Books, 1960.

Bein, Alexander. "Der Moderne Antisemitismus und Seine Bedeutung für die Judenfrage," *Vierteljahreshefte für Zeitgeschichte* 6 (1958): 340–60.

Chazan, Robert. *In the Year 1096: The First Crusade and the Jews*. Philadelphia: Jewish Publication Society, 1996.

Cohn, Norman. *Pursuit of the Millennium*. Fairlawn, N.J.: Essential Books, 1957.

———. *Warrant for Genocide: The Myth of the Jewish World Conspiracy*. Chico, Calif.: Judaic Studies, 1981.

Dimont, Max I. *Jews, God and History*. New York: Mentor, 1994; orig. published, 1962.

Gager, John. *Origins of Christian Anti-Semitism*. New York: Oxford University. 1983.

Gilman, Sander. *Jewish Self-Hatred: Anti-Semitism and the Hidden Language of the Jews*. Baltimore: Johns Hopkins University Press, 1986.

Hasan-Roken, G., and A. Dundes, eds. *The Wandering Jew: Essays in the Interpretation of a Christian Legend*. Bloomington: Indiana University Press, 1986.

Isaac, Jules. *The Teaching of Contempt: Christian Roots of Anti-Semitism*. New York: Holt, Rinehart and Winston, 1964.

Johnson, Paul. *A History of the Jews*. New York: Harper & Row, 1988.

Katz, Jacob. *From Prejudice to Destruction: Anti-Semitism, 1700–1933*. Cambridge, Mass.: Harvard University Press, 1981.

Katz, Steven T. *The Holocaust in Historical Perspective*. New York: Oxford University Press, 1994.

Langmuir, Gavin I. *Toward a Definition of Anti-Semitism*. Los Angeles: University of California Press, 1996.

Lindemann, Albert. *The Jew Accused: Three Anti-Semitic Affairs*. New York: Cambridge University Press, 1991.

————. *Esau's Tears: Modern Anti-Semitism and the Rise of the Jews.* New York: Cambridge University Press, 1997.

Littell, Franklin. *The Crucifixion of the Jews: The Failure of the Christian to Understand the Jewish Experience.* Detroit: Wayne State University Press, 1974.

Mann, G. *Der Antisemitismus: Wurzeln, Wirkung und Uberwindung.* Munich: New Tamid Verlag, 1971.

Manuel, Frank E. *The Broken Staff: Judaism through Christian Eyes.* Cambridge, Mass.: Harvard University Press, 1992.

Meier, Kurt. "Zur Interpretation von Luthers Judenschriften," in *Vierhundertfünfzig Jahre lutherische Reformation, 1517–1967.* Göttingen: Vandenhoeck & Ruprecht, 1967.

Poliakov, Léon. *History of Anti-Semitism.* 5 vols. New York: Schocken, 1974.

————. *The Aryan Myth.* Trans. Edmund Howard. New York: American Library, 1977.

Ruether, Rosemary R. *Faith and Fratricide: The Theological Roots of Anti-Semitism.* New York: Seabury Press, 1974.

Russell, Jeffrey Burton. *A History of Witchcraft.* London: Thomas and Hudson, 1982.

————. *Lucifer: The Devil in the Middle Ages.* Ithaca, N.Y.: Cornell University Press, 1984.

Schäfer, Peter. *Judeophobia: Attitudes towards the Jews in the Ancient World.* Cambridge, Mass.: Harvard University Press, 1997.

Tejirian, Edward J. *Sexuality and the Devil.* New York: Routledge, 1990.

Trachtenberg, Joshua. *The Devil and the Jews: The Medieval Conception of the Jew and Its Relation to Modern Anti-Semitism.* New Haven: Yale University Press, 1943.

Sartre, Jean-Paul. *Anti-Semite and Jew.* Trans. George J. Becker. New York: Schocken, 1948.

Wistrich, Robert S. *Between Redemption and Perdition: Antisemitism and Jewish Identity.* London: Routledge, 1990.

————. *Antisemitism: The Longest Hatred.* New York: Schocken, 1994.

German Judeophobia

Adler-Rudel, S. *Ostjuden in Deutschland, 1880–1940.* Tübingen: J. C. B. Mohr, 1959.

Angress, Werner T. *Between Fear and Hope: Jewish Youth in the Third Reich.* Trans. Christine Granger. New York: Columbia University Press, 1988.

Aschheim, Steven E. *Culture and Catastrophe: German and Jewish Confrontation with National Socialism and Other Crises.* New York: New York University Press, 1996.

Baker, Leonard. *Days of Sorrow and Pain: Leo Baeck and the Berlin Jews.* New York: Macmillan, 1978.

Ball-Kaduri, Kurt J. *Das Leben der Juden in Deutschland im Jahre 1933: Ein Zeitbericht.* Frankfurt: Europäische Verlagsanstalt, 1963.

————. *Vor der Katastrophe: Juden in Deutschland, 1934–1939.* Tel Aviv: Olamenu, 1967.

Baum, Rainer C. *The Holocaust and the German Elite: Genocide and National Suicide in Germany 1871–1945*. Towata, N.J.: Rowman, 1981.

Benz, Wolfgang, ed. *Die Juden in Deutschland, 1933–45*. Munich: C. H. Beck, 1993.

Berghahn, Klaus, ed. *The German-Jewish Dialogue Reconsidered: A Symposium in Honor of George L. Mosse*. New York: Peter Lang, 1996.

Berghash, Mark W. *Jews and Germans: Aspects of the True Self*. Los Angeles: University of California Press, 1985.

Brenner, Michael. *The Renaissance of Jewish Culture in Weimar Germany*. New Haven: Yale University Press, 1996.

Chernow, Ron. *The Warburgs: The Twentieth Century Odyssey of a Remarkable Jewish Family*. New York: Random House, 1993.

Craig, Gordon. *The Germans*. New York: New American Library, 1982.

Deak, Istvan. *Weimar Germany's Left-Wing Intellectuals: A Political History of the Weltbühne and Its Circle*. Berkeley: University of California Press, 1968.

Dippel, John V. H. *Bound upon a Wheel of Fire: Why So Many Jews Made the Tragic Decision to Remain in Nazi Germany*. New York: Basic Books, 1996.

Drobisch, Klaus, ed. *Juden unterm Hakenkreuz: Verfolgung und Ausrottung der deutschen Juden, 1933–45*. Frankfurt: Roderberg-Verlag, 1973.

Dunker, Ulrich. *Der Reichsbund deutscher Frontsoldaten: Geschichte eines jüdischen Abwehrverein*. Düsseldorf: Droste, 1977.

Dwork, Deborah. *Children with a Star: Jewish Youth in Nazi Europe*. New Haven: Yale University Press, 1991.

Elias, Norbert. *The Germans*. New York: Columbia University Press, 1996.

Felden, Klemens. "Die Übernahme des antisemitischen Stereotyps als soziale Norm durch die bürgerliche Gesellschaft Deutschlands." Diss. Heidelberg, 1963.

Flade, Roland. *Die Würzburger Juden: Ihre Geschichte vom Mittelalter bis zur Gegenwart*. Würzburg: Sturtz, 1987.

Freeden, Herbert. *Die jüdische Presse im Dritten Reich*. Frankfurt: Jüdischer Verlag bei Athenaeum, 1987.

Friedländer, Saul. *Nazi Germany and the Jews: The Years of Persecution, 1933–1939*. New York: HarperCollins, 1997.

Fromm, Bella. *Blood and Banquets: A Berlin Social Diary*. New York: Car Publishing Group, 1990.

Gay. Peter. *Weimar Culture: The Outsider as Insider*. New York: Harper & Row, 1968.

———. *Freud, Jews and Other Germans*. New York: Oxford University Press, 1978.

Gay, Ruth. *The Jews of Germany: A Historical Portrait*. New Haven: Yale University Press, 1992.

Gilman, Sander L. *Jews in Today's German Culture*. Bloomington: Indiana University Press, 1995.

Gordon, Sarah. *Hitler, Germans, and the Jewish Question*. Princeton, N.J.: Princeton University Press, 1984.

Greive, Hermann. *Geschichte des modernen Antisemitismus in Deutschland.* Darmstadt: Wissenschaftliche Buchhandlung, 1983.

Grunfeld, Frederic V. *Prophets without Honor: Freud, Kafka, Einstein, and Their World.* New York: Kodansha International, 1996.

Hanke, Peter. *Zur Geschichte der Juden in München zwischen 1933 und 1945.* Munich: Schriftreihe des Staatsarchivs München, Heft 3, 1967.

Heuberger, Rachel, and Helga Krohn. *Hinaus aus dem Ghetto: Juden in Frankfurt am Main, 1800–1950.* Frankfurt: Fischer, 1978.

Kahler, Erich. *Deutsche und Juden.* Darmstadt: Erato-Presse, 1964.

Kater, Michael. "Everyday Anti-Semitism in Prewar Nazi Germany: The Popular Bases," *Yad Vashem Studies* 14 (1984): 129–59.

Laqueur, Walter. "The German Youth Movement and the Jewish Question," *Leo Baeck Year Book* 6 (1961): 193–205.

Levy, Richard. *The Downfall of the Anti-Semitic Parties of Imperial Germany.* New Haven: Yale University Press, 1975.

Lorenz, Dagmar C. G., and Gabriele Weinberger. *Insiders and Outsiders: Jewish and Gentile Culture in Germany and Austria.* Detroit: Wayne State University Press, 1994.

Lowenthal, Marvin. *The Jews of Germany: A History of Sixteen Centuries.* Philadelphia: Jewish Publication Society, 1939.

Massing, Paul W. *Rehearsal for Destruction: A Study of Political Anti-Semitism in Imperial Germany.* New York: Harper, 1949.

Maurer, Trude. *Ostjuden in Deutschland, 1918–1933.* Hamburg: H. Christians Verlag, 1986.

Meyer, Michael, ed. *German-Jewish History in Modern Times.* New York: Columbia University Press, 1996.

Milfull, John, ed. *Why Germany? National Socialist Anti-Semitism and the European Context.* New York: Berg, 1993.

Mosse, George L. *The Crisis of German Ideology.* New York: Grosset and Dunlap, 1964.

———. *Germans: The Right, the Left, and the Search for a Third Force in Pre-Nazi Germany.* New York: Grosset and Dunlap, 1970.

———. *Toward the Final Solution: A History of European Racism.* New York: Harper & Row, 1978.

———. *German Jews beyond Judaism.* Cincinnati: Hebrew Union College Press, 1985.

Mosse, Werner. "Rudolf Mosse and the House of Mosse, 1867–1920," in *Yearbook of the Leo Baeck Institute* 4 (1958).

———. *Jews in the German Economy: The German-Jewish Economic Elite, 1820–1935.* Oxford: Clarendon Press, 1987.

———, ed. *Deutsches Judenstum in Krieg und Revolution, 1916–1923.* Tübingen: J. C. B. Mohr, 1971.

Mosse, Werner, and Arnold Paucker, eds. *Entscheidungsjahr 1932: Zur Judenfrage in der Endphase der Weimarer Republik.* Tübingen: Mohr, 1965.

Müller-Claudius, Michael. *Der Antisemitismus und das deutsche Verhängnis.* Frankfurt: J. Knecht, 1948.

Nebel, Theobald. *Die Geschichte der Jüdischen Gemeinde Talheim: Ein Beispiel für das Schicksal des Judentums in Württemberg.* Heilbronn: Gemeinde Talheim, 1963.

Niewyk, Donald L. *The Jews in Weimar Germany.* Baton Rouge: Louisiana State University Press, 1980.

Paucker, Arnold. *Deutsches Judentum im Krieg und Revolution.* Tübingen: Mohr, 1971.

———. *Juden im Wilhelminischen Deutschland,* 1976.

———. *Die Juden im Nationalsozialistischen Deutschland.* Tübingen: Mohr, 1986.

Pauley, Bruce F. *From Prejudice to Persecution: A History of Austrian Antisemitism.* Chapel Hill: University of North Carolina Press, 1992.

Peck, Abraham J. *Radicals and Reactionaries: The Crisis of Conservatism in Wilhelmine Germany,* 1978.

Pulzer, Peter. *The Rise of Political Anti-Semitism in Germany and Austria.* New York: Wiley, 1964.

———. *Jews and the German State: The Political History of a Minority, 1848–1933.* Oxford: Blackwell, 1992.

Reichmann, Eva G. *Hostages to Civilization: The Social Sources of National Socialist Anti-Semitism.* London: Gollancz, 1950.

Reinharz, Jehuda, and Walter Schatzberg, eds. *The Jewish Response to German Culture.* Hanover, N.H.: University Press of New England, 1985.

Richarz, Monika, ed. *Jewish Life in Germany: Memoirs from Three Centuries.* Bloomington: Indiana University Press, 1991.

Rose, Paul Laurence. *German Question/Jewish Question: Revolutionary Anti-Semitism from Kant to Wagner.* Princeton, N.J.: Princeton University Press, 1990.

Rürup, Reinhard. *Emanzipation und Antisemitismus.* Göttingen: Vandenhoeck, 1975.

Schorsch, Ismar. *Jewish Reactions to German Anti-Semitism, 1870–1914.* New York: Columbia University Press, 1972.

Schütz, Hans-Jürgen. *Juden in der deutschen Literatur.* Munich: Piper, 1990.

Serkin, David. *The Transformation of German Jewry, 1780–1840.* New York: Oxford University Press, 1987.

Showalter, Dennis E. *Little Man, What Now?* Hamden, Conn.: Archon Books, 1982.

Sterling, Eleonore. *Judenhass: Die Anfänge des politischen Antisemitismus in Deutschland.* Frankfurt: Europäische Verlagsanstalt, 1969.

Stern, Fritz. *The Politics of Cultural Despair: A Study in the Rise of the German Ideology.* New York: Doubleday, 1963.

———. *Gold and Iron: Bismarck, Bleichröder and the Building of the German Empire.* New York: Knopf, 1977.

———. *Dreams and Delusions: National Socialism in the Drama of the German Past.* New York: Vintage Books, 1989.

Tal, Uriel. *Christians and Jews in Germany: Religion, Politics and Ideology in the Second Reich, 1870–1914.* Ithaca, N.Y.: Cornell University Press, 1975.

Uthmann, Jörg. *Doppelgänger, du bleicher Geselle: Zur Pathologie der deutsch-jüdischen Verhältnisse.* Stuttgart: Seewald Verlag, 1976.

Volkov, Shulamit. "Kontinuität und Diskontinuität im deutschen Antisemitismus, 1878–1945, *Vierteljahreshefte für Zeitgeschichte* 33 (1985): 221–43.

Weltsch, Robert, ed. *Deutsches Judentum: Aufstieg und Krise.* Stuttgart: Deutsche Verlags-Anstalt, 1963.

Wertheimer, Jack. *Unwelcome Strangers: East European Jews in Imperial Germany.* New York: Oxford University Press, 1987.

Weinreich, Max. *Hitler's Professors: The Part of Scholarship in Germany's Crimes against the Jewish People.* New York: Yiddish Scientific Institute, YIVO, 1946.

Wistrich, Robert S. *The Jews of Vienna in the Age of Franz Joseph.* Oxford: Littman Library, 1989.

Hitler's Judeophobia

Baldwin, Peter, ed. *Reworking the Past: Hitler, the Holocaust and the Historians' Debate.* Boston: Beacon Press, 1990.

Baynes, Norman, ed. *The Speeches of Adolf Hitler: April 1922–August 1939.* London: Oxford University Press, 1942.

Binion, Rudolph. *Hitler among the Germans.* New York: Elsevier, 1979.

Bromberg, Norbert, and Verna Volz Small. *Hitler's Psychopathology.* New York: International Universities Press, 1983.

Bullock, Alan. *Hitler: A Study in Tyranny.* New York: Harper & Row, 1962.

———. *Hitler and Stalin: Parallel Lives.* New York: Knopf, 1992.

Burrin, Philippe. *Hitler and the Jews: The Genesis of the Holocaust.* London: Edward Arnold, 1994.

Domarus, Max, ed. *Hitler: Reden und Proklamationen, 1932–1945.* 4 vols. in 2. Wiesbaden: R. Löwit, 1973.

Fest, Joachim. *Hitler.* Trans. Richard and Clara Winston. New York: Harcourt, Brace & Jovanovich, 1973.

Haffner, Sebastian. *Anmerkungen zu Hitler.* Düsseldorf: Tholenaar, 1973.

Heer, Friedrich. *Der Glaube des Adolf Hitlers: Anatomie einer politischen Religiosität.* Munich: Bechtle, 1968.

Hitler, Adolf. *Mein Kampf.* New York: Reynal & Hitchcock, 1941.

———. *Hitler's Secret Book.* Trans. Salvator Attanasio. New York: Grove Press, 1961.

Jäckel, Eberhard. *Hitlers Weltanschauung: Entwurf einer Herrschaft.* Stuttgart: Deutsche Verlags-Anstalt, 1983.

———, ed. *Sämtliche Aufzeichnungen: 1905–1924.* Stuttgart: Deutsche Verlags-Anstalt, 1980.

Jenks, W. A. *Vienna and the Young Hitler.* New York: Columbia University Press, 1960.

Jetzinger, Franz. *Hitler's Youth.* Trans. Lawrence Wilson. London: Hutchison, 1958.

Jones, Sydney J. *Hitler in Vienna, 1907–13: Clues to the Future.* London: Blond & Briggs, 1983.

Kershaw, Ian. *The Hitler Myth: Image and Reality in the Third Reich*. Oxford: Oxford University Press, 1987.

Langer, Walter. *The Mind of Adolf Hitler*. New York: Basic Books, 1982.

Maser, Werner. *Hitler*. Trans. Peter and Betty Ross. London: Allen Lane, 1973.

————. *Hitlers Briefe und Notizen*. Düsseldorf: Econ Verlag, 1973.

————. *Mein Kampf: Der Fahrplan eines Welteroberers*. Esslingen: Bechtle, 1974.

Picker, Henry, ed. *Hitlers Tischgespräche im Führerhauptquartier*. Stuttgart: Goldmann Verlag, 1981.

Rauschning, Hermann. *Gespräche mit Hitler*. New York: Europa Verlag, 1940.

Smith, Bradley. *Hitler: His Family, Childhood and Youth*. Stanford, Calif.: Hoover Institution Press, 1967.

Stern, J. P. *The Führer and His People*. Glasgow: William Collins Sons, 1975.

Stierlin, Helm. *Adolf Hitler: A Family Perspective*. New York: Psychohistory Press, 1976.

Toland, John. *Hitler*. 2 vols. New York: Doubleday, 1976.

Trevor-Roper, H. R. *The Last Days of Adolf Hitler*. New York: Macmillan, 1947.

Waite, Robert G. L. *The Psychopathic God Adolf Hitler*. New York: Basic Books, 1977.

Wistrich, Robert. *Hitler's Apocalypse: Jews and Nazi Germany*. London: Weidenfeld & Nicholson, 1985.

The Totalitarian Racial State and Its Institutions

Aronson, Shlomo. *Reinhard Heydrich und die Frühgeschichte von Gestapo und SD*. Stuttgart: Deutsche Verlags-Anstalt, 1971.

Bartov, Omer. *Hitler's Army: Soldiers, Nazis, and War in the Third Reich*. New York: Oxford University Press, 1992.

Breitling, Rupert. *Die Nazionalsozialistische Rassenlehre*. Meisenheim: Hain 1971.

Browder, George C. *Foundations of the Nazi Police State: The Formation of Sipo and SD*. Lexington: University of Kentucky Press, 1990.

Browning, Christopher. *The Final Solution and the German Foreign Office*. New York: Holmes & Meier, 1978.

Buchheim, Hans, et al. *Anatomie des SS Staates*, 2 vols. Freiburg: Walter-Verlag, 1965).

Burleigh, Michael, and Wolfgang Wippermann. *The Racial State: Germany, 1933–1945*. Cambridge: Cambridge University Press, 1988.

Cecil, Robert. *The Myth of the Master Race: Alfred Rosenberg and Nazi Ideology*. New York: Dodd and Mead, 1972.

Cocks, Geoffrey. *Psychotherapy in the Third Reich: The Göring Institute*. New York: Oxford University Press, 1985.

Deichmann, Ute. *Biologists under Hitler*. Trans. Thomas Dunlap. Cambridge, Mass.: Harvard University Press, 1996.

Dicks, H. V. *Licensed Mass Murder: A Socio-Psychological Study of Some SS Killers*. New York: Basic Books, 1972.

Gellately, Robert. *The Gestapo and German Society: Enforcing Racial Policy 1933–1945.* Oxford: The Clarendon Press, 1990.

Hamburger Institut für Sozialforschung, ed. *Vernichtungskrieg: Verbrechen der Wehrmacht 1941 bis 1944.* Hamburg: HIS Verlages.mbH, 1996.

Heiber, Helmut. "Der Fall Grünspan," *Vierteljahreshefte für Zeitgeschichte 5* (1957): 154–72.

Hillel, Marc, and Clarissa Henry. *Of Pure Blood.* Trans. Eric Mossbacher. New York: McGraw-Hill, 1976.

Höhne, Heinz. *The Order of the Death's Head.* Trans. Richard Berry. New York: Ballantine, 1971.

Kater, M. H. *Das "Ahnenerbe" der SS 1935–1945.* Stuttgart: Deutsche Verlags-Anstalt, 1974.

———. *Doctors under Hitler: The German Medical Profession in Crisis during the Third Reich.* Chapel Hill: University of North Carolina Press, 1988.

Karski, Jan. *The Story of a Secret State.* London: Hodder, 1945.

Kogon, Eugen. *The Theory and Practice of Hell: The German Concentration Camps and the System behind Them.* Trans. Heinz Norden. New York: Berkeley Publications, 1958.

Krausnick, Helmut, and Hans-Heinrich Wilhelm. *Die Truppe des Weltanschauungskrieges: Die Einsatzgruppen der Sicherheitspolizei und des SD, 1938–1942.* Stuttgart: Deutsche Verlags-Anstalt, 1981.

Koehl, Robert. *RKFDV: German Resettlement and Population Policy 1939–45.* Cambridge, Mass.: Harvard University Press, 1957.

Lilienthal, Georg. *Der Lebensborn e.V.: Ein Instrument Nationalsozialistischer Rassenpolitik.* Mainz: Akademie der Wissenschaften und der Literatur, 1985.

Lösener, Bernhard. "Als Rassereferat im Reichsministerium des Innern," *Vierteljahreshefte für Zeitgeschichte 9* (July 1961): 264–313.

Manoschek, Walter, ed. *Die Wehrmacht im Rassenkrieg. Der Vernichtungskrieg hinter der Front.* Vienna: Picus Verlag, 1996.

Mommsen, Hans. "Dokumentation: Der nationalsozialistische Polizeistaat und die Judenverfolgung vor 1938," *Vierteljahreshefte für Zeitgeschichte 10* (January 1962): 68–87.

Müller-Hill, Benno. *Murderous Science: Elimination by Scientific Selection of Jews, Gypsies and Others, Germany 1933–1945.* Oxford: Oxford University Press, 1988.

Pendorf, Robert. *Mörder und Ermordete: Eichmann und die Juden-politik des Dritten Reiches.* Hamburg: Rütten und Loening Verlag, 1961.

Proctor, Robert N. *Racial Hygiene: Medicine under the Nazis.* Cambridge, Mass.: Harvard University Press, 1988.

Reitlinger, Gerald. *The SS: Alibi of a Nation, 1922–1945.* Englewood-Cliffs, N.J.: Prentice-Hall, 1981.

Safrian, Hans. *Eichmann und seine Gehilfen.* Frankfurt: Fischer, 1995.

Saller, K. *Die Rassenlehre des Nationalsozialismus.* Darmstadt: Progress, 1961.

Sofsky, Wolfgang. *The Order of Terror: The Concentration Camp.* Trans. William Templer. Princeton, N.J.: Princeton University Press, 1997.

Vogelsang, R. *Der Freundeskreis Himmler.* Göttingen: Musterschmidt, 1972.

Weindling, Paul. *Health, Race and German Politics between National Unification and Nazism, 1870–1945.* New York: Cambridge University Press, 1989.

Emigration and Aryanization

Adler, H. G. *Der verwaltete Mensch: Studien zur Deportation der Juden aus Deutschland.* Tübingen: J. C. B. Mohr, 1974.

Barkai, Avraham. *From Boycott to Annihilation: The Economic Struggles of German Jews.* Hanover, N.H.: Brandeis University Press, 1989.

Genschel, Helmut. *Die Verdrängung der Juden aus der Wirtschaft im Dritten Reich.* Göttingen: Musterschmidt, 1966.

Graml, Hermann. *Die Auswanderung der Juden aus Deutschland-zwischen 1933 und 1939: Gutachten des Instituts für Zeitgeschichte.* Munich: Selbstverlag, 1958, pp. 79–85.

Marcus, Ernst. "The German Foreign Office and the Palestine Question in the Period 1933–1939," *Yad Vashem Studies* 2 (1958): 179–204.

Euthanasia

Burleigh, Michael. *Death and Deliverance: Euthanasia in Germany, 1914–1945.* Cambridge: Cambridge University Press, 1994.

Ehrhardt, Helmut. *Euthanie and Vernichtung "lebensunwerten" Lebens.* Stuttgart: F. Enke, 1965.

Friedlander, Henry. *The Origins of Nazi Genocide from Euthanasia to the Final Solution.* Chapel Hill: University of North Carolina Press, 1995.

Klee, Ernst. *Euthanasie im N.S. Staat.* Frankfurt: Fischer, 1983.

Nowak, Kurt. *Euthanie und Sterilisierung im Dritten Reich.* Göttingen: Vandenhoeck & Ruprecht, 1978.

Schmuhl, Hans-Walter. *Rassenhygiene, Nationalsozialismus, Euthanasie: Von der Verhütung zur Vernichtung "lebensunwerten Lebens," 1890–1945.* Göttingen: Vandenhoeck & Ruprecht, 1987.

Ghettoization

Adler, H. G. *Theresienstadt, 1941–1945.* Tübingen: J. C. B. Mohr, 1960.

Arad, Yitzak. *Ghetto in Flames.* New York: Ktav, 1982.

Dobroszycki, Lucian, ed. *The Chronicle of the Lodz Ghetto.* New Haven: Yale University Press, 1984.

Trunk, Isaiah. *Judenrat: The Jewish Councils in Eastern Europe under Nazi Occupation.* New York: Macmillan, 1972.

General Holocaust

Adam, Uwe Dietrich. *Judenpolitik im Dritten Reich.* Düsseldorf: Droste, 1972.

Aly, Götz. *Vordenker der Vernichtung.* Frankfurt: Fischer, 1995.

Aly, Götz, and Susanne Heim. "The Economics of the Final Solution: A Case study from the General Government," *Simon Wiesenthal Center Annual 5* (1988): 3–48.

———. "Die Ökonomie der Endlösung: Menschenvernichtung und wirtschaftliche Neuordnung," *Beiträge zur nationalsozialistischen Gesundheits- und Sozialpolitik*, vol. 5: *Sozialpolitik und Judenvernichtung: Gibt es eine Ökonomie der Endlösung?* Berlin: Rotbuch, 1987, pp. 7–10.

———. "The Holocaust and Population Policy: Remarks on the Decision on the Final Solution," *Yad Vashem Studies* 24 (1994): 45–70.

Arad, Yitzak. *Belzec, Sobibor, Treblinka: The Operation Reinhard Death Camps*. Bloomington: Indiana University Press, 1987.

Bauer, Yehuda. *They Chose Life: Jewish Resistance in the Holocaust*. New York: American Jewish Committee, 1973.

———. *The Jewish Emergence from Powerlessness*. Toronto: University of Toronto Press, 1979.

———. *A History of the Holocaust*. New York: Franklin Watts, 1982.

———. *Jews for Sale: Nazi Jewish Negotiations, 1933–1945*. New Haven: Yale University Press, 1994.

Benz, Wolfgang. *Der Holocaust*. Munich: C. H. Beck, 1995.

———, ed. *Dimension des Völkermords: Die Zahl der jüdischen Opfer des Nationalsozialimus*. Munich: Oldenbourg, 1991.

Bosmajian, Hamida. *Metaphors of Evil: Contemporary German Literature and the Shadow of Nazism*. Iowa City: University of Iowa Press, 1979.

Bower, Tom. *Nazi Gold*. New York: HarperCollins, 1997.

Braham, Randolph L. *The Politics of Genocide: The Holocaust in Hungary*. 2 vols. New York: Columbia University Press, 1981.

Browning, Christopher R. *The Fateful Months: Essays on the Emergence of the Final Solution*. New York: Holmes & Meier, 1985.

———. *Ordinary Men: Reserve Police Battalion 101 and the Final Solution in Poland*. New York: HarperCollins, 1992.

———. *The Path to Genocide: Essays on Launching the Final Solution*. Cambridge: Cambridge University Press, 1992.

Burleigh, Michael. *Germany Turns Eastward: A Study of Ostforschung in the Third Reich*. Cambridge: Cambridge University Press, 1988.

Buscher, Frank M., and Michael Phayer. "German Bishops and the Holocaust," *German Studies Review* (1988): 463–85.

Cesarini, David, ed. *The Final Solution: Origins and Implementation*. London: Routledge, 1994.

Chary, Frederick B. *The Bulgarian Jews and the Final Solution, 1940–44*. Pittsburgh: University of Pittsburgh Press, 1972.

Dawidowicz, Lucy. *The War against the Jews, 1933–1945*. New York: Bantam, 1975.

———. *The Holocaust and the Historians*. Cambridge, Mass.: Harvard University Press, 1981.

Diner, Dan. "Rationalization and Method: Critique of a New Approach in Understanding the Final Solution," *Yad Vashem Studies* 24 (1994): 71–108.

Ezrahi, Sidre. *By Words Alone: The Holocaust in Literature.* Chicago: University of Chicago Press, 1980.

Fein, Helen. *Accounting for Genocide.* New York: Free Press, 1976.

Fleming, Gerald. *Hitler and the Final Solution.* Los Angeles: University of California Press, 1982.

Fackenheim, Emil L. *To Mend the World: Foundation of Post-Holocaust Jewish Thought.* Bloomington: Indiana University Press, 1988.

Friedlander, Henry, and Sybil Milton, eds. *The Holocaust, Ideology, Bureaucracy, and Genocide.* New York: Kraus International Publications, 1980.

Friedländer, Saul. "From Anti-Semitism to Extermination: A Historiographical Study of Nazi Policies toward the Jews and an Essay in Interpretation," *Yad Vashem Studies* 16 (1984).

———. *Memory, History and the Extermination of the Jews of Europe.* Bloomington: Indiana University Press, 1993.

———. *Reflections of Nazism: An Essay on Kitsch and Death.* Bloomington: Indiana University Press, 1993.

———. *Nazi Germany and the Jews. The Years of Persecution, 1933–1945.* New York: HarperCollins, 1997.

Furet, François, ed. *Unanswered Questions: Nazi Germany and the Genocide of the Jews.* New York: Schocken, 1989.

Gilbert, Martin. *Auschwitz and the Allies.* New York: Holt, Rinehart and Winston, 1981.

———. *The Holocaust: A History of the Jews of Europe during the Second World War.* New York: Holt, Rinehart Winston, 1985.

Goldhagen, David Jonah. *Hitler's Willing Executioners: Ordinary Germans and the Holocaust.* New York: Knopf, 1996.

Goldhagen, Erich. *"Weltanschauung und Endlösung: Zum Antisemitismus der nationalsozialistischen Führungsschicht."* Vierteljahreshefte für Zeitgeschichte 24 (1974): 379–405.

Graml, Hermann. *Antisemitism in the Third Reich.* Oxford: Blackwell, 1988.

Gutman, Ysrael. *The Jews of Warsaw 1939–1943: Ghetto, Underground Revolt.* Bloomington: Indiana University Press, 1982.

Haas, Peter J. *Morality after Auschwitz.* Philadelphia: Fortress Press, 1988.

Hartman, Geoffrey H. *The Longest Shadow: In the Aftermath of the Holocaust.* Bloomington: Indiana University Press, 1996.

Hausner, Gideon. *Justice in Jerusalem.* New York: Harper & Row, 1966.

Headland, Roland. "The Einsatzgruppen: The Question of Their Initial Operations," *Holocaust and Genocide Studies* 4, no. 4 (1989): 401–12.

Hilberg, Raul. *The Destruction of the European Jews.* 3 vols. New York: Holmes and Meier, 1985.

———. *Perpetrators, Victims, Bystanders: The Jewish Catastrophe, 1933–1945.* New York: HarperCollins, 1993.

Insdorf, Annette, *Indelible Shadows: Film and the Holocaust.* New York: Random House, 1983.

Jäckel, Eberhard, and Jürgen Rohwer, eds. *Der Mord an den Juden im Zweiten Weltkrieg.* Stuttgart: Deutsche Verlags-Anstalt, 1985.

Kulka, Otto Dov. "Major Trends and Tendencies in German Historiography on National Socialism and the Jewish Question, 1924–1984." *Yearbook of the Leo Baeck Institute* 30 (1985).

Krakowski, Shmuel. *The War of the Doomed: Jewish Armed Resistance in Poland 1942–44.* Jerusalem: Holmes & Meier, 1977.

La Copra, Dominick. *Representing the Holocaust: History, Theory, Trauma.* Ithaca, N.Y.: Cornell University Press. 1994.

Laqueur, Walter. *The Terrible Secret: Suppression of the Truth about Hitler's "Final Solution."* New York: Penguin, 1982.

Langer, Lawrence L. *The Holocaust and the Literary Imagination.* New Haven: Yale University Press, 1975.

Levin, N. *The Holocaust: The Destruction of European Jewry 1933–1945.* New Haven: Yale University Press, 1975.

Longerich, Peter, ed. *Die Ermordung Europäischer Juden.* Munich: Piper, 1989.

Lozowick, Yaacov. "Rollbahn Mord: The Early Activities of Einsatzgruppe C," *Holocaust and Genocide Studies* 2, no. 2 (1987): 221–41.

Luel, Steven A., and Paul Marcus. *Psychoanalytic Reflections on the Holocaust: Selected Essays.* Denver: Holocaust Awareness Institute, Center for Judaic Studies, University of Denver; New York: Ktav, 1984.

Marrus, Michael R. *The Holocaust in History.* New York: Meridian, 1989.

Marrus, Michael, and Robert O. Paxton. *Vichy France and the Jews.* Stanford: Stanford University Press, 1995.

Mayer, Arno J. *Why Did the Heavens Not Darken? The "Final Solution" in History.* New York: Pantheon, 1988.

Milfull, John, ed. *Why Germany? National Socialist Anti-Semitism and the European Context.* Providence: Berg, 1993.

Mommsen, Hans. "Die Realisierung des Utopischen: Die Endlösung der Judenfrage im dritten Reich," *Geschichte und Gesellschaft* 9, no. 2 (Autumn 1983).

Pätzold, Kurt, and Erika Schwarz. *Tagesordnung: Judenmord. Die Wannseekonferenz am 20. Januar 1942.* Berlin: Metropol, 1992.

Pehle, Walter H., ed. *November 1938: From Kristallnacht to Genocide.* New York: Berg, 1991.

Pohl, Dieter. *Von der Judenpolitik zum Judenmord.* Frankfurt: Peter Lang, 1993.

Pressac, Jean-Claude. *Auschwitz: Technique and Operation of the Gas Chambers.* New York: Bete Klarsfeld Foundation, 1989.

Reichmann, Eva G. *Hostages of Civilization: The Social Sources of National Socialist Anti-Semitism.* London: V. Gollancz, 1950.

Reitlinger, Gerald. *The Final Solution: The Attempt to Exterminate the Jews of Europe.* New York: Beechhurst, 1953.

Rosenfeld, Alvin H. *A Double Dying: Reflection on Holocaust Literature.* Bloomington: Indiana University Press, 1980.

Roth, John K., and Michael Berenbaum. *Holocaust: Religious and Philosophical Implications.* New York: Paragon House, 1989.

Rückerl, Adalbert, ed. *NS Vernichtungslager im Spiegel deutscher Strafprozesse: Belzec, Sobibor, Treblinka, Chelmo.* Munich: DTV, 1977.

Scheffler, Wolfgang. *Judenverfolgung im Dritten Reich, 1933–1945.* Berlin: Colloquium, 1964.

Schleunes, Karl A. *The Twisted Road to Auschwitz.* Urbana: University of Illinois Press, 1990.

Sereny, Gitta. *Into That Darkness: From Mercy Killing to Mass Murder.* New York: McGraw Hill, 1974.

Streim, Alfred. "The Tasks of the Einsatzgruppen," *Simon Wiesenthal Center Annual* 4 (1987): 309–28.

Weiss, John. *Ideology of Death: Why the Holocaust Happened in Germany.* Chicago: Ivan R. Dee, 1996.

Yahil, Leni. *The Holocaust: The Fate of the European Jews.* New York: Oxford University Press, 1990.

Young, James E. *Writing and Re-thinking the Holocaust.* Bloomington: Indiana University Press, 1988.

Perpetrators, Victims, Bystanders

Ball-Kaduri, K. J. "Testimonies and Recollections about Activities Organized by German Jewry during the Years 1933–1945," *Yad Vashem Studies* 4 (1960): 242–60.

———. *Das Leben der Juden in Deutschland im Jahre 1933: Ein Zeitbericht.* Frankfurt: Europäische Verlagsanstalt, 1963.

———. "Zum Leben der Juden in Deutschland während des zweiten Weltkrieges, *Zeitschrift für die Gesammelte Staatswissenschaft* 10, no. 1.2 (1973): 33–38.

Breitman, Richard. *The Architect of Genocide: Heinrich Himmler and the Final Solution.* New York: Knopf, 1991.

Friedländer, Saul. *Kurt Gerstein: The Ambiguity of Good.* New York: Knopf, 1969.

Klee, Ernst, et al. *The Good Old Days: The Holocaust as Seen by Its Perpetrators and Bystanders.* Trans. Deborah Burnstone. New York: Free Press, 1991.

Lang, Jochen von. *Eichmann Interrogated: Transcripts from the Archives of the Israeli Police.* New York: Farrar, Straus & Giroux, 1983.

Safrian, Hans. *Eichmann und seine Gehilfen.* Frankfurt: Fischer, 1995.

Zofka, Zdenek. "Der KZ-Arzt Josef Mengele: Zur Typologie eines NS Verbrechers," *Vierteljahreshefte für Zeitgeschichte* 34 (1986): 245–68.

Deniers

Anti-Defamation League. *Hitler's Apologists: The Anti-Semitic Propaganda of Holocaust "Revisionism."* New York: Anti-Defamation League, 1993.

Butz, A. R. *The Hoax of the Twentieth Century.* Torrance, Calif.: Institute for Historical Review, 1976.

Lipstadt, Deborah. *Denying the Holocaust: The Growing Assault on Truth and Memory.* New York: Penguin, 1994.

Stäglich, Wilhelm. *Der Auschwitz-Mythos.* Tübingen: Grabert, 1979.

Stern, Kenneth. *Holocaust Denial.* New York: American Jewish Committee, 1993.

Germans and the Holocaust: The Aftermath

Augstein, Rudolf, et al. *Historikerstreit: Die Dokumentation der Kontroverse um die Einzigartigkeit der nationalsozialistischen Judenvernichtung.* Munich: Piper, 1987.

Bankier, David. "The Germans and the Holocaust," *Jewish Quarterly* (Autumn 1990).

———. "The Germans and the Holocaust: What Did They Know?" *Yad Vashem Studies* 20 (1990): 68–98.

———. *The Germans and the Final Solution: Public Opinion under Nazism.* Oxford: Blackwell, 1996.

Bergmann, Werner, and Rainer Erb. "Public Beliefs about Anti-Jewish Attitudes in West Germany," *Patterns of Prejudice* 24, no. 1 (1990): 3–18.

———. *Antisemitismus in der Bundesrepublik Deutschland.* Opladen: Leske und Budrich, 1991.

Bodemann, Michal Y. *Jews, Germans, Memory.* Ann Arbor: University of Michigan Press, 1996.

Bower, Tom. *The Pledge Betrayed: America, Britain and the Denazification of Postwar Germany.* London: Andre Deutsch, 1981.

Browning, Christopher R. "Dämonisierung erklärt nichts," *Die Zeit* (April 26, 1996): 5.

Brumlik, Micha, ed. *Jüdisches Leben in Deutschland seit 1945.* Frankfurt: Jüdischer Verlag bei Athenäum, 1986.

Bubis, Ignatz. *Juden in Deutschland.* Berlin: Aufbau Verlag, 1996.

Cohn, Michal. *The Jews in Germany, 1945–1993.* Westport, Conn.: Praeger, 1994.

Craig, Gordon A. "The War of the German Historians," *New York Review of Books* (January 15, 1987).

———. "How Hell Worked," *New York Review of Books* (April 18, 1996): 4–8.

Diner, Dan, ed. *Ist der Nationalsozialismus Geschichte? Zur Historisierung und Historikerstreit.* Frankfurt: Fischer, 1987.

Dressen, Willi. "The Role of the Wehrmacht and the Police in the Annihilation of the Jews; the Prosecution and Postwar Careers of Perpetrators in the Police Force of the Federal Republic of Germany," *Yad Vashem Studies* 23 (1993): 295–319.

Elsässer, Jürgen. *Antisemitismus das alte Gesicht des neuen Deutschland.* Berlin: Dietz Verlag, 1992.

Engelmann, Bert. *Germany without Jews.* Trans. D. J. Beer. New York: Bantam, 1984.

Geiss, Immanuel. *Die Habermas-Kontroverse: Ein deutscher Streit.* Berlin: Siedler, 1987.

Habermas, Jürgen. *Eine Art Schadensabwicklung.* Frankfurt: Suhrkamp, 1987.

Hoffmann, Hilmar, ed. *Gegen den Versuch, Vergangenheit zu verbiegen.* Frankfurt: Athenäum, 1987.

Jaspers, Karl. *The Question of German Guilt.* Trans. E. B. Ashton. New York: Capricorn, 1961.

Kershaw, Ian. "The Persecution of the Jews and German Popular Opinion in the Third Reich." *Yearbook of the Leo Baeck Institute* 26 (1981): 261–84.

———. *Popular Opinion and Political Dissent in the Third Reich: Bavaria, 1933–45.* Oxford: Clarendon Press, 1983.

Kramer, Jane. "The Politics of Memory," *New Yorker* (August 14, 1995): 48–65.

Krondorfer, Björn. *Remembrance and Reconciliation: Encounters between Young Jews and Germans.* New Haven: Yale University Press, 1995.

Kulka, Otto D. "Die deutsche Geschichtsschreibung über Nationalsozialismus und die Endlösung," *Historische Zeitschrift* 240 (1985): 399–640.

Kurthen, Hermann, Werner Bergmann, and Rainer Erb, eds. *Antisemitism and Xenophobia in Germany after Reunification.* New York: Oxford University Press, 1997.

Lavy, George. *Germany and Israel: Moral Debt and National Interest.* London: Frank Cass, 1996.

Marin, Bernd. "Ein historisch neuartiger Antisemitismus ohne Antisemiten?" *Geschichte und Gesellschaft* 5 (1979): 545–69.

Moltmann, Bernhard, et al., eds. *Erinnerung zur Gegenwart des Holocausts in Deutschland-West und Deutschland-Ost.* Frankfurt: Hagg & Harchen Verlag, 1993.

Mommsen, Hans. *Auf der Suche nach historischer Normalität: Beiträge zum Geschichtsbildstreit in der Bundesrepublik.* Berlin: Argon, 1987.

———. "Was haben die deutschen vom Völkermord an den Juden gewusst? in Werner H. Pehle, ed. *Der Judenpogrom 1938. Von der Reichskristallnacht zum Völkermord.* Frankfurt: Fischer, 1988.

Mommsen, Hans, and Dieter Obst. "Die Reaktion der deutschen Bevölkerung auf die Verfolgung der Juden," in Hans Mommsen and Susanne Willems, eds., *Herrschaftsalltag im Dritten Reich: Studien und Texte.* Düsseldorf: Schwenn, 1989.

Noelle, Elizabeth, and Erich Peter Naumann, eds. *The Germans: Public Opinion Polls 1947–1966.* Westport, Conn.: Greenwood Press, 1981.

Nolte, Ernst. *Das Vergehen der Vergangenheit: Antwort an meine Kritiker im sogenannten Historikerstreit.* Berlin: Ullstein, 1988.

Pross, Harry. *Vor und nach Hitler: Zur deutschen Sozialpathologie.* Olten: Walter, 1962.

Pulzer, Peter. "Erasing the Past: German Historians Debate the Holocaust," *Patterns of Prejudice* 21, no. 3 (1987): 4–13.

Rabinbach, Anson, and Jack Zipes, eds. *Germans and Jews since the Holocaust.* New York: Holmes and Meier, 1986.

Reinharz, Jehuda, and Walter Schatzberg, eds. *The Jewish Response to German Culture.* Hanover, N.H.: University Press of New England, 1985.

Schneider, Peter. "Hitler's Shadow: On Being a Self-Conscious German," *Harper's Magazine* (September 1987): 49–54.

Schulze, Hagen. *Wir sind was wir geworden sind: Vom Nutzen der Geschichte für die deutsche Gegenwart.* Munich: Piper, 1987.

Silbermann, Alphons. *Sind wir Antisemiten?* Cologne: Verlag Wissenschaft und Politik, 1982.

Steinert, Marlis. *Hitler's War and the Germans.* Athens, Ohio: Ohio University Press, 1977.

Sterling, Eleonore. "Judenfreunde-Judenfeinde: Fragwürdiger Philosemitismus in der Bundesrepublik," *Die Zeit* (December 10, 1965).

Stern, Susan, ed. *Speaking Out: Jewish Voices from United Germany.* Chicago: Edition q, 1995.

Stokes, Lawrence D. "The German People and the Destruction of the European Jews." *Central European History* 6, no. 2 (1973): 167–91.

Ullrich, Volker. "Hitlers willige Mordgesellen," *Die Zeit* (April 19, 1996): 1.

Wehler, Hans-Ulrich, ed. *Entsorgung der deutschen Vergangenheit? Ein polemischer Essay zum Historikerstreit.* Munich: C. H. Beck, 1988.

———. "Wie ein Stachel im Fleisch," *Die Zeit* (1996): 16.

Weil, Frederick D. "The Imperfectly Mastered Past: Anti-Semitism in West Germany since the Holocaust," *New German Critique* 29 (1980): 135–53.

Wilhelm, Hans H. "The Holocaust in National Socialist Rhetoric and Writing," *Yad Vashem Studies* 16 (1984): 95–128.

Wolffsohn, Michael. *Ewige Schuld: 40 Jahre Deutsch-Jüdisch-Israelische Beziehungen.* Munich: Piper, 1988.

———. *Verwirrtes Deutschland? Provokative Zwischenrufe eines deutsch-jüdischen Patrioten.* Munich: Bruckmann, 1993.

———. *Die Deutschland Akte: Juden und Deutsche in Ost und West. Tatsachen und Legenden.* Munich: Bruckmann, 1995.

Wollenberg, Jörg, ed. *Niemand war dabei und keiner hat's gewusst: Die deutsche Öffentlichkeit und die Judenverfolgung.* Munich: Piper, 1989.

Evil, Genocidal Mentality, and Modern Bureaucracy

Adorno, Theodor, et al., *The Authoritarian Personality.* New York: W. W. Norton, 1969.

Allport, Gordon. *The Nature of Prejudice.* New York: Doubleday, 1958.

Barber, Zevedei. *Democracy and Dictatorship: Their Psychology and Patterns of Life.* New York: Grove Press, 1956.

Bartov, Omer. *Murder in our Midst: The Holocaust, Industrial Killing, and Representation.* New York: Oxford University Press, 1966.

Bauman, Zygmunt. *Modernity and the Holocaust.* Ithaca, N.Y.: Cornell University Press, 1989.

Becker, Ernest. *The Structure of Evil.* New York: Free Press, 1961.

———. *Escape from Evil.* New York: Free Press, 1975.

Burleigh, Michael. *Ethics and Extermination: Reflections on Nazi Genocide.* Cambridge: Cambridge University Press, 1997.

Cohn, Norman. *The Pursuit of the Millennium: Revolutionary Messianism in Medieval and Reformation Europe and Its Bearing on Modern Totalitarian Movements.* New York: Harper & Row, 1961.

Fackenheim, Emil. "Holocaust and Weltanschauung: Philosophical Reflections on Why They Did It," *Holocaust and Genocide Studies* (1988): 197–208.

Fromm, Erich. *The Anatomy of Human Destructiveness.* New York: Holt, Rinehart and Winston, 1973.

Hoffer, Eric. *The True Believer.* New York: Harper & Row, 1951.

Lifton, Robert J. *The Nazi Doctors: Medical Killing and the Psychology of Genocide.* New York: Basic Books, 1986.

Lifton, Robert J., and Eric Markusen. *The Genocidal Mentality: Nazi Holocaust and Nuclear Threat.* New York: Basic Books, 1990.

Miale, Florence R. and Michael Selzer. *The Nuremberg Mind: The Psychology of the Nazi Leaders.* New York: Quadrangle Books, 1976.

Milgram, Stanley. *Obedience to Authority.* New York: Harper & Row, 1974.

Mumford, Lewis. *The Myth of the Machine: The Pentagon of Power.* New York: Harcourt Brace, Jovanovich, 1964.

Rappoport, Leon, and George Kren. *The Holocaust and the Crisis of Human Behavior.* New York: Holmes and Meier, 1980.

Rhodes, James M. *The Hitler Movement: A Modern Millenarian Revolution.* Stanford, Calif.: Stanford University Press, 1980.

Russell, Jeffrey Burton. *Mephistopheles: The Devil in the Modern World.* Ithaca, N.Y.: Cornell University Press, 1986.

———. *The Prince of Darkness: Radical Evil and the Power of Good in History.* Ithaca, N.Y.: Cornell University Press, 1988.

Thompson, William Irwin. *Evil and the World Order.* New York: Harper & Row, 1976.

Voegelin, Eric. *The New Science of Politics.* Chicago: University of Chicago Press, 1952.

Wilson, James Q. *Crime and Human Nature.* New York: Simon and Schuster, 1986.

Yochelson, Samuel, and Stanton E. Samenow. *The Criminal Personality.* 2 vols. New York: Jason Aronson, 1977.

Zimbardo, Philip. "Interpersonal Dynamics in a Simulated Prison," *International Journal for Criminality and Penology* (1983): 64–97.

Index